International Law

Fourth Edition

International Law

Fourth Edition

Valerie Epps
Professor of Law
Director of the International Law Concentration
Suffolk University Law School
Boston, MA, U.S.A.

Carolina Academic Press
Durham, North Carolina

Library of Congress Cataloging-in-Publication Data

Epps, Valerie, 1943-
International law / Valerie Epps. -- 4th ed.
p. cm.
Includes bibliographical references and index.
ISBN 978-1-59460-551-2 (alk. paper)
1. International law. I. Title. II. Series.

KZ1242.E67 2009
341--dc22

2009019317

CAROLINA ACADEMIC PRESS
700 Kent Street
Durham, North Carolina 27701
Telephone (919) 489-7486
Fax (919) 493-5668
www.cap-press.com

Printed in the United States of America

For all my students, past and future, in the hope and belief that the development of a just system of international law can contribute to a better world for everyone.

Contents

Table of Cases

Bold type indicates that the whole case or a large excerpt of the case appears in the text.

Acknowledgments

I would like to thank the President and Trustees of Suffolk University who granted me a sabbatical leave, without which this book would never have been completed. The Legal Studies Department at Brandeis University kindly allowed me to test out the text in an international law course. My students at Suffolk University Law School have been a source of much inspiration and proved a spur to develop better materials for teaching. My research assistants, Tracy Devlin, Kristine Hung, Frank Maniscalco, Halim Moris, and Maureen Pomeroy have all been diligent, prompt, and creatively cheerful. Joan Comer typed, retyped, and then repeated that process many times, always with speed and much grace and Patricia McLaughlin provided excellent secretarial assistance throughout the original project. To them all I owe a great debt. The second edition would not have been completed without the efficiency, grace and calming influence of Mishell Fortes who corrected, changed and inserted all the additions to the new edition. In working on the third edition I was aided by Rita Mercardo, my research assistant, and by the ever patient and tireless Mishell Fortes. The fourth edition, once again, was only possible with the detailed and meticulous help of Mishell Fortes.

International Law

Fourth Edition

Preface

The purpose of this book is to introduce students, with little legal training, to the study of public international law. Within North America law is normally taught at the graduate level in a professional law school. Yet there is a long and honorable tradition of teaching international law at the undergraduate or postgraduate level, particularly within the larger framework of international relations, generally in departments of government or political science. Throughout most of the rest of the world, law, including international law, is taught at the undergraduate level.

The need for a book specifically designed for students with limited legal knowledge became apparent to me when I was asked to teach such a course at Brandeis University. I reviewed the available literature and, apart from the standard, narrative form introductions to international law, there was little available. There are, of course, a number of well known case books, widely used in the professional law schools, which I have used for many years teaching in law schools, but all of them were both too detailed for introductory courses and assumed a fairly large legal background. Almost invariably international law is taught as an upper level course in law schools and the authors of texts for such courses can reasonably count on students having a fairly comprehensive grasp of all the core subjects of law.

I concluded that teaching a course at the undergraduate level or to graduate nonlegal specialists required a somewhat different approach and somewhat different materials and so I set about to construct my own book. The result appears in the pages that follow. It should be added that these materials do not assume that such students are less able than graduate law students to grasp difficult issues nor does it assume that they cannot deal with a variety of complex instruments that bear on a particular problem. Rather the book focusses on the central problems of international law, assumes no prior legal knowledge except that gathered by living in a society organized under a legal system, and encourages students to work through a number of problems that present a variety of international issues. The overriding aspiration of this book is that students will acquire a general understanding of the mechanisms and concepts of the international legal system and that they will find encouragement to pursue further study of the area.

Valerie Epps
Professor of Law
Director of the International Law Concentration
Suffolk University Law School
Boston, Massachusetts, U.S.A.

Electronic Research Resources for International Law

There are an ever expanding number of sites for conducting international law research electronically. It is fair to say that the availability of international law materials electronically has revolutionized research in international law. There are a number of guides to such research. The citations to, or web site addresses of two excellent guides are listed below:

ASIL Guide to Electronic Resources for International Law, available at: www-asil.org/erg home.cfrs. **Electronic Information System for International Law**, available at: ww.eisil.org/. **International Law Guides**, available at: www.llrx.com/international_law.html, has links to many useful sites. Many law schools also maintain useful sites. Go to the particular law school's web site and click on Library. Cornell has a Legal Information Institute: http://www.law.cornell.edu/world/. Duke has an International Legal Research Tutorial: http://www.law.duke.edu/ilrt/. The Fletcher School of Law and Diplomacy has a useful treaty site at http://www.fletcher.tufts.edu.multi/multilaterals.html. **The United Nations web site, www.un.org** will connect you to the internet sites for the International Court of Justice, The International Criminal Tribunal for the Former Yugoslavia, The International Criminal Tribunal for Rwanda, The International Criminal Court, The International Tribunal for the Law of the Sea, the United Nations Treaty Collection, the United Nations Documentation Research Guide and a large amount of information on Peace and Security, Economic and Social Development, Human Rights and Humanitarian Affairs.

International Law

Fourth Edition

International Law

Introduction

What Is It?

When students are considering whether to take a course labeled "International Law" quite naturally they wish to know, in general terms, what the course covers. The dilemma faced by anyone seeking to answer this question is how to convey a broad sense of the subject matter to someone who has not yet studied the specifics of the course. Perhaps the best answer would be: "Wait and see," but that would probably infuriate a good number of potential students. This introduction will, however, be very brief. The book will then plunge into some of the specific issues addressed by international law. By the end of the book many questions about the nature of international law will have been tackled, by which time the student should have the necessary background to begin to appreciate the underlying concepts critically.

Traditional Definition

A traditional definition of international law is that it concerns the legal relationships between sovereign states and covers a wide variety of topics such as the law of the sea or the laws of war. More modern definitions would wish to include the legal relationships that exist not simply between states but also between and among international organizations, individuals, groups, multinational corporations and other entities that are considered capable of possessing the characteristics of international personality. For centuries the field of international law was only open to states, not because there was anything in the real world that prevented other entities from being players in this arena but simply because the theory of international law, in those centuries, had defined the field with a neat precision: only states possess international legal rights and duties: therefore no other entities are capable of possessing international legal rights and obligations. As the role of the nation state evolved and states took on an ever widening array of activities and as the corporation, international organizations and the individual came to occupy a radically different place in the legal spectrum it was clear that many subjects, originally considered as being outside the scope of international law, would have to be included in it. More recently, the rise of the paramilitary international non-state actor has again challenged the framework of international law.

Traditionally, the way in which a state treated its own citizens was considered to be a subject of that state's law alone. If state A passed laws allowing it to chop off a petty thief's hands, there was no body of law outside the municipal law of state A that exerted authority over the state. Most writers on international law would now maintain that every state is subject to a body of law, broadly called human rights, that would prohibit such treatment because it would violate the individual's right to be free from cruel or excessive punishments, and bodily dismemberment would be considered cruel and excessive for a petty thief. The individual is now seen as possessing international rights and also some international obligations.

As new entities and new concepts have gained acceptance in the international arena so the scope of international law has changed and broadened. The process will doubtless continue. The lesson it teaches us is that we must constantly ask ourselves why we define legal concepts in a particular way and what are the consequences of our insistence on a particular definition.

Chapter I

Sources of International Law

Who Makes Up International Law?
The Doctrine of Sources

Most students have a fairly good notion of how law gets made in their own country. They know that the legislature enacts laws and that often legislative power is divided between federal, state and local authorities. They also know that a variety of entities, broadly known as the executive branch of government, have the authority to carry out or enforce the laws and that judges, who may be elected or appointed, interpret and apply the law in cases before them. But who makes international law? The answer is that states and other international entities largely make international law for themselves through a variety of mechanisms that will be studied in the next section.

International law comes about in a number of ways. The most prominent sources are custom, treaties, general principles of law, judicial decisions and the work of scholars and writers. With respect to the work of writers and scholars, their work is regarded as evidence of what the law is, rather than strictly a source of law itself, but such work is often quite influential in shaping the development of international law. Each one of these sources will be studied separately though often a number of sources combine to create international law.

Custom

What is custom? It is a practice of states (or other international legal entities) engaged in by them out of a sense of legal obligation rather than out of a sense of kindness, courtesy or convenience. This latter element, namely that the practice be regarded as law, is spoken of as *opinio juris* in many cases and texts. Below are cases where courts have faced the task of determining whether a particular state practice amounts to a binding custom.

The Paquete Habana

The Supreme Court of the United States
175 U.S. 677 (1900)

Note

In 1898 war broke out between the U.S. and Spain, which then ruled Cuba as a colony. The U.S. imposed a blockade around Cuba. Two small Cuban fishing vessels, who did not know of the blockade, were catching fish on the high seas off the coast of Cuba. They were captured as prize of war by American warships and condemned by the U.S. district court in Florida. Later the boats were auctioned with the proceeds going to the U.S. government. The Cuban owners of the boats argued that, as fishing vessles, they were exempt from capture by virtue of customary international law. Below is the U.S. Supreme Court's decision in the case.

Mr. Justice Gray delivered the opinion of the court:

These are two appeals from decrees of the district court of the United States for the southern district of Florida condemning two fishing vessels and their cargoes as prize of war.

Each vessel was a fishing smack, running in and out of Havana, and regularly engaged in fishing on the coast of Cuba; sailed under the Spanish flag; was owned by a Spanish subject of Cuban birth, living in the city of Havana; was commanded by a subject of Spain, also residing in Havana.... Her cargo consisted of fresh fish, caught by her crew from the sea, put on board as they were caught, and kept and sold alive. Until stopped by the blockading squadron she had no knowledge of the existence of the war or of any blockade. She had no arms or ammunition on board, and made no attempt to run the blockade after she knew of its existence, nor any resistance at the time of the capture.

On April 25, 1898, about 2 miles off Mariel, and 11 miles from Havana, she was captured by the United States gunboat Castine.

We are then brought to the consideration of the question whether, upon the facts appearing in these records, the fishing smacks were subject to capture by the armed vessels of the United States during the recent war with Spain.

By an ancient usage among civilized nations, beginning centuries ago, and gradually ripening into a rule of international law, coast fishing vessels, pursuing their vocation of catching and bringing in fresh fish, have been recognized as exempt, with their cargoes and crews, from capture as prize of war.

This doctrine, however, has been earnestly contested at the bar; and no complete collection of the instances illustrating it is to be found, so far as we are aware, in a single published work, although many are referred to and discussed by the writers on international law, notably in 2 Ortolan, Règles Internationales et Diplomatie de la Mer, (4th ed.) lib. 3, c.2, pp. 51–56; in 4 Calvo, Droit International, (5th ed.) §§2367–2373; in De Boeck, Propriété Privée Ennemie sous Pavillon Ennemi, §§191–196; and in Hall, International Law, (4th ed.) §148. It is therefore worthwhile to trace the history of the rule, from the earliest accessible sources, through the increasing recognition of it, with occasional setbacks, to what we may now justly consider as its final establishment in our own country and generally throughout the civilized world.

The earliest acts of any government on the subject, mentioned in the books, either emanated from, or were approved by, a King of England.

In 1403 and 1406, Henry IV issued orders to his admirals and other officers, entitled "Concerning Safety of Fishermen—*De Securitate pro Piscatoribus.*" By an order of October 26, 1403, reciting that it was made pursuant to a treaty between himself and the King of France; and for the greater safety of the fishermen of either country, and so that they could be, and carry on their industry, the more safely on the sea, and deal with each other in peace; and that the French King had consented that English fishermen should be treated likewise,—it was ordained that French fishermen might, during the then pending season for the herring fishery, safely fish for herrings and all other fish, from the harbor of Gravelines and the island of Thanet to the mouth of the Seine and the harbor of Hautoune. And by an order of October 5, 1406, he took into his safe conduct and under his special protection, guardianship, and defense, all and singular the fishermen of France, Flanders, and Brittany, with their fishing vessels and boats, everywhere on the sea, through and within his dominions, jurisdictions, and territories, in regard to their fishery, while sailing, coming, and going, and, at their pleasure, freely and lawfully fishing, delaying, or proceeding, and returning homeward with their catch of fish, without any molestation or hindrance whatever; and also their fish, nets, and other property and goods soever; and it was therefore ordered that such fishermen should not be interfered with, provided they should comport themselves well and properly, and should not, by color of these presents, do or attempt, or presume to do or attempt, anything that could prejudice the King, or his Kingdom of England, or his subjects. 8 Rymer's Foedera, 336, 451.

The treaty made October 2, 1521, between the Emperor Charles V and Francis I of France, through their ambassadors, recited that a great and fierce war had arisen between them, because of which there had been, both by land and by sea, frequent depredations and incursions on either side, to the grave detriment and intolerable injury of the innocent subjects of each; and that a suitable time for the herring fishery was at hand, and, by reason of the sea being beset by the enemy, the fishermen did not dare to go out, whereby the subject of their industry bestowed by heaven to allay the hunger of the poor, would wholly fail for the year, unless it were otherwise provided.... And it was therefore agreed that the subjects of each sovereign, fishing in the sea, or exercising the calling of fishermen, could and might, until the end of the next January, without incurring any attack, depredation, molestation, trouble, or hindrance soever, safely and freely, everywhere in the sea, take herrings and every other kind of fish, the existing war by land and sea notwithstanding; and, further, that during the time aforesaid no subject of either sovereign should commit, or attempt or presume to commit, any depredation, force, violence, molestation, or vexation to or upon such fishermen or their vessels, supplies, equipments, nets, and fish, or other goods soever truly appertaining to fishing. The treaty was made at Calais, then an English possession.

* * *

France, from remote times, set the example of alleviating the evils of war in favor of all coast fishermen.

The same custom would seem to have prevailed in France until towards the end of the seventeenth century. For example, in 1675, Louis XIV and the States General to Holland by mutual agreement granted to Dutch and French fishermen the liberty, undisturbed by their vessels of war, of fishing along the coasts of France, Holland, and England. D'Hauterive et De Cussy, Traités de Commerce, pt.1, vol. 2, p. 278. But by the ordinances of 1681 and 1692 the practice was discontinued, because, Valin says, of the faithless conduct of the enemies of France, who, abusing the good faith with which she had always observed the treaties, habitually carried off her fishermen, while their own fished in safety.

The doctrine which exempts coast fishermen with their vessels and cargoes, from capture as prize of war, has been familiar to the United States from the time of the War of Independence.

* * *

In the treaty of 1785 between the United States and Prussia, article 23 (which was proposed by the American Commissioners, John Adams, Benjamin Franklin, and Thomas Jefferson, and is said to have been drawn up by Franklin), provided that, if war should arise between the contracting parties, "all women and children, scholars of every faculty, cultivators of the earth, artisans, manufacturers, and fishermen, unarmed and inhabiting unfortified towns, villages or places, and in general all others whose occupations are for the common subsistence and benefit of mankind, shall be allowed to continue their respective employments, and shall not be molested in their persons, nor shall their houses or goods be burnt or otherwise destroyed, nor their fields wasted by the armed force of the enemy into whose power, by the events of war, they may happen to fall; but if anything is necessary to be taken from them for the use of such armed force, the same shall be paid for at a reasonable price." 8 Stat. at 96....

Since the United States became a nation, the only serious interruptions, so far as we are informed, of the general recognition of the exemption of coast fishing vessels from hostile capture, arose out of the mutual suspicions and recriminations of England and France during the wars of the French Revolution.

Lord Stowell's judgment in *The Young Jacob and Johanna,* 1 C. Rob. 20, ... was much relied on by the counsel for the United States, and deserves careful consideration.

The vessel there condemned is described in the report as "a small Dutch fishing vessel taken April, 1798, on her return from the Dogger bank to Holland;" and Lord Stowell, in delivering judgment, said: "In former wars it has not been usual to make captures of these small fishing vessels; but this rule was a rule of comity only, and not of legal decision; it has prevailed from views of mutual accommodation between neighboring countries, and from tenderness to a poor and industrious order of people. In the present war there has, I presume, been sufficient reason for changing this mode of treatment; and as they are brought before me for my judgment they must be referred to the general principles of this court; they fall under the character and description of the last class of cases; that is, of ships constantly and exclusively employed in the enemy's trade." And he added: "It is a further satisfaction to me in giving this judgment, to observe that the facts also bear strong marks of a false and fraudulent transaction."

Both the capture and the condemnation were within a year after the order of the English government of January 24, 1798, instructing the commanders of its ships to seize French and Dutch fishing vessels, and before any revocation of that order. Lord Stowell's judgment shows that his decision was based upon the order of 1798, as well as upon strong evidence of fraud. Nothing more was adjudged in the case.

But some expressions in his opinion have been given so much weight by English writers that it may be well to examine them particularly. The opinion begins by admitting the known custom in former wars not to capture such vessels; adding, however, "but this was a rule of comity only, and not of legal decision." Assuming the phrase "legal decision" to have been there used, in the sense in which courts are accustomed to use it, as equivalent to "judicial decision," it is true that, so far as appears, there had been no such decision on the point in England. The word "comity" was apparently used by Lord Stowell as synonymous with courtesy or goodwill. But the period of a hundred years which has since elapsed is amply sufficient to have enabled what originally may have rested in custom or comity, courtesy or concession, to grow, by the general assent of civilized nations, into a settled rule of international law. As well said by Sir James Mackintosh: "In the present century a slow and silent, but very substantial, mitigation has taken place in the practice of war; and in proportion as that mitigated practice has received the sanction of time it is raised from the rank of mere usage, and becomes part of the law of nations." Discourse on the Law of Nations, 38; 1 Miscellaneous Works, 360.

* * *

In the treaty of peace between the United States and Mexico in 1848, were inserted the very words of the earlier treaties with Prussia, already quoted, forbidding the hostile molestation or seizure in time of war of the persons, occupations, houses, or goods of fishermen. 9 Stat. 939, 940.

France in the Crimean war in 1854, and in her wars with Austria in 1859 and with Germany in 1870, by general orders, forbade her cruisers to trouble the coast fisheries, or to seize any vessel or boat engaged therein, unless naval or military operations should make it necessary....

And the Empire of Japan (the last State admitted into the rank of civilized nations,) by an ordinance promulgated at the beginning of its war with China in August, 1894, established prize courts, and ordained that "the following enemy's vessels are exempt from detention," including in the exemption "boats engaged in coast fisheries," as well as "ships engaged exclusively on a voyage of scientific discovery, philanthropy, or religious mission." Takahashi, International Law, 11, 178.

International law is part of our law, and must be ascertained and administered by the courts of justice of appropriate jurisdiction as often as questions of right depending upon it are duly presented for their determination. For this purpose, where there is no treaty and no controlling executive or legislative act or judicial decision, resort must be had to the customs and usages of civilized nations, and as evidence of these, to the works of jurists and commentators who by years of labor, research and experience have made themselves peculiarly well acquainted with the subject of which they treat. Such works are resorted to by judicial tribunals, not for the speculations of their authors concerning what the law ought to be, but for trustworthy evidence of what the law really is. *Hilton v Guyot,* 159 U.S. 113, 163, 164, 214, 215.

Wheaton places, among the principal sources of international law, "Text-writers of authority, showing what is the approved usage of nations, or the general opinion respecting their mutual conduct, with the definitions and modifications introduced by general consent." As to these he forcibly observes: "Without wishing to exaggerate the importance of these writers, or to substitute, in any case, their authority for the principles of reason, it may be affirmed that they are generally impartial in their judgment. They are witnesses of the sentiments and usages of civilized nations and the weight of their testimony increases every time their authority is invoked by statesmen, and every year that passes without the rules laid down in their works being impugned by the avowal of contrary principles." Wheaton's, International Law (8th ed.), § 15.

Chancellor Kent says: "In the absence of higher and more authoritative sanctions, the ordinances of foreign states, the opinions of eminent statesmen, and the writings of distinguished jurists, are regarded as of great consideration on questions not settled by conventional law. In cases where the principal jurists agree, the presumption will be very great in favor of the solidity of their maxims; and no civilized nation that does not arrogantly set all ordinary law and justice at defiance, will venture to disregard the uniform sense of the established writers on international law." 1 Kent, Com. 18.

No international jurist of the present day has a wider or more deserved reputation than Calvo, who, though writing in French, is a citizen of the Argentine Republic, employed in its diplomatic service abroad.... [He states:] "Notwithstanding the hardships to which maritime wars subject private property, notwithstanding the extent of the recognized rights of belligerents, there are generally exempted, from seizure and capture, fishing vessels."

The modern German books on international law, cited by the counsel for the appellants, treat the custom, by which the vessels and implements of coast fishermen are exempt from seizure and capture, as well established by the practice of nations....

To this subject, in more than one aspect, are singularly applicable the words uttered by Mr. Justice Strong, speaking for this court: "Undoubtedly no single nation can change the law of the sea. The law is of universal obligation and no statute of one or two nations can create obligations for the world. Like all the laws of nations, it rests upon the common consent of civilized communities. It is of force, not because it was prescribed by any superior power, but because it has been generally accepted as a rule of conduct.... This is not giving to the statutes of any nation extraterritorial effect. It is not treating them as general maritime laws; but it is recognition of the historical fact that by common consent of mankind these rules have been acquiesced in as of general obligation...."

Mr. Chief Justice *Fuller*, with whom concurred Mr. Justice *Harlan* and Mr. Justice *McKenna*, **dissenting**:

The District Court held these vessels and their cargoes liable because not "satisfied that as a matter of law, without any ordinance, treaty, or proclamation, fishing vessels of this class are exempt from seizure."

This court holds otherwise, not because such exemption is to be found in any treaty, legislation, proclamation, or instruction granting it, but on the ground that the vessels were exempt by reason of an established rule of international law applicable to them, which it is the duty of the court to enforce.

I am unable to conclude that there is any such established international rule, or that this court can properly revise action which must be treated as having been taken in the ordinary exercise of discretion in the conduct of war....

In truth, the exemption of fishing craft is essentially an act of grace, and not a matter of right, and it is extended or denied as the exigency is believed to demand.

QUESTIONS

1. What was the custom that the Court found applicable in the *Paquete Habana* case?
2. What persuaded the Court that the practice was indeed a binding international custom?
3. Why are United States courts obliged to follow international custom?
4. Would the Court have followed the custom if Congress had passed a law indicating that no vessels were exempt from capture as prize of war?
5. If indeed there is an international custom, are states completely free to pass contrary legislation?
6. If states are free to pass legislation contrary to an international custom, won't that mean that custom will only exist if national legislatures either approve (overtly or tacitly) of the custom or if they fail to enact contrary legislation?
7. Are there any international customary laws from which states are not free to derogate? See note on *Jus Cogens* below, page 21.

Note: The Relationship of International Law to Domestic (National) Law

A number of issues are presented by the question of the relationship of international law to domestic law. The *Paquete Habana Case* states the U.S. approach which incorporates international customary law into U.S. domestic law, provided it does not conflict with pre-existing domestic law. Most other common law and civil law countries take this approach.[1] For example, a number of the judges in the *Ex Parte Pinochet* litigation in the U.K. expressed the view that international law was part of British common law.[2] Similar expressions can be found in the Supreme Court of Canada's discussion in *Reference re Secession of Quebec.*[3] Germany's Basic Law 25 specifically incorporates "general rules of public international law...." Further, such rules are stated to "take precedence over the laws...." Professor Shaw sums up his survey on this issue: "Most countries accept the operation of customary rules within their own jurisdictions, providing [*sic*] there is no conflict with existing laws, and some will allow international law to prevail over municipal provisions."[4]

With respect to the role that treaties play in national law, the answer is complicated by the variety of ways that treaties are made, as well as the possibility of constitutional provisions addressing the role of treaties. Some states, such as the U.K., always require an act of parliament before a treaty can be operative as municipal law. Other states, such as the U.S., often require a certain percentage of legislators to vote in favor of a treaty before the treaty can be ratified by the President. For example, under article II, section 2, of the U.S. Constitution, the President is given the "power, by and with the advice and consent of the Senate, to make treaties, provided two-thirds of the senators present concur;...." This power is again complicated by the Executive's centuries-old practice of entering into Executive Agreements (another term for international agreements) without the advice and consent of the Senate. Article VI of the U.S. Constitution makes "all treaties ... the supreme law of the land....", and has generally been interpreted as making treaties self-executing, that is, not requiring further legislation to become operative at the national level, but this view has recently been challenged in the case of *Medellin v. Texas.*[5]

A further question is whether subsequent legislation can override treaties. (Below it is noted that states are generally free to disregard customary law by passing contrary legislation, except where the customary rule is *jus cogens*. See note on *Jus Cogens*, below, page 21.) There is no general approach to this issue and different states exhibit different stances. The U.S. follows a "latter in time" rule so that the last item to become operative, whether a treaty or a regular piece of legislation will prevail. Other states hold that treaties prevail over regular legislation regardless of the date of the treaty or the contrary legislation.[6]

Despite all of these different ways of melding international law into domestic law while preserving the right to pass contrary legislation, it should be remembered that at the international level a state may not rely on its internal law to excuse the non-performance of an international obligation.[7]

---

1. For an excellent survey of a number of countries' approaches to this issue, see, Malcolm N. Shaw, International Law 138–179 (6th ed. 2008) [hereinafter Shaw].
2. See, e.g., [2000] 1 AC 61, 98; [2000] 1 AC 147, 276; see also, IV Blackstone's Commentaries, ch. 5; but cf., Regina v. Jones, [2006] UKHL 16.
3. 161 DLR (4th) 385, 399, 2 S.C.R. 217 (1998).
4. Shaw, supra note 1, at 177.
5. 128 S. Ct. 1346 (2008).
6. Shaw, supra note 1, at 178.
7. See Vienna Convention on the Law of Treaties, arts. 27 & 46, 1155 U.N.T.S. 331, signed 23 May 1969, entered into force 27 January 1980, reprinted at 8 I.L.M. 679 (1969); Cameroon v. Nige-

Abdullahi v. Pfizer, Inc.

562 F.3d 163 (2d Cir. 2009) (most footnotes omitted)

Before: Pooler, B.D. Parker, and Wesley, *Circuit Judges.*

Plaintiffs-Appellants appeal from judgments of the United States District Court for the Southern District of New York (Pauley, J.) dismissing complaints for lack of subject matter jurisdiction.... Reversed and Remanded.

Judge Wesley dissents in a separate opinion.

Barrington D. Parker, *Circuit Judge:*

This consolidated appeal is from the judgments of the United States District Court for the Southern District of New York (Pauley, J.) dismissing two complaints for lack of subject matter jurisdiction under the Alien Tort Statute, 28 U.S.C. § 1350 ("ATS").... Plaintiffs-Appellants Rabi Abdullahi and other Nigerian children and their guardians sued Defendant-Appellee Pfizer, Inc. Under the ATS ("the *Abdullahi* action"). They alleged that Pfizer violated a customary international law norm prohibiting involuntary medical experimentation on humans when it tested an experimental antibiotic on children in Nigeria, including themselves, without their consent of knowledge. Pfizer moved to dismiss both actions for lack of subject matter jurisdiction.... The district court granted the motion ... and both sets of plaintiffs have appealed.

As explained below, we conclude ... that the district court incorrectly determined that the prohibition in customary international law against nonconsensual human medical experimentation cannot be enforced through the ATS.... Consequently, we reverse and remand the cases to the district court for further proceedings.

BACKGROUND

A. Pfizer's Trovan Test in Nigeria

On review of a district court's grant of a motion to dismiss, we assume as true the facts alleged in the complaints, construing them in the light most favorable to the appellants.... The central events at issue in these cases took place in 1996, during an epidemic of bacterial meningitis in northern Nigeria. The appellants allege that at that time, Pfizer, the world's largest pharmaceutical corporation, sought to gain the approval of the U.S. Food and Drug Administration ("FDA") for the use on children of its new antibiotic, Trovafloxacin Mesylate, marketed as "Trovan." They contend that in April 1996, Pfizer, dispatched three of its American physicians to work with four Nigerian doctors to experiment with Trovan on children who were patients in Nigeia's Infectious Disease Hospital ("IDH") in Kano, Nigeria. Working in concert with Nigerian government officials, the team allegedly recruited two hundred sick children who sought treatment at the IDH and gave half of the children Trovan and the other half Ceftriaxone, an FDA-approved antibiotic the safety and efficacy of which was well-established. Appellants contend that Pfizer knew that Trovan had never previously been tested on children in the form being used and that animal tests showed that Trovan had life-threatening side effects, including joint disease, abnormal cartilage growth, liver damage, and a degenerative bone condition. Pfizer pur-

---

ria, 2002 I.C.J. 303, 430–431; Request for Interpretation of Judgment of 31 March 2004 (Mex. v. U.S.) 2009 I.C.J. ___, at para. 47.

portedly gave the children who were in the Ceftriaxone control group a deliberately low dose in order to misrepresent the effectiveness of Trovan in relation to Ceftriaxone. After approximately two weeks, Pfizer allegedly concluded the experiment and left without administering follow-up care. According to the appellants, the tests caused the deaths of eleven children, five of whom had taken Trovan and six of whom had taken the lowered dose of Ceftriaxone, and left many others blind, deaf, paralyzed, or brain-damaged.

Appellants claim that Pfizer, working in partnership with the Nigerian government, failed to secure the informed consent of either children or their guardians and specifically failed to disclose or explain the experimental nature of the study or the serious risks involved. Although the treatment protocol required the researchers to offer or read the subjects documents requesting and facilitating their informed consent, this was allegedly not done in either English or the subjects' native language of Hausa. The appellants also contend that Pfizer deviated from its treatment protocol by not alerting the children or their guardians to the side effects of Trovan or other risks of the experiment, not providing them with the option of choosing alternative treatment, and not informing them that the non-governmental organization Médecins Sans Frontières (Doctors without Borders) was providing a conventional and effective treatment for bacterial meningitis, free of charge, at the same site.

The appellants allege that, in an effort to rapidly secure FDA approval, Pfizer hastily assembled its test protocol at its research headquarters in Groton, Connecticut, and requested and received permission to proceed from the Nigerian government in March 1996. At the time, Pfizer also claimed to have secured approval from an IDH ethics committee. Appellants allege, however, that the March 1996 approval letter was backdated by Nigerian officials working at the government hospital well after the experiments had taken place and that at the time the letter was purportedly written, the IDH had no ethics committee. Appellants also contend that the experiments were condemned by doctors, including one on Pfizer's staff at the time of the Kano trial.

In 1998, the FDA approved Trovan for use on adult patients only. After reports of liver failure in patients who took Trovan, its use in America was eventually restricted to adult emergency care. In 1999, the European Union banned its use.

B. The Proceedings Below

In August 2001, the *Abdullahi* plaintiffs sued Pfizer under the ATS, alleging that the experiments violated international law....

In November 2002, following the dismissal of the *Zango* lawsuit, a number of the *Zango* plaintiffs filed the *Adamu* action. They alleged that in planning the Trovan experiment in Connecticut and in conducting the tests in Nigeria without informed consent, Pfizer violated the ... the ATS.

* * *

In *Abdullahi III*, Judge Pauley held that while "[p]laintiffs correctly state that nonconsensual medical experimentation violates the law of nations and, therefore, the laws of the United States," they failed to identify a source of international law that "provide[s] a proper predicate for jurisdiction under the ATS." 2005 WL 1870811, at *9, 14. Noting that "a decision to create a private right of action is one better left to legislative judgment in the great majority of cases," he concluded that "[a] cause of action for Pfizer's failure to get any consent, informed or otherwise, before performing medical experiments on the subject children would expand customary international law far beyond that contemplated by the ATS." *Id.* at 13–14 ...

* * *

DISCUSSION

The district court dismissed both actions based on its determination that it lacked subject matter jurisdiction because plaintiffs failed to state claims under the ATS. We review dismissal on this ground *de novo. Rweyemamu v. Cote*, 520 F.3d 198, 201 (2d Cir. 2008). "To survive dismissal, the plaintiff[s] must provide the grounds upon which [their] claim rests through factual allegations sufficient 'to raise a right to relief above the speculative level.'" *ATSI Commc'ns, Inc. V. Shaar Fund, Ltd.*, 493 F.3d 87, 98 (2d Cir. 2007) (quoting *Bell Atl. Corp v. Twombly*, 550 U.S. 544, 127 S. Ct. 1955, 1965 (2007)).

I. The Alien Tort Statute

The Alien Tort Statute, 28 U.S.C. § 1350, provides that "[t]he district courts shall have original jurisdiction of any civil action by an alien for a tort only, committed in violation of the law of nations or a treaty of the United States." Included in the Judiciary Act of 1789, the statute provided jurisdiction in just two cases during the first 191 years after its enactment. *See Taveras v. Taveraz*, 477 F. 3d 767, 771 (6th Cir. 2007). In the last thirty years, however the ATS has functioned slightly more robustly, conferring jurisdiction over a limited category of claims.

We first extensively examined the ATS in *Filartiga v. Pena-Irala*, 630 F.2d 876 (2d Cir. 1980), where we held that conduct violating the law of nations is actionable under the ATS "only where the nations of the world have demonstrated that the wrong is of mutual, and not merely several, concern, by means of express international accords." *Id.* at 888. Following *Filartiga*, we concluded that ATS claims may sometimes be brought against private actors, and not only state officials, *see Kadic v. Karadzic*, 70 F.3d 232, 239 (2d Cir. 1995), when the tortious activities violate norms of "universal concern" that are recognized to extend to the conduct of private parties—for example, slavery, genocide, and war crimes, *id.* at 240. This case involves allegations of both state and individual action. In *Flores v. Southern Peru Copper Corp.*, 414 F.3d 233 (2d Cir. 2003), we clarified that "the law of the nations" in the ATS context "refers to the body of law known as customary international law," which "is discerned from myriad decisions made in numerous and varied international and domestic arenas" and "does not stem from any single, definitive, readily-identifiable source." *Id.* at 247–48. These principles are rejected in their entirety by our dissenting colleague. In *Flores,* we concluded that ATS jurisdiction is limited to alleged violations of "those clear and unambiguous rules by which States universally abide, or to which they accede, out of a sense of legal obligation and mutual concern." *Id.* at 252. Applying this standard, we held that the appellants' claim that pollution from mining operations caused lung disease failed to state a violation of customary international law. We reasoned that the "right to life" and the "right to health" were insufficiently definite to constitute binding customary legal norms and that there was insufficient evidence to establish the existence of a narrower norm prohibiting intranational pollution. *Id.* at 254–55.

In 2004, the Supreme Court comprehensively addressed the ATS for the first time in *Sosa v. Alvarez-Machain*, 542 U.S. 692. Justice Souter, writing for the majority, clarified that the ATS was enacted to created jurisdiction over "a relatively modest set of actions alleging violations of the law of nations" and with "the understanding that the common law would provide a cause of action." *Id.* at 720, 723. The Supreme Court confirmed that federal courts retain a limited power to "adapt[] the law of nations to private rights" by recognizing "a narrow class of international norms" to be judicially enforceable through our residual common law discretion to create causes of action. *Id.* at 728–729. It cautioned, however, that courts must exercise this power with restraint and "the understanding that the door [to actionable violations] is still ajar subject to vigilant doorkeeping," permitting only those claims that "rest on a norm of international character accepted by the civilized world and defined with a specificity comparable to the features of the 18th-century paradigms [the Supreme Court has] recognized." *Id.* at 724. The common theme among these offenses is that they contravened the law of nations, admitted of a judicial remedy, and simultaneously threatened serious consequences in international affairs. *Id.* at 715 ...

In this way *Sosa* set a "high bar to new private causes of action" alleging violations of customary international law. *Id.* at 727 ...

Since *Sosa*, this Court has reviewed three judgments dismissing claims under the ATS. In *Khulumani v. Barclay National Bank, Ltd.*, 504 F.3d 254 (2d Cir. 2007) (per curiam), we held that the ATS conferred jurisdiction over multinational corporations that purportedly collaborated with the government of South Africa in maintaining apartheid because they aided and abetted violations of customary international law. *Id.* at 260. In *Vietnam Ass'n for Victims of Agent Orange v. Dow Chemical Co.*, 517 F.3d 104 (2d Cir. 2008), we concluded that the ATS did not support a claim that the defendants violated international law by manufacturing and supplying Agent Orange and other herbicides used by the United States military during the Vietnam War. *Id.* at 123. We reasoned that the sources of law on which the appellants relied did not define a norm prohibiting the wartime use of Agent Orange that was both universal and sufficiently specific to satisfy the requirements of *Sosa. Id.* at 119–23. Similarly, in *Mora v. People of the State of New York*, 524 F.3d 183 (2d Cir. 2008), we held that the norm at issue—one that prohibits the detention of a foreign national without informing him of the requirement of consular notifications and access under Article 36(1)(b)(3) of the Vienna Convention on Consular Relations—was insufficiently universal to support a claim under the ATS. *Id.* at 208–209.

Turning now to this appeal, and remaining mindful of our obligation to proceed cautiously and self-consciously in this area, we determine whether the norm alleged (1) is defined with a specificity comparable to the 18th-century paradigms discussed in *Sosa*, (2) is based upon a norm of international character accepted by the civilized world, and (3) is one that States universally abide by, or accede to, out of a sense of legal obligation and mutual concern.

A. The Prohibition of Nonconsensual Medical Experimentation on Humans

Appellants' ATS claims are premised on the existence of a norm of customary international law prohibiting medical experimentation on non-consenting human subjects. To determine whether this prohibition constitutes a universally accepted norm of customary international law, we examine the current state of international law by consulting the sources identified by Article 38 of the Statute of the International Court of Justice ("ICJ Statute"), to which the United States and all members of the United Nations are parties. *Flores*, 414 F.3d at 250; *see, e.g., United States v. Yousef*, 317 F.3d 56, 100–01 (2d Cir. 2003). Article 38 identifies the authorities that provide "competent proof of the content of ... international law." *Flores*, 414 F.3d at 251. These sources consist of:

> (a) international conventions, whether general or particular, establishing rules expressly recognized by the contesting states;
>
> (b) international custom, as evidence of a general practice accepted as law;
>
> (c) the general principles of law recognized by civilized nations;

(d) ... judicial decisions and the teachings of the most highly qualified publicists of the various nations, as subsidiary means for the determination of rules of law.

Statute of the International Court of Justice, art. 38(1), June 26, 1945, 59 Stat. 1055, 1060, T.S. No. 993 [hereinafter ICJ Statute].

The appellants ground their claims in four sources of international law that categorically forbid medical experimentation on non-consenting human subjects: (1) the Nuremberg Code, which states as its first principle that "[t]he voluntary consent of the human subject is absolutely essential"; (2) the World Medical Association's Declaration of Helsinki, which sets forth ethical principles to guide physicians world-wide and provides that human subjects should be volunteers and grant their informed consent to participate in research; (3) the guidelines authored by the Council for International Organizations of Medical Services ("CIOMS"), which require "the voluntary informed consent of [a] prospective subject"; and (4) Article 7 of the International Covenant on Civil and Political Rights ("ICCPR"), which provides that "no one shall be subjected without his free consent to medical or scientific experimentation."[8]

The district court found that "non-consensual medical experimentation violates the law of nations and, therefore, the laws of the United States" and cited the Nuremberg Code for support. *Abdullahi III*, 2005 WL 1870811, at 9. It then noted that "[w]hile federal courts have the authority to imply the existence of a private right of action for violations of *jus cogens* norms of international law, federal courts must consider whether there exist special factors counseling hesitation in the absence of affirmative action by Congress." *Id.* (internal citations and quotation marks omitted). The district court then separately analyzed the four sources of international law that prohibit nonconsensual medical experimentation on humans and the Universal Declaration of Human Rights. *Id.* at 11–13. It found that with the exception of the Nuremberg Code, these sources contain only aspirational or vague language lacking the specificity required for jurisdiction. *Id.* at 12–13. It also determined that because the United States did not ratify or adopt any of these authorities except the ICCPR, and because even the ICCPR is not self-executing, none of them create binding international legal obligations that are enforceable in federal court. *Id.* at 11–13. Finally, the district court concluded that the plaintiffs failed to provide a proper predicate for ATS jurisdiction because none of the sources independently authorizes a private cause of action and the inference of such a cause of action is a matter best left to Congress. *Id.* at 13–14.

The district court's approach misconstrued both the nature of customary international law and the scope of the inquiry required by *Sosa*. It mistakenly assumed that the question of whether a particular customary international law norm is sufficiently specific, universal, and obligatory to permit the recognition of a cause of action under the ATS is resolved essentially by looking at two things: whether each source of law referencing the norm is binding and whether each source expressly authorizes a cause of action to enforce the norm. But *Sosa*, as we have seen, requires a more fulsome and nu-

8. [Case footnote 7] These sources are located respectively at (1) *United States v. Brandt*, 2 Trials of War Criminals Before the Nuremberg Military Tribunals Under Control Council No. 10, 181 (1949)[hereinafter Nuremberg Trials]; (2) World Med. Ass'n, *Declaration of Helsinki: Ethical Principles for Medical Research Involving Human Subjects*, art. 20, 22, G.A. Res. (adopted 1964, amended 1975, 1983, 1989, 1996, and 2000), http://www.wma.net/e/policy/pdf/17c.pdf [hereinafter Declaration of Helsinki]; (3) Council for International Organizations of Medical Services [CIOMS], International Ethical Guidelines for Biomedical Research Involving Human Subjects, guideline 4 (3rd ed. 2002), *superseding id.* at guideline 1 (2nd ed. 1993); (4) International Covenant on Civil and Political Rights, art. 7, Dec. 19, 1966, 999 U.N.T.S. 171 [hereinafter ICCPR].

anced inquiry. Courts are obligated to examine how the specificity of the norm compares with 18th-century paradigms, whether the norm is accepted in the world community, and whether States universally abide by the norm out of a sense of mutual concern. By eschewing this inquiry, the district court did not engage the fact that norms of customary international law are "discerned from myriad decisions made in numerous and varied international and domestic arenas" and "[do] not stem from any single, definitive, readily-identifiable source." *Flores*, 414 F.3d at 247–48.

* * *

In sum, it was inappropriate for the district court to forego a more extensive examination of whether treaties, international agreements, or State practice have ripened the prohibition of nonconsensual medical experimentation on human subjects into a customary international law norm that is sufficiently (i) universal and obligatory, (ii) specific and definable, and (iii) of mutual concern, to permit courts to infer a cause of action under the ATS. *See Sosa*, 542 U.S. at 732–35. We now proceed with such an examination.

i. Universality

The appellants must allege the violation of a norm of customary international law to which States universally subscribe. *See Sosa*, 542 U.S. at 732; *Vietnam Ass'n for Victims of Agent Orange*, 517 F.3d at 117. The prohibition on nonconsensual medical experimentation on human beings meets this standard because, among other reasons, it is specific, focused and accepted by nations around the world without significant exception.

The evolution of the prohibition into a norm of customary international law began with the war crimes trials at Nuremberg. The United States, the Soviet Union, the United Kingdom and France "acting in the interest of all the United Nations," established the International Military Tribunal ("IMT") through entry into the London Agreement of August 8, 1945 ... According to the Charter, the IMT had the "power to try and punish persons who, acting in the interests of the European Axis countries, whether as individuals or as members of organisations, committed," among other offenses, war crimes and crimes against humanity. *Id.* at art. 6.

The IMT tried 22 "major" Nazi war criminals leaving "lower-level" war criminals, including "[l]eading physicians ... and leading German industrialists," to be tried in subsequent trials by U.S. military tribunals acting "under the aegis of the IMT" ... Consequently, the U.S. military tribunals effectively operated as extensions of the IMT ...

In August 1947, Military Tribunal 1, staffed by American judges and prosecutors and conducted under American procedural rules, *see* George J. Annas, *The Nuremberg Code in U.S. Courts: Ethics versus Expediency in The Nazi Doctors and the Nuremberg Code* 201, 201 (George J. Annas & Michael A. Grodin eds., 1992), promulgated the Nuremberg Code as part of the tribunal's final judgment against fifteen doctors who were found guilty of war crimes and crimes against humanity for conducting medical experiments without the subjects' consent, *Brandt*, 2 Nuremberg Trials, at 181–82. Among the nonconsensual experiments that the tribunal cited as a basis for their convictions were the testing of drugs for immunization against malaria, epidemic jaundice, typhus, smallpox and cholera. *Id.* at 175–178. Seven of the convicted doctors were sentenced to death and the remaining eight were sentenced to varying terms of imprisonment. *Id.* at 298–300. The tribunal emphasized that

> [i]n every single instance appearing in the record, subjects were used who did not consent to the experiments; indeed, as to some of the experiments, it is not even contended by the defendants that the subjects occupied the status of volunteers.

Id. at 183. The judgment concluded that "[m]anifestly human experiments under such conditions are *contrary to the principles of the law of nations* as they result from usages established among civilized peoples, from the laws of humanity, and from the dictates of public conscience." *Id.* (emphasis added and internal quotation marks omitted). The Code created as part of the tribunal's judgment therefore emphasized as its first principle that "[t]he voluntary consent of the human subject is absolutely essential." *Id.* at 181.

The American tribunal's conclusion that action that contravened the Code's first principle constituted a crime against humanity is a lucid indication of the international legal significance of the prohibition on nonconsensual medical experimentation. As Justices of the Supreme Court have recognized, "[t]he medical trials at Nuremberg in 1947 deeply impressed *upon the world* that experimentation with unknowing human subjects is morally and legally unacceptable." *United States v. Stanley*, 483 U.S. 669, 687 (1987) (Brennan, J., concurring in part and dissenting in part) (emphasis added); *see also id.* At 709–10 (O'Connor, J., concurring in part and dissenting in part)....

Consistent with this view, the Code's first principle has endured: "[S]ignificant world opinion has not come to the defense of the nature or manner in which the experiments were conducted in the Nazi concentration camps." Bassiouni et al., *supra*, at 1641. Rather, since Nuremberg, states throughout the world have shown through international accords and domestic law-making that they consider the prohibition on nonconsensual medical experimentation identified at Nuremberg as a norm of customary international law.

[Article 7 of the ICCPR states:] The clause was later revised to offer the simpler and sweeping prohibition that "no one shall be subjected without his free consent to medical or scientific experimentation." ICCPR, *supra*, at art. 7. This prohibition became part of Article 7 of the ICCPR, which entered into force in 1976, and is legally binding on the more than 160 States-Parties that have ratified the convention without reservation to the provision.10 By its terms this prohibition is not limited to state actors; rather, it guarantees individuals the right to be free from nonconsensual medical experimentation by any entity-state actors, private actors, or state and private actors behaving in concert....

The informed consent provision [of the World Medical Association's Declaration of Helsinki: Code of Ethics (1964)] now provides that "subjects must be volunteers and informed participants in the research project." Declaration of Helsinki, *supra*, at art. 20. The Declaration also requires that "[i]n any research on human beings, each potential subject must be adequately informed of the aims, methods, ... anticipated benefits and potential risks of the study, and the discomfort it may entail" and that researchers "obtain the subject's freely-given informed consent, preferably in writing." *Id.* at art. 22....

Currently, the laws and regulations of at least eighty-four countries, including the United States, require the informed consent of human subjects in medical research. That this conduct has been the subject of domestic legislation is not, of course, in and of itself proof of a norm. *See Flores*, 414 F.3d 249. However, the incorporation of this norm into the laws of this country and this host of others is a powerful indication of the international acceptance of this norm as a binding legal obligation, where, as here, states have shown that the norm is of mutual concern by including it in a variety of international accords.

The history of the norm in United States law demonstrates that it has been firmly embedded for more than 45 years and—except for our dissenting colleague—its validity has never been seriously questioned by any court. The importance that the United

States government attributes to this norm is demonstrated by its willingness to use domestic law to coerce compliance with the norm throughout the world. United States law requires that, as a predicate to FDA approval of any new drug, both American and foreign sponsors of drug research involving clinical trials, whether conducted here or abroad, procure informed consent from human subjects.

Additional international law sources support the norm's status as customary international law. The European Union embraced the norm prohibiting nonconsensual medical experimentation through a 2001 Directive passed by the European Parliament and the Council of the European Union....

Since 1997, thirty-four member States of the Council of Europe have also signed the Convention on Human Rights and Biomedicine, a binding convention and a source of customary international law. Convention for the Protection of Human Rights and Dignity of the Human Being with regard to the Application of Biology and Medicine: Convention on Human Rights and Biomedicine, art. 5, 15–16, *opened for signature* Apr. 4, 1997, E.T.S. No. 164,....

This history illustrates that from its origins with the trial of the Nazi doctors at Nuremburg through its evolution in international conventions, agreements, declarations, and domestic laws and regulations, the norm prohibiting nonconsensual medical experimentation on human subjects has become firmly embedded and has secured universal acceptance in the community of nations. Unlike our dissenting colleague's customary international law analysis, which essentially rests on the mistaken assumption that ratified international treaties are the only valid sources of customary international law for ATS purposes, *see* Dissent at 19–20, we reach this conclusion as a result of our review of the multiplicity of sources—including international conventions, whether general or particular, and international custom as identified through international agreements, declarations and a consistent pattern of action by national law-making authorities—that our precedent requires us to examine for the purpose of determining the existence of a norm of customary international law. Our dissenting colleague's reasoning fails to engage the incompatibility of nonconsensual human testing with key sources of customary international law identified in Article 38 of the ICJ's statute, most importantly international custom, as evidence of a general practice accepted as law, as well as the general principles of law recognized by civilized nations.

* * *

CONCLUSION

For the foregoing reasons, we REVERSE the judgments of the district court and REMAND for further proceedings.

WESLEY, *Circuit Judge*, dissenting:

The majority has undertaken to define a "firmly established" norm of international law, heretofore unrecognized by any American court or treaty obligation, on the basis of materials inadequate for the task. In deviating from our settled case law, the majority *identifies* no norm of customary international law, it creates a new norm out of whole cloth. Because the majority's analysis misconstrues—rather than vindicates—customary international law, I respectfully dissent....

The majority relies on eight sources of customary international law to support its determination that a norm against non-consensual medical experimentation on humans by private actors is universal and obligatory. However, this evidence falls far short of the quantum necessary to establish the existence of such a norm: (1) the International Covenant on Civil and Political Rights has been described by the Supreme Court as a "well-known international agreement[] that despite [its] moral authority, ha[s] little utility," in defining international obligations, *Sosa*, 542 U.S. at 734, and moreover, it does not apply to private actors, such as the Defendant in this action; (2) the Council of Europe's Convention on Human Rights and Biomedicine—a regional convention—[that] was not ratified by the most influential nations in the region, such as France, Germany, Italy, the Netherlands, Russia and the United Kingdom, and it was promulgated on April 4, 1997, one year *after* the conduct at issue in this litigation; (3) the UNESCO Universal Declaration of Bioethics and Human Rights of 2005 and (4) the European Parliament Clinical Trial Directive of 2001 both also post-date the relevant time period by several years; (5) the Declaration of Helsinki issued by the World Medical Association, a private entity, and (6) the International Ethical Guidelines for Research Involving Human Subjects promulgated by the Council for International Organizations for Medical Sciences, another private entity, [that] "express[] the sensibilities and the asserted aspirations and demands of some countries or organizations" but are not "statements of universally-recognized legal obligations," *Flores*, 414 F.3d at 262; (7) states' domestic laws, which, unsupported by express international accords, are not "significant or relevant for purposes of customary international law," *id.* at 249; and (8) the so-called Nuremberg Code, a statement of principles that accompanied a criminal verdict, possesses at best "subsidiary" value as a judicial decision, Statute of the International Court of Justice art. 38, June 26, 1945, 59 Stat. 1031, 33 U.N.T.S. 993 ("ICJ Statute"). Taken together, this evidence falls short of charting the existence of a universal and obligatory international norm actionable against non-government actors under the ATS....

For these reasons, I conclude that non-consensual medical experimentation by private actors, though deplorable, is not actionable under international law and would therefore affirm the district court's dismissal of Plaintiff's complaints.

QUESTIONS

1. Exactly what was the binding international custom found by the court in the *Abdullahi* case?
2. What sources did the majority rely on to find a customary international law binding in the U.S.?
3. Why did the dissenting judge disagree?

See note on *Jus Cogens* below, page 21.

Regional Custom

The Court has also accept the idea of regional custom, that is the idea that a practice among states within a particular area of the world can be sufficiently well established and accepted as law that it is binding among the states of that region but not elsewhere. In the *Asylum Case* (Columbia v. Peru) 1950 I.C.J. 266, the International Court of Justice stated:

> The Colombian government has finally invoked 'American international law in general'. In addition to the rules arising from agreements which have already been considered, it has relied on an alleged regional or local custom peculiar to Latin-American States. The Party which relies on a custom of this kind must

> prove that this custom is established in such a manner that it has become binding on the other Party.[9]

Ultimately, the Court determined that Colombia had failed to establish a regional custom because of "so much uncertainty and contradiction, so much fluctuation and discrepancy ... that it is not possible to discern in all this any constant and uniform usage, accepted as law...." Id. at 277.

Special or Local Custom

Where two states have engaged in a practice with respect to each other over a long period of time, the Court may also be willing to find that this practice meets the requirements of customary law and has become binding on the states concerned as a special custom. In the *Right of Passage Case* (Portugal v. India) 1960 I.C.J. 6, the Court stated:

> With regard to Portugal's claim ... on the basis of local custom, it is objected on behalf of India that no local custom could be established between only two States.... The Court sees no reason why long continued practice between two States accepted by them as regulating their relations should not form the basis of mutual rights and obligations.[10]

Jus Cogens

Although customary international law comes about by a consistent practice of states accepted as law, states are generally free to reject these rules by passing contrary laws. Such states are described as "persistent objectors" and they will not be bound by the custom. Are there, however, some customary rules which states are not free to reject? For some time, international law has accepted the notion of peremptory norms, or *jus cogens,* which bind all states, although there has been disagreement about which norms fall into this category. The Vienna Convention on the Law of Treaties, 1155 U.N.T.S. 331, article 53 provides: "a peremptory norm ... is a norm accepted and recognized by the international community of States as a whole as a norm from which no derogation is permitted...." Some candidates for *jus cogens* are: the prohibition on the use of force by one state against another; the prohibition against torture; the prohibition against racial discrimination; genocide; war crimes; crimes against humanity; slavery; and piracy.

The International Tribunal for the Former Yugoslavia explained the concept of *jus cogens* in the context of the prohibition on torture in *Prosecutor v. Furundzija,* Case No. 17-95-17/1-T, Judgment of the Trial Chamber, 10 Dec. 1998, at para. 153:

> "Because of the importance of the values it protects, [the prohibition of torture] ... has evolved into a peremptory norm or jus cogens, that is, a norm that enjoys a higher rank in the international hierarchy than treaty law and even 'ordinary' customary rules. The most conspicuous consequence of this higher rank is that the principle at issue cannot be derogated from by States through international treaties or local or special customs or even general customary rules not endowed with the same normative force." (Footnotes omitted).

---

9. 1950 I.C.J. 266, at 276.
10. 1960 I.C.J. 6, at 39.

Treaties

There has been a great deal of arcane debate over whether treaties simply create binding obligations between states which are parties to the particular treaty in question or whether a treaty itself can create obligations not just for the treaty partners but also for the international community as a whole and thus serve as a source of international law. Treaties most certainly do create obligations for states that choose to become parties to treaties. (In chapter III we shall study the law of treaties which has many analogies to the law of contracts found in national law.) Can treaties serve as a source of law for non-parties? The answer to this question is "yes", but most writers are then insistent that if a particular precept in a treaty is binding on non-parties it will be so because the precept itself has become part of customary law, so it will be the customary law (also expressed in the treaty), not the treaty as such, that will bind the non-parties. The process whereby treaties are expressive of pre-existing custom or where, over time, treaty concepts become binding customary norms has been expressly recognized by the International Court of Justice in the *North Sea Continental Shelf Cases*, see below. In the current era a great number of areas of international concern have been codified in multi-lateral treaties and often these treaties exert a powerful influence on the development of customary law and on national law. (See for example, The U.N. Law of the Sea Convention discussed in greater detail in chapter V.) Before WWII, treaties that were open to ratification by all states were a rarity. Treaties were more often signed by a limited number of states with similar interests. It was unlikely, therefore, that these treaties would give rise to the creation of a customary norm or were themselves expressive of existing universal norms. Since WWII, the number of treaties open for universal signature has proliferated. These treaties often combine large sections that are simply a codification of pre-existing customary law and sections that are new law for the treaty partners but which may rapidly come to express customary norms. This rapid progression towards a binding customary norm occurs because, where many states sign on to the treaty, other non-parties quickly recognize that the treaty provisions have become the way that the international community organizes itself on that particular matter.

North Sea Continental Shelf Cases

(Federal Republic of Germany v. Denmark)
(Federal Republic of Germany v. Netherlands)
International Court of Justice
1969 I.C.J. 3

Note

At the time of the Court's decision, Germany was still divided into two states, West Germany, here called The Federal Republic of Germany, and East Germany, known as The German Democratic Republic. East Germany was not involved in this case. West and East Germany were reunited in 1990. The Federal Republic of Germany is bordered to the north by Denmark and to the south by the Netherlands. The three countries all have coastlines on the North Sea and each country has a continental shelf projecting from its coast. Disputes broke out between Germany and both her neighbors concerning the method to be used to mark the boundary of each country's continental shelf. Denmark and the Netherlands wanted the Court to rule that the "equidistance principle" articulated in Article 6(2) of the 1958 Geneva Convention on the Continental Shelf was the correct method to be applied. The problem for Denmark and the Netherlands was that Germany was not a party to the 1958 Geneva Convention, so Denmark and the Netherlands argued that the method of delimiting continental shelves articulated in Article 6(2) was nevertheless expressive of customary law and therefore binding on Germany. The Court rejected the argument in this specific case for the reasons given below. Nonetheless, the Court made it quite clear that the premise of the argument, namely that treaty provisions could be a codification of existing customary law or might rapidly become expressive of a new customary norm, was entirely acceptable. The Court came to the conclusion that at the time the 1958 Geneva Convention was written it did not embody a pre-existing rule of customary law. The Court then went on to examine whether the rule expressed in Article 6(2) had since become a rule of customary law binding on Germany even though she was not a party to the Convention.

To understand the case you do not need to understand the precise dimensions of the "equidistance principle." Such precise knowledge is probably only understood by oceanographic cartographers. All you need to understand is that the principle is a method employed to delimit adjacent continental shelves.

Article 6, paragraph 2 states:

> 2. Where the same continental shelf is adjacent to the territories of two adjacent states, the boundary of the continental shelf shall be determined by agreement between them. In the absence of agreement, and unless another boundary line is justified by special circumstances, the boundary shall be determined by application of the principle of equidistance from the nearest points of the baseline from which the breadth of the territorial sea is measured.

Opinion of the Court

70. The Court must now proceed to the last stage in the argument put forward on behalf of Denmark and the Netherlands. This is to the effect that even if there was at the date of the Geneva Convention no rule of customary international law in favour of the equidistance principle, and no such rule was crystallized in Article 6 of the Convention, nevertheless such a rule has come into being since the Convention, partly because of its own impact, partly on the basis of subsequent State practice,—and that this rule, being now a rule of customary international law binding on all States, including therefore the Federal Republic, should be declared applicable to the delimitation of the boundaries between the Parties' respective continental shelf areas in the North Sea.

71. In so far as this contention is based on the view that Article 6 of the Convention has had the influence, and has produced the effect, described, it clearly involves treating that Article as a norm-creating provision which has constituted the foundation of, or has generated a rule which, while only conventional or contractual in its origin, has since passed into the general *corpus* of international law, and is now accepted as such by the *opinio juris,* so as to have become binding even for countries which have never, and do not, become parties to the Convention. There is no doubt

that this process is a perfectly possible one and does from time to time occur: it constitutes indeed one of the recognized methods by which new rules of customary international law may be formed. At the same time this result is not lightly to be regarded as having been attained.

72. It would in the first place be necessary that the provision concerned should, at all events potentially, be of a fundamentally norm-creating character such as could be regarded as forming the basis of a general rule of law. Considered *in abstracto* the equidistance principle might be said to fulfil this requirement. Yet in the particular form in which it is embodied in Article 6 of the Geneva Convention, and having regard to the relationship of that Article to other provisions of the Convention, this must be open to some doubt. In the first place, Article 6 is so framed as to put second the obligation to make use of the equidistance method, causing it to come after a primary obligation to effect delimitation by agreement. Such a primary obligation constitutes an unusual preface to what is claimed to be a potential general rule of law. Without attempting to enter into, still less pronounce upon any question of *jus cogens,* it is well understood that, in practice, rules of international law can, by agreement, be derogated from in particular cases, or as between particular parties,—but this is not normally the subject of any express provision, as it is in Article 6 of the Geneva Convention. Secondly the part played by the notion of special circumstances relative to the principle of equidistance as embodied in Article 6, and the very considerable, still unresolved controversies as to the exact meaning and scope of this notion, must raise further doubts as to the potential norm-creating character of the rule.

73. With respect to the other elements usually regarded as necessary before a conventional rule can be considered to have become a general rule of international law, it might be that, even without the passage of any considerable period of time, a very widespread and representative participation in the convention might suffice of itself, provided it included that of States whose interests were specially affected. In the present case however, the Court notes that, even if allowance is made for the existence of a number of States to whom participation in the Geneva Convention is not open, or which, by reason for instance of being land-locked States, would have no interest in becoming parties to it, the number of ratifications and accessions so far secured is, though respectable, hardly sufficient. That non-ratification may sometimes be due to factors other than active disapproval of the convention concerned can hardly constitute a basis on which positive acceptance of its principles can be implied: the reasons are speculative, but the facts remain.

74. As regards the time element, the Court notes that it is over ten years since the Convention was signed, but that it is even now less than five since it came into force in June 1964, and that when the present proceedings were brought it was less than three years, while less than one had elapsed at the time when the respective negotiations between the Federal Republic and the other two Parties for a complete delimitation broke down on the question of the application of the equidistance principle. Although the passage of only a short period of time is not necessarily, or of itself, a bar to the formation of a new rule of customary international law on the basis of what was originally a purely conventional rule, an indispensable requirement would be that within the period in question, short though it might be, State practice, including that of States whose interests are specially affected, should have been both extensive and virtually uniform in the sense of the provision invoked;—and should moreover have occurred in such a way as to show a general recognition that a rule of law or legal obligation is involved.

75. The Court must now consider whether State practice in the matter of continental shelf delimitation has, subsequent to the Geneva Convention, been of such a kind as to satisfy this requirement. Leaving aside cases, which, for various reasons, the Court does not consider to be reliable guides as precedents, such as delimitations affected between the present Parties themselves, or not relating to international boundaries, some fifteen cases have been cited in the course of the present proceedings, occurring mostly since the signature of the 1958 Geneva Convention, in which continental shelf boundaries have been delimited according to the equidistance principle—in the majority of the cases by agreement, in a few others unilaterally—or else the delimitation was foreshadowed but has not yet been carried out. Amongst these fifteen are the four North Sea delimitations United Kingdom/Norway-Denmark-Netherlands, and Norway/Denmark already mentioned in paragraph 4 of this Judgment. But even if these various cases constituted more than a very small proportion of those potentially calling for delimitation in the world as a whole, the Court would not think it necessary to enumerate or evaluate them separately, since there are, *a priori,* several grounds which deprive them of weight as precedents in the present context.

76. To begin with, over half the States concerned, whether acting unilaterally or conjointly, were or shortly became parties to the Geneva Convention, and were therefore presumably, so far as they were concerned, acting actually or potentially in the application of the Convention. From their action no inference could legitimately be drawn as to the existence of a rule of customary international law in favour of the equidistance principle. As regards those States, on the other hand, which were not, and have not become parties to the Convention, the basis of their action can only be problematical and must remain entirely speculative. Clearly, they were not applying the Convention. But from that no inference could justifiably be drawn that they believed themselves to be applying a mandatory rule of customary international law. There is not a shred of evidence that they did and, as has been seen (paragraphs 22 and 23), there is no lack of other reasons for using the equidistance method, so that acting, or agreeing to act in a certain way, does not of itself, demonstrate anything of a juridical nature.

77. The essential point in this connection—and it seems necessary to stress it—is that even if these instances of action by non-parties to the Convention were much more numerous than they in fact are, they would not, even in the aggregate, suffice in themselves to constitute the *opinio juris;*—for, in order to achieve this result, two conditions must be fulfilled. Not only must the acts concerned amount to settled practice, but they must also be such, or be carried out in such a way, as to be evidence of a belief that this practice is rendered obligatory by the existence of a rule of law requiring it. The need for such a belief, i.e., the existence of a subjective element, is implicit in the very notion of the *opinio juris sive necessitatis.* The States concerned must therefore feel that they are conforming to what amounts to a legal obligation. The frequency, or even habitual character of the acts is not in itself enough. There are many international acts, i.e., in the field of ceremonial and protocol, which are performed almost invariably, but which are motivated only by consideration of courtesy, convenience or tradition, and not by any sense of legal duty.

78. [T]he position is simply that in certain cases—not a great number—the States concerned agreed to draw or did draw the boundaries concerned according to the principle of equidistance. There is no evidence that they so acted because they felt legally compelled to draw them in this way by reason of a rule of customary law obliging them to do so—especially considering that they might have been motivated by other obvious factors.

79. Finally, it appears that in almost all of the cases cited, the delimitations concerned were median-line delimitations between opposite States, not lateral delimitations between adjacent States. For reasons which have already been given (paragraph 57) the Court regards the case of median-line delimitations between opposite states as different in various respects, and as being sufficiently distinct not to constitute a precedent for the delimitation of lateral boundaries. In only one situation discussed by the Parties does there appear to have been a geographical configuration which to some extent resembles the present one, in the sense that a number of States on the same coastline are grouped around a sharp curve or bend of it. No complete delimitation in this area has however yet been carried out. But the Court is not concerned to deny to this case, or any other of those cited, all evidential value in favour of the thesis of Denmark and the Netherlands. It simply considers that they are inconclusive, and insufficient to bear the weight sought to be put upon them as evidence of such a settled practice, manifested in such circumstances, as would justify the inference that delimitation according to the principle of equidistance amounts to a mandatory rule of customary international law,—more particularly where lateral delimitations are concerned.

81. The Court accordingly concludes that if the Geneva Convention was not in its origins or inception declaratory of a mandatory rule of customary international law enjoining the use of the equidistance principle for the delimitation of continental self areas between adjacent States, neither has its subsequent effect been constitutive of such a rule; and that State practice up-to-date has equally been insufficient for the purpose.

QUESTIONS

1. Why did the Court not accept the argument made by Denmark and the Netherlands that the equidistance principle, as articulated in Article 6(2) of the 1958 Geneva Convention on the Continental Shelf, had become a rule of customary law?
2. What do you understand the term "*opinio juris*" to mean?
3. How much state practice would satisfy the Court that the practice had become a customary rule?

Note

For further materials on the continental shelf see chapter V.

General Principles of Law

The International Court of Justice, which is the judicial arm of the United Nations, operates under provisions in the U.N. Charter and its own statute which is annexed to the Charter. Article 38 of the Court's statute lists the sources of law upon which the Court may rely when it is deciding cases that come before it. Article 38 states that the Court is to apply:

a) international conventions, whether general or particular, establishing rules expressly recognized by the contesting states;

b) international custom, as evidence of a general practice accepted as law;

c) the general principles of law recognized by civilized nations;

d) subject to the provisions of Article 59, judicial decisions and the teachings of the most highly qualified publicists of the various nations, as subsidiary means for the determination of rules of law.

Although this article governs a particular international court it has been widely regarded as an authoritative statement on the sources of international law. The article does not purport to indicate which of the listed sources should be resorted to first but most writers assume that the order in the article was meant to indicate a hierarchy of sources. If that is the case, then "general principles" will only come into play in the absence of a treaty or custom on a particular point.[11] The term "recognized by civilized nations" has a paternalistic air to it and was obviously a product of the colonial era during which the Charter and statute were drafted. Nowadays we tend to refer to general principles recognized by developed legal systems. What are these "general principles"? Nothing too startling. Occasionally an international court will find that it needs to resort to a legal precept found in national legal systems but never before used in an international court. Allowing international judges to rely on concepts common to the major national legal systems means that where there is a gap in international law the judges have some ability to fill it rather than simply announcing that the case cannot be decided because no international law currently exists on the topic. Examples of reliance on "general principles" have generally came from procedural or administrative areas of the law or notions of general legal liability. In the *Chórzow Factory Case*,[12] the Permanent Court of International Justice[13] stated that "a party cannot take advantage of his own wrong" and that "every violation of an engagement involves an obligation to make reparation." Some international tribunals have applied the concept of limitation (i.e. a claim is barred because too much time has passed between the alleged wrong doing and the presentation of the claim.)[14] The International Court of Justice has also used the principle of estoppel to bar a claim.[15] None of the above principles comes as a surprise to any one versed in even a smattering of law, but allowing international courts to resort to these general principles has proved useful in a system that operates without a legislative system that might otherwise be relied on to fill in legal gaps. Sometimes an international court will also refer to equity or fairness as guiding its decision either to find an international obligation or to refuse to do so.[16] Some writers maintain that equity is not as such a source of law but rather simply influences the way the court applies the law.

Judicial Decisions

It was noted earlier that at least for the International Court of Justice, its decisions are only binding on the parties before it in respect of the particular case.[17] One might expect

11. Article 59 of the Statute of the International Court of Justice states: "The decision of the Court has no binding force except between the parties and in respect of the particular case". In practice the Court either follows the rules laid down in similar cases or seeks to distinguish the case before it from previous cases.

12. P.C. I. J., Ser. A, No. 9, p. 31 (1927).

13. The Permanent Court was the judicial arm of the League of Nations. When the League was disbanded, the Permanent Court ceased to exist but the Statute of the International Court of Justice is based upon the Statute of the Permanent Court.

14. *Italy* (Gentini) *v. Venezuela*, Mixed Claims Commission, 1903 (Ralston, Venezuelan Arbitrations of 1903 at 720 (1904)).

15. *Temple Case* (Cambodia v. Thailand) 1962 I.C.J. 6, at 33.

16. *North Sea Continental Shelf Cases*, 1969 I.C.J. 3, at paras. 88ff.

17. See art. 59 of the Statute of the I.C.J., supra note 11.

therefore that the Court would approach each case on a clean slate regardless of whether the issues raised were similar to ones presented in an earlier case. Nothing could be further from the truth. In fact, if a case raises issues discussed in a previous case, the Court is often at pains to explain either why the issue will be resolved in the same way or why it should be distinguished. This approach makes sense as the Court obviously does not invent new law for each case before it. Why then was article 59 drafted as it was? The answer has at least two facets. Firstly, the drafters of article 59 were convinced that cases that arise between states are, to some extent, unique. It is true they are not like the everyday automobile accident that bears the characteristics of thousands of other similar accidents, but, taking an historical perspective, inter-state disputes often, in fact, share common characteristics. Secondly, it was well known that in the common-law legal systems precedent is relied upon rather more heavily than in civil law systems. The civil law countries did not want the International Court taking off down the common-law precedential road. As a result the Court does not apply the rule of *stare decisis*. Nonetheless, international judicial decisions often influence future decisions and the International Court often cites earlier cases.[18]

Writers and Scholars

National judicial decisions are often replete with long strings of citations to the works of eminent legal writers. This has been particularly so in recent decades in the developed world in part because of the advent of the law clerk or judge's assistant and in part because of the availability of sophisticated electronic data retrieval systems. International decisions refer to authors' works much less frequently. This may be due in part to the comparative dearth of law clerks in the international arena but is much more probably due to the judges' fears of being perceived as relying too heavily on authors from one particular country or one particular legal system. If the American judge on the International Court of Justice started authoring opinions peppered with citations only to American scholars, fellow judges might not be willing to join his opinions and he would rapidly get the reputation of deciding cases according to American notions rather than international norms. International judges have therefore often, been more sparing in their citations to scholars' works,[19] but this does not mean that international judges do not read scholars and other writers works nor does it mean they are not influenced by this body of work. National courts often rely on international scholars to support their determination of international law as two of the previous cases amply demonstrate.[20]

Concluding Remarks

In this section, most of the international law making process examined has been generated by states but, of course, with the very rapid expansion of the movement of goods,

18. See cases cited in 3 Shabtai Rosenne, The Law and Practice of the International Court, 1920–1996 at 1609–1615 (3d ed. 1997).

19. For an opinion of the International Court of Justice where the Court, the separate opinions and the dissenters cited extensively from a variety of sources including writers and scholars, see, *Legality of the Threat or Use of Nuclear Weapons*, 1996 I.C.J. 226 (Advisory Opinion of July 8), reprinted at 35 I.L.M. 1343 (1996).

20. See, *The Paquete Habana*, *supra* pages 5–10 and *Abdullahi v. Pfizer, Inc.*, *supra* pages 12–20.

services and people since the middle of the twentieth century, a whole host of international entities have grown up, or expanded, to deal with everything from postal services, air and sea travel, health standards, environmental standards, transfer of currencies and many other topics. All of the international structures established to regulate these fields, and many more, also contribute to the creation of international law. The United Nations remains the pre-eminent international governmental organization and its many organs and subsidiary organs have created a great web of international law. The U.N. Security Council can issue binding resolutions on all member states[21] and, in recent years, it has begun to use these powers almost like a super-legislature on an ever increasing variety of topics.

All of the methods of creating international law outlined in this chapter are at work within the rapidly expanding number of international regulatory systems to produce a highly dynamic system of international law creation.

Suggested Further Readings

Ian Brownlie, Principles of Public International Law, chapter 1 (7th ed. 2008).

D.J. Harris, Cases and Materials on International Law, chapters 1 & 2 (6th ed. 2004).

Sean D. Murphy, Principles of International Law, chapter 3 (2006).

Malcolm N. Shaw, International Law, chapter 3 (6th ed. 2008).

Rebecca M. M. Wallace, International Law, chapter 3 (5th ed. 2005).

21. U.N. Charter, art. 25.

Chapter II

Title to Territory

Modern national systems of law have a method for recording title to territory in some official register. Buyers of property receive a title which furnishes proof of ownership. Unfortunately there is no such system operative in the international arena and disputes over title to territory are frequent and often give rise to devastating wars. Some of the international rules concerning title to territory may seem antiquated and to hark back to the time when intrepid discoverers roamed the globe in search of lands that they could claim for their sovereign. While some of the cases definitely have an ancient ring to them, it is well to remember that without a thorough understanding of the international rules used to determine title to territory it will often be impossible to determine whether one side or the other (or both) has violated international law when conflicts erupt over territorial disputes.

Terra Nullius

If land is occupied by no one and not claimed by any state, no state owns the territory and it is said to be *terra nullius.* Such land is open to an ownership claim. In previous centuries powerful states sent out envoys to discover areas of the globe and claim them for the sending sovereign. Often the areas claimed would in fact be inhabited by tribes or groups of native peoples. The inhabitants would be subjugated and frequently forced to sign treaties of cession or required to acknowledge the sovereignty of the foreign intruder. This process represented the age old example of more technologically advanced people subjecting less technologically advanced people to their rule. The general name for this process was colonialism. The United Nations has spoken out against colonialism in recent decades and now international law prohibits "[t]he subjection of peoples to alien subjugation, domination and exploitation...." Declaration on the Granting of Independence to Colonial Territories and Peoples, G.A. Res. 1514 (XV) Dec.14, 1960, G.A. O.R., 15th Sess., Supp. 16, p.66. That same declaration asserts that "[a]ll peoples have the right to self-determination; by virtue of that right they freely determine their political status...." Since the 1960's virtually all of the former colonies of the few remaining empires have achieved independence though a few territories remain in a dependent status.

If an unoccupied territory was discovered, or in earlier centuries an occupied territory became subject to foreign domination, how did the discoverer or dominator acquire title to the territory?

Discovery

From the fifteenth century onwards many of the great empires sent envoys on long voyages to discover new lands and claim them for their sovereigns. The mere fact of finding an island or an unoccupied area of land was apparently never considered sufficient to establish sovereignty. It seems that some sort of ceremony claiming sovereignty over the territory in the name of a particular sovereign was necessary to establish a claim to title to the territory. Such a claim "was deemed good against all subsequent claims set up in opposition thereto unless, perhaps, transferred by conquest or treaty, relinquished, abandoned, or successfully opposed by continued occupation on the part of some other state."[1] Arbitrator Huber discussing Spain's claim to title through discovery of the Island of Palmas states: "The title of discovery ... would, under the most favorable and most extensive interpretation, exist only as an inchoate title, as a claim to establish sovereignty by effective occupation. An inchoate title however cannot prevail over a definite title founded on continuous and peaceful display of sovereignty."[2]

Occupation

If unoccupied territory was claimed by a state and occupied by that state then the occupation operated to confer title on the claimant. But what if the territory was inhabited by tribes of indigenous peoples? The International Court of Justice has stated that: "territories inhabited by tribes or peoples having a social and political organization were not regarded as *terra nullius*."[3] Technically then territory that was already inhabited by people (I have never heard of people, apart from reclusive hermits, living without social and political organizations) was not subject to occupation since a requirement of title through occupation was that the area be *terra nullius*. If settlement by the intruder occurred in such inhabited areas, title could only be acquired by treaties of cession or conquest.

Island of Palmas (Miangas) Case

Netherlands v. United States
Permanent Court of Arbitration (1928)
Sole Arbitrator: Max Huber
2 U.N. Rep. Int'l Arbitral Awards 829

By an agreement between the Netherlands and the U.S. (Jan. 23rd 1925) it was agreed that: "The sole duty of the Arbitrator shall be to determine whether the Island of Palmas (or Miangas) in its entirety forms a part of territory belonging to the United States of America or of Netherlands territory."

---

1. Arthur Keller et al., Creation of Rights of Sovereignty through Symbolic Acts 1400–1800, 148–149 (1938) (reprinted 1974).
2. *Island of Palmas Case*, (Neth. v. U.S.) 2 R.I.A.A. 829 (1928).
3. *Western Sahara Case*, 1975 I.C.J. 12, at 39 (Oct. 16).

Award of the Arbitrator

The *subject of the dispute* is the sovereignty over the Island of Palmas (or Miangas). [P]almas (or Miangas) is a single, isolated island, not one of several islands clustered together. It lies about half way between Cape San Augustin (Mindanao, Philippine Islands) and the most northerly island of the Nanusa (Nanoesa) group (Netherlands East Indies).

Before 1906 no dispute had arisen between the United States or Spain, on the one hand, and the Netherlands, on the other, in regard specifically to the Island of Palmas (or Miangas), on the ground that these powers put forward conflicting claims to sovereignty over the said island.

The two Parties claim the island in question as a territory attached for a very long period to territories relatively close at hand which are incontestably under the sovereignty of the one or the other of them.

The *United States*, as successor to the rights of Spain over the Philippines, bases its title in the first place on discovery. The existence of sovereignty thus acquired is, in the American view, confirmed not merely by the most reliable cartographers and authors, but also by treaty, in particular by the Treaty of Munster, of 1648, to which Spain and the Netherlands are themselves Contracting Parties. As, according to the same argument, nothing has occurred of a nature, in international law, to cause the acquired title to disappear, this latter title was intact at the moment when, by the Treaty of December 10th, 1898, Spain ceded the Philippines to the United States. In these circumstances, it is, in the American view, unnecessary to establish facts showing the actual display of sovereignty precisely over the Island of Palmas (or Miangas). The United States Government finally maintains that Palmas (or Miangas) forms a geographical part of the Philippine group and in virtue of the principle of contiguity belongs to the Power having the sovereignty over the Philippines.

According to the Netherlands Government, on the other hand, the fact of discovery by Spain is not proved, nor yet any other form of acquisition, and even if Spain had at any moment a title, such title had been lost. The principle of contiguity is contested.

The Netherlands Government's main argument endeavors to show that the Netherlands, represented for this purpose in the first period of colonization by the East India Company, have possessed and exercised rights of sovereignty from 1677, or probably from a date prior even to 1648, to the present day. This sovereignty arose out of conventions entered into with native princes of the Island of Sangi (the main island of Talautse (Sangi) Isles), establishing the suzerainty of the Netherlands over the territories of these princes, including Palmas (or Miangas). The state of affairs thus set up is claimed to be validated by international treaties.

The facts alleged in support of the Netherlands arguments are, in the United States Government's view, not proved, and even if they were proved, they would not create a title of sovereignty, or would not concern the Island of Palmas.

In the first place the Arbitrator deems it necessary to make some general remarks on *sovereignty in its relation to territory.*

Sovereignty in the relations between States signifies independence. Independence in regard to a portion of the globe is the right to exercise therein, to the exclusion of any other State, the functions of a State. The development of the national organization of States during the last few centuries and, as a corollary, the development of international law, have established this principle of the exclusive competence of the State in regard to its own territory in such a way as to make it the point of departure in settling most questions that concern international relations.

If a dispute arises as to the sovereignty over a portion of territory, it is customary to examine which of the States claiming sovereignty possesses a title—cession, conquest, occupation, etc.—superior to that which the other State might possibly bring forward against it. However, if the contestation is based on the fact that the other Party has actually displayed sovereignty, it cannot be sufficient to establish the title by which territorial sovereignty was validly acquired at a certain moment; it must also be shown that the territorial sovereignty has continued to exist and did exist at the moment which for the decision of the dispute must be considered as critical. This demonstration consists in the actual display of State activities, such as belongs only to the territorial sovereign.

Titles of acquisition of territorial sovereignty in present-day international law are either based on an act of effective apprehension, such as occupation or conquest, or, like cession, presuppose the ceding and the cessionary Powers or at least one of them, have the faculty of effectively disposing of the ceded territory.... It seems therefore natural that an element which is essential for the constitution of sovereignty should not be lacking in its continuation. So true is this, that practice, as well as doctrine, recognizes ... that the continuous and peaceful display of territorial sovereignty (peaceful in relation to other States) is as good as a title. The growing insistence with which international law, ever since the middle of the 18th century, has demanded that the occupation shall be effective would be inconceivable, if effectiveness were required only for the act of acquisition and not equally for the maintenance of the right. If the effectiveness has above all been insisted on in regard to occupation, this is because the question rarely arises in connection with territories in which there is already an established order of things.

Territorial sovereignty, as has already been said, involves the exclusive right to display the activities of a State. This right has a corollary, a duty: the obligation to protect within the territory the rights of other States, in particular their right to integrity and inviolability in peace and in war, together with the rights which each State may claim for its nationals in foreign territory. Without manifesting its territorial sovereignty in a manner corresponding to circumstances, the State cannot fulfil this duty. Territorial sovereignty cannot limit itself to its negative side, i.e. to excluding the activities of other States....

The principle that continuous and peaceful display of the functions of State within a given region is a constituent element of territorial sovereignty is not only based on the conditions of the formation of independent States and their boundaries (as shown by the experience of political history) ... [but also] on an international jurisprudence and doctrine widely accepted....

Manifestations of territorial sovereignty assume, it is true, different forms, according to conditions of time and place. Although continuous in principle, sovereignty cannot be exercised in fact at every moment on every point of a territory. The intermittence and discontinuity compatible with the maintenance of the right necessarily differ according as inhabited or uninhabited regions are involved, or regions enclosed within territories in which sovereignty is incontestably displayed or again regions accessible from, for instance, the high seas.

The *title alleged by the United States of America* as constituting the immediate foundation of its claim is that of *cession,* brought about by the Treaty of Paris, which cession transferred all rights of sovereignty which Spain may have possessed in the region indicated in Article III of the said Treaty and therefore also those concerning the Island of Palmas (or Miangas).

It is evident that Spain could not transfer more rights than she herself possessed.

Whilst there existed a divergence of views as to the extension of the cession to certain Spanish islands outside the treaty limits, it would seem that the cessionary Power never envisaged that the cession, in spite of the sweeping terms of Article III, should comprise territories on which Spain had not a valid title, though falling within the limits traced by the Treaty.

As pointed out above, the United States bases its claim, as successor of Spain, in the first place on *discovery.* In this connection a distinction must be made between the discovery of the Island of Palmas (or Miangas) as such, or as a part of the Philippines, which, beyond doubt, were discovered and even occupied and colonized by the Spaniards. This latter point, however, will be considered with the argument relating to contiguity; the problem of discovery is considered only in relation to the island itself which forms the subject of the dispute.

The documents supplied to the Arbitrator with regard to the discovery of the island in question consist in the first place of a communication made by the Spanish Government to the United States Government as to researches in the archives concerning expeditions and discoveries in the Moluccas, the "Talaos" Islands, the Palos Islands and the Marianes.

The above mentioned communication of the Spanish Government does not give any details as to the date of the expedition, the navigators or the circumstances in which the observations were made; it is not supported by extracts from the original reports on which it is based, nor accompanied by reproductions of the maps therein mentioned.

In any case for the purpose of the present affair it may be admitted that the original title derived from discovery belonged to Spain....

The fact that the island was originally called, not, as customarily, by a native name, but by a name borrowed from a European language, and referring to the vegetation, serves perhaps to show that no landing was made or that the island was uninhabited at the time of discovery. Indeed, the reports on record which concern the discovery of the Island of Palmas state only that an island was "seen", which island, according to the geographical data, is probably identical with that in dispute. No mention is made of landing or of contact with the natives. And in any case no signs of taking possession or of administration by Spain have been shown or even alleged to exist until the very recent date to which the reports of Captain Malone and M. Alvarez, of 1919, contained in the United States Memorandum, relate.

It is admitted by both sides that international law underwent profound modifications between the end of the Middle-Ages and the end of the 19th century, as regards the rights of discovery and acquisition of uninhabited regions or regions inhabited by savages or semicivilized peoples. Both Parties are also agreed that a juridical fact must be appreciated in the light of the law contemporary with it, and not of the law in force at the time when a dispute in regard to it rises or falls to be settled. The effect of discovery by Spain is therefore to be determined by the rules of international law in force in the first half of the 16th century—or (to take the earliest date) in the first quarter of it, i.e., at the time when the Portuguese or Spaniards made their appearance in the Sea of Celebes.

If the view most favorable to the American arguments is adopted—with every reservation as to the soundness of such view—that is to say, if we consider as positive law at the period in question the rule that discovery as such, i.e. the mere fact of seeing land, without any act, even symbolical, of taking possession, involved *ipso jure* territorial sovereignty and not merely an "inchoate title", a *jus ad rem,* to be completed eventually by an actual and durable taking of possession within a reasonable time, the question arises whether sovereignty yet existed at the critical date, i.e. the moment of conclusion and coming into force of the Treaty of Paris.

As regards the question which of different legal systems prevailing at successive periods is to be applied in a particular case (the so-called intertemporal law), a distinction must be made between the creation of rights and the existence of rights. The same principle which subjects the act creative of a right to the law in force at the time the right arises, demands that the existence of the right, in other words its continued manifestation, shall follow the conditions required by the evolution of law. International law in the 19th century, having regard to the fact that most parts of the globe were under the sovereignty of states members of the community of nations, and that territories without a master had become relatively few, took account of a tendency already existing and especially developed since the middle of the 18th century, and laid down the principle that occupation, to constitute a claim to territorial sovereignty, must be effective, that is, offer certain guarantees to other States and their nationals. It seems therefore incompatible with this rule of positive law that there should be regions which are neither under the effective sovereignty of a State, nor without a master, but which are reserved for the exclusive influence of one State, in virtue solely of a title of acquisition which is no longer recognized by existing law, even if such a title ever conferred territorial sovereignty. For these reasons, discovery alone, without any subsequent act, cannot at the present time suffice to prove sovereignty over the Island of Palmas (or Miangas); and in so far as there is no sovereignty, the question of an abandonment properly speaking of sovereignty by one State in order that the sovereignty of another may take its place does not arise.

If on the other hand the view is adopted that discovery does not create a definitive title of sovereignty, but only an "inchoate" title, such a title exists, it is true, without external manifestation. However, according to the view that has prevailed at any rate since the 19th century, an inchoate title of discovery must be completed within a reasonable period by the effective occupation of the region claimed to be discovered. This principle must be applied in the present case, for the reasons given above in regard to the rules determining which of successive legal systems is to be applied (the so-called intertemporal law). Now, no act of occupation nor, except as to a recent period, any exercise of sovereignty at Palmas by Spain has been alleged. But even admitting that the Spanish title still existed as inchoate in 1898 and must be considered as included in the cession under Article III of the Treaty of Paris, an inchoate title could not prevail over the continuous and peaceful display of authority by another State; for such display may prevail even over a prior, definitive title put forward by another State. This point will be considered, when the Netherlands argument has been examined and the allegations of either Party as to the display of their authority can be compared.

As it is not proved that Spain, at the beginning of 1648 or in June 1714, was in possession of the Island of Palmas (or Miangas), there is no proof that Spain acquired by the Treaty of Munster or the Treaty of Utrecht a title to sovereignty over the island which, in accordance with the said Treaties, and as long as they hold good, could have been modified by the Netherlands only in agreement with Spain.

It is, therefore, unnecessary to consider whether subsequently Spain by any express or conclusive action, abandoned the right, which the said Treaties may have conferred upon her in regard to Palmas (or Miangas). Moreover even if she had acquired a title she never intended to abandon, it would remain to be seen whether continuous and peaceful display of sovereignty by any other Power at a later period might not have superseded even conventional rights.

It appears further to be evident that Treaties concluded by Spain with third Powers recognizing her sovereignty over the "Philippines" could not be binding upon the Netherlands and as such Treaties do not mention the island in dispute, they are not available even as indirect evidence.

We thus come back to the question whether, failing any Treaty which, as between the States concerned, decides unequivocally what is the situation as regards the island, the existence of territorial sovereignty is established with sufficient soundness by other facts.

Although the United States Government does not take up the position that Spanish sovereignty must be recognized because it was actually exercised, the American Counter-Case none the less states that "there is at least some evidence of Spanish activities in the Island". In these circumstances it is necessary to consider *whether and to what extent the territorial sovereignty of Spain was manifested* in or in regard to the Island of Palmas (or Miangas).

Apart from the facts already referred to concerning the period of discovery, ... the documents laid before the Arbitration contain no trace of Spanish activities of any kind specifically on the Island of Palmas.

Neither is there any official document mentioning the Island of Palmas as belonging to an administrative or judicial district of the former Spanish government in the Philippines.

In the last place there remains to be considered *title arising out of contiguity.* Although States have in certain circumstances maintained that islands relatively close to their shores belonged to them in virtue of their geographical situation, it is impossible to show the existence of a rule of positive international law to the effect that islands situated outside territorial waters should belong to a State from the mere fact that its territory forms the *terra firma* (nearest continent or island of considerable size).

Nor is this principle of contiguity admissible as a legal method of deciding questions of territorial sovereignty; for it is wholly lacking in precision and would in its application lead to arbitrary results. This would be especially true in a case such as that of the island in question, which is not relatively close to one single continent, but forms part of a large archipelago in which strict delimitations between the different parts are not naturally obvious.

There lies, however, at the root of the idea of contiguity one point which must be considered also in regard to the Island of Palmas (or Miangas). It has been explained above that in the exercise of territorial sovereignty there are necessarily gaps, intermittence in time and discontinuity in space. This phenomenon will be particularly noticeable in the case of colonial territories, partly uninhabited or as yet partly unsubdued. The fact that a State cannot prove display of sovereignty as regards such a portion of territory cannot forthwith be interpreted as showing that sovereignty is inexistent. Each case must be appreciated in accordance with the particular circumstances.

As regards the territory forming the subject of the present dispute, it must be remembered that it is a somewhat isolated island, and therefore a territory clearly delimited and individualized. It is moreover an island permanently inhabited, occupied by a population sufficiently numerous for it to be impossible that acts of administration could be lacking for very long periods. The memoranda of both Parties assert that there is communication by boat and even with native craft between the Island of Palmas (or Miangas) and neighboring regions. The inability in such a case to indicate any acts of public administration makes it difficult to imagine the actual display of sovereignty, even if the sovereignty be regarded as confined within such narrow limits as would be supposed for a small island inhabited exclusively by natives.

The *Netherlands' arguments* contend that the East India Company established Dutch sovereignty over the Island of Palmas (or Miangas) as early as the 17th century, by means of conventions with the princes of Tabukan (Taboekan) and Taruna (Taroena), two native chieftains of the Island of Sangi (Groot Sangihe), the principal Island of the Talautse Isles (Sangi Islands), and that sovereignty has been displayed during the past two centuries.

Even the oldest contract, dated 1677, contains clauses binding the vassal of the East India Company to refuse to admit the nationals of other States, in particular Spain, into his territories, and to tolerate no religion other than protestantism, reformed according to the doctrine of the Synod of Dordrecht. Similar provisions are to be found in the other contracts of the 17th and 18th centuries. If both Spain and the Netherlands had in reality displayed their sovereignty over Palmas (or Miangas), it would seem that, during so long a period, collisions between the two Powers must almost inevitably have occurred.

The questions to be solved in the present case are the following:

Was the island of Palmas (or Miangas) in 1898 a part of the territory under Netherlands' sovereignty?

Did this sovereignty actually exist in 1898 *in regard to Palmas (or Miangas) and are the facts proved which were alleged on this subject?*

If the claim to sovereignty is based on the continuous and peaceful display of State authority, the fact of such display must be shown precisely in relation to the disputed territory. It is not necessary that there should be a special administration established in this territory; but it cannot suffice for the territory to be attached to another by a legal relation which is not recognized in international law as valid against a State contesting this claim to sovereignty; what is essential in such a case is the continuous and peaceful display of actual power in the contested region.

The acts of the *East India Company* . . . in view of occupying or colonizing the regions at issue in the present affair must, in international law, be entirely assimilated to acts of the Netherlands State itself.

[The] documentary evidence, taken together with the fact that no island called Miangas or bearing a similar name other than Palmas (or Miangas) seems to exist north of the Talautse (Sangi) and Talauer Isles, leads to the conclusion that the island Palmas (or Miangas) was in the early part of the 18th century considered by the Dutch East India Company as a part of their vassal State of Tabukan. This is the more probable for the reason that in later times, notably in an official report of 1825 the "far distant island Melangis" is mentioned again as belonging to Tabukan.

There is a considerable gap in the documentary evidence laid before the Tribunal by the Netherlands Government, as far as concerns not the vassal State of Tabukan in general, but Palmas (or Miangas) in particular. There is however no reason to suppose, when the Resident van Delden, in a report of 1825, mentioned the island "Melangis" as belonging to Tabukan, that these relations has not existed between 1726 and 1825.

It would however seem that before 1895 the direct relations between the island and the colonial administration were very loose. The documents relating to the time before 1895 are indeed scanty, but they are not entirely lacking. The most important fact is however the existence of documentary evidence as to the taxation of the people of Miangas by the Dutch authorities. Whilst in earlier times the tribute was paid in mats, rice and other objects, it was, in conformity with the contract with Taruna of 1885, replaced by a capitation, to be paid in money (one florin for each native man above 18 years). A table has been produced by the Netherlands Government which contains for all the dependencies of the Sangi States situated in the Talauer Islands the number of taxpayers and the amount to be paid. There "Menagasa" ranks as a part of the "Djoegoeschap" (Presidency) of the Nanusa under the dependencies of Taruna, with 88 "Hassiplichtigen" (taxpayers), paying each Fl. 1

The conclusions to be derived from the above examination of the arguments of the Parties are the following:

The claim of the United States to sovereignty over the Island of Palmas (or Miangas) is derived from Spain by way of cession under the Treaty of Paris. The latter Treaty, though it comprises the island in dispute within the limits of cession, and in spite of the absence of any reserves or protest by the Netherlands as to these limits, has not created in favour of the United States any title of sovereignty such as was not already vested in Spain. The essential point is therefore to decide whether Spain had sovereignty over Palmas (or Miangas) at the time of the coming into force of the Treaty of Paris.

The United States base their claim on the titles of discovery, of recognition by treaty and of contiguity, i.e. titles relating to acts or circumstances leading to the acquisition of sovereignty; they have however not established the fact that sovereignty so acquired was effectively displayed at any time.

The Netherlands on the contrary found their claim to sovereignty essentially on the title of peaceful and continuous display of State authority over the island. Since this title would in international law prevail over a title of acquisition of sovereignty not followed by actual display of State authority, it is necessary to ascertain in the first place, whether the contention of the Netherlands is sufficiently established by evidence, and if so, for what period of time.

The acts of indirect or direct display of Netherlands sovereignty at Palmas (or Miangas), especially in the 18th and early 19th centuries are not numerous, and there are considerable gaps in the evidence of continuous display. But apart from the consideration that the manifestations of sovereignty over a small and distant island, inhabited only by natives, cannot be expected to be frequent, it is not necessary that the display of sovereignty should go back to a very far distant period. It may suffice that such display existed in 1898, and had already existed as continuous and peaceful before that date long enough to enable any Power who might have considered herself as possessing sovereignty over the island, or having a claim to sovereignty, to have, according to local conditions, a reasonable possibility for ascertaining the existence of a state of things contrary to her real or alleged rights.

It is not necessary that the display of sovereignty should be established as having begun at a precise epoch; it suffices that it had existed at the critical period preceding the year 1898. It is quite natural that the establishment of sovereignty may be the outcome of a slow evolution, of a progressive intensification of State control. This is particularly the case, if sovereignty is acquired by the establishment of the suzerainty of a colonial Power over a native State, and in regard to outlying possessions of such a vassal State.

Now the evidence relating to the period after the middle of the 19th century makes it clear that the Netherlands Indian Government considered the island distinctly as a part of its possessions and that, in the years immediately preceding 1898, an intensification of display of sovereignty took place.

Since the moment when the Spaniards, in withdrawing from the Moluccas in 1666, made express reservations as to the maintenance of their sovereign rights, up to the contestation made by the United States in 1906, no contestation or other action whatever or protest against the exercise of territorial rights by the Netherlands over the Talautse (Sangi) Isles and their dependencies (Miangas included) has been recorded. The peaceful character of the display of Netherlands sovereignty for the entire period to which the evidence concerning acts of display relates (1700–1906) must be admitted.

As to the conditions of acquisition of sovereignty by way of continuous and peaceful display of State authority (so-called prescription), some of which have been discussed in the United States Counter-Memorandum, the following must be said:

The display has been open and public, that is to say that it was in conformity with usages as to exercise of sovereignty over colonial States.

There can further be no doubt that the Netherlands exercised the State authority over the Sangi States as sovereign in their own right, not under a derived or precarious title.

The conditions of acquisition of sovereignty by the Netherlands are therefore to be considered as fulfilled. It remains now to be seen whether the United States as successors of Spain are in a position to bring forward an equivalent or stronger title. This is to be answered in the negative.

The title of discovery ... would ... exist only as an inchoate title, as a claim to establish sovereignty by effective occupation. An inchoate title however cannot prevail over a definite title founded on continuous and peaceful display of sovereignty.

The title of contiguity, understood as a basis of territorial sovereignty, has no foundation in international law.

The Netherlands title of sovereignty, acquired by continuous and peaceful display of State authority during a long period of time going probably back beyond the year 1700, therefore holds good.

For these reasons the Arbitrator, ... decides that: The Island of Palmas (or Miangas) forms in its entirety a part of Netherlands territory.

QUESTIONS

1. What type of acts made the Dutch occupation of the Island of Palmas sufficient to demonstrate sovereignty?
2. What does Arbitrator Huber mean by the critical date?
3. What is meant by the application of intertemporal law?
4. Why was the U.S. claim not successful?

Case Concerning Sovereignty over Pedra Branca/Pulau Batu Puteh, Middle Rocks and South Ledge (Malaysia v. Singapore)

International Court of Justice
2008 I.C.J. ___

Note

This case concerns a sovereignty dispute over a small island, a cluster of small rocks, and another rock that is only visible at low-tide. The case is exhaustive (not to say exhausting) in its details of history, treaties, correspondence and conduct of the parties relating to the disputed areas. The excerpt below only relates to the island and largely presents the conclusions of the Court in order to demonstrate that even good title can be lost.

THE COURT, ...

delivers the following Judgment:

1. By joint letter dated 24 July 2003, filed in the Registry of the Court on the same day, the Ministers for Foreign Affairs of Malaysia and the Republic of Singapore (hereinafter "Singapore") notified to the Registrar a Special Agreement between the two States,....

2. The text of the Special Agreement reads as follows:

> "The Government of Malaysia and the Government of the Republic of Sinagpore (hereinafter referred to as 'the Parties');
>
> Considering that a dispute has arisen between them regarding sovereignty over Pedra Branca/Pulau Batu Puteh, Middle Rocks and South Ledge;
>
> Desiring that this dispute should be settled by the International Court of Justice (hereinafter referred to as 'the Court');
>
> Have agreed as follows: ...
>
> The Parties agree to submit the dispute to the Court under the terms of Article 36 (1) of its Statute....
>
> The Court is requested to determine whether sovereignty over:
>
> (a) Pedra Branca/Pulau Batu Puteh;
>
> (b) Middle Rocks;
>
> (c) South Ledge,
>
> belongs to Malaysia or the Republic of Singapore

* * *

2. Geographical location characteristics

16. Pedra Branca/Pulau Batu Puteh is a granite island, measuring 137 m long, with an average width of 60 m and covering an area of about 8,560 sq m at low tide. It is situated at the eastern entrance of the Straits of Singapore, at the point where the Straits open up into the South China Sea. Pedra Branca/Pulau Batu Puteh is located at 1° 19' 48" N and 104° 24' 27" E. It lies approximately 24 nautical miles to the east of Singapore, 7.7 nautical miles to the south of the Malaysian state of Johor and 7.6 nautical miles to the north of the Indonesian island of Bintan.

17. The names Pedra Branca and Batu Puteh mean "white rock" in Portuguese and Malay respectively. On the island stands Horsburgh lighthouse, which was erected in the middle of the nineteenth century.

* * *

3. General historical background

20. The Sultanate of Johor was established following the capture of Malacca by the Portuguese in 1511. Portugal's dominance in the 1500s as a colonial Power in the East Indies began to wane in the 1600s. By the mid-1600s the Netherlands had wrested control over various regions in the area from Portugal. In 1795, France occupied the Netherlands which prompted the British to establish rule over several Dutch possessions in the Malay archipelago. In 1813, the French left the Netherlands. Under the terms of the Anglo-Dutch Treaty of 1814 (also known as the Convention of London) the United Kingdom agreed to return the former Dutch possessions in the Malay archipelago to the Netherlands.

21.... This situation led to negotiations beginning in 1820 which culminated in the signing, on 17 March 1824, of a treaty between the United Kingdom and the Netherlands (entitled "Treaty between His Britannic Majesty and the King of the Netherlands, Respecting Territory and Commerce in the East Indies" and hereinafter referred to as "the 1824 Anglo-Dutch Treaty"). Under the terms of this Treaty, the Dutch withdrew their opposition to the occupation of Singapore by the United Kingdom and the latter agreed not to establish any trading post on any islands south of the Straits of Singapore. The Treaty had the practical effect of broadly establishing the spheres of influence of the two colonial Powers in the East Indies. As a consequence, one part of the Sultanate of Johor fell within a British sphere of influence while the other fell within a Dutch sphere of influence.

* * *

5. Sovereignty over Pedra Branca/Pulau Batu Putch

* * *

5.2 The question of the burden of proof

45. It is a general principle of law, confirmed by the jurisprudence of this Court, that a party which advances a point of fact in support of its claim must establish that fact (*Application of the Convention on the Prevention and Punishment of the Crime of Genocide (Bosnia and Herzegovina v. Serbia and Montenegro)*, Judgment of 26 February 2007, para. 204, citing *Military and Paramilitary Activities in and against Nicaragua (Nicaragua v. United States of America), Jurisdiction and Admissibility, Judgment, I.C.J. Reports 1984,* p. 437, para. 101).

5.3 Legal status of Pedra Branca/Pulau Batu Puteh before the 1840s

* * *

[After examining various types of evidence, the Court concluded:]

59. Thus from at least the seventeenth century until early in the nineteenth it was acknowledged that the territorial and maritime domain of the Kingdom of Johor comprised a considerable portion of the Malaya Peninsula, straddled the Straits of Singapore and included islands and islets in the area of the Straits. Specifically, this domain included the area where Pedra Branca/Pulau Batu Puteh is located.

62. Another factor of significance which the Court has to take into consideration in assessing the issue of the original title in the present case is the fact that throughout the entire history of the old Sultanate of Johor, there is no evidence that any competing claim had ever been advanced over the islands in the area of the Straits of Singapore.

67. The Court further recalls that, as expounded in the *Eastern Greenland* case ... [(Den. v. Nor.), 1933 P.C.I.J. (ser. A/B) No. 53 (April 5)] international law is satisfied with varying degrees in the display of State authority, depending on the specific circumstances of each case.

68. Having considered the actual historical and geographical context of the present case relating to the old Sultanate of Johor, the Court concludes that as far as the territorial domain of the Sultanate of Johor was concerned, it did cover in principle all the islands and islets within the Straits of Singapore, which lay in the middle of this Kingdom, and did thus include the island of Pedra Branca/Pulau Batu Puteh. The possession of the islands by the old Sultanate of Johor was never challenged by any other Power in the region and can in all the circumstances be seen as satisfying the condition of "continuous and peaceful display of territorial sovereignty (peaceful in relation to other States)" (... [Island of Palmas Case, 2 R.I.A.A. 839 (1949)].)

69. The Court thus concludes that the Sultanate of Johor had original title to Pedra Branca/Pulau Batu Puteh.

5.3.5. Conclusion

117. In the light of the foregoing, the Court concludes that Malaysia has established to the satisfaction of the Court that as of the time when the British started their preparations for the construction of the lighthouse on Pedra Branca/Pulau Batu Puteh in 1844, this island was under the sovereignty of the Sultan of Johor.

5.4 Legal status of Pedra Branca/Pulau Batu Puteh after the 1840s

* * *

123. One feature of the arguments on the law presented by the Parties should be mentioned at this point. Singapore, as has already been discussed, contended that Pedra Branca/Pulau Batu Puteh was *terra nullius* in 1847 (see paragraph 40 above). Recognizing however that the Court might reject that contention, Singapore submitted that even in that event, that is to say on the basis that "Malaysia could somehow show an historic title over the island, Singapore would still possess sovereignty over Pedra Branca since Singapore has exercised continuous sovereignty over the island while Malaysia has done nothing". It is true that it had shortly before said that "the notion of prescription ... has no role to play in the present case" but that was said on the basis that, as Singapore saw the case, Malaysia had not made out its historic title.

[The Court then examined the construction of a lighthouse on the island, 1850–1851, and the conduct of the parties from that date until the dispute arose].

5.5 Conclusion

273. The question to which the Court must now respond is whether in the light of the principles and rules of international law it stated earlier and of the assessment it has undertaken of the relevant facts, particularly the conduct of the Parties, sovereignty over Pedra Branca/Pulau Batu Puteh passed to the United Kingdom or Singapore.

274. The conduct of the United Kingdom and Singapore was, in many respects, conduct as operator of Horsburgh lighthouse, but that was not the case in all respects. Without being exhaustive, the Court recalls their investigation of marine accidents, their control over visits, Singapore's installation of naval communication equipment and its reclamation plans, all of which include acts *à titre de souverain*, the bulk of them after 1953. Malaysia and its predecessors did not respond in any way to that conduct, or the other conduct with that character identified earlier in this Judgment, of all of which (but for the installation of the naval communication equipment) it had notice.

275. Further, the Johor authorities and their successors took no action at all on Pedra Branca/Pulau Batu Puteh from June 1850 for the whole of the following century or more. And, when official visits (in the 1970s for instance) were made, they were subject to express Singapore permission. Malaysia's official maps of the 1960s and 1970s also indicate an appreciation by it that Singapore had sovereignty. Those maps, like the conduct of both Parties which the Court has briefly recalled, are fully consistent with the final matter the Court recalls. It is the clearly stated position of the Acting Secretary of the State of Johor in 1953 that Johor did not claim ownership of Pedra Branca/Pulau Batu Puteh. That statement has major significance.

276. The Court is of the opinion that the relevant facts, including the conduct of the Parties, previously reviewed and summarized in the two preceding paragraphs, reflect a convergent evolution of the positions of the Parties regarding title to Pedra Branca/Pulau Batu Puteh. The Court concludes, especially by reference to the conduct of Singapore and its predecessors *à titre de souverain*, taken together with the conduct of Malaysia and its predecessors including their failure to respond to the conduct of Singapore and its predecessors, that by 1980 sovereignty over Pedra Branca/Pulau Batu Puteh had passed to Singapore.

277. For the foregoing reasons, the Court concludes that sovereignty over Pedra Branca/Pulau Batu Puteh belongs to Sinagpore.

300. For these reasons,

THE COURT,

(1) By twelve votes to four,

Finds that sovereignty over Pedra Branca/Pulau Batu Puteh belongs to the Republic of Singapore.

[The Court also found, by fifteen votes to one, that "sovereignty over Middle Rocks belongs to Malayasia" and that "sovereignty over South Ledge belongs to the State in the territorial waters of which it is located." Because the Court had not been asked to draw a line delimiting the territorial seas in the area, it did not determine this issue.]

QUESTIONS

1. What persuaded the Court that in 1844 the island of Pedra Branca/Pulau Batu Puteh belonged to the Sultanate of Johor (which ultimately became part of Malaysia)?
2. What persuaded the Court that the island now belongs to Singapore?
3. If State A has good title to territory at a particular point in time, what is the least it must do to ensure the continuance of that good title into the future? What sort of information would you need to discover to answer this question?

Conquest

If one state invaded another state and defeated it in war, the most usual outcome was that the victor forced the vanquished to sign a treaty ceding the territory to the victorious party. Before the twentieth century conquest was a frequent mode of acquiring territory. Now a number of international agreements and the Charter of the United Nations prohibit the use of force in international relations.[4] The result of this prohibition is that generally a state may not now acquire territory through the use of force.

It has been suggested that if force is used in self-defense, as permitted by article 51 of the U.N. Charter, and if the exercise of self-defense results in the acquisition of territory such acquisition is valid. This argument has been roundly criticized as contrary to the Declaration on Friendly Relations which states that: "No territorial acquisition resulting from the threat or use of force shall be recognized as legal."[5] It has also been argued that under the laws of war the right of self-defense only continues until the armed attack (or possibly the threat of armed attack) has been repelled. Once the danger has been contained, the right to use force in self-defense evaporates and with it the right to retain any territory taken while exercising the right of self-defense. The Security Council has criticized Israel's retention of areas captured during the 1967 war which are currently gradually being returned to Arab control.

In July 2004, the International Court of Justice issued an Advisory Opinion: *Legal Consequences of the Construction of a Wall in the Occupied Palestinian Territory* (2004 I.C.J. 136) (Advisory Opinion 9 July 2004). The General Assembly of the United Nations had asked the Court to answer the following question:

> What are the legal consequences arising from the construction of the wall being built by Israel, the occupying Power, in the Occupied Palestinian Territory, including in and around East Jerusalem, as described in the report of the Secretary-General, considering the rules and principles of international law, including the Fourth Geneva Convention of 1949, and relevant Security Council and General Assembly Resolutions?

In the course of its opinion, the Court stated:

> On 24 October 1970, the General Assembly adopted resolution 2625 (XXV), entitled "Declaration on Principles of International Law concerning Friendly Relations and Co-operation among States" (hereinafter "resolution 2625 (XXV)"), in which it emphasized that "No territorial acquisition resulting from the threat or use of force shall be recognized as legal." As the Court stated in is Judgment in the case concerning *Military and Paramilitary Activities in and against Nicaragua (Nicaragua v. United States of America)*, the principles as to the use of force incorporated in the Charter reflect customary international law (see *I.C.J. Reports 1986*, pp. 98–101, paras. 187–190); the same is true of its corollary entailing the illegality of territorial acquisition resulting from the threat or use of force. (At para. 87).

Later, the Court added that "both the General Assembly and the Security Council have referred, with regard to Palestine, to the customary rule of 'the inadmissibility of the acquisition of territory by war'...." (at para. 117).

It should be noted, however, that there are several areas of the world which many people would characterize as having been taken by force even after WWII but which re-

4. U.N. Charter, art. 2(4), c.f., art.51; Covenant of the League of Nations, art. 10; Manley O. Hudson, International Legislation 1 (1931); Treaty Providing For the Renunciation of War as an Instrument of National Policy (the Kellogg-Briand Pact or the Pact of Paris), signed Aug. 27, 1928, entered into force, July 24, 1929, 94 L.N.T.S. 57; 1970 Declaration on Principles of International Law Concerning Friendly Relations and Co-operation Among States in Accordance with the Charter of the U.N., G.A. Res. 2625, U.N. GAOR, Supp. No. 28 25th Sess. (1970).

5. Id.

main in the hands of the user of force. India took over the Portuguese enclaves of Goa, Danao and Diu in 1961 and still controls them. China moved into Tibet in 1950 and, despite fairly widespread protests, shows no indication of relinquishing the territory. Both India and China claimed that they were "liberating" the respective territories which they maintain have always belonged to them.

Cession

Cession is the process whereby one sovereign gives title to territory to another sovereign. The process is usually effected by a treaty of cession. Sometimes land is acquired by purchase such as the United States' Louisiana purchase from France in 1803 and its Alaskan purchase from Russia in 1867. Today, treaties that are entered into under coercion are stated to be void (Vienna Convention on the Law of Treaties, articles 51 and 52) but in the past, the use of force was not prohibited by international law and thus many conquered nations were forced to sign treaties of cession. Sometimes, because of changes in the relative power of states, a country may successfully reacquire territory that it considered wrongfully taken from it, even if, at the time that the territory was ceded, such conduct did not violate international law. Hong Kong was ceded by China to Britain in the middle of the nineteenth century after the Opium Wars. Part was ceded under a ninety-nine year lease and part was ceded "in perpetuity." Nonetheless, Britain returned Hong Kong to China in 1997.

Prescription

In many municipal systems of law there is a provision for the acquisition of real property through the continuous and open use of it for a prescribed number of years despite the fact that the property is registered in another owner's name. In the common-law tradition this is known as "adverse possession" and normally takes at least twenty years. The question of whether one state can acquire title to territory despite an earlier recognized title vested in another state is much debated in international law. The *Malaysia v. Singapore Case* (see page 41ff.) addresses some aspects of this issue. Of course, if the earlier title holder abandoned the territory there is nothing to stop a subsequent claim to title, but exactly what constitutes abandonment is again debatable. A classic example of these dilemmas is provided by the materials on the Falkland Islands/Islas Malvinas dispute.

The Falkland Islands/Islas Malvinas Dispute

The dispute between Argentina and the United Kingdom over the ownership of the Falkland Islands/Islas Malvinas is an example of a territorial dispute escalating into a war. The discussion below will only focus on the main West Falkland and East Falkland Islands and will not include the dependencies of South Georgia and South Sandwich which have somewhat different histories.[6]

---

6. This section of the book relies on a variety of material: Julius Gorbel, Jr., The Struggle for the Falklands (rev. ed. 1982); Lowell Gustafson, The Sovereignty Dispute over the Falkland (Malvinas) Islands (1988); Michael Akehurst, A Modern Introduction to International Law (Appendix to the

The Islands lie about three hundred miles off the east coast of Argentina in the Southern Atlantic Ocean. They are thousands of miles from the United Kingdom.

The Discovery Claims

The British claim that Captain John Davis of the ship Desire discovered the Islands in 1592. The Argentines claim that various Spanish sailors discovered the Islands as far back as 1523 and that Argentina succeeded to the Spanish claims when she became independent from Spain in 1816. There were, however, a number of other nations that came to the area in the sixteenth century. A Dutch sailor sighted the Islands in 1599 and an Italian may have charted the Island as early as 1501, but the Dutch and Italians do not seem to have made claims of sovereignty.

Claims that rest on centuries old documents are necessarily difficult to prove but even in the early seventeenth century most writers on international law seemed to agree that discovery alone was not sufficient to confer title. At best discovery was seen as conferring an inchoate title which needed settlement or administration or some other displays of sovereignty to perfect title. Applying the principle of intertemporal law (the legal significance of a fact should turn on the law that was in existence at the time that the fact occurred) to the Spanish and British claims of discovery results in neither state acquiring sovereignty by discovery alone.

The Spanish also based their claim on Papal Bulls. Under the Roman Catholic Doctrine at that time the Pope was perceived to have the power to allocate unoccupied lands. A Papal Bull of 1493 appeared to divide up the area between Spain and Portugal and threatened excommunication to anyone who violated the allocation. Of course Britain was not a party to any discussions that may have preceded the issuance of the Bull and obviously by the time Henry VIII had rejected Rome it would have been foolish to expect that Britain would comply with Vatican dictates.

The Settlement Claims

During the seventeenth and eighteenth centuries there were a number of visits to the Islands by both British and Spanish sailors but these visits probably have no legal significance because no title was claimed on the basis of these expeditions. It was, in fact, the French who first settled on East Falkland in 1764. They built a fort and rough huts and by 1765 claimed to have a population of about 150 persons. In 1764 the British sent an expedition to the Islands and by 1766 a Captain McBride began to arrive with settlers on Saunders Island, a small island to the north of West Falkland. The Spanish returned at this point and ousted both the French and the British. The French sold their so-called settlement rights on East Falkland to the Spanish in 1766 and exacted considerable compensation from them for their withdrawal. The British did not surrender until 1770 and returned to Britain by 1771. In that year an agreement was entered into between Spain and Britain requiring Spain to restore the fort and the port but it was stated that the agreement "cannot affect the question of the prior right of sovereignty." Under this

5th ed.1984); Report on the Falkland Islands, Fifth Rep. of the Foreign Affairs Committee of the House of Commons, Sess. 1983–84, 1 H.C. Papers 268, xiv–xvii; Misc. 1 (1985), Cmnd. 9447.

agreement the claims to sovereignty were not settled and both parties retained whatever rights they may have previously acquired. The Spanish also apologized for using force against the settlers. There may have been a secret oral agreement between the parties that Britain would withdraw entirely. The British did eventually dismantle the colony by 1774 but they left a British flag and a plaque on Saunders Island stating that the Falkland Islands were the property of George III. The Spanish later removed the flag and the plaque.

By the late eighteenth century, Spanish claims were based on discovery, papal bulls, a treaty of succession to French settlement rights on East Falkland together with the possible secret oral agreement by the British to withdraw from the Islands. The Spanish had also exercised superior military force in ousting all other settlers. The British claim at this time was based on discovery, settlement on Saunders Island, a treaty with Spain apologizing for the ouster of the British and a plaque announcing British sovereignty over the Islands.

After 1774 the Spanish administered the Islands as part of the province of Buenos Aires. They appointed governors of the Islands and probably used it as a penal colony. By 1811 the Spanish garrison left the Islands and the Islands were then unoccupied. In 1816 the United Province of the River Plate, later to become Argentina, became independent from Spain and succeeded to Spanish claims. In 1820 the new republic sent a Colonel Jewitt to claim the Islands for Argentina. Britain recognized the newly declared republic in 1825 and the two states entered into a treaty of friendship, commerce and navigation in the same year but this treaty did not mention the Falklands. When the Argentines created a new governor of the Malvinas in 1828 the British protested but took no further action.

At this time some seal fishermen started to visit the Islands. In 1831 the American Captain Duncan of the warship Lexington landed, repulsed some resistance and declared the Island to be free from any government.

In 1832, the Argentines again sent out a governor but his soldiers mutinied and he was murdered. In December of the same year, a Captain Onslow arrived from England with instructions to "exercise Britain's rights of Sovereignty." The British claim that Onslow captured the port and "peacefully persuaded the remainder of the Argentine garrison to leave." The Argentines maintain that they were forcibly ousted by the British. By 1833, the British were firmly in possession and in 1843, the Islands became a British Crown Colony which they have remained since then with the exception of ten weeks Argentine forcible occupation during the 1982 war with Britain. Groups of sheep farming immigrants from Britain began arriving in the 1860's.

Summing up what happened in the Falklands/Malvinas prior to 1833, we find that there are some forty-seven years of Spanish occupation, two concurrent with the British, and two of those claimed through succession from France. The Argentines themselves have eleven years of occupation and they also claim succession from the Spanish. The British had at most, seven years occupation, two during the French settlement, plus a possible three years dismantling the colony. Up until 1833, the Argentines probably would have had a superior claim based on discovery followed by settlement. Disregarding discovery, prior to 1833 Argentina probably has a superior settlement claim, especially as she claims succession to the Spanish settlement claims. If the case had been presented to an international tribunal in 1832, however, it is doubtful whether either side would have engaged in enough undisputed displays of sovereignty to warrant a ruling of title to either claimant. Certainly the Spanish/Argentine claim was more established than the British claim but an international tribunal would probably have come to the conclusion that neither had a sufficient claim, although the Spanish/Argentine claim was clearly the stronger.

Occupation and Administration Since 1833: Title by Prescription

Britain claims that whatever rights existed in 1833, over a century and a half of administration and occupation of the territory, coupled with general recognition of British sovereignty by the international community, with the exception of most members of the Organization of American States, results in sovereignty by prescription. Argentina claims that since she was illegally ousted and has continually protested the British occupation, no title has been acquired by Britain.

It is difficult to document fully the Argentines' objections to British occupation, but there seems to be evidence of official protests in 1833, 1841, 1849, 1884, 1908, 1927, 1933, 1946, and by 1965 the General Assembly had called upon both parties to negotiate the issue. The crux of the legal issue then seems to turn on the question of the possibility under international law of prescriptive rights to title despite continual protest by another claimant who had previous established superior settlement rights perhaps amounting to sovereignty and it is here that we find a dearth of definitive principles and a paucity of precedents. Can a state acquire good title by forcibly ousting a previous title holder (assuming for the moment the Argentina had good title) and by administering the territory for a long period of time with nothing other than that paper protests by the other claimant? Could Britain claim title by conquest in light of the fact that the use of force was not prohibited by international law in 1833?

The Falklands/Malvinas dispute could not be resolved today without also addressing the issue of self-determination, that is the right of a people to choose their own form of government. The war that took place between Argentina and Britain in 1982 over the Falklands/Malvinas also raises substantial issues on the use of force and the conduct of war. For materials on war see chapter X.

QUESTIONS

1. Who had title to the Falklands/Malvinas in 1833?
2. If a state other than Britain had title to the Falklands/Malvinas in 1833 did Britain's ouster of the Argentinians and subsequent occupation for more than one hundred and fifty years result in Britain's acquiring title to the Islands?
3. What are the similarities and differences between the Falkland/Malvinas dispute and the *Island of Palmas* case?
4. Is the *Malaysia v. Singapore* case helpful?
5. If a court awarded title to the Malvinas to Argentina how many other states would be subject to being reclaimed by a former owner?
6. If a court awarded title to the Falklands to Britain would that encourage states to conquer other lands and settle them?

Uti Possidetis

Although the rule of *uti possidetis* (as you did possess, so you shall possess) traces its root to Roman civil law, it has been adapted in international law to provide a rule for states emerging from colonial rule. Colonial powers often drew the borders of colonized countries to suit their own purposes with little regard for ethnic, racial, religious or even natural geographic divisions. After World War II, almost all colonized states claimed independence. The rule of *uti possidetis* required the newly independent states to accept the boundaries as they had been drawn up by the colonical administrators. The International Court of Justice has often incorporated the *uti possidetis* rule into decisions on territorial disputes. In the frontier dispute between Burkina Faso and Mali, the Court stated that the purpose of *uti possidetis* "is to prevent the independence and stability of new States being endangered by fratricidal struggles provoked by the challenging of frontiers following the withdrawal of the administering power." *Case Concerning the Frontier Dispute (*Burkina Faso v. Mali) 1986 I.C.J. 554, at para. 23. The rule was expressly accepted by African states in the Cairo Declaration of 1964, and has also been applied in the European context. See, e.g., Statement of the European Arbitration Commission relating to the break up of the former Yugoslavia: "it is well established that, whatever the circumstances, the right to self-determination must not involve changes to existing frontiers at the time of independence (*uti possidetis juris*) except where the States concerned agree otherwise." 92 I.L.R. 168 (1992). The rule has also been applied in South America. See, e.g., *Case Concerning the Land, Island and Maritime Frontier Dispute*(El Salvador v. Honduras*)* 1992 I.C.J. 351.

Some scholars point out that the rule of *uti possidetis* directly conflicts with another rule of international law, the right of peoples to self-determination (see *infra* pages 246–257). They argue that the rigidity of the rule has often given rise to ethnic conflicts and may in fact be one of the main exacerbators of civil wars.[7]

Accretion and Avulsion

Occasionally natural events occur to the geography of a region to alter the shape of the territory. There may be a gradual increase in the land through silt deposits or shifts in the sea shore or river beds. These processes are known as accretion. Violent sub-terranian eruptions also cause the emergence of territory or the alteration in the shape of existing land. This activity is known as avulsion. Usually states must just put up with the configuration of the land that nature ascribes to them (although the Dutch have rather successfully resisted this type of resignation). If accretion occurs on an international boundary, as on a boundary river, the general view is that the international boundary will shift. If avulsion occurs on an international boundary the general view is that the boundary will not be altered. Such occurrences are rare. See *Case Concerning Kasikili/Sedudu Island* (Botswana v. Namibia) 1999 I.C.J. 1045. The U.S. Supreme Court is sometimes asked to rule on issues of accretion and avulsion in boundary disputes between different states within the U.S. In 1998, the Supreme Court stated: "We have long recognized that a sudden shoreline change known as avulsion (as distinct from accretion, or gradual change in configuration) 'has no effect on boundary'... and that this 'is the received rule of law of nations on this point, as laid down by all the writers of authority', ... including Sir William Blackstone...." *New Jersey v. New York*, 523 U.S. 767, 784 (1998) (citations omitted).

7. Joshua Castellino and Steve Allen, Title to Territory in International Law A Temporal Analysis Ch. 1 (2003).

The Arctic

Most of the Arctic is a solid mass of ice or ice-floes, rather than land as such. This raises the question as to whether any states can claim sovereignty over the area. Many environmentalists would like to see the area declared incapable of acquisition but several states have laid claim to the Arctic, including Canada, Denmark, Finland, Iceland, Norway, Russia, Sweden and the U.S. Some of these states claim areas of the Arctic based on the sector system. By this system a state pinpoints its most easterly and westerly claims to territory and draws a triangle from these points to the pole, claiming all the territory within the triangle. These claims have not been recognized by the world community and there is some hope that interested nations will work co-operatively to achieve an internationally protected conservation area in the Arctic. Recently, scientists seem to agree that the Arctic ice cap is melting. Mining for minerals and regular sea lanes may become possible. If so, territorial disputes are likely to increase. On May 28, 2008, the five states that border the Arctic Ocean, Canada, Denmark, Norway, the Russian Federation and the U.S. issued the *Ilulissat Declaration* in which they pledged to work cooperatively in the region. They stated: "By virtue of their sovereignty, sovereign rights and jurisdiction in large areas of the Arctic Ocean the five coastal states are in a unique position to address ... challenges." They also declared that they "see no need to develop a new comprehensive international legal regime to govern the Arctic Ocean."[8]

The Antarctic

Numerous states have claimed various portions of the Antarctic and many of these claims are overlapping. Some states refuse to recognize any land claims to the Antarctic while others have recognized some claims but not others. In an effort to stabilize the operative regime in the area, the Antarctic Treaty was signed in 1959 and entered into force in 1961.[9] All of the states currently claiming territory in the Antarctic are parties to the Treaty (Argentina, Australia, Chile, France, New Zealand, Norway and the United Kingdom). In addition a number of other states are also parties to the treaty. The Treaty requires that "Antarctica shall be used for peaceful purposes only" and prohibits "any measures of a military nature...." (art. I). The Treaty also guarantees "[f]reedom of scientific investigation" (art. II) and prohibits "nuclear explosions" and "disposal ... of radioactive waste material..."(art. V). Territorial claims are frozen (!) "while the present Treaty is in force." (art. VI). The Treaty has two amendment procedures. First, it may be amended by a unanimous vote of all the treaty partners named in the preamble to the Treaty and second, it provides that after thirty years from the Treaty's entry into force (i.e. 1991) any such treaty partner may call for a conference to review the Treaty (art. XII).

There have also been a large number of measures taken to protect the Antarctic environment including the Convention for the Conservation of Antarctic Marine Living Resources, signed in 1980 and entered into force in 1982[10] and the Protocol on Environ-

8. The Ilulissat Declaration, 28 May 2008, available at: www.um.dk/nr/rdonlyres/BE00B850-D278-4989-A6BE-6AE230415546/0/ArcticOceanConference.pdf; See also, United Nations Convention on the Law of the Sea, 1833 U.N.T.S. 3, Annex 2, art. 4. (Discussed in chapter V).

9. 402 U.N.T.S. 71, 12 U.S.T. 794, T.I.A.S. No. 4780.

10. 1329 U.N.T.S. 47, 33 U.S.T. 3476, reprinted at 19 I.L.M. 837, 841 (1980).

mental Protection to the Antarctic Treaty, signed in 1991 and entered into force in 1998, which imposes a moratorium on mining in Antarctica.[11] At the moment the world community seems unwilling to treat the territory of Antarctica as regular territory subject to claims of sovereignty and exploitation. The increased understanding both of the fragility of the environment and of global environmental interdependence may preserve for the polar regions a legal regime different from the traditional notion of state sovereignty.

Celestial Bodies and Space

The major treaty operative in this arena, the Treaty on Principles Governing the Activities of States in the Exploration and Uses of Outer Space, Including the Moon and other Celestial Bodies,[12] creates a regime that is described as "the province of all mankind" (art. I). This Treaty entered into force in 1967 and has been ratified by over ninety states. The Outer Space Treaty, as it is known, states that all exploration shall be carried out "for the benefit and in the interests of all countries...." (art. I) and that outer space "is not subject to national appropriation by claim of sovereignty, by means of use or occupation, or by any other means." (art. II). The area is to be used "exclusively for peaceful purposes" (art. IV) and nuclear weapons are prohibited (art. IV). A later treaty, the Agreement Governing the Activities of States on the Moon and Other Celestial Bodies,[13] entered into force in 1984 and emphasizes that the natural resources of the area are the common heritage of mankind. This treaty has only been ratified by thirteen states however.

Other recent agreements include the 1968 Agreement on the Rescue of Astronauts, the Return of Astronauts and the Return of Objects Launched into Outer Space[14] which governs cooperation in rescuing and returning astronauts and the 1972 Convention on International Liability for Damage Caused by Objects Launched into Outer Space[15] which imposes strict liability on the launching state for "damage caused by its space object on the surface of the earth or to aircraft in flight" (art. II) and fault liability for "damage being caused elsewhere than on the surface of the earth to a space object of one launching state or to persons or property on board such space object by a space object of another launching state...." (Art. III). It is clear from the above treaties that the traditional notions of sovereignty and ownership are not operative in outer space or on the moon or other celestial bodies.

Problem

The State of Alba claims to have discovered the island of Manca in the sixteenth century. Alba has various state documents describing the discovery that date back to 1560. At that time Manca was inhabited by a tribe known as the Mancans. The island is five miles in length and three miles in width and is blessed by a temperate climate and much nutritious vegetation. It lies two hundred miles off the south coast of Alba which is the

11. S. Treaty Doc. No. 102-22 (1991); reprinted at 30 I.L.M. 1455 (1991).

12. 610 U.N.T.S. 205, 18 U.S.T. 2410, T.I.A.S. No. 6347, reprinted at 6 I.L.M. 386 (1967).

13. 1363 U.N.T.S.3, 22 (E), 29 (F), signed Dec. 5, 1979, entered into force July 11, 1984, G.A. Res. 34/86, U.N. GAOR, Supp. No. 46, at 77, U.N. Doc. A/34/46 (1979); reprinted at 18 I.L.M. 1434 (1979).

14. 672 U.N.T.S. 119, 19 U.S.T. 7570, reprinted at 7 I.L.M. 149 (1968).

15. 961 U.N.T.S. 187, 24 U.S.T. 2389, T.I.A.S. No.7762, reprinted at 10 I.L.M. 965 (1971).

nearest mainland. Recently large deposits of gold have been found on the eastern tip of the island.

During the sixteenth and seventeenth centuries Alba occasionally sent settlers to Manca. The Albanese flag was planted near the main settlement and an Albanese official was sent to the island for two months every year to carry out geographic surveys and to write a report on the state of the indigenous population. Some time towards the end of the seventeenth century this official was conferred the title "Governor of Manca" though his activities remained the same as they had been previously.

In 1714 a naval vessel from the State of Benir came across the island by accident after a storm had blown the ship off course. The crew went ashore and finding only indigenous Mancans, the captain of the ship planted Benir's flag and the crew built several log cabins. No evidence was found of Albanese presence. Presumably the Albanese flag had succumbed to a storm or otherwise been removed and any Albanese settlers who might have lived there had either returned home or died. The captain of the Beniri ship left several crew members on the island and returned to Benir, a state seven hundred miles to the west. Later that year, seventy five Beniri settlers were sent to the island. They quickly established homes and farms and, apart from a few skirmishes with the Mancan tribesmen, seemed to enjoy a pleasant existence. A Beniri governor was installed a few months later.

Later in the year, when the Albanese governor came for his annual two month long trip to the island, he was amazed to find the Beniri settlement. He immediately protested to the Beniri governor who dismissed Albanese claims to the territory as "fanciful."

Six months later the Albanese navy launched an attack on the island in an attempt to retake it. The Albanese navy was soundly defeated by the Beniri settlers and some tribesmen who had been persuaded to join the Beniris in the fight.

Since then Benir has ruled Manca as a colony. The settlers have multiplied and intermarried with the tribesmen and the governor remains in residence. Alba has issued official protests from time to time in any forum willing to listen and, since 1945, when both Alba and Benir joined the United Nations, has frequently filed protests with the General Assembly. No action has ever been taken by the General Assembly on the matter.

Alba and Benir have recently agreed to submit the territorial dispute for resolution to the International Court of Justice.

Alba asks the Court to declare that Alba has good title to the island of Manca. Benir asks the Court to declare that Benir has good title to the island of Manca.

QUESTION

Please write an opinion for the Court *either* declaring that Alba has good title to Manca *or* that Benir has good title to Manca. You should set out your reasoning fully and explain why the losing party was not successful.

Suggested Further Readings

Ian Browlie, Principles of Public International Law, chapter 7 (7th ed. 2008).

Joshua Castellino & Steve Allen, Title to Territory in International Law: A Temporal Analysis (2003).

D.J. Harris, Cases and Materials on International Law, chapter 5 (6th ed. 2004).

R.Y. Jennings, The Acquisition of Territory in International Law (1962).

Malcolm N. Shaw, International Law, chapter 10 (6th ed. 2008).

Rebecca M. M. Wallace, International Law, chapter 5 (5th ed. 2005).

Chapter III

The Law of Treaties

All modern states have an internal system of law designed to determine when agreements between people or organizations are to be considered binding and enforceable in court. This body of law is known as contract law. It is replete with rules about when there is a binding agreement and when there is not; when the agreement has been breached; what actions or events may make the agreement invalid; and when it may be terminated or suspended. On the international plane there is a similar body of law known as the law of treaties which addresses many of the same types of issues.

We are fortunate that the international community has concluded a major convention setting out the rules for treaty law. The Vienna Convention on the Law of Treaties, which was drafted by the International Law Commission, was concluded in 1969 and came into force in 1980.[1] One hundred and eight states have become parties to the Vienna Convention. Even those who have not actually ratified the treaty, such as the United States, have issued statements to the effect that they consider large portions of the Convention to be declaratory of customary law and therefore binding regardless of ratification.

The Vienna Convention covers a great variety of the subtleties of treaty law but we shall only study the main elements.

What Is a Treaty? Definition

The Vienna Convention contains its own definition of a treaty in article 2(1)(a):

> "treaty" means an international agreement concluded between states in written form and governed by international law, whether embodied in a single instrument or in two or more related instruments and whatever its particular designation.

That last phrase simply means that the document does not have to be called a treaty in order to be binding. Indeed you will find a plethora of names for such documents, such as convention, pact, protocol, charter, act, concordat, declaration, exchange of notes or agreement. Agreements that are not between states or not in written form are not necessarily non-binding agreements. Oral agreements between state representatives may well be binding.[2] A state's unilateral statement may also be binding[3] and agreements between

1. 1155 U.N.T.S. 331, signed 23 May 1969; entered into force on 27 Jan. 1980, reprinted at 8 I.L.M. 679 (1969) [hereinafter Vienna Convention]. For a description of the International Law Commission see p. 286 n. 15.

2. See *Legal Status of Eastern Greenland* (Norway v. Denmark) 1933 P.C.I.J. (ser. A/B) No. 53, at 194 (Apr. 5).

3. *The Nuclear Tests Case* (Australia v. France) 1974 I.C.J. 253, at para. 51.

states and other organizations may well be enforceable under international or municipal law. The Vienna Convention's definition simply means that such agreements are not governed by the Vienna Convention. Agreements between states and international organizations are governed by another treaty, the Convention on Treaties between States and International Organizations or between International Organizations which was concluded in 1986 but has not yet entered into force.[4] Conversely agreements between states in writing may not be governed by international law. For example, the agreement may state that it is to be governed by municipal law or it may be written as a standard form contract for the shipment and delivery of goods where neither party expected international law to govern the agreement. It should be noted, however, that the Vienna Convention does apply to "any treaty which is the constituent instrument of an international organization"[5] such as the United Nations Charter.

Capacity to Conclude a Treaty

States are free to designate anyone to represent the state for the purpose of concluding a treaty provided s/he has been duly authorized with "full powers". The term "full powers" means that the person concerned will have been issued an appropriate document indicating such powers have been conferred upon him/her. Certain representatives of a state are automatically considered to have "full powers" by virtue of their office: a head of state, a leader of the government or a foreign affairs minister. (Article 7(2)(a)). Even if such persons do not in fact possess such powers under their own municipal law, if they hold themselves out as having the power to bind their country, international law will hold that other states have every right to rely on such representation and will find any agreement concluded by such a person binding.

Ratification

Internal Ratification: U.S. Procedure

Every state has its own internal law for determining which organs of government are empowered to make a treaty binding on the state. In the United States, for example, the executive branch negotiates and signs the treaty. From that point on the U.S. "is obliged to refrain from acts which would defeat the object and purpose of [the] treaty" (article 18). When the text is agreed upon, the treaty is presented to the Senate for its advice and consent[6] by a two-thirds vote. After the Senate has given its consent, the treaty is returned to the President for his ratification, which he may complete, or refuse to complete, as he sees fit. The President is also empowered to conclude Executive Agreements to which Senate consent is not necessary. These agreements are equally binding upon

4. Reprinted at 25 I.L.M. 543 (1986).
5. Vienna Convention, art. 5.
6. U.S. Const. art. II, § 2, cl. 2. The Senate has no power to ratify treaties under the U.S. Constitution although many authorities speak loosely (and inaccurately) of the Senate "ratifying" a treaty.

the United States. The distinction between "treaties" which require Senate consent and "executive agreements" which do not is entirely unclear in U.S. Constitutional Law, although a fair amount of historic practice often dictates the route to be employed.

International Ratification

After internal ratification has occurred, the state will send a formal indication of consent to be bound by the treaty either to the other states parties to the treaty or by depositing its consent with the depository organization designated by the treaty. If the state is also a member of the United Nations, the U.N. Charter requires the state to register the treaty with the U.N. Secretariat.[7]

Reservations

Article 2(1)(d) defines a reservation as:

> a unilateral statement, however phrased or named, made by a state, when signing, ratifying, accepting, approving or acceding to a treaty, whereby it purports to exclude or to modify the legal effect of certain provisions of the treaty in their application to that state.

In other words, a reservation allows a treaty party who does not like all of the terms of a treaty unilaterally to announce that certain parts of the treaty will not apply to it. At first blush, you might well think that such a system spells potential chaos. States being allowed to opt out of onerous parts of obligations at will hardly comports with the overarching principle of treaty law, *pacta sunt servanda*: treaties are binding and to be performed in good faith. A little history will shed some light.

First, there can be no reservations to bi-lateral (two party) treaties for the simple reason that if the two parties do not agree on any particular provision then there is no agreement on that provision, that is, there is no binding obligation on that point. But what if there are more than two states, for example, five states who wish to conclude a treaty? What if all five agree on nine out of the ten articles of the treaty and four of the five states agree on the tenth article but the fifth state does not agree with the tenth article? Two questions arise. Can the fifth state become a party to the treaty? And if so, what are the treaty relationships between the fifth state and the other states? These two questions were addressed by the International Court of Justice in the *Reservations to the Genocide Convention Case*,[8] reproduced below. Prior to this case the rule had been that states were not permitted to make reservations to treaties unless all of the other parties to the treaty accepted the reservation. In many ways the old system was much more orderly and predictable. Because of the new rule, reflected in the *Genocide Case* and in the Vienna Convention, articles 19 through 23, many modern treaties spell out whether parties are permitted to make reservations or not and if so usually indicate to which articles

7. U.N. Charter, art.102, para. 1.
8. 1951 I.C.J. 15.

reservations may be made and which articles do not permit reservations. Where a treaty has such a provision it will govern the question of the permissibility of reservations.

Reservations to the Convention on the Prevention and Punishment of the Crime of Genocide

1951 I.C.J. 15 (Advisory Opinion)

Note

The Convention on the Prevention and Punishment of the Crime of Genocide was adopted by the General Assembly of the U.N. on December 9, 1948, and entered into force on January 12, 1951.[9] A number of states appended reservations to the Convention upon ratification. The most divisive of the reservations were the ones that sought to exclude the operation of Article IX. That article provides:

> Disputes between the Contracting Parties relating to the interpretation, application or fulfillment of the present Convention, including those relating to the responsibility of a state for genocide or any of the other acts enumerated in Article III, shall be submitted to the International Court of Justice at the request of any of the parties to the dispute.

The effect of this article is to confer jurisdiction upon the International Court of Justice over any state party to the Convention if a complaint, arising under the Convention, is filed against that party by another party to the Convention. Obviously some states were not too keen to have the International Court of Justice investigate complaints under the Convention against them and so they sought to eliminate the effect of Article IX by adding a reservation to the Convention stating, in various ways, that Article IX was not to be operative with respect to their state. These reservations infuriated some Convention parties who felt that the enforcement mechanism provided by an international forum for the resolution of complaints was an essential feature of the Convention. As a result, the U.N. General Assembly adopted a resolution on November 16, 1950, asking the International Court of Justice to give an advisory opinion answering certain questions. The first two questions asked were:

In so far as concerns the Convention on the Prevention and Punishment of the Crime of Genocide in the event of a State ratifying or acceding to the Convention subject to a reservation made either on ratification or on accession, or on signature followed by ratification:

I. Can the reserving State be regarded as being a party to the Convention while still maintaining its reservation if the reservation is objected to by one or more of the parties to the convention but not by others?

II. If the answer to Question I is in the affirmative, what is the effect of the reservation as between the reserving State and:
(a) The parties which object to the reservation?
(b) Those which accept it?

---

9. 78 U.N.T.S. 277, G.A. Res. 2670, U.N. GAOR, 3d Comm, 3d Sess., pt. 1, U.N. Doc. A/810, at 174 (1948), 78 U.N.T.S. 277, signed 9 Dec. 1948, entered into force 12 Jan. 1951.

Opinion of the Court

The Court observes that the ... questions which have been referred to it for an Opinion have certain common characteristics.

[The] questions are expressly limited by the terms of the Resolution of the General Assembly to the Convention on the Prevention and Punishment of the Crime of Genocide, and the same Resolution invites the International Law Commission to study the general question of reservations to multilateral conventions both from the point of view of codification and from that of the progressive development of international law. The questions thus having a clearly defined object, the replies which the Court is called upon to give to them are necessarily and strictly limited to that Convention. The Court will seek these replies in the rules of law relating to the effect to be given to the intention of the parties to multilateral conventions.

Question I is framed in the following terms:

> Can the reserving State be regarded as being a party to the Convention while still maintaining its reservation if the reservation is objected to by one or more of the parties to the Convention but not by others?

The Court observes that this question refers, not to the possibility of making reservations to the Genocide Convention, but solely to the question whether a contracting State which has made a reservation can, while still maintaining it, be regarded as being a party to the Convention, when there is a divergence of views between the contracting parties concerning this reservation, some accepting the reservation, others refusing to accept it.

It is well established that in its treaty relations a State cannot be bound without its consent, and that consequently no reservation can be effective against any State without its agreement thereto. It is also a generally recognized principle that a multilateral convention is the result of an agreement freely concluded upon its clauses and that consequently none of the contracting parties is entitled to frustrate or impair, by means of unilateral decisions or particular agreements, the purpose and *raison d'etre* of the convention. To this principle was linked the notion of the integrity of the convention as adopted, a notion which in its traditional concept involved the proposition that no reservation was valid unless it was accepted by all the contracting parties without exception, as would have been the case if it had been stated during the negotiations.

This concept, which is directly inspired by the notion of contract, is of undisputed value as a principle. However, as regards the Genocide Convention, it is proper to refer to a variety of circumstances which would lead to a more flexible application of this principle. Among these circumstances may be noted the clearly universal character of the United Nations under whose auspices the Convention was concluded, and the very wide degree of participation envisaged by Article XI of the Convention. Extensive participation in conventions of this type has already given rise to greater flexibility in the international practice concerning multilateral conventions. More general resort to reservations, very great allowance made for tacit assent to reservations, the existence of practices which go so far as to admit that the author of reservations which have been rejected by certain contracting parties is nevertheless to be regarded as a party to the convention in relation to those contracting parties that have accepted the reservations—all these factors are manifestations of a new need for flexibility in the operation of multilateral conventions.

[The Court] must now determine what kind of reservations may be made and what kind of objections may be taken to them. The solution of these problems must be found in the special characteristics of the Genocide Convention. The origins and character of that Convention, the objects pursued by the General Assembly and the contracting parties, the relations which exist between the provisions of the Convention, inter se, and between those provisions and these objects, furnish elements of interpretation of the will of the General Assembly and the parties. The origins of the Convention show that it was the intention of the United Nations to condemn and punish genocide as a 'crime under international law' involving a denial of the right of existence of entire human groups, a denial which shocks the conscience of mankind and results in great losses to humanity, and which is contrary to moral law and to the spirit and aims of the United Nations (Resolution 96(I) of the General Assembly, December 11th, 1946). The first consequence arising from this conception is that the principles underlying the Convention are principles which are recognized by civilized nations as binding on States, even without any conventional obligation. A second consequence is the universal character both of the condemnation of genocide and of the co-operation required 'in order to liberate mankind from such an odious scourge' (Preamble to the Convention). The Genocide Convention was therefore intended by the General Assembly and by the contracting parties to be definitely universal in scope. It was in fact approved on December 9th, 1948, by a resolution which was unanimously adopted by fifty-six States.

The objects of such a convention must also be considered. The Convention was manifestly adopted for a purely humanitarian and civilizing purpose. It is indeed difficult to imagine a convention that might have this dual character to a greater degree, since its object on the one hand is to safeguard the very existence of certain human groups and on the other to confirm and endorse the most elementary principles of morality. In such a convention the contracting States do not have any interests of their own; they merely have, one and all, a common interest, namely, the accomplishment of those high purposes which are the *raison d'etre* of the convention. Consequently, in a convention of this type one cannot speak of individual advantages or disadvantages to States, or of the maintenance of a perfect contractual balance between rights and duties. The high ideals which inspired the Convention provide, by virtue of the common will of the parties, the foundation and measure of all its provisions.

The foregoing considerations, when applied to the question of reservations, and more particularly to the effects of objections to reservations, lead to the following conclusions.

The object and purpose of the Genocide Convention imply that it was the intention of the General Assembly and of the States which adopted it that as many States as possible should participate. The complete exclusion from the Convention of one or more States would not only restrict the scope of its application, but would detract from the authority of the moral and humanitarian principles which are its basis. It is inconceivable that the contracting parties readily contemplated that an objection to a minor reservation should produce such a result. But even less could the contracting parties have intended to sacrifice the very object of the Convention in favour of a vain desire to secure as many participants as possible. The object and purpose of the Convention thus limit both the freedom of making reservations and that of objecting to them. It follows that it is the compatibility of a reservation with the object and purpose of the Convention that must furnish the criterion for the attitude of a State in making the reservation on accession as well as for the appraisal by a State in objecting to the reservation. Such is the rule of conduct which must guide every State in the appraisal which it must make, individually and from its own standpoint, of the admissibility of any reservation.

It has nevertheless been argued that any State entitled to become a party to the Genocide Convention may do so while making any reservation it chooses by virtue of its sovereignty. The Court cannot share this view. It is obvious that so extreme an application of the idea of State sovereignty could lead to a complete disregard of the object and purpose of the Convention.

On the other hand, it has been argued that there exists a rule of international law subjecting the effect of a reservation to the express or tacit assent of all the contracting parties. This theory rests essentially on a contractual conception of the absolute integrity of the convention as adopted. This view, however, cannot prevail if, having regard to the character of the convention, its purpose and its mode of adoption, it can be established that the parties intended to derogate from that rule by admitting the faculty to make reservations thereto.

It results from the foregoing considerations that Question I, on account of its abstract character, cannot be given an absolute answer. The appraisal of a reservation and the effect of objections that might be made to it depend upon the particular circumstances of each individual case.

Having replied to Question I, the Court will now examine Question II, which is framed as follows:

> If the answer to Question I is in the affirmative, what is the effect of the reservation as between the reserving State and:
>
> (a) the parties which object to the reservation?
>
> (b) those which accept it?

The considerations which form the basis of the Court's reply to Question I are to a large extent equally applicable here. As has been pointed out above, each State which is a party to the Convention is entitled to appraise the validity of the reservation, and it exercises this right individually and from its own standpoint. As no State can be bound by a reservation to which it has not consented, it necessarily follows that each State objecting to it will or will not, on the basis of its individual appraisal within the limits of the criterion of the object and purpose stated above, consider the reserving State to be a party to the Convention. In the ordinary course of events, such a decision will only affect the relationship between the State making the reservation and the objecting State; on the other hand, as will be pointed out later, such a decision might aim at the complete exclusion from the Convention in a case where it was expressed by the adoption of a position on the jurisdictional plane.

The disadvantages which result from this possible divergence of views—which an article concerning the making of reservations could have obviated—are real; they are mitigated by the common duty of the contracting States to be guided in their judgment by the compatibility of the reservation with the object and purpose of the Convention. It must clearly be assumed that the contracting States are desirous of preserving intact at least what is essential to the object of the Convention; should this desire be absent, it is quite clear that the Convention itself would be impaired both in its principle and in its application.

It may be that the divergence of views between parties as to the admissibility of a reservation will not in fact have any consequences. On the other hand, it may be that certain parties who consider that the assent given by other parties to a reservation is incompatible with the purpose of the Convention, will decide to adopt a position on the jurisdictional plane in respect of this divergence and to settle the dispute which thus arises either by special agreement or by the procedure laid down in Article IX of the Convention.

Finally, it may be that a State, whilst not claiming that a reservation is incompatible with the object and purpose of the Convention, will nevertheless object to it, but that an understanding between that State and the reserving State will have the effect that the Convention will enter into force between them, except for the clauses affected by the reservation.

For these reasons,

THE COURT IS OF OPINION,

In so far as concerns the Convention on the Prevention and Punishment of the Crime of Genocide, in the event of a State ratifying or acceding to the Convention subject to a reservation made either on ratification or on accession, or on signature followed by ratification,

On Question I:

by seven votes to five,

that a state which has made and maintained a reservation which has been objected to by one or more of the parties to the Convention but not by others, can be regarded as being a party to the Convention if the reservation is compatible with the object and purpose of the Convention; otherwise, that State cannot be regarded as being a party to the Convention.

On Question II:

by seven votes to five,

(a) that if a party to the Convention objects to a reservation which it considers to be incompatible with the object and purpose of the Convention, it can in fact consider that the reserving State is not a party to the Convention;
(b) that if, on the other hand, a party accepts the reservation as being compatible with the object and purpose of the Convention, it can in fact consider that the reserving State is a party to the Convention.

Dissenting Opinion of Judges Guerrero, McNair, Read and Hsu Mo

We regret that we are unable to concur in the Opinion of the Court, while agreeing that the Court has competence to give an opinion.

We also consider that the role of the Court in this matter is a limited one. The Court is not asked to state which is in its opinion the best system for regulating the making of reservations to multilateral conventions. States engaged in the preparation of a multilateral convention, by means either of a diplomatic conference or of the machinery of the United Nations, are free to insert in the text provisions defining the limits within which, and the means by which, reservations can be proposed and can take effect. With these questions of policy the Court is not concerned. Its opinion is requested as to the existing law and its operation upon reservations to the Genocide Convention, which contains no express provisions to govern this matter. But the Court cannot overlook the possibility that its opinion may have a wider effect—more particularly having regard to the fact that Dr. Kerno, the representative of the Secretary-General of the United Nations, in addressing the Court, treated the matter generally and expressed the hope that the opinion would be useful in dealing with the general problem of reservations to multilateral conventions.

In considering the requirements of international law as to the proposal of reservations and the conditions of their effectiveness, the Court is not confronted with a legal vacuum. The consent of the parties is the basis of treaty obligations. The law governing reservations is only a particular application of this fundamental principle, whether the consent of the parties to a reservation is given in advance of the proposal of the reservation or at the same time or later. The fact that in so many of the multilateral conventions of the past hundred years, whether negotiated by groups of States or the League of Nations or the United Nations, the parties have agreed to create new rules of law or to declare existing rules of law, with the result that this activity is often described as 'legislative' or 'quasi-legislative', must not obscure the fact that the legal basis of these conventions, and the essential thing that brings them into force, is the common consent of the parties.

The practice of proposing reservations to treaties (though the word 'reservation' is not always used) is at least a century old, but it did not receive much attention from legal writers until the present century. The following quotations show clearly that the practice of governments has resulted in a rule of law requiring the unanimous consent of all the parties to a treaty before a reservation can take effect and the State proposing it can become a party.

* * *

This attempt to classify reservations into 'compatible' and 'incompatible' would involve a corresponding classification of the provisions of the Convention into two categories—of minor and major importance; when a particular provision formed part of 'the object and purpose of the Convention' a reservation made against it would be regarded as 'incompatible', and the reserving State would not be considered as a party to the Convention; when a particular provision did not form part of 'the object and purpose', any party which considered a reservation made against it to be 'compatible' might regard the reserving State as a party. Any State desiring to become a party to the Convention would be at liberty to assert that a particular provision was not a part of 'the object and purpose', that a reservation against it was 'compatible with the object and purpose of the Convention' and that it had therefore a right to make that reservation—subject always to an objection by any of the existing parties on the ground that the reservation is not 'compatible'.

We regret that ... we are unable to accept this doctrine.

* * *

We believe that the integrity of the terms of the Convention is of greater importance than mere universality in its acceptance. While is it undoubtedly true that the representatives of the governments, in drafting and adopting the Genocide Convention, wished to see as many States become parties to it as possible, it was certainly not their intention to achieve universality at any price. There is no evidence to show that they desired to secure wide acceptance of the Convention even at the expense of the integrity or uniformity of its terms, irrespective of the wishes of those States which have accepted all the obligations under it.

* * *

In conclusion, the enormity of the crime of genocide can hardly be exaggerated, and any treaty for its repression deserves the most generous interpretation; but the Genocide Convention is an instrument which is intended to produce legal effects by creating legal obligations between the parties to it, and we have therefore felt it necessary to examine it against the background of law.

Judge M. Alvarez also filed a dissenting opinion.

Problems

1. When the U.S. Senate gave its advice and consent to ratification of the Genocide Convention in 1986 it appended two reservations. One reservation provided that the U.S. must give its specific consent to the jurisdiction of International Court of Justice before the Court would have the power to render a decision under a complaint filed against the U.S. pursuant to Article IX of the Convention. The other reservation stated: "That nothing in the Convention requires or authorizes legislation or other action by the United States of America prohibited by the Constitution of the United States as interpreted by the United States"

   If you were representing the State of Alpha which had become a party to the Convention many years ago and you were now informed by the U.N. Secretary-General that the United States had ratified the Convention subject to the above reservations, what response would you advise your state to make to these reservations? Remember that if you do nothing for twelve months you will be treated as having accepted the reservation. Vienna Convention art. 20(5).
2. If you were drafting a multi-lateral convention and you wished to include an article on the permissibility or impermissibility of reservations what factors would influence whether you would allow reservations to certain articles or whether you would ban them?

Entry into Force

States are free to choose the manner and date in which a treaty enters into force. Most modern treaties have a provision specifying how and when the treaty enters into force, usually upon the ratification of a specified number of states. For example the U.N. Convention on the Law of the Sea[10] states that the treaty will enter into force one year after the deposit of the sixtieth ratification.[11] If a treaty does not specify when entry into force occurs then it will occur "as soon as consent to be bound by the treaty has been established for all the negotiating states" (article 24(2)).

Observance and Application of Treaties

The great overriding principle of treaty law is often expressed in Latin: *pacta sunt servanda*, which article 26 of the Vienna Convention translates as "Every treaty in force is binding upon the parties to it and must be performed by them in good faith." Article 27 makes it clear that internal law cannot be raised as a justification for the failure to keep a treaty. Article 46 makes that limitation specifically applicable with respect to competence to conclude a treaty unless it is objectively manifest that the party purporting to

10. 1833 U.N.T.S. 3, signed 10 Dec. 1982, entered into force 16 Nov. 1994, reprinted at 21 I.L.M. 1261 (1982).

11. Id. at art. 308. The sixtieth state deposited its ratification on 16 November 1993, and the Convention entered into force on 16 November 1994.

bind the state had no such authority. Treaties are deemed to be prospective and are applicable to the state's entire territory unless they indicate otherwise.

Interpretation of Treaties

When the Vienna Convention was being drafted by the International Law Commission two schools of treaty interpretation emerged. One group wished to concentrate on *the meaning of the text.* It was assumed that most treaties are negotiated by educated and sophisticated people, so that by the time a text is arrived at the ambiguities will have been largely eliminated and the text will in fact reflect the intention of the parties. Such a view leads naturally to rules of interpretation that restrict quite severely the types and occasions on which extrinsic evidence (evidence arising outside the four corners of the document) may be introduced to prove the meaning of the treaty. The other group focused on *the intention of the parties* and were much more willing to establish rules that would allow the introduction of a broad array of evidence that might throw light upon the intention of the parties. It is fair to say that the first group largely won the day. Both groups were sometimes willing to take into account the overall object and purpose of the treaty.

Article 31 of the Convention establishes the rule of interpreting a treaty in accordance with its ordinary meaning but adds that this rule operates in light of the treaty's context and its overall objective. The meaning given to context and objective is fairly limited. The only occasions when supplementary means of interpretation may be resorted to, such as "travaux preparatoires" (preparatory works) are when the ordinary meaning method "leaves the meaning ambiguous or obscure" or when that method of interpretation leads to an "absurd or unreasonable" result (article 32(a)&(b)). See *Case Concerning Kasikili/Sedudu Island* (Botswana v. Nambia), 1999 I.C.J. 1045.

The Court has relied upon Article 31 in a number of cases. In the *Case Concerning the Territorial Dispute* (Libyan Arab Jamahiriya v. Chad) 1994 I.C.J. 6, at paragraph 41, the Court stated:

> in accordance with customary international law, reflected in Article 31 of the 1969 Vienna Convention on the Law of Treaties, a treaty must be interpreted in good faith in accordance with the ordinary meaning to be given to its terms in their context and in light of its object and purpose. Interpretation must be based above all upon the text of the treaty. As a supplementary measure recourse may be had to means of interpretation such as the preparatory works of the treaty and the circumstances of its conclusion.

Again, in the *Case Concerning Maritime Delimitation and Territorial Questions* (Qatar v. Bahrain), 1995 I.C.J. 6, at paragraph 40, the Court made it clear that it had interpreted the disputed text in question:

> "in accordance with the ordinary meaning to be given to its terms in their context and in light of the object and purpose of the said [text].... In these circumstances, the Court does not consider it necessary to resort to supplementary means of interpretation in order to determine the meaning of the [text]....; however, as in other cases..., it considers that it can have recourse to such supplementary means in order to seek a possible confirmation of its interpretation of the text.

Case Concerning Avena and Other Mexican Nationals (Mexico v. United States of America)

2004 I.C.J. 12

Note

The facts of the *Avena* case are explained in the judgment below.

In the *Avena* case, the I.C.J. frequently refers to the *LaGrand* case (Germany v. U.S.) 2001 I.C.J. 466. That case concerned two German brothers who had been sentenced to death in the U.S. Germany filed suit against the U.S. in the I.C.J. arguing that the brothers' treaty rights under the Vienna Convention on Consular Relations had been violated. The Court ruled that the Vienna Convention on Consular Relations created rights for the individual criminal defendants as well as rights for states that are party to the treaty. It stated that the U.S. must provide review and reconsideration of both the convictions and the sentences of the criminal defendants by taking into consideration the violations of the rights set forth in the treaty.

The Court ... delivers the following Judgment:

1. On 9 January 2003 the United Mexican States (hereinafter referred to as "Mexico") filed in the Registry of the Court an Application instituting proceedings against the United States of America (hereinafter referred to as the "United States") for "violations of the Vienna Convention on Consular Relations" of 24 April 1963 (hereinafter referred to as the "Vienna Convention") allegedly committed by the United States.

In its Application, Mexico based the jurisdiction of the Court on Article 36, paragraph 1, of the Statute of the Court and on Article I of the Optional Protocol concerning the Compulsory Settlement of Disputes, which accompanies the Vienna Convention (hereinafter referred to as the "Optional Protocol").

* * *

15. The present proceedings have been brought by Mexico against the United States on the basis of the Vienna Convention, and of the Optional Protocol providing for the jurisdiction of the Court over "disputes arising out of the interpretation or application" of the Convention. Mexico and the United States are, and were at all relevant times, parties to the Vienna Convention and to the Optional Protocol. Mexico claims that the United States has committed breaches of the Vienna Convention in relation to the treatment of a number of Mexican nationals who have been tried, convicted and sentenced to death in criminal proceedings in the United States. The original claim related to 54 such persons, but as a result of subsequent adjustments to its claim made by Mexico..., only 52 individual cases are involved. These criminal proceedings have been taking place in nine different States of the United States, namely California (28 cases), Texas (15 cases), Illinois (three cases), Arizona (one case), Arkansas (one case), Nevada (one case), Ohio (one case), Oklahoma (one case) and Oregon (one case), between 1979 and the present.

* * *

17. The provisions of the Vienna Convention of which Mexico alleges violations are contained in Article 36.... Article 36 relates, according to its title, to "Communication and contact with nationals of the sending State". Paragraph 1*(b)* of that Article provides

that if a national of that State "is arrested or committed to prison or to custody pending trial or is detained in any other manner", and he so requests, the local consular post of the sending State is to be notified. The Article goes on to provide that the "competent authorities of the receiving State" shall "inform the person concerned without delay of his rights" in this respect. Mexico claims that in the present case these provisions were not complied with by the United States authorities in respect of the 52 Mexican nationals the subject of its claim. As a result, the United States has according to Mexico committed breaches of paragraph 1*(b)*; moreover, Mexico claims, for reasons to be explained below ... that the United States is also in breach of paragraph 1*(a)* and*(c)* and of paragraph 2 of Article 36, in view of the relationship of these provisions with paragraph 1*(b)*.

* * *

19. The underlying facts alleged by Mexico may be briefly described as follows: some are conceded by the United States, and some disputed. Mexico states that all the individuals the subject of its claims were Mexican nationals at the time of their arrest. It further contends that the United States authorities that arrested and interrogated these individuals had sufficient information at their disposal to be aware of the foreign nationality of those individuals. According to Mexico's account, in 50 of the specified cases, Mexican nationals were never informed by the competent United States authorities of their rights under Article 36, paragraph 1*(b)*, of the Vienna Convention and, in the two remaining cases, such information was not provided "without delay", as required by that provision. Mexico has indicated that in 29 of the 52 cases its consular authorities learned of the detention of the Mexican nationals only after death sentences had been handed down. In the 23 remaining cases, Mexico contends that it learned of the cases through means other than notification to the consular post by the competent United States authorities under Article 36, paragraph 1*(b)*. It explains that in five cases this was too late to affect the trials, that in 15 cases the defendants had already made incriminating statements, and that it became aware of the other three cases only after considerable delay.

20. Of the 52 cases referred to in Mexico's final submissions, 49 are currently at different stages of the proceedings before United States judicial authorities at state or federal level, and in three cases, those of Mr. Fierro (case No. 31), Mr. Moreno (case No. 39) and Mr. Torres (case No. 53), judicial remedies within the United States have already been exhausted. The Court has been informed of the variety of types of proceedings and forms of relief available in the criminal justice systems of the United States, which can differ from state to state. In very general terms, and according to the description offered by both Parties in the pleadings, it appears that the 52 cases may be classified into three categories: 24 cases which are currently in direct appeal; 25 cases in which means of direct appeal have been exhausted, but post-conviction relief *(habeas corpus)*, either at State or at federal level, is still available; and three cases in which no judicial remedies remain. The Court also notes that, in at least 33 cases, the alleged breach of the Vienna Convention was raised by the defendant either during pre-trial, at trial, on appeal or in *habeas corpus* proceedings, and that some of these claims were dismissed on procedural or substantive grounds and others are still pending. To date, in none of the 52 cases have the defendants had recourse to the clemency process.

* * *

40. In its final submissions Mexico asks the Court to adjudge and declare that the United States, in failing to comply with Article 36, paragraph 1, of the Vienna Convention, has "violated its international legal obligations to Mexico, in its own right and in the exercise of its right of diplomatic protection of its nationals".

The Court would first observe that the individual rights of Mexican nationals under subparagraph 1*(b)* of Article 36 of the Vienna Convention are rights which are to be asserted, at any rate in the first place, within the domestic legal system of the United States. Only when that process is completed and local remedies are exhausted would Mexico be entitled to espouse the individual claims of its national through the procedure of diplomatic protection.

In the present case Mexico does not, however, claim to be acting solely on that basis. It also asserts its own claims, basing them on the injury which it contends that *it has itself suffered, directly and through its nationals,* as a result of the violation by the United States of the obligations incumbent upon it under Article 36, paragraph 1*(a), (b)* and*(c)*.

The Court would recall that, in the *LaGrand* case, it recognized that "Article 36, paragraph 1 [of the Vienna Convention], creates individual rights [for the national concerned], which ... may be invoked in this Court by the national State of the detained person" (*I.C.J. Reports 2001*, p. 494, para. 77). It would further observe that violations of the rights of the individual under Article 36 may entail a violation of the rights of the sending State, and that violations of the rights of the latter may entail a violation of the rights of the individual. In these special circumstances of interdependence of the rights of the State and of individual rights, Mexico may, in submitting a claim in its own name, request the Court to rule on the violation of rights which it claims to have suffered both directly and through the violation of individual rights conferred on Mexican nationals under Article 36, paragraph 1*(b)*. The duty to exhaust local remedies does not apply to such a request.

* * *

Article 36, paragraph 1 [of the Vienna Convention on Consular Relations]

49. In its final submissions Mexico asks the Court to adjudge and declare that,

> "the United States of America, in arresting, detaining, trying, convicting, and sentencing the 52 Mexican nationals on death row described in Mexico's Memorial, violated its international legal obligations to Mexico, in its own right and in the exercise of its right to diplomatic protection of its nationals, by failing to inform, without delay, the 52 Mexican nationals after their arrest of their right to consular notification and access under Article 36 (1)*(b)* of the Vienna Convention on Consular Relations, and by depriving Mexico of its right to provide consular protection and the 52 nationals' right to receive such protection as Mexico would provide under Article 36 (1)*(a)* and*(c)* of the Convention".

50. The Court has already in its Judgment in the *LaGrand* case described Article 36, paragraph 1, as "an interrelated régime designed to facilitate the implementation of the system of consular protection"*(I.C.J. Reports 2001*, p. 492, para. 74). It is thus convenient to set out the entirety of that paragraph.

> "With a view toward facilitating the exercise of consular functions relating to nationals of the sending State:
>
> *(a)* consular officers shall be free to communicate with nationals of the sending State and to have access to them. Nationals of the sending State shall have the same freedom with respect to communication with and access to consular officers of the sending State;
>
> *(b)* if he so requests, the competent authorities of the receiving State shall, without delay, inform the consular post of the sending State if, within its consular dis-

trict, a national of that State is arrested or committed to prison or to custody pending trial or is detained in any other manner. Any communication addressed to the consular post by the person arrested, in prison, custody or detention shall be forwarded by the said authorities without delay. The said authorities shall inform the person concerned without delay of his rights under this subparagraph;

(c) consular officers shall have the right to visit a national of the sending State who is in prison, custody or detention, to converse and correspond with him and to arrange for his legal representation. They shall also have the right to visit any national of the sending State who is in prison, custody or detention in their district in pursuance of a judgment. Nevertheless, consular officers shall refrain from taking action on behalf of a national who is in prison, custody or detention if he expressly opposes such action."

* * *

57.... The Court therefore finds that, as regards the 52 persons listed ... above, the United States had obligations under Article 36, paragraph 1*(b)*.

58. Mexico asks the Court to find that

> "the obligation in Article 36, paragraph 1, of the Vienna Convention requires notification of consular rights and a reasonable opportunity for consular access before the competent authorities of the receiving State take any action potentially detrimental to the foreign national's rights".

59. Mexico contends that, in each of the 52 cases before the Court, the United States failed to provide the arrested persons with information as to their rights under Article 36, paragraph 1*(b)*, "without delay". It alleges that in one case, Mr. Esquivel (case No. 7), the arrested person was informed, but only some 18 months after the arrest, while in another, that of Mr. Juárez (case No. 10), information was given to the arrested person of his rights some 40 hours after arrest. Mexico contends that this still constituted a violation, because "without delay" is to be understood as meaning "immediately", and in any event before any interrogation occurs.

* * *

61. The Court thus now turns to the interpretation of Article 36, paragraph 1*(b)*, having found in paragraph 57 above that it is applicable to the 52 persons listed in paragraph 16. It begins by noting that Article 36, paragraph 1*(b)*, contains three separate but interrelated elements: the right of the individual concerned to be informed without delay of his rights under Article 36, paragraph 1*(b)*; the right of the consular post to be notified without delay of the individual's detention, if he so requests; and the obligation of the receiving State to forward without delay any communication addressed to the consular post by the detained person.

* * *

63. The Court finds that the duty upon the detaining authorities to give the Article 36, paragraph 1*(b)*, information to the individual arises once it is realized that the person is a foreign national, or once there are grounds to think that the person is probably a foreign national. Precisely when this may occur will vary with circumstances. The United States Department of State booklet, *Consular Notification and Access—Instructions for Federal, State and Local Law Enforcement and Other Officials Regarding Foreign Nationals in the United States and the Rights of Consular Officials to Assist Them*, issued to federal, state and local authorities in order to promote compliance with Article 36 of

the Vienna Convention points out in such cases that: "most, but not all, persons born outside the United States are not [citizens]. Unfamiliarity with English may also indicate foreign nationality." The Court notes that when an arrested person himself claims to be of United States nationality, the realization by the authorities that he is not in fact a United States national, or grounds for that realization, is likely to come somewhat later in time.

64. The United States has told the Court that millions of aliens reside, either legally or illegally, on its territory, and moreover that its laws concerning citizenship are generous. The United States has also pointed out that it is a multicultural society, with citizenship being held by persons of diverse appearance, speaking many languages. The Court appreciates that in the United States the language that a person speaks, or his appearance, does not necessarily indicate that he is a foreign national. Nevertheless, and particularly in view of the large numbers of foreign nationals living in the United States, these very circumstances suggest that it would be desirable for enquiry routinely to be made of the individual as to his nationality upon his detention, so that the obligations of the Vienna Convention may be complied with. The United States has informed the Court that some of its law enforcement authorities do routinely ask persons taken into detention whether they are United States citizens. Indeed, were each individual to be told at that time that, should he be a foreign national, he is entitled to ask for his consular post to be contacted, compliance with this requirement under Article 36, paragraph 1*(b)*, would be greatly enhanced. The provision of such information could parallel the reading of those rights of which any person taken into custody in connection with a criminal offence must be informed prior to interrogation by virtue of what in the United States is known as the "Miranda rule"; these rights include, *inter alia*, the right to remain silent, the right to have an attorney present during questioning, and the right to have an attorney appointed at government expense if the person cannot afford one. The Court notes that, according to the United States, such a practice in respect of the Vienna Convention rights is already being followed in some local jurisdictions.

65. Bearing in mind the complexities explained by the United States, the Court now begins by examining the application of Article 36, paragraph 1 *(b)*, of the Vienna Convention to the 52 cases.

* * *

75. The question nonetheless remains as to whether, ... the United States did provide the required information to the arrested persons "without delay". It is to that question that the Court now turns.

76. The Court has been provided with declarations from a number of the Mexican nationals concerned that attest to their never being informed of their rights under Article 36, paragraph 1*(b)*. The Court at the outset notes that, in 47 such cases, the United States nowhere challenges this fact of information not being given. Nevertheless, in the case of Mr. Hernández (case No. 34), the United States observes that

> "Although the [arresting] officer did not ask Hernández Llanas whether he wanted them to inform the Mexican Consulate of his arrest, it was certainly not unreasonable for him to assume that an escaped convict would not want the Consulate of the country from which he escaped notified of his arrest."

The Court notes that the clear duty to provide consular information under Article 36, paragraph 1*(b)*, does not invite assumptions as to what the arrested person might prefer, as a ground for not informing him. It rather gives the arrested person, once informed, the right to say he nonetheless does not wish his consular post to be notified. It necessarily follows that in each of these 47 cases, the duty to inform "without delay" has been violated.

77. In four cases, namely Ayala (case No. 2), Esquivel (case No. 7), Juárez (case No. 10) and Solache (case No. 47), some doubts remain as to whether the information that was given was provided without delay. For these, some examination of the term is thus necessary.

* * *

83. The Court now addresses the question of the proper interpretation of the expression "without delay" in the light of arguments put to it by the Parties. The Court begins by noting that the precise meaning of "without delay", as it is to be understood in Article 36, paragraph 1*(b)*, is not defined in the Convention. This phrase therefore requires interpretation according to the customary rules of treaty interpretation reflected in Articles 31 and 32 of the Vienna Convention on the Law of Treaties.

84. Article 1 of the Vienna Convention on Consular Relations, which defines certain of the terms used in the Convention, offers no definition of the phrase "without delay". Moreover, in the different language versions of the Convention various terms are employed to render the phrases "without delay" in Article 36 and "immediately" in Article 14. The Court observes that dictionary definitions, in the various languages of the Vienna Convention, offer diverse meanings of the term "without delay" (and also of "immediately"). It is therefore necessary to look elsewhere for an understanding of this term.

85. As for the object and purpose of the Convention, the Court observes that Article 36 provides for consular officers to be free to communicate with nationals of the sending State, to have access to them, to visit and speak with them and to arrange for their legal representation. It is not envisaged, either in Article 36, paragraph 1, or elsewhere in the Convention, that consular functions entail a consular officer himself or herself acting as the legal representative or more directly engaging in the criminal justice process. Indeed, that is confirmed by the wording of Article 36, paragraph 2, of the Convention. Thus, neither the terms of the Convention as normally understood, nor its object and purpose, suggest that "without delay" is to be understood as "immediately upon arrest and before interrogation".

86. The Court further notes that, notwithstanding the uncertainties in the *travaux préparatoires*, they too do not support such an interpretation.

* * *

87. The Court thus finds that "without delay" is not necessarily to be interpreted as "immediately" upon arrest. It further observes that during the Conference debates on this term, no delegate made any connection with the issue of interrogation. The Court considers that the provisions in Article 36, paragraph 1*(b)*, that the receiving State authorities "shall inform the person concerned without delay of his rights" cannot be interpreted to signify that the provision of such information must necessarily precede any interrogation, so that the commencement of interrogation before the information is given would be a breach of Article 36.

88. Although, by application of the usual rules of interpretation, "without delay" as regards the duty to inform an individual under Article 36, paragraph 1*(b)*, is not to be understood as necessarily meaning "immediately upon arrest", there is nonetheless a duty upon the arresting authorities to give that information to an arrested person as soon as it is realized that the person is a foreign national, or once there are grounds to think that the person is probably a foreign national.

89. With one exception, no information as to entitlement to consular notification was given in any of the cases ... within any of the various time periods suggested by the delegates to the Conference on the Vienna Convention, or by the United States itself.... Indeed, the information was given either not at all or at periods very significantly removed from the time of arrest.

* * *

90. The Court accordingly concludes that with respect to each of the individuals listed ... the United States has violated its obligation under Article 36, paragraph 1*(b)*, of the Vienna Convention to provide information to the arrested person.

* * *

98. In the first of its final submissions, Mexico also asks the Court to find that the violations it ascribes to the United States in respect of Article 36, paragraph 1*(b)*, have also deprived "Mexico of its right to provide consular protection and the 52 nationals' right to receive such protection as Mexico would provide under Article 36 (1) *(a)* and *(c)* of the Convention".

99. The relationship between the three subparagraphs of Article 36, paragraph 1, has been described by the Court in its Judgment in the *LaGrand* case (*I.C.J. Judgements 2001*, p. 492, para. 74) as "an interrelated régime". The legal conclusions to be drawn from that interrelationship necessarily depend upon the facts of each case. In the *LaGrand* case, the Court found that the failure for 16 years to inform the brothers of their right to have their consul notified effectively prevented the exercise of other rights that Germany might have chosen to exercise under subparagraphs*(a)* and*(c)*.

100. It is necessary to revisit the interrelationship of the three subparagraphs of Article 36, paragraph 1, in the light of the particular facts and circumstances of the present case.

101. The Court would first recall that, in the case of Mr. Juárez (case No. 10)..., when the defendant was informed of his rights, he declined to have his consular post notified. Thus in this case there was no violation of either subparagraph *(a)* or subparagraph*(c)* of Article 36, paragraph 1.

102. In the remaining cases, because of the failure of the United States to act in conformity with Article 36, paragraph 1*(b)*, Mexico was in effect precluded (in some cases totally, and in some cases for prolonged periods of time) from exercising its right under paragraph 1*(a)* to communicate with its nationals and have access to them. As the Court has already had occasion to explain, it is immaterial whether Mexico would have offered consular assistance, "or whether a different verdict would have been rendered. It is sufficient that the Convention conferred these rights"*(I.C.J. Reports 2001,* p. 492, para. 74), which might have been acted upon.

103. The same is true, *pari passu*, of certain rights identified in subparagraph *(c)*: "consular officers shall have the right to visit a national of the sending State who is in prison, custody or detention, and to converse and correspond with him ..."

* * *

106. On this aspect of the case, the Court thus concludes:

(1) that the United States committed breaches of the obligation incumbent upon it under Article 36, paragraph 1*(b)*, of the Vienna Convention to inform detained Mexican nationals of their rights under that paragraph, in case of the following 51 individuals: [the names of the 51 individuals are listed];

(2) that the United States committed breaches of the obligation incumbent upon it under Article 36, paragraph 1*(b)* to notify the Mexican consular post of the detention of the Mexican nationals listed in subparagraph (1) above, except in [the case of two individuals];

(3) that by virtue of its breaches of Article 36, paragraph 1*(b)*, as described in subparagraph (2) above, the United States also violated the obligation incumbent upon it under Article 36, paragraph 1*(a)*, of the Vienna Convention to enable Mexican consular officers to communicate with and have access to their nationals, as well as its obligation under paragraph 1*(c)* of that Article regarding the right of consular officers to visit their detained nationals;

(4) that the United States, by virtue of these breaches of Article 36, paragraph 1*(b)*, also violated the obligation incumbent upon it under paragraph 1*(c)* of that Article to enable Mexican consular officers to arrange for legal representation of their nationals in the case of the following individuals: [the names of 34 individuals are listed];

* * *

Legal consequences of the breach

115. Having concluded that in most of the cases brought before the Court by Mexico in the 52 instances, there has been a failure to observe the obligations prescribed by Article 36, paragraph 1*(b)*, of the Vienna Convention, the Court now proceeds to the examination of the legal consequences of such a breach and of what legal remedies should be considered for the breach.

* * *

119. The general principle on the legal consequences of the commission of an internationally wrongful act was stated by the Permanent Court of International Justice in the *Factory at Chorzów* case as follows: "It is a principle of international law that the breach of an engagement involves an obligation to make reparation in an adequate form."*(Factory at Chorzów, Jurisdiction, 1927,* P.C.I.J., *Series* A, *No. 9,* p.21) What constitutes "reparation in an adequate form" clearly varies depending upon the concrete circumstances surrounding each case and the precise nature and scope of the injury, since the question has to be examined from the viewpoint of what is the "reparation in an adequate form" that corresponds to the injury. In a subsequent phase of the same case, the Permanent Court went on to elaborate on this point as follows:

> "The essential principle contained in the actual notion of an illegal act—a principle which seems to be established by international practice and in particular by the decisions of arbitral tribunals—is that reparation must, as far as possible, wipe out all the consequences of the illegal act and reestablish the situation which would, in all probability, have existed if that act had not been committed."*(Factory at Chorzów, Merits, 1928, P.C.I.J., Series A, No. 17,* p. 47.)

* * *

121. Similarly, in the present case the Court's task is to determine what would be adequate reparation for the violations of Article 36. It should be clear from what has been observed above that the internationally wrongful acts committed by the United States were the failure of its competent authorities to inform the Mexican nationals concerned, to notify Mexican consular posts and to enable Mexico to provide consular assistance. It follows that the remedy to make good these violations should consist in an obligation on the United States to permit review and reconsideration of these nationals'

cases by the United States courts, as the Court will explain further in paragraphs 128 to 134 below, with a view to ascertaining whether in each case the violation of Article 36 committed by the competent authorities caused actual prejudice to the defendant in the process of administration of criminal justice.

122. The Court reaffirms that the case before it concerns Article 36 of the Vienna Convention and not the correctness as such of any conviction or sentencing. The question of whether the violations of Article 36, paragraph 1, are to be regarded as having, in the causal sequence of events, ultimately led to convictions and severe penalties is an integral part of criminal proceedings before the courts of the United States and is for them to determine in the process of review and reconsideration. In so doing, it is for the courts of the United States to examine the facts, and in particular the prejudice and its causes, taking account of the violation of the rights set forth in the Convention.

123. It is not to be presumed, as Mexico asserts, that partial or total annulment of conviction or sentence provides the necessary and sole remedy.

* * *

131. In stating in its Judgment in the *LaGrand* case that "the United States of America, *by means of its own choosing,* shall allow the review and reconsideration of the conviction and sentence"*(I.C.J. Reports 2001,* p. 516, para. 128; emphasis added), the Court acknowledged that the concrete modalities for such review and reconsideration should be left primarily to the United States. It should be underlined, however, that this freedom in the choice of means for such review and reconsideration is not without qualification: as the passage of the Judgment quoted above makes abundantly clear, such review and reconsideration has to be carried out "by taking account of the violation of the rights set forth in the Convention" *(I.C.J. Reports 2001*, p. 514, para. 125), including, in particular, the question of the legal consequences of the violation upon the criminal proceedings that have followed the violation.

* * *

138. The Court would emphasize that the "review and reconsideration" prescribed by it in the *LaGrand* case should be effective. Thus it should "tak[e] account of the violation of the rights set forth in [the] Convention"*(I.C.J. Reports 2001*, p. 516, para. 128 (7)) and guarantee that the violation and the possible prejudice caused by that violation will be fully examined and taken into account in the review and reconsideration process. Lastly, review and reconsideration should be both of the sentence and of the conviction.

* * *

140. As has been explained ... above, the Court is of the view that, in cases where the breach of the individual rights of Mexican nationals under Article 36, paragraph 1*(b)*, of the Convention has resulted, in the sequence of judicial proceedings that has followed, in the individuals concerned being subjected to prolonged detention or convicted and sentenced to severe penalties, the legal consequences of this breach have to be examined and taken into account in the course of review and reconsideration. The Court considers that it is the judicial process that is suited to this task.

* * *

144. Finally, the Court will consider the eighth submission of Mexico, in which it asks the Court to adjudge and declare:

> "That the [United States] shall cease its violations of Article 36 of the Vienna Convention with regard to Mexico and its 52 nationals and shall provide

appropriate guarantees and assurances that it shall take measures sufficient to achieve increased compliance with Article 36 (1) and to ensure compliance with Article 36 (2)."

* * *

149. The Mexican request for guarantees of non-repetition is based on its contention that beyond these 52 cases there is a "regular and continuing" pattern of breaches by the United States of Article 36. In this respect, the Court observes that there is no evidence properly before it that would establish a general pattern. While it is a matter of concern that, even in the wake of the *LaGrand* Judgment, there remain a substantial number of cases of failure to carry out the obligation to furnish consular information to Mexican nationals, the Court notes that the United States has been making considerable efforts to ensure that its law enforcement authorities provide consular information to every arrested person they know or have reason to believe is a foreign national. Especially at the stage of pre-trial consular information, it is noteworthy that the United States has been making good faith efforts to implement the obligations incumbent upon it under Article 36, paragraph 1, of the Vienna Convention, through such measures as a new outreach programme launched in 1998, including the dissemination to federal, state and local authorities of the State Department booklet mentioned above.... The Court wishes to recall in this context what it has said in paragraph 64 about efforts in some jurisdictions to provide the information under Article 36, paragraph 1 *(b)*, in parallel with the reading of the "Miranda rights".

* * *

151. The Court would now re-emphasize a point of importance. In the present case, it has had occasion to examine the obligations of the United States under Article 36 of the Vienna Convention in relation to Mexican nationals sentenced to death in the United States. Its findings as to the duty of review and reconsideration of convictions and sentences have been directed to the circumstance of severe penalties being imposed on foreign nationals who happen to be of Mexican nationality. To avoid any ambiguity, it should be made clear that, while what the Court has stated concerns the Mexican nationals whose cases have been brought before it by Mexico, the Court has been addressing the issues of principle raised in the course of the present proceedings from the viewpoint of the general application of the Vienna Convention, and there can be no question of making an *a contrario* argument in respect of any of the Court's findings in the present Judgment. In other words, the fact that in this case the Court's ruling has concerned only Mexican nationals cannot be taken to imply that the conclusions reached by it in the present Judgment do not apply to other foreign nationals finding themselves in similar situations in the United States.

* * *

153. For these reasons,

THE COURT,

* * *

(4) By fourteen votes to one,

Finds that, by not informing, without delay upon their detention, the 51 Mexican nationals referred to ... above of their rights under Article 36, paragraph 1*(b)*, of the Vienna Convention on Consular Relations of 24 April 1963, the United States of America breached the obligations incumbent upon it under that subparagraph; ...

(5) By fourteen votes to one,

Finds that, by not notifying the appropriate Mexican consular post without delay of the detention of the 49 Mexican nationals referred to ... above and thereby depriving the United Mexican States of the right, in a timely fashion, to render the assistance provided for by the Vienna Convention to the individuals concerned, the United States of America breached the obligations incumbent upon it under Article 36, paragraph 1 *(b)*; ...

(6) By fourteen votes to one,

Finds that, in relation to the 49 Mexican nationals referred to ... above, the United States of America deprived the United Mexican States of the right, in a timely fashion, to communicate with and have access to those nationals and to visit them in detention, and thereby breached the obligations incumbent upon it under Article 36, paragraph 1 *(a)* and*(c)*, of the Convention; ...

(7) By fourteen votes to one,

Finds that, in relation to the 34 Mexican nationals referred to ... above, the United States of America deprived the United Mexican States of the right, in a timely fashion, to arrange for legal representation of those nationals, and thereby breached the obligations incumbent upon it under Article 36, paragraph 1*(c)*, of the Convention; ...

(8) By fourteen votes to one,

Finds that, by not permitting the review and reconsideration, in the light of the rights set forth in the Convention, of the conviction and sentences of Mr. César Roberto Fierro Reyna, Mr. Roberto Moreno Ramos and Mr. Osvaldo Torres Aguilera, after the violations referred to in subparagraph (4) above had been established in respect of those individuals, the United States of America breached the obligations incumbent upon it under Article 36, paragraph 2, of the Convention; ...

(9) By fourteen votes to one,

Finds that the appropriate reparation in this case consists in the obligation of the United States of America to provide, by means of its own choosing, review and reconsideration of the convictions and sentences of the Mexican nationals referred to in subparagraphs (4), (5), (6) and (7) above, by taking account both of the violation of the rights set forth in Article 36 of the Convention and of paragraphs 138 to 151 of this Judgment;

(10) Unanimously,

Takes note of the commitment undertaken by the United States of America to ensure implementation of the specific measures adopted in performance of its obligations under Article 36, paragraph 1*(b)*, of the Vienna Convention; and *finds* that this commitment must be regarded as meeting the request by the United Mexican States for guarantees and assurances of non-repetition;

(11) Unanimously,

Finds that, should Mexican nationals nonetheless be sentence to severe penalties, without their rights under Article 36, paragraph 1*(b)*, of the Convention having been respected, the United States of America shall provide, by means of its own choosing, review and reconsideration of the conviction and sentence, so as to allow full weight to be given to the violation of the rights set forth in the Convention....

* * *

QUESTIONS

1. Which obligations under the Vienna Convention on Consular Relations was the U.S. held to have violated with respect to Mexico?
2. Which obligations had the United States failed to keep with respect to the Mexican defendants?
3. How did the Court interpret the Consular Convention phrase "without delay"?
4. If, in the future, a Mexican national (or indeed a national of any state which is a party to the Vienna Convention on Consular Relations) is not informed by the U.S. (or any state party to the Convention) of his/her rights under the Convention and is detained by the government or convicted and sentenced to jail, what must the U.S.(or any other state party to the Convention) do to remedy the situation and what rights would the individual have?

Note

The *Avena* litigation was the third time that a country had brought a suit against the United States for violations of the Vienna Convention on Consular Relations. The first was Paraguay,[12] followed by Germany[13] and then Mexico.

The cases in the ICJ were primarily treaty violation cases....

> The factual question of whether the United States had violated its obligations under the VCCR was hardly at issues in any of these cases. For the most part, the United States admitted its failures, apologized to the States concerned, and promised to do a better job of complying with the treaty in the future. The major arguments at the international level addressed whether individual prisoners could claim remedies for the treaty violation and, if so, what the scope of the remedy would be. The ICJ ruled in the German *LaGrand* case that individuals could claim rights under the treaty, and Mexico argued in the *Avena* case that the remedy should be the partial, or total, nullification of all convictions or sentences where the treaty had been violated. If the ICJ had completely agreed with Mexico, the effect in the United States, and in all the other countries who are party to the VCCR, might have been vast.
>
> The criminal bar in the United States rapidly realized that for their foreign clients they had a new, and possibly winning, argument. Literally hundreds of cases in the United States either raised the treaty defense at trial, on direct appeal, or on collateral review.
>
> The ICJ finally rejected blanket nullification of convictions and determined that the United States must provide "review and reconsideration" of all convictions and sentences of the foreigners represented in the litigation to determine whether the failure to inform the defendants of their treaty rights "caused actual prejudice to the defendant[s]" and whether "in the causal sequence of events" the violations of the VCCR "ultimately led to convictions and severe penalties...." The Court, moreover, indicated that this review and reconsideration must be carried out by the judicial branch of government, not by clemency boards or pardoning commissions.

---

12. Convention on Consular Relations Case (Paraguay v. U.S.), 1998 I.C.J. 248 (Interim Protection Order of Apr. 9).

13. LaGrand (Germany v. U.S.) 2001 I.C.J. 466 (June 27).

> Almost all of the defendants had been procedurally barred from raising the treaty issue because, being ignorant of their treaty rights, they had failed to raise the issue at the first possible opportunity. The ICJ ruled, however, that courts in the United States could not use the procedural default bar to prevent defendants from raising the treaty issue because it was the United States itself, or the individual states as the agents of the United States, who had the obligation to inform the defendants of their rights.
>
> The stage was thus set for addressing the issue of the extent to which U.S. courts must comply with rulings by an international court, particular when the ruling reaches far into the criminal justice process of U.S. state courts....
>
> The United States has historically been, at best, ambivalent about the binding nature of international law but never before has the federal government been ordered by an international court to enforce a treaty obligation through the mechanism of its state courts, requiring the state courts to disregard some of their criminal procedure rules. It came as a great surprise, therefore, when, after the ICJ's judgment in the Mexican case, President Bush issued a memorandum on February 28, 2005 telling the states that they must comply with the *Avena* decision. Texas promptly replied that the President had no power to interfere with the running of the state's criminal courts.... This ushered in the next phase of controversy which has raised large Constitutional questions revolving around the allocation of power between various branches of the government and between federal and state governments.
>
> *Medellin* [v. *Texas*, 128 S.Ct. 1346 (2008)] was the first case to make its way to the Supreme Court raising this vast array of hugely significant issues,.... The Supreme Court's decision ultimately refused to enforce the ICJ's *Avena* decision either as a result of obligations under treaties or in compliance with the President's memorandum. The states remain free to comply with the decision as Justice Steven's concurring opinion invites them to do so. Although the Court does imply that the Senate has the power to make clear that treaties are self executing and that Congress is free to pass implementing legislation, the impact of this decision on the way that the rest of the world views the United States' compliance with its international obligations is likely to be severe.[14]

There has been further litigation in the I.C.J. relating to the *Avena Case*, most recently in *Request for Interpretation of Judgment of 31 March 2004* (Mexico v. U.S.), 2009 I.C.J. ___, where the Court found that by executing José Medellin the United States had violated the Court's order of 16 July 2008 and again reaffirmed "the continuing binding character of the obligations of the United States under ... the *Avena* Judgment...." (Dispositive, paras. 2 & 3). (Jan. 19).

States that are parties to the Vienna Convention on the Law of Treaties will try to use the Convention's rules on treaty interpretation (articles 31–33) when such issues arise in their own courts but there may be disagreement among judges about the meaning of the Convention's rules.

---

14. Valerie Epps, The *Medellin v. Texas* Symposium: A Case Worthy of Comment, 31 Suffolk Transnat'l L. Rev. 209, 210–213 (footnotes omitted)(2008).

The United States is not a party to the Vienna Convention on the Law of Treaties and has generally followed a fairly liberal path in allowing the introduction of extrinsic evidence to interpret treaties. The excerpts from the cases below are designed to highlight the various approaches to treaty interpretation followed by different members of the United States Supreme Court.

Olympic Airways v. Husain, 504 U.S. 644, 649–650 (2004), was a case which turned on the interpretation of the word "accident" in the Warsaw Convention.[15] Justice Thomas, writing for the majority said:

> We begin with the language of ... the Convention.... In [an earlier case], the Court recognized that the text of the Convention does not define the term "accident" and that the context in which it is used is not "illuminating.".... The Court nevertheless discerned the meaning of the term "accident" from the Convention's text, structure, and history as well as from the subsequent conduct of the parties to the Convention. (Citations omitted).

In his dissent, however, Justice Scalia stated:

> When we interpret a treaty, we accord the judgments of sister signatories "'considerable weight'" .... True to that canon, our previous Warsaw Convention opinions have carefully considered foreign case law.... Today's decision stands out for its failure to give any serious consideration to how the courts of our treaty partners have resolved the legal issues before us....
>
> One would have thought that foreign courts' interpretations of a treaty that their governments adopted jointly with ours, and that they have an actual role in applying, would be (to put it mildly) all the more relevant. Id. at 658. (Citations omitted).

In *Medellin v. Texas*, 128 S.Ct 1346, at 1357–1358 (2008) Chief Justice Roberts, in his majority opinions concluded that because various treaties were interpreted as non-self executing (i.e. they needed further legislation to be domestically enforceable), the I.C.J.'s decision in *Avena* could not be enforced in state courts where state law was contrary to the judgment. He stated:

> The interpretation of a treaty, like the interpretation of a statute, begins with the text.... Because a treaty ratified by the United States is "an agreement among sovereign powers," we have also considered as "aids to its interpretation" the negotiation and drafting history of the treaty as well as "the postratification understanding" of signatory nations. (Citations omitted).

Justice Breyer, in his vigorous dissent disagreed with the focus of the majority's interpretative methodology:

> For these reasons, I would find the United State's treaty obligation to comply with the ICJ judgment in *Avena* is enforceable in court in this case without further congressional action beyond Senate ratification (*sic*) of the relevant treaties. The majority reaches a different conclusion because it looks for the wrong thing (explicit textual expression about self-execution) using the wrong standard (clarity) in the wrong place (the treaty language). Id. At 1389.

---

15. Convention for the Unification of Certain Rules Relating to International Transportation by Air, signed 12 Oct. 1929, entered into force 12 Feb. 1933 (later amended by the Hague Protocol of 1955, and the Montreal Protocol of 1975), 49 Stat. 3000, T.S. No. 876 (1934).

Justice Breyer would have looked to the Supremacy Clause, Article VI, of the U.S. Constitution to determine the self-execution issue.

Invalidity

Several grounds are listed in the Convention which may result in a treaty's being found invalid.

Error

This ground of invalidity has seldom been invoked. One can reasonably expect that State negotiators of a treaty will be properly informed about the subject under discussion. This article does not include errors in the wording of a treaty which is covered by article 79. To be invoked as a ground of invalidity the error must relate "to a fact or situation which was assumed by the State to exist at the time when the treaty was concluded and formed an essential basis of its consent to be bound by the treaty." (Article 48(1)). If the State claiming error "contributed by its own conduct to the error" or had notice of the error then the state is not permitted to claim invalidity. Occasionally this ground has been raised with respect to the alleged inaccuracy of maps that were relied upon in settling a border dispute.[16]

Fraud and Corruption

Article 49 provides that a state may claim invalidity of a treaty if it "has been induced to conclude a treaty by the fraudulent conduct of another ... state...." The Vienna Convention does not define fraud and the International Law Commission decided that it would not attempt to define the term but rather "leave its precise scope to be worked out in practice...."[17]

If a treaty has been procured by the corruption of its representative by another negotiating state that may be grounds for invalidity. Again there are few cases. Not too many states will admit to, or leave evidence of, attempts at corruption and those who may have succumbed to such attempts are unlikely to reveal it willingly. The International Law Commission was aware of the practice of some states to give and receive gifts when treaties are signed, sometimes on quite a lavish scale. Although it did not address this practice directly, it did note that the article "did not mean to imply that ... a small courtesy or favour shown to a representative in connection with the conclusion of a treaty may be invoked as a pretext for invalidating the treaty."[18]

16. In the *Case Concerning the Temple of Preah Vihear*, (Cambodia v. Thailand) 1962 I.C.J. 6, Thailand claimed that a map which showed the border between Thailand and Cambodia contained an error. The Court refused to accept this argument because Thai members of the border Commission of Delimitation had seen and approved the map.

17. 1966, II Y.B. Int'l L. Comm'n 244.

18. Id. at 245.

Coercion

Article 51 declares that if a treaty has been "procured by the coercion of its representative through acts or threats directed against him [it] shall be without any legal effect." There are only a few examples of such coercion which have come to light. The threats referred to in article 51 have to be directed against the representative personally rather than against his/her state. In 1939 the representatives of Czechoslovakia were subject to extreme pressure to sign a treaty establishing German control over their state.

> "The German ministers [Goering and Ribbentrop] were pitiless.... They literally hunted Dr. Hácha [the President of Czechoslovakia] and M. Chavlkovsky [the Foreign Minister] round the table on which the documents were lying, thrusting them continually before them, pushing pens into their hands...."[19]

During these proceedings Dr. Hácha fainted and was revived by an injection from Dr. Morell, Hitler's physician.

Article 52 declares a treaty void if it is the result of "the threat or use of force in violation of the principles of international law embodied in the Charter of the United Nations." This article refers directly to the prohibition contained in article 2(4) of the U.N. Charter. Historically international law had not prohibited the use of force and indeed throughout the centuries force had been a principal method of settling interstate disputes with the victor imposing its wishes on the vanquished. During the twentieth century a movement was begun to bring the use of force within the umbrella of international law. This movement culminated in the adoption of the U.N. Charter in 1945. The limits on the use of force contained in the Charter are now established as customary law. (See chapter X.) Some of the members of the International Law Commission had wanted to include other forms of coercion, such as economic coercion, as falling within article 52 but this proposal was rejected.

Conflict with a Peremptory Norm (*Jus Cogens*)

Article 53 declares a treaty void "if, at the time of its conclusion, it conflicts with a peremptory norm of general international law." Article 64 states that if an existing treaty conflicts with a newly emerged peremptory norm, the treaty "becomes void and terminates." Article 53 defines a peremptory norm as "a norm accepted and recognized by the international community of States as a whole as a norm from which no derogation is permitted...." While there is often disagreement about whether a particular rule has reached the level of a peremptory norm, a number of international rules have clearly reached that status, such as the prohibition of the use of force found in article 2(4) of the U.N. Charter and the prohibition of genocide reflected in the Genocide Convention.[20]

---

19. Dispatch by the French Ambassador to Berlin, M. Coulondre, as quoted in William L. Shirer, The Rise and Fall of the Third Reich 446 (1960).

20. 78 U.N.T.S. 277, adopted by the U.N. General Assembly on 9 Dec.1948, G.A. Res. 2670, U.N. GAOR, 3d. Sess., pt. 1, U.N. Doc. A/810 at 174 (1948), entered into force 12 Jan. 1951. For other examples of peremptory norms see The International Law Commission's Commentary to the Vienna Convention, 1966, II Y.B. Int'l L. Comm'n 247–248.

Termination and Suspension

Modern treaties almost always have a termination article, unless they deal with certain fundamental rights, such as human rights. A termination clause would typically provide that upon the giving of a specified term of notice any party to the treaty may terminate its consent to be bound and withdraw from the treaty. Article 54 makes it clear that termination is perfectly permissible provided it is done in conformity with the terms of the treaty or with the consent of all the other treaty partners. If a treaty does not contain a termination provision, article 56 states that "it is not subject to denunciation or withdrawal unless" the parties intended to allow such or such a right can be implied from the treaty, in which case the parties must give at least a year's notice of their intent to withdraw from the treaty. If all the parties to an existing treaty conclude a later treaty on the same subject matter, the earlier treaty is terminated if that was the intent of the parties or if the provisions of the later treaty are incompatible with the earlier treaty (article 59).

Material Breach

It is important to note that not all breaches of treaties give rise to a right to terminate. Many treaties are full of technical provisions and to allow termination for minor breaches would undermine the principle of *pacta sunt servanda.* The Vienna Convention defines a material breach as either "a repudiation of the treaty not sanctioned by the present Convention" or "the violation of a provision essential to the accomplishment of the object or purpose of the treaty." (Article 60(3)(a)&(b)). These termination provisions are specifically stated not to apply "to provisions relating to the protection of the human person contained in treaties of a humanitarian character...." (Article 60(5)). The notion here is that if, for example, a state party to the Torture Convention[21] suddenly starts practicing torture on its citizens, that does not permit other parties to the Convention to terminate their obligations under the Treaty and start torturing their own citizens.

In both the *LaGrand Case*[22] and the *Avena Case*[23] the United States was found to have breached the Vienna Convention on Consular Relations. The main issue for the I.C.J was whether the Convention created individual rights and, if so, what remedies should be afforded both to the individuals who had not been informed of their rights and to their countries. Neither Germany, nor Mexico, contemplated arguing that, as a consequence of the United States' breach of the Convention, they had a right to refuse consular notification to U.S. citizens in their countries, nor did they suggest that their obligations under the Convention were wholly terminated with respect to the United States.

---

21. 1465 U.N.T.S. 85, adopted by the General Assembly, 10 Dec. 1984, G.A. Res. 46, U.N. GAOR, 39th Sess., Annex, reprinted at 23 I.L.M. 1027 (1984), as modified 24 I.L.M. 535 (1985), entered into force 26 June 1987.

22. (Germany v. U.S.) 2001 I.C.J. 466, para. 67.

23. (Mexico v. U.S.) 2004 I.C.J. 12, para. 106.

Legal Consequences for States of the Continued Presence of South Africa in Namibia (South West Africa) Notwithstanding Security Council Resolution 276 (1970)

1971 I.C.J. 16 (Advisory Opinion)

Note

The League of Nations had set up a system of Mandates under which developed nations exercised administrative powers over less developed states. These Mandates were absorbed within the United Nations after the League collapsed. The United Kingdom was granted a Mandate over South West Africa [later to become Namibia] to be carried out for the United Kingdom by the government of the Union of South Africa. The Mandatory Power was "to ensure the moral and material well-being and security of the indigenous inhabitants of South West Africa [Namibia]." South Africa had pursued a policy of apartheid, not only within South Africa, but also within South West Africa, which had been widely condemned by the international community. After lengthy and fruitless negotiations, the General Assembly adopted a resolution deciding that South Africa's Mandate over South West Africa was terminated.[24] This resolution was reaffirmed by Security Council Resolution 276.[25] South Africa refused to abide by the resolutions and the Security Council requested an advisory opinion from the International Court of Justice on the following question:

> What are the legal consequences for States of the continued presence of South Africa in Namibia, notwithstanding Security Council resolution 276 (1970)?

In the course of deciding that South Africa's continued presence in Namibia was illegal and that it should immediately withdraw from the area, the Court discussed the topic of material breach of a treaty.

Opinion of the Court

In paragraph 3 of the operative part of the resolution the General Assembly, "*Declares* that South Africa has failed to fulfil its obligations in respect of the administration of the Mandated Territory and to ensure the moral and material well-being and security of the indigenous inhabitants of South West Africa and has, in fact, disavowed the Mandate". In paragraph 4 the decision is reached, as a consequence of the previous declaration "that the Mandate conferred upon His Britannic Majesty to be exercised on his behalf by the Government of the Union of South Africa is *therefore* terminated...." (Emphasis added.) It is this part of the resolution which is relevant in the present proceedings.

---

24. Terminating South Africa's Mandate Over South West Africa, 27 Oct. 1966, G.A. Res. 2145, U.N. GAOR, 21st Sess., (1966), reprinted at 5 I.L.M. 1190 (1966).

25. The Situation in Namibia, 30 Jan. 1970, S.C. Res. 276, U.N. SCOR, U.N. Doc. S/INF/25, at 1 (1970).

In examining this action of the General Assembly it is appropriate to have regard to the general principles of international law regulating termination of a treaty relationship on account of breach.... As the Court indicated in 1962 "this Mandate, like practically all other similar Mandates" was "a special type of instrument composite in nature and instituting a novel international régime. It incorporates a definite agreement...." (I.C.J. Reports 1962, p. 331). The Court stated conclusively in that Judgment that the Mandate "in fact and in law, is an international agreement having the character of a treaty or convention" (I.C.J. Reports 1962, p. 330). The rules laid down by the Vienna Convention on the Law of Treaties concerning termination of a treaty relationship on account of breach (adopted without a dissenting vote) may in many respects be considered as a codification of existing customary law on the subject. In the light of these rules, only a material breach of a treaty justifies termination, such breach being defined as:

(a) a repudiation of the treaty not sanctioned by the present Convention; or
(b) the violation of a provision essential to the accomplishment of the object or purpose of the treaty (Art. 60, para. 3).

General Assembly resolution 2145 (XXI) determines that both forms of material breach had occurred in this case. By stressing that South Africa "has, in fact, disavowed the Mandate", the General Assembly declared in fact that it had repudiated it. The resolution in question is therefore to be viewed as the exercise of the right to terminate a relationship in case of a deliberate and persistent violation of obligations which destroys the very object and purpose of that relationship.

* * *

It has been contended that the Covenant of the League of Nations did not confer on the Council of the League power to terminate a mandate for misconduct of the Mandatory and that no such power could therefore be exercised by the United Nations, since it could not derive from the League greater powers than the latter itself had. For this objection to prevail it would be necessary to show that the mandates system, as established under the League, excluded the application of the general principle of law that a right of termination on account of breach must be presumed to exist in respect of all treaties, except as regards provisions relating to the protection of the human person contained in treaties of a humanitarian character (as indicated in Art. 60, para. 5, of the Vienna Convention). The silence of a treaty as to the existence of such a right cannot be interpreted as implying the exclusion of a right which has its source outside of the treaty, in general international law, and is dependent on the occurrence of circumstances which are not normally envisaged when a treaty is concluded.

QUESTIONS

1. How had the agreement in the case above been breached?
2. Why was the breach considered material?
3. What is a party to a treaty permitted to do once it has decided that the other party has materially breached the treaty?

Supervening Impossibility of Performance

Occasionally it will be impossible to carry out a treaty because "an object indispensable for the execution of the treaty" (article 61) has permanently disappeared or been destroyed. Article 61 recognizes these conditions as permitting termination or withdrawal from a treaty. The International Law Commission's Commentary supplies some examples: "the submergence of an island, the drying up of a river or the destruction of a dam or hydro-electric installation indispensable for the execution of the treaty."[26] If the condition creating the impossibility is only temporary, then the treaty will be suspended until conditions have returned to the *status quo ante*. Impossibility of performance may not be invoked by a party to the treaty where the impossibility results from a breach of that party's obligations under the treaty. If a state party to the treaty ceases to exist the rules of state succession to treaties apply. (See pages 92–95.)

Fundamental Change of Circumstances

It was with some reluctance that the International Law Commission included a provision for invalidity of treaties on the basis of a fundamental change of circumstances. It was well understood that if this provision were drafted too broadly it would provide an easy escape route for those wishing to break treaties. At the same time most modern scholars accept the principle of *rebus sic stantibus* which posits a tacit implied clause in all treaties which rests the treaty's validity on "things remaining as they are." This idea essentially means that if the conditions under which the treaty was negotiated change radically, then the whole basis of the treaty is vitiated. The problem for the drafters of the Vienna Convention was to keep this principle within reasonable bounds. Article 62 states that a fundamental change of circumstances can only be invoked as a ground for terminating or withdrawing from a treaty when: "(a) the existence of those circumstances constituted an essential basis of the consent of the parties ... and (b) the effect of the change is radically to transform the extent of the obligations still to be performed...." Specifically excluded from this doctrine are boundary treaties or where "the fundamental change is a result of a breach by the party invoking it...." (Article 62 (2)(a)&(b)).

Case Concerning Gabcíkovo-Nagymaros Project

Hungary v. Slovakia
1997 I.C.J. 7

Note

"Hungary and Czechoslovakia in 1977 concluded a treaty for the building of dam structures in Slovakia and Hungary for the production of electric power, flood control and improvement of navigation on the Danube. In 1989 Hungary suspended and subsequently abandoned completion of the project alleging that it entailed grave risks to the Hungarian environment and the water supply of Budapest. Slovakia (successor to Czechoslovakia['s treaty obligations, para. 123]) denied these allegations and insisted that Hungary carry out its treaty obligations. It planned and subsequently put into operation an alternative project only on Slovak territory, [referred to as Variant C] whose

26. Reports of the Commission to the General Assembly, 1966, II Y.B. Int'l L. Comm'n 256.

operation had effects on Hungary's access to the waters of the Danube."[27] Hungary argued, *inter alia,* that she was not required to comply with the treaty because of supervening impossibility of performance, fundamental change of circumstances and material breach of the treaty by Czechoslovakia. The portions of the Court's opinion dealing with those issues appear below.

Opinion of the Court

94. Hungary's second argument relied on the terms of Article 61 of the Vienna Convention, which is worded as follows:

"Article 61
Supervening impossibility of performance

1. A party may invoke the impossibility of performing a treaty as a ground for terminating or withdrawing from it if the impossibility results from the permanent disappearance or destruction of an object indispensable for the execution of the treaty. If the impossibility is temporary, it may be invoked only as a ground for suspending the operation of the treaty.

2. Impossibility of performance may not be invoked by a party as a ground for terminating, withdrawing from or suspending the operation of a treaty if the impossibility is the result of a breach by that party either of an obligation under the treaty or of any other international obligation owed to any other party to the treaty".

Hungary declared that it could not be "obliged to fulfil a practically impossible task, namely to construct a barrage system on its own territory that would cause irreparable environmental damage". It concluded that:

> By May 1992 the essential object of the Treaty—an economic joint investment which was consistent with environmental protection and which was operated by the two parties jointly—had permanently disappeared, and the Treaty had thus become impossible to perform.

In Hungary's view, the "object indispensable for the execution of the treaty", whose disappearance or destruction was required by Article 61 of the Vienna Convention, did not have to be a physical object, but could also include, in the words of the International Law Commission, "a legal situation which was the raison d'être of the rights and obligations".

Slovakia claimed that Article 61 was the only basis for invoking impossibility of performance as a ground for termination, that paragraph 1 of that Article clearly contemplated physical "disappearance or destruction" of the object in question, and that, in any event, paragraph 2 precluded the invocation of impossibility "if the impossibility is the result of a breach by that party ... of an obligation under the treaty".

95. As to "fundamental change of circumstances", Hungary relied on Article 62 of the Vienna Convention on the Law of Treaties which states as follows:

"Article 62
Fundamental change of circumstances

1. A fundamental change of circumstances which has occurred with regard to those existing at the time of the conclusion of a treaty, and which was not foreseen by the par-

27. Unofficial Communiqué prepared by the Registry of the Court, No. 97/10, Sept. 25, 1997.

ties, may not be invoked as a ground for terminating or withdrawing from the treaty unless:

(a) the existence of those circumstances constituted an essential basis of the consent of the parties to be bound by the treaty; and

(b) the effect of the change is radically to transform the extent of obligations still to be performed under the treaty.

2. A fundamental change of circumstance may not be invoked as a ground for terminating or withdrawing from a treaty:

(a) if the treaty establishes a boundary; or

(b) if the fundamental change is the result of a breach by the party invoking it either of an obligation under the treaty or of any other international obligation owed to any party to the treaty.

3. If, under the foregoing paragraphs, a party may invoke a fundamental change of circumstances as a ground for terminating or withdrawing from a treaty it may also invoke the change as a ground for suspending the operation of the treaty."

Hungary identified a number of "substantive elements" present at the conclusion of the 1977 Treaty which it said had changed fundamentally by the date of notification of termination. These included the notion of "socialist integration", for which the Treaty had originally been a "vehicle", but which subsequently disappeared; the "single and indivisible operational system", which was to be replaced by a unilateral scheme; the fact that the basis of the planned joint investment had been overturned by the sudden emergence of both States into a market economy; the attitude of Czechoslovakia which had turned the "framework treaty" into an "immutable norm"; and finally, the transformation of a treaty consistent with environmental protection into "a prescription for environmental disaster."

Slovakia, for its part, contended that the changes identified by Hungary had not altered the nature of the obligations under the Treaty from those originally undertaken, so that no entitlement to terminate it arose from them.

96. Hungary further argued that termination of the Treaty was justified by Czechoslovakia's material breaches of the Treaty, and in this regard it invoked Article 60 of the Vienna Convention on the Law of Treaties, which provides:

"Article 60

Termination or suspension of the operation of a treaty as a consequence of its breach

1. A material breach of a bilateral treaty by one of the parties entitles the other to invoke the breach as a ground for terminating the treaty or suspending its operation in whole or in part.

2. A material breach of a multilateral treaty by one of the parties entitles:

(a) the other parties by unanimous agreement to suspend the operation of the treaty in whole or in part or to terminate it either;

(i) in the relations between themselves and the defaulting State, or

(ii) as between all the parties;

(b) a party specially affected by the breach to invoke it as a ground for suspending the operation of the treaty in whole or in part in the relations between itself and the defaulting State;

(c) any party other than the defaulting State to invoke the breach as a ground for suspending the operation of the treaty in whole or in part with respect to itself if the treaty is of such a character that a material breach of its provisions by one party radically changes the position of every party with respect to the further performance of its obligations under the treaty.

3. A material breach of a treaty, for the purposes of this article, consists in:

(a) a repudiation of the treaty not sanctioned by the present Convention; or

(b) the violation of a provision essential to the accomplishment of the object or purpose of the treaty.

4. The foregoing paragraphs are without prejudice to any provision in the treaty applicable in the event of a breach.

5. Paragraphs 1 to 3 do not apply to provisions relating to the protection of the human person contained in treaties of a humanitarian character, in particular to provisions prohibiting any form of reprisals against persons protected by such treaties."

Hungary claimed in particular that Czechoslovakia violated the 1977 Treaty by proceeding to the construction and putting into operation of Variant C, as well as failing to comply with its obligations under Articles 15 and 19 of the Treaty. Hungary further maintained that Czechoslovakia had breached other international conventions (among them the Convention of 31 May 1976 on the Regulation of Water Management Issues of Boundary Waters) and general international law.

Slovakia denied that there had been, on the part of Czechoslovakia or on its part, any material breach of the obligations to protect water quality and nature, and claimed that Variant C, far from being a breach, was devised as "the best possible approximate application" of the Treaty. It furthermore denied that Czechoslovakia had acted in breach of other international conventions or general international law.

97. Finally, Hungary argued that subsequently imposed requirements of international law in relation to the protection of the environment precluded performance of the Treaty. The previously existing obligation not to cause substantive damage to the territory of another State had, Hungary claimed, evolved into an *erga omnes* obligation of prevention of damage pursuant to the "precautionary principle". On this basis, Hungary argued, its termination was "forced by the other party's refusal to suspend work on Variant C".

Slovakia argued, in reply, that none of the intervening developments in environmental law gave rise to norms of *jus cogens* that would override the Treaty. Further, it contended that the claim by Hungary to be entitled to take action could not in any event serve as legal justification for termination of the Treaty under the law of treaties, but belonged rather "to the language of self-help or reprisals".

98. The question, as formulated in Article 2, paragraph 1 (*c*), of the Special Agreement, deals with treaty law since the Court is asked to determined what the legal effects are of the notification of termination of the Treaty. The question is whether Hungary's notification of 19 May 1992 brought the 1977 Treaty to an end, or whether it did not meet the requirements of international law, with the consequence that it did not terminate the Treaty.

99. The Court has referred earlier to the question of the applicability to the present case of the Vienna Convention of 1969 on the Law of Treaties. The Vienna Convention is not directly applicable to the 1977 Treaty inasmuch as both States ratified that Convention only after the treaty's conclusion. Consequently only those rules which are declaratory of customary law are applicable to the 1977 Treaty. As the Court has already stated

above (see paragraph 46), this is the case, in many respects, with Articles 60 to 62 of the Vienna Convention, relating to termination or suspension of the operation of a treaty. On this, the Parties, too, were broadly in agreement.

100. The 1977 Treaty does not contain any provision regarding its termination. Nor is there any indication that the parties intended to admit the possibility of denunciation or withdrawal. On the contrary, the Treaty establishes a long-standing and durable régime of joint investment and joint operation. Consequently, the parties not having agreed otherwise, the Treaty could be terminated only on the limited grounds enumerated in the Vienna Convention.

102. Hungary also relied on the principle of the impossibility of performance as reflected in Article 61 of the Vienna Convention on the Law of Treaties. Hungary's interpretation of the wording of Article 61 is, however, not in conformity with the terms of that Article, nor with the intentions of the diplomatic Conference which adopted the Convention. Article 61, paragraph 1, requires the "permanent disappearance or destruction of an object indispensable for the execution" of the treaty to justify the termination of a treaty on grounds of impossibility of performance. During the conference, a proposal was made to extend the scope of the article by including in it cases such as the impossibility to make certain payments because of serious financial difficulties (*Official Records of the United Nations Conference on the Law of Treaties, First Session, Vienna, 26 March–24 May 1968*, Doc. A/CONF.39/11, Summary records of the plenary meetings and of the meetings of the Committee of the Whole, 62nd Meeting of the Committee of the Whole, pp. 361–365). Although it was recognized that such situations could lead to a preclusion of the wrongfulness of non-performance by a party of its treaty obligations, the participating States were not prepared to consider such situations to be a ground for terminating or suspending a treaty, and preferred to limit themselves to a narrower concept.

103. Hungary contended that the essential object of the Treaty—an economic joint investment which was consistent with environmental protection and which was operated by the two contracting parties jointly—had permanently disappeared and that the Treaty had thus become impossible to perform. It is not necessary for the Court to determine whether the term "object" in Article 61 can also be understood to embrace a legal régime as in any event, even if that were the case, it would have to conclude that in this instance that régime had not definitively ceased to exist. The 1977 Treaty—and in particular its Articles 15, 19 and 20—actually made available to the parties the necessary means to proceed at any time, by negotiation, to the required readjustments between economic imperatives and ecological imperatives. The Court would add that, if the joint exploitation of the investment was no longer possible, this was originally because Hungary did not carry out most of the works for which it was responsible under the 1977 Treaty; Article 61, paragraph 2, of the Vienna Convention expressly provides that impossibility of performance may not be invoked for the termination of a treaty by a party to that treaty when it results from that party's own breach of an obligation flowing from that treaty.

104. Hungary further argued that it was entitled to invoke a number of events which, cumulatively, would have constituted a fundamental change of circumstances. In this respect it specified profound changes of a political nature, the Project's diminishing economic viability, the progress of environmental knowledge and the development of new norms and prescriptions of international environmental law....

The Court recalls that in the *Fisheries Jurisdiction* case (*I.C.J. Reports 1973*, p. 63, para. 36), it stated that,

> "Article 62 of the Vienna Convention on the Law of Treaties, ... may in many respects be considered as a codification of existing customary law on the subject of the termination of a treaty relationship on account of change of circumstances".

The prevailing political situation was certainly relevant for the conclusion of the 1977 Treaty. But the Court will recall that the Treaty provided for a joint investment programme for the production of energy, the control of floods and the improvement of navigation on the Danube. In the Court's view, the prevalent political conditions were thus not so closely linked to the object and purpose of the Treaty that they constituted an essential basis of the consent of the parties, and in changing, radically altered the extent of the obligations still to be performed. The same holds good for the economic system in force at the time of the conclusion of the 1977 Treaty. Besides, even though the estimated profitability of the Project might have appeared less in 1992 than in 1977, it does not appear from the record before the Court that it was bound to diminish to such an extent that the treaty obligations of the parties would have been radically transformed as a result.

The changed circumstances advanced by Hungary are, in the Court's view, not of such a nature, either individually or collectively, that their effect would radically transform the extent of the obligations still to be performed in order to accomplish the Project. A fundamental change of circumstances must have been unforeseen; the existence of the circumstances at the time of the Treaty's conclusion must have constituted an essential basis of the consent of the parties to be bound by the Treaty. The negative and conditional wording of Article 62 of the Vienna Convention on the Law of Treaties is a clear indication moreover that the stability of treaty relations requires that the plea of fundamental change of circumstances be applied only in exceptional cases.

105. The Court will now examine Hungary's argument that it was entitled to terminate the 1977 Treaty on the ground that Czechoslovakia had violated its Articles 15, 19 and 20 (as well as a number of other conventions and rules of general international law); and that the planning, construction and putting into operation of Variant C also amounted to a material breach of the 1977 Treaty.

106. As to that part of Hungary's argument which was based on other treaties and general rules of international law, the Court is of the view that it is only a material breach of the treaty itself, by a State party to that treaty, which entitles the other party to rely on it as a ground for terminating the treaty. The violation of other treaty rules or of the rules of general international law may justify the taking of certain measures, including countermeasures, by the injured State, but it does not constitute a ground for termination under the law of treaties.

* * *

108. Hungary's main argument for invoking a material breach of the Treaty was the construction and putting into operation of Variant C. As the Court has found in paragraph 79 above, Czechoslovakia violated the Treaty only when it diverged the waters of the Danube into the bypass canal in October 1992. In constructing the works which would lead to the putting into operation of Variant C, Czechoslovakia did not act unlawfully.

In the Court's view, therefore, the notification of termination by Hungary on 19 May 1992 was premature. No breach of the Treaty by Czechoslovakia had yet taken place and consequently Hungary was not entitled to invoke any such breach of the Treaty as a ground for terminating it when it did.

* * *

For these reasons,

THE COURT ...

(2) ... B. Finds, by thirteen votes to two that Hungary and Slovakia must negotiate in good faith in light of the prevailing situation, and must take all necessary measures to ensure the achievement of the objectives of the Treaty of 16 September 1977, in accordance with such modalities as they may agree upon....

QUESTIONS

1. Why did the Court reject Hungary's argument that supervening impossibility of performance released Hungary from carrying out the 1977 treaty?
2. Why did the Court reject Hungary's argument that a fundamental change of circumstances had occurred sufficient to release Hungary from her treaty obligations?
3. Why did the Court reject Hungary's argument that a material breach of the treaty by Czechoslovakia entitled Hungary to declare the treaty terminated.

In 1998, Slovakia filed for an additional judgment on the grounds of "the unwillingness of Hungary to implement the Judgment...." The Court ordered Hungary to file a reply to this request by 7 December 1998. No further information appears on the Court's website.

Note

In *The Fisheries Case* (Jurisdiction) (U.K. v. Iceland) 1973 I.C.J. 3, para. 43 the Court outlined another requirement before a fundamental change of circumstances can be successfully invoked to terminate a treaty:

> "Moreover, in order that a change of circumstances may give rise to a ground for invoking the termination of a treaty it is also necessary that it should have resulted in a radical transformation of the extent of the obligations to be performed. The change must have increased the burden of the obligations to be executed to the extent of rendering the performance something essentially different from that originally undertaken."

Procedure for Termination

The International Law Commission was concerned that the rules on invalidity might provoke a plethora of unilateral claims of termination of treaties so it laid down stringent rules to be followed by parties invoking grounds for termination. First the party invoking termination, withdrawal or suspension must notify in writing the other parties and indicate what measures it intends to take. Three months after notification, if no objection has been registered, the party making the notification may go ahead with its measures. If objection has been raised then the parties are required to use the means indicated under Article 33 of the U.N. Charter ("negotiation, inquiry, mediation, conciliation, arbitration, judicial settlement..." etc.) If no solution is reached within twelve months from the raising of an objection then any party to a dispute arising under Article 53 (treaties conflicting with a peremptory norm) or Article 54 (termination under a treaty's provisions or consent of the parties) may submit it to the International Court of

Justice for resolution. Any party to a dispute arising under any other part of Part V of the Vienna Convention (invalidity, termination and suspension) may "set in motion the procedure specified in the Annex to the Convention...." (The procedure outlined in the Annex provides for the creation of a conciliation commission).

State Succession in Respect of Treaties

The question of what happens to a state's obligations under treaties when it ceases to exist, becomes a new entity, separates from a part of its territory, acquires more territory, declares its independence from a former ruler or somehow evolves into a different entity is a hotly disputed question in international law. This issue has become particularly important with the reunification of the two Germanies, the disintegration of the former Yugoslavia and the break up of the Soviet Union.

The Vienna Convention on Succession of States in Respect of Treaties[28] was signed in 1978 and entered into force in 1996 but has received only a very modest number of ratifications. The two competing views on this issue are generally termed "the clean slate theory" and "the continuity theory." The clean slate view basically allows a new entity to start on a clean slate, that is to adopt only those treaties it wishes to be bound by and to reject the others. The continuity view holds the new entity to the obligations that attached to the same territory under the old entity. The Vienna Convention largely adopts the clean slate approach but with some notable exceptions. The clean slate theory does not apply to boundary treaties (article 11), treaties relating to the use of, or restrictions upon territory for the benefit of another state or for the establishment of foreign military bases on the territory (article 12).[29] There are also special rules for uniting or separating states (Part IV).[30]

Case Concerning Application of the Convention on the Prevention and Punishment of the Crime of Genocide Bosnia-Herzegovina v. Yugoslavia*

1996 I.C.J. 595 (Preliminary Objections)

Opinion of the Court

1. On 20 March 1993, the Government of the Republic of Bosnia-Herzegovina (hereinafter called "Bosnia-Herzegovina") filed in the Registry of the Court an Application instituting proceedings against the Government of the Federal Republic of Yugoslavia

28. 1946 U.N.T.S. 3, adopted 22 Aug. 1978, entered into force 6 Nov. 1996, reprinted at 17 I.L.M. 1488 (1978).

29. See *Case Concerning Gabcíkovo-Nagymaros Project* (Hungary v. Slovakia) 1997 I.C.J. 7, at para. 123.

30. For a helpful overview of the problem of state succession see Peter Malanczuk, Akehurst's Modern Introduction to International Law, 161–172 (7th rev. ed. 1997).

* In 2003, the area in question was renamed The Union of Serbia and Montenegro. In 2006, Montenegro separated from Serbia. The official name of Serbia is now The Republic of Serbia.

(hereinafter called "Yugoslavia") in respect of a dispute concerning alleged violations of the Convention on the Prevention and Punishment of the Crime of Genocide (hereinafter called "the Genocide Convention"), adopted by the General Assembly of the United Nations on 9 December 1948, as well as various matters which Bosnia-Herzegovina claims are connected therewith. The Application invoked Article IX of the Genocide Convention as the basis of the jurisdiction of the Court.

* * *

16. Bosnia-Herzegovina has principally relied, as a basis for the jurisdiction of the Court in this case, on Article IX of the Genocide Convention. The Court will initially consider the preliminary objections raised by Yugoslavia on this point.... In its third objection, Yugoslavia, on various grounds, has disputed the contention that the Convention binds the two Parties or that it has entered into force between them; and in its fifth objection, Yugoslavia has objected, for various reasons, to the argument that the dispute submitted by Bosnia-Herzegovina falls within the provisions of Article IX of the Convention. The Court will consider these two alleged grounds of lack jurisdiction in turn.

17. The proceedings instituted before the Court are between two States whose territories are located within the former Socialist Federal Republic of Yugoslavia. That Republic signed the Genocide Convention on 11 December 1948 and deposited its instrument of ratification, without reservation, on 29 August 1950. At the time of the proclamation of the Federal Republic of Yugoslavia, on 27 April 1992, a formal declaration was adopted on its behalf to the effect that:

> "The Federal Republic of Yugoslavia, continuing the State, international legal and political personality of the Socialist Federal Republic of Yugoslavia, shall strictly abide by all the commitments that the Socialist Federal Republic of Yugoslavia assumed internationally."

This intention thus expressed by Yugoslavia to remain bound by the international treaties to which the former Yugoslavia was party was confirmed in an official Note of 27 April 1992 from the Permanent Mission of Yugoslavia to the United Nations, addressed to the Secretary-General. The Court observes, furthermore, that it has not been contested that Yugoslavia was party to the Genocide Convention. Thus, Yugoslavia was bound by the provisions of the Convention on the date of the filing of the Application in the present case, namely, on 20 March 1993.

18. For its part, on 29 December 1992, Bosnia-Herzegovina transmitted to the Secretary-General of the United Nations, as depositary of the Genocide Convention, a Notice of Succession in the following terms:

> "the Government of the Republic of Bosnia and Herzegovina, having considered the Convention on the Prevention and Punishment of the Crime of Genocide, of December 9, 1948, to which the former Socialist Federal Republic of Yugoslavia was a party, wishes to succeed to the same and undertakes faithfully to perform and carry out all the stipulations therein contained with effect from March 6, 1992, the date on which the Republic of Bosnia and Herzegovina became independent".

On 18 March 1993, the Secretary-General communicated the following Depositary Notification to the parties to the Genocide Convention:

> "On 29 December 1992, the notification of succession by the Government of Bosnia and Herzegovina to the above-mentioned Convention was deposited

> with the Secretary-General, with effect from 6 March 1992, the date on which Bosnia and Herzegovina assumed responsibility for its international relations."

19. Yugoslavia has contested the validity and legal effect of the Notice of 29 December 1992, contending that, by its acts relating to its accession to independence, the Republic of Bosnia-Herzegovina had flagrantly violated the duties stemming from the "principle of equal rights and self-determination of peoples". According to Yugoslavia, Bosnia-Herzegovina was not, for this reason, qualified to become a party to the convention. Yugoslavia subsequently reiterated this objection in the third preliminary objection which it raised this case.

The Court notes that Bosnia-Herzegovina became a Member of the United Nations following the decisions adopted on 22 May 1992 by the Security Council and the General Assembly, bodies competent under the Charter. Article XI of the Genocide Convention opens it to "any Member of the United Nations"; from the time of its admission to the Organization, Bosnia-Herzegovina could thus become a party to the Convention. Hence the circumstances of its accession to independence are of little consequence.

20. It is clear from the foregoing that Bosnia-Herzegovina could become a party to the Convention through the mechanism of State succession. Moreover, the Secretary-General of the United Nations considered that this had been the case, and the Court took note of this in its Order of 8 April 1993 (*I.C.J. Reports 1993,* p. 16, para. 25).

21. The Parties to the dispute differed as to the legal consequences to be drawn from the occurrence of a State succession in the present case. In this context, Bosnia-Herzegovina has, among other things, contended that the Genocide Convention falls within the category of instruments for the protection of human rights, and that consequently the rule of "automatic succession" necessarily applies. Bosnia-Herzegovina concluded therefrom that it became a party to the Convention with effect from its accession to independence. Yugoslavia disputed any "automatic succession" of Bosnia-Herzegovina to the Genocide Convention on this or any other basis.

22. As regards the nature of the Genocide Convention, the Court would recall what it stated in its Advisory Opinion of 28 May 1951 relating to the *Reservations to the Convention on the Prevention and Punishment of the Crime of Genocide:*

> "In such a convention the contracting States do not have any interests of their own; they merely have, one and all, a common interest, namely, the accomplishment of those high purposes which are the *raison d'etre* of the convention. Consequently, in a convention of this type one cannot speak of individual advantages or disadvantages to States, or of the maintenance of a perfect contractual balance between rights and duties." (I.C.J. Reports 1951, p. 23.)

The Court subsequently noted in that Opinion that:

> "The object and purpose of the Genocide Convention imply that it was the intention of the General Assembly and of the States which adopted it that as many States as possible should participate. The complete exclusion from the Convention of one or more States would not only restrict the scope of its application, but would detract from the authority of the moral and humanitarian principles which are its basis." (*Ibid.*, p. 24.)

23. Without prejudice as to whether or not the principle of "automatic succession" applies in the case of certain types of international treaties or conventions, the Court does not consider it necessary, in order to decided on its jurisdiction in this case, to make a determination on the legal issues concerning State succession in respect to treaties which have

been raised by the Parties. Whether Bosnia-Herzegovina automatically became party to the Genocide Convention on the date of its accession to independence on 6 March 1992, or whether it became a party as a result—retroactive or not—of its Notice of Succession of 29 December 1992, at all events it was a party to it on the date of the filing of its Application on 20 March 1993. These matters might, at the most, possess a certain relevance with respect to the determination of the scope *ratione temporis* of the jurisdiction of the Court, a point which the Court will consider later (paragraph 34 below).

* * *

26.... In the present case, even if it were established that the Parties, each of which was bound by the Convention when the Application was filed, had only been bound as between themselves with effect from 14 December 1995, the Court could not set aside its jurisdiction on this basis, inasmuch as Bosnia-Herzegovina might at any time file a new application, identical to the present one, which would be unassailable in this respect.

In the light of the foregoing, the Court considers that it must reject Yugoslavia's third preliminary objection.

QUESTION

Why did the Court decide that both Yugoslavia and Bosnia-Herzegovina were bound by the Genocide Convention?

The Court decided the merits of the case in 2007, *Bosnia and Herzegovina v. Serbia and Montenegro*, 2007 I.C.J. ___.

The Effect of War on Treaties

The Vienna Convention does not address the question of the effect of war on treaties. The International Law Commission considered that:

> the study of this topic would inevitably involve a consideration of the effect of the provisions of the Charter concerning the threat or use of force upon the legality of the recourse to the particular hostilities in question; and it did not feel that this question could conveniently be dealt with in the context of its present work upon the law of treaties.[31]

Techt v. Hughes

Court of Appeals of New York, 1920
229 N.Y. 222, 128 N.E. 185, cert. den. 254 U.S. 643

Note

An American citizen died in New York without a will in 1917. His estate consisted of some real estate located in New York City. His death occurred shortly after the United

31. 1996, II Y.B. Int'l L. Comm'n 176 (para.29).

States had declared war on Austria-Hungary. The decedent had two daughters. One daughter, Mrs. Techt, had married a citizen of the Austria-Hungarian Empire and as a result of the existing laws had lost her U.S. citizenship and become a citizen of Austria-Hungary. The other daughter, Ms. Hughes, was a U.S. Citizen. Ms. Hughes argued that she should inherit the whole of her father's property because her sister was now an "enemy alien." The lower court classified Mrs. Techt as an "alien friend" and ruled that she could inherit half the property. Ms. Hughes appealed and the Court of Appeals agreed with her that Mrs. Techt was not an alien friend, but Mrs. Techt had brought to the court's attention a treaty of 1848 between the United States and Austria-Hungary[32] which provided that citizens of either state could inherit property in the other state and were permitted to sell the property within two years and take the proceeds. The Court of Appeals therefore had to address the question of whether the 1848 treaty was still effective, permitting Mrs. Techt to inherit her father's property, or whether the outbreak of war between the treaty partners had resulted in the termination or suspension of the treaty.

CARDOZO, J.

The support of the statute failing, there remains the question of the treaty. The treaty, if in force, is the supreme law of the land (Const. U.S. art.6) and supersedes all local laws inconsistent with its terms. The right which it secures is in form a right of sale. In substance, it is a right of ownership. The fee [ownership right in land] descends, subject to the condition that it shall be disposed of within the 'term of two years, which term may be reasonably prolonged according to circumstances.'

The effect of war upon the existing treaties of belligerents is one of the unsettled problems of the law. The older writers sometimes said that treaties ended ipso facto when war came. 3 Phillimore, Int. L. 794. The writers of our time reject these sweeping statements. 2 Oppenheim, Int. L. §99; Hall, Int. L. 398, 401; Fiore, Int.L. (Borchard's Transl.) §845. International law to-day does not preserve treaties or annul them, regardless of the effects produced. It deals with such problems pragmatically, preserving or annulling as the necessities of war exact. It establishes standards, but it does not fetter itself with rules. When it attempts to do more, it finds that there is neither unanimity of opinion nor uniformity of practice. 'The whole question remains as yet unsettled.' Oppenheim, supra. This does not mean, of course, that there are not some classes of treaties about which there is general agreement. Treaties of alliance fall. Treaties of boundary or cession, 'dispositive' or 'transitory' conventions, survive. Hall, Int. L. pp. 398, 401; 2 Westlake, Int. L. 34; Oppenheim, supra. So, of course, do treaties which regulate the conduct of hostilities. Hall, supra; 5 Moore, Dig. Int. L. 372; Society for Propagation of the Gospel v Town of New Haven, 8 Wheat. 464, 494, 5 L.Ed. 662.

Intention in such circumstances is clear. These instances do not represent distinct and final principles. They are illustrations of the same principle. They are applications of a standard. When I ask what that principle or standard is, and endeavor to extract it from the long chapters in the books, I get this, and nothing more: That provisions compatible with a state of hostilities, unless expressly terminated, will be enforced, and those incompatible rejected.

'Treaties lose their efficacy in war only if their execution is incompatible with war.' Bluntschli, Droit International Codifie, sec. 538.

32. Convention between United States and Austria, concluded 8 May 1848, proclaimed, 25 Oct. 1850; 9 Stat. 944.

That in substance was Kent's view, here as often in advance of the thought of his day:

'All those duties, of which the exercise is not necessarily suspended by the war, subsist in their full force. The obligation of keeping faith is so far from ceasing in time of war that its efficacy becomes increased, from the increased necessity of it.' 1 Kent, Comm. p. 176.

That, also, more recently, is the conclusion embodied by the Institute of International Law in the rules voted at Christiania in 1912, which defined the effects of war on international conventions. In these rules, some classes of treaties are dealt with specially and apart. Treaties of alliance, those which establish a protectorate or a sphere of influence, and generally treaties of a political nature, are, it is said, dissolved. Dissolved, too, are treaties which have relation to the cause of war. But the general principle is declared that treaties which it is reasonably practicable to execute after the outbreak of hostilities must be observed then, as in the past. The belligerents are at liberty to disregard them only to the extent and for the time required by the necessities of war.

This, I think, is the principle which must guide the judicial department of the government when called upon to determine during the progress of a war whether a treaty shall be observed, in the absence of some declaration by the political departments of the government that it has been suspended or annulled. A treaty has a twofold aspect. In its primary operation, it is a source of private rights for individuals within states. Head Money Cases, 112 U.S. 580, 598, 5 Sup. Ct. 247, 28 L.Ed. 798. Granting that the termination of the compact involves the termination of the rights, it does not follow, because there is a privilege to rescind, that the privilege has been exercised. The question is not what states may do after war has supervened, and this without breach of their duty as members of the society of nations. The question is what courts are to presume that they have done.

'Where the department authorized to annul a voidable treaty shall deem it most conducive to the national interest that it should longer continue to be obeyed and observed, no right can be incident to the judiciary to declare it void in a single instance.' Jay, C.J., in Jones v Walker, 2 Paine, 688, 701, Fed. Cas. No. 7, 507.

Cf. The Legal Nature of Treaties, vol. 10, American Journal of Int. Law (1916), pp. 721, 722.

President and Senate may denounce the treaty, and thus terminate its life. Congress may enact an inconsistent rule, which will control the action of the courts. Fong Yue Ting v U.S., 149 U.S. 698, 13 Sup. Ct. 1016, 37 L.Ed. 905. The treaty of peace itself may set up new relations, and terminate earlier compacts, either tacitly or expressly. The proposed treaties with Germany and Austria give the victorious powers the privilege of choosing the treaties which are to be kept in force or abrogated. But until some one of these things is done, until some one of these events occurs, while war is still flagrant, and the will of the political departments or the government unrevealed, the courts, as I view their function, play a humbler and more cautious part. It is not for them to denounce treaties generally en bloc. Their part it is, as one provision or another is involved in some actual controversy before them, to determine whether, alone or by force of connection with an inseparable scheme, the provision is inconsistent with the policy or safety of the nation in the emergency of war, and hence presumably intended to be limited to times of peace. The mere fact that other portions of the treaty are suspended, or even abrogated, is not conclusive. The treaty does not fall in its entirety unless it has the character of an indivisible act.

To determine whether it has this character, it is not enough to consider its name or label. No general formula suffices. We must consult in each case the nature and purpose of the specific articles involved.

I find nothing incompatible with the policy of the government, with the safety of the nation, or with the maintenance of the war in the enforcement of this treaty, so as to sustain the plaintiff's title.

Note

Techt v. Hughes, supra, was decided before the promulgation of the U.N. Charter which seeks, among other things, to outlaw the use of force. In earlier centuries war was often a limited engagement largely carried on between the armed forces of the combatants. World War II changed that pattern dramatically with both sides engaging in widespread bombing of civilian areas. The concept of "total" war was born so that the notion of continuing treaty relationships between belligerents becomes less acceptable. The Vienna Convention, article 63, makes it clear that the mere severance of diplomatic or consular relations between treaty partners does not terminate or suspend treaties between them "except in so far as the existence of diplomatic or consular relations is indispensable for the application of the treaty." On the effect of hostilities between treaty partners the Restatement Third, § 336, Comment e states:

> Under traditional international law, the outbreak of war between states terminated or suspended agreements between them. However, not all agreements were necessarily affected. In particular, agreements governing the conduct of hostilities survived, since they were designed for application during war. However, the United Nations Charter prohibits the use of armed force between states except in limited circumstances, and was intended to outlaw war.... The consequences of these principles for the law as to the effect of hostilities on treaties remains uncertain.[33]

Reporters' Note 4 to § 336 elaborates further:

> Since 1945, when the United Nations Charter came into effect, there has been uncertainty about the impact of hostilities upon international agreements. The Vienna Convention, Article 73, disclaims any judgment on the question. The full import of the provisions of the Charter prohibiting the use of force is debated, but the Charter clearly intended to outlaw war. See § 905, Comment *g*. It has been suggested that it effectively abolished war as a legal regime (although, for humanitarian reasons, it has been accepted that the Geneva Conventions on the Law of War continue to be applicable). However, since the traditional effect of war on treaties derived from the fact that continuing treaty relations generally were deemed inconsistent with the state of war, perhaps as a special application of the doctrine of *rebus sic stantibus*, it is arguable that major hostilities are "changed circumstances" providing a basis for suspending or terminating a treaty, regardless of whether there is a lawful state of war. In any event, the victim of aggression in violation of Article 2(4) of the Charter can surely be justified in treating treaty obligations as suspended. On the other hand, the aggressor may not invoke his own unlawful act as a basis for exemption from the obligation of treaties and would be liable for consequent violation of treaty

33. Restatement (Third) of the Foreign Relations Law of the United States, § 336, cmt. e (1987).

obligations (as well as for violation of the Charter), but not for violation of an agreement of the type not applicable during hostilities.

The Effect of War on Human Rights Treaties

Recently, considerable attention has been given to the question of the effect of war on human rights treaties. One view is that once international armed conflict occurs, then the conflict is entirely governed by the laws of armed conflict, including the four Geneva Conventions of 1949. This area of law is known as humanitarian law, which is applicable during armed conflict and distinct from human rights law. Another view is that human rights treaties continue throughout war unless they conflict with the specific provisions of a law regulating war. The International Court of Justice has addressed this issue in two of its opinions, as the excerpt below explains.

Legal Consequences of the Construction of a Wall in the Occupied Palestinian Territory

2004 I.C.J. 136 (Advisory Opinion)

Note

For the introduction to this case see page 45 *supra.*

* * *

102. The participants in the proceedings before the Court also disagree whether the international human rights conventions to which Israel is party apply within the Occupied Palestinian Territory. Annex I to the report of the Secretary-General states:

> "4. Israel denies that the International Covenant on Civil and Political Rights and the International Covenant on Economic, Social and Cultural Rights, both of which it has signed, are applicable to the occupied Palestinian territory. It asserts that humanitarian law is the protection granted in a conflict situation such as the one in the West Bank and Gaza Strip, whereas human rights treaties were intended for the protection of citizens from their own Government in times of peace."

Of the other participants in the proceedings, those who addressed this issue contend that, on the contrary, both Covenants are applicable within the Occupied Palestinian Territory.

103. On 3 October 1991 Israel ratified both the International Covenant on Economic, Social and Cultural Rights of 19 December 1966 and the International Covenant on Civil and Political Rights of the same date, as well as the United Nations Convention on the Rights of the Child of 20 November 1989. It is a party to these three instruments.

104. In order to determine whether these texts are applicable in the Occupied Palestinian Territory, the Court will first address the issue of the relationship between international humanitarian law and human rights law and then that of the applicability of human rights instruments outside national territory.

105. In its Advisory Opinion of 8 July 1996 on the *Legality of the Threat or Use of Nuclear Weapons*, the Court had occasion to address the first of these issues in relation to the International Covenant on Civil and Political Rights. In those proceedings certain States had argued that "the Covenant was directed to the protection of human rights in peacetime, but that questions relating to unlawful loss of life in hostilities were governed by the law applicable in armed conflict" (*I.C.J. Reports 1996 (I)*, p. 239, para. 24)

The Court rejected this argument, stating that:

> "the protection of the International Covenant of Civil and Political Rights does not cease in times of war, except by operation of Article 4 of the Covenant whereby certain provisions may be derogated from in a time of national emergency. Respect for the right to life is not, however, such a provision. In principle, the right not arbitrarily to be deprived of one's life applies also in hostilities. The test of what is an arbitrary deprivation of life, however, then falls to be determined by the applicable *lex specialis*, namely, the law applicable in armed conflict which is designed to regulate the conduct of hostilities." (*Ibid.*, p. 240, para. 25).

106. More generally, the Court considers that the protection offered by human rights conventions does not cease in case of armed conflict, save through the effect of provisions for derogation of the kind to be found in Article 4 of the International Covenant on Civil and Political Rights. As regards the relationship between international humanitarian law and human rights law, there are thus three possible situations: some rights may be exclusively matters of international humanitarian law; others may be exclusively matters of human rights law; yet others may be matters of both these branches of international law. In order to answer the question put to it, the Court will have the take into consideration both these branches of international law, namely human rights law and, as *lex specialis*, international humanitarian law.

See also, the Court's discussion of the application of the Vienna Convention on Diplomatic Relations during armed conflict in *Case Concerning Armed Activities on the Territory of the Congo* (Democratic Republic of The Congo v. Uganda) 2005 I.C.J. ___, pages 149-150 *infra*.

Suggested Further Readings

Ian Brownlie, Principles of Public International Law, chapter 27 (7th ed. 2008).

D.J. Harris, Cases and Materials on International Law, chapter 10 (6th ed. 2004).

Lord McNair, The Law of Treaties (1986).

Macolm N. Shaw, International Law, chapter 16 (6th ed. 2008).

I.M. Sinclair, The Vienna Convention on the Law of Treaties (2 ed. 1984).

Rebecca M.M. Wallace, International Law, chapter 10 (5th ed. 2005).

Chapter IV

Jurisdiction

American law students usually spend part of their first year at law school learning about civil procedure. One of the topics studied is the question of when a state (such as California or Massachusetts) within the United States may exercise jurisdiction (broadly speaking—power) over a person or entity. It is accepted that if the person or entity has no connection with a state, that state may not exercise jurisdiction over the person or entity. For example, if one resident of California killed another resident of California in Los Angeles, the State of Massachusetts could not exercise its criminal jurisdiction over the alleged murderer. But what would be the case if the victim normally lived in Massachusetts and was simply on a short vacation in Los Angeles? There is a long line of United States Supreme Court cases that seek to identify the *minimum level of contacts* that the persons, entities or transactions involved must have with the forum state in order for the state to exercise jurisdiction. This body of law has grown up out of the Supreme Court's interpretation of the Due Process clause of the Fourteenth Amendment to the United States Constitution. International law has a similar counterpart. Broadly it addresses the question of when a nation state may exercise its jurisdiction. Jurisdiction is divided into three categories: (a) jurisdiction to prescribe ("the authority of a state to make its law applicable to persons or activities");[1] (b) jurisdiction to adjudicate ("to subject particular persons or things to its judicial process"); (c) jurisdiction to enforce or execute ("to use the resources of government to induce or compel compliance with its law.")

The international law relating to jurisdiction is by no means complete and has usually arisen in the criminal as opposed to the civil context. No state is obliged to exercise its jurisdiction even if international law would raise no objection to its doing so. Each state passes its own internal laws indicating in what circumstances it will exercise jurisdiction. There are five bases of jurisdiction recognized in international law. Some of the categories are more broadly accepted than others.

The Territorial Principle

International law permits a state to exercise its *jurisdiction to legislate* (prescribe) with respect to:

(a) conduct that, wholly or in substantial part, takes place within its territory;
(b) the status of persons, or interests in things, present within its territory;
(c) conduct outside its territory that has or is intended to have substantial effect within its territory.[2]

1. Restatement (Third) The Foreign Relations Law of the United States, Introductory Note to Part IV, at 231 (1987) [hereinafter Restatement Third]. The three categories of jurisdiction in the text are those outlined in the Restatement Third.

2. Restatement Third at § 402(1).

The state will also have *jurisdiction to adjudicate* under the territorial principle if the exercise of jurisdiction is "reasonable".[3] What constitutes reasonableness is fairly vague[4] but again basically takes into account how closely the person or entity is connected with the territory of the state. Again, *jurisdiction to enforce,* under the territorial principle, is limited by reasonableness measured by connection to the territory.[5]

If you ask yourself the question: "Could the French legislature pass laws making it a crime for one Englishman to kill another Englishman in London?" You will immediately sense that the answer to this question is "No." If you ask "Why not?" the answer is that the murder has no connection with France. On the other hand if you ask "Could the French legislature make it a crime for a Frenchman (or a citizen of any other country) to kill another Frenchman (or citizen of any other country) in Paris?" you would immediately answer "Yes." Again, if asked "Why?" you would reply that the activity took place on French soil and may have involved French citizens. Suppose the murder took place in Paris but the culprit and the victim were Spanish citizens? Then France would have legislative jurisdiction on the basis of the territorial principle and Spain would have legislative jurisdiction on the basis of the nationality principle (see p. 105ff). Where more than one state has a basis on which to claim jurisdiction, the conflicting claims will usually be settled between the two states. In the example above doubtless the French authorities would try the culprit and if convicted, he would probably (though not definitely) be protected from subsequent prosecution by Spanish authorities, if he ever returned to Spain.[6]

Most of the instances where a state asserts jurisdiction on the basis of the territorial principle are not particularly controversial. There is no disagreement that the state has the right to assert jurisdiction where the conduct being regulated takes place within a state (e.g., murder) or when the state regulates persons or entities within the state (e.g., people's status, such as the definition of a minor) or interests in things (e.g., a shareholder's rights in a corporation). More controversial are some of the instances where the state attempts to regulate "conduct outside its territory that has or is intended to have substantial effect within its territory."[7] No one disputes that if a person stands on the Canadian side of the U.S.-Canadian border and aims a gun at a person standing on the American side of the border injuring or killing that person, that both Canada and the United States may assert jurisdiction on the basis of the territorial principle; Canada may do so because the conduct took place substantially within Canadian territory and the United States may do so because the conduct outside its territory was intended to have, and did have, a substantial effect within its territory. The more difficult cases involve a state's attempt to regulate the conduct of persons or entities outside its territory where the conduct has an economic effect within the state's territory. A 1945 case in the U.S. court of appeals for the second circuit interpreted the U.S. anti-trust laws as having an extremely broad sweep which evoked widespread criticism.

---

3. Id at §421(1).
4. Id. at §421(2) (a)-(k).
5. Id. at §431(1) & (2).
6. Most developed criminal legal systems have a principle of double jeopardy which prevents a person from being tried twice for the same offense. This may, or may not apply in the case of foreign convictions. International law does not yet have such a principle though it has certainly been suggested, See Harvard Research Draft Convention of 1935, arts. 13–14 which only apply to aliens, reprinted at 29 Am. J. Int'l L. 971, 972 (Supp. 1935).
7. Restatement Third at §402(1).

United States v. Aluminum Co. of America [a Canadian corporation]

148 F.2d 416 (2d Cir. 1945)

Note

The anti-trust laws of the United States are designed to prevent restraints of trade and to prohibit activity that limits competition. Section 1 of the Sherman Act[8] provides: "every contract, combination ... or conspiracy, in restraint of trade or commerce among the several States, or with foreign nations, is declared to be illegal." One of the defendants in the case was ... [Aluminum Company of America], a Canadian corporation. It was alleged that this foreign corporation had formed an "alliance" with a number of other foreign producers of aluminum and that they had agreed upon quotas and fixed prices. In other words the foreign corporations were alleged to have formed a cartel to regulate the production and price of aluminum. The issue before the court was whether Congress intended to include foreign cartels within the prohibitions contained in the Sherman Act where those cartels, acting outside the territory of the United States, intended their activities to have an effect on trade in the United States.

Opinion of the Court

Before L. Hand, Swan and A. Hand, Circuit Judges.

Whether ... [Aluminum Company] itself violated [section 1 of the Sherman Act] depends upon the character of the "Alliance." It [the Alliance] was a Swiss corporation, created in pursuance of an agreement entered into on July 3, 1931, the signatories to which were a French corporation, two German, one Swiss, a British, and [Aluminum Company]. The original agreement, or "cartel," provided for the formation of a corporation in Switzerland which should issue shares, to be taken up by the signatories. This corporation was from time to time to fix a quota of production for each share, and each shareholder was to be limited to the quantity measured by the number of shares it held, but was free to sell at any price it chose. The corporation fixed a price every year at which it would take off any shareholder's hands any part of its quota which it did not sell. No shareholder was to "buy, borrow, fabricate or sell" aluminum produced by anyone not a shareholder except with the consent of the board of governors, but that must not be "unreasonably withheld." However ... until 1936, when the new arrangement was made, imports into the United States were not included in the quotas....

The agreement of 1936 abandoned the system of unconditional quotas, and substituted a system of royalties. Each shareholder was to have a fixed free quota for every share it held, but as its production exceeded the sum of its quotas, it was to pay a royalty, graduated progressively in proportion to the excess; and these royalties the "Alliance" divided among the shareholders in proportion to their shares.... Although this agreement, like its predecessor, was silent as to imports into the United States, when that question arose during its preparation as it did, all the shareholders agreed that such imports should be included in the quotas....

8. 15 U.S.C.A.§ 1 (1890).

Did either the agreement of 1931 or that of 1936 violate § 1 of the Act? The answer does not depend upon whether we shall recognize as a source of liability a liability imposed by another state. On the contrary we are concerned only with whether Congress chose to attach liability to the conduct outside the United States of persons not in allegiance to it. That being so, the only question open is whether Congress intended to impose the liability, and whether our own Constitution permitted it to do so: as a court of the United States, we cannot look beyond our own law. Nevertheless, it is quite true that we are not to read general words, such as those in this Act, without regard to the limitations customarily observed by nations upon the exercise of their powers.... We should not impute to Congress an intent to punish all whom its courts can catch, for conduct which has no consequences within the United States.... On the other hand, it is settled law—as ... [Aluminum Company] itself agrees—that any state may impose liabilities, even upon persons not within its allegiance, for conduct outside its borders that has consequences within its borders which the state reprehends; and these liabilities other states will ordinarily recognize.... Restatement of Conflict of Laws § 65. It may be argued that this Act extends further. Two situations are possible. There may be agreements made beyond our borders not intended to affect imports, which do affect them, or which affect exports. Almost any limitation of the supply of goods in Europe, for example, or in South America, may have repercussions in the United States, if there is trade between the two. Yet when one considers the international complications likely to arise from an effort in this country to treat such agreements as unlawful, it is safe to assume that Congress certainly did not intend the Act to cover them. Such agreements may on the other hand intend to include imports into the United States, and yet it may appear that they have had no effect upon them. That situation might be thought to fall within the doctrine that intent may be a substitute for performance in the case of a contract made within the United States; or it might be thought to fall within the doctrine that a statute should not be interpreted to cover acts abroad which have no consequence here. We shall not choose between these alternatives; but for argument we shall assume that the Act does not cover agreements, even though intended to affect imports or exports, unless its performance is shown actually to have had some effect upon them. Where both conditions are satisfied, the situation certainly falls within such decisions as *United States v. Pacific & Arctic R. & Navigation Co.*, 228 U.S. 87, 33 S.Ct. 443, 57 L.Ed. 742; *Thomsen v. Cayser*, 243 U.S. 66, 37 S.Ct. 353, 61 L.Ed. 597, Ann.Cas.1917D, 322 and *United States v. Sisal Sales Corporation*, 274 U.S. 268, 47 S.Ct. 592, 71 L.Ed. 1042.... It is true that in those cases the persons held liable had sent agents into the United States to perform part of the agreement; but an agent is merely an animate means of executing his principal's purposes, and, for the purposes of this case, he does not differ from an inanimate means; besides, only human agents can import and sell ingot.

Both agreements would clearly have been unlawful, had they been made within the United States; and it follows from what we have just said that both were unlawful, though made abroad, if they were intended to affect imports and did affect them.

[The court found that the 1936 agreement had intended to set a quota for imports to the United States and that as ... [Aluminum Company] had not shown that imports were not affected, that agreement violated section one of the Sherman Act.]

QUESTION

In the age of a globalized economy, what problems might arise if each country decided to regulate economic activities outside its own country that were perceived as have an effect in its country?

Note

The world wide scope of U.S. anti-trust laws has resulted in a considerable backlash of laws passed by other countries designed to undo the effects of the extra-territorial reach of the laws which many believe go well beyond what is permissible under the "effects" component of the territorial basis for the assertion of jurisdiction.

See, e.g., United Kingdom Protection of Trading Interests Act of 1980, reprinted at 21 I.L.M. 834 (1982); Uranium Information Security Regulation, CAN. STAT. O & REGS. 76-644 (P.C. 1976-2368, Sept. 21, 1976), promulgated under the authority of Atomic Energy Control Act, CAN. REV. STAT. ch. A-19 (1970); Business Records Protection Act, Ont. Rev. Stat. c. 54 (1970) (Ontario, Canada).

The Nationality Principle

This principle permits a state to exercise jurisdiction over a person or entity on the basis of the nationality of the person or entity. For example, in the United States all male U.S. citizens are required to register under the military service laws when they reach the age of eighteen years regardless of where in the world they might be living at the time. 50 U.S.C.A. App. § 453. Similarly the U.S. tax code makes all income of U.S. citizens taxable regardless of the location of the source of the income or the location of the citizen. Internal Revenue Code § 1.[9] For example, a U.S. citizen living and earning wages in the United Kingdom has an obligation to pay taxes both to the U.S. (nationality principle) and to the U.K. (territorial principle). Such double taxation obligations would obviously be burdensome, so many countries (including the U.S. and the U.K.) have entered into Double Taxation Treaties, which would be better named "Anti-Double Taxation Treaties." See e.g., U.S.-U.K. Treaty.[10] These treaties essentially allow the treaty parties to collect taxes on the basis of the place from where the income is generated and the parties agree to forgo collecting taxes on the basis of citizenship.

Common law countries exercise jurisdiction on the basis of nationality very sparingly with few of their laws applying to a citizen while the citizen is outside the country. Civil law countries tend to use this basis of jurisdiction more frequently and a few countries make their criminal law entirely applicable to all of their citizens no matter where they were when they committed the offense. For example, if a citizen of India murdered someone in New York city that person would certainly have violated the laws of New York but the Indian citizen would also have violated the laws of India because India's criminal law applies to all Indian citizens where ever they may be in the world. Indian Penal Code § 4 (3d ed. Raju 1965). Here again we have an example of two nations with concurrent jurisdiction. No doubt the New York authorities would arrest and try the culprit and India would probably respect that decision and not retry the offender should s/he ever return to India. If however New York did not assert jurisdiction over the offender, India could certainly do so under the nationality principle.

9. 26 U.S.C. § 1 (1986).

10. Convention for Avoidance of Double Taxation and the Prevention of Fiscal Evasion with Respect to Taxes on Income and Capital Gains (U.S.-U.K.), signed 31 Dec. 1975, entered into force together with three additional protocols, 25 April 1980, 31 U.S.T. 5668, T.I.A.S. No. 9682.

QUESTION

Can you think of reasons why a state might be hesitant to assert jurisdiction on the basis of nationality where the person is living abroad and the activities take place outside the state?

The Passive Personality Principle

This principle affirms that a state may assert jurisdiction on the basis of the nationality of the victim of an offence regardless of where the offence occurs or the nationality of the perpetrator. The principle has not been widely accepted but recently a number of international treaties, designed to curb various types of terrorism, have incorporated the principle.[11] The Restatement Third, § 402, Comment g states that the principle "is increasingly accepted as applied to terrorist and other organized attacks on a state's nationals by reason of their nationality, or to assassination of a state's diplomatic representative or other officials."

United States v. Fawaz Yunis, a/k/a Nazeeh

924 F.2d 1086 (D.C. Cir. 1991)

Before MIKVA, Chief Judge, WALD and RUTH BADER GINSBERG, Circuit Judges.

Opinion for the Court filed by Chief Judge MIKVA.

MIKVA, Chief Judge:

Appellant Fawaz Yunis [a citizen of Lebanon] challenges his convictions on conspiracy, aircraft piracy, and hostage-taking charges stemming from the hijacking of a Jordanian passenger aircraft in Beirut, Lebanon. He appeals from orders of the district court denying his pretrial motions relating to jurisdiction, illegal arrest, alleged violations of the Posse Comitatus Act,[12] and the government's withholding of classified documents during discovery. Yunis also challenges the district court's jury instructions as erroneous and prejudicial.

Although this appeal raises novel issues of domestic and international law, we reject Yunis' objections and affirm the convictions.

I. BACKGROUND

On June 11, 1985, appellant and four other men boarded Royal Jordanian Airlines Flight 402 ("Flight 402") shortly before its scheduled departure from Beirut, Lebanon. They wore civilian clothes and carried military assault rifles, ammunition bandoleers, and hand grenades. Appellant took control of the cockpit and forced the pilot to take off immediately. The remaining hijackers tied up Jordanian air marshals assigned to the

---

11. E.g., Convention on Offenses and Certain Other Acts Committed on Board Aircraft, art. 4(b), 704 U.N.T.S. 219, 20 U.S.T. 2941, T.I.A.S. No. 6768, signed 14 Sept 1963; entered into force, 4 Dec. 1969. See also Omnibus Diplomatic Security and Anti-terrorism Act of 1986, 18 U.S.C. § 2231 (1986).

12. The Posse Comitatus Act, 18 U.S.C. § 1385 "establishes criminal penalties for willful use of 'any part of the Army or the Air Force' in law enforcement, unless expressly authorized by law." *U.S. v. Yunis*, at 1093.

flight and held the civilian passengers, including two American citizens, captive in their seats. The hijackers explained to the crew and passengers that they wanted the plane to fly to Tunis, where a conference of the Arab League was under way. The hijackers further explained that they wanted a meeting with delegates to the conference and that their ultimate goal was removal of all Palestinians from Lebanon.

After a refueling stop in Cyprus, the airplane headed for Tunis but turned away when authorities blocked the airport runway. Following a refueling stop at Palermo, Sicily, another attempt to land in Tunis, and a second stop in Cyprus, the plane returned to Beirut, where more hijackers came aboard. These reinforcements included an official of Lebanon's Amal Militia, the group at whose direction Yunis claims he acted. The plane took off for Syria, but was turned away and went back to Beirut. There, the hijackers released the passengers, held a press conference reiterating their demand that Palestinians leave Lebanon, blew up the plane, and fled from the airport.

An American investigation identified Yunis as the probable leader of the hijackers and prompted U.S. civilian and military agencies, led by the Federal Bureau of Investigation (FBI), to plan Yunis' arrest. After obtaining an arrest warrant, the FBI put "Operation Goldenrod" into effect in September 1987. Undercover FBI agents lured Yunis onto a yacht in the eastern Mediterranean Sea with promises of a drug deal, and arrested him once the vessel entered international waters. The agents transferred Yunis to a United States Navy munitions ship and interrogated him for several days as the vessel steamed toward a second rendezvous, this time with a Navy aircraft carrier. Yunis was flown to Andrews Air Force Base from the aircraft carrier, and taken from there to Washington, D.C. In Washington, Yunis was arraigned on an original indictment charging him with conspiracy, hostage taking, and aircraft damage. A grand jury subsequently returned a superseding indictment adding additional aircraft damage counts and a charge of air piracy.

* * *

Yunis admitted participation in the hijacking at trial but denied parts of the government's account and offered the affirmative defense of obedience to military orders, asserting that he acted on instructions given by his superiors in Lebanon's Amal Militia. The jury convicted Yunis of conspiracy, 18 U.S.C. § 371 (1988), hostage taking, 18 U.S.C. § 1203 (1988), and air piracy, 49 U.S.C. App. § 1472(n) (1988). However, it acquitted him of three other charged offences that went to trial: violence against people on board an aircraft, 18 U.S.C. § 32(b)(1) (1988), aircraft damage, 18 U.S.C. § 32(b)(2) (1988), and placing a destructive device aboard an aircraft, 18 U.S.C. § 32(b)(3) (1988). The district court imposed concurrent sentences of five years for conspiracy, thirty years for hostage taking, and twenty years for air piracy. Yunis appeals his convictions and seeks dismissal of the indictment.

II. ANALYSIS

Yunis argues that the district court lacked subject matter and personal jurisdiction to try him on the charges of which he was convicted, that the indictment should have been dismissed because the government seized him in violation of the Posse Comitatus Act and withheld classified materials useful to his defense, and that the convictions should be reversed because of errors in the jury instructions. We consider these claims in turn.

A. *Jurisdictional Claims*

Yunis appeals first of all from the district court's denial of his motion to dismiss for lack of subject matter and personal jurisdiction. *See United States v. Yunis,* 681 F.Supp. 896 (D.D.C. 1988). Appellant's principal claim is that, as a matter of domestic law, the federal hostage taking and air piracy statutes do not authorize assertion of federal jurisdiction over him. Yunis also suggests that a contrary construction of these statutes would conflict with established principles of international law, and so should be avoided by this court. Finally, appellant claims that the district court lacked personal jurisdiction because he was seized in violation of American law.

1. Hostage Taking Act

The Hostage Taking Act provides, in relevant part:

> (a) [W]hoever, whether inside or outside the United States, seizes or detains and threatens to kill, to injure, or to continue to detain another person in order to compel a third person or a governmental organization to do or to abstain from any act ... shall be punished by imprisonment by any term of years or for life.
>
> (b)(1) It is not an offence under this section if the conduct required for the offence occurred outside the United States unless—
>
> (A) the offender or the person seized or detained is a national of the United States;
>
> (B) the offender is found in the United States; or
>
> (C) the governmental organization sought to be compelled is the Government of the United States.

18 U.S.C. § 1203. Yunis claims that this statute cannot apply to an individual who is brought to the United States by force, since those convicted under it must be "found in the United States." But this ignores the law's plain language. Subsections (A), (B), and (C) of section 1203(b)(1) offer independent bases for jurisdiction where "the offence occurred outside the United States." Since two of the passengers on Flight 402 were U.S. citizens, section 1203(b)(1)(A), authorizing assertion of U.S. jurisdiction where "the offender or the person seized or detained is a national of the United States," is satisfied. The statute's jurisdictional requirement has been met regardless of whether or not Yunis was "found" within the United States under section 1203(b)(1)(B).

Appellant's argument that we should read the Hostage Taking Act differently to avoid tension with international law falls flat. Yunis points to no treaty obligations of the United States that give us pause. Indeed, Congress intended through the Hostage Taking Act to execute the International Convention Against the Taking of Hostages, which authorizes any signatory state to exercise jurisdiction over persons who take its nationals hostage "if that State considers it appropriate." International Convention Against the Taking of Hostages, *opened for signature* Dec. 18, 1979, art. 5, para. 1, 34 U.N. GAOR Supp. (No. 39), 18 I.L.M. 1456, 1458. *See* H.R. CONF. Rep. No. 1159, 98th Cong., 2d Sess. 418 (1984), *reprinted in* 1984, U.S. CODE CONG. & ADMIN. NEWS 3182, 3710, 3714.

Nor is jurisdiction precluded by norms of customary international law. The district court concluded that two jurisdictional theories of international law, the "universal principle" and the "passive personal principle," supported assertion of U.S. jurisdiction to prosecute Yunis on hijacking and hostage-taking charges. *See Yunis,* 681 F.Supp. at 899–903. Under the universal principle, states may prescribe and prosecute "certain offences recognized by the community of nations as of universal concern, such as piracy, slave trade, attacks on or hijacking of aircraft, genocide, war crimes, and perhaps certain acts of terrorism," even absent any special connection between the state and the offence. *See* RESTATEMENT (THIRD) OF THE FOREIGN RELATIONS LAW OF THE UNITED STATES §§ 404, 423, (1987) [hereafter RESTATEMENT]. Under the passive personal principle, a state may punish non-nationals for crimes committed against its nationals outside of its territory, at least where the state has a particularly strong interest in the crime. *See id.* at §402 comment g; *United States v. Benitez,* 741 F.2d. 1312, 1316 (11th Cir. 1984) (passive personal principle invoked to approve prosecution of Colombian citizen convicted of shooting U.S. drug agents in Colombia), *cert. denied,* 471 U.S. 1137, 105 S.Ct. 2679, 86 L.Ed.2d 698 (1985).

Relying primarily on the RESTATEMENT, Yunis argues that hostage taking has not been recognized as a universal crime and that the passive personal principle authorizes assertion of jurisdiction over alleged hostage takers only where the victims were seized because they were nationals of the prosecuting state. Whatever merit appellant's claims may have as a matter of international law, they cannot prevail before this court. Yunis seeks to portray international law as a self-executing code that trumps domestic law whenever the two conflict. That effort misconceives the role of judges as appliers of international law and as participants in the federal system. Our duty is to enforce the Constitution, laws, and treaties of the United States, not to conform the law of the land to norms of customary international law. *See* U.S. CONST. art.VI. As we said in *Committe of U.S. Citizens Living in Nicaragua v Reagan,* 859 F.2d 929 (D.C.Cir. 1988): "Statutes inconsistent with principles of customary international law may well lead to international law violations. But within the domestic legal realm, that inconsistent statute simply modifies or supersedes customary international law to the extent of the inconsistency." *Id.* at 938. *See also Federal Trade Comm'n v Compagnie de Saint-Gabain-Pont-a-Mousson,* 636 F.2d 1300, 1323 (D.C. Cir. 1980) (U.S. courts "obligated to give effect to an unambiguous exercise by Congress of its jurisdiction to prescribe even if such an exercise would exceed the limitations imposed by international law").

To be sure, courts should hesitate to give penal statutes extraterritorial effect absent a clear congressional directive. *See Foley Bros. v. Filardo,* 336 U.S. 281, 285, 69 S.Ct. 575, 577, 93 L.Ed 680 (1949); *United States v. Bowman,* 260 U.S. 94, 98, 43 S.Ct. 39, 41, 67 L.Ed. 149 (1922). Similarly, courts will not blind themselves to potential violations of international law where legislative intent is ambiguous. *See Murray v. The Schooner Charming Betsy,* 6 U.S. (2 Cranch) 64, 118, 2 L.Ed. 208 (1804) ("[A]n act of congress ought never to be construed to violate the law of nations, if any other possible construction remains...."). But the statute in question reflects an unmistakable congressional intent, consistent with treaty obligations of the United States, to authorize prosecution of those who take Americans hostage abroad no matter where the offence occurs or where the offender is found. Our inquiry can go no further.

* * *

III. Conclusion

For the foregoing reasons, the convictions are confirmed. [The arguments relating to the Anti-hijacking Act, the legality of seizure, the Posse Comitatus Act, the discovery claims, the jury instructions and the obedience to military orders claims are all omitted].

QUESTIONS

1. On what bases did the court justify the exercise of jurisdiction over Yunis?
2. Which other states would have had a basis for the exercise of jurisdiction?
3. In general, do you think a state should assert jurisdiction over an offence when the perpetrator is a non-national and all the elements of the crime took place abroad?

4. If states are indeed free to pass laws contrary to international law, as the court indicates, how can international law ever be binding upon states? Is there any forum where a violation of international law can be remedied?

Note

For further discussion of the validity of the court's jurisdiction if the defendant has been brought before the court by illegal means see *Attorney General of the Government of Israel v. Eichmann*, below at pp. 115–122 and *U.S. v. Alvarez-Machain*, below at pp. 128–138.

The Protective Principle

This principle permits a state to exercise jurisdiction over "certain conduct outside its territory by persons not its nationals that is directed against the security of the State or against a limited class of other state interests."[13] A state may well pass laws prohibiting espionage, counterfeiting or falsifying official documents and make the legislation applicable not only to activity within the state but also to activities abroad carried out by non-nationals.[14] Nations may be tempted to define their security interests too broadly and may provoke the wrath of other nations if this principle is used excessively.[15] Where the activities in question are clearly directed against the security of the state, its property or citizens, the principle is less controversial.

United States v. Bin Laden

92. F. Supp.2d 189
(S.D.N.Y. 2000) (footnotes omitted)

OPINION

Hon. Leonard B. Sand, U.S.D.J.

Opinion as to Jurisdiction

The sixth superseding indictment in this case ("the Indictment") charges fifteen defendants with conspiracy to murder United States nationals, to use weapons of mass de-

13. Restatement Third at §402(3).

14. See, e.g., U.S. v. Birch, 470 F. 2d 808 (4th Cir. 1972).

15. Canada, Mexico, the European Union and many other countries protested the passage of the United States Cuban Liberty and Democratic Solidarity (LIBERTAD) Act of 1996, 22 U.S.C. §§6021–6091 (1996) U.S. Pub. L. 104-114, 110 Stat. 785 (Mar. 12, 1996), reprinted at 35 I.L.M. 357 (1996), which, among other things, permits the U.S. to deny entry visas to the executives of foreign companies that own, lease or have other property interests in Cuban property that is the subject of an unsettled claim for compensation after expropriation by the Cuban government. Id. §401. When asked to justify such denials of visas, the United States Trade Representative, Mikey Cantor, cited United States security interests. Richard W. Stevenson, Canada, Backed by Mexico, Protests to U.S. on Cuba Sanctions, N.Y. Times, March 15, 1996, at A7, cols. 1–6. §302 of the Act permits suits by U.S. nationals to recover damages for property confiscated by the Cuban government after Jan. 1, 1959. §306 of the Act permits the President to suspend the right to bring suit, which so far has been continuously invoked. This statute, known as the Helms-Burton Act, has provoked widespread criticism.

struction against the United States nationals, to destroy United States buildings and property, and to destroy United States defense utilities. The Indictment also charges defendants Mohamed Sadeek Odeh, Mohamed Rashed Daoud al-'Owahli, and Khalfan Khamis Mohamed, among others, with numerous crimes in connection with the August 1998 bombings of the United States Embassies in Nairobi, Kenya, and Dar es Salaam, Tanzania, including 223 counts of murder. The Indictment also charges defendant Wadih el Hage with numerous perjury and false statement counts. Six of the Defendants are presently in the custody of the Bureau of Prisons: Mamdouh Mahmud Salim, Ali Mohamed, Wadih El Hage, Mohamed Rashed Daoud Al-Owhali, Khalfan Khamis Mohamed, and Mohamed Sadeek Odeh ("Odeh"). Presently before the Court is Odeh's Motion to Dismiss Counts 5–244 for Lack of Jurisdiction, in which the other defendants join. For the reasons given below, we grant Odeh's Motion as to Counts 234, 235, 240, and 241, but deny it as to Counts 5–233, 236–239, and 242–244.

Discussion

Odeh argues that most of the counts charged in the Indictment must be dismissed by this Court because they are based on statutes that are inapplicable to the acts he is alleged to have performed. In support of this position, Odeh advances six arguments, which we address seriatim.

I. Extraterritorial Application

Odeh argues that Counts 5–8, 11–237, and 240–244 must be dismissed because (a) they concern acts allegedly performed by Odeh and his co-defendants outside United States territory, yet (b) are based on statues that were not intended by Congress to regulate conduct outside United States territory. More specifically, Odeh argues that "the following statutes that form the basis for the indictment fail clearly and unequivocally to regulate the conduct of foreign nationals for conduct outside the territorial boundaries of the United States: ... Whether Congress intended several of these provisions (viz.,Sections 844(f)[malicious damage to U.S. property], (h) [carrying explosives during commission of a felony], and (n) [conspiring to commit the above offenses]; 930(c) [use or possession of firearm in commission of another offense], and 2155 [obstructing the national defense of the U.S. or destroying national defense premises]) to apply extraterritorially present issues of first impression.

A. General Principles of Extraterritorial Application

It is well-established that Congress has the power to regulate conduct performed outside United States territory. See EEOC v. Arabian Am. Oil Co., 499 U.S. 244, 248, 113 L. Ed. 2d 272, 111 S. Ct. 1227 (1991) ("Congress has the authority to enforce its laws beyond the territorial boundaries of the United States."). It is equally well-established, however, that courts are to presume that Congress has not exercised this power—i.e., that statutes apply only to acts performed within United States territory—unless Congress manifests an intent to reach acts performed outside United States territory. See Sale v. Haitian Ctrs. Council, Inc., 509 U.S. 155, 188, 125 l. Ed. 2d 128, 113 S. Ct. 2549 (1993) ("Acts of Congress normally do not have extraterritorial application unless such an intent is clearly manifested."); Arabian Am. Oil Co., 499 U.S. at 248 (quoting Foley Bros v. Filardo, 336 U.S. 281, 285, 93 L. Ed. 680, 69 S. Ct. 575 (1949)) ("It is a longstanding principle of American law 'that legislation of Congress, unless a contrary intent appears, is meant to apply only within the territorial jurisdiction of the United States.'"). This "clear manifestation" requirement does not require that extraterritorial coverage should be found only if the statute itself explicitly provides for extraterritorial application. Rather, courts should consider "all available evidence about the meaning" of the statute, e.g., its text, structure, and legislative history. Sale, 509 U.S. at 177; See also Smith v. United States, 507 U.S. 197, 201–03, 122 L. Ed. 2d 548, 113 S. Ct. 1178 (1993) (examining text, structure, and legislative history).

Furthermore, the Supreme Court has established a limited exception to this standard approach for "criminal statutes which are, as a class, not logically dependent on their locality for the Government's jurisdiction, but are enacted because of the right of the Government to defend itself against obstruction, or fraud where perpetrated, especially if committed by its own citizens, officers, or agents." United States v. Bowman. 260 U.S. 94, 98. 43 S. Ct. 39, 67 L. Ed. 149 (1922). As regards statutes of this type, courts may infer the requisite intent "from the nature of the offence" described in the statute, and thus need not examine its legislative history. Id. The Court further observed that "to limit the [] locus [of such a statute] to the strictly territorial jurisdiction [of the United States] would be greatly to curtail the scope and usefulness of the statute and leave open a large immunity for frauds as easily committed by citizens on the seas and in foreign countries as at home." Id. Bowman concerned a statute making it illegal knowingly to "present [] a false claim against the United States, ... to any officer of the civil, military or naval service or to any department...." Id. at 101 ... In concluding that Congress intended this statute to apply extraterritorially, the Court reasoned that it "cannot [be] supposed that when Congress enacted the statute or amended it, it did not have in mind that a wide field for such frauds upon the Government ... [existed] in private and public vessels of the United States on the high seas and in foreign ports beyond the land jurisdiction of the United States ..." Id. at 102.

Odeh argues that Bowman is "not controlling precedent" because it "involved the application of [a] penal statute [] to United States citizens," i.e., not to foreign nationals such as himself. Odeh's Memo. At 17. This argument is unavailing for three reasons. First, although Bowman "is expressly limited by its *facts* to prosecutions of United States citizens," Odeh's Reply Memo. at 3 (emphasis added), its underlying rationale is not dependent on the nationality of the offender. Rather, Bowman rests on two factors: (1) the right of the United States to protect itself from harmful conduct—irrespective of the locus of this conduct, and (2) the presumption that Congress would not both (a) enact a statute designed to serve this protective function, and—where the statute proscribes acts that could just as readily be performed outside the United States as within it—(b) undermine this protective intention by limiting the statute's application to United States territory. Give that foreign nationals are in at least as good a position to perform extraterritorial conduct as are United States nationals, it would make little sense to restrict such statutes to United States nationals. To paraphrase Bowman, "to limit [a statute's coverage to United States nationals] would be greatly to curtail the scope and usefulness of the statute and leave open a large immunity for frauds as easily committed [by foreign nationals] as [by United States nationals]." Bowman, 260 U.S. at 98.

Second, the Courts of Appeals—focusing on Bowman's general rule rather than its peculiar facts—have applied this rule to reach conduct by foreign nationals on foreign soil. For example, the Court of Appeals for this Circuit has held that 18 U.S.C. § 1546, which criminalizes the making of false statements with respect to travel documents, was intended by Congress to apply extraterritorially to the conduct of foreign nationals. See United States v. Pizzarusso, 388 F.2d 8. 9 (2d Cir.), cert. denied, 392 U.S. 936, 20 L. Ed. 2d 1395, 88 S. Ct. 2306 (1968); see also United States v. Larsen, 952 F.2d 1099, 1101 (9th Cir. 1991) (18 U.S.C. § 841 (a)(1)—possession of narcotics with intent to distribute); United States v. Wright-Barker, 784 F.2d 167 (3d Cir. 1986) (same); United States v. Orozco-Prada, 732 F.2d 1076, 1088 (2d Cir.), cert. denied, 469 U.S. 845 (1984) (same);

United States v. Benitez, 741 F.2d 1312, 1317 (11th Cir. 1984), cert. denied, 471 U.S. 1137, 86 L.Ed 2d 698, 105 S. Ct. 2679 (1985) (18 U.S.C. §2112—theft of personal property of the United States); United States v. Zehe, 601 F. Supp. 196, 200 (D. Mass. 1985) (18 U.S.C. §§792–799—espionage). Indeed, the Eleventh Circuit has held that one of the statutes targeted by Odeh, viz., 18 U.S.C. §1114—which penalizes murder and attempted murder of officers and employees of the United States—applies to conduct by foreign nationals on foreign soil. See Benitez, 741 F.2d at 1317. Correlatively, no court, to date, has refused to apply the Bowman rule on the ground that the defendant was a foreign national.

Third, the irrelevance of the defendant's nationality to the Bowman rule is reinforced by a consideration of the relationship between this rule and the principles of extraterritorial jurisdiction recognized by international law. Under international law, the primary basis of jurisdiction is the "subjective territorial principle," under which "a state has jurisdiction to prescribe law with respect to ... conduct that, wholly or in substantial part, takes place within its territory." Restatement (Third) of the Foreign Relations Law of the United States §402(1)(a) (1987); see also Christopher L. Blakesley, Extraterritorial Jurisdiction in M. Cherif Bassiouni (ed.), International Criminal Law 47–50 (2d ed. 1999). International law recognizes five other principles of jurisdiction by which a state may reach conduct outside its territory: (1) the objective territorial principle; (2) the protective principle; (3) the nationality principle; (4) the passive personality principle; and (5) the universality principle. See id. at 50–81. The objective territoriality principle provides that a state has jurisdiction to prescribe law with respect to "conduct outside its territory that has or is intended to have substantial effect within its territory." Restatement §402(1)(c). The protective principle provides that a state has jurisdiction to prescribe law with respect to "certain conduct outside its territory by persons not its nationals that is directed against the security of the state or against a limited class of other state interests." Id §402(3) (emphasis added). The nationality principle provides that a state has jurisdiction to prescribe law with respect to "the activities, interests, status, or relations of its nationals outside as well as within its territory." Id. §402(2). The passive personality principle provides that "a state may apply law—particularly criminal law—to an act committed outside its territory by a person not its national where the victim of the act was its national." Id. §402, cmt.g. The universality principle provides that, "[a] state has jurisdiction to define and prescribe punishment for certain offenses recognized by the community of nations as of universal concern, such as piracy, slave trade, attacks on or hijacking of aircraft, genocide, war crimes, and perhaps certain acts of terrorism," regardless of the locus of their occurrence. Id. §404 (emphasis added). Because Congress has the power to override international law if it so chooses, see United States v. Yunis, 288 U.S. App. D.C. 129, 924 F.2d 1086, 1091 (D.C. Cir. 1991); United States v. Aluminum Co. of Am., 148 F.2d 416, 443 (2d Cir. 1945); Restatement §402, cmt. i., none of these five principles places ultimate limits on Congress's power to reach extraterritorial conduct. At the same time, however, in "in determining whether a statute applies extraterritorially, [courts] presume that Congress does not intend to violate principles of international law.... [and] in the absence of an explicit Congressional directive, courts do not give extraterritorial effect to any statute that violates principles of international law." United States v. Vasquez-Velasco, 15 F.3d 833, 839 (9th Cir. 1994) (citing McCulloch v. Sociedad Nacional de Marineros de Honduras, 372 U.S. 10, 21–22, 9 L. Ed. 2d 547, 83 S. Ct. 671 (1963). Hence, courts that find that a given statute applies extraterritorially typically pause to note that this finding is consistent with one or more of the five principles of extraterritorial jurisdiction under international law. See, e.g.,

United States v. MacAllister, 160 F. 3d 1304, 1308 (11th Cir. 1998), cert. denied, 145 L. Ed. 2d 114, 120 S. Ct. 318 (1999) (objective territorial principle); Vasquez-Velasco, 15 F.3d at 841 (objective territoriality principle, protective principle, and passive personality principle); Benitez, 741 F.2d at 1316 (protective principle and passive personality principle); Pizzarusso, 388 F.2d at 11 (protective principle).

The Bowman rule would appear to be most directly related to the protective principle, which, as noted, explicitly authorizes a state's exercise of jurisdiction over "conduct outside its territory by persons not its nationals." Restatement § 402(3). Hence, an application of the Bowman rule that results in the extraterritorial application of a statute to the conduct of foreign nationals is consistent with international law. Therefore, it is not surprising that the lower courts have shown no hesitation to apply the Bowman rule in cases involving foreign defendants.

Odeh attempts to distinguish the preceding lower federal court cases—with the exception of Benitez—by arguing that they concern a special category of "inherently extraterritorial" statutes....

This attempt to distinguish the preceding lower federal court cases fails for two reasons. First, it fails for basically the same reason that Odeh's attempt to distinguish Bowman itself fails: It fixates on the peculiar facts of these cases rather than on the underlying Bowman rationale on which the courts base their respective holdings. Again, this rationale depends in no way on the nationality of the perpetrator. Rather, it depends on the right of the United States to defend itself from harmful conduct regardless of its locus, and a presumption that Congress would not undercut the effectiveness of statutes intended to serve this protective purpose by limited them to United States territory and United States nationals.

Second, as detailed below, most of the statutes targeted by Odeh are more clearly designed to protect the United States than is the drug smuggling statute, viz., 18 U.S.C. § 841(a)(1), that is on Odeh's list of "inherently extraterritorial" statues; and, similarly, most of these statutes protect United States interests that are arguably of more importance than the interest protected by the fraudulent visa application statute, viz., 18 U.S.C. § 1546, which is likewise on that list. Surely it would be an anomalous state of affairs if, on the one hand, a statute that provides merely that "it shall be unlawful ... to manufacture, distribute, or dispense, or possess with intent to manufacture, distribute, or dispense, a controlled substance," 18 U.S.C. § 841(a)(1), were an "inherently extraterritorial" statute; while, on the other hand, a statute that makes it unlawful to "kill or attempt to kill any officer of employee of the United States," 18 U.S.C. § 1114, were an "inherently domestic" statute. Yet it is precisely this anomalous state of affairs that Odeh invites this Court to establish. We decline to do so.

* * *

Note

After much further litigation, Odeh's conviction was affirmed and his case remanded for resentencing, U.S. v. Odeh, 548 F.3d 276 (2d Cir. 2008).

QUESTIONS

1. Why did the court find that Odeh's participation in blowing up the U.S. embassies in Kenya and Tanzania fell within the scope of prohibited activities

under statutes outlawing malicious damage to U.S. property even though Odeh was not a citizen of the U.S. and the activities did not take place in the U.S.?

2. Using the protective principle, do you think that the U.S. could pass laws making it an offense for anyone to destroy U.S. government owned property or U.S. citizen owned property anywhere in the world?

The Universality Principle

Certain activities have been considered so reprehensible by the international community that the usual rules of jurisdiction are waived and any state apprehending the alleged perpetrator is deemed competent to exercise its jurisdiction. The obligations not to engage in such activities is said to be an obligation *erga omnes*: that is, the obligagion is owed to the entire international community, not just the victim or the state representing the victim and consequently, all states have the right to complain of a breach of such an obligation. There is a certain amount of agreement over core activities that trigger universal jurisdiction. Piracy, slave trade, operating a "stateless vessel," (see chapter V) genocide, torture, crimes against humanity, and war crimes have all reached the level of being defined as "universal crimes." Other activities such as hijacking of aircraft and various forms of terrorism are not so widely accepted as conferring universal jurisdiction though such jurisdiction has often been conferred by states entering into an international treaty on the subject.[16]

Attorney General of the Government of Israel v. Eichmann

Judgment of the Supreme Court of Israel
MAY 29, 1962[17]

I.

The appellant, Adolf Eichmann, was found guilty by the District Court of Jerusalem of offences of the most extreme gravity against the Nazi and Nazi Collaborators (Punishment) Law, 1950 (hereinafter referred to as "the Law") and was sentenced to death.

These offences may be divided into four groups:

(a) Crimes against the Jewish people, contrary to Section I(a)(I) of the Law;
(b) Crimes against humanity, contrary to Section I(a)(2);
(c) War Crimes, contrary to Section I(a)(3);

* * *

(d) Membership of hostile organizations, contrary to Section 3.

[*The Jurisdiction of the Court*]

6. Most of the legal contentions of counsel for the appellant revolve around the argument that in assuming jurisdiction to try the appellant the District Court acted contrary to the principles of international law. These contentions are as follows.

---

16. E.g., The Hague Convention on the Suppression of Unlawful Seizure of Aircraft, 860 U.N.T.S. 105, 22 U.S.T. 1641, T.I.A.S. No. 7192, reprinted at 10 I.L.M. 133 (1971), entered into force, 14 Oct. 1971; International Convention Against the Taking of Hostages, 1316 U.N.T.S. 205, T.I.A.S. No. 11081, reprinted at 18 I.L.M. 1456 (1979), entered into force, 3 June 1983.

17. 16 Piske Din 2033 (1962) (in Hebrew, translated by the Ministry of Justice of Israel) reprinted in 36 Int'l L. Rep. at 277 (E. Lauterpacht ed. 1968).

(1) The Law of 1950, which is the only source of the jurisdiction of the Court in this case, constitutes *ex post facto* penal legislation which prescribes as offences acts that were committed before the State of Israel came into existence; therefore the validity of this Law is confined to its citizens alone.

(2) The offences for which the appellant was tried are "extra-territorial offences", that is to say, offences that were committed outside the territory of Israel by a citizen of a foreign State, and even though the Law confers jurisdiction in respect of such offences, it conflicts in so doing with the principle of territorial sovereignty, which postulates that only the country within whose territory the offence was committed or to which the offender belongs—in this case, Germany—has the right to punish therefor.

(3) The acts constituting the offence of which the appellant was convicted were at the time of their commission Acts of State.

(4) The appellant was brought to Israel territory, to be tried for the offences in question, unwillingly and without the consent of the country in which he resided, and this was done through agents of the State of Israel, who acted on the orders of their Government.

* * *

(7) We reject all these contentions.

[*Retroactive Penal Legislation in International Law*]

(8).... As to the first argument, the answer must be that the principle *nullum crimen sine lege, nulla poena sine lege*, in so far as it negates penal legislation with retroactive effect, has not yet become a rule of customary international law:

"There is no rule of general customary international law forbidding the enactment of norms with retrospective force, so called ex post facto laws." (Kelsen, *Peace through Law* (1944), p. 87).

"There is clearly no principle of international law embodying the maxim against retroactivity of criminal law." (Stone, *Legal Controls of International Conflict* (1959), p. 369.)

It is true that in many countries the said principle has been embodied in the constitution of the State or in its criminal code, because of the considerable moral value inherent in it, and in such countries the Court may not depart from it by one iota. (See Cr.A. 53/54: *Eshed, Merkaz Amani L'Tahbura v. Attorney-General*, (1954) 8 Piske Din 785, 819, 830–832.) But this state of affairs is not universal. Thus in the United Kingdom, a country whose system of law and justice is universally recognized as being of a high standard, there is no constitutional limitation of the power of the Legislature to vest its criminal laws with retrospective effect, and should it do so the court will have no power to deny them this force (Allen, *Law in the Making*, 5th ed., p.444). Certainly, there too, general recognition prevails of the moral value of the principle embodied in the above-mentioned maxim. But that recognition has become legally effective to the extent only that that maxim constitutes a rule for the construction of statutes, that is to say, where doubt exists as to the intention of the Legislature the court is directed not to construe the criminal statute with which it is dealing so as to include within its purview an act committed prior to its enactment. (*Queen v. Griffiths* [1891] 2 Q.B. 145; Allen, op. cit.,pp. 443–444.) Similarly, the British Parliament usually avoids passing a criminal statue with retroactive effect, and it will only do so exceptionally where the object of salus populi compels the taking of this course (Willes J. in *Phillips v. Eyre* (1871) L.R. 6 Q.B. 1, 25, cited in paragraph 7 of the judgment—p. 179, above).

Accordingly, if it is the contention of counsel for the appellant that we must apply international law as it is, and not as it ought to be from the moral point of view, then we must reply that precisely from a legal point of view, no such rule in international law is to be found; and *ipso facto* the said principle cannot be deemed to be part of the Israel municipal legal order by virtue of international law, but the extent of its application in this country is the same as in England.

* * *

[*Criminal Jurisdiction over Acts Committed by Foreign Nationals Abroad*]

9. The same applies to the second argument also. As will be recalled, this argument is to the effect that the enactment of a criminal law applicable to an act committed in a foreign country by a foreign national conflicts with the principle of territorial sovereignty. But here too we must hold that there is no such rule in customary international law, and that to this day it has not obtained general international agreement. Evidence of this is to be found in the Judgment of the Permanent Court of International Justice in the *Lotus* case (P.C.I.J., Series A, No. 10, 1927. [1]) There the majority of the Judges recognized the competence of the State of Turkey to enact a criminal statute covering the negligent conduct of a French citizen while on duty as officer-of-the-watch of a French ship at the time of her collision on the high seas—and therefore outside Turkey's territorial waters—with a ship flying the Turkish flag. The collision caused the sinking of the Turkish ship and also the death of eight of her passengers who were of Turkish nationality. It was held in that case that the principle of territorial sovereignty merely requires that a State exercise its penal power within its own borders and not outside them; that subject to this restriction every State has a wide discretion as to the application of its laws and the jurisdiction of its courts in respect of acts committed outside the State; and that only in so far as it is possible to point to a specific rule prohibiting the exercise of this discretion—a rule agreed upon by international treaty—is a State prevented from exercising it. That view was based on the following two grounds; (a) it is precisely the conception of State sovereignty which demands the preclusion of any presumption that there is a restriction on its independence; and (b) even if it is true that the principle of the territorial character of criminal law is firmly established in various States, it is no less true that in almost all such States penal jurisdiction has been extended, in ways that vary from state to state, so as to embrace offences committed outside its territory.

* * *

[*Conformity of the Nazi and Nazi Collaborators (Punishment) Law with Principles of International Law*]

10. We have thus far stated our reasons for dismissing the first two contentions of counsel for the appellant in reliance upon the rules that determine the relationship between Israel municipal law and international law. Our principal object was to make it clear—and this by way of a negative approach—that under international law no *prohibition* whatsoever falls upon the enactment of the Law of 1950 either because it created *ex post facto* offences or because such offences are of an extra-territorial character. Nevertheless, like the District Court, we too do not content ourselves with this solution but have undertaken the task of showing that it is impossible to justify these contentions even from a positive approach—that in enacting the said Law the Knesset only sought to set out the principle of international law and embody its aims. The two propositions on which we propose to rely will therefore be as follows:

(1) The crimes created by the Law and of which the appellant was convicted must be deemed today as having always borne the stamp of international crimes, banned by the law of nations and entailing individual criminal responsibility.

(2) It is the peculiarly universal character of these crimes that vests in every State the authority to try and punish anyone who participated in their commission.

* * *

[*The Character of International Crimes*]

II. *The first proposition.* Our view that the crimes in question must today be regarded as crimes which were also in the past banned by the law of nations and entailed individual criminal responsibility, is based upon the following reasons:

(a) As is well known, the rules of the law of nations are not derived solely from international treaties and crystallized international custom. In the absence of a supreme legislative authority and international codes the process of its evolution resembles that of the common law; in other words, its rules are fashioned piecemeal by analogy with the rules embedded in treaties and custom, on the basis of the "general principles of law recognized by civilized nations" and having regard to vital international needs that compel an immediate solution. A principle which constitutes a common denominator of the legal systems current in many countries must clearly be regarded as a "general principle of law recognized by civilized nations".

* * *

(b) When we turn to consider—with reference to the crimes with which we are here concerned—how the method explained ... above actually works in practice, it becomes essential to dwell first on the features which identify crimes that have long been recognized by customary international law. In doing this, we shall find that these include, among others, the following features: these crimes constitute acts which damage vital international interests; they violate the universal moral values and humanitarian principles that lie hidden in the criminal law systems adopted by civilized nations. The underlying principle in international law regarding such crimes is that the individual who has committed any of them and who, when doing so, may be presumed to have fully comprehended the heinous nature of this act, must account for his conduct. It is true that international law does not prescribe explicit and scaled criminal sanctions; that there still does not exist either an International Criminal Court or even international penal machinery. For the time being, however, international law surmounts these difficulties—which merely reflect its present retarded stage of development—by authorizing the countries of the world to mete out punishment for the violation of its provisions, which is effected by putting these provisions into operation either directly or by virtue of municipal legislation which has adopted and integrated them.

* * *

Secondly, and this is most important, the interest in preventing and punishing acts belonging to the category in question—especially when they are perpetrated on a very large scale—must necessarily extend beyond the borders of the State to which the perpetrators belong and which evinced tolerance or encouragement of their outrages; for such acts can undermine the foundations of the international community as a whole and impair its very stability.

* * *

What is more, in the wake of Resolution 96 (I) of December 1, 1946, the United Nations General Assembly unanimously adopted on December 9, 1948, the Convention for the Prevention and Punishment of the Crime of Genocide. Article I of this Convention provides:

> The Contracting Parties confirm that genocide, whether committed in time of peace or in time of war, is a crime under international law.

As the District Court has shown, relying on the Advisory Opinion of the International Court of Justice dated May 28, 1951, the import of this provision is that the principles inherent in the Convention—as distinct from the contractual obligations embodied therein—"were already part of customary international law when the dreadful crimes were perpetrated, which led to the United Nations Resolution and the drafting of the Convention—the crimes of Genocide committed by the Nazis" (paragraph 21 of the judgment....).

The outcome of the above analysis is that the crimes set out in the Law of 1950, which we have grouped under the inclusive caption "crimes against humanity", must be seen today as acts that have always been forbidden by customary international law—acts which are of a "universal" criminal character and entail individual criminal responsibility. That being so, the enactment of the Law was not from the point of view of international law a legislative act which conflicted with the principle *nulla poena* or the operation of which was retroactive, but rather one by which the Knesset gave effect to international law and its objectives. For this reason also, therefore, the first contention of counsel for the appellant rests on shaky foundations.

[Universal Jurisdiction]

12. *The second proposition.* It will be recalled that according to this proposition it is the universal character of the crimes in question which vests in every State the authority to try and punish those who participated in their commission. This proposition is closely linked with the one advanced in the preceding paragraph, from which indeed it follows as a logical outcome. The grounds upon which it rests are as follows:

(a) One of the principles whereby States assume in one degree or another the power to try and punish a person for an offence is the principle of universality. Its meaning is substantially that such power is vested in every State regardless of the fact that the offence was committed outside its territory by a person who did not belong to it, provided he is in its custody when brought to trial. This principle has wide currency and is universally acknowledged with respect to the offence of piracy *jure gentium.* But while general agreement exists as to this offence, the question of the scope of its application is in dispute (see *Harvard Research* (1935), pp. 503 ff).

* * *

(b) The brief survey of views set out above shows that, notwithstanding the differences between them, there is full justification for applying here the principle of universal jurisdiction since the international character of "crimes against humanity" (in the wide meaning of the term) dealt with in this case is no longer in doubt while the unprecedented extent of their injurious and murderous effects is not to be disputed at the present time. In other words, the basic reason for which international law recognizes the right of each State to exercise such jurisdiction in piracy offences—notwithstanding the fact that its own sovereignty does not extend to the scene of the commission of the offence (the high seas) and the offender is a national of another State or is stateless—applies with even greater force to the above-mentioned crimes. That reason is, it will be recalled, that the interest to prevent bodily and material harm to those who sail the seas and to persons engaged in trade between nations, is a vital interest common to all civilized States and of universal scope....

* * *

The above explanation of the substantive basis upon which the exercise of the principle of universal jurisdiction in respect of the crime of piracy rests, justifies its exercise in regard also to the crimes which are the subject of the present case.

(c) The truth is—and this further supports our conclusion—that the application of this principle has for some time been moving beyond the international crime of piracy.

* * *

In his Note on the legal basis of jurisdiction over war crimes in the *British Year Book of International Law,* XXVIII (1951), p. 382, at pp. 390, 391, Baxter stated that at the end of the Second World War cases of war crimes were tried by the British Military Tribunal in Germany in which the victims were not British subjects but nationals of Allied countries.... Baxter indeed concluded, on the basis of these cases and also of those that were tried by the American tribunals in Germany under Control Council Law No. 10, that:

> International law also surmounts the jurisdictional barrier, as municipal law cannot, by recognizing the universality of jurisdiction enjoyed by war crimes tribunals.

Moreover, accordingly to this expert's opinion even a neutral country has jurisdiction to try a person for a war crime (*loc. cit., p. 392*).

* * *

(e) Counsel for the appellant has further submitted that under Article 6 of the Genocide Convention a person accused of this crime shall be tried by a court of competent jurisdiction of the State in which it was committed. According to his submission, that article has affirmed the application of the "territorial" principle, and the "universal" principle is therefore implicitly negated. The reply to this contention was given by the District Court in paragraph 21 *et seq.* of its judgment. It is that Article 6 imposes upon the parties contractual obligations with future effect, that is to say, obligations which bind them to prosecute for crimes of genocide which may be committed within their territories in the future. This obligation, however, has nothing to do with the universal *power* vested in every State to prosecute for crimes of this type committed in the past—a power which is based on *customary* international law.

(f) We sum up our views on this subject as follows. Not only do all the crimes attributed to the appellant bear an international character, but their harmful and murderous effects were so embracing and widespread as to shake the international community to its very foundations. The State of Israel therefore was entitled, pursuant to the principle of universal jurisdiction and in the capacity of a guardian of international law and an agent for its enforcement, to try the appellant. That being the case, no importance attaches to the fact that the State of Israel did not exist when the offences were committed. Here therefore is an additional reason—and one based on a positive approach—for rejecting the second, "jurisdictional", submission of counsel for the appellant.

[The "Protective" and "Passive Personality" Principles]

We wish to add one further observation. In regard to the crimes directed against the Jews the District Court found additional support for its jurisdiction in the connecting link between the State of Israel and the Jewish people—including that between the State of Israel and the Jewish victims of the holocaust—and the National Home in Palestine, as is explained in its judgment. It therefore upheld its criminal and penal jurisdiction by virtue also of the "protective" principle and the principle of "passive personality". It should be made clear that we fully agree with every word said by the Court on this subject in paragraphs 31–38 of its judgment. If in our judgment we have concentrated on the international and universal character of the crimes of which the appellant has been convicted, one of the reasons for our so doing is that some of them were directed against non-Jewish groups (Poles, Slovenes, Czechs and gipsies).

[Abduction]

13. It will be convenient if at this point we proceed to consider the fourth submission of counsel for the appellant, which is also jurisdictional. It will be recalled that he argued that his client was brought to this country against his will, without the consent of his country of residence (Argentina) and by agents of the State of Israel. Counsel for the appellant has complained to us that the District Court refused to grant his application for the hearing of evidence to prove that the Government of Israel was implicated in the act of abduction, and he repeated his application in this Court.

This submission is unconnected with the preceding two, since it denies the right of the State of Israel to try the appellant for the crimes in question because of the circumstances under which he was brought here, while the others deny such right even if he were to be tried in this country after having arrived here of his own free will. We have no intention of dealing with this contention at any great length, for it has been analyzed with great thoroughness by the District Court (paragraphs 41–52 of its judgment). Relying on a long line of local, British, American and Continental precedents, which were cited extensively in its judgment, the District Court reached the following conclusions:

(1) In the absence of an extradition agreement between the State to which a "fugitive offender" has been brought for trial and the country of "asylum" (from which he was removed by force or by stratagem)—and even if such an agreement existed between the two countries but the offender was not extradited to the first country in accordance therewith—the Court will not investigate the circumstances in which he was detained and brought into the area of jurisdiction.

(2) This also applies if the offender's contention is that the abduction was carried out by agents of the State prosecuting him, since in such a case the right violated is not that of the offender but the sovereign right of the State aggrieved. In other words, the violation of the right raises a question—either political or one of a breach of international law—between the two countries concerned and it must therefore find its solution at this international level. It is not, however, justiciable before the Court into whose area of jurisdiction the offender has been brought.

(3) From the point of view of international law the aggrieved State may condone the violation of its sovereignty and waive its claims, including the claim for the return of the offender to its territory, and such waiver may be explicit or by acquiescence.

(4) Only in one eventuality has a fugitive offender a right of immunity, namely, when he has been extradited by the country of asylum to the country requesting his extradition for a specific offence which is not the offence for which he is tried.

(5) The appellant was not extradited to Israel by Argentina and the State of Israel is not bound by any agreement with Argentina to try him for a specific offence or not to try him for the offences involved in this case.

(6) Moreover, following upon the Resolution of the Security Council of the United Nations of June 23, 1960 (Exhibit T/1), the Governments of Argentina and Israel settled the dispute between them when they issued, on August 3, 1960—before the indictment was presented—a joint communiqué (Exhibit T/4) stating that they "have resolved to regard as closed the incident that arose out of the action taken by citizens of Israel, which infringed the fundamental rights of the State of Argentina". This means that Argentina has condoned the violation of her sovereignty and has waived her claims, including that for the return of the appellant. Any violation therefore of international law that may have been involved in this accident has thus been remedied.

(7) The rights of asylum and immunity belong to the country of asylum and not to the offender. It was not for the appellant to force Argentina, a foreign sovereign State, to give him asylum against its will, especially when at the time of entering upon its territory he was a "wanted war criminal", concealed his true identity and resided there subsequently "under an assumed name and on forged papers". It follows therefore that the State of Argentina gave him no asylum or refuge from the outset, while by the declaration of the settlement of the incident and the waiver of the claim for his return, it finally refused to grant him asylum.

(8) In view of the foregoing there was no room for hearing the evidence which counsel for the appellant sought to adduce on the circumstances of the abduction.

* * *

We have therefore decided to dismiss the appeal as to both the conviction and sentence, and to affirm the judgment and the sentence of the District Court.

* * *

Note

After conviction, Eichmann appealed to the President of Israel for clemency, but this appeal was rejected. On May 31, 1962, Eichmann was executed by hanging; his body was cremated, and the ashes were scattered over the sea.

QUESTIONS

1. Run through all of the possible bases for Israel's jurisdiction over Eichmann's offences—territorial, nationality, passive personality, protective, universal—what problems do you find with each of these bases? Which basis of jurisdiction seems to present the least problems?
2. Why did the Court refuse to accept Eichmann's argument that because he had been unlawfully captured and forcibly brought before the lower court, the court had no jurisdiction to try him?
3. Which other States might have had a stronger basis of jurisdiction for trying Eichmann? Do you think any of those countries would have provided a preferable forum?

For a case that finds individual rights arising under a treaty see *LaGrand Case* (Germany v. United States) 2001 I.C.J. 466, paras. 75–77; and the *Avena Case* (Mexico v. United States) 2004 I.C.J. 12, paras. 57, 61, 63 & 76 at pp. 66–77 *supra*.

Case Concerning the Arrest Warrant of 11 April 2000 (Democratic Republic of the Congo v. Belgium)

2002 I.C.J. 3

Note

In this case Belgium had issued an international arrest warrant for Mr. Abdulaye Yerodia Ndombasi, the Congo's incumbent Minister for Foreign Affairs, for alleged crimes constituting serious violations of international humanitarian law occurring outside Belgium against non Belgian victims. Congo brought suit against Belgium in the I.C.J. The Court held that an incumbent Foreign Minister of a foreign country is entitled to immunity from the jurisdiction of Belgium's national courts but the Court did not address the issue of whether Belgium had the right to assert universal jurisdiction over such crimes. Some judges on the Court thought that the opinion should have first addressed the issue of universal jurisdiction. The excerpt that appears below surveys the development of the concept of universal jurisdiction. For the Court's decision on the merits, see pp. 164–170 *infra.*

Joint Separate Opinion of Judges Higgins, Kooijmans and Buergenthal

* * *

6. As Mr. Yerodia was a non-national of Belgium and the alleged offences described in the arrest warrant occurred outside of the territory over which Belgium has jurisdiction, the victims being non-Belgians, the arrest warrant was necessarily predicated on a universal jurisdiction. Indeed, both it and the enabling legislation of 1993 and 1999 expressly say so. Moreover, Mr. Yerodia himself was outside of Belgium at the time the warrant was issued.

7. In its Application instituting proceedings (p. 7), the Democratic Republic of the Congo complained that Article 7 of the Belgian Law:

> *"establishes the universal applicability of the Law and the universal jurisdiction of the Belgian courts in respect of 'serious violations of international humanitarian law', without even making such applicability and jurisdiction conditional on the presence of the accused on Belgian territory.*

* * *

16. [T]he Court should have "found it appropriate" to deal with the question of whether the issue and international circulation of a warrant based on universal jurisdiction in the absence of Mr. Yerodia's presence on Belgian territory was unlawful. This should have been done before making a finding on immunity from jurisdiction, and the Court should indeed have "examined in some detail various problems raised" by the request as formulated by the Congo in its final submissions.

* * *

19. We therefore turn to the question whether States are entitled to exercise jurisdiction over persons having no connection with the forum State when the accused is not present in the State's territory. The necessary point of departure must be the sources of international law identified in Article 38, paragraph 1*(c)*, of the Statute of the Court, together with obligations imposed upon all United Nations Members by Security Council resolutions, or by such General Assembly resolutions as meet the criteria enunciated by the Court in the case concerning *Legality of the Threat or Use of Nuclear Weapons, Advisory Opinion (I.C.J. Reports 1996*, p. 226, para. 70).

20. Our analysis may begin with national legislation, to see if it evidences a State practice. Save the Belgian legislation of 10 February 1999, national legislation, whether in fulfilment of international treaty obligations to make certain international crimes offences also in national law, or otherwise, does not suggest a universal jurisdiction over these offences. Various examples typify the more qualified practice. The Australian War Crimes Act of 1945, as amended in 1988, provides for the prosecution in Australia of crimes committed between 1 September 1939 and 8 May 1945 by persons who were Australian citizens or residents at the times of being charged with the offences (ss. 9 and 11). The United Kingdom War Crimes Act of 1991 enables proceedings to be brought

for murder, manslaughter or culpable homicide, committed between 1 September 1935 and 5 June 1945, in a place that was part of Germany or under German occupation, and in circumstances where the accused was at the time, or has become, a British citizen or resident of the United Kingdom. The statutory jurisdiction provided for by France, Germany and (in even broader terms) the Netherlands, refer for their jurisdictional basis to the jurisdictional provisions in those international treaties to which the legislation was intended to give effect. It should be noted, however, that the German Government on 16 January 2002 has submitted a legislative proposal to the German Parliament, section 1 of which provides:

> "This Code governs all the punishable acts listed herein violating public international law, [and] in the case of felonies listed herein [this Code governs] even if the act was committed abroad and does not show any link to [Germany]."

The Criminal Code of Canada 1985 allows the execution of jurisdiction when at the time of the act or omission the accused was a Canadian citizen or "employed by Canada in a civilian or military capacity"; or the "victim is a Canadian citizen or a citizen of a State that is allied with Canada in an armed conflict", or when "at the time of the act or omission Canada could, in conformity with international law, exercise jurisdiction over the person on the basis of the person's presence in Canada" (Art.7).

21. All of these illustrate the trend to provide for the trial and punishment under international law of certain crimes that have been committed extraterritorially. But none of them, nor the many others that have been studied by the Court, represent a classical assertion of a universal jurisdiction over particular offences committed elsewhere by persons having no relationship or connection with the forum State.

22. The case law under these provisions has largely been cautious so far as reliance on universal jurisdiction is concerned. In the *Pinochet* case in the English courts, the jurisdictional basis was clearly treaty based, with the double criminality rule required for extradition being met by English legislation in September 1988, after which date torture committed abroad was a crime in the United Kingdom as it already was in Spain. In Australia the Federal Court referred to a group of crimes over which international law granted universal jurisdiction, even though national enabling legislation would also be needed (*Nulyarimma*, 1999: genocide). The High Court confirmed the authority of the legislature to confer jurisdiction on the courts to exercise a universal jurisdiction over war crimes (*Polyukhovich*, 1991). In Austria (whose Penal Code emphasizes the double-criminality requirement), the Supreme Court found that it had jurisdiction over persons charged with genocide, given that there was not a functioning legal system in the State where the crimes had been committed nor a functioning international criminal tribunal at that point in time (*Cvjetkovic*, 1994). In France it has been held by a *juge d'instruction* that the Genocide Convention does not provide for universal jurisdiction (*in re Javor*, reversed in the *Cour d'Appel* on other grounds. The *Cour de Cassation* ruling equally does not suggest universal jurisdiction). The *Munyeshyaka* finding by the *Cour d'Appel* (1998) relies for a finding—at first sight inconsistent—upon cross-reference into the Statute of the International Tribunal for Rwanda as the jurisdictional basis. In the *Qaddafi* case the *Cour d'Appel* relied on passive personality and not on universal jurisdiction (in the *Cour de Cassation* it was immunity that assumed central importance).

23. In the *Bouterse* case the Amsterdam Court of Appeal concluded that torture was a crime against humanity, and as such an "extraterritorial jurisdiction" could be exercised over a non-national. However, in the *Hoge Road*, the Dutch Supreme Court attached

conditions to this exercise of extraterritorial jurisdiction (nationality, or presence within the Netherlands at the moment of arrest) on the basis of national legislation.

24. By contrast, a universal jurisdiction has been asserted by the Bavarian Higher Regional Court in respect of a prosecution for genocide (the accused in this case being arrested in Germany). And the case law of the United States has been somewhat more ready to invoke "universal jurisdiction", though considerations of passive personality have also been of key importance (*Yunis,* 1988; *Bin Laden,* 2000).

25. An even more ambiguous answer is to be derived from a study of the provisions of certain important treaties of the last 30 years, and the obligations imposed by the parties themselves.

26. In some of the literature on the subject it is asserted that the great international treaties on crimes and offences evidence universality as a ground for the exercise of jurisdiction recognized in international law. (See the interesting recent article of Luis Benavides "The Universal Jurisdiction Principle: Nature and Scope", *Anuario Mexicano de Derecho Internacional,* Vol. 1, p. 58 (2001).) This is doubtful.

27. Article VI of the Convention on the Prevention and Punishment of the Crime of Genocide, 9 December 1948, provides:

> "Persons charged with genocide or any of the other acts enumerated in Article III shall be tried by a competent tribunal of the State in the territory of which the act was committed, or by such international penal tribunal as may have jurisdiction with respect to those Contracting Parties which shall have accepted its jurisdiction."

This is an obligation to assert territorial jurisdiction, though the *travaux préparatoires* do reveal an understanding that this obligation was not intended to affect the right of a State to exercise criminal jurisdiction on its own nationals for acts committed outside the State (A/C 6/SR, 134; p. 5). Article VI also provides a potential grant of non-territorial competence to a possible future international tribunal—even this not being automatic under the Genocide Convention but being restricted to those Contracting Parties which would accept its jurisdiction. In recent years it has been suggested in the literature that Article VI does not prevent a State from exercising universal jurisdiction in a genocide case. (And see, more generally, *Restatement (Third) of the Foreign Relations Law of the United States (1987),* § 404.)

28. Article 49 of the First Geneva Convention, Article 50 of the Second Geneva Convention, Article 129 of the Third Geneva Convention and Article 146 of the Fourth Geneva Convention, all of 12 August 1949, provide:

> "Each High Contracting Party shall be under the obligation to search for persons alleged to have committed, or to have ordered to be committed, ... grave breaches, and shall bring such persons, regardless of their nationality, before its own courts. It may also, if it prefers, and in accordance with the provisions of its own legislation, hand such persons over for trial to another High Contracting Party concerned, provided such High Contracting Party has made out a *prima facie* case."

29. Article 85, paragraph 1, of the First Additional Protocol to the 1949 Geneva Convention incorporates this provision by reference.

30. The stated purpose of the provision was that the offences would not be left unpunished (the extradition provisions playing their role in this objective). It may imme-

diately be noted that this is an early form of the *aut dedere aut prosequi* to be seen in later conventions. But the obligation to prosecute is primary, making it even stronger.

* * *

40. This short historical survey [of jurisdictional provisions in a number of treaties] may be summarized as follows:

41. The parties to these treaties [The Single Convention on Narcotics and Drugs, 1961; the Hague Convention for the Suppression of Unlawful Seizure of Aircraft, 1970; the International Convention Against the Taking of Hostages, 1979; and the Convention Against Torture, 1984] agreed both to grounds of jurisdiction and as to the obligation to take the measures necessary to establish such jurisdiction. The specified grounds relied on links of nationality of the offender, or the ship or aircraft concerned, or of the victim. See, for example, Article 4(1) Hague Convention; Article 3 (1) Tokyo Convention; Article 5, Hostages Convention; Article 5, Torture Convention. These may properly be described as treaty-based broad extraterritorial jurisdiction. But in addition to these were the parallel provisions whereby a State party in whose jurisdiction the alleged perpetrator of such offences is found, shall prosecute him or extradite him. By the loose use of language the latter has come to be referred to as "universal jurisdiction", though this is really an obligatory territorial jurisdiction over persons, albeit in relation to acts committed elsewhere.

42. Whether this obligation (whether described as the duty to establish universal jurisdiction, or, more accurately, the jurisdiction to establish a territorial jurisdiction over persons for extraterritorial events) is an obligation only of treaty law, *inter partes or*, whether it is now, *at least as regards the offences articulated in the treaties*, an obligation of customary international law was pleaded by the Parties in this case but not addressed in any great detail.

43. Nor was the question of whether any such general obligation applies to crimes against humanity, given that those too are regarded everywhere as comparably heinous crimes. Accordingly, we offer no view on these aspects.

44. However, we note that the inaccurately termed "universal jurisdiction principle" in these treaties is a principle of *obligation,* while the question in this case is whether Belgium had the right to issue and circulate the arrest warrant if it so chose.

If a dispassionate analysis of State practice and Court decisions suggests that no such jurisdiction is presently being exercised, the writings of eminent jurists are much more mixed. The large literature contains vigorous exchanges of views (which have been duly studied by the Court) suggesting profound differences of opinion. But these writings, important and stimulating as they may be, cannot of themselves and without reference to the other sources of international law, evidence the existence of a jurisdictional norm. The assertion that certain treaties and court decisions rely on universal jurisdiction, which in fact they do not, does not evidence an international practice recognized as custom. And the policy arguments advanced in some of the writings can certainly suggest why a practice or a court decision should be regarded as desirable, or indeed lawful; but contrary arguments are advanced, too, and in any event these also cannot serve to substantiate an international practice where virtually none exists.

45. That there is no established practice in which States exercise universal jurisdiction, properly so called, is undeniable. As we have seen, virtually all national legislation envisages links of some sort to the forum State; and no case law exists in which pure universal jurisdiction has formed the basis of jurisdiction. This does not necessarily in-

dicate, however, that such an exercise would be unlawful. In the first place, national legislation reflects the circumstances in which a State provides in its own law the ability to exercise jurisdiction. But a State is not required to legislate up to the full scope of the jurisdiction allowed by international law. The war crimes legislation of Australia and the United Kingdom afford examples of countries making more confined choices for the exercise of jurisdiction. Further, many countries have no national legislation for the exercise of well recognized forms of extraterritorial jurisdiction, sometimes notwithstanding treaty obligations to enable themselves so to act. National legislation may be illuminating as to the issue of universal jurisdiction, but not conclusive as to its legality. Moreover, while none of the national case law to which we have referred happens to be based on the exercise of a universal jurisdiction properly so called, there is equally nothing in this case law which evidences an *opinio juris* on the illegality of such a jurisdiction. In short, national legislation and case law,—that is, State practice—is neutral as to exercise of universal jurisdiction.

46. There are, moreover, certain indications that a universal criminal jurisdiction for certain international crimes is clearly not regarded as unlawful. The duty to prosecute under those treaties which contain the *aut dedere aut prosequi* provisions opens the door to a jurisdiction base on the heinous nature of the crime rather than on links of territoriality or nationality (whether as perpetrator or victim). The 1949 Geneva Conventions lend support to this possibility, and are widely regarded as today reflecting customary international law. (See, e.g., Cherif Bassiouni, *International Criminal Law, Volume III: Enforcement*, 2nd Edition, (1999), p. 228; Theodor Meron "International Criminalization of Internal Atrocities" 89 *AJIL*(1995), at 576.)

47. The contemporary trends, reflecting international relations as they stand at the beginning of the new century, are striking. The movement is towards bases of jurisdiction other than territoriality. "Effects" or "impact" jurisdiction is embraced both by the United States and, with certain qualifications, by the European Union. Passive personality jurisdiction, for so long regarded as controversial, is now reflected not only in the legislation of various countries (the United States, Ch. 113A, 1986 Omnibus Diplomatic and Antiterrorism Act; France, Art. 689, Code of Criminal Procedure, 1975), and today meets with relatively little opposition, at least so far as a particular category of offences is concerned.

* * *

52. We may thus agree with the authors of the Oppenheim, 9th Edition, at page 998, that:

> "While no general rule of positive international law can as yet be asserted which gives to states the right to punish foreign nationals for crimes against humanity in the same way as they are, for instance, entitled to punish acts of piracy, there are clear indications pointing to the gradual evolution of a significant principle of international law to that effect."

* * *

QUESTION

If the ICJ had ruled on the legality of the prosecution (not simply the issuance of an arrest warrant) of a Congolese citizen (not the Foreign Minister) for crimes against humanity where neither the accused, nor the victims, nor the location of the alleged atrocities had any connection with Belgium, but the accused was found in, or properly extradited to, Belgium, and Belgian had a statute permitted such prosecution, do you think the Court would have upheld such an assertion of jurisdiction?

Extradition

If someone commits a crime in state A and flees to state B, State A may request the extradition of the offender. Extradition is the process by which one state hands over an alleged offender to another state. Some states engage in this practice on an informal, reciprocal basis but most states spell out their respective duties in bi-lateral or multi-lateral extradition treaties. These treaties usually list the offences for which extradition is required (usually more serious offences) though they often allow each state to refuse to extradite their own nationals. Common law countries are usually prepared to extradite their own nationals but civil law countries often have specific statutes forbidding the extradition of nationals. If a state refuses extradition of a national, the extradition treaty usually imposes an obligation on that state to try the offender. You may wonder how a state can try someone who committed an offence in another state but you should bear in mind that civil law countries exercise jurisdiction on the basis of nationality much more frequently than common law countries.

There have been a number of cases where a serious offender has fled from the place of the crime and extradition has been requested but refused. If the case is considered serious enough the state may seek other means to bring the offender back for trial. The *Eichmann* case is a famous example of the forcible abduction of an offender. Argentina originally filed a complaint with the United Nations Security Council claiming a violation of her sovereignty but the claim was dropped when Israel and Argentina mutually agreed to declare the incident closed. (See *Eichmann* case, pp. 115–122 *supra.*)

United States v. Humberto Alvarez-Machain

Supreme Court of the United States
504 U.S. 655(1992)

The **Chief Justice** [Rehnquist] delivered the opinion of the Court.

The issue in this case is whether a criminal defendant, abducted to the United States from a nation with which it has an extradition treaty, thereby acquires a defense to the jurisdiction of this country's courts. We hold that he does not, and that he may be tried in federal district court for violations of the criminal law of the United States.

Respondent, Humberto Alvarez-Machain, is a citizen and resident of Mexico. He was indicted for participating in the kidnap and murder of United States Drug Enforcement Administration (DEA) special agent Enrique Camarena-Salazar and a Mexican pilot working with Camarena, Alfredo Zavala-Avelar. The DEA believes that respondent, a medical doctor, participated in the murder by prolonging agent Camarena's life so that others could further torture and interrogate him. On April 2, 1990, respondent was forcibly kidnapped from his medical office in Guadalajara, Mexico, to be flown by private plane to El Paso, Texas, where he was arrested by DEA officials. The District Court concluded the DEA agents were responsible for respondent's abduction, although they were not personally involved in it. *United States v. Caro-Quintero,* 745 F.Supp. 599, 602–604, 609 (C.D. Cal. 1990).[18]

Respondent moved to dismiss the indictment, claiming that his abduction constituted outrageous governmental conduct, and that the District Court lacked jurisdiction to try him because he was abducted in violation of the extradition treaty between the United States and Mexico. Extradition Treaty, May 4, 1978, [1979] United States-United Mexican States, 31 U.S.T. 5059, T.I.A.S. No. 9656 (Extradition Treaty or Treaty). The District Court rejected the outrageous governmental conduct claim, but held that it lacked jurisdiction to try respondent because his abduction violated the Extradition Treaty. The district court discharged respondent and ordered that he be repatriated to Mexico. *Caro-Quintero,* supra, 614. The Court of Appeals affirmed the dismissal of the indictment and the repatriation of respondent, relying on its decision in *United States v. Verdugo-Urquidez,* 939 F.2d 1341 (CA9 1991), cert pending, No. 91-670. 946 F.2d 1466 (1991). In *Verdugo,* the Court of Appeals held that the forcible abduction of a Mexican national with the authorization or participation of the United States violated the Extradition Treaty between the United States and Mexico. Although the Treaty does not expressly prohibit such abductions, the Court of Appeals held that the "purpose" of the Treaty was violated by a forcible abduction, 939 F.2d, at 1350, which, along with a formal protest by the offended nation, would give a defendant the right to invoke the Treaty violation to defeat jurisdiction of the district court to try him. The Court of Appeals further held that the proper remedy for such a violation would be dismissal of the indictment and repatriation of the defendant to Mexico.

In the instant case, the Court of Appeals affirmed the district court's finding that the United States had authorized the abduction of respondent, and that letters from the Mexican government to the United States government served as an official protest of the Treaty violation. Therefore, the Court of Appeals ordered that the indictment against respondent be dismissed and that respondent be repatriated to Mexico. 946 F. 2d, at 1467. We granted certiorari, 502 US 1024 (1992), and now reverse.

Although we have never before addressed the precise issue raised in the present case, we have previously considered proceedings in claimed violation of an extradition treaty, and proceedings against a defendant brought before a court by means of a forcible abduction. We addressed the former issue in *United States v. Rauscher,* 119 U.S. 407 (1886); more precisely, the issue of whether the Webster-Ashburton Treaty of 1842, 8 Stat. 576, which governed extraditions between England and the United States, prohibited the prosecution of defendant Rauscher for a crime other than the crime for which he had been extradited. Whether this prohibition, known as the doctrine of specialty, was an intended part of the treaty had been disputed between the two nations for some time. *Rauscher,* 119 U.S. at 411. Justice Miller delivered the opinion of the Court, which carefully examined the terms and history of the treaty; the practice of nations in regards to extradition treaties; the case law from the states; and the writings of commentators, and reached the following conclusion:

> [A] person who has been within the jurisdiction of the court by *virtue of proceedings under an extradition treaty,* can only be tried for one of the offences

18. Apparently, DEA officials had attempted to gain respondent's presence in the United States through informal negotiations with Mexican officials, but were unsuccessful. DEA officials then, through a contact in Mexico, offered to pay a reward and expenses in return for the delivery of respondent to the United States. *United States v. Caro-Quintero,* 745 F. Supp. 599, 602–604 (C.D. Cal. 1990).

> described in the treaty, and for the offence with which he is charged in the proceedings for his extradition, until a reasonable time and opportunity have been given him, after his release or trial upon such charge, to return to the country from whose asylum he had been forcibly taken under those proceedings" Id., at 430 (emphasis added).

In addition, Justice Miller's opinion noted that any doubt as to this interpretation was put to rest by two federal statutes which imposed the doctrine of specialty upon extradition treaties to which the United States was a party. Id., at 423. Unlike the case before us today, the defendant in *Rauscher* had been brought to the United States by way of an extradition treaty; there was no issue of a forcible abduction.

In *Ker v. Illinois,* 119 U.S. 436 (1886), also written by Justice Miller and decided the same day as *Rauscher*, we addressed the issue of a defendant brought before the court by way of a forcible abduction. Frederick Ker had been tried and convicted in an Illinois court for larceny; his presence before the court was procured by means of forcible abduction from Peru. A messenger was sent to Lima with the proper warrant to demand *Ker* by virtue of the extradition treaty between Peru and the United States. The messenger, however, disdained reliance on the treaty processes, and instead forcibly kidnapped *Ker* and brought him to the Unites States. We distinguished Ker's case from *Rauscher,* on the basis that Ker was not brought into the United States by virtue of the extradition treaty between the United States and Peru, and rejected Ker's argument that he had a right under the extradition treaty to be returned to this country only in accordance with its terms. We rejected Ker's due process argument more broadly, holding in line with "the highest authorities" that "such forcible abduction is no sufficient reason why the party should not answer when brought within the jurisdiction of the court which has the right to try him for such an offence, and presents no valid objection to his trial in such court." *Ker, supra,* at 444.

In *Frisbie v. Collins,* 342 U.S. 519, rehearing denied, 343 U.S. 937 (1952), we applied the rule in *Ker* to a case in which the defendant had been kidnapped in Chicago by Michigan officers and brought to trial in Michigan. We upheld the conviction over objections based on the due process clause and the Federal Kidnapping Act and stated:

> This Court has never departed from the rule announced in [*Ker*] that the power of a court to try a person for crime is not impaired by the fact that he had been brought within the court's jurisdiction by reason of a "forcible abduction." No persuasive reasons are now presented to justify overruling this line of cases. They rest on the sound basis that due process of law is satisfied when one present in court is convicted of crime after having been fairly apprized of the charges against him and after a fair trial in accordance with constitutional procedural safeguards. There is nothing in the Constitution that requires a court to permit a guilty person rightfully convicted to escape justice because he was brought to trial against his will." *Frisbie, supra,* at 522 (citation and footnote omitted).

The only differences between *Ker* and the present case are that *Ker* was decided on the premise that there was no governmental involvement in the abduction, 119 U.S. at 443; and Peru, from which Ker was abducted, did not object to his prosecution. Respondent finds these differences to be dispositive, as did the Court of Appeals in *Verdugo,* 939 F.2d, at 1346, contending that they show that respondent's prosecution, like the prosecution of Rauscher, violates the implied terms of a valid extradition treaty. The Government, on the other hand argues that *Rauscher* stands as an "exception" to the rule in *Ker* only when an extradition treaty is invoked, and the terms of the treaty provide that its breach will limit the jurisdiction of a court. Brief for United States 17. Therefore, our first inquiry must be whether the abduction of respondent from Mexico violated the extradition treaty between the United States and Mexico. If we conclude that the Treaty does not prohibit respondent's abduction, the rule in *Ker* applies, and the court need not inquire as to how respondent came before it.

In construing a treaty, as in construing a statute, we first look to its terms to determine its meaning. *Air France v. Saks*, 470 U.S. 392, 397 (1985); *Valentine v. United States ex rel. Neidecker,* 299 U.S. 5, 11 (1936). The Treaty says nothing about the obligations of the United States and Mexico to refrain from forcible abductions of people from the territory of the other nation, or the consequences under the Treaty if such an abduction occurs. Respondent submits that Article 22(1) of the Treaty which states that it "shall apply to offences specified in Article 2 [including murder] committed before and after this Treaty enters into force," 31 U.S.T., at 5073–5074, evidences an intent to make application of the Treaty mandatory for those offences. However, the more natural conclusion is that Article 22 was included to ensure that the Treaty was applied to extradition requested after the Treaty went into force, regardless of when the crime of extradition occurred.

More critical to respondent's argument is Article 9 of the Treaty which provides:

1. Neither Contracting Party shall be bound to deliver up its own nationals, but the executive authority of the requested Party shall, if not prevented by the laws of that Party, have the power to deliver them up if, in its discretion, it be deemed proper to do so.
2. If extradition is not granted pursuant to paragraph 1 of this Article, the requested Party shall submit the case to its competent authorities for the purpose of prosecution provided that Party has jurisdiction over the offence." *Id.*, at 5065.

According to respondent, Article 9 embodies the terms of the bargain which the United States struck: If the United States wishes to prosecute a Mexican national, it may request that individual's extradition. Upon a request from the United States, Mexico may either extradite the individual, or submit the case to the proper authorities for prosecution in Mexico. In this way, respondent reasons, each nation preserved its right to choose whether its nationals would be tried in its own courts or by the courts of the other nation. This preservation of rights would be frustrated if either nation were free to abduct nationals of the other nation for the purposes of prosecution. More broadly, respondent reasons, as did the Court of Appeals, that all the processes and restrictions on the obligation to extradite established by the Treaty would make no sense if either nation were free to resort to forcible kidnapping to gain the presence of an individual for prosecution in a manner not contemplated by the Treaty. *Verdugo, supra,* at 1350.

We do not read the Treaty in such a fashion. Article 9 does not purport to specify the only way in which one country may gain custody of a national of the other country for the purposes of prosecution. In the absence of an extradition treaty, nations are under no obligation to surrender those in their country to foreign authorities for prosecution. *Rauscher,* 119 U.S., at 411–412; *Factor v. Laubenheimer*, 290 U.S. 276, 287 (1933); cf. *Valentine v. United States ex rel. Neidecker, supra*, 299 U.S., at 8–9 (United States may not extradite a citizen in the absence of a statute or treaty obligation). Extradition treaties exist so as to impose mutual obligations to surrender individuals in certain defined sets of circumstances, following established procedures. See 1 J. Moore, A Treatise on Extradition and Interstate Rendition, §72 (1891). The Treaty thus provides a mechanism which would not otherwise exist, requiring, under certain circumstances, the United States and Mexico to extradite individuals to the other country, and establishing the procedures to be followed when the Treaty is invoked.

The history of negotiation and practice under the Treaty also fails to show that abductions outside of the Treaty constitute a violation of the Treaty. As the Solicitor General notes, the Mexican government was made aware, as early 1906, of the *Ker* doctrine, and the United States' position that it applied to forcible abductions made outside of the terms of the United States-Mexico extradition treaty. Nonetheless, the current version of the Treaty, signed in 1978, does not attempt to establish a rule that would in any way curtail the effect of *Ker*. Moreover, although language which would grant individuals exactly the right sought by respondent had been considered and drafted as early as 1935 by a prominent group of legal scholars sponsored by the faculty of Harvard Law School, no such clause appears in the current treaty.

Thus, the language of the Treaty, in the context of its history, does not support the proposition that the Treaty prohibits abductions outside of its terms. The remaining question, therefore, is whether the Treaty should be interpreted so as to include an implied term prohibiting prosecution where the defendant's presence is obtained by means other than those established by the Treaty. See *Valentine*, 299 U.S., at 17. ("Strictly the question is not whether there had been a uniform practical construction denying the power, but whether the power had been so clearly recognized that the grant should be implied").

Respondent contends that the Treaty must be interpreted against the backdrop of customary international law, and that international abductions are "so clearly prohibited in international law" that there was no reason to include such a clause in the Treaty itself. Brief for Respondent 11. The international censure of international abductions is further evidenced, according to respondent, by the United Nations Charter and The Charter of the Organization of American States. *Id.*, at 17. Respondent does not argue that these sources of international law provide an independent basis for the right respondent asserts not to be tried in the United States, but rather that they should inform the interpretation of the Treaty terms.

The Court of Appeals deemed it essential in order for the individual defendant to assert a right under the Treaty, that the affected foreign government had registered a protest. *Verdugo*, 939 F.2d, at 1357 ("in the kidnapping case there must be a formal protest from the offended government after the kidnapping"). Respondent agrees that the right exercised by the individual is derivative of the nation's right under the Treaty, since nations are authorized, notwithstanding the terms of an extradition treaty, to voluntarily render an individual to the other country on terms completely outside of those provided in the Treaty. The formal protest, therefore, ensures that the "offended" nation actually objects to the abduction and has not in some way voluntarily rendered the individual for prosecution. Thus the Extradition Treaty only prohibits gaining the defendant's presence by means other than those set forth in the Treaty when the nation from which the defendant was abducted objects.

This argument seems to us inconsistent with the remainder of respondent's argument. The Extradition Treaty has the force of law, and if, as respondent asserts, it is self-executing, it would appear that a court must enforce it on behalf of an individual regardless of the offensiveness of the practice of one nation to the other nation. In *Rauscher*, the Court noted that Great Britain had taken the position in other cases that the Webster-Ashburton Treaty included the doctrine of specialty, but no importance was attached to whether or not Great Britain had protested the prosecution of *Rauscher* for the crime of cruel and unusual punishment as opposed to murder.

More fundamentally, the difficulty with the support respondent garners from international law is that none of it relates to the practice of nations in relation to extradition treaties. In *Rauscher*, we implied a term in the Webster-Ashburton Treaty because of the practice of nations with regard to extradition treaties. In the instant case, respondent would imply terms in the extradition treaty from the practice of nations with regards to international law more generally. Respondent would have us find that the Treaty acts as a prohibition against a violation of the general principle of international law that one government may not "exercise its police power in the territory of another state". Brief for Respondent 16. There are many actions which could be taken by a nation that would violate this principle, including waging war, but it cannot seriously be contended that an invasion of the United States by Mexico would violate the terms of the Extradition Treaty between the two nations.

In sum, to infer from this Treaty and its terms that it prohibits all means of gaining the presence of an individual outside of its terms goes beyond established precedent and practice. In *Rauscher*, the implication of a doctrine of specialty into the terms of the Webster-Ashburton treaty which, by its terms, required the presentation of evidence establishing probable cause of the crime of extradition before extradition was required, was a small step to take. By contrast, to imply from the terms of this Treaty that it prohibits obtaining the presence of an individual by means outside of the procedures the Treaty establishes requires a much larger inferential leap, with only the most general of international law principles to support it. The general principles cited by respondent simply fail to persuade us that we should imply in the United States-Mexico Extradition Treaty a term prohibiting international abductions.

Respondent and his *amici* may be correct that respondent's abduction was "shocking," Tr. of Oral Arg. 40, and that it may be in violation of general international law principles. Mexico has protested the abduction of respondent through diplomatic notes, App. 33–38, and the decision of whether respondent should be returned to Mexico, as a matter outside of the Treaty, is a matter for the Executive Branch. We conclude, however, that respondent's abduction was not in violation of the Extradition Treaty between the United States and Mexico, and therefore the rule of *Ker v. Illinois* is fully applicable to this case. The fact of respondent's forcible abduction does not therefore prohibit his trial in a court in the United States for violations of the criminal laws of the United States.

The Judgment of the Court of Appeals is therefore reversed, and the case is remanded for further proceedings consistent with this opinion.

So ordered.

Justice **Stevens**, with whom Justice **Blackmun** and Justice **O'Connor** join, dissenting.

The Court correctly observes that this case raises a question of first impression. See *ante*, at 659. The case is unique for several reasons. It does not involve an ordinary abduction by a private kidnaper, or bounty hunter, as in *Ker v. Illinois*, 119 U.S. 436 (1886); nor does it involve the apprehension of an American fugitive who committed a crime in one State and sought asylum in another, as in *Frisbie v. Collins*, 342 U.S. 519 (1952). Rather it involves this country's abduction of another country's citizen; it also involves a violation of the territorial integrity of that other country, with which this country has signed an extradition treaty.

A Mexican citizen was kidnapped in Mexico and charged with a crime committed in Mexico; his offence allegedly violated both Mexican and American law. Mexico has formally demanded on at least two separate occasions that he be returned to Mexico and has represented that he will be prosecuted and punished for his alleged offence. It is clear that Mexico's demand must be honored if this official abduction violated the 1978 Extradition Treaty between the United States and Mexico. In my opinion, a fair reading of the treaty in light of our decision in *United States v. Rauscher*, 119 U.S. 407 (1886), and applicable principles of international law, leads inexorably to the conclusion that the District Court, *United States v. Caro-Quintero*, 745 F. Supp. 599 (CD Cal 1990), and the Court of Appeals for the Ninth Circuit, 946 F.2d 1466 (1991) (*per curiam*), correctly construed that instrument.

I.

The Extradition Treaty with Mexico is a comprehensive document containing 23 articles and an appendix listing the extraditable offences covered by the agreement. The parties announced their purpose in the preamble: The two Governments desire "to cooperate more closely in the fight against crime and, to this end, to mutually render better assistance in matters of extradition." From the preamble, through the description of the parties' obligations with respect to offences committed within as well as beyond the territory of a requesting party, the delineation of the procedures and evidentiary requirements for extradition, the special provisions for political offences and capital punishment, and other details, the Treaty appears to have been designed to cover the entire subject of extradition. Thus, Article 22, entitled "Scope of Application" states that the "Treaty shall apply to offences specified in Article 2 committed before and after this Treaty enters into force," and Article 2 directs that "[e]xtradition shall take place, subject to this Treaty, for willful acts which fall within any of [the extraditable offences listed in] the clauses of the Appendix." Moreover, as noted by the Court, *ante*, at 663, Article 9 expressly provides that neither Contracting Party is bound to deliver up its own nationals, although it may do so in its discretion but if it does not do so, it "shall submit the case to its competent authorities for purposes of prosecution."

Petitioner's claim that the Treaty is not exclusive, but permits forcible governmental kidnapping, would transform these, and other, provisions into little more than verbiage. For example, provisions requiring "sufficient" evidence to grant extradition (Art.3), withholding extradition for political or military offences (Art.5), withholding extradition when the person sought has already been tried (Art. 6), withholding extradition when the statute of limitations for the crime has lapsed (Art.7), and granting the requested State discretion to refuse to extradite an individual who would face the death penalty in the requesting country (Art. 8), would serve little purpose if the requesting country could simply kidnap the person. As the Court of Appeals for the Ninth Circuit recognized in a related case, "[e]ach of these provisions would be utterly frustrated if a kidnapping were held to be a permissible course of governmental conduct." *United States v. Verdugo-Urquidez*, 939 F.2d 1341, 1349 (1991). In addition, all of these provisions "only make sense if they are understood as *requiring* each treaty signatory to comply with those procedures whenever it wishes to obtain jurisdiction over an individual who is located in another treaty nation." *Id.*, at 1351

It is true, as the Court notes, that there is no express promise by either party to refrain from forcible abduction in the territory of the other nation. See *ante*, at 664, 665–666. Relying on that omission, the Court, in effect, concludes that the Treaty merely creates an optional method of obtaining jurisdiction over alleged offenders, and that the parties silently reserved the right to resort to self help whenever they deem force more expeditious than legal process. If the United States, for example, thought it more expedient to torture or simply to execute a person rather than to attempt extradition, these options would be equally available because they, too, were not explicitly prohibited by the Treaty. That, however, is a highly improbable interpretation of a consensual agreement, which on its face appears to have been intended to set forth comprehensive and exclusive rules concerning the subject of extradition. In my opinion, "the manifest scope and object of the treaty itself," *Rauscher*, 119 U.S., at 422, plainly imply a mutual undertaking to respect the territorial integrity of the other contracting party. That opinion is confirmed by a consideration of the "legal context" in which the Treaty was negotiated. *Cannon v. University of Chicago*, 441 U.S. 677, 699 (1979).

In *Rauscher*, the Court construed an extradition treaty that was far less comprehensive than the 1978 Treaty with Mexico. The 1842 Treaty with Great Britain determined the boundary between the United States and Canada, provided for the suppression of the African slave trade, and also contained one paragraph authorizing the extradition of fugitives "in certain cases." 8 Stat. 576. In Article X, each Nation agreed to "deliver up to justice all persons" properly charged with any one of seven specific crimes, including murder. 119 U.S., at 421. After Rauscher had been extradited for murder, he was charged with the lesser offence of inflicting cruel and unusual punishment on a member of the crew of a vessel on the high seas. Although the treaty did not purport to place any limit on the jurisdiction of the demanding State after acquiring custody of the fugitive, this Court held that he could not be tried for any offence other than murder. Thus, the treaty constituted the exclusive means by which the United States could obtain jurisdiction over a defendant within the territorial jurisdiction of Great Britain.

The Court noted that the Treaty included several specific provisions, such as the crimes for which one could be extradited, the process by which the extradition was to be carried out, and even the evidence that was to be produced, and concluded that "the fair purpose of the treaty is, that the person shall be delivered up to be tried for that offence and for no other." *Id.*, at 423. The Court reasoned that it did not make sense for the Treaty to provide such specifics only to have the person "pas[s] into the hands of the country which charges him with the offence, free from all the positive requirements and just implications of the treaty under which the transfer of his person takes place." *Id.*, at 421. To interpret the Treaty in a contrary way would mean that a country could request extradition of a person for one of the seven crimes covered by the Treaty, and then try the person for another crime, such as a political crime, which was clearly not covered by the Treaty; this result, the Court concluded, was clearly contrary to the intent of the parties and the purpose of the Treaty.

Rejecting an argument that the sole purpose of Article X was to provide a procedure for the transfer of an individual from the jurisdiction of one sovereign to another, the Court stated:

> No such view of solemn public treaties between the great nations of the earth can be sustained by a tribunal called upon to give judicial construction to them.
>
> The opposite view has been attempted to be maintained in this country upon the ground that there is no express limitation in the treaty of the right of the country in which the offence was committed to try the person for the crime alone for which he was extradited, and that once being within the jurisdiction of that country, no matter by what contrivance or fraud or by what pretence of

> establishing a charge provided for by the extradition treaty he may have been brought within the jurisdiction, he is, when here, liable to be tried for any offence against the laws as though arrested here originally. This proposition of the absence of express restriction in the treaty of the right to try him for other offences than that for which he was extradited, is met by the manifest scope and object of the treaty itself. *Id.*, at 422.

Thus, the Extradition Treaty, as understood in the context of cases that have addressed similar issues, suffices to protect the defendant from prosecution despite the absence of any express language in the Treaty itself purporting to limit this Nation's power to prosecute a defendant over whom it had lawfully acquired jurisdiction.

Although the Court's conclusion in *Rauscher* was supported by a number of judicial precedents, the holdings in these cases were not nearly as uniform as the consensus of international opinion that condemns one Nation's violation of the territorial integrity of a friendly neighbor. It is shocking that a party to an extradition treaty might believe that it has secretly reserved the right to make seizures of citizens in the other party's territory. Justice Story found it shocking enough that the United States would attempt to justify an American seizure of a foreign vessel in a Spanish port:

> But, even supposing, for a moment, that our laws had required an entry of the Apollon, in her transit, does it follow, that the power to arrest her was meant to be given, after she had passed into the exclusive territory of a foreign nation? We think not. *It would be monstrous* to suppose that our revenue officers were authorized to enter into foreign ports and territories, for the purpose of seizing vessels which had offended against our laws. It cannot be presumed that Congress would voluntarily justify such a clear violation of the laws of nations. *The Apollon*, 9 Wheat. 362, 370–371 (1824) (emphasis added).

The law of nations, as understood by Justice Story in 1824, has not changed. Thus, a leading treatise explains:

> A State must not perform acts of sovereignty in the territory of another State.
>
> * * *
>
> It is ... a breach of International Law for a State to send its agents to the territory of another State to apprehend persons accused of having committed a crime. Apart from other satisfaction, the first duty of the offending State is to hand over the person in question to the State in whose territory he was apprehended. 1 Oppenheim's International Law 295, and n. 1 (H. Lauterpacht 8th ed. 1955).

Commenting on the precise issue raised by this case, the chief reporter for the American Law Institute's Restatement of Foreign Relations used language reminiscent of Justice Story's characterization of an official seizure in a foreign jurisdiction as "monstrous."

> When done without consent of the foreign government, abducting a person from a foreign country is a gross violation of international law and gross disrespect for a norm high in the opinion of mankind. It is a blatant violation of the territorial integrity of another state; it eviscerates the extradition system (established by a comprehensive network of treaties involving virtually all states). [Quoting Louis Henkin, A Decent Respect to the Opinions of Mankind, 25 John Marshall L. J. 215, 231 (1992)].

In the *Rauscher* case, the legal background that supported the decision to imply a covenant not to prosecute for an offence different from that for which extradition had been granted was far less clear than the rule against invading the territorial integrity of a treaty partner that supports Mexico's position in this case. If *Rauscher* was correctly decided—and I am convinced that it was—its rationale clearly dictates a comparable result in this case.

* * *

As the Court observes at the outset of its opinion, there is reason to believe that respondent participated in an especially brutal murder of an American law enforcement agent. That fact, if true, may explain the Executive's intense interest in punishing respondent in our courts. Such an explanation, however, provides no justification for disregarding the Rule of Law that this Court has a duty to uphold. That the Executive may wish to reinterpret the Treaty to allow for an action that the Treaty in no way authorizes should not influence this Court's interpretation. Indeed, the desire for revenge exerts "a kind of hydraulic pressure ... before which even well settled principles of law will bend," *Northern Securities Co. v. United States,* 193 U.S. 197, 401 (1904) (Holmes, J., dissenting), but it is precisely at such moments that we should remember and be guided by our duty "to render judgment evenly and dispassionately according to law, as each is given understanding to ascertain and apply it." *United States v. Mine Workers,* 330 U.S. 258, 342 (1947) (Rutledge, J., dissenting). The way that we perform that duty in a case of this kind sets an example that other tribunals in other countries are sure to emulate.

The significance of this Court's precedents is illustrated by a recent decision of the Court of Appeal of the Republic of South Africa. Based largely on its understanding of the import of this Court's cases—including our decision in *Ker v. Illinois*—that court held that the prosecution of a defendant kidnapped by agents of South Africa in another country must be dismissed. *S v. Ebrahim,* S. Afr. L. Rep. (Apr–June 1991). The Court of Appeal of South Africa—indeed, I suspect most courts throughout the civilized world—will be deeply disturbed by the "monstrous" decision the Court announces today. For every Nation that has an interest in preserving the Rule of Law is affected, directly or indirectly, by a decision of this character. As Thomas Paine warned, an "avidity to punish is always dangerous to liberty" because it leads a Nation "to stretch, to misinterpret, and to misapply even the best of laws." To counter that tendency, he reminds us:

> He that would make his own liberty secure must guard even his enemy from oppression; for if he violates this duty he establishes a precedent that will reach to himself.

I respectfully dissent.

QUESTIONS

1. Why did the Court decide that the forcible abduction of Alvarez-Machain did not violate the U.S.-Mexican Extradition Treaty?
2. Did the Court follow the general rules of treaty interpretation as laid down in the Vienna Convention on the Law of Treaties, articles 31 and 32? (See, chapter III.)
3. Suppose the Court had found that the kidnapping of Alvarez-Machain did violate the Treaty, would the Court have automatically decided that the breach of the treaty resulted in a lack of jurisdiction in U.S. Courts?

4. What remedies does the Vienna Convention on the Law of Treaties suggest once a breach has been found?
5. What entity has the right to complain about the violation of a treaty?
6. If the Court had found that the kidnapping and forcible abduction by persons paid by the United States government violated customary international law (see chapter X on the Use of Force) what remedies would be available? To whom would the remedies run?

For a case that finds individual rights arising under a treaty see *LaGrand Case* (Germany v. United States) 2001 I.C.J. 466, paras. 75–77; and the *Avena Case* (Mexico v. United States) 2004 I.C.J. 12, paras. 57, 61, 63 & 76 at pp. 66–76 *supra*.

Problem

Suppose that you are the chief legal adviser to the Foreign Ministry of the country of Padora and that Padora has an extradition treaty with the U.S. exactly similar to the U.S.-Mexican treaty discussed in the *Alvarez-Machain* case above. Your government is not happy with the decision in that case and has asked you to draft amended language to the U.S.-Padoran extradition treaty which will ensure that if the U.S. should ever abduct a citizen from Padora, the U.S. courts would not have jurisdiction over that person and the U.S. would be required to repatriate the abducted Padoran. Please draft some paragraphs to achieve these purposes to be inserted in a new treaty to be negotiated between the U.S. and Padora.

Immunity from Jurisdiction

Diplomatic Immunity

There is a long history of one state granting immunity to accredited diplomats from another state. There is no obligation on the part of any state to engage in relations of any sort with other nations but, if a state does enter into diplomatic relations with another state and receives an accredited diplomat, international law clearly requires almost total immunity from civil and criminal jurisdiction for the diplomat. If the host state disapproves of the diplomat's activities or otherwise wishes to break relations with the diplomat's state, the host state's only remedy is to ask the diplomat to leave and to give him/her a reasonable amount of time to get out of the country.[19] The Vienna Convention on Diplomatic Relations[20] has been ratified by a great number of countries and many of its provisions are declaratory of customary law. The Convention provides differing levels of immunity for the diplomat, his or her family, the administrative and technical staff, the service staff and private servants. The main idea behind the Convention was that diplomats needed immunity in order to carry out their functions freely and without fear of reprisal.

---

19. Vienna Convention on Diplomatic Relations, *infra* note 20, at art. 9.

20. 500 U.N.T.S. 95, 23 U.S.T. 3227, T.I.A.S. No. 7502, signed 19 April 1961; entered into force, 24 April 1964.

From time to time relations between states may become strained and, without immunity, it would be far too easy for the host state to seize the diplomats on some trumped up charges and use them as bargaining chips in any ensuing negotiations. You may well wonder what happens if in fact a diplomat does break the criminal law of the host country. Suppose the diplomat is suspected of murdering someone. First, the Vienna Convention puts a positive obligation on diplomats to observe the laws of the host state[21] but it is clear that immunity from arrest and criminal prosecution attaches to the diplomat even for the most heinous of crimes.[22] The host state may at any time declare any diplomat a *persona non grata* in which case the sending state must either recall the person or terminate his/her functions within the mission.[23] Even if the person is no longer regarded as a diplomat by either the sending or the receiving state immunity still attaches to those official activities carried out while the person was a diplomat.[24]

The persons accredited as diplomatic agents are declared "inviolable" and the host state is obligated to treat the diplomat with "due respect and ... take all appropriate steps to prevent any attack on his person, freedom, or dignity."[25] The premises of the diplomatic mission are declared inviolable under the Convention[26] and the host state has an obligation to protect the premises "against any intrusion or damage and to prevent any disturbance of the peace of the mission or impairment of its dignity."[27] The mission's official correspondence is also declared inviolable[28] and the diplomatic bag "shall not be opened or detained."[29]

You may wonder why a state would grant diplomats total immunity from criminal jurisdiction and almost total immunity from its civil jurisdiction.[30] The answer lies in examining how the host state would like its own diplomats treated when they are abroad and by bearing in mind that although there have been some celebrated accusations of criminal activity on the part of diplomats,[31] these are few and far between. Occasionally there have been suggestions that the scope of immunity should be narrowed but so far these suggestions have not met with success. There are also some notorious examples of a host state failing to live up to its obligations under the Convention.

---

21. Id. art. 41(1).
22. Id. art. 29 & 31.
23. Id. art. 9.
24. Id. art. 39(2).
25. Id. art 29.
26. Id. art 22(1).
27. Id. art. 22(2).
28. Id. art. 27(2).
29. Id. art 27(3).
30. For exceptions to immunity from civil jurisdiction see Vienna Convention, art. 31(1). For a recent application of civil immunity see *Tabion v. Mufti*, 73 F. 3d 535 (4th Cir. 1996) (suit for violation of the Fair Labor Standards Act by a servant against a Jordanian Embassy official dismissed on the basis of diplomatic immunity).
31. A person within the Libyan People's Bureau (Embassy) in London, U.K., shot and killed a British policewoman and wounded ten protesters outside the Bureau on April 17, 1984. The British police surrounded the Bureau and it would have been relatively easy either to storm it or lay siege to it. There was no doubt that someone in the Bureau had fired the shot. Nevertheless, the British government respected the inviolability of the mission and the immunity from criminal jurisdiction of the diplomatic agents. The diplomats were given two weeks to leave the country and diplomatic relations were broken off between Libya and the U.K. After two weeks all the diplomats had left and the British police took over the Bureau. See, Jon Nordheimer, Gunman in London in Libyan Embassy Fires into Crowd, N.Y. Times, April 18, 1984, at A1; R.W. Apple, Jr., Searching of Bags of Libyans Barred, N.Y. Times, April 26, 1984, at A12.

Case Concerning United States Diplomatic and Consular Staff in Tehran

United States of America v. Iran
1980 I.C.J. 3

Note

During 1979 the Shah of Iran was deposed. The Shah's family had to flee the country and the United States agreed to admit the Shah, ostensibly for medical treatment. This action provoked protests in Iran specifically at the U.S. Embassy in Tehran and at some U.S. consulates in other Iranian cities. On November 4, 1979 a crowd of students and protesters took over the U.S. Embassy. The Iranian security forces offered no assistance in curbing the demonstration or in restoring the Embassy to the Americans once it had been taken by force. The Embassy staff and two private American citizens who were visiting the Embassy were seized by the protesters. After some negotiations the women and black hostages were released, leaving fifty remaining diplomatic and consular staff and two private citizens still in custody. The Embassy premises, archives and documents were ransacked. The United States applied to the International Court of Justice for interim measures of protection asking for the return of the Embassy, the release of the hostages and safe passage out of the country for all personnel being held. The Court promptly granted all of the U.S. requests. (Order of Provisional Measures, 15 December, 1979 1. C. J. 7). Iran refused to comply with the order. (While the Court was considering the case on the merits, U.S. military forces entered Iran and attempted to rescue the hostages. The attempt was unsuccessful and eight U.S. military personnel were killed in a collision between two U.S. aircraft.) The U.S. claim for relief was based on a number of treaties to which both the U.S. and Iran were parties, including the Vienna Convention on Diplomatic Relations of 1961 and the Vienna Convention on Consular Relations of 1963.[32]

Judgment of the Court

56.... The events which are the subject of the United States' claims fall into two phases which it will be convenient to examine separately.

57. The first of these phases covers the armed attack on the United States Embassy by militants on 4 November 1979, the overrunning of its premises, the seizure of its inmates as hostages, the appropriation of its property and archives and the conduct of the Iranian authorities in the face of those occurrences....

58. No suggestion has been made that the militants, when they executed their attack on the Embassy, had any form of official status as recognized "agents" or organs of the Iranian State. Their conduct in mounting the attack, overrunning the Embassy and seizing its inmates as hostages cannot, therefore, be regarded as imputable to that State on that basis.... Their conduct might be considered as itself directly imputable to the Iranian State only if it were established that, in fact, on the occasion in question the militants acted on behalf of the State, having been charged by some competent organ of the

32. See *infra* note 36.

Iranian State to carry out a specific operation. The information before the Court does not, however, suffice to establish with the requisite certainty the existence at that time of such a link between the militants and any competent organ of the state.

59. Previously, it is true, the religious leader of the country, the Ayatollah Khomeini, had made several public declarations inveighing against the United States as responsible for all his country's problems.... In [a November 1, 1979] message the Ayatollah Khomeini had declared that it was "up to the dear pupils, students and theological students to expand with all their might their attacks against the United States and Israel, so they may force the United States to return the deposed and criminal Shah, and to condemn this great plot".... In the view of the Court, however, it would be going too far to interpret such general declarations of the Ayatollah Khomeini to the people or students of Iran as amounting to an authorization from the State to undertake the specific operation of invading and seizing the United States Embassy....

61. [This] ... does not mean that Iran is, in consequence, free of any responsibility in regard to those attacks; for its own conduct was in conflict with its international obligations. By a number of provisions of the Vienna Conventions of 1961 and 1963, Iran was placed under the most categorical obligations, as a receiving State, to take appropriate steps to ensure the protection of the United States Embassy and Consulates, their staffs, their archives, their means of communication and the freedom of movement of the members of their staffs.

62. ... In the view of the Court, the obligations of the Iranian Government here in question are not merely contractual obligations established by the Vienna Conventions of 1961 and 1963, but also obligations under general international law.

63. The facts ... above establish to the satisfaction of the Court that on 4 November 1979 the Iranian Government failed altogether to take any "appropriate steps" to protect the premises, staff and archives of the United States' mission against attack by the militants, and to take any steps either to prevent this attack or to stop it before it reached its completion. They also show that on 5 November 1979 the Iranian Government similarly failed to take appropriate steps for the protection of the United States Consulates at Tabriz and Shiraz. In addition they show, in the opinion of the Court, that the failure of the Iranian Government to take such steps was due to more than mere negligence or lack of appropriate means.

67. This inaction of the Iranian Government by itself constituted clear and serious violation of Iran's obligations to the United States under the provisions of Article 22, paragraph 2, and Articles 24, 25, 26, 27 and 29 of the 1961 Vienna Convention on Diplomatic Relations, and Articles 5 and 36 of the 1963 Vienna Convention on Consular Relations. Similarly, with respect to the attacks of the Consulates at Tabriz and Shiraz, the inaction of the Iranian authorities entailed clear and serious breaches of its obligations under the provisions of several further articles of the 1963 Convention on Consular Relations....

68. The Court is therefore led inevitably to conclude, in regard to the first phase of the events which has so far been considered, that on 4 November 1979 the Iranian authorities:

(a) were fully aware of their obligations under the conventions in force to take appropriate steps to protect the premises of the United States Embassy and its diplomatic and consular staff from any attack and from any infringement of their inviolability, and to ensure the security of such other persons as might be present on the said premises;

(b) were fully aware, as a result of the appeals for help made by the United States Embassy, of the urgent need for action on their part;

(c) had the means at their disposal to perform their obligations;
(d) completely failed to comply with these obligations.

Similarly, the Court is led to conclude that the Iranian authorities were equally aware of their obligations to protect the United States Consulates at Tabriz and Shiraz, and of the need for action on their part, and similarly failed to use the means which were at their disposal to comply with their obligations.

69. The second phase of the events which are the subject of the United States' claims comprises the whole series of facts which occurred following the completion of the occupation of the United States Embassy by the militants, and the seizure of the Consulates at Tabriz and Shiraz. The occupation having taken place and the diplomatic and consular personnel of the United States' mission having been taken hostage, the action required of the Iranian Government by the Vienna Conventions and by general international law was manifest. Its plain duty was at once to make every effort, and to take every appropriate step, to bring these flagrant infringements of the inviolability of the premises, archives and diplomatic and consular staff of the United States Embassy to a speedy end, to restore the Consulates at Tabriz and Shiraz to United States control, and in general to re-establish the status quo and to offer reparation for the damage.

70. No such step was, however, taken by the Iranian authorities....

73. The seal of official government approval was finally set on this situation by a decree issued on 17 November 1979 by the Ayatollah Khomeini. His decree began with the assertion that the American Embassy was "a centre of espionage and conspiracy" and that "those people who hatched plots against our Islamic movement in that place do not enjoy international diplomatic respect." He went on expressly to declare that the premises of the Embassy and the hostages would remain as they were until the United States had handed over the former Shah for trial and returned his property to Iran. This statement of policy the Ayatollah qualified only to the extent of requesting the militants holding the hostages to "hand over the blacks and the women, if it is proven that they did not spy, to the Ministry of Foreign Affairs so that they may be immediately expelled from Iran"....

74. ... The approval given to these facts by the Ayatollah Khomeini and other organs of the Iranian State, and the decision to perpetuate them, translated continuing occupation of the Embassy and detention of the hostages into acts of that State. The militants, authors of the invasion and jailers of the hostages, had now become agents of the Iranian State for whose acts the State itself was internationally responsible....

76. The Iranian authorities' decision to continue the subjection of the premises of the United States Embassy to occupation by militants and of the Embassy staff to detention as hostages, clearly gave rise to repeated and multiple breaches of the applicable provisions of the Vienna Conventions even more serious than those which arose from their failure to take any steps to prevent the attacks on the inviolability of these premises and staff.

80. [T]he Court considers that it should examine ... [the question whether] the conduct of the Iranian Government ... might be justified by the existence of special circumstances.

81. In his letters of 9 December 1979 and 16 March 1980, ... Iran's Minister for Foreign Affairs referred to the present case as only "a marginal and secondary aspect of an overall problem". This problem, he maintained, "involves, *inter alia*, more than 25 years of continual interference by the United States in the internal affairs of Iran, the shameless

exploitation of our country, and numerous crimes perpetrated against the Iranian people, contrary to and in conflict with all international and humanitarian norms". In the first of the two letters he indeed singled out amongst the "crimes" which he attributed to the United States an alleged complicity on the part of the Central Intelligence Agency in the coup d'état of 1953 and in the restoration of the Shah to the throne of Iran.

82. ... The Court, in its Order of 15 December 1979, pointed out that if the Iranian Government considered the alleged activities of the United States in Iran legally to have a close connection with the subject-matter of the Application it was open to Iran to present its own case regarding those activities to the Court by way of defence to the United States' claims.

83. In any case, even if the alleged criminal activities of the United States in Iran could be considered as having been established, the question would remain whether they could be regarded by the Court as constituting a justification of Iran's conduct and thus a defence to the United States' claims in the present case. The Court, however, is unable to accept that they can be so regarded. This is because diplomatic law itself provides the necessary means of defence against, and sanction for, illicit activities by members of diplomatic or consular missions.

84. The Vienna Conventions of 1961 and 1963 contain express provisions to meet the case when members of an embassy staff, under the cover of diplomatic privileges and immunities, engage in such abuses of their functions as espionage or interference in the internal affairs of the receiving State....

85. Thus, it is for the very purpose of providing a remedy for such possible abuses of diplomatic functions that Article 9 of the 1961 Convention on Diplomatic Relations stipulates:

> 1. The receiving State may at any time and without having to explain its decision, notify the sending State that the head of the mission or any member of the diplomatic staff of the mission is *persona non grata* or that any other member of the staff of the mission is not acceptable. In any such case, the sending State shall, as appropriate, either recall the person concerned or terminate his functions with the mission....
>
> 2. If the sending State refuses or fails with a reasonable period to carry out its obligations under paragraph 1 of this Article, the receiving State may refuse to recognize the person concerned as a member of the mission.

The 1963 Convention contains, in Article 23, paragraphs 1 and 4, analogous provision in respect of consular officers and consular staff.... Beyond that remedy for dealing with abuses of the diplomatic function by individual members of a mission, a receiving State has in its hands a more radical remedy if abuses of their functions by members of a mission reach serious proportions. This is the power which every receiving State has, at its own discretion, to break off diplomatic relations with a sending State and to call for the immediate closure of the offending mission.

89. Accordingly, the Court finds that no circumstances exist in the present case which are capable of negativing the fundamentally unlawful character of the conduct pursued by the Iranian State on 4 November 1979 and thereafter....

91. ... Wrongfully to deprive human beings of their freedom and to subject them to physical constraint in conditions of hardship is in itself manifestly incompatible with the principles of the Charter of the United Nations, as well as with the fundamental principles enunciated in the Universal Declaration of Human Rights. But what has

above all to be emphasized is the extent and seriousness of the conflict between the conduct of the Iranian State and its obligations under the whole corpus of the international rules of which diplomatic and consular law is comprised, rules the fundamental character of which the Court must here again strongly affirm....

92. ... The frequency with which at the present time the principles of international law governing diplomatic and consular relations are set at nought by individuals or groups of individuals is already deplorable. But this case is unique and of very particular gravity because here it is not only private individuals or groups of individuals that have disregarded and set at nought the inviolability of a foreign embassy, but the government of the receiving State itself.... Such events cannot fail to undermine the edifice of law carefully constructed by mankind over a period of centuries, the maintenance of which is vital for the security and well-being of the complex international community of the present day, to which it is more essential than ever that the rules developed to ensure the ordered progress of relations between its members should be constantly and scrupulously respected.

93. [T]he Court considers that it cannot let pass without comment the incursion into the territory of Iran made by United States military units on 24–25 April 1980.... No doubt the United States Government may have had understandable preoccupations with respect to the well-being of its nationals held hostage in its Embassy for over five months. No doubt also the United States Government may have had understandable feelings of frustration at Iran's long-continued detention of the hostages, notwithstanding two resolutions of the Security Council as well as the Court's own Order of 15 December 1979 calling expressly for their immediate release. Nevertheless ... the Court cannot fail to express its concern in regard to the United States' incursion into Iran.... [T]he Court was in course of preparing the present judgment adjudicating upon the claims of the United States against Iran when the operation of 24 April 1980 took place. The Court therefore feels bound to observe that an operation undertaken in those circumstances, from whatever motive, is of a kind calculated to undermine respect for the judicial process in international relations and to recall that in paragraph 47, 1 B, of its Order of 15 December 1979 the Court had indicated that no action was to be taken by either party which might aggravate the tension between the two countries.

94. At the same time, however, the Court must point out that neither the question of the legality of the operation of 24 April 1980, under the Charter of the United Nations and under general international law, nor any possible question of responsibility flowing from it, is before the Court....

95. For these reasons,

THE COURT,

1. By thirteen votes to two,

Decides that the Islamic Republic of Iran ... has violated ... obligations owed by it to the United States of America under international conventions in force between the two countries, as well as under long-established rules of general international law;....

3. Unanimously,

Decides that the Government of the Islamic Republic of Iran must immediately take all steps to redress the situation resulting from the events of 4 November 1979....

Note

The Court also ruled that Iran must "terminate the unlawful detention" of the hostages; must provide the hostages with means to leave the country; must restore the seized premises, property, archives and documents to the U.S.; and must make reparations to the U.S. either by mutual agreement or through proceedings before the Court.

Not until seven months after the Court's judgment did Iran release the hostages. That release was brought about by an agreement between the U.S. and Iran known as the Declaration of Algeria, reprinted at 20 I.L.M. 223 (1981). The agreement provided a mechanism for the settlement of claims by both states. The United States also agreed to withdraw all pending claims against Iran in the International Court of Justice.

QUESTIONS

1. Why did the Court find the state of Iran responsible for the students' and other protesters' actions?
2. Which provisions of the Vienna Convention on Diplomatic Relations and the Vienna Convention on Consular Relations did the Court find were violated by Iran?
3. Why did the Court refuse to accept Iran's argument that the U.S. interference in Iran's internal affairs justified the Embassy seizure? In letters to the Court Iran had stated that the U.S. had engineered the overthrow of the Iranian government headed by Dr. Mossadegh in 1953, had restored the Shah and that his regime was directly under American control.

If a particularly serious crime is committed by a diplomat, the host state may request a waiver of immunity from the sending state and the sending state is free to grant a waiver should it deem it appropriate.[33] Sometimes it is difficult to work out how broad a waiver has been granted by the diplomat's state.

Knab v. Republic of Georgia

No. 97-CV-03118 (TFH), 1998 U.S. Dist.
LEXIS 8820 (D.D.C. May 29, 1998) (mem.)
(Some footnotes omitted)

* * *

OPINION BY: Thomas F. Hogan, United States District Judge.

I Background

This case stems from a traffic accident that occurred on January 3, 1997. That evening, defendant Makharadze was involved in an accident and collision that resulted in the death of Joviane Waltrick, as well as injuries to several other people. It is undisputed that, at the time of the accident, defendant Makharadze was a diplomat with the Mission for the Republic of Georgia. Plaintiff's Amended Complaint in this case asserts that defendant Makharadze was acting in his official capacity when he allegedly caused the accident....

33. Id. art. 32(1). It is only the diplomat's state that has the power to insist on immunity or waive immunity, not the diplomat.

On January 14, 1997, the State Department formally requested that the Republic of Georgia waive Makharadze's immunity from prosecution. Specifically, the State Department's request described some of the criminal charges that the U.S. Attorney proposed to bring, and the Department requested a "waiver of Mr. Makharadze's immunity to enable the U.S. Attorney to pursue this matter in accordance with local law." ... The request did not explicitly discuss a waiver of civil liability.

On February 14, 1997, the Republic of Georgia agreed to the State Department's request. Specifically, the Republic stated that, on consideration of the request, and in accordance with Article 32 of the Vienna Convention, it "waived diplomatic immunity for Mr. George Makharadze, so that he can be prosecuted in the United States, for the accident that took place on January 3, 1997, in Washington, D.C." ...

Defendant Makharadze faced criminal charges in District of Columbia Superior Court. On October 8, 1997, defendant pled guilty to all charges. Defendant is currently incarcerated, serving his sentence on those convictions.

Plaintiff [Personal representative of the estate of Joviane Waltrick who was killed in the accident] served the Complaint in this case on December 31, 1997 [seeking damages for the death of Waltrick] . On January 9, 1998, plaintiff asked the State Department to request a waiver from the Republic of Georgia for Mr. Makharadze's civil immunity. The State Department replied that it was not its practice to seek waiver of immunity for civil cases.... The State Department also stated its opinion that, pursuant to Article 39(2) of the Vienna Convention on Diplomatic Relations, defendant Makharadze "has residual immunity from the civil jurisdiction of U.S. courts only 'with respect to acts performed ... in the exercise of his functions as a member of the mission.'" Id. The Department noted, however, that defendant Makharadze would be amenable to suit if the Court determined that "his actions were nondiplomatic in nature."

II Discussion

Defendant Makharadze has filed a motion to dismiss the claims against him. A motion to dismiss is appropriate "only if 'it is clear that no relief could be granted under any set of facts that could be proven consistent with the allegations.'" ...

Defendant argues that the Court must dismiss the claims against him because he enjoys diplomatic immunity from civil suit. It is undisputed that, at the time of the accident, Makharadze was a diplomatic officer of the Georgian Mission. Under the Diplomatic Relations Act of 1978, diplomatic officers are entitled to the full privileges and immunities granted by the Vienna Convention on Diplomatic Relations. 22 U.S.C. § 254b. Pursuant to that statute, the Court must dismiss civil action against an officer who has immunity under the Convention, because the Court lacks jurisdiction. 22 U.S.C. § 254d. See also Carrera v. Carrera, 84 U.S. App. D.C. 333, 174 F.2d 496 (D.C. Cir. 1949); Aidi v. Yaron, 672 F.Supp. 516, 518 (D.D.C. 1987). Thus, the Court must determine whether defendant Makharadze enjoys civil immunity for his actions.

The Vienna Convention provides diplomatic officers with immunity against most actions in United States courts. Specifically Article 31(1) of the Convention provides a diplomatic officer with "immunity from the criminal jurisdiction of the receiving State." It then provides the officer with "immunity from its civil and administrative jurisdiction."[34] Defendant Makharadze was clearly entitled to this immunity on January 3, 1997.

---

34. [Case footnote 1] The Convention excepts immunity in certain civil actions, but there is no allegation that any exception applies to this case.

However, in response to the request of the State Department, the Republic of Georgia executed a waiver of defendant's immunity. Defendant argues that this waiver applied only to his immunity from criminal jurisdiction, and not to his immunity from civil jurisdiction. Plaintiff argues that the Republic of Georgia waived all of defendant Makharadze's immunity. Plaintiff also argues that, even if defendant's immunity has not been waived, it no longer shields him from liability, because he has ceased to perform diplomatic functions.

A. Republic of Georgia's Waiver

Under Article 32(1) of the Vienna Convention, a sending state may waive the immunity of its diplomatic officers, if it wishes.[35] However, such a waiver must be "express," Vienna Convention Art. 32(2). The burden of establishing a waiver lies on the party asking the Court to assert jurisdiction, which in this case is plaintiff. See e.g., Hellenic Lines, Ltd. v. Moore, 120 U.S. App. D.C. 288, 345 F.2d 978, 980 n.3 (D.C. Cir. 1965).

There is no doubt that the Republic of Georgia expressly waived Makharadze's immunity from criminal jurisdiction when it waived "the diplomatic immunity for Mr. George Makharadze, so that he can be prosecuted in the United States, for the accident that took place on January 3, 1997, in Washington, D.C." However, the waiver does not explicitly discuss immunity from civil jurisdiction. Thus, the crucial question is whether the Republic of Georgia has waived defendant's civil immunity as well as his criminal immunity. The Court has been unable to find any published precedent that is directly germane to this issue; surprisingly, it appears to be a question of first impression.

Plaintiff primarily argues that the Vienna Convention does not contemplate a "limited waiver" of immunity; that is, plaintiff asserts that a waiver of any diplomatic immunity waives all diplomatic immunity. In support of this argument, plaintiff analogizes to the attorney-client privilege, which cannot be waived by a client in one forum and then asserted in another. See e.g., Permian Corp. v. United States, 214 U.S. App. D.C. 396, 665 F.2d 1214 (D.C. Cir. 1981) (If privilege is waived as to a document in one case, it is waived as to that document in any future cases).

The Court agrees with plaintiff that a "limited waiver" does not seem possible under the Vienna Convention. For example, the Republic of Georgia could not waive defendant's immunity from criminal jurisdiction for purposes of one criminal prosecution and then seek to assert it in another criminal prosecution. However, Article 31 of the Convention does not confer immunity in a single blanket statement, but confers criminal immunity in one sentence and civil and administrative immunity separately, in another sentence. This suggests that the Convention considers immunity from criminal jurisdiction and immunity from civil and administrative jurisdiction to be distinct privileges. Therefore, it is possible that a state may waive one immunity and not waive the other, just as a person may waive his attorney-client privilege as to one document but not as to another. Such a waiver of criminal, but not civil, immunity is not a "limited waiver," but is instead a complete waiver of one immunity, which does not necessarily affect the other, distinct immunity. For this reason, the Republic of Georgia's waiver of defendant Makharadze's criminal immunity does not necessarily affect his civil immunity.

---

35. [Case footnote 2] It appears, however, that a diplomatic officer may not, of his own accord, waive his immunity. See e.g., Logan v. Dupuis, 990 F. Supp. 26, 31 (D.D.C. 1997). Therefore, defendant Makharadze has not waived his immunity by appearing in this action, as plaintiff argues, because he lacks the authority to execute such a waiver. Furthermore, even if defendant could waive his immunity, the Court finds that defendant's appearance would not serve as a sufficient waiver.

Plaintiff also argues that the Republic of Georgia has, in fact, waived defendant's civil immunity as well as his criminal immunity. While the evidence could perhaps support an inference of such a waiver, however, it certainly does not establish an explicit waiver. The Republic of Georgia waived "the diplomatic immunity for Mr. George Makharadze, so that he can be prosecuted in the United States, for the accident that took place on January 3, 1997, in Washington, D.C." Because the waiver itself does not mention civil immunity, plaintiff urges the Court to read the word "prosecuted" to encompass both civil and criminal actions. Legal etymology hardly compels such a reading, and the Court cannot infer this meaning from the circumstances of the waiver. The Republic of Georgia's statement of waiver explicitly refers to the State Department's request for waiver, which discussed criminal prosecution and only criminal prosecution. Because there is no express evidence that the waiver covered civil actions, the Court cannot find the required "express" waiver of civil immunity from plaintiff's speculative construction of the word "prosecuted." ...

B. Defendant's Current Diplomatic Status

It is undisputed that defendant Makharadze no longer performs diplomatic functions in this country. Plaintiff argues that, even if defendant's immunity from civil jurisdiction is not waived, it does not protect him from suit because he no longer enjoys diplomatic status.

Again, the Court is faced with an issue rarely discussed by American courts. Article 39 of the Vienna Convention states that an official's privileges and immunities end when his diplomatic functions cease. Because defendant Makharadze's diplomatic functions ceased in October of 1997, he no longer enjoys the blanket, functional immunities conferred by the Vienna Convention. However, Article 39 provides that a residual immunity subsists with respect to "acts performed by such a person in the exercise of his functions as a member of the mission." Therefore, defendant's immunity remains intact for acts performed in the exercise of his duties as a diplomatic officer of the Republic of Georgia.

Plaintiff does not contend that the accident on January 3, 1997, occurred outside the scope of those duties; indeed, the Amended Complaint explicitly asserts that defendant Makharadze was acting within the scope of his duty. Thus, there is no reason to suppose that this accident lies outside the protection of defendant's residual immunity. For this reason, defendant's current status does not affect the force of his immunity from civil jurisdiction.

C. Conclusion

Plaintiff has not established a waiver of defendant Makharadze immunity from civil jurisdiciton. Neither the Republic of Georgia's explicit waiver of criminal immunity, nor the circumstances surrounding that waiver, supports such a conclusion. Furthermore, although defendant Makharadze no longer enjoys the blanket immunity granted to acting diplomatic officers, he enjoys residual immunity for actions taken in performance of his former duties. Because plaintiff explicitly pleads that the accident occurred in the course of defendant Makharadze' official duties, the Court must conclude that residual immunity attaches. Therefore, because defendant Makharadze enjoys immunity from the civil jurisdiction of this Court, the Court must dismiss him from the case....

* * *

Ordered that all claims against defendant Mackharadze are dismissed....

Case Concerning Armed Activities on the Territory of The Congo

(Democratic Republic of Congo v. Uganda)
2005 I.C.J. ___

Note

This case mainly concerned claims by the Democratic Republic of Congo (Congo) about Uganda's military activities and support of irregular forces in Congo but there was also a counter-claim by Uganda against Congo relating to the treatment by Congo of Uganda's Embassy, diplomats located at the Embassy and at an airport, and other persons on the Embassy premises. The excerpt below only deals with Uganda's claims relating to violations of diplomatic immunity.

Second Counter-Claim

306. In its second counter-claim, Uganda claims that Congolese armed forces carried out three separate attacks on the Ugandan Embassy in Kinshasa in August, September and November 1998; confiscated property belonging to the Government of Uganda, Ugandan diplomats and Ugandan nationals; and maltreated diplomats and other Ugandan nationals present on the premises of the mission

* * *

323. The Court first recalls that the Vienna Convention on Diplomatic Relations continues to apply notwithstanding the state of armed conflict that existed between the Parties at the time of the alleged maltreatment. The Court recalls that, according to Article 44 of the Vienna Convention on Diplomatic Relations:

"The receiving State must, even in case of armed conflict, grant facilities in order to enable persons enjoying privileges and immunities, other than nationals of the receiving State, and members of the families of such persons irrespective of their nationality, to leave at the earliest possible moment. It must, in particular, in case of need, place at their disposal the necessary means of transport for themselves and their property."

324. Further, Article 45 of the Vienna Convention provides as follows:

"If diplomatic relations are broken off between two States, or if a mission is permanently or temporarily recalled:

(a) the receiving State must, even in case of armed conflict, respect and protect the premises of the mission, together with its property and archives;
(b) the sending State may entrust the custody of the premises of the mission, together with its property and archives, to a third State acceptable to the receiving State;
(c) the sending State may entrust the protection of its interests and those of its nationals to a third State acceptable to the receiving State."

In the case concerning *United States Diplomatic and Consular Staff in Tehran,* the Court emphasized that "[e]ven in the case of armed conflict or in the case of a breach in diplomatic relations those provisions require that both the inviolability of the members of a diplomatic mission and of the premises, ... must be respected by the receiving State" (Judgment, I.C.J. Reports 1980, p. 40, para 86).

* * *

334. Regarding the merits of Uganda's second counter-claim, the Court finds that there is sufficient evidence to prove that there were attacks against the Embassy and acts of maltreatment against Ugandan diplomats at Ndjili International Airport.

* * *

337. Therefore, the Court finds that, as regards the attacks on Uganda's diplomatic premises in Kinshasa, the DRC has breached its obligations under Article 22 of the Vienna Convention on Diplomatic Relations.

338. Acts of maltreatment by DRC forces of persons within the Ugandan Embassy were necessarily consequential upon a breach of the inviolability of the Embassy premises prohibited by Article 22 of the Vienna Convention on Diplomatic Relations. This is true regardless of whether the persons were or were not nationals of Uganda or Ugandan diplomats. In so far as the persons attacked were in fact diplomats, the DRC further breached its obligations under Article 29 of the Vienna Convention.

339. Finally, there is evidence that some Ugandan diplomats were maltreated at Ndjili International Airport when leaving the country.... The Court therefore finds that, through acts of maltreatment inflicted on Ugandan diplomats at the airport when they attempted to leave the country, the DRC acted in violation of its obligations under international law on diplomatic relations.

* * *

345. For these reasons,

THE COURT,

* * *

(12) Unanimously,

Finds that the Democratic Republic of the Congo, by the conduct of its armed forces, which attacked the Ugandan Embassy in Kinshasa, maltreated Ugandan diplomats and other individuals on the Embassy premises, maltreated Ugandan diplomats at Ndjili International Airport, as well as by its failure to provide the Ugandan Embassy and Ugandan diplomats with effective protection and by its failure to prevent archives and Ugandan property from being seized from the premises of the Ugandan Embassy, violated obligations owed to the Republic of Uganda under the Vienna Convention on Diplomatic Relations of 1961;

(13) Unanimously,

Finds that the Democratic Republic of the Congo is under obligation to make reparation to the Republic of Uganda for the injury caused;

(14) Unanimously,

Decides that, failing agreement between the Parties, the question of reparation due to the Republic of Uganda shall be settled by the Court, and reserves for this purpose the subsequent procedure in the case.

* * *

QUESTIONS

1. Does diplomatic protection and immunity, as outlined in the Vienna Convention on Diplomatic Relations apply during armed conflict? If so, why? See also, The Effect of War on Treaties, chapter III, pp. 95–100.

2. The Court found that the rights of non-Ugandans on Ugandan Embassy premises were violated. How could Uganda represent the rights of non-nationals at the international level?

See *Nottebohm Case* (Liechtenstein v. Guatemala) 1955 I.C.J. 4, chapter VII.

Consular Immunity

The traditional role of the consul was to represent his/her state abroad, usually not in the capital city, and to deal with administrative and trade matters as opposed to political and foreign relations issues that were handled by the embassy. Today there is a great deal of overlap in the functions carried out in consulates and embassies. Consular staff enjoy a more limited immunity from the host state's jurisdiction than diplomatic staff.

The Vienna Convention on Consular Relations was signed in 1963 and entered into force in 1967.[36] It provides for immunity from civil and criminal jurisdiction for consular officers "in respect of acts performed in the exercise of consular functions."[37] When the criminal act did not arise from official actions, the consular officer may not be arrested or detained pending trial "except in the case of a grave crime and pursuant to a decision by the competent judicial authority."[38] Note that this provision only relates to arrest and detention before trial. It does not prohibit a trial. For grave crimes, not arising out of official duties, consular officers can be detained pending trial after a judicial order for such detention.

The consular officers' accompanying family members have very limited immunity extending only to taxes,[39] customs duties on articles for personal use,[40] immigration controls[41] and military obligations.[42] The sending state has the authority to waive all immunities under the Convention should it wish to do so.[43]

The Convention also provides for the inviolability of consular premises,[44] the inviolability of consular archives and documents,[45] freedom of movement for members of the consular post[46] and freedom of communication by means of official correspondence, including the consular bag.[47] For other aspects of a consul's rights and duties with respect to citizens of the consul's state detained in the foreign country where the consul is serving see the *Avena Case* (Mexico v. United States) 2004 I.C.J. 12, pp. 66–76 *supra.*

36. 596 U.N.T.S. 261, 21 U.S.T. 77, T.I.A.S. No. 6820, signed 24 April 1963, entered into force, 19 Mar. 1967.

37. Id. art. 43(1). There are two minor exceptions to the immunity from civil jurisdiction for official acts: actions arising out of contracts where the official was not acting as an agent of the sending state, art. 43(2)(a); and actions for damages arising from a vehicular accident in the receiving state, art. 43(2)(b). The latter situation is normally taken care of by mandatory insurance, see art. 56.

38. Id. art. 41(1).

39. Id. art. 49 (paras. (a)–(f) of art. 49 list exemptions to this immunity).

40. Id. art 50.

41. Id. art. 46.

42. Id. art. 52.

43. Id. art. 45.

44. Id. art. 31.

45. Id. art. 33.

46. Id. art. 34.

47. Id. art. 35.

There are very few cases where consular officials are prosecuted largely because, if they are suspected of illegal activity, the host state will request their removal and the case will never find its way to court. Occasionally, however, a host state will prosecute a more egregious crime. See, for example, U.S. v. Sihadej Chindawongse/U.S. v. Boripat Siripan, 771 F.2d 840 (4th Cir. 1985) (no immunity for consular officers for conspiring to distribute heroin).

For a case interpreting some of the substantive obligations of a state party to the Vienna Convention on Consular Relations see the *LaGrand Case* (Germany v. United States) 2001 I.C.J. 466, and the *Avena Case* (Mexico v. United States) 2004 I.C.J.12, pp. 66–76 *supra*.

Head of State and Other Ministers' Immunity

Regina v. Bartle and the Commissioner of Police for the Metropolis and Others Ex Parte Pinochet

House of Lords, U.K. (24 March 1999)

Lord Browne-Wilkinson,

My Lords,

As is well known, this case concerns an attempt by the Government of Spain to extradite Senator Pinochet from this country to stand trial in Spain for crimes committed (primarily in Chile) during the period when Senator Pinochet was head of state in Chile. The interaction between the various legal issues which arise is complex. I will therefore seek, first, to give a short account of the legal principles which are in play in order that my exposition of the facts will be more intelligible.

Outline of the law

In general, a state only exercises criminal jurisdiction over offences which occur within its geographical boundaries. If a person who is alleged to have committed a crime in Spain is found in the United Kingdom, Spain can apply to the United Kingdom to extradite him to Spain. The power to extradite from the United Kingdom for an "extradition crime" is now contained in the Extradition Act 1989. That Act defines what constitutes an "extradition crime." For the purposes of the present case, the most important requirement is that the conduct complained of must constitute a crime under the law of both Spain and of the United Kingdom. This is known as the double criminality rule.

Since the Nazi atrocities and the Nuremberg trials, international law has recognized a number of offences as being international crimes. Individual states have taken jurisdiction to try some international crimes even in cases where such crimes were not committed within the geographical boundaries of such states. The most important of such international crimes for present purposes is torture which is regulated by the International Convention Against Torture and other Cruel, Inhuman or Degrading Treatment or Punishment, 1984. The obligations placed on the United Kingdom by that Convention (and on the other 110 or more signatory states who have adopted the Convention) were incorporated into the law of the United Kingdom by section 134 of the Criminal Justice Act 1988. That Act came into force on 29 September 1988. Section 134 created a new crime under United Kingdom law, the crime of torture. As required by the Torture Convention "all" torture wherever committed world-wide was made criminal under United Kingdom law and triable in the United Kingdom. No one has suggested that before section 134 came into effect torture committed outside the United Kingdom was a crime under United Kingdom law. Nor is it suggested that section 134 was retrospective so as to make torture committed outside the United Kingdom before 29 September 1988 a United Kingdom crime. Since torture outside the United Kingdom was not a crime under U.K. law until 29 September 1988, the principle of double criminality which requires an Act to be a crime under both the law of Spain and of the United Kingdom cannot be satisfied in relation to conduct before that date if the principle of double criminality requires the conduct to be criminal under United Kingdom law *at the date it was committed*. If, on the other hand, the double criminality rule only requires the conduct be criminal under U.K. law *at the date of extradition* the rule was satisfied in relation to all torture alleged against Senator Pinochet whether it took place before or after 1988. The Spanish courts have held that they have jurisdiction over all the crimes alleged.

In these circumstances, the first question that has to be answered is whether or not the definition of an "extradition crime" in the Act of 1989 requires the conduct to be criminal under U.K. law at the date of commission or only at the date of extradition.

This question, although raised, was not decided in the Divisional Court. At the first hearing in this House it was apparently conceded that all the matters charged against Senator Pinochet were extradition crimes. It was only during the hearing before your Lordships that the importance of the point became fully apparent. As will appear, in my view only a limited number of the charges relied upon to extradite Senator Pinochet constitute extradition crimes since most of the conduct relied upon occurred long before 1988. In particular, I do not consider that torture committed outside the United Kingdom before 29 September 1988 was a crime under U.K. law. It follows that the main question discussed at the earlier stages of this case—is a former head of state entitled to sovereign immunity from arrest or prosecution in the U.K. for acts of torture—applies to far fewer charges. But the question of state immunity remains a point of crucial importance since, in my view, there is certain conduct of Senator Pinochet (albeit a small amount) which does constitute an extradition crime and would enable the Home Secretary (if he thought fit) to extradite Senator Pinochet to Spain unless he is entitled to state immunity. Accordingly, having identified which of the crimes alleged is an extradition crime, I will then go on to consider whether Senator Pinochet is entitled to immunity in respect of those crimes. But first I must state shortly the relevant facts.

The facts

On 11 September 1973 a right-wing coup evicted the left-wing regime of President Allende. The coup was led by a military junta, of whom Senator (then General) Pinochet was the leader. At some stage he became head of state. The Pinochet regime remained in power until 11 March 1990 when Senator Pinochet resigned.

There is no real dispute that during the period of the Senator Pinochet regime appalling acts of barbarism were committed in Chile and elsewhere in the world: torture, murder and the unexplained disappearance of individuals, all on a large scale. Although it is not alleged that Senator Pinochet himself committed any of those acts, it is alleged that they were done in pursuance of a conspiracy to which he was a party, at his instigation and with his knowledge. He denies these allegations. None of the conduct alleged was committed by or against citizens of the United Kingdom or in the United Kingdom.

In 1998 Senator Pinochet came to the United Kingdom for medical treatment. The judicial authorities in Spain sought to extradite him in order to stand trial in Spain on a large number of charges. Some of those charges had links with Spain. But most of the charges had no connection with Spain. The background to the case is that to those of left-wing political convictions Senator Pinochet is seen as an arch-devil: to those of right-wing persuasions he is seen as the saviour of Chile. It may well be thought that the trial of Senator Pinochet in Spain for offences all of which related to the state of Chile and most of which occurred in Chile is not calculated to achieve the best justice. But I cannot emphasize too strongly that that is no concern of your Lordships. Although others perceive our task as being to choose between the two sides on the grounds of personal preference or political inclination, that is an entire misconception. Our job is to decide two questions of law: are there any extradition crimes and, if so, is Senator Pinochet immune from trial for committing those crimes. If, as a matter of law, there are not extradition crimes or he is entitled to immunity in relation to whichever crimes there are, then there is no legal right to extradite Senator Pinochet to Spain or, indeed, to stand in the way of his return to Chile. If, on the other hand, there are extradition crimes in relation to which Senator Pinochet is not entitled to state immunity then it will be open to the Home Secretary to extradite him. The task of this House is only to decide those points of law.

On 16 October 1998 an international warrant for the arrest of Senator Pinochet was issued in Spain. On the same day, a magistrate in London issued a provisional warrant ("the first warrant") under section 8 of the Extradition Act 1989. He was arrested in a London hospital on 17 October 1998. On 18 October the Spanish authorities issued a second international warrant. A further provisional warrant ("the second warrant") was issued by the magistrate at Bow Street Magistrates Court on 22 October 1998 accusing Senator Pinochet of:

> "(1) Between 1 January 1988 and December 1992 being a public official intentionally inflicted severe pain or suffering on another in the performance or purported performance of his official duties;
>
> (2) Between the first day of January 1988 and 31 December 1992 being a public official, conspired with persons unknown to intentionally inflict severe pain or suffering on another in the performance or purported performance of his official duties;
>
> (3) Between the first day of January 1982 and 31 January 1992 he detained other persons (the hostages) and in order to compel such persons to do or to abstain from doing any act threatened to kill, injure or continue to detain the hostages;
>
> (4) Between the first day of January 1982 and 31 January 1992 conspired with persons unknown to detain other persons (the hostages) and in order to compel such persons to do or to abstain from doing any act, threatened to kill, injure or continue to detain the hostages;
>
> (5) Between January 1976 and December 1992 conspired together with persons unknown to commit murder in a Convention country."

Senator Pinochet started proceedings for habeas corpus and for leave to move for judicial review of both the first and second provisional warrants.

* * *

The appeal came on again for rehearing on 18 January 1999 before your Lordships. In the meantime the position had changed yet again. First, the Home Secretary had issued to the magistrate authority to proceed under section 7 of the Act of 1989. In deciding to permit the extradition to Spain to go ahead he relied in part on the decision of this

House at the first hearing that Senator Pinochet was not entitled to immunity. He did not authorize the extradition proceedings to go ahead on the charge of genocide: accordingly no further arguments were addressed to us on the charge of genocide which has dropped out of the case.

Secondly, the Republic of Chile applied to intervene as a party. Up to this point Chile had been urging that immunity should be afforded to Senator Pinochet, but it now wished to be joined as a party. Any immunity precluding criminal charges against Senator Pinochet is the immunity not of Senator Pinochet but of the Republic of Chile. Leave to intervene was therefore given to the Republic of Chile. The same amicus, Mr. Lloyd Jones, was heard as at the first hearing as were counsel for Amnesty International. Written representations were again put in on behalf of Human Rights Watch.

Thirdly, the ambit of the charges against Senator Pinochet had widened yet again. Chile had put in further particulars of the charges which they wished to advance. In order to try to bring some order to the proceedings, Mr. Alun Jones Q.C., for the Crown Prosecution Service, prepared a schedule of the 32 U.K. criminal charges which correspond to the allegations made against Senator Pinochet under Spanish law, save that the genocide charges are omitted. The charges in that schedule are fully analyzed and considered in the speech of my noble and learned friend, Lord Hope of Craighead who summarizes the charges as follows:

Charges 1, 2 and 5: conspiracy to torture between 1 January 1972 and 20 September 1973 and between 1 August 1973 and 1 January 1990;

Charge 3: conspiracy to take hostages between 1 August 1973 and 1 January 1990;

Charge 4: conspiracy to torture in furtherance of which murder was committed in various countries including Italy, France, Spain and Portugal, between 1 January 1972 and 1 January 1990.

Charges 6 and 8: torture between 1 August 1973 and on 11 September 1973.

Charges 9 and 12: conspiracy to murder in Spain between 1 January 1975 and 31 December 1976 and in Italy on 6 October 1975.

Charges 10 and 11: attempted murder in Italy on 6 October 1975.

Charges 13–29; and 31–32: torture on various occasions between 11 September 1973 and May 1977.

Charge 30: torture on 24 June 1989

I turn then to consider which of those charges are extradition crimes.

Extradition Crimes

As I understand the position, at the first hearing in the House of Lords the Crown Prosecution Service did not seek to rely on any conduct of Senator Pinochet occurring before 11 September 1973 (the date on which the coup occurred) or after 11 March 1990 (the date when Senator Pinochet retired as head of state.) Accordingly, as the case was then presented, if Senator Pinochet was entitled to immunity such immunity covered the whole period of the alleged crimes. At the second hearing before your Lordships, however, the Crown Prosecution Service extended the period during which the crimes were said to have been committed: for example, see charges 1 and 4 where the conspiracies are said to have started on 1 January 1972, i.e. at a time before Senator Pinochet was head of state and therefore [before he] could be entitled to immunity. In consequence at the second hearing counsel for Senator Pinochet revived the submission that certain of the charges, in particular those relating to torture and conspiracy to torture, were not "extradition crimes" because *at the time the acts were done* the acts were not criminal under the law of the United Kingdom. Once raised, this point could not be confined simply to the period (if any) before Senator Pinochet became head of state. If the double criminality rule requires it to be shown that at the date of the conduct such conduct would have been criminal under the law of the United Kingdom, any charge based on torture or conspiracy to torture occurring before 29 September 1988 (when section 134 of the Criminal Justice Act came into force) could not be an "extradition crime" and therefore could not in any event found an extradition order against Senator Pinochet.

* * *

It is therefore quite clear from the words I have emphasized that under the Act of 1870 the double criminality rule required the conduct to be criminal under English law at the conduct date not at the request date.

* * *

Therefore in this class of case regulated by Schedule 1 to the Act of 1989 the same position applies as it formerly did under the Act of 1870, i.e. the conduct has to be a crime under English law at the conduct date.

* * *

The charges which allege extradition crimes

The consequences of requiring torture to be a crime under U.K. law at the date the torture was committed are considered in Lord Hopes's speech. As he demonstrates, the charges of torture and conspiracy to torture relating to conduct before 29 September 1988 (the date on which section 134 came into effect) are not extraditable, i.e. only those parts of the conspiracy to torture alleged in charge 2 and of torture and conspiracy to torture alleged in charge 4 which relate to the period after that date and the single act of torture alleged in charge 30 are extradition crimes relating to torture.

Lord Hope also considers, and I agree, that the only charge relating to hostage-taking (charge 3) does not disclose any offence under the Taking of Hostages Act 1982. The statutory offence consists of taking and detaining a person (the hostage,) so as to compel someone who is not the hostage to do or abstain from doing some act: section 1. But the only conduct relating to hostages which is charged alleges that the person detained (the so-called hostage) was to be forced to do something by reason of threats to injure other non-hostages which is the exact converse of the offence. The hostage charges therefore are bad and do not constitute extradition crimes.

Finally, Lord Hopes' analysis shows that the charge of conspiracy in Spain to murder in Spain (charge 9) and such conspiracies in Spain to commit murder in Spain, and such conspiracies in Spain prior to 29 September 1988 to commit acts of torture in Spain, as can be shown to form part of the allegations in charge 4 are extradition crimes.

I must therefore consider whether, in relation to these two surviving categories of charge, Senator Pinochet enjoys sovereign immunity. But first it is necessary to consider the modern law of torture.

Torture

Apart from the law of piracy, the concept of personal liability under international law for international crimes is of comparatively modern growth. The traditional subjects of international law are states not human beings. But consequent upon the war crime trials after the 1939–45 World War, the international community came to recognize that there could be criminal liability under international law for a class of crimes such as war crimes and crimes against humanity. Although there may be legitimate doubts as to the legality of the Charter of the Nuremberg Tribunal, in my judgement those doubts were stilled by the Affirmation of the Principles of International Law recognized by the Charter of the Nuremberg Tribunal adopted by the United Nations General Assembly on 11 December 1946. That Affirmation affirmed the principles of international law recognized by the Charter of the Nuremberg Tribunal and the judgement of the Tribunal and directed the Committee on the codification of international law to treat as a matter of primary importance plans for the formulation of the principles recognized in the Charter of the Nuremberg Tribunal. At least from that date onwards the concept of personal liability for a crime in international law must have been part of international law. In the early years state torture was one of the elements of a war crime. In consequence torture, and various other crimes against humanity, were linked to war or at least to hostilities of some kind. But in the course of time this linkage with war fell away and torture, divorced from war or hostilities, became an international crime on its own: see *Oppenheim's International Law* (Jennings and Watts edition) vol. 1, 996; note 6 to Article 18 of the *I.L.C. Draft Code of Crimes Against Peace; Prosecutor v. Furundzija* Tribunal for Former Yugoslavia, Case No. 17-95-17/1-T. Ever since 1945, torture on a large scale has featured as one of the crimes against humanity: see, for example, U.N. General Assembly Resolutions 3059, 3452 and 3453 passed in 1973 and 1975; Statutes of the International Criminal Tribunals for former Yugoslavia (Article 5) and Rwanda (Article 3.)

Moreover, the Republic of Chile accepted before your Lordships that the international law prohibiting torture has the character of jus cogens or a peremptory norm, i.e. one of those rules of international law which have a particular status. In *Furundzija (supra)* at para. 153, the Tribunal said:

> "Because of the importance of the values it protects, [the prohibition of torture] has evolved into a peremptory norm or jus cogens, that is, a norm that enjoys a higher rank in the international hierarchy than treaty law and even 'ordinary' customary rules. The most conspicuous consequence of this higher rank is that the principle at issue cannot be derogated from by states through international treaties or local or special customs or even general customary rules not endowed with the same normative force.... Clearly, the jus cogens nature of the prohibition against torture articulates the notion that the prohibition has now become one of the most fundamental standards of the international community. Furthermore, this prohibition is designed to produce a deterrent effect, in that it signals to all member of the international community and the individuals over whom they wield authority that the prohibition of torture is an absolute value from which nobody must deviate." (See also the cases cited in Note 170 to the *Furundzija* case.)

The jus cogens nature of the international crime of torture justifies states in taking universal jurisdiction over torture wherever committed. International law provides that offences jus cogens may be punished by any state because the offenders are "common enemies of all mankind and all nations have an equal interest in their apprehension and prosecution": *Demjanjuk v. Petrovsky* (1985) 603 F. Supp. 1468; 776 F. 2d 571.

It was suggested by Miss Montgomery, for Senator Pinochet, that although torture was contrary to international law it was not strictly an international crime in the highest sense. In the light of the authorities to which I have referred (and there are many others) I have no doubt that long before the Torture Convention of 1984 state torture was an international crime in the highest sense.

But there was no tribunal or court to punish international crimes of torture. Local courts could take jurisdiction: see *Demjanjuk* (supra); *Attorney-General of Israel v. Eichmann* (1962) 36 I.L.R.S. But the objective was to ensure a general jurisdiction so that the torturer was not safe wherever he went. For example, in this case it is alleged that during the Pinochet regime torture was an official, although unacknowledged, weapon of government and that, when the regime was about to end, it passed legislation designed to afford an amnesty to those who had engaged in institutionalized torture. If these allegations are true, the fact that the local court had jurisdiction to deal with the international crime of torture was nothing to the point so long as the totalitarian regime remained in power: a totalitarian regime will not permit adjudication by its own courts on its own shortcomings. Hence the demand for some international machinery to repress state torture which is not dependent upon the local courts where the torture was committed. In the event, over 110 states (including Chile, Spain and the United Kingdom) became state parties to the Torture Convention. But it is far from clear that none of them practiced state torture. What was needed therefore was an international system which could punish those who were guilty of torture and which did not permit the evasion of punishment by the torturer moving from one state to another. The Torture Convention was agreed not in order to create an international crime which had not previously existed but to provide an international system under which the international criminal—the torturer—could find no safe haven. Burgers and Danelius (respectively the chairman of the United Nations Working Group on the 1984 Torture Convention and the draftsmen of its first draft) say, at p. 131, that it was "an essential purpose [of the Convention] to ensure that a torturer does not escape the consequences of his act by going to another country."

The Torture Convention

Article 1 of the Convention defines torture as the intentional infliction of severe pain and of suffering with a view to achieving a wide range of purposes "when such pain or suffering is inflicted by or at the instigation of or with the consent or acquiescence of a public official or other person acting in an official capacity." Article 2(1) requires each state party to prohibit torture on territory within its own jurisdiction and Article 4 requires each state party to ensure that "all" acts of torture are offences under its criminal law. Article 2(3) outlaws any defense of superior orders. Under Article 5(1) each state party has to establish its jurisdiction over torture (a) when committed within territory under its jurisdiction (b) when the alleged offender is a national of that state, and (c.) in certain circumstances, when the victim is a national of that state. Under Article 5(2) a state party has to take jurisdiction over any alleged offender who is found within its territory. Article 6 contains provisions for a state in whose territory an alleged torturer is found to detain him, inquire into the position and notify the states referred to in Article 5(1) and to indicate whether it intends to exercise jurisdiction. Under Article 7 the state in whose territory the alleged torturer is found shall, if he is not extradited to any of the states mentioned in Article 5(1), submit him to its authorities for the purpose of prosecution. Under Article 8(1) torture is to be treated as an extraditable offence and under Article 8(4) torture shall, for the purposes of extradition, be treated as having been committed not only in the place where it occurred but also in the state mentioned in Article 5(1.)

Who is an "official" for the purposes of the Torture Convention?

The first question on the Convention is to decide whether acts done by a head of state are done by "a public official or a person acting in an official capacity" within the meaning of Article 1. The same question arises under section 134 of the Criminal Justice Act 1988. The answer to both questions must be the same. In his judgement at the first hearing (at pp. 1476–1477E) Lord Slynn held that a head of state was neither a public official nor a person acting in an official capacity within the meaning of Article 1: he pointed out that there are a number of international conventions (for example the Yugoslav War Crimes Statute and the Rwanda War Crimes Statute) which refer specifically to heads of state when they intend to render them liable. Lord Lloyd apparently did not agree with Lord Slynn on this point since he thought that a head of state who was a torturer could be prosecuted in his own country, a view which could not be correct unless such head of state had conducted himself as a public official or in an official capacity.

It became clear during the argument that both the Republic of Chile and Senator Pinochet accepted that the acts alleged against Senator Pinochet, if proved, were acts done by a public official or person acting in an official capacity within the meaning of Article 1. In my judgment these concessions were correctly made. Unless a head of state authorizing or promoting torture is an official or acting in an official capacity within Article 1, then he would not be guilty of the international crime of torture even within his own state. That plainly cannot have been the intention. In my judgment it would run completely contrary to the intention of the Convention if there was anybody who could be exempt from guilt. The crucial question is not whether Senator Pinochet falls within the definition in Article 1: he plainly does. The question is whether, even so, he is procedurally immune from process. To my mind the fact that a head of state can be guilty of the crime casts little, if any, light on the question whether he is immune from prosecution for that crime in a foreign state.

Universal jurisdiction

There was considerable argument before your Lordships concerning the extent of the jurisdiction to prosecute torturers conferred on states other than those mentioned in Article 5(1). I do not find it necessary to seek an answer to all points raised. It is enough that it is clear that in all circumstances, if the Article 5(1) states do not choose to seek extradition or to prosecute the offender, other states must do so. The purpose of the Convention was to introduce the principle aut dedere aut punire—either you extradite or you punish: Burgers and Danelius p. 131. Throughout the negotiation of the Convention certain countries wished to make the exercise of jurisdiction under Article 5(2) dependent upon the state assuming jurisdiction having refused extradition to an Article 5(1) state. However, at a session in 1984 all objections to the principle of aut dedere aut punire were withdrawn. "The inclusion of universal jurisdiction in the draft convention was no longer opposed by any delegation": Working Group on the Draft Convention U.N. Doc. E/CN. 4/1984/72, para. 26. If there is no prosecution by, or extradition to, an Article 5(1) state, the state where the alleged offender is found (which will have already taken him into custody under the Article 6) must exercise the jurisdiction under Article 5(2) by prosecuting him under Article 7(1).

I gather the following important points from the Torture Convention:

1) Torture within the meaning of the Convention can only be committed by "a public official or person acting in an official capacity," but these words include a head of state. A single act of official torture is "torture" within the Convention;

2) Superior orders provide no defense;

3) If the states with the most obvious jurisdiction (the Article 5(1) states) do not seek to extradite, the state where the alleged torturer is found must prosecute or, apparently, extradite to another country, i.e. there is universal jurisdiction.

4) There is no express provision dealing with state immunity of heads of state, ambassadors or other officials.

5) Since Chile, Spain and the United Kingdom are all parties to the Convention, they are bound under treaty by its provisions whether or not such provisions would apply in the absence of treaty obligation. Chile ratified the Convention with effect from 30 October 1988 and the United Kingdom with effect from 8 December 1988.

State immunity

This is the point around which most of the argument turned. It is of considerable general importance internationally since, if Senator Pinochet is not entitled to immunity in relation to the acts of torture alleged to have occurred after 29 September 1988, it will be the first time so far as counsel have discovered when a local domestic court has refused to afford immunity to a head of state or former head of state on the grounds that there can be no immunity against prosecution for certain international crimes.

Given the importance of the point, it is surprising how narrow is the area of dispute. There is general agreement between the parties as to the rules of statutory immunity and the rationale which underlies them. The issue is whether international law grants state immunity in relation to the international crime of torture and, if so, whether the Republic of Chile is entitled to claim such immunity even though Chile, Spain and the United Kingdom are all parties to the Torture Convention and therefore "contractually" bound to give effect to its provisions from 8 December 1988 at the latest.

It is a basic principle of international law that one sovereign state (the forum state) does not adjudicate on the conduct of a foreign state. The foreign state is entitled to procedural immunity from the processes of the forum state. This immunity extends to both criminal and civil liability. State immunity probably grew from the historical immunity of the person of the monarch. In any event, such personal immunity of the head of state persists to the present day: the head of state is entitled to the same immunity as the state itself. The diplomatic representative of the foreign state in the forum state is also afforded the same immunity in recognition of the dignity of the state which he represents. This immunity enjoyed by a head of state in power and an ambassador in post is a complete immunity attaching to the person of the head of state or ambassador and rendering him immune from all actions or prosecutions whether or not they relate to matters done for the benefit of the state. Such immunity is said to be granted ratione personae.

What then when the ambassador leaves his post or the head of state is deposed? The position of the ambassador is covered by the Vienna Convention on Diplomatic Relations, 1961. After providing for immunity from arrest (Article 29) and from criminal and civil jurisdiction (Article 31), Article 39(1) provides that the ambassador's privileges shall be enjoyed from the moment he takes up post; and subsection (2) provides:

> "(2) When the functions of a person enjoying privileges and immunities have come to an end, such privileges and immunities shall normally cease at the moment when he leaves the country, or on expiry of a reasonable period in which to do so, but shall subsist until that time, even in the case of armed conflict. However, with respect to acts performed by such a person in the exercise of his functions as a member of the mission, immunity shall continue to subsist."

The continuing partial immunity of the ambassador after leaving post is of a different kind from that enjoyed ratione personae while he was in post. Since he is no longer the representative of the foreign state he merits no particular privileges or immunities as a person. However in order to preserve the integrity of the activities of the foreign state during the period when he was ambassador, it is necessary to provide that immunity is afforded to his *official* acts during his tenure in post. If this were not done the sovereign immunity of the state could be evaded by calling in question acts done during the previous ambassador's time. Accordingly under Article 39(2) the ambassador, like any other official of the state, enjoys immunity in relation to his official acts done while he was an official. This limited immunity, ratione materiae, is to be contrasted with the former immunity ratione personae which gave complete immunity to all activities whether public or private.

In my judgment at common law a former head of state enjoys similar immunities, ratione materiae, once he ceases to be head of state. He too loses immunity ratione personae on ceasing to be head of state: see Watts *The Legal Position in International Law of Heads of States, Heads of Government and Foreign Ministers* p. 88 and the cases there cited. He can be sued on his private obligations: *Ex-King Farouk of Egypt v. Christian Dior* (1957) 24 I.L.R.228; *Jimenez v. Aristeguieta* (1962) 311 F. 2d 547. As ex head of state he cannot be sued in respect of acts performed whilst head of state in his public capacity: *Hatch v. Baez* [1876] 7 Hun. 596. Thus, at common law, the position of the former ambassador and the former head of state appears to be much the same: both enjoy immunity for acts done in performance of their respective functions whilst in office.

I have belaboured this point because there is a strange feature of the United Kingdom law which I must mention shortly. The State Immunity Act 1978 modifies the traditional complete immunity normally afforded by the common law in claims for damages against foreign states. Such modifications are contained in Part I of the Act.

* * *

Accordingly, "the necessary modifications" which need to be made will produce the result that a former head of state has immunity in relation to acts done as part of his official functions when head of state. Accordingly, in my judgement, Senator Pinochet as former head of state enjoys immunity ratione materiae in relation to acts done by him as head of state as part of his official functions as head of state.

The question then which has to be answered is whether the alleged organization of state torture by Senator Pinochet (if proved) would constitute an act committed by Senator Pinochet as part of his official functions as head of state. It is not enough to say that it cannot be part of the functions of the head of state to commit a crime. Actions which are criminal under the local law can still have been done officially and therefore give rise to immunity ratione materiae. The case needs to be analyzed more closely.

Can it be said that the commission of a crime which is an international crime against humanity and jus cogens is an act done in an official capacity on behalf of the state? I believe there to be strong ground for saying that the implementation of torture as defined by the Torture Convention cannot be a state function. This is the view taken by Sir Arthur Watts (supra) who said (at p. 82):

* * *

> "The idea that individuals who commit international crimes are internationally accountable for them has now become an accepted part of international law. Problems in this area—such as the non-existence of any standing international tribunal to have jurisdiction over such crimes, and the lack of agreement as to what acts are internationally criminal for this purpose—have not affected

> the general acceptance of the principle of individual responsibility for international criminal conduct."

Later, at p. 84, he said:

> "It can no longer be doubted that as a matter of general customary international law a head of state will personally be liable to be called to account if there is sufficient evidence that he authorized or perpetrated such serious international crimes."

It can be objected that Sir Arthur was looking at those cases where the international community has established an international tribunal in relation to which the regulating document *expressly* makes the head of state subject to the tribunal's jurisdiction: see, for example, the Nuremberg Charter Article 7; the Statute of the International Tribunal for former Yugoslavia; the Statute of the International Tribunal for Rwanda and the Statute of the International Criminal Court. It is true that in these cases it is expressly said that the head of state or former head of state is subject to the court's jurisdiction. But those are cases in which a new court with no existing jurisdiction is being established. The jurisdiction being established by the Torture Convention and the Hostages Convention is one where existing domestic courts of all the countries are being authorized and required to take jurisdiction internationally. The question is whether, in this new type of jurisdiction, the only possible view is that those made subject to the jurisdiction of each of the state courts of the world in relation to torture are not entitled to claim immunity.

I have doubts whether, before the coming into force of the Torture Convention, the existence of the international crime of torture as jus cogens was enough to justify the conclusion that the organization of state torture could not rank for immunity purposes as the performance of an official function. At that stage there was no international tribunal to punish torture and no general jurisdiction to permit or require its punishment in domestic courts. Not until there was some form of universal jurisdiction for the punishment of the crime of torture could it really be talked about as a fully constituted international crime. But in my judgment the Torture Convention did provide what was missing: a worldwide universal jurisdiction. Further, it required all member states to ban and outlaw torture: Article 2. How can it be for international law purposes an official function to do something which international law itself prohibits and criminalizes? Thirdly, an essential feature of the international crime of torture is that it must be committed "by or with the acquiescence of a public official or other person acting in an official capacity." As a result all defendants in torture cases will be state officials. Yet, if the former head of state has immunity, the man most responsible will escape liability while his inferiors (the chiefs of police, junior army officers) who carried out his orders will be liable. I find it impossible to accept that this was the intention.

Finally, and to my mind decisively, if the implementation of a torture regime is a public function giving rise to immunity ratione materiae, this produces bizarre results. Immunity ratione materiae applies not only to ex-heads of state and ex-ambassadors but to all state officials who have been involved in carrying out the functions of the state. Such immunity is necessary in order to prevent state immunity being circumvented by prosecuting or suing the official who, for example, actually carried out the torture when a claim against the head of state would be precluded by the doctrine of immunity. If that applied to the present case, and if the implementation of the torture regime is to be treated as official business sufficient to found an immunity for the former head of state, it must also be official business sufficient to justify immunity for his inferiors who actually did the torturing. Under the Convention the international crime of torture can only be committed by an official or someone in an official capacity. They would all be entitled to immunity. It would follow that there can be no case outside Chile in which a successful prosecution for torture can be brought unless the State of Chile is prepared to waive its right to its officials' immunity. Therefore the whole elaborate structure of universal jurisdiction over torture committed by officials is rendered abortive and one of the main objectives of the Torture Convention—to provide a system under which there is no safe haven for torturers—will have been frustrated. In my judgment all these factors together demonstrate that the notion of continued immunity for ex-heads of state is inconsistent with the provisions of the Torture Convention.

For these reasons in my judgment if, as alleged, Senator Pinochet organized and authorized torture after 8 December 1988, he was not acting in any capacity which gives rise to immunity ratione materiae because such actions were contrary to international law, Chile had agreed to outlaw such conduct and Chile had agreed with the other parties to the Torture Convention that all signatory states should have jurisdiction to try official torture (as defined in the Convention) even if such torture were committed in Chile.

As to the charges of murder and conspiracy to murder, no one has advanced any reason why the ordinary rules of immunity should not apply and Senator Pinochet is entitled to such immunity.

For these reasons, I would allow the appeal so as to permit the extradition proceedings to proceed on the allegation that torture in pursuance of a conspiracy to commit torture, including the single act of torture which is alleged in charge 30, was being committed by Senator Pinochet after 8 December 1988 when he lost his immunity.

In issuing to the magistrate an authority to proceed under section 7 of the Extradition Act 1989, the Secretary of State proceeded on the basis that the whole range of torture charges and murder charges against Senator Pinochet would be the subject matter of the extradition proceedings. Your Lordships' decision excluding from consideration a very large number of those charges constitutes a substantial change in the circumstances. This will obviously require the Secretary of State to reconsider his decision under section 7 in the light of the changed circumstances.

Note

The opinions of the other five justices are omitted. The final vote was 6–1 in favor of no immunity for conspiracy to torture or torture after 8 December 1988. (There was a minority view that the immunity should have been lifted as of 29 September 1988 and one judge thought that no immunity could be claimed even as far back as 1973.)

The British Home Secretary eventually decided that Senator Pinochet could be extradited to Spain on the torture charges but later, evidence of Senator Pinochet's deteriorating health was presented to the Home Office and he was determined to be medically unfit to stand trial. He returned to Chile on March 3, 2000. There are currently criminal charges pending against him in the Chilean courts.

QUESTIONS

1. What do you understand the double criminality requirement to be for extradition from the U.K.?
2. Why is torture considered to be a crime that confers upon states the right to prosecute the torturer regardless of any connection with the prosecuting state?

3. Why did the Court decided that Senator Pinochet could not claim immunity for acts of torture occurring after the date that Britain made the prohibition of torture as found in the Torture Convention part of its legislation even though Pinochet was still President of Chile at that time?
4. Why did the Court uphold immunity for Senator Pinochet with respect to the charges of murder and conspiracy to murder?

Case Concerning the Arrest Warrant of 11 April 2000 (Democratic Republic of the Congo v. Belgium)

2002 I.C.J. 3

Note

The facts of the case appear in the body of the opinion.

* * *

THE COURT, ...

delivers the following Judgment:

1. On 17 October 2000 the Democratic Republic of the Congo (hereinafter referred to as "the Congo") filed in the Registry of the Court an Application instituting proceedings against the Kingdom of Belgium (hereinafter referred to as "Belgium") in respect of a dispute concerning an "international arrest warrant issued on 11 April 2000 by a Belgian investigating judge ... against the Minister for Foreign Affairs in office of the Democratic Republic of the Congo, Mr. Abdulaye Yerodia Ndombasi".

In that Application the Congo contended that Belgium had violated the "principle that a State may not exercise its authority on the territory of another State", the "principle of sovereign equality among all Members of the United Nations, as laid down in Article 2, paragraph 1, of the Charter of the United Nations", as well as "the diplomatic immunity of the Minister for Foreign Affairs of a sovereign State, as recognized by the jurisprudence of the Court and following from Article 41, paragraph 2, of the Vienna Convention of 18 April 1961 on Diplomatic Relations".

* * *

10. In its Application, the Congo formulated the decision requested in the following terms:

> "The Court is requested to declare that the Kingdom of Belgium shall annul the international arrest warrant issued on 11 April 200 by a Belgian investigating judge, Mr. Vandermeersch, of the Brussels *tribunal de premiére instance* against the Minister for Foreign Affairs in office of the Democratic Republic of the Congo, Mr. Abdulaye Yerodia Ndombasi, seeking his provisional detention pending a request for extradition to Belgium for alleged crimes constituting 'serious violations of international humanitarian law', that warrant having been circulated by the judge to all States, including the Democratic Republic of the Congo, which received it on 12 July 2000."

* * *

13. On 11 April 2000 an investigating judge of the Brussels *tribunal de premiére instance* issued "an international arrest warrant *in absentia*" against Mr. Abdulaye Yerodia

Ndombasi, charging him, as perpetrator or co-perpetrator, with offences constituting grave breaches of the Geneva Conventions of 1949 and of the Additional Protocols thereto, and with crimes against humanity.

At the time when the arrest warrant was issued Mr. Yerodia was the Minister for Foreign Affairs of the Congo.

14. The arrest warrant was transmitted to the Congo on 7 June 2000, being received by the Congolese authorities on 12 July 2000. According to Belgium, the warrant was at the same time transmitted to the International Criminal Police Organization (Interpol), an organization whose function is to enhance and facilitate cross-border criminal police co-operation worldwide; through the latter, it was circulated internationally.

15. In the arrest warrant, Mr. Yerodia is accused of having made various speeches inciting racial hatred during the month of August 1998. The crimes with which Mr. Yerodia was charged were punishable in Belgium under the Law of 16 June 1993 "concerning the Punishment of Grave Breaches of the International Geneva Conventions of 12 August 1949 and of Protocols I and II of 8 June 1977 Additional Thereto", as amended by the Law of 19 February 1999 "concerning the Punishment of Serious Violations of International Humanitarian Law" (hereinafter referred to as the "Belgian Law").

Article 7 of the Belgian Law provides that "The Belgian courts shall have jurisdiction in respect of the offences provided for in the present Law, wheresoever they may have been committed". In the present case, according to Belgium, the complaints that initiated the proceedings as a result of which the arrest warrant was issued emanated from 12 individuals all resident in Belgium, five of whom were of Belgian nationality. It is not contested by Belgium, however, that the alleged acts to which the arrest warrant relates were committed outside Belgian territory, that Mr. Yerodia was not a Belgian national at the time of those acts, and that Mr. Yerodia was not in Belgian territory at the time that the arrest warrant was issued and circulated. That no Belgian nationals were victims of the violence that was said to have resulted from Mr. Yerodia's alleged offences was also uncontested.

Article 5, paragraph 3, of the Belgian Law further provides that "[i]mmunity attaching to the official capacity of a person shall not prevent the application of the present Law".

* * *

17. On 17 October 2000, the Congo filed in the Registry an Application instituting the present proceedings (see paragraph 1 above), in which the Court was requested "to declare that the Kingdom of Belgium shall annul the international arrest warrant issued on 11 April 2000". The Congo relied in its Application on two separate legal grounds. First, it claimed that "[t]he *universal jurisdiction* that the Belgian State attributes to itself under Article 7 of the Law in question" constituted a

> "[v]iolation of the principle that a State may not exercise its authority on the territory of another State and of the principle of sovereign equality among all Members of the United Nations, as laid down in Article 2, paragraph 1, of the Charter of the United Nations".

Secondly, it claimed that "[t]he non-recognition, on the basis of Article 5 ... of the Belgian Law, of the immunity of a Minister for Foreign Affairs in office" constituted a "[v]iolation of the diplomatic immunity of the Minister for Foreign Affairs of a sovereign State, as recognized by the jurisprudence of the Court and following from Article 41, paragraph 2, of the Vienna Convention of 18 April 1961 on Diplomatic Relations".

18. On the same day that it filed its Application instituting proceedings, the Congo submitted a request to the Court for the indication of a provisional measure under Article 41 of the Statute of the Court. During the hearings ... the Court was informed that in November 2000 a ministerial reshuffle had taken place in the Congo, following which Mr. Yerodia had ceased to hold office as Minister for Foreign Affairs and had been entrusted with the portfolio of Minister of Education....

19. From mid-April 2001, with the formation of a new Government in the Congo, Mr. Yerodia ceased to hold the post of Minister of Education. He no longer holds any ministerial office today.

* * *

45. As indicated above ... in its Application instituting these proceedings, the Congo originally challenged the legality of the arrest warrant of 11 April 2000 on two separate grounds: on the one hand, Belgium's claim to exercise a universal jurisdiction and, on the other, the alleged violation of the immunities of the Minister for Foreign Affairs of the Congo then in office. However, in its submissions in its Memorial, and in its final submissions at the close of the oral proceedings, the Congo invokes only the latter ground.

46. As a matter of logic, the second ground should be addressed only once there had been a determination in respect of the first, since it is only where a State has jurisdiction under international law in relation to a particular matter that there can be any question of immunities in regard to the exercise of that jurisdiction. However, in the present case, and in view of the final form of the Congo's submissions, the Court will address first the question whether, assuming that it had jurisdiction under international law to issue and circulate the arrest warrant of 11 April 2000, Belgium in so doing violated the immunities of the then Minister for Foreign Affairs of the Congo.

51. The Court would observe at the outset that in international law it is firmly established that, as also diplomatic and consular agents, certain holders of high-ranking office in a State, such as the Head of State, Head of Government and Minister for Foreign Affairs, enjoy immunities from jurisdiction in other States, both civil and criminal. For the purposes of the present case, it is only the immunity from criminal jurisdiction and the inviolability of an incumbent Minister for Foreign Affairs that fall for the Court to consider.

* * *

52.... [The Vienna Convention on Diplomatic Relations, 1961, and the New York Convention on Special Missions, 1969] provide useful guidance on certain aspects of the question of immunities. They do not, however, contain any provision specifically defining the immunities enjoyed by Ministers for Foreign Affairs. It is consequently on the basis of customary international law that the Court must decide the questions relating to the immunities of such Ministers raised in the present case.

53. In customary international law, the immunities accorded to Ministers for Foreign Affairs are not granted for their personal benefit, but to ensure the effective performance of their functions on behalf of their respective States. In order to determine the extent of these immunities, the Court must therefore first consider the nature of the functions exercised by a Minister for Foreign Affairs. He or she is in charge of his or her Government's diplomatic activities and generally acts as its representative in international negotiations and intergovernmental meetings. Ambassadors and other diplomatic agents carry out their duties under his or her authority. His or her acts may bind the State represented, and there is a presumption that Minister for Foreign Affairs, simply by virtue of that office, has full powers to act on behalf of the State (see, e.g., Art. 7,

para. 2*(a)*, of the 1969 Vienna Convention on the Law of Treaties). In the performance of these functions, he or she is frequently required to travel internationally, and thus must be in a position freely to do so whenever the need should arise. He or she must also be in constant communication with the Government, and with its diplomatic missions around the world, and be capable at any time of communicating with representatives of other States. The Court further observes that a Minister for Foreign Affairs, responsible for the conduct of his or her State's relations with all other States, occupies a position such that, like the Head of State or the Head of Government, he or she is recognized under international law as representative of the State solely by virtue of his or her office. He or she does not have to present letters of credence: to the contrary, it is generally the Minister who determines the authority to be conferred upon diplomatic agents and countersigns their letters of credence. Finally, it is to the Minister for Foreign Affairs that *chargés d'affaires* are accredited.

54. The Court accordingly concludes that the functions of a Minister for Foreign Affairs are such that, throughout the duration of his or her office, he or she when abroad enjoys full immunity from criminal jurisdiction and inviolability. That immunity and that inviolability protect the individual concerned against any act of authority of another State which would hinder him or her in the performance of his or her duties.

55. In this respect, no distinction can be drawn between acts performed by a Minister for Foreign Affairs in an "official" capacity, and those claimed to have been performed in a "private capacity", or, for that matter, between acts performed before the person concerned assumed office as Minister for Foreign Affairs and acts committed during the period of office. Thus, if a Minister for Foreign Affairs is arrested in another State on a criminal charge, he or she is clearly thereby prevented from exercising the functions of his or her office. The consequences of such impediment to the exercise of those official functions are equally serious, regardless of whether the Minister for Foreign Affairs was, at the time of arrest, present in the territory of the arresting State on an "official" visit or a "private" visit, regardless of whether the arrest relates to acts allegedly performed before the person became the Minister for Foreign Affairs or to acts performed while in office, and regardless of whether the arrest relates to alleged acts performed in an "official" capacity or a "private" capacity. Furthermore, even the mere risk that, by travelling to or transiting another State a Minister for Foreign Affairs might be exposing himself or herself to legal proceedings could deter the Minister from travelling internationally when required to do so for the purposes of the performance of his or her official functions.

56. The Court will now address Belgium's argument that immunities accorded to incumbent Ministers for Foreign Affairs can in no case protect them where they are suspected of having committed war crimes or crimes against humanity.

* * *

58. The Court has carefully examined State practice, including national legislation and those few decisions of national higher courts, such as the House of Lords or the French Court of Cassation. It has been unable to deduce from this practice that there exists under customary international law any form of exception to the rule according immunity from criminal jurisdiction and inviolability to incumbent Ministers for Foreign Affairs, where they are suspected of having committed war crimes or crimes against humanity.

The Court has also examined the rules concerning the immunity or criminal responsibility of persons having an official capacity contained in the legal instruments creating international criminal tribunals, and which are specifically applicable to the latter (see Charter of the International Military Tribunal of Nuremberg, Art. 7; Charter of the International Military Tribunal of Tokyo, Art. 6; Statute of the International Criminal Tribunal for the former Yugoslavia, Art. 7, para. 2; Statute of the International Criminal Tribunal for Rwanda, Art. 6, para. 2; Statute of the International Criminal Court, Art. 27). It finds that these rules likewise do not enable it to conclude that any such an exception exists in customary international law in regard to national courts.

Finally, none of the decisions of the Nuremberg and Tokyo international military tribunals, or of the International Criminal Tribunal for the former Yugoslavia, cited by Belgium deal with the question of the immunities of incumbent Ministers for Foreign Affairs before national courts where they are accused of having committed war crimes or crimes against humanity. The Court accordingly notes that those decisions are in no way at variance with the findings it has reached above.

* * *

59. It should further be noted that the rules governing the jurisdiction of national courts must be carefully distinguished from those governing jurisdictional immunities: jurisdiction does not imply absence of immunity, while absence of immunity does not imply jurisdiction. Thus, although various international conventions on the prevention and punishment of certain serious crimes impose on States obligations of prosecution or extradition, thereby requiring them to extend their criminal jurisdiction, such extension of jurisdiction in no way affects immunities under customary international law, including those of Ministers for Foreign Affairs. These remain opposable before the courts of a foreign State, even where those courts exercise such a jurisdiction under these conventions.

60. The Court emphasizes, however, that the *immunity* from jurisdiction enjoyed by incumbent Ministers for Foreign Affairs does not mean that they enjoy *impunity* in respect of any crimes they might have committed, irrespective of their gravity. Immunity from criminal jurisdiction and individual criminal responsibility are quite separate concepts. While jurisdictional immunity is procedural in nature, criminal responsibility is a question of substantive law. Jurisdictional immunity may well bar prosecution for a certain period or for certain offences; it cannot exonerate the person to whom it applies from all criminal responsibility.

61. Accordingly, the immunities enjoyed under international law by an incumbent or former Minister for Foreign Affairs do not represent a bar to criminal prosecution in certain circumstances.

First, such persons enjoy no criminal immunity under international law in their own countries, and may thus be tried by those countries' courts in accordance with the relevant rules of domestic law.

Secondly, they will cease to enjoy immunity from foreign jurisdiction if the State which they represent or have represented decides to waive that immunity.

Thirdly, after a person ceases to hold the office of Minister for Foreign Affairs, he or she will no longer enjoy all of the immunities accorded by international law in other States. Provided that it has jurisdiction under international law, a court of one State may try a former Minister for Foreign Affairs of another State in respect of acts committed prior or subsequent to his or her period of office, as well as in respect of acts committed during that period of office in a private capacity.

Fourthly, an incumbent or former Minister for Foreign Affairs may be subject to criminal proceedings before certain international criminal courts, where they have jurisdiction. Examples include the International Criminal Tribunal for the former Yugoslavia, and the International Criminal Tribunal for Rwanda, established pursuant to

Security Council resolutions under Chapter VII of the United Nations Charter, and the future International Criminal Court created by the 1998 Rome Convention. The latter's Statute expressly provides, in Article 27, paragraph 2, that "[i]mmunities or special procedural rules which may attach to the official capacity of a person, whether under national or international law, shall not bar the Court from exercising its jurisdiction over such a person".

* * *

71. ... Accordingly, the Court concludes that the circulation of the warrant, whether or not it significantly interfered with Mr. Yerodia's diplomatic activity, constituted a violation of an obligation of Belgium towards the Congo, in that it failed to respect the immunity of the incumbent Minister for Foreign Affairs of the Congo and, more particularly, infringed the immunity from criminal jurisdiction and the inviolability then enjoyed by him under international law.

72. The Court will now address the issue of the remedies sought by the Congo on account of Belgium's violation of the above-mentioned rules of international law.

* * *

76. [A]s the Permanent Court of International Justice stated in its Judgment of 13 September 1928 in the case concerning the *Factory at Chorzów:*

> "[t]he essential principle contained in the actual notion of an illegal act—a principle which seems to be established by international practice and in particular by the decisions of arbitral tribunals—is that reparation must, as far as possible, wipe out all the consequences of the illegal act and reestablish the situation which would, in all probability, have existed if that act had not been committed" *(P.C.I.J., Series A, No. 17,* p. 47).

In the present case, "the situation which would, in all probability, have existed if [the illegal act] had not been committed" cannot be re-established merely by a finding by the Court that the arrest warrant was unlawful under international law. The warrant is still extant, and remains unlawful, notwithstanding the fact that Mr. Yerodia has ceased to be Minister for Foreign Affairs. The Court accordingly considers that Belgium must, by means of its own choosing, cancel the warrant in question and so inform the authorities to whom it was circulated.

* * *

Joint Separate Opinion of Judges Higgins, Kooijmans and Burgenthal

80. Under traditional customary law the Head of State was seen as personifying the sovereign State. The immunity to which he was entitled was therefore predicated on status, just like the State he or she symbolised. Whereas State practice in this regard is extremely scarce, the immunities to which to other high State officials (like Heads of Government and Ministers for Foreign Affairs) are entitled have generally been considered in the literature as merely functional. (Cf. Arthur Watts, "The Legal Position in International Law of Head of States, Heads of Governments and Foreign Ministers", *Recueil des Cours 1994-III,* Vol. 247, pp. 102–103.)

81. We have found no basis for the argument that Ministers of Foreign Affairs are entitled to the same immunities as Heads of State. In this respect, it should be pointed out that paragraph 3.2 of the International Law *Commission's Draft Articles on Jurisdictional Immunities of States and their Property* Of 1991, which contained a saving clause for the privileges and immunities of Heads of State, failed to include a similar provision for those of Ministers for Foreign Affairs (or Heads of Government). In its commentary,

the ILC, stated that mentioning the privileges and immunities of Ministers for Foreign Affairs would raise the issues of the basis and the extent of their jurisdictional immunity. In the opinion of the ILC these immunities were clearly not identical to those of Heads of State.

82. The Institut de droit international took a similar position in 2001 with regard to Foreign Ministers. Its resolution on the Immunity of Heads of State, based on a thorough report on all relevant State practice, states expressly that these "shall enjoy, in criminal matters, immunity from jurisdiction before the courts of a foreign State for any crime he or she may have committed, regardless of its gravity". But the Institut, which in this resolution did assimilate the position of Head of Government to that of Head of State, carefully avoided doing the same with regard to the Foreign Minister.

83. We agree, therefore, with the Court that the purpose of the immunities attaching to Ministers for Foreign Affairs under customary international law is to ensure the free performance of their functions on behalf of their respective States (Judgment, para. 53). During their term of office, they must therefore be able to travel freely whenever the need to do so arises. There is broad agreement in the literature that a Minister for Foreign Affairs is entitled to full immunity during official visits in the exercise of his function. This was also recognized by the Belgian investigating judge in the arrest warrant of 11 April 2000. The Foreign Minister must also be immune whenever and wherever engaged in the functions required by his office and when in transit therefor.

84. Whether he is also entitled to immunities during private travels and what is the scope of any such immunities, is far less clear. Certainly, he or she may not be subjected to measures which would prevent effective performance of the functions of a Foreign Minister. Detention or arrest would constitute such a measure and must therefore be considered an infringement of the inviolability and immunity from criminal process to which a Foreign Minister is entitled. The arrest warrant of 11 April 2000 was directly enforceable in Belgium and would have obliged the police authorities to arrest Mr. Yerodia had he visited that country for non-official reasons. The very issuance of the warrant therefore must be considered to constitute an infringement on the inviolability to which Mr. Yerodia was entitled as long as he held the office of Minister for Foreign Affairs of the Congo.

85. Nonetheless, that immunity prevails only as long as the Minister is in office and continues to shield him or her after that time only for "official" acts. It is now increasingly claimed in the literature (see e.g., Andrea Bianchi "Denying State Immunity to Violators of Human Rights", 46 *Austrian Journal of Public and International Law* (1994), pp. 227–228) that serious international crimes cannot be regarded as official acts because they are neither normal State functions nor functions that a State alone (in contrast to an individual) can perform: (Goff, J. (as he then was) and Lord Wilberforce articulated this test in the case of *1° Congreso del Partido*(1978) QB 500 at 528 and (1983) AC 244 at 268, respectively). This view is underscored by the increasing realization that State-related motives are not the proper test for determining what constitutes public State acts. The same view is gradually also finding expression in State practice, as evidenced in judicial decisions and opinions. (For an early example, see the judgment of the Israel Supreme Court in the *Eichmann* case; Supreme Court, 29 May 1962, 36 *International Law Reports*, p. 312.) See also the speeches of Lords Hutton and Phillips of Worth Matravers in *R* v. *Bartle and the Commissioner of Police for the Metropolis and Others,* ex parte Pinochet ("Pinochet III"); and of Lords Steyn and Nicholls of Birkenhead in "Pinochet I", as well as the judgment of the Court of Appeal of Amsterdam in the *Bouterse* case (*Gerechtshof Amsterdam*, 20 November 2000, para. 4.2.)

* * *

QUESTIONS

1. What justifications does the Court articulate for finding that an incumbent foreign minister enjoys immunity from the jurisdiction of Belgium courts even for grave international crimes?
2. Do you agree with the decision?
3. If Iraq issued an international arrest warrant for U.S. President George W. Bush or U.S. Secretary of Defense Donald Rumsfeld when they were still in office, accusing them of war crimes, do you think an incumbent U.S. President or incumbent U.S. Secretary of Defense should be able to claim immunity from Iraq's national courts? What about a former U.S. President or a former U.S. Secretary of Defense?

Immunity for International Organizations

If a state decides to allow an international organization to operate from a base within its territory, that state will negotiate an agreement with the organization spelling out the scope of the immunities to be enjoyed. For example the United States entered into an agreement with the United Nations when it was decided that the United Nations was to be headquartered in New York City.[48] These immunities are those associated with facilitating the purposes of the international organization and will usually include immunity from taxes, immigration controls and military service and may include some immunity from legal process and criminal jurisdiction. There is also a General Convention on the Privileges and Immunities of the United Nations[49] which grants a broad based immunity to the assets and other property of the United Nations. Representatives of members of the United Nations are granted immunity "from personal arrest or detention and from seizure of their personal baggage, and, in respect of words spoken or written and all acts done by them in their capacity as representatives, immunity from legal process of every kind."[50] This latter type of immunity attaches while the representatives are "exercising their functions and during the journey to and from the place of meeting...."[51]

Sovereign Immunity

Absolute Theory

In the past most monarchs were held to represent the sovereignty of the state and to be above the law. They were not subject to any legal procedures within their own state and when they travelled abroad they enjoyed immunity from jurisdiction, largely based on a theory of the equality of sovereigns. If indeed sovereigns were equal, the theory stated, one sovereign could not subject another sovereign to its legal process. During this period the courts adhered to the theory of absolute sovereign immunity under

48. Agreement between the United Nations and the United States Regarding the Headquarters of the United Nations, 11 U.N.T.S. 11, 61 Stat. 3416, T.I.A.S. No. 1676.

49. Adopted by the General Assembly, Feb. 13, 1946, 1 U.N.T.S. 13, 21 U.S.T. 1418, T.I.A.S. No. 6900.

50. Id. art. IV § 11(a).

51. Id. art. IV § 11.

which foreign sovereigns or foreign governments were generally not subject to any legal proceedings.[52]

The modern state gradually evolved from absolute monarchy to constitutional monarchy (with severe limitations on the power of the crown) to a variety of republics with different representative forms of government. The role of the state expanded from mustering armies and carrying on foreign relations to engaging in a whole variety of enterprises from regulating trade, to running steel mills and trains, to providing pensions and health care. The modern state is often the largest single employer within a nation and generally engages in a host of activities both commercial and governmental.

As the state expanded its activities so it was more likely to find itself in legal disputes with the general population. On the domestic front people began to press for a waiver of their own state's immunity in their own local court system. Somehow it did not seem fair that, for example, a paper manufacturer who supplied paper to the Department of Agriculture should be unable to sue for the price of the goods delivered when the Department failed to pay just because the defendant in the case happened to be the government. The people's representatives soon got busy passing legislation that waived sovereign immunity for their own government on a fairly broad basis.[53]

There was a reluctance to tackle the issue of a foreign sovereign's immunity, however, because

(a) that might subject your own state to reciprocal treatment elsewhere under a legal system that might be very different from your own, and;
(b) such legislation, subjecting foreign sovereigns to jurisdiction, would certainly have a major impact on foreign relations.

The theory of many governmental systems was that foreign affairs were the province of the executive not the legislature, so that the people's representatives were without power to alter the system without executive consent.

In an era where most people did not have dealings with foreigners, sovereign or otherwise, the existence of immunity for foreign sovereigns did not weigh too heavily in the public consciousness. Gradually, however, as the role and activities of the state expanded and as international travel became commonplace, many more people and organizations began to have international contacts. Today the overwhelming majority of businesses in developed countries have some aspect of their enterprise that stretches beyond national borders. The result has been that more people and corporations have dealings with foreign governments. If a dispute arose with a foreign government, the government could always claim absolute immunity and avoid any type of settlement as long as the doctrine of absolute sovereign immunity prevailed. Sometimes the person could sue the foreign government in its own state courts but that would depend on the extent to which immunity had been repealed in the foreign state and anyway litigating claims abroad would inevitably be expensive. The cry went up to limit the scope of immunity afforded to foreign sovereigns in the courts.

---

52. For a discussion of absolute foreign sovereign immunity and a list of exceptions to that immunity, see *The Schooner Exchange v. McFaddon*, 11 U.S. (7 Cranch) 116 (1812).

53. See e.g., The Tucker Act, 28 U.S.C. § 1346(a)(2) (1982); The Federal Tort Claims Act, 28 U.S.C. § 1346(b) (1982); The Suits in Admiralty Act, 46 U.S.C. § 740 (1982 & Supp. 1 1983).

The Restrictive Theory

The doctrine of restrictive sovereign immunity states that foreign sovereigns will not be subject to suit in disputes involving governmental matters but will be subject to the courts' jurisdiction in commercial matters. Application of this doctrine began as early as 1886 in a case from the Court of Cassation in Naples, Italy. A number of other courts began to follow suit and by the middle of the twentieth century a sizable number of states had abandoned absolute sovereign immunity and embraced the restrictive theory.[54] The courts often referred to governmental activities as sovereign or public acts (*jure imperii*) and spoke of commercial activities as private acts (*jure gestionis*). The great task for the courts, once they had accepted the restrictive theory of sovereign immunity, was in sorting out the dividing line between governmental activities and commercial activities. Not an easy task.

At the beginning of the 1950s about the only major states still adhering to absolute sovereign immunity were the United States, the United Kingdom and the Soviet Union. These states were beginning to recognize the inequity of the situation. For example, a U.S. citizen who had a dispute with the Italian government concerning commercial activity could not sue the Italian government in U.S. Courts, whereas an Italian citizen who had a dispute with the U.S. government concerning commercial activity could sue the U.S. government in Italian courts. In 1952, Jack B. Tate, Acting Legal Adviser to the U.S. Department of State wrote a now famous letter to Acting Attorney General Philip B. Perlman of the Department of Justice. In the letter Mr. Tate reviews state practice of granting immunity to foreign sovereigns and concludes that his Department will henceforth follow the restrictive theory of sovereign immunity when advising U.S. courts on pleas of immunity from foreign sovereigns. Mr. Tate was well aware that the U.S. courts were not bound to follow the State Department's suggestions but, in light of the fact that the U.S. courts generally defer to the executive department in matters touching on international relations, he thought it likely that the courts might be willing to follow the State Department's advice. Mr. Tate's letter is reproduced below.

Letter Addressed to Acting Attorney General Philip B. Perlman from the Department of State's Acting Legal Adviser, Jack B. Tate, May 19, 1952

26 Dep't St. Bull. 984 (1952)

My Dear Mr. Attorney General:

The Department of State has for some time had under consideration the question whether the practice of the Government in granting immunity from suit to foreign governments made parties defendant in the courts of the United States without their consent should not be changed. The Department has now reached the conclusion that such immunity should no longer be granted in certain types of cases. In view of the obvious interest of your Department in this matter I should like to point out briefly some of the facts which influenced the Department's decision.

54. For an excellent mid-century review of state immunity practice see *Dralle v. Republic of Czechoslovakia*, Supreme Court of Austria, (1950) Int'l L. Rep. 155 (H. Lauterpacht ed.).

A study of the law of sovereign immunity reveals the existence of two conflicting concepts of sovereign immunity, each widely held and firmly established. According to the classical or absolute theory of sovereign immunity, a sovereign cannot, without his consent, be made a respondent in the courts of another sovereign. According to the newer or restrictive theory of sovereign immunity, the immunity of the sovereign is recognized with regard to sovereign or public acts (*jure imperii*) of a state, but not with respect to private acts (*jure gestionis*). There is agreement by proponents of both theories, supported by practice, that sovereign immunity should not be claimed or granted in actions with respect to real property (diplomatic and perhaps consular property excepted) or with respect to the disposition of the property of a deceased person even though a foreign sovereign is the beneficiary.

The classical or virtually absolute theory of sovereign immunity has generally been followed by the courts of the United States, the British Commonwealth, Czechoslovakia, Estonia, and probably Poland.

The decisions of the courts of Brazil, Chile, China, Hungary, Japan, Luxembourg, Norway, and Portugal may be deemed to support the classical theory of immunity if one or at most two old decisions anterior to the development of the restrictive theory may be considered sufficient on which to base a conclusion.

The position of the Netherlands, Sweden, and Argentina is less clear since although immunity has been granted in recent cases coming before the courts of those countries, the facts were such that immunity would have been granted under either the absolute or restrictive theory. However, constant references by the courts of these three countries to the distinction between public and private acts of the state, even though the distinction was not involved in the result of the case, may indicate an intention to leave the way open for a possible application of the restrictive theory of immunity if and when the occasion presents itself.

A trend to the restrictive theory is already evident in the Netherlands where the lower courts have started to apply that theory following a Supreme Court decision to the effect that immunity would have been applicable in the case under consideration under either theory.

The German courts, after a period of hesitation at the end of the nineteenth century have held to the classical theory, but it should be noted that the refusal of the Supreme Court in 1921 to yield to pressure by the lower courts for the newer theory was based on the view that that theory had not yet developed sufficiently to justify a change. In view of the growth of the restrictive theory since that time the German courts might take a different view today.

The newer or restrictive theory of sovereign immunity has always been supported by the courts of Belgium and Italy. It was adopted in turn by the courts of Egypt and of Switzerland. In addition, the courts of France, Austria and Greece, which were traditionally supporters of the classical theory, reversed their position in the 20's to embrace the restrictive theory. Rumania, Peru, and possibly Denmark also appear to follow this theory.

Furthermore, it should be observed that in most of the countries still following the classical theory there is a school of influential writers favoring the restrictive theory and the views of writers, at least in civil law countries, are a major factor in the development of the law. Moreover, the leanings of the lower courts in civil law countries are more significant in shaping the law than they are in common law countries where the rule of precedent prevails and the trend in these lower courts is to the restrictive theory.

Of related interest to this question is the fact that ten of the thirteen countries which have been classified above as supporters of the classical theory have ratified the Brussels Convention of 1926 under which immunity for government owned merchant vessels is waived. In addition the United States, which is not a party to the Convention, some years ago announced and has since followed, a policy of not claiming immunity for its public owned or operated merchant vessels. Keeping in mind the importance played by cases involving public vessels in the field of sovereign immunity, it is thus noteworthy that these ten countries (Brazil, Chile, Estonia, Germany, Hungary, Netherlands, Norway, Poland, Portugal, Sweden) and the United States have already relinquished by treaty or in practice an important part of the immunity which they claim under the classical theory.

It is thus evident that with the possible exception of the United Kingdom little support has been found except on the part of the Soviet Union and its satellites for continued full acceptance of the absolute theory of sovereign immunity. There are evidences that British authorities are aware of its deficiencies and ready for a change. The reasons which obviously motivate state trading countries in adhering to the theory with perhaps increasing rigidity are most persuasive that the United States should change its policy. Furthermore, the granting of sovereign immunity to foreign governments in the courts of the United States is most inconsistent with the action of the Government of the United States in subjecting itself to suit in these courts in both contract and tort and with its long established policy of not claiming immunity in foreign jurisdictions for its merchant vessels. Finally, the Department feels that the widespread and increasing practice on the part of governments of engaging in commercial activities makes necessary a practice which will enable persons doing business with them to have their rights determined in the courts. For these reasons it will hereafter be the Department's policy to follow the restrictive theory of sovereign immunity in the consideration of requests of foreign governments for a grant of sovereign immunity.

It is realized that a shift in policy by the executive cannot control the courts but it is felt that the courts are less likely to allow a plea of sovereign immunity where the executive has declined to do so. There have been indications that at least some Justices of the Supreme Court feel that in this matter courts should follow the branch of the Government charged with responsibility for the conduct of foreign relations.

In order that your Department, which is charged with representing the interests of the Government before the courts, may be adequately informed it will be the Department's practice to advise you of all requests by foreign governments for the grant of immunity from suit and of the Department's action thereon.

Sincerely yours,

For the Secretary of State:

Jack B. Tate

Acting Legal Adviser

After the Tate letter, both the Department of State and the courts struggled with drawing the line between those activities which merited immunity and those which did not. It is fair to say that there was little agreement on the matter. One line of argument was that the *purpose of the government's acts* should be examined. The problem with this approach was that all acts of government are presumably carried out for a public purpose with the result that all governmental activity ends up being immune from jurisdiction. Another line of argument was that *nature of the government's acts* should be examined. The problem with this approach is that it gives no guidance as to which acts are to be treated as private (and therefore subject to jurisdiction) and which acts are to be treated as public (and therefore not subject to jurisdiction). The courts in the U.S. and other countries struggled on with tenuous line drawing.[55]

QUESTIONS

Ask yourself whether you would define the following acts as public or private:

1. The Spanish government makes a contract with a U.S. vessel owner to transport surplus wheat from Alabama to Spanish ports to feed the Spanish people. The vessel owner sustains damages allegedly because of the unsafe Spanish docking facilities and sues the Spanish government in U.S. court. (*Victory Transport Inc. v. Comisaria General de Abastecimiento y Transportes*, 336 F.2d 354, 356–60 (2d Cir. 1964)).
2. The Bangladeshi government enters into a license agreement with a U.S. corporation permitting it to capture and export rhesus moneys from Bangladesh. The Bangladeshi government terminates the licensing agreement and the corporation sues in U.S. court. (*Mol Inc. v. People's Republic of Bangladesh*, 736 F.2d 1326 (9th Cir.) cert. den. 469 U.S. 1037 (1984)).
3. The Iranian government makes a contract with a German plumbing firm to repair the heating system in the Iranian Embassy in Cologne. The Embassy refuses payment and the plumbing firm sues in the German courts. (*Decision of April 30, 1963, West German Constitutional Court*, 45 Int'l L. Rep. 57 (1963)).
4. The U.S. government enters into a contract with an Italian company to build sewers for the U.S. Logistic Command in Italy. Contract disagreements erupt and the Italian firm sues the U.S. government in the Italian courts. (*Governo degli Stati Uniti di America c. Soc. I.R.S.A.* [1963] Foro Ital. 1405, 47 Revista de Diritto Internazionale 484 (May 13, 1963)).

Eventually the legislatures of various countries decided to enact statutes that were meant to resolve the difficulties the courts had been facing. In the United States for example, Congress passed the *Foreign Sovereign Immunities Act of 1976*.[56] In Britain, the government passed the *State Immunity Act of 1978*[57] and in Canada the legislature enacted the *State Immunity Act of 1982*.[58]

All of the above acts adopt the restrictive immunity principle and spell out which types of foreign governmental acts will be immune from jurisdiction and which types of acts will be subject to jurisdiction. The courts now struggle with the definitions provided by the statutes. There is still room for much disagreement but it is fair to say that foreign governments now have a much smaller scope for claiming immunity than previously.

The Act of State Doctrine

This doctrine states that the courts of the United States will not examine the validity of the acts of a recognized foreign government carried out within its own territory even

55. For a discussion of various approaches to the issue, see *Victory Transport, Inc. v. Comisaria General de Abastecimiento y Transportes*, 336 F.2d 354 (2d Cir. 1964), cert. den., 381 U.S. 934 (1965).

56. 28 U.S.C.A. §§ 1330, 1332, 1391, 1441, 1602–1611 (1976).

57. Reprinted at 17 I.L.M. 1123 (1978).

58. 29, 30 & 31 Eliz. 2, ch. 95; reprinted at 21 I.L.M. 798 (1982).

when it is claimed that those acts violate international law. The doctrine is similar to sovereign immunity but was created in American courts in deference to the U.S. Constitutional allocation of authority over foreign affairs to the executive branch of government. The most famous case in recent decades involved claims that the Cuban government had refused to pay compensation after expropriating private property.[59] It was argued that this refusal to pay compensation violated international law. At the time the case was filed, the United States still had diplomatic relations with Cuba. The United States Supreme Court refused to examine the validity of the Cuban government's acts largely to leave the executive branch free to conduct foreign relations as it saw fit. The Court indicated that those aggrieved by the actions of foreign governments should generally look to the executive branch for redress.

> Following an expropriation of any significance, the Executive engages in diplomacy aimed to assure that United States citizens who are harmed are compensated fairly. Representing all claimants of this country, it will often be able, either by bilateral or multilateral talks, by submission to the United Nations, or by the employment of economic and political sanctions, to achieve some degree of general redress.[60]

The United States Congress was infuriated by the Supreme Court's decision and passed legislation known as the Hickenlooper Amendments[61] to undo the Court's refusal to pass judgment on the validity of a foreign government's confiscation of property when it is claimed that the confiscation violates international law. As a result American courts are authorized to assess the validity of expropriations of American owned property by foreign governments that are alleged to violate international law.

The Act of State doctrine, like the doctrine of sovereign immunity, is based on the notion of the sovereign equality of states and on courts' deference to executive branch authority over foreign relations. The restrictive form of sovereign immunity allows courts to hear claims related to the commercial activities of a foreign government. In such cases the commercial activity will be carried on either directly in the forum state or be in some way related to the forum state. The activity in question in a case raising act of state issues, however, will be acts of the foreign government carried out within its own territory. International law does not require the application of the act of state doctrine, though many domestic courts have fashioned a similar doctrine.

The act of state doctrine is not applied by courts in cases raising allegations of war crimes, genocide, human rights violations, acts of terrorism or generally any crimes over which the state has asserted universal jurisdiction.

Problem

Jacob Hall is a citizen of the state of Alba by virtue of being born there. He spent the first three months of his life in Alba before his parents, both citizens of the state of Beta, moved back to Beta. Jacob lived in Beta until he was twenty when he joined an international art auction house located in Cetera, the capital of the state of Ceta. Since then Jacob has led a fast paced life moving in the world of buying and selling high priced art, sculpture and antique furniture. Over the course of his career three priceless Vermeer

59. *Banco National de Cuba v. Sabbatino*, 376 U.S. 398 (1964).

60. Id. at 431.

61. 22 U.S.C. § 2370(e)(2).

portraits, all owned by the State of Ceta National Gallery of Art, disappeared shortly after they were consigned to Jacob's portfolio at the auction house. Though the police never ruled him out as a suspect, no evidence ever came to light linking Jacob with the disappearances.

At the age of forty-five in 1993, Jacob suddenly retired from his job and went to live in the state of Delta. He is apparently living in great luxury. Six months after he arrived in Delta, the Delta legislature passed a special bill conferring citizenship upon Jacob. The usual requirement is five years residency.

Six months ago the Ceta police unearthed some evidence that directly linked Jacob to the disappearance of the Vermeers. The evidence seems to suggest that Jacob took the portraits back to Beta and that he was paid large amounts of money to deliver the Vermeers to a well known Betan criminal who promptly disappeared with the portraits. The Ceta authorities have indicted Jacob for the art thefts and have asked the Delta authorities to extradite Jacob to Ceta. Ceta and Delta are parties to a bilateral extradition treaty which obligates both parties to surrender criminally indicted fugitives to the other state. The treaty also provides that neither party is obligated to surrender its own citizens under the treaty. The treaty also stipulates that in the event of a dispute arising under the treaty either party may take the dispute to the International Court of Justice for resolution. Delta refuses to extradite Jacob on the grounds that he is a citizen of Delta.

QUESTIONS

(Before trying to answer this question please read *The Nottebohm Case* (*Liechtenstein v. Guatemala*) 1955 I.C.J. 4 at pp. 270–275).

1. Write an opinion for the Court ruling *either* that Delta must extradite Jacob *or* that Delta is under no obligation to extradite Jacob.
2. Assume for purposes of this sub-section only that in light of Delta's refusal to extradite Jacob, Ceta sent undercover agents to Delta who captured Jacob and forcibly brought him to Ceta. Jacob was then put on trial in Ceta for the art thefts. Please explain any defenses that Jacob could raise to his being tried in Ceta and write an opinion of the trial court either accepting or rejecting each of the defenses raised. You should assume that the Ceta courts may assert jurisdiction to the maximum amount permitted by international law.

Suggested Further Readings

Ian Brownlie, Principles of Public International Law, chapters 15, 16, & 17 (7th ed. 2008).

D.J. Harris, Cases and Materials on International Law, chapter 6 (6th ed. 2004).

Sean D. Murphy, Principles of International Law, chapters 8 & 9 (2006).

Malcolm N. Shaw, International Law, chapters 12 & 13 (6th ed. 2008).

Rebecca M. M. Wallace, International Law, chapter 6 (5th ed. 2005).

Chapter V

The Law of the Sea

Introduction

The law of the sea is one of the areas of international law where there was a good deal of settled customary law even before the twentieth century. It is also one of the great success stories of multi-lateral treaty making. In the 1950s important conventions were drafted by the International Law Commission. The first United Nations Conference on the Law of the Sea took place in 1958 and adopted four of the Commission's conventions: the Convention on the Territorial Sea and the Contiguous Zone;[1] the Convention on the High Seas[2] the Convention on the Continental Shelf;[3] and the Convention on Fishing and Conservation of the Living Resources of the High Seas.[4] All of these conventions received a fair number of ratifications and all have entered into force. Parts of the conventions represented existing customary law and parts have contributed to the development of customary law. Some pressing issues were, however, left unresolved by the conventions, such as the breadth of the territorial seas and who, if anyone, had rights to the resources of the deep seabed. To a large extent these conventions have been superseded by a convention adopted after a series of United Nations conferences on the law of the sea which took place between 1974 and 1982. The United Nations Convention on the Law of the Sea (UNCLOS)[5] was opened for signature in Jamaica in 1982 and one hundred and fifty-five states signed the Convention. The United States, which had been a major participant in all the preliminary conferences, refused to sign, largely because of its objections to the regime created for deep seabed mining (Part XI of the Convention). Even though UNCLOS had received the required number of ratifications to enter into force by November 16, 1994,[6] most of the industrialized states had initially refused to ratify the Convention. In order to accommodate the objections of the industrialized states, the United Nations Secretary-General initiated consultations which have resulted in a 1994 Agreement Relating to

1. 516 U.N.T.S. 205, 15 U.S.T. 1606, T.I.A.S. No. 5639, signed 29 April 1958, entered into force, 10 Sept. 1964.

2. 450 U.N.T.S. 82, 13 U.S.T. 2312, T.I.A.S. No. 5200, signed 29 April 1958, entered into force, Sept. 30, 1962.

3. 449 U.N.T.S. 311, 15 U.S.T. 471, T.I.A.S. No. 5578, signed 29 April 1958, entered into force, 10 June 1964.

4. 559 U.N.T.S. 285, 17 U.S.T. 138, T.I.A.S. No. 5969, signed 29 April 1958, entered into force, 20 Mar. 1966.

5. 1833 U.N.T.S. 3, signed 10 Dec. 1982, entered into force, 16 Nov. 1994, reprinted at 21 I.L.M. 1261 (1982) [hereinafter UNCLOS or 1982 Convention].

6. UNCLOS, art. 308 states that the Convention enters into force one year after the deposit of the sixtieth ratification.

the Implementation of Part XI of the United Nations Convention on the Law of the Sea of 10 December 1982.[7] This new Agreement went into force in 1996 and has received one hundred and thirty-five ratifications. The United States has signed but not yet ratified the Agreement. The Agreement modifies UNCLOS to the extent that the two documents are inconsistent. There is a complex series of provisions for states that have yet to ratify UNCLOS and states that have already ratified UNCLOS to become parties to the 1994 Agreement.[8] One hundred and fifty-six states have now ratified UNCLOS.

The legal regime that emerges from UNCLOS and the 1994 Agreement can best be studied by looking at various segments of the waters of the world: internal waters, bays, the territorial sea, archipelagos, straits, the contiguous zone, the exclusive economic zone, the continental shelf, the high seas and the deep seabed. This chapter will address each one of these areas and conclude with a section on jurisdiction over vessels.

Internal Waters

Internal waters are those waters that lie within a state such as lakes or rivers. The state exercises exclusive jurisdiction over these waters and can, if it wishes to do so, exclude other nations from entering these waters. The water that lies on the landward side of the baseline from which the territorial sea is measured[9] (generally the low-water line along the coast),[10] bays[11] and ports[12] are also controlled by the coastal state and form part of the state's internal waters (see Figure 1, p. 181).

Lakes, bays that meet the Convention's definition (see pp. 180–183 *infra*) and rivers are all internal waters controlled by the coastal state.

Bays

It was agreed that the waters within a bay are internal waters but the basic problem confronting the drafters of the Convention was what constituted a bay. Coastal states are generally eager to define as much water as possible as within their jurisdiction, so the tendency was to try to define even large, shallow curvatures of the coastline as bays and thus claim them as internal waters. Under this theory France and Spain, between them, could claim the whole of the Bay of Biscay and Mexico and the United States could claim the Gulf of Mexico. Obviously such inclusive claims would not be acceptable. Article 10 of UNCLOS defines a bay narrowly as:

7. Signed 28 July 1994, entered into force 28 July 1996, U.N. GAOR, 48th Sess., 101st plen. mtg., Annex, U.N. Doc. A/RES/48/263 (1994), reprinted at 33 I.L.M. 1309, Annex at 1313 (1994).

8. Id. at arts. 4, 7, annex, sec. 1, para. 12.

9. UNCLOS, art. 9(1).

10. Id. at art. 5.

11. Id. at art. 10.

12. Id. at art. 11.

Figure 1. Map of Internal Waters

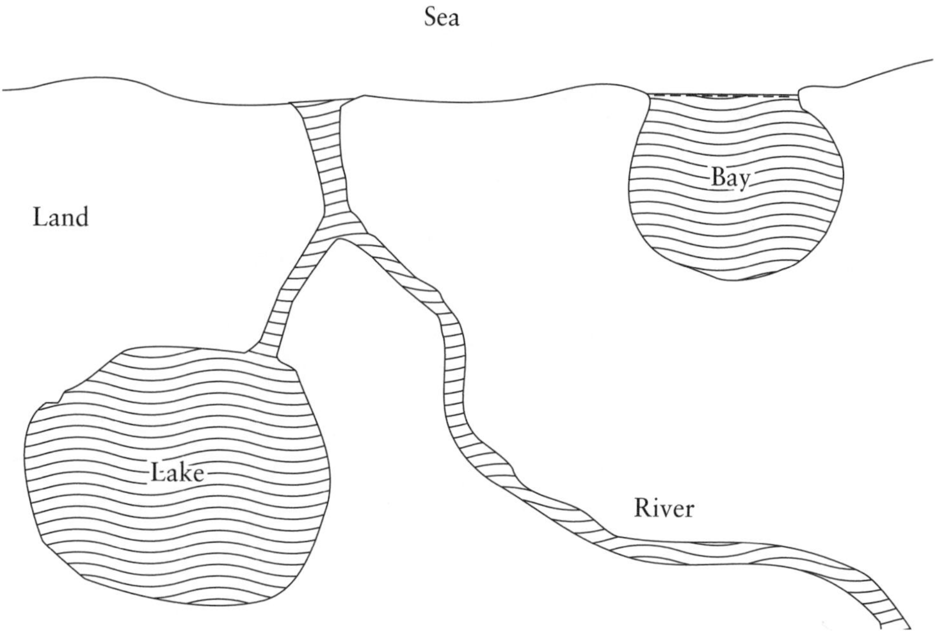

> a well-marked indentation whose penetration is in such proportion to the width of its mouth as to contain land-locked waters and constitute more than a mere curvature of the coast. An indentation shall not, however, be regarded as a bay unless its area is as large as, or larger than, that of the semi-circle whose diameter is a line drawn across the mouth of that indentation. (Article 10(2)).

To constitute a bay, therefore, a body of water first has to satisfy the semi-circular area test. This ensures that small coastal indentations are not counted as bays. The next problem was to decide from what point a bay's mouth would be measured and how wide the mouth could be. Article 10(3) states that "[f]or the purpose of measurement, the area of an indentation is that lying between the low-water mark around the shore of the indentation and a line joining the low-water mark of its natural entrance points." Article 10(4) provides: "If the distance between the low-water marks of the natural entrance points of a bay does not exceed 24 nautical miles, a closing line may be drawn between these two low water marks, and the waters enclosed thereby shall be considered as internal waters." Thus an indentation having the configuration below would constitute a bay and a straight line could be drawn across the entrance points so that all water on the landward side of the line would be internal waters (see Figure 2, p. 182).

But what about deep indentations whose mouths are greater than twenty-four nautical miles across? Article 10(5) provides: "Where the distance between the low-water mark of the natural entrance points of the bay exceeds 24 nautical miles, a straight baseline of 24 nautical miles shall be drawn within the bay in such a manner as to enclose the maximum area of water that is possible with a line of that length." Thus the straight line would be drawn some way up the indentation to determine which area constitutes internal waters, as set out in Figure 3.

Figure 2. Map of Bay

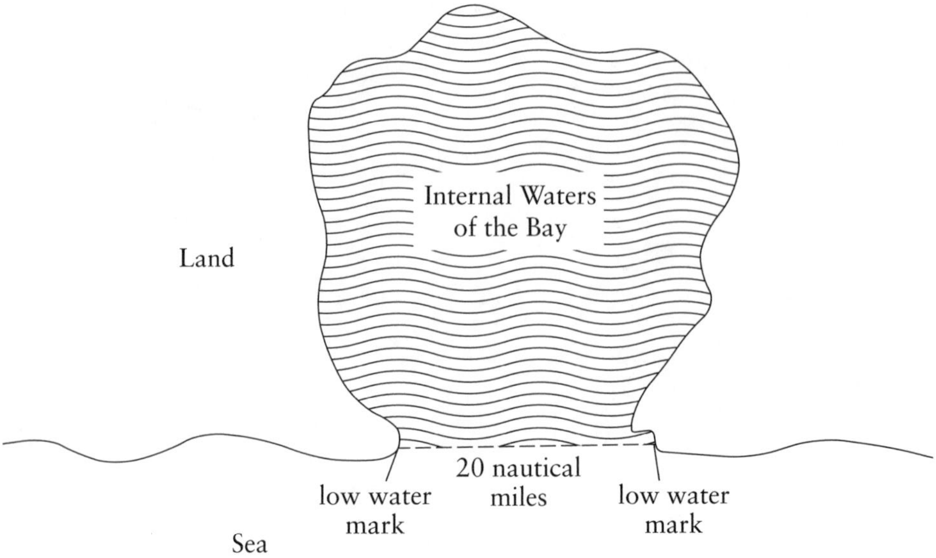

Historic Bays

Article 10 did not settle all issues related to bays and article 10(6) specifically states that the "foregoing provisions do not apply to so-called "historic" bays…." A number of

Figure 3. Map of Bay

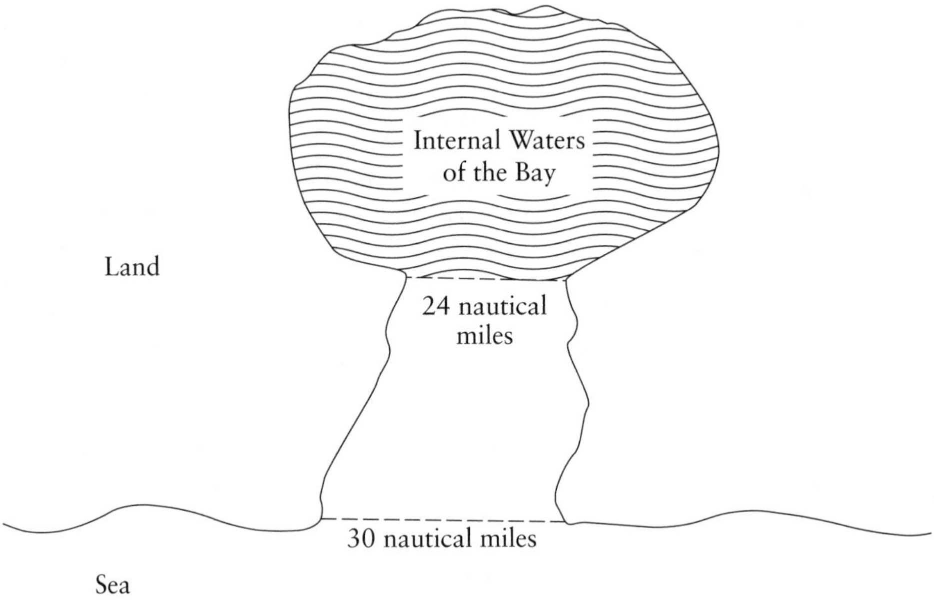

states have claimed large bodies of waters, some with entrance points hundreds of miles apart, as historic bays and entirely within the coastal state's internal waters. UNCLOS does not contain a definition of an historic bay and the determination of whether a body of water constitutes an historic bays probably turns upon the length of time that the state has claimed the water as a bay and exercised jurisdiction over it and the extent to which other nations have been willing to accept that characterization.[13] Canada claims as internal waters the whole of the Hudson Bay, which has entrance points fifty miles apart, though the United States disputes this claim. Libya claims the Gulf of Sidra (or Sirte) as an historic bay with a closing line of three hundred miles. This is disputed by a number of states including the United States.[14]

The Territorial Sea

Prior to UNCLOS there had been general agreement that a coastal state was entitled to claim a belt of waters around its coast as "territorial sea." It was agreed that the coastal state could exercise its jurisdiction over this belt of water even to the extent of excluding all fishing by foreigners in those waters. What was not agreed upon however was (a) the width of the territorial sea and (b) the extent to which the coastal state could prohibit foreign vessels from entering the territorial seas. The 1982 Convention resolved both issues. Article 2 of UNCLOS states:

1. The sovereignty of a coastal State extends, beyond its land territory and internal waters ... to an adjacent belt of sea, described as the territorial sea.
2. This sovereignty extends to the air space over the territorial sea as well as to its bed and subsoil.
3. The sovereignty over the territorial sea is exercised subject to this Convention and to other rules of international law.

Article 3 defines the breadth of the territorial sea as "not exceeding 12 nautical miles, measured from baselines determined in accordance with this Convention." Normally the baseline "for measuring the breadth of the territorial sea is the low-water line along the coast...." (Article 5).

For centuries states had disagreed about the breadth of the territorial sea. The Western industrialized states had generally claimed three nautical miles, the Scandinavian countries had claimed four nautical miles and certain South American countries had claimed up to two hundred nautical miles. Before the 1982 Convention, which for the first time permitted coastal states to claim up to two hundred nautical miles as an exclusive economic zone (article 57), the territorial sea was seen primarily in security terms or in terms of providing an exclusive fishing zone for the coastal state. (Can you think why the more powerful states should generally have favored a narrower territorial sea whereas the less powerful states generally wanted a broader territorial sea?). Once it was clear that the 1982 Convention was going to have a provision for a much expanded ex-

13. See, *Continental Shelf Case* (Tunisia v. Libya), 1982 I.C.J. 18, at 72–74.

14. The United States has challenged Libya's claims over the Gulf of Sidra on several occasions. In 1981, U.S. ships were in Gulf waters but beyond the twelve mile territorial sea limit. Libyan fighter planes were harassing the U.S. vessels and in retaliation U.S. jets shot down two Libyan planes. In 1986 U.S. navy ships entered the Gulf and fighting took place between the Libyan and the U.S. navies. See Yehuda Z. Blum, The Gulf of Sidra Incident, 80 Amer. J. Int'l L. 668 (1986).

clusive fishing (and other resources) zone it was easier to reach the compromise of twelve nautical miles as the breadth of the territorial sea.

Measuring the Territorial Sea

The normal point from which to measure the territorial sea was agreed upon as the low-water mark along the coast (article 5) but the International Court of Justice had permitted the drawing of straight baselines (that is, joining up certain low-water marks by straight lines rather than following every coastal indentation) in certain geographic circumstances.[15] The 1982 Convention adopts the Court's ruling and provides for straight baselines "where the coastline is deeply indented and cut into, or if there is a fringe of islands along the coast...." (article 7(1)). The same article also states that the "drawing of straight baselines must not depart to any appreciable extent from the general direction of the coast...." (article 7(3)) and that "account may be taken, in determining particular baselines, of economic interests peculiar to the region concerned...." (article 7(5)). A good number of states now employ the straight baseline method along portions of their coasts including the United Kingdom and the United States.

Powers of the Coastal State in the Territorial Sea and Foreign Ships' Right of Innocent Passage

Although article 2 of UNCLOS made it clear that the coastal state's sovereignty extends to the territorial sea, it also stated that the state's sovereignty had to be exercised "subject to this Convention...." (article 2(3)). A great debate had raged over whether foreign ships and in particular foreign warships had to ask permission of the coastal state before entering the territorial sea. Western nations tended to assert that all ships had the right to enter a coastal state's territorial sea provided the ship was exercising the right of "innocent passage." Eastern bloc countries tended to dispute this and argued either that all foreign vessels had to seek permission to enter the territorial sea or that foreign warships (as opposed to mercantile ships) could only enter the territorial sea after being granted permission by the coastal state. There was no general agreement on this issue but article 17 of UNCLOS resolves this long fought battle by stating that "ships of all states, whether coastal or land-locked, enjoy the right of innocent passage through the territorial sea." Notice that article 17 makes no distinction between warships and mercantile ships but simply refers to "ships of all states...." Note that there is no similar right of innocent passage for aircraft to fly over the territorial sea. Aircraft must receive permission to fly over a state's territory or its territorial sea.

The next battle was over the meaning of "innocent passage." Passage is defined in article 18 and article 19(1) states that "[p]assage is innocent so long as it is not prejudicial to the peace, good order or security of the coastal State." Article 19(2) contains a long list of activities that are automatically considered prejudicial to the peace of the coastal state, i.e., non-innocent. The activities listed include: the threat or use of force against

15. In the *Anglo-Norwegian Fisheries Case* (U.K. v. Norway) 1951 I.C.J. 116, the Court had allowed Norway to draw straight baselines along the seaward points of the island fringe which surrounds Norway because of the peculiarities of the Norwegian coastline and the economic dependence of the local population on the waters so enclosed.

the coastal state; practice with weapons; collecting information prejudicial to the security of the coastal state; launching or landing of aircraft or any military device; activities contrary to the customs, fiscal, immigration or sanitary laws; serious pollution; fishing; research or survey activities; interfering with communications or installations; and a final catch-all section, "any other activity not having a direct bearing on passage," (article 19(2)(l)).[16]

Article 20 requires submarines and other underwater vehicles "to navigate on the surface and to show their flag" when passing through the territorial sea. Article 23 requires "[f]oreign nuclear-powered ships and ships carrying nuclear or other inherently dangerous or noxious substances" to "carry documents and observe special precautionary measures established for such ships by international agreements."

Although the coastal state may not "hamper the innocent passage of foreign ships through the territorial seas...." (article 24), the coastal state can regulate passage in a number of ways. It can adopt laws and regulations to protect navigation, cables and pipelines, living resources of the sea, the environment and marine research and can prevent violations of its customs, fiscal, immigration and sanitary laws. (Article 21). It can also set up sea lanes and traffic separation schemes, particularly for inherently dangerous cargoes and nuclear vessels (article 22). The coastal state may take steps to prevent non-innocent passage (article 25(1)) or even suspend innocent passage rights temporarily if such suspension "is essential for the protection of its security, including weapons exercises." (Article 25(3)).

The coastal state may only exercise its criminal and civil jurisdiction over foreign vessels exercising the right of innocent passage in very limited circumstances. (Articles 27 and 28, see pp. 216–217).

One remaining difficulty is the question of what a state may do if it believes a foreign vessel is engaging in non-innocent activities in the territorial sea. Article 25(1) permits the coastal state to "take the necessary steps in its territorial sea to prevent passage which is not innocent." Article 30 states that "[i]f any warship does not comply with the laws and regulations of the coastal State concerning passage through the territorial sea and disregards any request for compliance therewith which is made to it, the coastal State may require it to leave the territorial sea immediately." Article 31 states that the flag state of a foreign warship shall bear the responsibility for any damage to the coastal state resulting from non compliance of the warship with the coastal state's laws or regulations when passing through the territorial sea.

Although it is not entirely clear, it looks as if the 1982 Convention intends that the coastal state shall first request a foreign warship to stop violating the requirements of innocent passage and that if the foreign warship refuses to comply, the coastal state can order it to leave the territorial sea. Article 25(1) does not distinguish between warships and commercial vessels and simply permits "necessary steps" to prevent non-innocent passage. Three questions present themselves. First, what is permitted under "necessary steps" to prevent non-innocent passage in the territorial sea? Second, must a foreign warship be asked to comply with regulations before being asked to leave the territorial

---

16. Whenever I read article 19(2)(l) I always wonder: if the captain of a vacation cruise ship throws a party for the passengers as the ship is going through a foreign state's territorial sea, is the ship engaging in non-innocent activities to the extent that it has forfeited its right to traverse the territorial sea? On the one hand, parties on board ship generally are "not prejudicial to the peace, good order or security of the coastal State" but, on the other hand, can scarcely be described as an activity "having a direct bearing on passage."

sea; and third, may the coastal state do anything to a ship engaging in non-innocent passage in the territorial sea beyond asking the foreign ship to leave and escorting it from the area?

Some scholars maintain that "necessary steps" "include the use of reasonable force as a last resort even against warships...."[17] Others have argued that "[i]n the absence of immediate threat of armed attack ... escorting foreign naval vessels out of territorial waters is the strongest action a coastal state should take. The seizure of foreign war ships or other attacks upon them are much too dangerous and provocative acts to be permitted under international law."[18]

When a coastal state determines that its security is threatened it may well wish to use the element of surprise rather than letting the foreign vessel know that it is aware of its presence by requesting it to leave. When Sweden found a Soviet submarine in one of its bays in 1981 it requested an apology from the U.S.S.R. It then impounded the submarine and interrogated the commander and the crew. After protracted negotiations, the U.S.S.R. apologized and the submarine was returned to the Soviets. By that time Swedish officials had a thorough knowledge of the workings of Soviet submarines. In 1982, the Swedish Navy dropped several depth charges in an attempt to make some foreign submarines surface that it thought it had detected in its internal and territorial waters. No submarines were discovered although the Swedish authorities concluded that foreign submarines had been in Swedish waters.[19] Had Sweden violated international law in either of these incidents?

Aircraft have no right to fly over foreign territory or foreign territorial seas. What may a state do if foreign planes violate its airspace? In February 1996, Cuba shot down two U.S. registered civilian planes that may have been in Cuban airspace killing the four people on board. The planes had been sent by a group called "Brothers to the Rescue" made up mainly of Cuban expatriates opposed to Fidel Castro's rule of Cuba. The group had previously dropped pamphlets over Cuba expressing its condemnation of the Castro regime. The Cuban government claims that protests had been sent to the U.S. government on previous occasions when U.S. planes had violated its airspace and that it warned the two planes to stay out of Cuban airspace. The U.S. Department of State asserts that no such warnings were received.[20] Did the U.S. registered planes violate international law? Did Cuba violate international law?

---

17. D.J. Harris, Cases and Materials on International Law 424 (6th ed. 2004).

18. Telegram sent by U.S. Secretary of State Dean Rusk to all diplomatic posts after the crew of the U.S. Navy intelligence ship *Pueblo* had been captured off North Korea allegedly for spying in North Korean territorial waters, reprinted at 62 Amer. J. Int'l L. 756 (1968). Although Secretary Rusk was basing his argument on the 1958 Convention on the Territorial Sea and the Contiguous Zone (to which North Korea was not a party) and customary law, the language of the 1982 Convention has not changed the law appreciably.

19. See Roma Sadurska, Foreign Submarines in Swedish Waters: The Erosion of an International Norm, 10 Yale J. Int'l L. 34 (1984).

20. CBS Evening News (CBS Television broadcast, April 30, 1996, Dan Rather reporting). By some estimates: "Cases of trespassing *civil* aircraft being shot down are not uncommon." D.J. Harris, Cases and Materials on International Law 242 (6th ed. 2004). There is some support for the view that military aircraft that enter foreign airspace can be shot down though such incidents would be governed by the rules relating to use of force and would have to meet the self-defence, proportionality and necessity requirement. (See chapter X.) Both Cuba and the United States are parties to The Chicago Convention on International Civil Aviation (15 U.N.T.S. 295, T.I.A.S. No. 1591, signed 7 Dec. 1944, entered into force 4 April 1947). Article 3 bis was adopted by the ICAO Assembly and entered into force 1 Oct. 1998. It states that "every State must refrain from resorting to the use of weapons against civil aircraft in flight ... [but] [t]his provision shall not be interpreted as modifying ... the rights and obligations of States set forth in the Charter of the United Nations." See related

United States v. Conroy
United States v. Walker

589 F.2d 1258 (5th Cir.) cert. den.
444 U.S. 831 (1979)

Before RONEY, RUBIN and VANCE, Circuit Judges.

ALVIN B. RUBIN, Circuit Judge:

If the Coast Guard cutter DAUNTLESS is not otherwise recorded in history, her forays to protect coasts of the United States from illicit imports will be commemorated in decisions of the Fifth Circuit. The defendants, convicted of either conspiracy or both conspiracy and attempting to import marijuana, charge that the zeal of her commanding officer exceeded his statutory authority and led him to violate their constitutional rights by boarding their American vessel in Haitian waters. Having recently attempted to chart the rules concerning coast guard authority with respect to domestic vessels in coastal waters as well as on the high seas, we now explore the same questions in the uncharted foreign domain.

I.

Once upon a time there was an informer, most of these tales begin. In this instance he was Flemming Larson Budal, a Danish citizen who was residing in the United States, had been an informer for several months, had worked on a number of other cases, and had been paid $200 a week by the Drug Enforcement Administration.

In December, 1975, Budal began a series of conversations with two of the defendants, Schubert and Conroy, in New England, and together they formulated a plan to smuggle a boatload of marijuana from Jamaica. During this time Budal was in constant communication with a special agent of the DEA.

Schubert obtained a 53-foot Gulfstar sailboat in Ft. Lauderdale. Soon afterwards Budal flew to Ft. Lauderdale where he was met by Dahl and Schubert, and another indictee who was separately tried. They were later joined by a fourth defendant, Jacobs, and together lived on the vessel, the NAHOA, [a U.S. registered vessel]until September 3, 1976, when they weighed anchor for Jamaica. Conroy remained in New England, allegedly to await the return of the other defendants with their cargo.

The DEA agent had furnished Budal two electronic detection devices of the kind known as beepers, one of which was to be turned on when the vessel was loaded. This device emits a signal by means of which its location can be determined by other electronic equipment. Rather then [sic] keep either on his person, Budal concealed one in the engine room and the other in an air vent on the NAHOA.

When the NAHOA was about 40 miles from Jamaica, the crew met the fifth defendant, Walker, who came out from the island on a small motorboat. Walker made four trips to the NAHOA ferrying marijuana.

---

litigation where several people have been convicted on multiple criminal charges including acting as unregistered Cuban intelligence agents and one has been convicted of "conspiracy to commit murder by supporting and implementing a plan to shoot down United States civilian aircraft outside of Cuban and United States airspace." U.S. v. Hernandez, 106 F.Supp. 2d 1317 (S.D. Fla. 2000). These convictions were reversed and remanded for new trial, sub nom., U.S. v. Campa, 419 F.3d 1219 (11th Cir. 2005). On rehearing *en banc*, the Court of Appeals affirmed both the trial court's denial of a change of venue and all of the convictions and remanded for consideration of remaining issues. 529 F.3d 980 (11th Cir. 2008), cert. den., 129 S. Ct. 2790 (2009).

The DAUNTLESS, under the command of Lieutenant Robert Council, was on border patrol in the Windward Passage between Haiti and Cuba, on guard for the NAHOA. When a DEA plane flying over nearby waters received an electronic signal from one of Budal's beepers, the DAUNTLESS attempted to establish a barrier patrol in the Windward Passage.

A day later the commanding officer of the DAUNTLESS recognized a radar beep on his scope as a vessel located about nine miles southwest of Haiti. He set his course for the vessel, and soon sighted her; it was, as anticipated, the NAHOA. He attempted to communicate with the vessel by radio, flag, and flashing lights, all signaling her to heave to. Nevertheless, those aboard the vessel set course straight for Haiti, and entered that nation's territorial waters.

Oral approval, later confirmed in writing, to enter Haitian waters and search the NAHOA was obtained from the Haitian Chief-of-Staff, and the DAUNTLESS continued in pursuit. When on further signals, the NAHOA did not halt, the flag Sierra Quebec III was raised: this signifies "stop or we'll shoot." The NAHOA then hove to, and Lieutenant Council pulled alongside her in a small boat. He smelled marijuana, and asked permission to board. Schubert denied his request, but Lieutenant Council went on the vessel and requested the ship's papers. Schubert prevented him from entering the ship's cabin; the lieutenant ordered a search, and found 7000 pounds of marijuana.

Defendants Conroy, Schubert, Dahl and Jacobs contend that in this dramatic encounter the Coast Guard were little better, legally, than pirates. The installation of the beeper was an illegal search; the boarding of the vessel in Haitian waters exceeded the statutory authority of the Coast Guard and violated their constitutional rights because it was unreasonable and warrantless. In addition, defendant Walker, who was separately tried, alleges that there was insufficient evidence to convict him of conspiracy, and that procedural errors denied him a fair trial.

[Arguments related to the installation of the beeper are omitted].

III. THE SEIZURE IN FOREIGN WATERS

The Fourth Amendment not only protects all within our bounds; it also shelters our citizens wherever they may be in the world from unreasonable searches by our own government. *Reid v. Covert*, 1957, 354 U.S. 1, 5–6, 77 S.Ct. 1222, 1225, 1 L.Ed.2d 1148, 1157. See Note, *The Applicability of the Exclusionary Rule in Federal Court to Evidence Seized and Confessions Obtained in Foreign Countries*, 16 Column. J. Transnat'l L. 495 (1977).[21] The mere consent of foreign authorities to a seizure that would be unconstitutional in the United States does not dissipate its illegality even though the search would be valid under local law. Indeed the United States does not here contend that those aboard the NAHOA were beyond the shield of the Fourth Amendment. The issue is whether the search was invalid because it was made without a warrant and by a federal agency, the Coast Guard, that lacked express statutory authority to conduct it.

A. Statutory Authority

In *United States v. Warren*, 5 Cir. en banc 1978, 578 F.2d 1058, we held that the Coast Guard has authority under 14 U.S.C. § 89(a)[10] to board American vessels on

---

21. Since *U.S. v. Conroy* was decided the U.S. Supreme Court has limited the protection of the U.S. Constitution outside U.S. borders. *U.S. v. Verdugo-Urquidez*, 494 U.S. 259 (1990) held that Fourth Amendment protections do not apply to the search and seizure by U.S. agents of property owned by a nonresident alien when the property is located in a foreign country.

10. *US v. Conroy*, footnote 10

14 U.S.C. § 89(a) provides in part:

the high seas beyond the twelve-mile limit not only to inspect for safety and documentation but also to "look for obvious customs and narcotics violations." 578 F.2d at 1065. In *United States v. Cadena*, 5 Cir. 1978, 585 F.2d 1252, we gave the same statutory provision, Section 89(a), a reading broad enough to cover the stop on the high seas of foreign vessels subject to extra-territorial application of domestic law. That statute in terms, however, would not reach the territorial waters of another nation for it relates only to "the high seas and waters over which the United States has jurisdiction."

Conceding that the statute per se would not authorize the Haitian search, the government urges that the phrase, "upon the high seas and waters over which the United States has jurisdiction," was not intended to be restrictive, and that the Coast Guard has implicit power to search an American vessel in foreign waters even in the absence of express statutory authority. We agree.

The legislative history of the present form of the statute leads to the conclusion that the high-seas phrase was not intended to be restrictive. Before it was amended to incorporate that phrase, the statutory authority of the Coast Guard was examined in *Maul v. United States*, 1927, 274 U.S. 501, 47 S.Ct. 735, 71 L.Ed. 1171. The majority opinion searched specific statutes to find express statutory authorization for the Coast Guard to seize domestic vessels on the high seas in enforcing the revenue laws. Mr. Justice Brandeis, with whom Mr. Justice Holmes joined, concurring, would not have rested on an interpretation of specific statutory authority because of his apprehension that "the construction adopted by the court may have in other cases far-reaching and regrettable results." 274 U.S. as 512, 47 S.Ct. at 739, 71 L.Ed. at 1176. He added that, notwithstanding what he perceived as lack of express statutory language, "authority [to seize American vessels beyond the territorial waters] exists because it is to be implied as an incident of the police duties of ocean patrol which Congress has imposed upon the Coast Guard." *Id.*

Thereafter, Congress amended Section 89(a) to incorporate the high-seas phrase in the hope of avoiding the problem foreseen by Mr. Justice Brandeis.

* * *

However, while affirmatively empowering the Coast Guard to engage in law enforcement activities on the high seas and in American territorial waters, the resultant statute was silent as to the role of the Coast Guard elsewhere. The reason for the omission is apparent: the authority of the Coast Guard to proceed in foreign territorial waters simply was not a matter entertained by Congress while deliberating upon the statute.

* * *

The Coast Guard may make inquiries, examinations, inspections, searches, seizures, and arrests upon the high seas and waters over which the United States has jurisdiction, for the prevention, detection, and suppression of violations of laws of the United States. For such purposes, commissioned, warrant, and petty officers may at any time go on board any vessel subject to the jurisdiction, or to the operation of any law, of the United States, address inquiries to those on board, examine the ship's documents and papers, and examine, inspect, and search the vessel and use all necessary force to compel compliance. When from such inquiries, examination, inspection, or search it appears that a breach of the laws of the United States rendering a person liable to arrest is being, or has been committed, by any person, such person shall be arrested ... ; or, if it shall appear that a breach of the laws of the United States has been committed so as to render such vessel, or the merchandise, or any part thereof, on board of, or brought into the United States by, such vessel, liable to forfeiture ... such vessel or such merchandise, or both, shall be seized.

Because neither mandate nor prohibition of search can be divined from Section 89(a), the Coast Guard's authority, if it exists, must be, as Mr. Justice Brandeis said, an incident of its other powers. The powers that Congress gives agencies in the executive branch are better when—as is usually the case—they are explicit. The statute that is express and unequivocal is least likely to be misunderstood or violated either by neglect or zealous overuse. Yet authority may be granted by inference as well; in its relationship with the executive branch, Congress is not bound by the strictures that apply to the criminal law, and require such statutes to be explicit. The pattern of legislation from 1790 to 1927 traced by Mr. Justice Brandeis and the subsequent congressional action we have here discussed, make it clear that, in the absence of objection by the sovereign power involved, Congress intended the Coast Guard to have authority to stop and search American vessels on foreign waters as well as on the high seas and in territorial waters even though it never said so with unequivocal didacticism.

B. International Law

Our statutory interpretation of Coast Guard authority, premised on the concurring opinion of Mr. Justice Brandeis in *Maul*, is implicitly supported by principles of international law that justify law enforcement activities by the Coast Guard in foreign waters. International law is part of our domestic law. *The Paquete Habana*, 1900, 175 U.S. 677, 700, 20 S. Ct. 290, 299, 44 L.Ed. 320, 328. The possible application of the law of nations to supplement the statute is consistent with the statement in the House of Representatives report, "The powers conferred by this act are not to be construed to affect any other powers conferred by existing law." H.R. Rep. No. 2452, at 4.

The law of nations classifies Coast Guard vessels as warships. Such vessels belong to the State, are under the direction of a military commander and manned by a military crew, and legally bear the ensign of the national navy. *See* II C. Hyde, International Law 395 (1922); Convention on the High Seas, 450 U.N.T.S. 82, 13 U.S.T. 2312, T.I.A.S. No. 5200, art. 8.

* * *

The United-Nations-sponsored Convention on the Territorial Sea and the Contiguous Zone entered into force in 1964; the United States Senate had previously ratified [*sic*] the Convention in 1960, and the President had signed [*sic*] it in 1961.[22] 15 U.S.T. 1606, T.I.A.S. No. 5639 (1958). Haiti is also a party to the Convention. Thus the Convention represents existing U.S. policy, at least with respect to other party nations.

After much debate, the draftsmen of the multilateral treaty rejected any requirement of previous authorization by a coastal state for the entry of a foreign warship into its territorial waters. *See* 4 Whiteman,[Digest of International Law] *supra*, at 415–16 [1965]. Article 14(1) of the Convention on the Territorial Sea and the Contiguous Zone states simply, "Subject to the provisions of these articles, ships of all States, whether coastal or not, shall enjoy the right of innocent passage through the territorial sea." 15 U.S.T. at 1610. Article 16(1) provides that the coastal state may take "the necessary steps in its territorial sea to prevent passage which is not innocent." No distinction is made between warships and other vessels.

At least between parties to the Convention, such as the United States and Haiti, a warship of one nation may enter the territorial waters of the other without first giving

22. The U.S. Senate does not ratify treaties. The Senate gives its advice and consent to the ratification of treaties. The President ratifies treaties for the U.S. See chapter III.

notification and receiving authorization. Ratification of the convention by the United States manifests implicit authorization for its warships to do what the warships of other nations might do. The DAUNTLESS was not, of course, on a hostile mission. Indeed, it bears emphasis again that, despite the fact that presumably no consent by Haitian authority was required under the terms of the treaty, permission was in fact obtained. Therefore, in the ensuing search, there was a conjunction of implicit recognition by the United States Government of the power of its warship to make the search, and explicit approval of the search by the Haitian government.

Even had we been provided no guidance by the implicit authorization granted warships under the treaty, we would still be compelled to conclude that the defendants can not assail the legality of the seizure of their vessel in Haitian waters. Since 1815 it has been established that redress for improper seizure in foreign waters is not due to the owner or crew of the vessel involved, but to the foreign government whose territoriality has been infringed by the action. In *The Richmond*, 1815, 13 U.S. (9 Cranch) 102, 3 L.Ed. 670, the Court rejected a challenge similar to the one we face here to the seizure of an American registered vessel in the territorial waters of Spain. Chief Justice Marshall explained, "The seizure of an American vessel, within the territorial jurisdiction of a foreign power, is certainly an offense against that power, which must be adjusted between the two governments. This court can take no cognisance of it." 13 U.S. at 103, 3 L.Ed. at 671. Here, where not even the foreign government complains of the American assertion of sovereignty over its own vessel, defendants have no basis for complaint unless the seizure was improper on some other grounds.

[Other Constitutional arguments are omitted].

QUESTIONS

1. Under the 1982 Convention did the DAUNTLESS have the right to enter Haitian territorial waters and search and seize the NAHOA without seeking permission from the Haitian authorities?
2. Suppose the DAUNTLESS had not sought permission to enter Haitian territorial waters, would that have altered the outcome of the case?
3. Suppose the DAUNTLESS had asked permission to enter Haitian territorial waters but the permission had been denied. Nonetheless, the DAUNTLESS seized the NAHOA. Would that have altered the outcome in the case?
4. Suppose the DAUNTLESS had sought permission from Haiti to enter her territorial waters and that permission had been denied but that the DAUNTLESS nonetheless seized the NAHOA. Haiti then delivered a protest to the U.S. government. Would that have altered the outcome of the case?

Archipelagos

After the International Court of Justice had permitted the drawing of straight baselines in certain geographic circumstances in the *Anglo-Norwegian Fisheries Case* of 1951[23] some archipelagic states began to wonder whether straight baselines could be

23. See *supra* note 15.

drawn around the outside of their outermost islands, thus enclosing all the waters between the islands as internal waters. In 1955 The Philippines made such a pronouncement[24] and in 1957 Indonesia followed suit.[25] Such developments did not please the international community because it meant that foreign vessels had no right of passage through the enclosed waters. The 1982 Convention tackled the subject by creating a new regime for mid-ocean archipelagic states (articles 46–54).

Article 46(a) defines an archipelagic state as "constituted wholly by one or more archipelagos [which] may include other islands." An archipelago is defined as "a group of islands, including parts of islands, interconnecting waters and other natural features which are so closely interrelated that [they] form an intrinsic geographical, economic and political entity, or which historically have been regarded as such." (Article 46(b)). States that form part of a mainland but have archipelagos lying off parts of their coasts are covered by article 7. The regime created for mid-ocean archipelagic states permits the drawing of straight baselines "joining the outermost points of the outermost islands and drying reefs" (article 47(1)) provided the baselines include the main islands, have a certain ratio of water to land and generally (with certain exceptions), do not exceed one hundred nautical miles. (Article 47).

The archipelagic waters enclosed by straight baselines are said to be within the sovereignty of the archipelagic state including the airspace (article 49) but "ships of all States enjoy the right of innocent passage through archipelagic waters" (article 52(1)) which passage may only be suspended if essential for security purposes. (Article 52(2)). The archipelagic state "may designate sea lanes and air routes ... through or over its archipelagic waters...." (Article 53(1)) This right of sea lane or air route passage to traverse archipelagic waters is "solely for the purpose of continuous, expeditious and unobstructed transit between one part of the high seas or an exclusive economic zone and another part of the high seas or an exclusive economic zone." (Article 53(3)). This right of passage seems similar to the right of transit passage through international straights, see pp. 194–195. There does not appear to be any right to suspend sea lane passage through archipelagic waters.

The regime thus created for mid-ocean archipelagos allows the drawing of straight baselines around the islands of the archipelago but gives both the right of innocent passage for ships through these waters and the right of sea lane passage for ships and aircraft through designated sea lanes or air routes through or over the enclosed waters.

International Straits

Before the 1982 Convention permitted a territorial sea of twelve nautical miles, many states only claimed three nautical miles for their territorial sea. At that time most states regarded everything beyond the territorial sea as high seas and open to the vessels of all nations. This meant that many of the world's straits had a high seas passage through them because they were wider than six nautical miles. A high seas route meant that ships and aircraft did not have to ask permission of the coastal states to pass through the strait, nor did the ships have to confine themselves to "innocent" activities. When it

24. Marjorie Whiteman, 4 Digest of International Law 282–83 (1965).
25. Id. at 284.

was agreed that the territorial sea would be widened to twelve nautical miles, it was immediately realized that many straits that previously had a high seas route through them would now be completely swallowed up by territorial sea.[26] While the territorial sea regime allowed innocent passage for all ships, the limitations imposed by innocent passage were a far cry from the virtually unfettered passage permitted through the previously existing high seas route. Aircraft were given no right of innocent passage over the territorial sea whereas they had been free to fly over a high seas route. A compromise was reached by the introduction of the concept of "transit" passage. First, however, a strait had to be defined and here the drafters of the new Convention had a fair amount of customary law upon which to draw.

Definition of an International Strait

Customary Law

Corfu Channel Case

(United Kingdom v. Albania)
1949 I.C.J. 4

Note

See also an excerpt of the case on pp. 240–242.

> "On May 15th, 1946, the British cruisers Orion and Superb, were fired at by an Albania battery in the vicinity of Saranda.... The United Kingdom Government at once protested to the Albania Government, stating that innocent passage through straits is a right recognized by international law." 1949 I.C.J. at 26.

Judgment of the Court

It is, in the opinion of the Court, generally recognized and in accordance with international custom that States in time of peace have a right to send their warships through straits used for international navigation between two parts of the high seas without the previous authorization of a coastal State, provided that the passage is innocent. Unless otherwise prescribed in an international convention, there is no right for a coastal State to prohibit such passage through straits in time of peace.

The Albanian Government does not dispute that the North Corfu Channel is a strait in the geographical sense; but it denies that this Channel belongs to the class of international highways through which a right of passage exists, on the grounds that it is only of secondary importance and not even a necessary route between two parts of the high seas, and that it is used almost exclusively for local traffic to and from the ports of Corfu and Saranda.

It may be asked whether the test is to be found in volume of traffic passing through the Strait or in its greater or lesser importance for international navigation. But in the

26. It has been estimated that there are over one hundred international straits that are less than twenty four nautical miles wide.

opinion of the Court the decisive criterion is rather its geographical situation as connecting two parts of the high seas and the fact of its being used for international navigation. Nor can it be decisive that this Strait is not a necessary route between two parts of the high seas, but only an alternative passage between the Aegean and the Adriatic Seas. It has nevertheless been a useful route for international maritime traffic.

* * *

Having regard to these various considerations, the Court has arrived at the conclusion that the North Corfu Channel should be considered as belonging to the class of international highways through which passage cannot be prohibited by a coastal State in time of peace.

Note

Even though the North Corfu Channel was within Albania's territorial sea and even though many states maintained at that time a requirement that foreign warships must seek permission before entering the territorial sea, the Court ruled that foreign warships had a right of innocent passage through international straits that connect one part of the high seas with another part of the high seas which could not be suspended by the coastal state in peacetime.

Treaty Law

The *Corfu Channel Case* did not settle the question of the rights of passage through straits that connect one part of the high seas to a territorial sea. Article 16(4) of the 1958 Convention on the Territorial Sea and the Contiguous Zone[27] provided a right of innocent passage through such straits but relatively few states had ratified this Convention.

The transit passage regime created in the 1982 Convention applies only to "straits which are used for international navigation between one part of the high seas or an exclusive economic zone and another part of the high seas or an exclusive economic zone." (Article 37). (For the rules relating to the exclusive economic zone see pp. 197–198. Article 55 defines the exclusive economic zone as "an area beyond and adjacent to the territorial sea. . . ." not extending "beyond two hundred nautical miles from the baselines. . . ." (article 57)).

Other types of straits are governed by different articles in the 1982 Convention. If, in a strait, there exists "a route through the high seas or through an exclusive economic zone of similar convenience with respect to navigational and hydrographical characteristics. . . ." (article 36) then there is no right of transit passage. Ships and aircraft must take the high seas or exclusive economic zone route and abide by the rules of those regimes, or if ships choose to traverse the territorial sea in such a strait they must abide by the rules of innocent passage. Article 38(1) provides that "if the strait is formed by an island of a State bordering the strait and its mainland, transit passage shall not apply if there exists seaward of the island a route through the high seas or through an exclusive economic zone of similar convenience with respect to navigational and hydrographical characteristics." The *Corfu Channel Case* presents an "island" situation like the one de-

27. See *supra* note 1.

scribed in article 38(1). The island of Corfu is owned by Greece which is "an island of a State bordering the strait and its mainland...." although the claim was against Albania, another state bordering the strait. Since transit passage does not apply in the island situation described in article 38(1), the right of innocent passage applies except that such a right of innocent passage through such a straight cannot be suspended (article 45(2)) as it can in the territorial sea when "such suspension is essential for the protection of [the coastal state's] security...." (article 25(3)). Where a strait connects the high seas or an exclusive economic zone and the territorial sea of another state (article 45(1)(b)) the regime of innocent passage applies which cannot be suspended (article 45(2)).

Article 38 provides a right of transit passage for all ships and aircraft through international straits that connect one part of the high seas or exclusive economic zone and another part of the high seas or exclusive economic zone. This right of transit passage means "the freedom of navigation and overflight solely for the purpose of continuous and expeditious transit of the strait...." (Article 38(2)). Such passage does not exclude "entering, leaving or returning from a State bordering the strait, subject to the conditions of entry to that state." (Article 28(2)). This right of transit passage "shall not be impeded...." (Article 38(1)). While exercising the right of transit passage ships and aircraft must "refrain from any activities other than those incident to their normal modes of continuous and expeditious transit unless rendered necessary by *force majeure* or by distress...." (Article 39(1)(c)).

How is the right of transit passage different from the right of innocent passage? Aircraft are given a right of transit passage through article 37 straits, whereas no such right of overflight is given to aircraft under innocent passage. This right of transit passage applies to military aircraft as well as civilian planes (article 38(1) refers to "all ... aircraft...."). Submarines must surface and show their flags when exercising the right of innocent passage (article 20) but no such requirement is stated for transit passage, so presumably submarines may exercise the right of transit passage underwater. Article 19 has a long list of prohibited activities for ships exercising innocent passage. Articles 39 to 41 list less stringent restrictions on ships and aircraft exercising transit passage. The regulatory powers of the coastal states in transit passage (articles 41 and 42) are more limited than those permitted in innocent passage (articles 21, 22, 23, 24, 25, 26).

QUESTION

Study the map in Figure 4 (p. 196) and determine what rights (1) a foreign ship and (2) a foreign aircraft has to pass through the Straits of Tiran. Can the coastal states suspend those rights and if so, in what circumstances?

The maximum width of the Gulf of Aquaba is seventeen nautical miles. The only navigable channel into the Gulf is through the Straits of Tiran which are three miles wide. All states bordering the Gulf claim the maximum territorial sea permissible under UNCLOS.

The Contiguous Zone

For centuries coastal states have asserted the right to exercise jurisdiction in the waters off their coasts in order to ensure their security or to protect other interests they deemed vital. In 1804 the United States Supreme Court stated "[A state's] power to secure itself from injury may certainly be exercised beyond the limits of its territory.... If

Figure 4. Straits of Tiran

this right be extended too far, the exercise of it will be resisted." *Church v. Hubbart*, 6 U.S. (2 Cranch) 187, at 234–35 (1804). The difficulty was in defining the limit of this authority. The Supreme Court noted: "[The exercise of this right] has occasioned long and frequent contests, which have sometimes ended in open war. The English, it will be recollected, complained of the right claimed by Spain to search their vessels on the high seas, which was carried so far, that the *guarda costas* of that nation seized vessels not in the neighborhood of their coasts. This practice was the subject of long and fruitless negotiations, and at length, of open war." *Church v. Hubbart*, at 235.

The 1958 Convention on the Territorial Sea included a provision permitting coastal states to exercise control necessary to prevent violations of its customs, fiscal, immigration or sanitary regulations in an area contiguous to its territorial sea but not to extend beyond twelve miles from the baselines. (Article 24). No agreement was reached on a security zone which, given the capacity of modern weapons, would probably need a global limit. The Commentary by the International Law Commission on its Draft Articles for the 1958 Convention noted: "In so far as measures of self-defence against an imminent and direct threat to the security of the State are concerned, the Commission refers to general principles of international law and the Charter of the United Nations."[28]

28. 1956 II Yr. Bk. Int'l L. Comm'n at 294–95.

The 1982 Convention uses the same approach as the 1958 Convention and provides in article 33(1): "[I]n a zone contiguous to its territorial sea" the state may:

> exercise the control necessary to:
>
> (a) prevent infringement of its customs, fiscal, immigration or sanitary laws and regulations within its territory or territorial sea;
>
> (b) punish infringement of the above laws and regulations committed within its territory or territorial sea.
>
> 2. The contiguous zone may not extend beyond 24 nautical miles from the baselines from which the breadth of the territorial sea is measured.

The contiguous zone gives a coastal state a grant of authority up to twenty-four nautical miles off its coasts but for very specific and limited reasons. If a state claims a territorial sea of twelve nautical miles it will be able to claim another twelve nautical miles for its contiguous zone. What exactly can a coastal state do to foreign vessels in its contiguous zone? How much power does the term "control" grant to the coastal state? Professor Shearer states:

> Since laws on the substantive subjects of customs, fiscal, immigration and sanitary matters cannot be applied to the contiguous zone, it follows that an offence cannot be committed until the boundary of territorial waters is crossed by inward-bound ships. "Control" therefore must be limited to such measures as inspections and warnings, and cannot include arrest or forcible taking into port. It is arguable, however, and probably sustainable on the history of the British Hovering Acts and similar legislation elsewhere, that a coastal State might lawfully legislate to make it an offence to hover or to tranship dutiable cargoes in the contiguous zone and to carry out an arrest there because these activities are within the connotations of "prevention."[29]

The Exclusive Economic Zone

Many states had enforced an exclusive fisheries zone in their territorial sea for decades. These coastal states simply prohibited all foreign vessels from fishing in their territorial seas. Before the middle of the twentieth century most fishermen were employed on small boats that only had the capacity to fish fairly close to the shore. The building of much larger boats and the availability of refrigeration changed the traditional fishing patterns. Large "fish factory" ships put to sea for several months and caught and processed fish all over the world. Fish stocks began to dwindle and nations with traditional fishing fleets were anxious to provide their fleets some protection. States began to make unilateral declarations extending their exclusive fishing zones beyond their territorial sea. Iceland claimed a twelve mile zone in 1958 which was recognized as legitimate by the International Court of Justice in 1974.[30] A number of Latin American states claimed a two hundred mile zone which were the subject of numerous protests.

The 1958 Conventions could reach no agreement on a fishing zone but, by the time the 1982 Convention was ready to be signed, more than fifty states claimed various

29. I.A. Shearer, Problems of Jurisdiction and Law Enforcement Against Delinquent Vessels, 35 Int. & Comp. L. Q. 320, at 330 (1986); see also, Restatement Third, § 513, cmt. f.

30. *Fisheries Jurisdiction Case* (Merits) (U.K. v. Iceland) 1974 I.C.J. 3.

types of exclusive zones beyond their territorial seas.[31] The 1982 Convention created a new exclusive economic zone:

> "The exclusive economic zone is an area beyond and adjacent to the territorial sea, subject to the specific legal regime established in this Part, under which the rights and jurisdiction of the coastal State and the rights and freedoms of other States are governed by the relevant provisions of this Convention." (Article 55).

This zone "shall not extend beyond 200 nautical miles from the baselines. . . ." (Article 57).

Rights Exercised in the Exclusive Economic Zone

Coastal States' Rights

The coastal state is given "sovereign rights" in the exclusive economic zone but only for certain purposes: "exploring and exploiting, conserving and managing the natural resources, whether living or non-living, of the waters ... and of the sea-bed and its subsoil. . . ." (Article 56(1)(a)). It is also given jurisdiction for the establishment of "installations and structures" and over "marine scientific research ... [and] the protection and preservation of the marine environment." (Article 56(1)(b)).

The coastal state is given the responsibility for determining "the allowable catch of living resources in its exclusive economic zone." (Article 61(1)) It must also undertake conservation and management measures to prevent over-exploitation of the zone (article 61(2)) and promote "optimum utilization of the living resources. . . ." (Article 62(1)). If the coastal state does not harvest the entire allowable catch it must give other states (including land-locked states) access to the resources by making agreements with other states. (Article 62(2), 69 & 70).

In order to enforce its rights in the exclusive economic zone, a coastal state may "take such measures, including boarding, inspection, arrest and judicial proceeding, as may be necessary to ensure compliance. . . ." (Article 73(1)). Arrested vessels and crews must be released upon the posting of a bond but penalties for violations of the exclusive economic zone regulations may not include imprisonment or corporal punishment and the flag state must be "promptly notified." (Article 73).

The delimitation of the exclusive economic zone between states with opposite and adjacent coasts is to be worked out by agreement "to achieve an equitable solution." (Article 74(1)).

Foreign States' Rights

All states are guaranteed the rights of "navigation and overflight in the exclusive economic zone and the "laying of submarine cables and pipelines ... compatible with ... this Convention." (Article 58(1)).

See also, *The Saiga Case* at pp. 218–234 *infra*.

31. X New Directions in the Law of the Sea, at 472 (Myron Nordquist, S. Houston Lay & Kenneth R. Simmonds eds., 1980–81).

The Continental Shelf

In 1945, U.S. President Harry S. Truman was the first to claim national rights in a continental shelf. Truman proclaimed that:

> the United States regards the natural resources of the subsoil and seabed of the continental shelf beneath the high seas but contiguous to the coasts of the United States as appertaining to the United States, subject to its jurisdiction and control. In cases where the continental shelf extends to the shores of another state, or is shared with an adjacent state, the boundary shall be determined by the United States and the state concerned in accordance with equitable principles. The character as high seas of the waters above the continental shelf and the right to their free and unimpeded navigation are in no way thus affected.[32]

The reason that this proclamation took place in the mid-nineteen forties was that oil and mineral resources had been discovered in the continental shelf and it had become technologically possible to harvest those resources.

The term "continental shelf" is used to describe the sloping ledge covered by water that projects from the coastline of many states. The breadth of the continental shelf varies very considerably, sometimes only projecting a few miles, sometimes extending hundreds of miles. The Truman proclamation encouraged other states to make similar claims which they did, in rapid succession. The International Law Commission drafted the Convention on the Continental Shelf which was signed in 1958 and entered into force in 1964.[33] The 1982 Convention builds on the 1958 Convention and defines the continental shelf as comprising:

> the sea-bed and subsoil of the submarine areas that extend beyond [the coastal State's] territorial sea throughout the natural prolongation of its land territory to the outer edge of the continental margin, or to a distance of 200 nautical miles from the baselines from which the breadth of the territorial sea is measured where the outer edge of the continental margin does not extent to that distance. (Article 76(1)).

There are provisions for measuring the continental shelf when it projects beyond two hundred nautical miles (articles 76 (4) and (7)) and wealth sharing provisions for resources harvested by the coastal state from its continental shelf between 200 nautical miles and three hundred and fifty nautical miles from the baselines (article 82). The continental shelf may not be claimed by any state beyond three hundred and fifty nautical miles (article 76(6)).

The 1982 Convention makes it clear that the coastal state's rights in the continental shelf do not affect the status of the waters above it (article 78). The coastal state's rights in the continental shelf are described as "sovereign" but only "for the purpose of exploring it and exploiting its natural resources." (Articles 7(1)). The coastal state is given exclusive rights to harvest the "mineral and other non-living resources of the sea-bed and subsoil together with living organisms belonging to sedentary species....," (article

32. 10 Fed. Reg. 12,303 (1945); reprinted in Marjorie Whitman, 4 Digest of International Law 756 (1965). A press release made it clear that the claim only extended to the shelf "which is covered by no more than 100 fathoms (600 feet) of water...." Id. at 758.

33. See *supra* note 3.

77(4)) and the right to "authorize and regulate drilling on the continental shelf...." (Article 81). Other states are however given the right "to lay submarine cables and pipelines on the continental shelf...." (article 79(1)) subject to the coastal state's right to "control ... pollution from pipelines...." (article 79(2)).

If the coastal state decides to exploit the non-living resources of its continental shelf beyond two hundred nautical miles from the baselines then a system of payments to the International Seabed Authority (see p. 190) is to be distributed "on the basis of equitable sharing criteria, taking into account the interests and needs of developing States, particularly the least developed and the land-locked among them." (Article 82(4)).

Delimitation of the Continental Shelf between States with Opposite or Adjacent Coasts

One of the most intractable problems surrounding the issue of continental shelves has been the question of delimitation of the shelf when it is claimed by more than one state. The issue has generated a number of cases before the International Court of Justice.

The 1958 Convention on the Continental Shelf stated that delimitation should take place by agreement or if that was not possible by using the equidistance principle, but the International Court of Justice had ruled that the equidistance principle did not represent binding customary law for non-parties to the Convention.[34] The 1982 Convention states that delimitation "shall be effected by agreement on the basis of international law ... in order to achieve an equitable solution." (Article 83(1)). "If no agreement can be reached within a reasonable period of time, the States concerned shall resort to the procedure provided for in Part XV." (Article 83(2)). Part XV permits parties to the Convention to chose one of a variety of dispute settlement mechanisms including the International Court of Justice or the International Tribunal for the Law of the Sea (article 287), which is established under the Convention (see Annex VI), or binding conciliation (article 284). A Commission on the limits of the Continental Shelf is also established under article 76(8) and Annex II and parties can request recommendations from the Commission which are binding.

There are three different types of decisions that have contributed to this growing area of continental shelf delimitation law: (1) agreements between states delimiting their continental shelves;[35] (2) decisions of the International Court of Justice;[36] and (3) decisions of *ad hoc* arbitral tribunals.[37] The late Professor Charney, a leading authority on the law of the sea, has summed up the jurisprudence of this area of law as follows:

34. *North Sea Continental Shelf Cases* (The Federal Republic of Germany v. Denmark; The Federal Republic of Germany v. The Netherlands) 1969 I.C.J. 3, see *supra* pp. 22–26.

35. See, International Maritime Boundaries (Jonathan I. Charney & Lewis M. Alexander eds. 1998). More than 130 maritime boundary delimitations are examined in this book.

36. See, e.g., *Continental Shelf* (Tunisia v. Libya) 1982 I.C.J. 18; *Delimitation of the Maritime Border in the Gulf of Maine Area* (Canada v. U.S.) 1984 I.C.J. 246; *Continental Shelf* (Libya v. Malta) 1985 I.C.J. 13; *Land, Island and Maritime Frontier Dispute* (El Salvador v. Honduras: Nicaragua intervening), 1990 I.C.J. 92; *Maritime Delimitation in the Area between Greenland and Jan Mayen* (Denmark v. Norway) 1993 I.C.J. 38.

37. See, e.g., *Delimitation of the Maritime Areas between Canada and France* (St. Pierre and Miquelon, (arbitral award of June 10, 1992), reprinted at 31 I.L.M. 1149 (1992); *Delimitation of the Maritime Boundary between Guinea and Guinea-Bissau*, reprinted at 25 I.L.M. 252 (1986).

> A primary criticism of the current state of this law is its indeterminacy. International law does not require that maritime boundaries be delimited in accordance with any particular method; rather, it requires that they be delimited in accordance with equitable principles, taking into account all of the relevant circumstances of the case so as to produce an equitable result. The equitable principles are indeterminate and the relevant circumstances are theoretically unlimited.[38]

Charney hoped that "the continuing series of judgments and awards ... [would] progressively refine the legal rules and their objectives."[39]

The High Seas

Under the 1958 Convention, the high seas were defined as any part of the sea that was not either territorial sea or internal waters.[40] Since the 1982 Convention added new areas of the sea that were subject to certain rights conferred upon coastal states, the definition had to be changed. Article 86 of the 1982 Convention now defines the high seas as: "all parts of the sea that are not included in the exclusive economic zone, in the territorial sea or the internal waters of a State, or in the archipelagic waters of an archipelagic State...."

By the early seventeenth century the idea that the high seas should be open to all nations had been clearly articulated by the great Dutch jurist Hugo Grotius in his seminal work *Mare Liberum* (1609). This ancient principle has been preserved in the 1982 Convention which states that "[n]o State may validly purport to subject any part of the high seas to its sovereignty." (Article 89). Article 87 reaffirms that "[t]he high seas are open to all States, whether coastal or landlocked...." This article also confirms "freedom of navigation," "freedom of overflight," "freedom to lay any submarine cables and pipelines," "freedom to construct artificial islands and other installations permitted by international law," "freedom of fishing" and "freedom of scientific research." These freedoms must "be exercised ... with due regard for the interests of other States ... and also with due regard for the rights under this Convention with respect to activities in the Area." (The Area covers the deep sea bed, ocean floor and subsoil, see pp. 202–204).

Article 88 of the 1982 Convention clearly states that "[t]he high seas shall be reserved for peaceful purposes." Many states engage in military maneuvers and the testing of conventional weapons on the high seas. The issue of testing nuclear weapons either on the sea, or land or underground has generated much controversy. The Comprehensive Test Ban Treaty[41] was opened for signature in 1996 and over one hundred and seventy states have signed it. One hundred and forty-eight states have already deposited their ratifications of the treaty. (See also section on Prohibited Activities on the High Seas, pp. 209–214.)

---

38. Jonathan I. Charney, Progress in International Maritime Boundary Delimitation Law, 88 Amer. J. Int'l L. 227, 230 (1994).

39. Id. at 233.

40. Convention on the High Seas, *supra* note 2, at art 1.

41. U.N. GAOR, 50th Sess., U.N. Doc. A/50/1027, Annex, 26 August 1996, opened for signature Sept. 24, 1996, reprinted at 35 I.L.M. 1439 (1996). For very useful current information on this treaty go to: http://www.ctbto.org. See p. 254.

The Deep Sea Bed

None of the 1958 Conventions had dealt with the deep sea bed largely because the possibility of economic activity on the sea bed was considered extremely remote. Rapid technological advances have made deep sea bed mining feasible. The discovery of manganese nodules and other minerals on the sea bed began to enhance the economic prospects for sea bed mining. In the early 1980s, this mining was thought to be imminent but a decade long depressed market for certain minerals reduced the immediate prospects for mining.

The regime created for the deep sea bed in the 1982 Convention appears at Part XI with annexes (articles 133–191). It is highly complex and only the briefest outline will be given here. The 1994 Agreement which seeks to modify key provisions of Part XI will also be sketched briefly.

The core dispute relating to the deep sea bed focusses on the issue of who owns the deep sea bed and who should control the assets resulting from any economic development of that area. Many developing countries felt that the deep sea bed was "the common heritage of mankind" (article 136) and that any activities carried out in such an area should be "carried out for the benefit of mankind as a whole ... taking into particular consideration the interests and needs of developing States...." (Article 104). The industrialized states with the technological capacity to engage in deep sea bed mining tended to favor a free enterprise system with the spoils going to whoever managed to exploit an area first, similar to the freedom to fish on the high seas. A type of compromise was worked out between these two positions in the 1982 Convention but the developed nations initially refused to ratify the Convention principally because of dissatisfaction with the deep sea bed regime.

The Deep Sea Bed Regime under the 1982 Convention

The 1982 Convention defines as the "Area" "the sea-bed and ocean floor and subsoil thereof, beyond the limits of national jurisdiction...." (Article 1(1)). All activities in the "Area" are controlled by the International Sea-Bed Authority (articles 1(2), 153, 156–158). The principal organs of the Authority are the Assembly,[42] the Council,[43] the Secretariat[44] and the Enterprise.[45] A system of "parallel access" is set up whereby either the Enterprise or a public or private entity can undertake economic development of the Area but all such entities must enter into agreements with the Authority in order to carry out any activities in the Area.

A public or private entity applying to develop a site in the Area is required to submit applications to work at two equally viable sites.[46] The Enterprise will award one site to the applicant and reserve the other site for itself or qualified applicants from developing states. This system essentially requires applicants to undertake site development work for their competitors. The applicant is also obliged to transfer any specialized technol-

42. 1982 Convention, arts. 159–60.
43. Id. arts. 161–65.
44. Id. arts. 166–69.
45. Id. art. 170 and Annex IV.
46. Id. Annex III, art. 8.

ogy used in the operation to the Enterprise and qualified developing states at reasonable rates.[47]

The transfer of technology requirement is mandatory and again requires the applicant to reveal valuable information to its competitors. The idea behind these two requirements, parallel access and technology transfer, was to provide access to the resources of the deep sea bed to developing nations, but the Convention specifies that these requirements only last for ten years once the Enterprise has begun development of the deep sea bed.[48]

There are also provisions for a heavy application fee of $500,000,[49] an annual fixed fee of not less than $1 million[50] and other complex details relating to the financial terms of the contracts to be made by the Enterprise with applicants.[51]

A number of industrialized states objected to many of the deep sea bed mining provisions. One category of objections related to the organizational structure of the various institutions created by the deep sea bed regime. The fear was that because key industrial states were not guaranteed seats on some of the constituent organs, those organs would be dominated by developing countries. The economic objections related to what was seen as discriminatory competitive advantage being given to the Enterprise at the cost of the applicants and the burden of heavy financial payments, limitations on production and revenues being distributed to developing countries.[52] It was hoped that the industrialized states would find enough advantage in the rest of the Convention to persuade them to accept the deep sea provisions, but this was not to be.

The Deep Sea Bed Regime under the 1994 Agreement

Under the auspices of the U.N. Secretary-General consultations took place to try to resolve the various objections. By the summer of 1994 an agreement had been reached to modify the deep sea bed provisions of the Convention.[53] This agreement went into force in 1996 and has been ratified by over one hundred and fifteen states. It modifies the 1982 Convention to the extent that the documents are inconsistent.[54] The new agreement alters various parts of the decision making process in certain sea bed institutions, limits the sea bed regime to the time when it becomes economically viable and then bases the regime on free-market principles. It also alters the fees and revenue structure of the Convention.[55] Interesting legal issues were raised concerning the question of

47. Id. Annex III, art. 5.
48. Id. Annex III, art. 5(7).
49. Id. Annex III, art. 13(2).
50. Id. Annex III, art 13(3).
51. Id. Annex III, art. 13.
52. See, e.g., Statement of David A. Colson, U.S. Deputy Asst. Sect. of State, Hearings before the Subcomm. on Oceanography, Gulf of Mexico, and the Outer Continental Shelf Deep Seabed Mining, 103rd Cong., 1st Sess. 37 (1994).
53. Agreement Relating to the Implementation of Part XI of the United Nations Convention on the Law of the Sea of 10 December, 1982, U.N. GAOR, 48th Sess., 101st plen. mtg., Annex, U.N. Doc. A/RES/48/263/Annex (1994), signed 28 July 1994, entered into force, 28 July 1996 reprinted at 33 I.L.M. 1309, Annex at 1313 (1994).
54. Id. art. 2.
55. See, generally, Jonathan I. Charney, Entry Into Force of the 1982 Convention on the Law of the Sea, 35 Va J. Int'l L. 381, 392–95 (1995).

whether states which had already ratified the 1982 Convention could be bound by the changes in the 1994 Agreement since the 1982 Convention's articles on amendment made no provisions for the modification procedure envisioned by the 1994 Agreement. The 1994 Agreement attempts to deal with this dilemma.[56]

Settlement of Maritime Disputes

The Convention also contains a mandatory dispute settlement mechanism for any disputes that arise out of the application or interpretation of the Convention.[57] Parties to disputes have a variety of fora in which to settle their differences. They may choose to go before the International Court of Justice if they are states,[58] or a newly created court, the International Tribunal for the Law of the Sea,[59] including a Sea-Bed Disputes Chamber,[60] or an arbitral tribunal,[61] or a specialized arbitral tribunal.[62] The International Tribunal for the Law of the Sea sits in Hamburg, Germany and is now hearing cases and issuing judgments.

Marine Pollution

Environmental law, like many other areas of law, has often made progress in the wake of crisis. The law relating to marine pollution is no exception to this rule. A series of treaties have come into existence to deal with particular problems. Three areas have been of special concern, oil spills, the dumping of various types of refuse and the release of nuclear waste. Each of these areas has generated multi-lateral and bilateral treaties and the brief descriptions below highlight some of the more important treaties.

The Convention for the Prevention of the Pollution of the Sea by Oil (OILPOL)[63] prohibited the discharge of oil at sea and gave the flag state jurisdiction to prosecute violators. These prohibitions have been extended to cover other noxious substances by the Convention for the Prevention of Pollution from Ships (MARPOL).[64]

When oil tankers ran aground and discharged large quantities of oil near a coastline, the coastal state was unsure what actions it was permitted to undertake to protect itself. In 1967, the *Torrey Canyon*, a Liberian registered tanker, ran aground off the south coast of England leaking massive amounts of oil into the sea. The British authorities bombed the tanker to minimize further damage. This incident gave rise

56. See, id. 395–400.
57. Id. Part XV.
58. Id. art. 287(b).
59. Id. art. 287(a) & Annex VI.
60. Id. art. 186–191 & Annex VI.
61. Id. art. 287(c) & Annex VII.
62. Id. art. 287(d) & Annex VIII.
63. 327 U.N.T.S. 3, 12 U.S.T. 2989, T.I.A.S. No. 4900, amended, 600 U.N.T.S. 332, 17 U.S.T. 1523, T.I.A.S. No. 6109, amended, 28 U.S.T. 1205, T.I.A.S. No. 8505, reprinted at 9 I.L.M. 1 (1970), signed on 12 May 1954, entered into force 26 July 1958.
64. U.N. Doc. MP/CONF/WP 35 (1973), reprinted at 12 I.L.M. 1319 (1973), signed on 2 Nov. 1973.

to the International Convention Relating to Intervention on the High Seas in Cases of Oil Pollution Casualties[65] which permits parties to the Convention to "take such measures on the high seas as may be necessary to prevent, mitigate or illiminate grave and imminent danger to their coastline or related interests from pollution or threat of pollution of the sea by oil, following upon a maritime casualty or acts related to such a casualty, which may reasonably be expected to result in major harmful consequences."[66]

The issue of compensation for damages caused by oil spills was addressed by the Convention on Civil Liability for Oil Pollution Damage[67] which imposes strict liability, with certain exceptions, on the vessel owners and requires compensation. An international fund was established by another Convention to provide for compensation where the polluting owner's assets proved insufficient.[68]

The Geneva Convention on the High Seas[69] requires states to take measures to prevent the dumping of radio-active waste in the sea.[70] There are also a number of conventions relating to dumping of different sorts of waste from ships and aircraft.

In 1978, another Liberian registered tanker, the *Amoco Cadiz*, foundered off the coast of Brittany, France. It released most of its cargo of 230,000 tons of crude oil. This accident proved influential in the drafting of the 1982 Convention. Part XII of the 1982 Convention contains detailed provisions on the "Protection and Preservation of the Marine Environment."[71] The obligation "to protect and preserve the marine environment"[72] is imposed on all parties and states must take measures "necessary to prevent, reduce and control pollution of the marine environment from any source...."[73] These measures include the control of pollution from vessels.[74] Enforcement of regulations can be carried out by the flag state,[75] port states[76] or coastal states.[77]

The Convention imposes obligations of "Global and Regional Co-operation,"[78] "Technical Assistance",[79] and "Monitoring and Environmental Assistance."[80] It also requires the regulation of pollution from land-based sources,[81] from sea-bed activities,[82]

65. 26 U.S.T. 765, T.I.A.S. No 8068, reprinted at 9 I.L.M. 25 (1970), signed 29 Nov. 1969, entered into force 6 May 1975.

66. Id. art. 1(1). A 1973 Protocol permits intervention for substances other than oil, reprinted at 13 I.L.M. 605(1974).

67. 973 U.N.T.S. 3, reprinted at 9 I.L.M. 45 (1970), signed 29 Nov. 1969, entered into force 19 June 1975.

68. International Convention on the Establishment of an International Fund for Compensation for Oil Pollution Damage, 1110 U.N.T.S. 47, signed 18 Dec. 1971, entered into force 16 Oct. 1978, reprinted at 11 I.L.M. 284 (1972).

69. See, *supra* note 2.

70. Id. art. 25.

71. 1982 Convention, arts. 192–237. Part XII contains provisions relating to "Marine Scientific Research," arts. 238–65.

72. Id. art. 194(1).

73. Id. art. 194(1).

74. Id. art. 211.

75. Id. art. 217.

76. Id. art. 218.

77. Id. art. 220(2).

78. Id. arts. 197–201.

79. Id. arts. 202–203.

80. Id. arts. 204–206.

81. Id. art. 207.

82. Id. art. 208.

from activities in the Area,[83] from dumping,[84] from vessels[85] and from or through the atmosphere.[86] Altogether the 1982 Convention provides an extremely comprehensive regime for the control of marine pollution.

Fishing

Before the United Nations Convention on the Law of the Sea, most nations only claimed three nautical miles of territorial sea. They could, and most did, prohibit foreign registered vessels from fishing in the territorial sea. Beyond the territorial seas, however, were the high seas which were open to all states' vessels and in which all ships were free to fish. During the twentieth century, advances in technology made the possibility of catching and refrigerating huge quantities of fish much easier. The result was a rapid depletion of fish stocks throughout the world. UNCLOS, through the Exclusive Economic Zone (EEZ), permitted coastal states the right to claim all the resources of the waters off their coasts up to two hundred nautical miles from the base lines. With this right came certain responsibilities to maintain living resources at "levels which can produce the maximum sustainable yield" UNCLOS, art. 61(3). Coastal states are required to establish a total allowable catch and either harvest the catch themselves or grant permits to other states to do so. Arts. 61–62, 69–70.

Problems arose with respect to fish that spent part of their lives within EEZ and part of their lives on the high seas. There was a fear that ships fishing on the high seas might decimate these stocks so that they would never live to return to the EEZ from which they had originated. As a result, so far seventy-five states have ratified the *Straddling Fish Stocks Agreement*[87] which seeks to manage the conservation and to limit the allowable catch of these fish.

Jurisdiction over Vessels

Nationality of Vessels

One of the pervasive problems connected with the law of the sea concerns the proper registration and control over vessels. For centuries, ships that have sought to evade the law have either shunned all registration (becoming a stateless vessel, see *infra* article 92(2) and pp. 209–214) or have found a "registration of convenience," that is they have registered in states that have the fewest regulations surrounding registration and exercise virtually no control over ships once they are registered. You may have wondered

83. Id. art. 209.
84. Id. art. 210.
85. Id. art. 211.
86. Id. art. 212.
87. Agreement for the Implementation of the Provisions of the United Nations Convention on the Law of the Sea of 10 December 1982 Relating to the Conservation and Management of Straddling Fish Stocks and Highly Migratory Fish Stocks, 2167 U.N.T.S. 88, signed, 4 Aug. 1995, entered into force, 11 Dec. 2001.

why almost every oil tanker involved in an accident is registered in Liberia, Panama or Honduras. The answer is that registration in these countries is relatively inexpensive and these states exercise much less control over their registered ships than many other states. The minimum wages for crews are far lower than minimum wages in many countries. The ship owners can, therefore, operate their ships much less expensively than if they were registered in a state with more rigorous regulations.

The 1982 Convention guarantees that "[e]very State, whether coastal or land-locked, has the right to sail ships flying its flag on the high seas." (Article 90). Article 91 describes the nationality of ships:

1. Every State shall fix the conditions for the grant of its nationality to ships, for the registration of ships in its territory, and for the right to fly its flag. Ships have the nationality of the State whose flag they are entitled to fly. There must exist a genuine link between the State and the ship.
2. Every State shall issue to ships to which it has granted the right to fly its flag documents to that effect.

Article 92 describes the status of ships:

1. Ships shall sail under the State of one flag only and, save in exceptional cases expressly provided for in international treaties or in this Convention, shall be subject to its exclusive jurisdiction on the high seas. A ship may not change its flag during a voyage or while in a port of call, save only in the case of a real transfer of ownership or change of registry.
2. A ship which sails under the flags of two or more States, using them according to convenience, may not claim any of the nationalities in question with respect to any other State, and may be assimilated to a ship without nationality.

Article 95, however provides warships with immunity from jurisdiction:

> Warships on the high seas have complete immunity from the jurisdiction of any State other than the flag State.

The articles above raised two related issues: (a) what exactly is a genuine link? and (b) what may a State do if it knows or suspects that a ship has no genuine link with the state of registration?

The Genuine Link Requirement

The 1982 Convention imposes a number of duties upon the flag state which are spelled out in article 94. In general a state is required to exercise "jurisdiction and control in administrative, technical and social matters over ships flying its flag." (article 94(1)). The state must "maintain a register of ships" and take jurisdiction over "the master, officers and crew" with respect to "administrative, technical and social matters concerning the ship." (Article 94(2)). States must "ensure safety at sea" of their ships (article 94(3)) and a detailed list of the measures to be taken to ensure safety are spelled out. (Article 94(3)(4)(5) & (7)). Clearly if all states complied with the requirements of article 94, the enforcement of the requirements would in themselves go some way to providing a genuine link between the vessel and the state of registration.

Other factors have also been looked at to determine a genuine link:

The Restatement Third § 501, Comment b states:

> "Genuine link." In general, a state has a "genuine link" entitling it to register a ship and to authorize the ship to use its flag if the ship is owned by nationals of

> the state, whether natural or juridical persons, and the state exercises effective control over the ship. In most cases a ship is owned by a corporation created by the state of registry. However, in determining whether a 'genuine link' with the state of registry exists, the following additional factors are to be taken into account: whether the officers and crew of the ship are nationals of the state; how often the ship stops in the ports of the state; and how extensive and effective is the control that the state exercises over the ship.

In 1987, during the Iran-Iraq war, Kuwait found that a number of its oil tankers were coming under fire as they crossed the Persian Gulf. The Kuwait government requested military protection from the United States (and the United Kingdom) government. Since a proportion of the oil shipped from Kuwait was destined for the U.S. market, the U.S. government agreed to provide protection for eleven ships but only if the Kuwaiti vessels were re-flagged as U.S. registered ships. The ships were Kuwaiti owned, built in Japan, with Arab and Filipino crews.

How was the re-flagging accomplished? A corporation, Chesapeake Shipping, Inc., was formed in Delaware. Its sole assets were the eleven tankers and its sole activity was to charter the tankers back to the original owner, the Kuwait Oil Tanker Company, a Kuwaiti corporation. A number of waivers were granted on "national security grounds" from U.S. safety and inspection requirements. Initially only the captain was going to be a U.S. citizen but after an outcry from the American maritime unions, the top five officers were required to be Americans.

The re-flagging of the Kuwaiti tankers caused a huge amount of criticism both from American and foreign maritime interests. After the cease fire in the Iran-Iraq war, the re-flagging was quietly dropped and the tankers reverted to their Kuwaiti registration.[88]

Remedy Where There Is No Genuine Link

Article 94(6) of the 1982 Convention provides:

> A State which has clear grounds to believe that proper jurisdiction and control with respect to a ship have not been exercised may report the facts to the flag state. Upon receiving such a report, the flag State shall investigate the matter and, if appropriate, take any action to remedy the situation.

The Restatement Third, § 501, Comment b states:

> Although international law requires a genuine link between the ship and the registering state, the lack of a genuine link does not justify another state in refusing to recognize the flag or in interfering with the ship. A state may, however, reject diplomatic protection by the flag state when the flag state has no genuine link with the ship. If another state doubts the existence of a genuine link, for instance, because there is evidence that the flag state has not been exercising its duties to control and regulate the ship (see § 502), it may request that

---

88. See, generally, Michael Isikoff, Delaware Firm is New Home of Kuwait Ships: With Whitehouse Support, Reflagging Has Sailed Through Regulatory Obstacles, The Wash. Post, July 5, 1987, at A21. See also, *Case Concerning Oil Platforms* (Iran v. U.S.) 2003 I.C.J. 161, at paras. 52ff., pp. 403–406 *infra*.

the flag state "investigate the matter and, if appropriate, take any action necessary to remedy the situation." LOS Convention, Article 94(6);....

In general only the flag state may exercise jurisdiction over its vessels on the high seas. The International Tribunal for the Law of the Sea addressed this issue in the *Saiga Case,* see case, *infra* at pp. 218–234.

QUESTIONS

1. Do you think there was a genuine link between the Kuwaiti tankers and the United States?
2. What might other nations have done if they determined that there was not a genuine link between the Kuwaiti tankers and the state of registration, the U.S.? (See *The Saiga Case*, pp. 218–234 *infra.*)
3. Suppose a Dutch ship and a re-flagged Kuwati oil tanker had collided in the Persian Gulf. The newly registered U.S. oil tanker accuses the Dutch vessel of negligence and both nations (the U.S. and the Netherlands) agree to submit the dispute to the International Court of Justice. Do you think the Dutch government could successfully reject the U.S. claim on the grounds that the U.S. had no right to represent the oil tanker at the international level? Compare, *The Nottebohm Case*(Liechtenstein v. Guatemala) 1955 I.C.J. 4., pp. 270–275, with *The Saiga Case*, (St. Vincent and the Grenadines v. Guinea) 1999 ITLOS No.2, pp. 218–234.

Prohibited Activities on the High Seas

Certain activities are prohibited on the high seas. Article 99 of the 1982 Convention prohibits the transportation of slaves and declares that any slave taking refuge on board a ship "shall *ipso facto* be free." Article 100 imposes the obligation on all states to "cooperate to the fullest extent in the repression of piracy on the high seas...." Piracy is given a highly technical definition in article 110.[89] States must also "cooperate in the suppression of illicit traffic in narcotic drugs and psychotropic substances...." (article 108) and "cooperate in the suppression of unauthorized broadcasting from the high seas." (Article 109(1)). Ships must also be registered and fly under the flag of the state of registration. (Articles 91 & 92).

What may a ship do if it comes across a vessel engaged in one of the prohibited activities?

89. "Piracy consists of any of the following acts:
(a) any illegal acts of violence or detention, or any act of depredation, committed for private ends by the crew or the passengers of a private ship or a private aircraft, and directed:
(I) on the high seas, against another ship or aircraft, or against persons or property on board such ship or aircraft;
(ii) against a ship, aircraft, persons or property in a place outside the jurisdiction of any State;
(b) any act of voluntary participation in the operation of a ship or of an aircraft with knowledge of facts making it a pirate ship or aircraft;
(c) any act of inciting or of intentionally facilitating an act described in subparagraph (a) or (b)." 1982 Convention, art. 110.

When we were examining the bases for the assertion of jurisdiction by a state, we examined the Universality Principle (see pp. 115–127). There it was stated that there are certain activities, including slavery, piracy or operating a stateless vessel, that are considered sufficiently heinous to confer universal jurisdiction on all states. In other words, any state that finds the perpetrator is authorized to apprehend, try and punish him/her, provided that the domestic laws of the particular state apprehending the suspect permit such a trial. Some scholars would add drug trafficking and hostage taking to the list. Although the 1982 Convention does not recognize this principle directly it does make certain provisions with respect to certain prohibited activities.

Article 105 provides that: "On the high seas ... every State may seize a pirate ship or aircraft ... [and] [t]he courts of the State which carried out the seizure may decide upon the penalties to be imposed...." Such seizures can only be carried out by "warships or military aircraft...." (Article 107).

Article 109 permits a number of different states the right to arrest and try those engaged in unauthorized broadcasting on the high seas: "(a) the flag state...."; "(b) the State of registry of the installation," if the broadcast is from an installation; "(c) the State of which the ... [broadcaster] is a national"; "(d) any State where the transmission can be received"; or "(e) any State where authorized radio communication is suffering interference."

With respect to narcotic trafficking, article 108 only provides that the flag state of the suspected vessel "may request the co-operation of other States to suppress such traffic."

Article 110 provides for a "right of visit" in certain circumstances:

1. Except where acts of interference derive from powers conferred by treaty, a warship which encounters on the high seas a foreign ship, other than a ship entitled to complete immunity in accordance with articles 95 and 96, is not justified in boarding it unless there is reasonable ground for suspecting that:
   (a) the ship is engaged in piracy:
   (b) the ship is engaged in the slave trade;
   (c) the ship is engaged in unauthorized broadcasting and the flag State of the warship has jurisdiction under article 109;
   (d) the ship is without nationality; or
   (e) though flying a foreign flag or refusing to show its flag, the ship is, in reality, of the same nationality as the warship.
2. In the cases provided for in paragraph 1, the warship may proceed to verify the ship's right to fly its flag. To this end, it may send a boat under the command of an officer to the suspected ship. If suspicion remains after the documents have been checked, it may proceed to a further examination on board the ship, which must be carried out with all possible consideration.
3. If the suspicions prove to be unfounded, and provided that the ship boarded has not committed any act justifying them, it shall be compensated for any loss or damage that may have been sustained.
4. These provisions apply *mutatis mutandis* to military aircraft.
5. These provisions also apply to any other duly authorized ships or aircraft clearly marked and identifiable as being on government service."

The above article obviously provides for a right of inspection in the circumstances outlined but it is not clear what powers the inspecting vessel has if its suspicions prove founded. May the inspecting ship arrest the crew and take them and the ship back to home port? May the crew be tried? If so, for what?

United States v. Garcia

182 Fed. Appx. 873 (11th Cir 2006)
cert. denied, 549 U.S. 1110 (2007)

PER CURIAM:

Adelso Torres Garcia ("Torres") and Oscar Manuel Garcia y Garcia ("Garcia") appeal their convictions for possession with intent to distribute cocaine while aboard a vessel subject to the jurisdiction of the United States. The Piracies and Felonies on the High Seas Clause of the Constitution ("the High Seas Clause") ["The Congress shall have the power to ... define and punish piracies and felonies committed on the high seas, and offenses against the law of nations;" U.S. Const. art. I, § 8, cls. 1 & 10], granted Congress the power to define and punish offenses committed on the high seas, and we have not required a nexus between the United States and offense conduct under the Maritime Drug Law Enforcement Act ("MDLEA") or its predecessor statute. We AFFIRM their convictions.

I. BACKGROUND

Torres and Garcia were indicted for, *inter alia,* possession with intent to distribute cocaine while aboard a vessel subject to the jurisdiction of the United States, in violation of 46 App. U.S.C. § 1093 (a), (g), and 21 U.S.C. § 960(b)(1) (B)(ii). R1-1 at 1–3. Garcia and Torres, who are both natives and citizens of Guatemala, were aboard the "*El Almirante,*" a Guatemalan registered boat, which the U.S. Coast Guard intercepted and boarded in international waters. The Coast Guard discovered more than 2,500 kilograms of cocaine aboard the *El Almirante.*

Garcia and codefendant Erick Armando Aguilar Ramirez filed a "Motion to Dismiss the Indictment for Lack of Subject Matter Jurisdiction"; Torres adopted the motion. R1-101, 112, 119. In the motion, Garcia argued that Congress exceeded its powers by enacting the MDLEA, under which it purported to criminalize drug smuggling by foreign nationals aboard foreign vessels. Following a hearing, the district court denied the motion. R1-140. Specifically, the district court found that Congress's enactment of the MDLEA was a constitutional exercise of power pursuant to the [High Seas] Clause, and, while the Clause did not give Congress the power to criminalize all conduct on the high seas, it also did not limit Congress's extraterritorial power as to those felonies only with a nexus to the United States. *Id.* at 2–8. The district court also found, however, that drug trafficking constituted an offense against the law of nations, and thus empowered Congress to criminalize it pursuant to the Clause. *Id.* 9–11.

Garcia and Torres subsequently entered conditional guilty pleas, reserving their rights (1) to appeal the denial of their motion to dismiss the indictment, and (2) if successful on appeal, to withdraw their pleas. Torres was sentenced to serve a term of imprisonment of 135 months, and Garcia was sentenced to serve 168 months.

On appeal, they argue that Congress exceeded its constitutional authority by punishing offenses committed in international waters by foreigners aboard a foreign vessel and that Congress's authority was limited to criminalizing certain offenses.

II. DISCUSSION

Torres contends that (1) the only source of constitutional authority for the Maritime Drug Law Enforcement Act is the High Seas Clause, which granted Congress the authority to define and punish piracy, felonies, and offenses against the law of nations committed on the high seas; (2) the meanings of "felonies" and "piracy" within the High Seas Clause are not synonymous; and (3) the authority to define and punish felonies is more limited in its extraterritorial scope than the authority to punish piracy. Appellant Torres' Brief at 4–6. Specifically, he asserts that, because piracy is the only "universal jurisdiction" offense, only piracy may be punished regardless of the nexus between the United States and the offender or the vessel. *Id.* at 6–8. Next, he argues that the purpose of the High Seas Clause was not to give Congress "general legislative authority over international waters," but to vest authority over United States vessels and nationals in the federal, rather than state, government. *Id.* at 8–9. Finally, Torres asserts that drug smuggling is not a universal jurisdiction offense because (1) it is not an international law crime, (2) it is not so shocking that it makes all jurisdictional limits moot, (3) only war crimes, genocide, and piracy are universal jurisdiction offenses, and (4) Congress, when enacting the MDLEA, did not expressly declare that it was legislating under its power to define international law offenses.

Garcia asserts that Congress has the authority to criminalize only the following offenses occurring on the high seas: (1) piracy, as universally defined; (2) felonies committed by a person aboard a stateless vessel; and (3) felonies committed by or against a United States citizen. He contends that a vessel flying a foreign flag remains under the jurisdiction of that nation, [over] which Congress has no authority to legislate. He asserts that the High Seas Clause was intended only to ensure that American citizens traveling on the high seas were subject to uniform criminal laws. Garcia also notes that those cases upholding the MDLEA's predecessor statute all dealt with stateless vessels. He then compares the nexus requirement imposed by due process principles with that imposed by the High Seas Clause, noting that they are distinct concepts and that other courts' discussions of due process requirements do not necessarily inform the analysis here. Next, Garcia argues that the "protective principle" of international law, which we have held provides a basis for the extraterritorial application of the MDLEA, also requires a nexus between the offense conduct and the United States. Appellant Garcia's Brief at 25–26. Finally, he asserts that drug smuggling is not an offense against the law of nations as it is private conduct which cannot constitute such an offense.

"We review the constitutionality of a statute *de novo.*" *United States v. Ballinger,* 395 F.3d 1218, 1225 (11th Cir. 2005) (*en banc*). The MDLEA makes it "unlawful for any person on board a vessel ... subject to the jurisdiction of the United States ... to knowingly or intentionally manufacture or distribute, or to possess with intent to manufacture or distribute, a controlled substance." 46 App. U.S.C.A. § 1903(a). A vessel subject to the jurisdiction of the United States is defined as, *inter alia,* "a vessel registered in a foreign nation where the flag nation has consented or waived objection to the enforcement of United States law by the United States." Id. At § 1903(c)(1)(C).

The High Seas Clause grants Congress the power "[t]o define and punish Piracies and Felonies committed on the high Seas, and Offences against the Law of Nations." U.S. Const. art I, § 8, cl. 10. While we have not addressed the precise question raised here and while there is little case law interpreting the scope of the High Seas Clause, other circuits have upheld the constitutionality of the MDLEA. Without specifically discussing the High Seas Clause's limits, the Ninth Circuit held that the MDLEA was a constitutional exercise of Congressional power pursuant to the High Seas Clause. *United States v. Moreno-Morillo*, 334 F.3d 819, 824 (9th Cir. 2003) (citing *United States v. Davis,* 905 F.2d 245, 248 (9th Cir. 1990), and *United States v. Aikins,* 946 F.2d 608, 613 (9th Cir. 1990)). The Third Circuit also held that the High Seas Clause provided Congress with the authority to enact the MDLEA and criminalize drug trafficking on the high seas, regardless of whether a nexus to the United States existed. *United States v. Martinez-Hidalgo,* 993 F.2d 1052, 1056 (3rd Cir. 1993).

We have previously rejected the argument that the MDLEA is unconstitutional because the conduct at issue lacks a nexus to the United States. *United States v. Rendon,* 354 F.3d 1320, 1325 (11th Cir. 2003), *cert. denied,* 541 U.S. 1035, 124 S.Ct. 2110, 158 L.Ed. 2d 720 (2004); see also *United States v. Marino-Garcia,* 679 F.2d 1373, 1383 (11th Cir. 1982) (holding that the predecessor statute to § 1903, 21 U.S.C. § 955a, did not require a nexus between stateless vessels and the United States). We have also observed that Congress has power to enact legislation pursuant to the "protective principle" of international law. *United States v. Gonzalez,* 776 F.2d 931, 939 (11th Cir. 1985). "Universal jurisdiction is a doctrine of international law allowing states to define and punish certain crimes considered to be of 'universal concern.'" *Herero People's Reparations Corp. v. Deutsche Bank,* A.G., 370 F.3d 1192, 1196 (D. C. Cir.), *cert. denied,* 543 U.S. 987, 125 S. Ct. 508, 160 L.Ed. 2d 371 (2004). In contrast, the protective principle "permits a nation to assert jurisdiction over a person whose conduct outside the nation's territory threatens the nation's security or could potentially interfere with the operation of its governmental functions." *Gonzalea,* 776 F.2d at 938. "The protective principle does not require that there be proof of an actual or intended effect inside the United States. The conduct may be forbidden if it has a potentially adverse effect and is generally recognized as a crime by nations that have reasonably developed legal systems." *Id.* at 939. Congress enacted the MDLEA because drug trafficking aboard vessels (1) "is a serious international problem and is universally condemned" and (2) "presents a specific threat to the security and societal well-being of the United States."46 App. U.S.C. § 1902. For these reasons, Congress could properly enact the MDLEA under the Constitution.

III. CONCLUSION

Because the High Seas Clause granted Congress the power to define and punish offenses committed on the high seas and because we have not required a nexus between the United States and the offense conduct under the MDLEA or its predecessor statute, we affirm the district court. [Convictions] [a]ffirmed.

QUESTIONS

1. What gave the U.S. coast guard the right to arrest Guatelman citizens sailing on the high seas in a Guatemalan registered ship? (Note: although the court states that the U.S. Coast Guard could subject a foreign vessel on the high seas to U.S. authority where the state of registration either granted permission or waived objection, the court does not find that Guatemala had consented or waived objection here).
2. Suppose the countries from which the "El Almirante"came and the countries to which she intended to travel did not prohibit shipment or use of cocaine. Why should the United States be allowed to try Garcia, Torres and Ramirez for the possession with intent to distribute cocaine when there was no evidence that they intended to distribute cocaine in the United States?
3. Suppose a coast guard vessel from a fundamentalist Muslim country that completely bans all liquor came across a U.S. vessel on the high seas. Suppose that the U.S. vessel embarked from Boston and was sailing to London, U.K. with the usual amount of liquor on board for consumption by the crew and

passengers. Could the coast guard vessel from the liquor banning country arrest the U.S. crew and try them for possession of intoxicating liquors with the intent to distribute?

Article 97 makes it clear that in the event of a collision on the high seas only the flag state or the state of nationality of the master or other responsible crew member may institute penal or disciplinary proceedings. This article effectively reversed a decision made in 1927 by the Permanent Court of International Justice. In the *Case of the S.S. Lotus*,[89] the Permanent Court had ruled that there was no rule of international law that prohibited Turkey from asserting penal jurisdiction over the French officer on watch on a French registered vessel after the French vessel and a Turkish vessel had collided on the high seas sinking the Turkish ship and killing eight Turkish nationals. This decision, which was decided by a split vote, eight to seven, provoked widespread criticism.

Jurisdiction over Foreign Vessels

Internal Waters and Ports

States may assert jurisdiction over foreign vessels in their internal waters on the basis of the Territorial Principle (see pp. 101–105). The Restatement Third, § 512, Comment c states: "the coastal state may exercise jurisdiction with respect to a ship in port and over activities on board such ship, but in practice coastal states usually have little interest in exercising jurisdiction over such activities, except when the peace of the port is disturbed." With respect to foreign vessels in port the coastal state would generally rather have the master of the ship or the flag state exercise jurisdiction over foreign vessels but there are exceptions to this disinclination to exercise jurisdiction.

Wildenhus' Case

120 U.S. 1 (1887)

Note

In this case, a Belgian registered ship had docked at Jersey City, New Jersey, U.S.A. While there, a member of the crew killed another member of the crew below decks. Both were Belgian nationals. The local police arrested crew member Wildenhus and charged him with homicide. The Belgian consul objected to the arrest and pointed to the bi-lateral treaty of March 9, 1880, entered into between Belgium and the United States, which provide that with respect to the internal order of merchant vessels docked in each other's ports,

> [t]he local authorities shall not interfere except when the disorder that has arisen is of such a nature as to disturb tranquility and public order on shore, or

89. (France v. Turkey) 1927 P.C.I.J. (ser. A.) No. 10.

in the port, or when a person of the country or not belonging to the crew shall be concerned therein.

Opinion of the Court: Waite, C.J.

* * *

[T]he only important question left for our determination is whether the thing which has been done—the disorder that has arisen—on board this vessel is of a nature to disturb the public peace, or, as some writers term it, the "public respose," of the people who look to the state of New Jersey for their protection. If the thing done—"the disorder," as it is called in the treaty—is of a character to affect those on shore or in the port when it becomes known, the fact that only those on the ship saw it when it was done, is a matter of no moment. Those who are not on the vessel pay no special attention to the mere disputes or quarrels of the seamen while on board, whether they occur under deck or above. Neither do they, as a rule, care for anything done on board which relates only to the discipline of the ship, or to the preservation of order and authority. Not so, however, with crimes which from their gravity awaken a public interest as soon as they become known, and especially those of a character which every civilized nation considers itself bound to provide a severe punishment for when committed within its own jurisdiction. In such cases inquiry is certain to be instituted at once to ascertain how or why the thing was done, and the popular excitement rises or falls as the news spreads, and the facts become known. It is not alone the publicity of the act, or the noise and clamor which attends it, that fixes the nature of the crime, but the act, itself. If that is of a character to awaken public interest when it becomes known, it is a "disorder," the nature of which is to affect the community at large, and consequently to invoke the power of the local government whose people have been disturbed by what was done. The very nature of such an act is to disturb the quiet of a peaceful community, and to create, in the language of the treaty, a "disorder" which will "disturb tranquillity [sic] and public order on shore or in the port." The principle which governs the whole matter is this: Disorders which disturb only the peace of the ship or those on board are to be dealt with exclusively by the sovereignty of the home of the ship, but those which disturb the public peace may be suppressed, and, if need be, the offenders punished, by the proper authorities of the local jurisdiction. It may not be easy at all times to determine to which of the two jurisdictions a particular act of disorder belongs. Much will undoubtedly depend on the attending circumstances of the particular case, but all must concede that felonious homicide is a subject for the local jurisdiction; and that, if the proper authorities are proceeding with the case in a regular way the consul has no right to interfere to prevent it.

* * *

The judgment of the circuit court is affirmed.

QUESTION

Do you think it likely that at the end of the nineteen century the people of Jersey City were in fact disturbed by the news that one Belgian crew member had killed another Belgian crew member on board a Belgian ship while in port?

By the time the *Wildenhus* case was decided the rule was fairly certain that murder would be interpreted to disturb the peace of the port and that almost no other acts would be considered sufficiently grave to trigger local jurisdiction.

The Territorial Sea

The 1982 Convention makes it clear that the coastal state's sovereignty extends to the territorial sea (article 2(1) & (2)) but that the sovereignty has to be exercised pursuant to the Convention and other rules of international law (article 2(3)). Foreign ships are given a right of innocent passage through the territorial sea (article 17) and we have already discussed what a state may do when it suspects a foreign ship is violating its right of innocent passage (see pp. 172–180).

The coastal state is free to extend its laws to the territorial sea and to the extent that it does so, ships that violate those laws are subject to arrest but with rather large exceptions carved out by the 1982 Convention. Article 27 provides:

> **Criminal jurisdiction on board a foreign ship**
>
> 1. The criminal jurisdiction of the coastal State should not be exercised on board a foreign ship passing through the territorial sea to arrest any person or to conduct any investigation in connection with any crime committed on board the ship during its passage, save only in the following cases:
>
> (a) if the consequences of the crime extend to the coastal State;
>
> (b) if the crime is of a kind to disturb the peace of the country or the good order of the territorial sea;
>
> (c) if the assistance of the local authorities has been requested by the master of the ship or by a diplomatic agent or consular officer of the flag State; or
>
> (d) if such measures are necessary for the suppression of illicit traffic in narcotic drugs or psychotropic substances.
>
> 2. The above provisions do not affect the right of the coastal State to take any steps authorized by its laws for the purpose of an arrest or investigation on board a foreign ship passing through the territorial sea after leaving internal waters.
>
> 3. In the cases provided for in paragraphs 1 and 2, the coastal State shall, if the master so requests, notify a diplomatic agent or consular officer of the flag State before taking any steps, and shall facilitate contact between such agent or officer and the ship's crew. In cases of emergency this notification may be communicated while the measures are being taken.
>
> 4. In considering whether or in what manner an arrest should be made, the local authorities shall have due regard to the interests of navigation.
>
> 5. Except as provided in Part XII or with respect to violations of laws and regulations adopted in accordance with Part V, the coastal State may not take any steps on board a foreign ship passing through the territorial sea to arrest any person or to conduct any investigation in connection with any crime committed before the ship entered the territorial sea, if the ship, proceeding from a foreign port, is only passing through the territorial sea without entering internal waters.

In general then, the coastal state may not assert its criminal jurisdiction over foreign vessels passing through its territorial sea, with the few exceptions noted above.

With respect to civil jurisdiction, Article 28 provides:

Civil jurisdiction in relation to foreign ships

1. The coastal State should not stop or divert a foreign ship passing through the territorial sea for the purpose of exercising civil jurisdiction in relation to a person on board the ship.

2. The coastal State may not levy execution against or arrest the ship for the purpose of any civil proceedings, save only in respect of obligations or liabilities assumed or incurred by the ship itself in the course or for the purpose of its voyage through the waters of the coastal State.

3. Paragraph 2 is without prejudice to the right of the coastal State, in accordance with its laws, to levy execution against or to arrest, for the purpose of any civil proceedings, a foreign ship lying in the territorial sea, or passing through the territorial sea after leaving internal waters.

Again, the power of the coastal state to assert civil jurisdiction over foreign vessels or persons aboard such vessels passing through the territorial sea is extremely limited.

The Right of Hot Pursuit

If a coastal state proclaims an exclusive economic zone of two hundred nautical miles and prohibits all fishing by foreign vessels in the zone but the coast guard finds a foreign vessel fishing within the zone, what may the coastal state authorities do?

Article 111 provides for the right of hot pursuit from the various zones created by the 1982 Convention.

Right of hot pursuit

1. The hot pursuit of a foreign ship may be undertaken when the competent authorities of the coastal State have good reason to believe that the ship has violated the laws and regulations of that State. Such pursuit must be commenced when the foreign ship or one of its boats is within the internal waters, the archipelagic waters, the territorial sea or the contiguous zone of the pursuing State, and may only be continued outside the territorial sea or the contiguous zone if the pursuit has not been interrupted. It is not necessary that, at the time when the foreign ship within the territorial sea or the contiguous zone receives the order to stop, the ship giving the order should likewise be within the territorial sea or the contiguous zone. If the foreign ship is within a contiguous zone, as defined in article 33, the pursuit may only be undertaken if there has been a violation of the rights for the protection of which the zone was established.

2. The right of hot pursuit shall apply *mutatis mutandis* to violations in the exclusive economic zone or on the continental shelf, including safety zones around continental shelf installations, of the laws and regulations of the coastal State applicable in accordance with this Convention to the exclusive economic zone or the continental shelf, including such safety zones.

3. The right of hot pursuit ceases as soon as the ship pursued enters the territorial sea of its own State or of a third State.

4. Hot pursuit is not deemed to have begun unless the pursuing ship has satisfied itself by such practicable means as may be available that the ship pursued or one of its boats or other craft working as a team and using the ship pursued

as a mother ship is within the limits of the territorial sea, or, as the case may be, within the contiguous zone or the exclusive economic zone or above the continental shelf. The pursuit may only be commenced after a visual or auditory signal to stop has been given at a distance which enables it to be seen or heard by the foreign ship.

5. The right of hot pursuit may be exercised only by warships or military aircraft, or other ships or aircraft clearly marked and identifiable as being on government service and authorized to that effect.

6. Where hot pursuit is effected by an aircraft:

(a) the provisions of paragraphs 1 to 4 shall apply *mutatis mutandis*;

(b) the aircraft giving the order to stop must itself actively pursue the ship until a ship or another aircraft of the coastal State, summoned by the aircraft, arrives to take over the pursuit, unless the aircraft is itself able to arrest the ship. It does not suffice to justify an arrest outside the territorial sea that the ship was merely sighted by the aircraft as an offender or suspected offender, if it was not both ordered to stop and pursued by the aircraft itself or other aircraft or ships which continue the pursuit without interruption.

7. The release of a ship arrested within the jurisdiction of a State and escorted to a port of that State for the purposes of an inquiry before the competent authorities may not be claimed solely on the ground that the ship, in the course of its voyage, was escorted across a portion of the exclusive economic zone or the high seas, if the circumstances rendered this necessary.

8. Where a ship has been stopped or arrested outside the territorial sea in circumstances which do not justify the exercise of the right of hot pursuit, it shall be compensated for any loss or damage that may have been thereby sustained.

QUESTION

Could the coast guard have relied upon hot pursuit in *United States v. Conroy*, pp. 187–191? (Careful, this may be a trick question).

The Saiga Case

(St. Vincent and the Grenadines v. Guinea)
1999 International Tribunal for the Law of the Sea (ITLOS) No. 2

* * *

Factual background

31. The *Saiga* is an oil tanker. At the time of its arrest on 28 October 1997, it was owned by Tabona Shipping Company Ltd. of Nicosia, Cyprus, and managed by Seascot Shipmanagement Ltd. of Glasgow, Scotland. The ship was chartered to Lemania Shipping Group Ltd. of Geneva, Switzerland. The *Saiga* was provisionally registered in Saint Vincent and the Grenadines on 12 March 1997. The Master and crew of the ship were all of Ukranian nationality. There were also three Senegalese nationals who were employed as painters. The *Saiga* was engaged in selling gas oil as bunker and occasionally water to

fishing and other vessels off the coast of West Africa. The owner of the cargo of gas oil on board was Addax BV of Geneva, Switzerland.

32. Under the command of Captain Orlov, the *Saiga* left Dakar, Senegal, on 24 October 1997 fully laden with approximately 5,400 metric tons of gas oil. On 27 October 1997, between 0400 and 1400 hours and at a point 10°25'03"N and 15°42'06"W, the *Saiga* supplied gas oil to three fishing vessels, the *Giuseppe Primo* and the *Kriti*, both flying the flag of Senegal, and the *Eleni S*, flying the flag of Greece. This point was approximately 22 nautical miles from Guinea's island of Alcatraz. All three fishing vessels were licensed by Guinea to fish in its exclusive economic zone. The *Saiga* then sailed in a southerly direction supply gas oil to other fishing vessels at a pre-arranged place. Upon instructions from the owner of the cargo in Geneva, it later changed course and sailed towards another location beyond the southern border of the exclusive economic zone of Guinea.

33. At 0800 hours on 28 October 1997, the *Saiga*, according to its log book, was at a point 09°00'01"N and 14°58'58"W. It had been drifting since 0420 hours while awaiting the arrival of fishing vessels to which it was to supply gas oil. This point was south of the southern limit of the exclusive economic zone of Guinea. At about 0900 hours the *Saiga* was attacked by a Guinean patrol boat (P35). Officers from that boat and another Guinean patrol boat (P328) subsequently boarded the ship and arrested it. On the same day, the ship and its crew were brought to Conakry, Guinea, where its Master was detained. The travel documents of the members of the crew were taken from them by the authorities of Guinea and armed guards were placed on board the ship. On 1 November 1997, two injured persons from the *Saiga*, Mr. Sergey Klyuyev and Mr. Djibril Niasse, were permitted to leave Conakry for Dakar for medical treatment. Between 10 and 12 November 1997, the cargo of gas oil on board the ship, amounting to 4,941.322 metic tons, was discharged on the orders of the Guinean authorities. Seven members of the crew and two painters left Conakry on 17 November 1997, one crew member left on 14 December 1997 and six on 12 January 1998. The Master and six crew members remained in Conakry until the ship was released on 28 February 1998.

34.... The criminal charges against the Master were specified in a schedule of summons (*cédule de citation)*, issued on 10 December 1997 under the authority of the Public Prosecutor (*Procureur de la République*), which additionally named the State of Saint Vincent and the Grenadines as civilly responsible to be summoned (*civilement responsable à citer*). Criminal proceedings were subsequently instituted by the Guinean authorities against the Master before the Tribunal of First Instance (*tribunal de première instance)* in Conakry.

35. On 13 November 1997, Saint Vincent and the Grenadines submitted to this Tribunal a Request for the prompt release of the *Saiga* and its crew under article 292 of the Convention. On 4 December 1997, the Tribunal delivered Judgment on the Request. The judgment ordered that Guinea promptly release the *Saiga* and its crew upon the posting of a reasonable bond or security by Saint Vincent and the Grenadines. The security consisted of the gas oil discharged from the *Saiga* by the authorities of Guinea plus an amount of US$ 400,000 to be posted in the form of a letter of credit or bank guarantee or, if agreed by the parties, in any other form.

36. On 17 December 1997, judgment was rendered by the Tribunal of First Instance in Conakry against the Master. The Tribunal of First Instance cited, as the basis of the charges against the Master, articles 111 and 242 of the Convention, articles 361 and 363 of the Penal Code of Guinea (hereinafter "the Penal Code"), article 40 of the Merchant Marine Code of Guinea (hereinafter the "Merchant Marine Code"), articles 34, 316 and

317 of the Customs Code of Guinea (hereinafter "the Customs Code") and articles 1 and 8 of Law L/94/007/CTRN of 15 March 1994 concerning the fight against fraud covering the import, purchase and sale of fuel in the Republic of Guinea (hereinafter "Law L/94/007"). The charge against the Master was that he had "imported, without declaring it, merchandise that is taxable on entering national Guinean territory, in this case diesel oil, and that he refused to comply with injunctions by Agents of the Guinean Navy, thus committing the crimes of contraband, fraud and tax evasion."

37. The Tribunal of First Instance in Conakry found the Master guilty as charged and imposed on him a fine of 15,354,024,040 Guinean francs. It also ordered the confiscation of the vessel and its cargo as a guarantee for payment of the penalty.

38. The Master appealed to the Court of Appeal *(cour d'appel)* in Conakry against his conviction by the Tribunal of First Instance. On 3 February 1998, judgment was rendered by the Court of Appeal. The Court of Appeal found the Master guilty of the offence of "illegal import, buying and selling of fuel in the Republic of Guinea" which it stated was punishable under Law L/94/007. The Court of Appeal imposed a suspended sentence of six months imprisonment on the Master, a fine of 15,354,040,000 Guinean francs and ordered that all fees and expenses be at his expense. It also ordered the confiscation of the cargo and the seizure of the vessel as a guarantee for payment of the fine.

39. On 11 March 1998, the Tribunal delivered the Order prescribing provisional measures, referred to in paragraph 8. Prior to the issue of its Order, the Tribunal was informed, by a letter dated 4 March 1998 sent on behalf of the Agent of Saint Vincent and the Grenadines, that the *Saiga* had been released from detention and had arrived safely in Dakar, Senegal. According to the Deed of Release signed by the Guinean authorities and the Master, the release was in execution of the Judgment of the Tribunal of 4 December 1997.

Jurisdiction

40. There is no disagreement between the parties regarding the jurisdiction of the Tribunal in the present case. Nevertheless, the Tribunal must satisfy itself that it has jurisdiction to deal with the case as submitted.

41. As stated in paragraph 1, the dispute was originally submitted by the Notification of 22 December 1997 to an arbitral tribunal to be constituted in accordance with Annex VII to the Convention. The parties subsequently agreed, by the 1998 Agreement, to transfer the dispute to the Tribunal. The 1998 Agreement provides, in paragraph 1, that "the dispute shall be deemed to have been submitted to the International Tribunal for the Law of the Sea on the 22 December 1997, the date of the Notification by St. Vincent and the Grenadines."

42. The Tribunal, in its Order dated 20 February 1998, stated that, having regard to the 1998 Agreement and article 287 of the Convention, it was "satisfied that Saint Vincent and the Grenadines and Guinea have agreed to submit the dispute to it".

43. The Tribunal finds that the basis of its jurisdiction in this case is the 1998 Agreement, which transferred the dispute to the Tribunal, together with articles 286, 287 and 288 of the Convention.

* * *

45. Accordingly, the Tribunal finds that it has jurisdiction over the dispute as submitted to it.

* * *

Challenges to admissibility

Registration of the *Saiga*

55. The first objection raised by Guinea to the admissibility of the claims set out in the application is that Saint Vincent and the Grenadines does not have legal standing to bring claims in connection with the measures taken by Guinea against the *Saiga*. The reason given by Guinea for its contention is that on the day of its arrest the ship was "not validly registered under the flag of Saint Vincent and the Grenadines" and that, consequently, Saint Vincent and the Grenadines is not legally competent to present claims either on its behalf or in respect of the ship, its Master and the other members of the crew, its owners or its operators.

56. This contention of Guinea is challenged by Saint Vincent and the Grenadines on several grounds.

57. The facts relating to the registration of the *Saiga*, as they emerge from the evidence produced before the Tribunal, are as follows:

(a) The *Saiga* was registered provisionally on 12 March 1997 as a Saint Vincent and the Grenadines ship under section 36 of the Merchant Shipping Act of 1982 of Saint Vincent and the Grenadines (hereinafter "the Merchant Shipping Act"). The Provisional Certificate of Registration issued to the ship on 14 April 1997 stated that it was issued by the Commissioner for Maritime Affairs of Saint Vincent and the Grenadines on behalf of the Government of Saint Vincent and the Grenadines under the terms of the Merchant Shipping Act. The Certificate stated: "This Certificate expires on 12 September 1997."

(b) The registration of the ship was recorded in the Registry Book of Saint Vincent and the Grenadines on 26 March 1997. The entry stated: "Valid thru: 12/09/1997".

(c) A Permanent Certificate of Registration was issued on 28 November 1997 by the Commissioner for Maritime Affairs of Saint Vincent and the Grenadines on behalf of that State. The Certificate stated: "This Certificate is permanent."

58. Guinea contends that the ship was unregistered between 12 September 1997 and 28 November 1997 because the Provisional Certificate of Registration expired on 12 September 1997 and the Permanent Certificate of Registration was issued on 28 November 1997. From this Guinea concludes: "It is thus very clear that the MV 'SAIGA was not validly registered' in the time period between 12 September 1997 and 28 November 1997. For this reason, the MV 'SAIGA' may [be] qualified to be **a ship without nationality** at the time of its attack." Guinea also questioned whether the ship had been deleted from the Maltese Register where it was previously registered.

59. Saint Vincent and the Grenadines controverts Guinea's assertion that the expiry of the Provisional Certificate of Registration implies that the ship was not registered or that it lost the nationality of Saint Vincent and the Grenadines. It argues that when a vessel is registered under its flag "it remains so registered until deleted from the registry". It notes that the conditions and procedures for deletion of ships from its Registry are set out in Part l, sections 9 to 42 and 59 to 61, of the Merchant Shipping Act, and emphasizes that none of these procedures was at any time applied to the *Saiga*. In support of its claim, Saint Vincent and the Grenadines refers to the declaration dated 27

October 1998 by the Commissioner for Maritime Affairs of Saint Vincent and the Grenadines which states that the ship was registered under the Saint Vincent and the Grenadines flag on 12 March 1997 "and is still today validly registered".

60. Saint Vincent and the Grenadines further contends that, under the Merchant Shipping Act, a ship does not lose Vincentian nationality because of the expiry of its provisional certificate of registration. In support of its contentions, Saint Vincent and the Grenadines refers to section 36(2) of the Merchant Shipping Act which states that a provisional certificate "shall have the same effect as the ordinary certificate of registration until the expiry of one year from the date of its issue". Saint Vincent and the Grenadines argues that, pursuant to this provision, a provisional certificate of registration remains in force until the expiry of one year from the date of its issue. In further support for this contention, Saint Vincent and the Grenadines points out that, under section 36 (3)(d) of the Merchant Shipping Act, payment of "the annual fee for one year" is required when an application is made for provisional registration. It further maintains that, just as a person would not lose nationality when his or her passport expires, a vessel would not cease to be registered merely because of the expiry of a provisional certificate. According to Saint Vincent and the Grenadines, the provisional certificate, like a passport, is evidence, but not the source, of national status. For these reasons, Saint Vincent and the Grenadines contends that the Provisional Certificate in this case remained in force after 12 September 1997 and at all times material to the present dispute. With regard to the question raised by Guinea concerning the previous registration of the ship, Saint Vincent and the Grenadines stated that its authorities had received from the owner of the ship "satisfactory evidence that the ship's registration in the country of last registration had been closed" as required by section 37 of the Merchant Shipping Act.

61. Guinea argues that automatic extensions of a provisional certificate of registration is neither provided for nor envisaged under the Merchant Shipping Act. In this connection, it argues that the declarations by the Commissioner for Maritime Affairs of 27 October 1998 and the Deputy Commissioner for Maritime Affairs of 1 March 1999, to the effect the *Saiga* "remained validly registered in the Register of Ships of Saint Vincent & the Grenadines as at 27th October 1997" do not suffice to fill the gap in registration between 12 September 1997 and 28 November 1997, when the Permanent Certificate of Registration of the *Saiga* was issued. It further argues that these declarations on the registration status cannot be accepted as independent documentary evidence in the context of the present proceedings. According to Guinea, the *Saiga's* registration could only have continued after the expiry of its Provisional Certificate if the Provisional Certificate had been replaced with another provisional certificate or its expiry date had been extended. Guinea points out that there is no evidence that any such action was taken after the Provisional Certificate expired. It states that a comparison of a provisional certificate of registration of a ship with a person's passport is misplaced, since a ship acquires nationality by registration and is required to have a certificate, while a person's nationality does not depend on the acquisition or retention of a passport. For these reasons, Guinea maintains that the *Saiga* did not have the nationality of Saint Vincent and the Grenadines during the period between the expiry of the Provisional Certificate on 12 September 1997 and the issue of the Permanent Certificate on 28 November 1997.

62. The question for consideration is whether the *Saiga* had the nationality of Saint Vincent and the Grenadines at the time of its arrest. The relevant provision of the Convention is article 91, which reads as follows

Article 91
Nationality of ships

1. Every State shall fix the conditions for the grant of its nationality to ships, for the registration of ships in its territory, and for the right to fly its flag. Ships have the nationality of the State whose flag they are entitled to fly. There must exist a genuine link between the State and the ship.

2. Every State shall issue to ships to which it has granted the right to fly its flag documents to that effect.

63. Article 91 leaves to each State exclusive jurisdiction over the granting of its nationality to ships. In this respect, article 91 codifies a well-established rule of general international law. Under this article, it is for Saint Vincent and the Grenadines to fix the conditions for the grant of its nationality to ships, for the registration of ships in its territory and for the right to fly its flag. These matters are regulated by a State in its domestic law. Pursuant to article 91, paragraph 2, Saint Vincent and the Grenadines is under an obligation to issue to ships to which it has granted the right to fly its flag documents to that effect. The issue of such documents is regulated by domestic law.

64. International law recognizes several modalities for the grant of nationality to different types of ships. In the case of merchant ships, the normal procedure used by States to grant nationality is registration in accordance with domestic legislation adopted for that purpose. This procedure is adopted by Saint Vincent and the Grenadines in the Merchant Shipping Act.

65. Determination of the criteria and establishment of the procedures for granting and withdrawing nationality to ships are matters within the exclusive jurisdiction of the flag State. Nevertheless, disputes concerning such matters may be subject to the procedures under Part XV of the Convention, especially in cases where issues of interpretation or application of provisions of the Convention are involved.

66. The Tribunal considers that the nationality of a ship is a question of fact to be determined, like other facts in dispute before it, on the basis of evidence adduced by the parties.

67. Saint Vincent and the Grenadines has produced evidence before the Tribunal to support its assertion that the *Saiga* was a ship entitled to fly its flag at the time of the incident giving rise to the dispute. In addition to making references to the relevant provisions of the Merchant Shipping Act, Saint Vincent and the Grenadines has drawn attention to several indications of Vincentian nationality on the ship or carried on board. These include the inscription of "Kingstown" as the port of registry on the stern of the vessel, the documents on board and the ship's seal which contained the words "SAIGA Kingstown" and the then current charter-party which recorded the flag of the vessel as "Saint Vincent and the Grenadines".

68. The evidence adduced by Saint Vincent and the Grenadines has been reinforced by its conduct. Saint Vincent and the Grenadines has at all times material to the dispute operated on the basis that the *Saiga* was a ship of its nationality. It has acted as the flag State of the ship during all phases of the proceedings. It was in that capacity that it invoked the jurisdiction of the Tribunal in its Application for the prompt release of the *Saiga* and its crew under article 292 of the Convention and in its Request for the prescription of provisional measures under article 290 of the Convention.

69. As far as Guinea is concerned, the Tribunal cannot fail to note that it did not challenge or raise any doubts about the registration or nationality of the ship at any time

until the submission of its Counter-Memorial in October 1998. Prior to this, it was open to Guinea to make inquiries regarding the registration of the *Saiga* or documentation relating to it. For example, Guinea could have inspected the Register of Ships of Saint Vincent and the Grenadines. Opportunities for raising doubts about the registration or nationality of the ship were available during the proceedings for prompt release in November 1997 and for the prescription of provisional measures in February 1998. It is also pertinent to note that the authorities of Guinea named Saint Vincent and the Grenadines as civilly responsible to be summoned in the schedule of summons by which the Master was charged before the Tribunal of First Instance in Conakry. In the ruling of the Court of Appeal, Saint Vincent and the Grenadines was stated to be the flag State of the *Saiga*.

70. With regard to the previous registration of the *Saiga*, the Tribunal notes the statement made by Saint Vincent and the Grenadines in paragraph 60. It considers this statement to be sufficient.

71. The Tribunal recalls that, in its Judgment of 4 December 1997 and in its Order of 11 March 1998, the *Saiga* is described as a ship flying the flag of Saint Vincent and the Grenadines.

72. On the basis of the evidence before it, the Tribunal finds that Saint Vincent and the Grenadines has discharged the initial burden of establishing that the *Saiga* had Vincentian nationality at the time it was arrested by Guinea. Guinea had therefore to prove its contention that the ship was not registered in or did not have the nationality of Saint Vincent and the Grenadines at that time. The Tribunal considers that the burden has not been discharged and that it has not been established that the *Saiga* was not registered in or did not have the nationality of Saint Vincent and the Grenadines at the time of the arrest.

73. The Tribunal concludes:

(a) it has not been established that the Vincentian registration or nationality of the *Saiga* was extinguished in the period between the date on which the Provisional Certificate of Registration was stated to expire and the date of issue of the Permanent Certificate of Registration;

(b) in the particular circumstances of this case, the consistent conduct of Saint Vincent and the Grenadines provides sufficient support for the conclusion that the *Saiga* retained the registration and the nationality of Saint Vincent and the Grenadines at all times material to dispute;

(c) in view of Guinea's failure to question the assertion of Saint Vincent and the Grenadines that it is the flag State of the *Saiga* when it had every reasonable opportunity to do so and its other conduct in the case, Guinea cannot successfully challenge the registration and nationality of the *Saiga* at this stage;

(d) in the particular circumstances of this case, it would not be consistent with justice if the Tribunal were to decline to deal with the merits of the dispute.

74. For the above reasons, the Tribunal rejects Guinea's objection to the admissibility of the claims of Saint Vincent and the Grenadines based on the ground that the *Saiga* was not registered in Saint Vincent and the Grenadines at the time of its arrest and that, consequently, the *Saiga* did not have Vincentian nationality at that time.

Genuine link

75. The next objection to admissibility raised by Guinea is that there was no genuine link between the *Saiga* and Saint Vincent and the Grenadines. Guinea contends that

"without a genuine link between Saint Vincent and the Grenadines and the M/V '*Saiga*', Saint Vincent and the Grenadines' claim concerning a violation of its right of navigation and the status of the ship is not admissible before the Tribunal vis-à-vis Guinea, because Guinea is not bound to recognise the Vincentian nationality of the M/V '*Saiga*', which forms a prerequisite for the mentioned claim in international law".

76. Guinea further argues that a State cannot fulfil its obligations as a flag State under the Convention with regard to a ship unless it exercises prescriptive and enforcement jurisdiction over the owner or, as the case may be, the operator of the ship. Guinea contends that, in the absence of such jurisdiction, there is no genuine link between the ship and Saint Vincent and the Grenadines and that, accordingly, it is not obliged to recognize the claims of Saint Vincent and the Grenadines in relation to the ship.

77. Saint Vincent and the Grenadines maintains that there is nothing in the Convention to support the contention that the existence of a genuine link between a ship and a State is a necessary precondition for the grant of nationality to the ship, or that the absence of such a genuine link deprives a flag State of the right to bring an international claim against another State in respect of illegal measures taken against the ship.

78. Saint Vincent and the Grenadines also challenges the assertion of Guinea that there was no genuine link between the *Saiga* and Saint Vincent and the Grenadines. It claims that the requisite genuine link existed between it and the ship. Saint Vincent and the Grenadines calls attention to various facts which, according to it, provide evidence of this link. These include the fact that the owner of the *Saiga* is represented in Saint Vincent and the Grenadines by a company formed and established in that State and the fact that the Saiga is subject to the supervision of the Vincentian authorities to secure compliance with the International Convention for the Safety of Life at Sea (SOLAS), 1960 and 1974, the International Convention for the Prevention of Pollution from Ships, 1973, as modified by the Protocol of 1978 relating thereto (MARPOL 73/78), and other conventions of the International Maritime Organization to which Saint Vincent and the Grenadines is a party. In addition, Saint Vincent and the Grenadines maintains that arrangements have been made to secure regular supervision of the vessel's seaworthiness through surveys, on at least an annual basis, conducted by reputable classification societies authorized for that purpose by Saint Vincent and the Grenadines. Saint Vincent and the Grenadines also points out that, under its laws, preference is given to Vincentian nationals in the manning of ships flying its flag. It further draws attention to the vigorous efforts made by its authorities to secure the protection of the *Saiga* on the international plane before and throughout the present dispute.

79. Article 91, paragraph 1, of the Convention provides: "There must exist a genuine link between the State and the ship." Two questions need to be addressed in this connection. The first is whether the absence of a genuine link between a flag State and a ship entitles another State to refuse to recognize the nationality of the ship. The second question is whether or not a genuine link existed between the *Saiga* and Saint Vincent and the Grenadines at the time of the incident.

80. With regard to the first question, the Tribunal notes that the provision in article 91, paragraph 1, of the Convention, requiring a genuine link between the State and the ship, does not provided the answer. Nor do articles 92 and 94 of the Convention, which together with article 91 constitute the context of the provision, provide the answer. The Tribunal, however, recalls that the International Law Commission, in article 29 of the Draft Articles on the Law of the Sea adopted by it in 1956, proposed the concept of a "genuine link" as a criterion not only for the attribution of nationality to a ship but also

for the recognition by other States of such nationality. After providing that "ships have the nationality of the State whose flag they are entitled to fly", the draft article continued: "Nevertheless, for purposes of recognition of the national character of the ship by other States, there must exist a genuine link between the State and the ship". This sentence was not included in article 5, paragraph 1, of the Convention on the High Seas of 29 April 1958 (hereinafter "the 1958 Convention"), which reads, in part, as follows:

> There must exist a genuine link between the State and the ship; in particular, the State must effectively exercise its jurisdiction and control in administrative, technical and social matters over ships flying its flag.

Thus, while the obligation regarding a genuine link was maintained in the 1958 Convention, the proposal that the existence of a genuine link should be a basis for the recognition of nationality was not adopted.

81. The Convention follows the approach of the 1958 Convention, Article 91 retains the part of the third sentence of article 5, paragraph 1, of the 1958 Convention which provides that there must be a genuine link between the State and the ship. The other part of that sentence, stating that the flag State shall effectively exercise its jurisdiction and control in administrative, technical and social matters over ships flying its flag, is reflected in article 94 of the Convention, dealing with the duties of the flag State.

82. Paragraphs 2 to 5 article 94 of the Convention outline the measures that a flag State is required to take to exercise effective jurisdiction as envisaged in paragraph 1. Paragraph 6 sets out the procedure to be followed where another State has "clear grounds to believe that proper jurisdiction and control with respect to a ship have not been exercised". That State is entitled to report the facts to the flag State which is then obliged to "investigate the matter and, if appropriate, take any action necessary to remedy the situation". There is nothing in article 94 to permit a State which discovers evidence indicating the absence of proper jurisdiction and control by a flag State over a ship to refuse to recognize the right of the ship to fly the flag of the flag State.

83. The conclusion of the Tribunal is that the purpose of the provisions of the Convention on the need for a genuine link between a ship and its flag State is to secure more effective implementation of the duties of the flag State, and not to establish criteria by reference to which the validity of the registration of ships in a flag State may be challenged by other States.

84. This conclusion is not put into question by the United Nations Convention on Conditions for Registration of Ships of 7 February 1986 invoked by Guinea. This Convention (which is not in force) sets out as one of its principal objectives the strengthening of "the genuine link between a State and ships flying its flag". In any case, the Tribunal observes that Guinea has not cited any provision in that Convention which lends support to its contention that "a basic condition for the registration of a ship is that also the owner or operator of the ship is under the jurisdiction of the flag State".

* * *

86. In the light of the above considerations, the Tribunal concludes that there is no legal basis for the claim of Guinea that it can refuse to recognize the right of the *Saiga* to fly the flag of Saint Vincent and the Grenadines on the ground that there was no genuine link between the ship and Saint Vincent and the Grenadines.

87. With regard to the second question, the Tribunal finds that, in any case, the evidence adduced by Guinea is not sufficient to justify its contention that there was no genuine link between the ship and Saint Vincent and the Grenadines at the material time.

88. For the above reasons, the Tribunal rejects the objection to admissibility based on the absence of a genuine link between *Saiga* and Saint Vincent and the Grenadines.

* * *

Nationality of claims

103. In its last objection to admissibility, Guinea argues that certain claims of Saint Vincent and the Grenadines cannot be entertained by the Tribunal because they relate to violations of the rights of persons who are not nationals of Saint Vincent and the Grenadines. According to Guinea, the claims of Saint Vincent and the Grenadines in respect of loss or damage sustained by the ship, its owners, the Master and other members of the crew and other persons, including the owners of the cargo, are clearly claims of diplomatic protection. In its view, Saint Vincent and the Grenadines is not competent to institute these claims on behalf of the persons concerned since none of them is a national of Saint Vincent and the Grenadines. During the oral proceedings, Guinea withdrew its objection as far as it relates to the shipowners, but maintained it in respect of the other persons.

104. In opposing this objection, Saint Vincent and the Grenadines maintains that the rule of international law that a State is entitled to claim protection only for its nationals does not apply to claims in respect of persons and things on board a ship flying its flag. In such cases, the flag State has the right to bring claims in respect of violations against the ship and all persons on board or interested in its operation. Saint Vincent and the Grenadines, therefore, asserts that it has the right to protect the ship flying its flag and those who served on board, irrespective of their nationality.

* * *

106. The provisions referred to in the preceding paragraph [articles 94, 217, 106, 110 para. 3, 111 para. 8 and 292] indicate that the Convention considers a ship as a unit, as regards the obligations of the flag State with respect to the ship and the right of a flag State to seek reparation for loss or damage caused to the ship by acts of other States and to institute proceedings under article 292 of the Convention. Thus the ship, every thing on it, and every person involved or interested in its operations are treated as an entity linked to the flag State. The nationalities of these persons are not relevant.

107. The Tribunal must also call attention to an aspect of the matter which is not without significance in this case. This relates to two basic characteristics of modern maritime transport: the transient and multinational composition of ships' crews and the multiplicity of interests that may be involved in the cargo on board a single ship. A container vessel carries a large number of containers, and the persons with interests in them may be of many different nationalities. This may also be true in relation to cargo on board a break-bulk carrier. Any of these ships could have a crew comprising persons of several nationalities. If each person sustaining damage were obliged to look for protection from the State of which such person is a national, undue hardship would endue.

108. The Tribunal is, therefore, unable to accept Guinea's contention that Saint Vincent and the Grenadines is not entitled to present claims for damages in respect of natural and juridical persons who are not nationals of Saint Vincent and the Grenadines.

109. In the light of the above considerations, the Tribunal rejects the objection to admissibility based on nationality of claims.

Arrest of the *Saiga*

110. Saint Vincent and the Grenadines asserts that the arrest of the *Saiga* and the subsequent actions of Guinea were illegal. It contends that the arrest of the *Saiga* was unlawful because the ship did not violate any laws or regulations of Guinea that were applicable to it. It further maintains that, if the laws cited by Guinea did apply to the activities of the *Saiga*, those laws, as applied by Guinea, were incompatible with the Convention.

111. The laws invoked by Guinea as the basis for the arrest of the *Saiga* and the prosecution and conviction of its Master are the following:

(a) Law L/94/007;

(b) The Merchant Marine Code;

(c) The Customs Code;

(d) The Penal Code.

* * *

116. The main charge against the *Saiga* was that it violated article 1 of Law L/94/007 by importing gas oil into the customs radius (*rayon des douanes*) of Guinea. Guinea justifies this action by maintaining that the prohibition in article 1 of Law L/94/007 "can be applied for the purpose of controlling and suppressing the sale of gas oil to fishing vessels in the customs radius according to article 34 of the Customs Code of Guinea". In support of this contention, Guinea declares that it is the consistent practice and the settled view of the courts of Guinea that the term "Guinea", referred to in article 1 of the Law L/94/007, includes the customs radius, and that, consequently, the prohibition of the import of gas oil into Guinea extends to the importation of such oil into any part of the customs radius. According to Guinea, the fact that the *Saiga* violated the laws of Guinea has been authoritatively established by the Court of Appeal. In its view, that decision cannot be questioned in this case because the Tribunal is not competent to consider the question whether the internal legislation of Guinea has been properly applied by the Guinean authorities or its courts.

117. Saint Vincent and the Grenadines contends that the *Saiga* did not violate Law L/94007 because it did not import oil into Guinea, as alleged by the authorities of Guinea. It points out that article 1 of the Customs Code defines the "customs territory" of Guinea as including "the whole of the national territory, the islands locate along the coastline and the Guinean territorial waters". It notes also that, according to articles 33 and 34 of the Customs Code, the customs radius is not part of the customs territory of Guinea but only a "special area of surveillance" and that Guinea is not entitled to enforce its customs laws in it. Saint Vincent and the Grenadines, therefore, argues that the *Saiga* could not have contravened Law L/94/007 since it did not at any time enter the territorial sea of Guinea or introduce, directly or indirectly, any gas oil into the customs territory of Guinea, as defined by the Customs Code.

118. For these reasons, Saint Vincent and the Grenadines maintains that, on a correct interpretation of Law L/94/007 read with articles 1 and 34 of the Customs Code, the *Saiga* did not violate any laws of Guinea when it supplied gas oil to the fishing vessels in the exclusive economic zone of Guinea.

119. In the alternative, Saint Vincent and the Grenadines contends that the extension of the customs laws of Guinea to the exclusive economic zone is contrary to the Convention. It argues that article 56 of the Convention does not give the right to Guinea to extend the application of its customs laws and regulations to that zone. It therefore con-

tends that Guinea's customs laws cannot be applied to ships flying its flag in the exclusive economic zone. Consequently, the measures taken by Guinea against the *Saiga* were unlawful.

* * *

123. Saint Vincent and the Grenadines claims that, in applying its customs laws to the *Saiga* in its customs radius, which includes parts of the exclusive economic zone, Guinea acted contrary to the Convention. It contends that in the exclusive economic zone Guinea is not entitled to exercise powers which go beyond those provided for in articles 56 and 58 of the Convention. It further asserts that Guinea violated its rights to enjoy the freedom of navigation or other internationally lawful uses of the sea in the exclusive economic zone, since the supply of gas oil by the *Saiga* falls within the exercise of those rights.

124. Guinea denies that the application of its customs and contraband laws in its customs radius is contrary to the Convention or in violation of any rights of Saint Vincent and the Grenadines. It maintains that it is entitled to apply its customs and contraband laws to prevent the unauthorized sale of gas oil to fishing vessels operating in its exclusive economic zone. It further maintains that such supply is not part of the freedom of navigation under the Convention or an internationally lawful use of the sea related to the freedom of navigation but a commercial activity and that it does not, therefore, fall within the scope of article 58 of the Convention. For that reason, it asserts that the Guinean action against the *Saiga* was taken not because the ship was navigating in the exclusive economic zone of Guinea but because it was engaged in "unwarranted commercial activities".

125. Guinea further argues that the exclusive economic zone is not part of the high seas or of the territorial sea, but a zone with its own legal status (*a sui generis zone*). From this it concludes that rights or jurisdiction in the exclusive economic zone, which the Convention does not expressly attribute to the coastal States, do not automatically fall under the freedom of the high seas.

126. The Tribunal needs to determine whether the laws applied or the measures taken by Guinea against the *Saiga* are compatible with the Convention. In other words, the question is whether, under the Convention, there was justification for Guinea to apply its customs laws in the exclusive economic zone within a customs radius extending to a distance of 250 kilometers from the coast.

127. The Tribunal notes that, under the Convention, a coastal State is entitled to apply customs laws and regulations in its territorial sea (articles 2 and 21). In the contiguous zone, a coastal State

> may exercise the control necessary to:
>
> (a) prevent infringement of its customs, fiscal, immigration or sanitary laws and regulations within its territory or territorial sea;
>
> (b) punish infringement of the above laws and regulations committed within its territory or territorial sea. (article 33, paragraph 1)

In the exclusive economic zone, the coastal State has jurisdiction to apply customs laws and regulations in respect of artificial islands, installations and structures (article 60, paragraph 2). In the view of the Tribunal, the Convention does not empower a coastal State to apply its customs laws in respect of any other parts of the exclusive economic zone not mentioned above.

* * *

136. The Tribunal, therefore, finds that, by applying its customs laws to a customs radius which includes parts of the exclusive economic zone, Guinea acted in a manner contrary to the Convention. Accordingly, the arrest and detention of the *Saiga*, the prosecution and conviction of its Master, the confiscation of the cargo and the seizure of the ship were contrary to the Convention.

* * *

Hot pursuit

139. Saint Vincent and the Grenadines contends that, in arresting the *Saiga*, Guinea did not lawfully exercise the right of hot pursuit under article 111 of the Convention. It argues that since the *Saiga* did not violate the laws and regulations of Guinea applicable in accordance with the Convention, there was no legal basis for the arrest. Consequently, the authorities of Guinea did not have "good reason" to believe that the *Saiga* had committed an offence that justified hot pursuit in accordance with the Convention.

140. Saint Vincent and the Grenadines asserts that, even if the *Saiga* violated the laws and regulations of Guinea as claimed, its arrest on 28 October 1997 did not satisfy the other conditions for hot pursuit under article 111 of the Convention. It notes that the alleged pursuit was commenced while the ship was well outside the contiguous zone of Guinea. The *Saiga* was first detected (by radar) in the morning of 28 October 1997 when the ship was either outside the exclusive economic zone of Guinea or about to leave that zone. The arrest took place after the ship had crossed the southern border of the exclusive economic zone of Guinea.

141. Saint Vincent and the Grenadines further asserts that, wherever and whenever the pursuit was commenced, it was interrupted. It also contends that no visual and auditory signals were given to the ship prior to the commencement of the pursuit, as required by article 111 of the Convention.

* * *

145. The relevant provisions of article 111 of the Convention which have been invoked by the parties are as follows:

Article 111

Right of hot pursuit

> 1. The hot pursuit of a foreign ship may be undertaken when the competent authorities of the coastal State have good reason to believe that the ship has violated the laws and regulations of that State. Such pursuit must be commenced when the foreign ship or one of its boats is within the internal waters, the archipelagic waters, the territorial sea or the contiguous zone of the pursuing State, and may only be continued outside the territorial sea or the contiguous zone if the pursuit has not been interrupted. It is not necessary that, at the time when the foreign ship within the territorial sea or contiguous zone receives the order to stop, the ship giving the order should likewise be within the territorial sea or the contiguous zone. If the foreign ship is within the contiguous zone, as defined in article 33, the pursuit may only be undertaken if there has been a violation of the rights for the protection of which the zone was established.
>
> 2. The right of hot pursuit shall apply *mutatis mutandis* to violations in the exclusice economic zone or on the continental shelf, including safety zones around continental shelf installations, of the laws and regulations of the coastal

> State applicable in accordance with this Convention to the exclusive economic zone or the continental shelf, including such safety zones.
>
> 3. The right of hot pursuit ceases as soon as the ship pursued enters the territorial sea of its own State or of a third State.
>
> 4. Hot pursuit is not deemed to have begun unless the pursing ship has satisfied itself by such practicable means as may be available that the ship pursued or one of its boats or other craft working as a team and using the ship pursued as a mother ship is within the limits of the territorial sea, or, as the case may be, within the contiguous zone or the exclusive economic zone or above the continental shelf. The pursuit may only be commenced after a visual or auditory signal to stop has been given at a distance which enables it to be seen or heard by the foreign ship.

146. The Tribunal notes that the conditions for the exercise of the right of hot pursuit under article 111 of the Convention are cumulative; each of them has to be satisfied for the pursuit to be legitimate under the Convention. In this case, the Tribunal finds that several of these conditions were not fulfilled.

147. With regard to the pursuit alleged to have commenced on 27 October 1997, the evidence before the Tribunal indicates that, at the time the Order for the Joint Mission of the Customs and Navy of Guinea was issued, the authorities of Guinea, on the basis of information available to them, could have had no more than a suspicion that a tanker had violated the laws of Guinea in the exclusive economic zone. The Tribunal also notes that, in the circumstances, no visual or auditory signals to stop could have been given to the *Saiga*. Furthermore, the alleged pursuit was interrupted. According to the evidence given by Guinea, the small patrol boat P35 that was sent out on 26 October 1997 on a northward course to search for the *Saiga* was recalled when information was received that the *Saiga* had changed course. This recall constituted a clear interruption of any pursuit, whatever legal basis might have existed for its commencement in the first place.

148. As far as the pursuit alleged to have commenced on 28 October 1998 is concerned, the evidence adduced by Guinea does not support its claim that the necessary auditory or visual signals to stop were given to the *Saiga* prior to the commencement of the alleged pursuit, as required by article 111, paragraph 4, of the Convention. Although Guinea claims that the small patrol boat (P35) sounded its siren and turned on its blue revolving light signals when it came within visual and hearing range of the *Saiga*, both the Master who was on the bridge at the time and Mr. Niasse who was on the deck, categorically denied that any such signals were given. In any case, any signals given at the time claimed by Guinea cannot be said to have been given at the commencement of the alleged pursuit.

149. The Tribunal has already concluded that no laws or regulations of Guinea applicable in accordance with the Convention were violated by the *Saiga*. It follows that there was no legal basis for the exercise of the right of hot pursuit by Guinea in this case.

150. For these reasons, the Tribunal finds that Guinea stopped and arrested the *Saiga* on 28 October 1997 in circumstances which did not justify the exercise of the right of hot pursuit in accordance with the Convention.

* * *

Use of force

153. Saint Vincent and the Grenadines claims that Guinea used excessive and unreasonable force in stopping and arresting the *Saiga*. It notes that the *Saiga* was an unarmed

tanker almost fully laden with gas oil, with a maximum speed of 10 knots. It also notes that the authorities of Guinea fired at the ship with live ammunition, using solid shots from large-calibre automatic guns.

154. Guinea denies that the force used in boarding, stopping and arresting the *Saiga* was either excessive or unreasonable. It contends that the arresting officers had no alternative but to use gunfire because the *Saiga* refused to stop after repeated radio messages to it to stop and in spite of visual and auditory signals from the patrol boat P35. Guinea maintains that gunfire was used as a last resort, and denies that large-calibre ammunition was used. Guinea places the responsibility for any damage resulting form the use of force on the Master and crew of the ship.

155. In considering the force used by Guinea in the arrest of the *Saiga*, the Tribunal must take into account the circumstances of the arrest in the context of the applicable rules of international law. Although the Convention does not contain express provisions on the use of force in the arrest of ships, international law, which is applicable by virtue of article 293 of the Convention, requires that the use of force must be avoided as far as possible and, when force is unavoidable, it must not go beyond what is reasonable and necessary in the circumstances. Considerations of humanity must apply in the law of the sea, as they do in other areas of international law.

156. These principles have been followed over the years in law enforcement operations at sea. The normal practice used to stop a ship at sea is first to give an auditory or visual signal to stop, using internationally recognized signals. Where this does not succeed, a variety of actions may be taken, including the firing of shots across the bows of the ship. It is only after the appropriate actions fail that the pursuing vessel may, as a last resort, use force. Even then, appropriate warning must be issued to the ship and all efforts should be made to ensure that life is not endangered (*S.S. "I'm Alone"* case*(Canada/United States, 1935)*, U.N.R.I.A.A., Vol. III, p. 1609; *The Red Crusader* case *(Commission of Enquiry, Denmark-United Kingdom, 1962)*, I.L.R., Vol. 35, p. 485). The basic principle concerning the use of force in the arrest of a ship at sea has been reaffirmed by the Agreement for the Implementation of the Provisions of the United Nations Convention on the Law of the Sea of 10 December 1982 Relating to the Conservation and Management of Straddling Fish Stocks and Highly Migratory Fish Stocks. Article 22, paragraph 1 (f), of the Agreement states:

> 1. The inspecting State shall ensure that its duly authorized inspectors:
>
> ...
>
> (f) avoid the use of force except when and to the degree necessary to ensure the safety of the inspectors and where the inspectors are obstructed in the execution of their duties. The degree of force used shall not exceed that reasonably required in the circumstances.

157. In the present case, the Tribunal notes that the *Saiga* was almost fully laden and was low in the water at the time it was approached by the patrol vessel. Its maximum speed was 10 knots. Therefore it could be boarded without much difficulty by the Guinean officers. At one stage in the proceedings Guinea sought to justify the use of gunfire with the claim that the *Saiga* had attempted to sink the patrol boat. During the hearing, the allegation was modified to the effect that the danger of sinking to the patrol boat was from the wake of the *Saiga* and not the result of a deliberate attempt by the ship. But whatever the circumstances, there is no excuse for the fact that the officers fired at the ship itself with live ammunition from a fast-moving patrol boat without issuing any of the signals and warnings required by international law and practice.

158. The Guinean officers also used excessive force on board the *Saiga*. Having boarded the ship without resistance, and although there is no evidence of the use or threat of force from the crew, they fired indiscriminately while on the deck and used gunfire to stop the engine of the ship. In using firearms in this way, the Guinean officers appeared to have attached little or no importance to the safety of the ship and the persons on board. In the process, considerable damage was done to the ship and to vital equipment in the engine and radio rooms. And, more seriously, the indiscriminate use of gunfire caused severe injuries to two of the persons on board.

* * *

Reparation

167. Saint Vincent and the Grenadines requests the Tribunal to declare that Guinea is liable, under article 111, paragraph 8, of the Convention and under international law which applies by virtue of article 304 of the Convention, for damages for violation of its rights under the Convention.

168. Saint Vincent and the Grenadines claims compensation for material damage in respect of natural and juridical persons. Compensation is claimed in respect of damage to the ship, financial losses of the shipowners, the operators of the *Saiga*, the owners of the cargo, and the Master, members of the crew and other persons on board the ship. Compensation is also claimed in respect of loss of liberty and personal injuries, including pain and suffering. Saint Vincent and the Grenadines requests that interest be given at the rate of 8% on the damages awarded for material damage.

169. Article 111, paragraph 8, of the Convention provides:

> Where a ship has been stopped or arrested outside the territorial sea in circumstances which do not justify the exercise of the right of hot pursuit, it shall be compensated for any loss or damage that may have been thereby sustained.

Reparation may also be due under international law as provided for in article 304 of the Convention, which provides:

> The provisions of this Convention regarding responsibility and liability for damage are without prejudice to the application of existing rules and the development of further rules regarding responsibility and liability under international law.

170. It is a well-established rule of international law that a State which suffers damage as a result of an internationally wrongful act by another State is entitled to obtain reparation for the damage suffered from the State which committed the wrongful act and that "reparation must, as far as possible, wipe out all the consequences of the illegal act and reestablish the situation which would, in all probability, have existed if that act had not been committed" (*Factory at Chorzów, Merits, Judgment No. 13, 1928, P.C.I.J., Series A, No. 17, p. 47).*

171. Reparation may be in the form of "restitution in kind, compensation, satisfaction and assurances and guarantees of non-repetition either singly or in combination" (article 42, paragraph 1, of the Draft Articles of the International Law Commission on State Responsibility). Reparation may take the form of monetary compensation for economically quantifiable damage as well as for non-material damage, depending on the circumstances of the case. The circumstances include such factors as the conduct of the State which committed the wrongful act and the manner in which the violation occurred. Reparation in the form of satisfaction may be provided by a judicial declaration that there has been a violation of a right.

172. In the view of the Tribunal, Saint Vincent and the Grenadines is entitled to reparation for damage suffered directly by it as well as for damage or other loss suffered by the *Saiga*, including all persons involved or interested in its operation. Damage or other loss suffered by the *Saiga* and all persons involved or interested in its operations comprises injury to persons, unlawful arrest, detention or other forms of ill-treatment, damage to or seizure of property and other economic losses, including loss of profit.

173. The Tribunal considers it generally fair and reasonable that interest is paid in respect of monetary losses, property damage and other economic losses. However, it is not necessary to apply a uniform rate of interest in all instances. In the present case, the Tribunal has set an interest rate of 6% in respect of award of compensation. In determining this rate, account has been taken, *inter alia*, of commercial conditions prevailing in the countries where the expenses were incurred or the principal operations of the party being compensated are located. A higher rate of 8% is adopted in respect of the value of the gas oil to include loss of profit. A lower rate of interest of 3% is adopted for compensation for detention and for injury, pain and suffering, disability and psychological damage, payable from three months after the date of the Judgment.

* * *

175. After a careful scrutiny of invoices and other documents submitted, the Tribunal decides to award compensation in the total amount of US$ 2,123,357 (United States Dollars Two Million One Hundred and Twenty-Three Thousand Three Hundred Fifty-Seven) with interest....

* * *

176. With regard to the claims of Saint Vincent and the Grenadines for compensation for violation of its rights in respect of ships flying its flag, the Tribunal has declared in paragraphs 136 and 159 that Guinea acted wrongfully and violated the rights of Saint Vincent and the Grenadines in arresting the *Saiga* in the circumstances of the case and in using excessive force. The Tribunal considers that these declarations constitute adequate reparation.

177. Saint Vincent and the Grenadines requests the Tribunal to award compensation for the loss of registration revenue resulting from the illegal arrest of the *Saiga* by Guinea, and for the expenses resulting from the time lost by its officials in dealing with the arrest and detention of the ship and its crew. The Tribunal notes that no evidence has been produced by Saint Vincent and the Grenadines that the arrest of the *Saiga* caused a decrease in registration activity under its flag, with resulting loss of revenue. The Tribunal considers that any expenses incurred by Saint Vincent and the Grenadines in respect of its officials must be borne by it as having been incurred in the normal functions of a flag State. For these reasons, the Tribunal does not accede to these requests for compensation made by Saint Vincent and the Grenadines.

* * *

QUESTIONS

1. What persuaded the Tribunal that the nationality of the *Saiga* was St. Vincent and the Grenadines?
2. Why did the Tribunal conclude that Guinea had no right to refuse to recognize the right of the *Saiga* to fly the flag of St. Vincent and the Grenadines even if there had been no genuine link between the ship and the state of St. Vincent and the Grenadines?

3. Why did the Tribunal permit St. Vincent and the Grenadines to represent the claims of all persons with an interest in the *Saiga*, including the crew, even though none of them was a national of St. Vincent and the Grenadines?
4. Why was Guinea's arrest, detention and seizure of the *Saiga*, the prosecution and conviction of its Master and the confiscation of the cargo illegal?
5. Why was Guinea's claim to have exercised the right of hot pursuit of the *Saiga* rejected?
6. Why was Guinea's use of force to arrest the *Saiga* and the crew considered illegal?
7. Why was Guinea required to pay reparations for the injury to the crew, damage to the ship, and financial losses of the shipowners and cargo owners?
8. What reparation did St. Vincent and the Grenadines receive?
9. In March 2009, a U.S. naval vessel was conducting sea-bed surveys about 75 miles south of China's Hainan Island within China's exclusive economic zone. The Chinese navy adopted several harrassment tactics. Thom Shanker & Mark Mazzeti; China and U.S. Clash on Naval Fracas, N.Y. Times, March 10, 2009. Are foreign naval survey activities permitted within a state's EEZ?

Fishing on the High Seas

Before the twentieth century activities on the high seas operated on the basis of freedom and commonage. The high seas were open to all states, as they still are (article 87(1)), and activities were largely unrestricted. Fishing was the main activity on the high seas and, in general, the level of fishing engaged in permitted fish and marine mammal stocks to replenish themselves, though there were notably exceptions, such as certain species of whale. With the vastly increased fishing capacity now available the balance has tipped very much against maintaining any sort of equilibrium of fish stock unless aggressive conservation and management is practiced. Many species have been fished either to extinction or almost to extinction and some nations have prohibited the fishing of certain species in their exclusive economic zones even for their own fishing fleets.

The 1982 Convention recognizes the necessity for the "conservation and management of the living resources of the high seas."[90] Articles 116 through 120 deal with states' obligations to practice conservation and management of the high seas' resources.

Article 116 reaffirms every state's right "to engage in fishing on the high seas...." but this right is made subject to a series of other obligations. First, states must abide by any existing treaty obligations they may have with other states relating to fishing. Second, the right to fish is subject to other articles in the 1982 Convention dealing with (I) fish that move from the exclusive economic zone to adjacent waters in the high seas (article 63(2)); (ii) highly migratory species (article 64); (iii) marine mammals (article 65); (iv) anadromous stock (article 66); and (v) catadromous species (article 67). Third, articles 117 through 120 provide further limitations on the right to fish. States are given the duty to take "such measures for their respective nationals as may be necessary for the conservation of the living resources of the high seas." (Article 117). They are required to "cooperate in the conservation and management of living resources in the area of the high seas...." (Article 118). Methods of "determining the allowable catch" are outlined

90. 1982 Convention, Part VII, section 2, title.

in article 119, and article 120 requires the "conservation and management of marine mammals in the high seas." A further treaty implementing certain provisions of the 1982 Convention relating to straddling fish stocks and highly migratory species of fish has now entered into force.[91] There are also numerous bilateral, regional and multi-lateral treaties relating to various aspects of conservation of the resources of the high seas.[92]

Problem

The south coast of the state of Zeta is riddled with tiny inlets only one of which has a mouth opening wider than ten nautical miles. (All miles referred to in this question are nautical miles.) The inlets are usually not very deep, stretching for only a couple of hundred yards inland from the main coastline. There is one inlet, however, with a fifteen mile wide mouth and which stretches inland maintaining that width for twenty miles before tapering into the estuary of a river. This inlet is known as the Isis Inlet.

The state of Omega borders Zeta to the West and both nations are heavily dependent on the fishing industry which flourishes off their southern coasts. Until recently both nations claimed a territorial sea of three miles. They excluded each other from this three mile zone but otherwise fished off each other's coasts.

In 1982 both Zeta and Omega signed the United Nations Law of the Sea Convention (UNCLOS) and both nations have since ratified the convention. Both states have taken full advantage of the various coastal zones permitted by the convention.

Some fishermen from Omega were seen by the Zetan coast guard fishing when they were one hundred and ninety five miles out at sea directly south from the mid-point of a straight line connecting the low-water marks at the East and West entrances to the mouth of the Isis Inlet. The Zetan coast guard were 193 miles from the mouth of the Isis Inlet when they began to chase the Omegan fishermen. The Zetan coast guard officers eventually caught up with and arrested the fishermen when they were 230 miles from the mouth of the Isis Inlet. At their criminal trial in the Zetan courts, the Omegan fishermen claimed they were fishing on the high seas and that they were arrested on the high seas contrary to international law.

QUESTIONS

1. Please explain whether you agree or disagree with the Omegan fishermen's claims that they were fishing on the high seas and that their arrest on the high seas was illegal.
2. Assume for purposes of this sub-section only that when the Zetan coast guard spotted the fishermen, 195 miles from the mouth of the Isis Inlet they radioed the Omegan registered fishing vessels to "heave to and await inspection." The Omegan boats heard the radio message but immediately headed south out to sea. The Zeta coast guard chased them for twenty miles but then the fishermen

91. Agreement for the Implementation of the Provisions of the Convention Relating to the Conservation and Management of Straddling Fish Stocks and Highly Migratory Fish Stocks, 2167 U.N.T.S. 3, signed 4 August 1995, entered into force 11 December 2001.

92. See e.g., International Convention for the Regulation of Whaling, 161 U.N.T.S. 72, signed 2 Dec. 1946, entered into force 10 Nov. 1948; Convention on Fishing and Conservation of Living Resources of the High Seas, 559 U.N.T.S. 285, signed 29 April 1958, entered into force, 20 March 1966.

headed inland. The Zetan coast guard finally arrested the Omegan boats when they were three miles off the coast of the state of Epsilon which lies to the east of Zeta. Epsilon is also a party to UNCLOS. Epsilon has protested to Zeta over the arrest of the Omegan boats "in our sovereign territorial sea." Nonetheless the fishermen were brought back to Zeta and tried for illegal fishing.

Please outline any defenses you would expect the Omegan fishermen to raise at their trial in Zeta and explain whether or not you would expect these defenses to be successful.

Suggested Further Readings

Ian Brownlie, Principles of Public International Law, chapters 9, 10 & 11 (7th ed. 2008).

D.J. Harris, Cases and Materials on International Law, chapter 7 (6th ed. 2004).

Sean D. Murphy, Principles of International Law, chapter 11 (2006).

Malcolm N. Shaw, International Law, chapter 11 (6th ed. 2008).

Louis B. Sohn, & John E. Noyes, Cases and Materials on the Law of the Sea (2004).

Rebecca M. M. Wallace, International Law, chapter 7 (5th ed. 2005).

Chapter VI

International Environmental Law

International environmental law has been an area of dynamic growth, particularly in the last forty years. During the pre-industrial era, states did not have much capacity to damage the globe but with the rise of the industrial state that changed. The mining of fossil fuels and the production of manufactured goods increased the capacity for environmental damage dramatically. Some decades passed before it was suspected that man's activities were the direct cause of changes in the environment and further decades went by before the scientific proof was forthcoming that these changes were harmful and the direct cause of damage. Even with solid scientific evidence, it is taking some time for the international community to develop standards for state responsibility, agree on prohibited activities and articulate remedies for violations of norms.

State Responsibility for Environmental Harm

Each state has a body of law describing what types of activities property owners are (a) required to engage in and (b) prohibited from undertaking. Early property law developed the notion of "nuisance" so that, for example, one property owner could sue his neighboring property owner for allowing thistles to grow in his fields. When the thistle seeds blew into the property owner's fields, implanted themselves and ruined his existing crop, the property owner argued that he was entitled to relief for the ensuing damage. The courts began to describe such thistle growing activity as negligent, that is not in conformity with the accepted standard of care. The courts awarded damages for the resulting harm and also issued orders prohibiting such activity or requiring the thistle grower to chop down the thistles before they went to seed. There was no such similar body of law at the international level until the twentieth century when states began to realize that the activity of a particular state could cause substantial damage not only to itself but also to other states.

The original notion was that if a state wished to allow massive air or water pollution within its own borders that was no concern of the international community, but that if pollution made its way into another state, that gave rise to a legitimate claim on the part of the harmed state. Of course, it soon became apparent that pollution, in whatever form, is no respecter of national boundaries and that effective relief for the international community could only be found in a comprehensive regime that regulated the activities of a state within its own borders.

Establishing the Standard for State Responsibility

Customary Law

The Corfu Channel Case (Merits)

United Kingdom v. Albania
1949 I.C.J. 4

Note

"On May 15, 1946, the British cruisers *Orion* and *Superb*, while passing southward through the North Corfu Channel, were fired at by an Albanian battery in the vicinity of Saranda...."[1] The Albanian authorities had characterized these waters as Albanian territorial waters and argued that foreign warships and merchant vessels had no right to pass through these waters without permission from Albania. The Court determined that the waters constituted an international strait and as such Albania could not prohibit international shipping through the straight in peace time. (See *Corfu Channel Case* at pp. 193–194.)

Later "[o]n October 22, 1946, a squadron of British warships, the cruisers *Mauritius* and *Leander* and the destroyers *Saumarez* and *Volage*, left the port of Corfu and proceeded northward through a channel previously swept for mines in the North Corfu Strait.... Outside the Bay of Saranda, *Saumarez* struck a mine and was heavily damaged.... Whilst towing the damaged ship, *Volage* struck a mine and was much damaged...."[2]

The United Kingdom filed a claim in the International Court of Justice against Albanian seeking compensation for damage caused by the mines.

Judgment of the Court

Three weeks later, on November 13th, the North Corfu Channel was swept by British minesweepers and twenty-two moored mines were cut.

On the evidence produced, the Court finds that the following facts are established:

In October, 1944, the North Corfu Channel was swept by the British Navy and no mines were found in the channel thus swept, whereupon the existence of a safe route through the Channel was announced in November 1944. It was in this swept channel that the minefield was discovered on November 13th, 1946.

It is further proved by evidence produced by the United Kingdom Government that the mining of *Saumarez* and *Volage* occurred in Albanian territorial waters, just at the place in the swept channel where the minefield was found....

The Court, consequently finds that the following facts are established. The two ships were mined in Albanian territorial waters in a previously swept and check-swept channel.... In such circumstances the Court arrives at the conclusion that the explosions were due to mines belonging to that minefield.

1. 1949 I.C.J. 4, 27.
2. Id. at 12–13.

* * *

Such are the facts upon which the Court must ... give judgment as to Albania's responsibility for the explosions on October 22nd, 1946, and for the damage and loss of human life which resulted, and for the compensation, if any, due in respect of such damage and loss.

To begin with, the foundation for Albania's responsibility, as alleged by the United Kingdom, must be considered. On this subject, the main position of the United Kingdom is to be found in its submission No. 2: that the minefield which caused the explosions was laid between May 15th, 1946, and October 22nd, 1946, by or with the connivance or knowledge of the Albanian Government.

* * *

In fact, although the United Kingdom Government never abandoned its contention that Albania herself laid the mines, very little attempt was made by the Government to demonstrate this point.

* * *

In these circumstances, the Court need pay no further attention to this matter.

The Court now comes to the second alternative argument of the United Kingdom Government, namely, that the minefield was laid with the connivance of the Albanian Government. According to this argument, the minelaying operation was carried out by two Yugoslav warships at a date prior to October 22nd, but very near that date. This would imply collusion between the Albanian and the Yugoslav Government for assistance, or of acquiescence by the Albanian authorities in the laying of the mines....

* * *

In light of the information now available to the Court, the authors of the minelaying remain unknown....

Finally, the United Kingdom Government put forward the argument that, whoever the authors of the minelaying were, it could not have been done without the Albanian Government's knowledge.

It is clear that knowledge of the minelaying cannot be imputed to the Albanian Government by reason merely of the fact that a minefield discovered in Albanian territorial waters caused the explosions of which the British warships were the victims. It is true, as international practice shows, that a State on whose territory or in whose waters an act contrary to international law has occurred, may be called upon to give an explanation. It is also true that that State cannot evade such a request by limiting itself to a reply that it is ignorant of the circumstances of the act and of its authors. The State may, up to a certain point, be bound to supply particulars of the use made by it of the means of information and inquiry at its disposal. But it cannot be concluded from the mere fact of the control exercised by a State over its territory and waters that that State necessarily knew, or ought to have known, of any unlawful act perpetrated therein, nor yet that it necessarily knew, or should have known, the authors. This fact, by itself and apart from other circumstances, neither involves *prima facie* responsibility nor shifts the burden of proof.

On the other hand, the fact of this exclusive territorial control exercised by a State within its frontiers has a bearing upon the methods of proof available to establish the knowledge of that State as to such events. By reason of this exclusive control, the other State, the victim of a breach of international law, is often unable to furnish direct proof of facts giving rise to responsibility. Such a State should be allowed a more liberal recourse to inferences of fact and circumstantial evidence. This indirect evidence is admitted in all systems of law, and its use is recognized by international decisions. It must be regarded as of special weight when it is based on a series of facts linked together and leading logically to a single conclusion.

The Court must examine therefore whether it has been established by means of indirect evidence that Albania has knowledge of minelaying in her territorial waters independently of any connivance on her part in this operation. The proof may be drawn from inferences of fact, provided that they leave *no room* for reasonable doubt....

* * *

The Court cannot fail to give great weight to the opinion of the Experts who examined the locality in a manner giving every guarantee of correct and impartial information. Apart from the existence of a look-out post at Cape Denta, which has not been proved, the Court, basing itself on the declarations of the Albanian Government that look-out posts were stationed at Cape Kiephali and St. George's Monastery, refers to the following conclusions in the Experts' Report: (1) that in the case of minelaying from the North towards the South, the minelayers would have been seen from Cape Kiephali; (2) in the case of minelaying from the South, the minelayers would have been seen from Cape Kiephali and St. George's Monastery.

From all the facts and observations mentioned above, the Court draws the conclusion that the laying of the minefield which caused the explosions on October 22, 1946, could not have been accomplished without the knowledge of the Albanian Government.

The obligations resulting for Albania from this knowledge are not disputed between the Parties. Counsel for the Albanian Government expressly recognized that [*translation*] "if Albania had been informed of the operation before the incidents of October 22nd, and in time to warn the British vessels and shipping in general of the existence of mines in the Corfu Channel, her responsibility would be involved...."

The obligations incumbent upon the Albanian authorities consisted in notifying, for the benefit of shipping in general, the existence of a minefield in Albanian territorial waters and in warning the approaching British warships of the imminent danger to which the minefield exposed them. Such obligations are based, not in the Hague Convention of 1907, No. VIII, which is applicable in time of war, but on certain general and well-recognized principles, namely: elementary considerations of humanity, even more exacting in peace than in war; the principle of the freedom of maritime communication; and every State's obligation not to allow knowingly its territory to be used for acts contrary to the rights of other States.

In fact, Albania neither notified the existence of the minefield, nor warned the British warships of the danger they were approaching....

* * *

In fact, nothing was attempted by the Albanian authorities to prevent the disaster. These grave omissions involve the international responsibility of Albania.

The Court therefore reaches the conclusion that Albania is responsible under international law for the explosions which occurred on October 22nd, 1946, in Albanian waters, and for the damage and loss of human life which resulted from them, and that there is a duty upon Albania to pay compensation to the United Kingdom....

* * *

QUESTIONS

1. The United Kingdom failed to prove either that Albania laid the mines or that the mines were laid with the connivance of the Albanian Government. Why then was Albania held responsible for the explosion of the mines and the resulting damage?
2. If Albania had known of the existence of the mines, what could she have done, short of removing them, to avoid responsibility for the explosions?
3. How would you phrase, in generally terms, the principle of state responsibility which this case articulates?

Trail Smelter Case
United States v. Canada

3 U.N. Rep. Int'l Arb. Awards 1938 (1941)

Note

A Canadian company was engaged in smelting zinc and lead in the town of Trail, British Columbia, on the banks of the Columbia River about eleven miles upstream from the United States border. Over the years the smelting production increased and by the 1930s more than 300 tons of sulphur were being released into the air daily. These fumes were alleged to be blowing into the United States and causing damage to property in the state of Washington. The United States and Canada referred the case to the International Joint Commission, an entity established to resolve such problems by a United States-Canadian Treaty. In 1931, the Commission awarded $350,000 to the United States in damages, which Canada agreed to pay. The Trail Smelter continued its operations and a Special Arbitral Tribunal reached a decision in 1941 that compensation was due for the pollution between 1932 and 1937 and that in the future the Trail Smelter was required to refrain from causing any damage to the State of Washington by smelting fumes. The Tribunal was required to apply the "law and practice followed in dealing with cognate questions in the United States of America as well as international law and practice...."[3]

Decision of the Tribunal

The first problem which arises is whether the question should be answered on the basis of the law followed in the United States or on the basis of international law. The Tribunal, however, finds that this problem need not be solved here as the law followed in the United States in dealing with the quasi-sovereign rights of the States of the Union, in the matter of air pollution, whilst more definite, is in conformity with the general rules of international law....

As Professor Eagleton puts it (*Responsibility of States in International Law,* 1928, p. 80): "A State owes at all times a duty to protect other States against injurious acts by individuals from within its jurisdiction." A great number of such general pronouncements

3. Art. IV, Convention for Settlement of Difficulties Arising from Operations of Smelter at Trail, B.C. April 15, 1935, T.S. No. 893, 49 Stat. 3241, 3 R.I.A.A. 1905 (1908).

by leading authorities concerning the duty of a State to respect other States and their territory have been presented to the Tribunal. These and many others have been carefully examined. International decisions, in various matters, from the Alabama case onward, and also earlier ones, are based on the same general principle, and, indeed, this principle, as such, has not been questioned by Canada. But the real difficulty often arises rather when it comes to determine what, *pro subjecta materie,* is deemed to constitute an injurious act.

* * *

No case of air pollution dealt with by an international tribunal has been brought to the attention of the Tribunal nor does the Tribunal know of any such case. The nearest analogy is that of water pollution. But, here also, no decision of an international tribunal has been cited or has been found.

There are, however, as regards both air pollution and water pollution, certain decisions of the Supreme Court of the United States which may legitimately be taken as a guide in this field of international law, for it is reasonable to follow by analogy, in international cases, precedents established by that court in dealing with controversies between States of the Union or with other controversies concerning the quasi-sovereign rights of such States, where no contrary rule prevails in international law and no reason for rejecting such precedents can be adduced from the limitations of sovereignty inherent in the Constitution of the United States.

* * *

The Tribunal, therefore, finds that the above [U.S. Supreme Court] decisions, taken as a whole, constitute an adequate basis for its conclusions, namely, that, under the principles of international law, as well as of the law of the United States, no State has the right to use or permit the use of its territory in such a manner as to cause injury by fumes in or to the territory of another or the properties or persons therein, when the case is of serious consequence and the injury is established by clear and convincing evidence.

* * *

Considering the circumstances of the case, the Tribunal holds that the Dominion of Canada is responsible in international law for the conduct of the Trail Smelter.... [I]t is, therefore, the duty of the Government of the Dominion of Canada to see to it that this conduct should be in conformity with the obligation of the Dominion under international law as herein determined.

The Tribunal, therefore, ... [decides]: So long as the present conditions in the Columbia River Valley prevail, the Trail Smelter shall be required to refrain from causing any damage through fumes in the State of Washington; the damage herein referred to and its extent being such as would be recoverable under the decisions of the courts of the United States in suits between private individuals....

QUESTIONS

1. The Trail Smelter was not violating any laws of British Columbia or Canada. Why then was Canada held responsible for the damage caused in the state of Washington?
2. How would you restate the rule of international law that Canada was found to have violated?

3. What sources did the tribunal rely upon in finding the above rule of international law?

Note

The standard of care owed by a state to the international community has often been described as "due diligence" but recently there have been suggestions that a "strict liability" standard should be applied in the case of activities recognized as ultra-hazardous. Under a strict liability standard states are liable for damage caused by their activity regardless of whether they exercised due diligence when undertaking the activity. Some conventions now apply a strict liability standard for certain dangerous activities.[4]

Declarations and Treaty Law

In the latter half of the twentieth century individual states began to enact legislation to curb environmental damage within their own borders but the success of these efforts was dependent upon the particular political climate of the individual state. It soon became apparent that however stringent a state was in curbing its own activities, internal legislation could not protect it against environmental damage emanating from less responsible states. Thus a massive international effort was begun to draft principles and conventions in the environmental area.

The United Nations Conference on the Human Environment met in 1972 in Stockholm, Sweden and issued a Declaration.[5] This type of Declaration is often characterized by grand statements of purpose. For example, Principle 2 of the Declaration states:

> The natural resources of the earth, including the air, water, land, flora and fauna and especially representative samples of natural ecosystems, must be safeguarded for the benefit of present and future generations through careful planning or management as appropriate.

Such statements are known as "soft law," in so far as they are not meant to create immediately enforceable legal rights. Rather, they represent the direction in which the international community is seeking to move and may in time come to represent the underlying norms that give rise to specific binding obligations upon states.

After the Stockholm Conference, the United Nations Environment Programme (UNEP) was created.[6] Although this is one of the smaller U.N. agencies, it has been very influential in drafting a whole array of environmental treaties some of which have received widespread ratification. For example, the Convention on International Trade in Endangered Species of Wild Fauna and Flora (CITES)[7] has received one hundred and seventy-five ratifications.

---

4. See e.g., Convention on International Liability for Damage Caused by Space Objects, art. II, 961 U.N.T.S. 187, 24 U.S.T. 2389, T.I.A.S. No. 7762, signed 29 March 1972, entered into force, 1 Sept. 1972, reprinted at 10 I.L.M. 965 (1971).

5. Stockholm Declaration of the U.N. Conference on the Human Environment, June 16, 1972, U.N. Doc. A/CONF. 48/14/Rev. 1 at 3 (1972), U.N. Sales No. E. 73. II. A. 14 (1973), reprinted at 11 I.L.M. 1416 (1972).

6. UNEP's web site provides much useful information: http://www.unep.org.

7. 993 U.N.T.S. 243, 27 U.S.T. 1087, T.I.A.S. No. 8249, (1973) signed 3 March 1973, entered into force, 1 July 1975, reprinted at 12 I.L.M. 1085 (1973). See also Lusaka Agreement on Co-operative

More recently the international community met at the Rio Summit in Brazil in 1992 at the United Nations Conference on Environment and Development. More than one hundred and seventy nations and a host of non-governmental organizations met to create a framework for the environment for the next several decades. A Declaration on Environment and Development[8] was issued which affirmed that "Human beings are at the centre of concerns for sustainable development. They are entitled to a healthy and productive life in harmony with nature." (Principle I). The conference also adopted Agenda 21[9] which provides a broad ranging framework for the protection of the global environment. The Convention on Biological Diversity[10] has received over one hundred and ninety ratifications and the United Nations Framework Convention on Climate Change currently has one hundred and ninety-two parties.[11]

Gradually the international community has come to articulate a number of areas of environmental concern and each of these areas has spawned its own declarations and treaties. It should be noted that the non-governmental organizations have been incredibly active and persuasive in the environmental arena. States often drag their feet in agreeing to norms and in enforcing them because large industrial interests argue that stricter regimes will be too costly. Non-governmental groups such as the World Wide Fund for Nature or Greenpeace International have no such constraints.

Below are listed some of the areas that have given rise to new legal regimes together with some of the treaties which have created the legal framework.

Hazardous Waste

The Basel Convention on the Control of Transboundary Movements of Hazardous Wastes and Their Disposal[12] defines hazardous wastes and sets controls and limitations on the transfer of such wastes between treaty partners. There is a similar convention applying specifically to Africa: the Bamako Convention on the Ban of the Import into Africa and the Control of Transboundary Movement and Management of Hazardous Wastes Within Africa.[13] More recently, the Rotterdam Convention on the Prior Informed Consent Procedure for Certain Hazardous Chemicals and Pesticides in International Trade[14] went into force in 2004 and currently has one hundred and twenty-seven parties.

Enforcement Operations Directed at Illegal Trade in Wild Flora and Fauna, 1950 U.N.T.S. 35, signed 8 Sept. 1994, entered into force, 10 Dec. 1996 (open to African states).

8. [Rio] Declaration on Environment and Development, signed 14 June 1992, U.N. GAOR, 47th Sess., U.N. Doc. A/CONF. 151/5/Rev.1 (1992), reprinted at 31 I.L.M. 874 (1992).

9. Report of the Sect.-Gen. of the Conference, U.N. Doc. A/CONF. 151/PC/100 (1992).

10. 1760 U.N.T.S. 79, signed 5 June 1992, entered into force, 29 Dec. 1993, reprinted at 31 I.L.M. 818 (1992). See also, Cartagena Protocol on Biosafety to the Convention on Biological Diversity, ___ U.N.T.S. ___, signed 29 Jan. 2000, entered into force, 11 Sept. 2003.

11. 1771 U.N.T.S. 107, signed 9 May 1992, entered into force 21 March 1994, reprinted at 31 I.L.M. 818 (1992). See also, Kyoto Protocol to the U.N. Framework Convention on Climate Change, ___ U.N.T.S. ___ signed 11 Dec. 1997, entered into force, 16 Feb. 2005. Currently 184 states have ratified the Protocol.

12. 1673 U.N.T.S. 57, signed 22 Mar. 1989, entered into force, 5 May 1992, reprinted at 28 I.L.M. 657 (1989). See also Amendment to the Basal Convention, adopted 22 Sept. 1995, not yet in force.

13. 2101 U.N.T.S. 242, signed 30 Jan. 1991, entered into force 22 April 1998, reprinted at 30 I.L.M. 773 (1991).

14. 2244 U.N.T.S. 337, adopted 10 Sept. 1998, entered into force 24 Feb. 2004.

Atmosphere, Ozone and Climate

The principle first announced in the *Trail Smelter Case* has found much more concrete expression in the Convention on Long-Range Transboundary Air Pollution[15] which calls on parties to limit, gradually reduce and prevent long-range transboundary air pollution. The Vienna Convention for the Protection of the Ozone Layer[16] provides a mechanism for exchange of information and scientific research. The 1987 Montreal Protocol on Substances that Deplete the Ozone Layer[17] together with various adjustments and amendments sets permissible levels of chlorofluorocarbon (CFC) consumption and freezes the use of halons. The Helsinki Declaration on the Protection of the Ozone Layer[18] called for the phasing out of CFCs by the year 2000.

The pressing issue of global warming has received attention in the United Nations Framework Convention on Climate Change,[19] and the Kyoto Protocol[20] to that Convention. The Stockholm Convention on Persistent Organic Pollutants[21] also entered into force in 2004 and currently has one hundred and sixty-two parties.

Nature, Flora, Fauna and Other Resources

Mention has already been made of the Convention on Biological Diversity[22] and the CITES[23] convention. A recent non binding statement on the world's forests addresses management, conservation and sustainable development of these vital resources.[24] The 1972 Convention for the Protection of the World Cultural and Natural Heritage[25] imposes upon members "the duty of ensuring identification, protection, conservation, presentation and transmission to future generations of ... cultural and natural heritage...." Article 4.

In a recent case in the International Court of Justice, *Case Concerning Gabcíkovo-Nagymaros Project*,[26] which concerned treaty obligations relating to the construction and operation of dams on the Danube river, Hungary argued that she was entitled to terminate a treaty with Slovakia because of "new requirements of international law for the protection of the environment...."[27] The Court determined that "newly developed norms of environmental law [were] relevant for the implementation of the Treaty.... [and that the Treaty] require[d] the parties ... to ensure that the quality of

15. 1302 U.N.T.S. 217, T.I.A.S. No. 10541, 18 I.L.M. 1442 (1979), signed 13 Nov. 1979, entered into force, 16 Mar. 1983. For subsequent Protocols see 27 I.L.M. 707 (1988).

16. 1513 U.N.T.S. 293, signed 22 March 1985, entered into force, 22 Sept. 1988, reprinted at 26 I.L.M. 1516 (1987).

17. 1522 U.N.T.S. 3, signed 16 Sept. 1987, entered into force, 1 Jan. 1989, reprinted at 26 I.L.M. 1550 (1987).

18. Signed 2 May 1989, reprinted at 28 I.L.M. 1335 (1989).

19. See *supra* note 11.

20. Id.

21. ___ U.N.T.S. ___, adopted 22 May 2001, entered into force 17 May 2004.

22. See *supra* note 10.

23. See *supra* note 7.

24. Non-Legally Binding Authorative Statement of Principles for a Global Consensus on the Management, Conservation and Sustainable Development of All Types of Forests, signed 13 June 1992, U.N. Doc. A/CONF. 151/6 Rev. 1, (1992), reprinted at 31 I.L.M. 887 (1992).

25. 1037 U.N.T.S. 151, 27 U.S.T. 37, T.I.A.S. No. 8226, signed 23 Nov. 1972, entered into force 17 Dec. 1975.

26. (Hungary v. Slovakia), 1997 I.C.J. 7.

27. Id. at para. 111.

water in the Danube is not impaired and that nature is protected, to take new environmental norms into consideration...."[28] The Court also noted that the "awareness of the vulnerability of the environment and the recognition that environmental risks have to be assessed on a continuous basis have become much stronger in [recent] years...."[29]

Nuclear Fallout

The possibility of radioactive fallout from nuclear devices has caused concern for some decades. In 1961 the General Assembly of the United Nations issued a Declaration on the Prohibition of the Use of Nuclear and Thermo-Nuclear Weapons[30] which stated that the use of such weapons "is contrary to the spirit, letter and aims of the United Nations and, as such, a direct violation of the Charter of the United Nations." In 1963 the Treaty Banning Nuclear Weapon Tests in the Atmosphere, in Outer Space and Under Water[31] was signed and entered into force the same year. In 1991 the General Assembly overwhelmingly endorsed "the complete cessation of nuclear-weapon tests and a comprehensive test ban...."[32]

In 1973 France indicated that she would carry out atmospheric nuclear testing in the South Pacific in the near future. Australia and New Zealand brought the *Nuclear Tests Cases*[33] against France asking the International Court of Justice to declare that international law prohibited atmospheric nuclear testing. The Court ultimately dismissed the cases after France had unilaterally announced that the 1974 tests would be the last. The Court declared that:

> 51. In announcing the 1974 series of atmospheric tests would be the last the French Government conveyed to the world at large ... its intention effectively to terminate these tests.... It is from the actual substance of these statements, and from the circumstances attending their making, that the legal implications of the unilateral act must be deduced. The objects of these statements are clear and they were addressed to the international community as a whole, and the Court holds that they constitute an undertaking possessing legal effect....
>
> 52. Thus the Court faces a situation in which the objective of the Applicant has in effect been accomplished, inasmuch as the Court finds that France has undertaken the obligation to hold no further nuclear tests in the atmosphere in the South Pacific.[34] The Court added that "if the basis of this Judgment were to be affected, the Applicant could request an examination of the situation in accordance with the provisions of the Statute...."[35]

---

28. Id. at para. 112.
29. Id.
30. G.A. Res. 1653, U.N. GAOR, 16th Sess., 1063d plen. mtg., at 236, U.N. Doc. A/RES/1653 (1961).
31. 480 U.N.T.S. 43, 14 U.S.T. 1313, T.I.A.S. No. 5433, signed 5 August 1963, entered into force, 10 Oct. 1963, reprinted at 2 I.L.M. 883 (1963).
32. G.A. Res. 46/29, U.N. GAOR, 46th Sess., 65th plen. mtg., U.N. Doc. A/RES/46/29 (1991).
33. *Nuclear Tests Cases* (Australia v. France), 1974 I.C.J. 253; (New Zealand v. France), 1974 I.C.J. 457.
34. *Nuclear Tests Case* (Australia v. France), 1974 I.C.J. 253, at paras. 51 & 52.
35. Id. at para. 60.

In 1995 France carried out a series of underground nuclear tests in the South Pacific which provoked widespread protests throughout the world. New Zealand, relying on the language of the Court's 1974 judgment, filed a "Request for an Examination of the Situation," asking the Court to declare that "the proposed nuclear tests will constitute a violation of the rights under international law of New Zealand, as well as of other States; ... [and] that it is unlawful for France to conduct such nuclear tests before it has undertaken an Environmental Impact Assessment according to accepted international standards. Unless such an assessment establishes that the tests will not give rise, directly or indirectly, to radioactive contamination of the marine environment the rights under international law of New Zealand, as well as the rights of other States, will be violated."[36]

The Court dismissed New Zealand's request stating that "in analyzing its Judgment of 1974, the Court has reached the conclusion that the Judgment dealt exclusively with atmospheric nuclear tests; ... consequently it is not possible for the Court now to take into consideration questions relating to underground nuclear tests...."[37] As a result the Court has not, as yet, delivered an opinion on the legality of nuclear testing. The Comprehensive Nuclear-Test Ban Treaty was opened for signature on September 24, 1996. States parties to this treaty "undertake[] not to carry out any nuclear weapon test explosion ... at any place under [their] jurisdiction or control."[38] One hundred and eighty states have signed this treaty and one hundred and forty-eight states have ratified the treaty. To enter into force the treaty requires that forty-four designated states ratify the treaty (article XIV). To date forty-one of the forty-four states have signed the treaty and thirty-five of those have ratified the treaty including France, the Russian Federation and the United Kingdom.

In 1986 an explosion at the Chernobyl (at that time in the U.S.S.R.) atomic power plant caused large amounts of radioactive emissions. The U.S.S.R. was slow to admit that anything untoward had occurred and only when other countries presented evidence of increased levels of radioactivity did the U.S.S.R. reluctantly agree that an accident had occurred. This incident led to the Convention on Early Notification of a Nuclear Accident[39] which requires parties, in the event of a radioactive accident, to "notify, directly or through the International Atomic Energy Agency ... those states which are or may be physically affected...." (Article 2). The Convention on Assistance in Case of a Nuclear Accident or Radiological Emergency[40] provides for cooperation between the parties in order "to minimize its [the accident's] consequences and to protect life, property and the environment from the effects of radioactive releases." (Article 1 (1)).

---

36. Request for an Examination of the Situation in Accordance with Paragraph 63 of the Court's Judgment of 20 December 1974 in the Nuclear Tests (New Zealand v. France) Case, 1995 I.C.J. 288, 291 (order of Sept. 22).

37. Id. at 306. Shortly after the Court's 1974 decisions, France withdrew its acceptance of the Court's compulsory jurisdiction. New Zealand and Australia could not, therefore, bring a new claim against France.

38. U.N. Doc. A/50/1027, signed 26 Aug. 1996, reprinted at 35 I.L.M. 1439 (1996). For very useful current information on this treaty go to: http://www.ctbto.org.

39. 1439 U.N.T.S. 275, signed 26 Sept. 1986, entered into force, 27 Oct. 1986, reprinted at 25 I.L.M. 1370 (1986).

40. 1457 U.N.T.S. 133, signed 26 Sept. 1986, entered into force, 26 Feb. 1987, reprinted at 25 I.L.M. 1377 (1986).

Legality of the Threat or Use of Nuclear Weapons

International Court of Justice, Advisory Opinion, 1996.
1996 I.C.J. 226, reprinted at 35 I.L.M. 809 (1996)

Note

The General Assembly of the United Nations submitted the following question to the Court for an advisory opinion: "Is the threat or use of nuclear weapons in any circumstances permitted under international law?" The main body of the opinion appears at pages 454–475 below. In the course of the Court's opinion it examined the effect of nuclear weapons on the environment and discussed whether environmental treaties or customary law prohibited the threat or use of nuclear weapons.

The Court found that "the most directly relevant applicable law governing the question of which it was seized, is that relating to the use of force enshrined in the United Nations Charter and the law applicable in armed conflict which regulates the conduct of hostilities, together with any specific treaties on nuclear weapons that the court might determine to be relevant." (Opinion at paragraph 34). Nonetheless, the Court found that the unique destructive capacity of nuclear weapons had to be taken into account in examining the relevant law. The section of the Court's opinion focusing on environmental issues is reproduced below.

Opinion of the Court

27. In both their written and oral statements, some States furthermore argued that any use of nuclear weapons would be unlawfully by reference to existing norms relating to the safeguarding and protection of the environment, in view of their essential importance.

Specific references were made to various existing international treaties and instruments. These included Additional Protocol I of 1977 to the Geneva Conventions of 1949, Article 35, paragraph 3 of which prohibits the employment of "methods or means of warfare which are intended, or may be expected, to cause widespread, long-term and severe damage to the natural environment"; and the Convention of 18 May 1977 on the Prohibition of Military or Any Other Hostile Use of Environmental Modification Techniques, which prohibits the use of weapons which have "widespread, long-lasting or severe effects" on the environment (Art. 1). Also cited were Principle 21 of the Stockholm Declaration of 1972 and Principle 2 of the Rio Declaration of 1992 which express the common conviction of the States concerned that they have a duty "to ensure that activities within their jurisdiction or control do not cause damage to the environment of other States or of areas beyond the limits of national jurisdiction". These instruments and other provisions relating to the protection and safeguarding of the environment were said to apply at all times, in war as well as in peace, and it was contended that they would be violated by the use of nuclear weapons whose consequences would be widespread and would have transboundary effects.

28. Other States questioned the binding legal quality of these precepts of environmental law; or, in the context of the Convention on the Prohibition of Military or Any Other Hostile Use of Environmental Modification Techniques, denied that it was con-

cerned at all with the use of nuclear weapons in hostilities; or, in the case of Additional Protocol I, denied that they were generally bound by its terms, or recalled that they had reserved their position in respect of Article 35, paragraph 3, thereof.

It was also argued by some States that the principal purpose of environmental treaties and norms was the protection of the environment in time of peace. It was said that those treaties made no mention of nuclear weapons. It was also pointed out that warfare in general, and nuclear warfare in particular, were not mentioned in their texts and that it would be destabilizing to the rule of law and to confidence in international negotiations if those treaties were now interpreted in such a way as to prohibit the use of nuclear weapons.

29. The Court recognizes that the environment is under daily threat and that the use of nuclear weapons could constitute a catastrophe for the environment. The Court also recognizes that the environment is not an abstraction but represents the living space, the quality of life and the very health of human beings, including generations unborn. The existence of the general obligation of States to ensure that activities within their jurisdiction and control respect the environment of other States or of areas beyond national control is now part of the corpus of international law relating to the environment.

30. However, the Court is of the view that the issue is not whether the treaties relating to the protection of the environment are or not applicable during an armed conflict, but rather whether the obligations stemming from these treaties were intended to be obligations of total restraint during military conflict.

The Court does not consider that the treaties in question could have intended to deprive a State of the exercise of its right of self-defence under international law because of its obligations to protect the environment. Nonetheless, States must take environmental considerations into account when assessing what is necessary and proportionate in the pursuit of legitimate military objectives. Respect for the environment is one of the elements that go to assessing whether an action is in conformity with the principles of necessity and proportionality.

This approach is supported, indeed, by the terms of Principle 24 of the Rio Declaration, which provides that:

> Warfare is inherently destructive of sustainable development. States shall therefore respect international law providing protection for the environment in times of armed conflict and cooperate in its further development, as necessary.

31. The Court notes furthermore that Article 35, paragraph 2, and 55 of Additional Protocol I provide additional protection for the environment. Taken together, these provisions embody a general obligation to protect the natural environment against widespread, long-term and severe environmental damage; the prohibition of methods and means of warfare which are intended, or may be expected, to cause such damage; and the prohibition of attacks against the natural environment by way of reprisals.

These are powerful constraints for all the States having subscribed to these provisions.

32. General Assembly resolution 47/37 of 25 November 1992 on the Protection of the Environment in Times of Armed Conflict, is also of interest in this context. It affirms the general view according to which environmental considerations constitute one of the elements to be taken into account in the implementation of the principles of the law applicable in armed conflict; it states that "destruction of the environ-

ment, not justified by military necessity and carried out wantonly, is clearly contrary to existing international law." Addressing the reality that certain instruments are not yet binding on all States, the General Assembly in this resolution "*[a]ppeals* to all States that have not yet done so to consider becoming parties to the relevant international conventions."

In its recent Order in the *Request for an Examination of the Situation in Accordance with Paragraph 63 of the Court's Judgment of 20 December 1974 in the Nuclear Tests*(New Zealand v. France) *Case*, the Court stated that its conclusion was "without prejudice to the obligations of States to respect and protect the natural environment" (*Order of 22 September 1995, I.C.J. Reports 1995*, p. 306, para. 64). Although that statement was made in the context of nuclear testing, it naturally also applies to the actual use of nuclear weapons in armed conflict.

33. The Court thus finds that while the existing international law relating to the protection and safeguarding of the environment does not specifically prohibit the use of nuclear weapons, it indicates important environmental factors that are properly to be taken into account in the context of the implementation of the principles and rules of the law applicable in armed conflict.

35. In applying this law [relating to the use of force and the conduct of hostilities] to the present case, the Court cannot however fail to take into account certain unique characteristics of nuclear weapons.

The Court has noted the definitions of nuclear weapons contained in various treaties and accords. It also notes that nuclear weapons are explosive devices whose energy results from the fusion or fission of the atom. By its very nature, that process, in nuclear weapons as they exist today, releases not only immense quantities of heat and energy, but also powerful and prolonged radiation. According to the material before the Court, the first two causes of damage are vastly more powerful than the damage caused by other weapons, while the phenomenon of radiation is said to be peculiar to nuclear weapons. These characteristics render the nuclear weapon potentially catastrophic. The destructive power of nuclear weapons cannot be contained in either space or time. They have the potential to destroy all civilization and the entire ecosystem of the planet.

The radiation released by a nuclear explosion would affect health, agriculture, natural resources and demography over a very wide area. Further, the use of nuclear weapons would be a serious danger to future generations. Ionizing radiation has the potential to damage the future environment, food and marine ecosystem, and to cause genetic defects and illness in future generations.

36. In consequence, in order correctly to apply to the present case the Charter law on the use of force and the law applicable in armed conflict, in particular humanitarian law, it is imperative for the Court to take account of the unique characteristics of nuclear weapons, and in particular their destructive capacity, their capacity to cause untold human suffering, and their ability to cause damage to generations to come.

See also dissenting opinion of Judge Koroma pages 471–473 *infra*.

Other Regimes

The Outerspace treaties,[41] the Antarctic Treaty[42] and the Law of the Sea Convention[43] have been mentioned in other chapters. There are also a number of treaties and declarations relating to water courses most notably the Convention and Statute on the Regime of Navigable Waterways of International Concern;[44] the Helsinki Rules on the Uses of the Waters of International Rivers;[45] and the Convention on the Protection and Use of Transboundary Watercourses and International Lakes[46] which states that it is "intended to strengthen national measures for the protection and ecologically sound management of transboundary surface waters and ground waters."

There has recently been a movement to require states and other agencies to undertake environmental impact assessments prior to entering upon any major project. The Convention on Environmental Impact Assessment in a Transboundary Context[47] requires parties to establish "an environmental impact assessment procedure that permits public participation and preparation of ... environmental impact assessment documentation...." for activities "that are likely to cause significant adverse transboundary impact...." (Article 2). The World Bank now requires an environmental impact assessment for all projects that use Bank funds and effect any natural resources.

Developing nations have often complained that they have more pressing needs than environmental concerns and that they should be subject to more relaxed standards while they are trying to supply basic necessities to their peoples and exercising their right to development. Some treaties recognize the special needs of developing nations and provide less stringent standards for such states.[48] There is also resentment at the application of a so-called double standard. For example, it is argued, Europe chopped down all her forests centuries ago to engage in agriculture; now, when developing countries wish to do the same thing, they are told that they must not do so because it is bad for the environment.

The growth of international environmental law in recent decades has been phenomenal. The world still lacks effective enforcement mechanisms and relies primarily on the good faith of states to carry out their obligations under the various treaties. Some

41. See, e.g., Treaty on Principles Governing the Activities of States in the Exploration and Uses of Outer Space, Including the Moon and Other Celestial Bodies, 610 U.N.T.S. 205, 18 U.S.T. 2410, T.I.A.S. No. 6347, opened for signature 27 Jan. 1967, entered into force 10 Oct. 1967, reprinted at 6 I.L.M. 386 (1967). (See chapter II.)

42. 402 U.N.T.S. 71, 12 U.S.T. 794, T.I.A.S. No. 4780, signed 1 Dec. 1959, entered into force 23 June 1961. (See chapter II.)

43. U.N. Convention on the Law of the Sea, 1833 U.N.T.S. 3, signed 10 Dec. 1982, entered into force 16 Nov. 1994, reprinted at 21 I.L.M. 1261 (1982). (See chapter V.)

44. 7 L.N.T.S. 35, signed 20 April 1921, entered into force, 31 Oct. 1922.

45. International Law Association, Report of the Fifty-Second Conference, Helsinki, 1966 at 484, 52 Int'l L. Ass'n 484 (1987).

46. 1936 U.N.T.S. 269, signed 17 March 1992, entered into force, 6 Oct. 1996, reprinted at 31 I.L.M. 1312 (1992).

47. 1989 U.N.T.S. 309, adopted 25 Feb. 1991, entered into force, 10 Sept. 1997, reprinted at 30 I.L.M. 800 (1991). See also Amendment to the Convention on Environmental Impact Assessment in a Transboundary Context, adopted 27 Feb. 2001, not yet in force, and Protocol on Strategic Environmental Assessment to the Convention on Environmental Impact Assessment in a Transboundary Context, adopted on 21 May 2003, not yet in force.

48. See, e.g., Montreal Protocol on Substances That Deplete the Ozone Layer, art. 5, 1522 U.N.T.S. 3, signed 16 Sept. 1987, entered into force, 1 Jan. 1989, reprinted at 26 I.L.M. 1550 (1987).

treaties have created their own inspection and verification systems[49] and some international agencies undertake monitoring and reporting activities.[50] The continuing success of this remarkable movement will ultimately depend upon the willingness of the world's population to put long term protection of the environment ahead of short term economic success.

Suggested Further Readings

Ian Browlie, Principles of Public International Law, chapter 12 & 13 (7th ed. 2008).

Mark W. Janis & John E. Noyes, Cases and Commentary on International Law, chapter 10 (3d ed. 2006).

Alexandre Kiss & Dinah Shelton, Guide to International Environmental Law (2007).

Ved P. Nanda & George Pring, International Environmental Law and Policy for the 21st Century (2004).

Malcolm N. Shaw, International Law, chapter 15 (6th ed. 2008).

Philippe Sands, Principles of International Environmental Law (2d ed. 2003).

---

49. See e.g., Treaty on the Southeast Asia Nuclear Weapon-Free Zone, signed 15 Dec. 1995, entered into force, 27 March 1997,reprinted at 35 I.L.M. 635 (1996); African Nuclear-Weapon-Free Zone Treaty, signed 13 Sept. 1995, U.N. Doc. A/50/426, reprinted at 35 I.L.M. 698 (1996).

50. See, e.g., Use of the Atomic Energy Agency in the Convention on Early Notification of a Nuclear Accident, art. 2, 1439 U.N.T.S. 275, signed Sept. 26, 1986, entered into force, 27 Oct. 1986, reprinted at 25 I.L.M. 1370 (1986).

Chapter VII

International Legal Personality: States, International Organizations, Non-State Groups, Individuals, and Multi-National Corporations

In chapter I it was stated that the classic definition of international law was that it encompassed the legal relationships between sovereign states. Unless an entity could claim statehood it could not claim any international rights or responsibilities. The classic definition has altered considerably in the last half century. Now international organizations and individuals have gained international legal status for certain purposes. This chapter will take a brief look at the following subjects: the definition of a state; secession and self-determination; state responsibility; a state's capacity to bring international claims on behalf of an individual; the international status of international organizations (including a description of the structure of the United Nations); non-state groups; and the international status of individuals.

The Definition of a State

Since states are still the principal actors in international law it is as well to discuss the definition of the state. Most definitions of a state set out four requirements: a defined territory; a permanent population; a government; and the capacity to enter into relations with other states.[1]

A Defined Territory

Most states have well defined boundaries accepted by other states. Within their boundaries states have the exclusive right to display sovereignty and the corollary duty to protect the international rights of individuals, whether nationals or aliens, within the state and to protect the rights of other states as they interact with the state.

A number of states either have been, or are currently, embroiled in territorial disputes. These disputes may emanate from within the state or from other states. Within

1. See Convention on Rights and Duties of States, 165 L.N.T.S. 19, art. 1, signed 26 Dec. 1933, entered into force 26 Dec. 1934; Restatement Third § 201 (1987).

the state, various groups may be claiming that they have been unjustly deprived of their lands. Such issues will ultimately be settled by the internal dispute settlement machinery. Those claims do not impinge upon the question of statehood. If a particular group not only claims territory but also asserts a right to secession, then the state's boundaries are indeed questionable just as they would be if another state laid claim to part of the state's territory. Provided a state has some area of land that it definitely controls, international law is usually willing to treat the entity as a state. Israel was admitted to the United Nations in 1948 when its borders were far from clear. Negotiations concerning the ultimate status of the Palestinian occupied territories means that Israel's borders and the extent of the territory she occupies are likely to alter, but no one doubts that Israel is a state. What indicia of statehood the Palestinians will have to demonstrate before the world decides to recognize Palestine as a state is yet to be determined.

A Permanent Population

All populations are always in flux in terms of numbers but in order to be considered a state, the entity must have some people. Earlier in the century there were suggestions that an entity must have a certain minimum number of inhabitants to qualify for statehood but that view has now been rejected. A number of micro-states have been admitted to the United Nations such as Liechtenstein with a population of roughly 31,000 and Nauru with roughly 12,000 inhabitants. A number of states also have nomadic populations who spend part of the year in one state and part in another. Again this is not considered to negate statehood provided the state always has a core of inhabitants.

Some areas of the globe are very inhospitable to human habitation such as the Arctic and Antarctic regions. The Antarctic is subject to a number of overlapping territorial claims on the part of several states. See pp. 51–52 *supra*. There is no permanent population in the Antarctic. Its status is now governed by The Antarctic Treaty,[2] but it is not considered a state.

A Government

A state must have an organized governmental structure which is largely independent from outside authority. States are of course free to enter into alliances with other states and to make agreements with other states promising to perform or refrain from performing certain acts. Most states have always entered into a whole variety of different networks of international agreements on a host of topics. No one suggests that these agreements jeopardize an entity's statehood. If, however, aspects of a state's foreign, defense, monetary or domestic policy are governed by another state, the international community may be unwilling to treat the entity as a state. After Finland declared its independence from the Soviet Union following the revolution of 1917, chaos erupted which the new Finnish government was only able to subdue with difficulty. The League of Nations Commission of Jurists discussed the question of when Finland became a state in the course of its decision in the *Aaland Islands Case*. The Commission stated:

2. 402 U.N.T.S. 71, 12 U.S.T. 794, T.I.A.S. No. 4780, signed Dec. 1, 1959, entered into force June 23, 1961.

> In the midst of revolution and anarchy, certain elements essential to the existence of a State, even some elements of fact, were lacking for a considerable period. Political and social life was disorganized; the authorities were not strong enough to assert themselves ... the Government had been chased from the capital and forcibly prevented from carrying out its duties.... It is, therefore, difficult to say at what exact date the Finnish Republic, in the legal sense of the term, actually became a definitely constituted sovereign State. This certainly did not take place until a state political organization had been created, and until the public authorities had become strong enough to assert themselves throughout the territories of the State without the assistance of foreign troops.[3]

Many governments undergo rebel attacks or civil wars. The British government was attacked by the Irish Republican Army for several decades but the turmoil was insufficient to persuade the international community that the United Kingdom no longer existed as a state. At various times, Lebanon has undergone severe internal strife as well as outside control of certain areas by both Syria and Israel and yet Lebanon continued to be recognized as a state. A civil war may simply result in a new government's coming to power but sometimes it results in the creation of a new entity. The civil war in Ethiopia eventually resulted in the new state of Eritrea being created out of the northern part of the country in 1993.[4] In Nigeria, however, the break away state of Biafra was ultimately unsuccessful in achieving statehood and returned to the Nigerian Federation in 1970.

Capacity to Enter into Relations with Other States

An entity that wishes to enter into relationships with other states obviously needs a fairly high degree of governmental organization. Those persons conducting the external relationships on behalf of the entity have to be perceived by other states as having a credible claim to represent the entity. Ultimately, an entity's ability actually to enter into relationships with other states depends only in part on its capacity to conduct such relationships. Other states must be willing to treat the entity as a state and to conduct relationships with the entity on a state-to-state basis.

There have been a number of entities throughout history that have possessed all four indicia of statehood but the international community has nevertheless refused to recognize them as states or to have any dealings with them. In 1965, Ian Smith, the Prime Minister of the British self-governing colony of Rhodesia declared independence from Great Britain. The Smith government wanted to retain a system of government that kept almost all governing powers in the hands of the minority white population. The British government insisted on universal suffrage and no white racial preferences, although it is fair to say that such a position was of recent origin and that prior to the 1960s the British government had not objected to white domination in Rhodesia. Britain refused to recognize Smith's declaration of independence and the rest of the world followed suit. The U.N. imposed broad based economic sanctions of the Smith government[5] and called upon all states "not to recognize this illegal racist minority

3. League of Nations O.J., Spec. Supp. 3, 4 at 8–9 (1920).

4. See, Minasse Haile, Legality of Secessions: The Case of Eritrea, 8 Emory Int'l L. Rev. 479 (1994).

5. S.C Res. 253, U.N. SCOR, 23rd Sess., Resolutions and Decisions (1968).

regime...."[6] By 1979, the guerilla independence movement had toppled the Smith Government and the independent State of Zimbabwe was declared and rapidly recognized by the international community.

There was no doubt that the Smith regime possessed all of the requirements of statehood in an objective sense but the world community had condemned the regime for its racist politics and refused to recognize it as a state. Some authors have used the example of the Smith regime to argue that there is a fifth requirement for statehood, namely that the entity should meet with the approval (either on moral and/or legal grounds) of the world community before it fully possesses the requirements for statehood. When the apartheid government of South Africa created the so-called independent states of Transkei, Bophutgatswana, Venda and Ciskei, in the 1970–80s these states were perceived by the world as manifesting the racial separation policies of the South African government. As a result no other state was willing to recognize them as international entities.

Secession and Self-Determination

Reference re Secession of Quebec

Supreme Court of Canada
2 S.C.R. 217 (1998)

* * *

Pursuant to s. 53 of the *Supreme Court Act,* the Governor in Council referred the following questions to this Court:

1. Under the Constitution of Canada, can the National Assembly, legislature or government of Quebec effect the secession of Quebec from Canada unilaterally?

2.Does international law give the National Assembly, legislature or government of Quebec the right to effect the secession of Quebec from Canada unilaterally? In this regard, is there a right to self-determination under international law that would give the National Assembly, legislature or government of Quebec the right to effect the secession of Quebec from Canada unilaterally?

3.In the event of a conflict between domestic and international law on the right of the National Assembly, legislature or government of Quebec to effect the secession of Quebec from Canada unilaterally, which would take precedence in Canada?

Issues regarding the Court's reference jurisdiction were raised by the *amicus curiae.* He argued that s. 53 of the *Supreme Court Act* was unconstitutional; that, even if the Court's reference jurisdiction was constitutionally valid, the questions submitted were outside the scope of s. 53; and, finally, that these questions were not justiciable.

Held: Section 53 of the *Supreme Court Act* is constitutional and the Court should answer the Reference questions.

> [On question 1, the Court held that under the Canadian Constitution there was no right to unilateral secession.]

---

6. Question Concerning the Situation in Southern Rhodesia, Nov. 12, 1965, S.C. Res. 216, U.N. SCOR, 20th Sess., Resolutions ad Decisions at 8 (1965).

* * *

B. *Question 2*

Does international law give the National Assembly, legislature or government of Quebec the right to effect the secession of Quebec from Canada unilaterally? In this regard, is there a right to self-determination under international law that would give the National Assembly, legislature or government of Quebec the right to effect the secession of Quebec from Canada unilaterally?

* * *

110. The argument before the Court on Question 2 has focused largely on determining whether, under international law, a positive legal right to unilateral secession exists in the factual circumstances assumed for the purpose of our response to Question 1. Arguments were also advanced to the effect that, regardless of the existence or non-existence of a positive right to unilateral secession, international law will in the end recognize effective political realities—including the emergence of a new state—as facts. While our responses to Question 2 will address considerations raised by this alternative argument of "effectivity", it should first be noted that the existence of a positive legal entitlement is quite different from a prediction that the law will respond after the fact to a then existing political reality. These two concepts examine different points in time. The questions posed to the Court address legal rights in advance of a unilateral act of purported secession. While we touch below on the practice governing the international recognition of emerging states, the Court is a wary of entertaining speculation about the possible future conduct of sovereign states on the international level as it was under Question 1 to speculate about the possible future course of political negotiations among the participants in the Canadian federation. In both cases, the reference questions are directed only to the legal framework within which the political actors discharge their various mandates.

(1) *Secession at International Law*

111. It is clear that international law does not specifically grant component parts of sovereign states the legal right to secede unilaterally from their "parent" state. This is acknowledged by the experts who provided their opinions on behalf of both the *amicus curiae* and the Attorney General of Canada. Given the lack of specific authorization for unilateral secession, proponents of the existence of such a right at international law are therefore left to attempt to found their argument (I) on the proposition that unilateral secession is not specifically prohibited and that what is not specifically prohibited is inferentially permitted; or (ii) on the implied duty of states to recognize the legitimacy of secession brought about by the exercise of the well-established international law right of "a people" to self-determination. The *amicus curiae* addressed the right of self-determination, but submitted that it was not applicable to the circumstances of Quebec within the Canadian federation, irrespective of the existence or non-existence of a referendum result in favour of secession. We agree on this point with the *amicus curiae*, for reasons that we will briefly develop.

(a) *Absence of a Specific Prohibition*

112. International law contains neither a right of unilateral secession nor the explicit denial of such a right, although such a denial is, to some extent, implicit in the exceptional circumstances required for secession to be permitted under the right of the people to self-determination, e.g., the right of secession that arises in the exceptional situation of an oppressed or colonial people, discussed below. As will be seen, interna-

tional law places great importance on the territorial integrity of nation states and, by and large, leaves the creation of a new state to be determined by the domestic law of the existing state of which the seceding entity presently forms a part (r). Y. Jennings, *The Acquisition of Territory in International Law* (1963), at pp. 8–9). Where, as here, unilateral secession would be incompatible with the domestic Constitution, international law is likely to accept that conclusion subject to the right of peoples to self-determination, a topic to which we now turn.

(b) *The Right of a people to Self-determination*

113. While international law generally regulates the conduct of nation states, it does, in some specific circumstances, also recognize the "rights" of entities other than nation states—such as the right of a people to self-determination.

114. The existence of the right of a people to self-determination is now so widely recognized in international conventions that the principle has acquired a status beyond "convention" and is considered a general principle of international law. (A. Cassese, *Self-determination of peoples: A legal reappraisal* (1995), at pp. 171–72; K. Doehring, "Self-Determination", in B. Simma, ed., *The Charter of the United Nations: A Commentary* (1994), at p. 70.)

115. Article 1 of the *Charter of the United Nations*, Can. T.S. 1945 No. 7, states in part that one of the purposes of the United Nations (U.N.) is:

> *Article 1*
>
> ...
>
> 2. To develop friendly relations among nations based on respect for the principle of equal rights and self-determination of peoples, and to take other appropriate measures to strengthen universal peace;

116. Article 55 of the U.N. Charter further states that the U.N. shall promote goals such as higher standards of living, full employment and human rights "[w]ith a view to the creation of conditions of stability and well-being which are necessary for peaceful and friendly relations among nations based on respect for the principle of equal rights and self-determination of peoples".

117. This basic principle of self-determination has been carried forward and addressed in so many U.N. conventions and resolutions that, as noted by Doehring, *supra*, at p. 60:

The sheer number of resolutions concerning the right of self-determination makes their enumeration impossible.

118. For our purposes, reference to the following conventions and resolutions is sufficient. Article 1 of both the U.N.'s *International Covenant on Civil and Political Rights,* 999 U.N.T.S. 171, and its *International Covenant on Economic, Social and Cultural Rights,* 993 U.N.T.S. 3, states:

> 1. All peoples have the right of self-determination. By virtue of that right they freely determine their political status and freely pursue their economic, social and cultural development.

119. Similarly, the U.N. General Assembly's *Declaration on Principles of International Law concerning Friendly Relations and Co-operation among States in accordance with the Charter of the United Nations,* GA Res. 2625 (XXV), 24 October 1970 *(Declaration on Friendly Relations), States:*

> By virtue of the principle of equal rights and self-determination of peoples enshrined in the Charter of the United Nations, all peoples have the right freely to

> determine, without external interference, their political status and to pursue their economic, social and cultural development, and every State has the duty to respect this right in accordance with the provisions of the Charter.

120. In 1993, the U.N. World Conference of Human Rights adopted the *Vienna Declaration and Programme of Action*, A/Conf.157/24, 25 June 1993, that reaffirmed Article 1 of the two above-mentioned convenants. The U.N. General Assembly's *Declaration on the Occasion of the Fiftieth Anniversary of the United Nations*, GA Res. 50/6, 9 November 1995, also emphasizes the right to self-determination by providing that the U.N.'s member states will:

> 1 . . .
>
> Continue to reaffirm the right of *self-determination of all peoples*, taking into account the particular situation of peoples under colonial or other forms of alien domination or foreign occupation, and recognize the right of peoples to take legitimate action in accordance with the Charter of the United Nations to realize their inalienable right of self-determination. *This shall not be construed as authorizing* or encouraging any action that would dismember or impair, totally or in part, the *territorial integrity or political unity of sovereign and independent States* conducting themselves in compliance with the principle of equal rights and self-determination of people and thus possessed of a Government representing the whole people belonging to the territory without distinction of any kind. . . . [Emphasis added.]

121. The right to self-determination is also recognized in other international legal documents. For example, the *Final Act of the Conference on Security and Co-operation in Europe*, 14 I.L.M. 1292 (1975) *(Helsinki Final Act)*, states (in Part VIII):

> The participating States will respect the equal rights of peoples and *their right to self-determination*, acting at all times in conformity with the purposes and principles of the Charter of the United Nations and with the relevant norms of international law, including those relating to territorial integrity of States. By virtue of the principle of equal rights and self-determination of peoples, all peoples always have the right, in full freedom, to determine, when and as they wish, their internal and external political status, without external interference, and to pursue as they wish their political, economic, social and cultural development. [Emphasis added.]

122. As will be seen, international law expects that the right to self-determination will be exercised by the peoples within the framework of existing sovereign states and consistent with the maintenance of the territorial integrity of those states. Where this is not possible, in the exceptional circumstances discussed below, a right of secession may arise.

(I) Defining "Peoples"

123. International law grants the right to self-determination to "peoples". Accordingly, access to the right requires the threshold step of characterizing as a people the group seeking self-determination. However, as the right to self-determination has developed by virtue of a combination of international agreements and conventions, coupled with state practice, with little formal elaboration of the definition of "peoples", the result has been that the precise meaning of the term "peoples" remains somewhat uncertain.

124. It is clear that "a people" may include only a portion of the population of an existing state. The right to self-determination has developed largely as a human right, and is generally used in documents that simultaneously contain references to "nation"

and "state". The juxtaposition of these terms is indicative that the reference to "people" does not necessarily mean the entirety of a state's population. To restrict the definition of the term to the population of existing states would render the granting of a right to self-determination largely duplicative, given parallel emphasis within the majority of the source documents on the need to protect the territorial integrity of existing states, and would frustrate its remedial purpose.

125. While much of the Quebec population certainly shares many of the characteristics (such as a common language and culture) that would be considered in determining whether a specific group is a "people", as do other groups within Quebec and/or Canada, it is not necessary to explore this legal characterization to resolve Question 2 appropriately. Similarly, it is not necessary for the Court to determine whether, should a Quebec people exist within the definition of public international law, such a people encompasses the entirety of the provincial population or just a portion thereof. Nor is it necessary to examine the position of the aboriginal population within Quebec. As the following discussion of the scope of the right to self-determination will make clear, whatever be the correct application of the definition of people(s) in this context, their right of self-determination cannot in the present circumstances be said to ground a right to unilateral secession.

(ii) Scope of the Right to Self-determination

126. The recognized sources of international law establish that the right to self-determination of a people is normally fulfilled through *internal* self-determination—a people's pursuit of its political, economic, social and cultural development within the framework of an existing state. A right to *external* self-determination (which in this case potentially takes the form of the assertion of a right to unilateral secession) arises in only the most extreme cases and, even then, under carefully defined circumstances. *External* self-determination can be defined as in the following statement from the *Declaration on Friendly Relations* as

> [t]he establishment of a sovereign and independent State, the free association or integration with an independent State or the emergence into any other political status freely determined by a *people* constitute modes of implementing the right of self-determination by *that people.* [Emphasis added.]

127. The international law principle of self-determination has evolved within a framework of respect for the territorial integrity of existing states. The various international documents that support the existence of a people's right to self-determination also contain parallel statements supportive of the conclusion that the exercise of such a right must be sufficiently limited to prevent threats to an existing state's territorial integrity or the stability of relations between sovereign states.

128. The *Declaration on Friendly Relations,* the *Vienna Declaration* and the *Declaration on the Occasion of the Fiftieth Anniversary of the United Nations* are specific. They state, immediately after affirming a people's right to determine political, economic, social and cultural issues, that such rights are *not* to

> be construed as authorizing or encouraging any action that would dismember or *impair, totally or in part, the territorial integrity or political unity of sovereign and independent States conducting themselves in compliance with the principle of equal rights and self-determination of peoples* and thus possessed of a Government representing the whole people belonging to the territory without distinction.... [Emphasis added.]

129. Similarly, while the concluding document of the Vienna Meeting in 1989 of the Conference on Security and Co-operation in Europe on the follow-up to the *Helsinki*

Final Act again refers to peoples having the right to determine "their international and *external* political status" (emphasis added), that statement is immediately followed by express recognition that the participating states will at all times act, as stated in the *Helsinki Final Act,* "in conformity with the purposes and principles of the Charter of the United Nations and with the relevant norms of international law, *including those relating to territorial integrity of States*" (emphasis added). Principle 5 of the concluding document states that the participating states (including Canada):

> ... confirm their commitment strictly and effectively to observe the principle of the territorial integrity of States. They will refrain from any violation of this principle and thus from any action aimed by direct or indirect means, in contravention of the purposes and principles of the Charter of the United Nations, other obligations under international law or the provisions of the [Helsinki] Final Act, at violating the territorial integrity, political independence or the unity of a State. *No actions or situations in contravention of this principle will be recognized as legal by the participating States.* [Emphasis added.]

Accordingly, the reference in the *Helsinki Final Act* to a people determining its external political status is interpreted to mean the expression of a people's external political status through the government of the existing state, save in the exceptional circumstances discussed below. As noted by Cassese, *supra,* at p. 287, given the history and textual structure of this document, its reference to external self-determination simply means that "no territorial or other change can be brought about by the central authorities of a State that is contrary to the will of the whole people of that State".

130. While the *International Covenant on Economic, Social and Cultural Rights* and the *International on Covenant Civil and Political Rights* do not specifically refer to the protection of territorial integrity, they both define the ambit of the right to self-determination in terms that are normally attainable within the framework of an existing state. There is no necessary incompatibility between the maintenance of the territorial integrity of existing states, including Canada, and the right of a "people" to achieve a full measure of self-determination. A state whose government represents the whole of the people or peoples resident within its territory, on a basis of equality and without discrimination, and respects the principles of self-determination in its own internal arrangements, is entitled to the protection under international law of its territorial integrity.

(iii) Colonial and Oppressed Peoples

131. Accordingly, the general state of international law with respect to the right to self-determination is that the right operates within the overriding protection granted to the territorial integrity of "parent" states. However, as noted by Cassese, *supra*, at p. 334, there are certain defined contexts within which the right to the self-determination of peoples does allow that right to be exercised "externally", which, in the context of this reference, would potentially mean secession:

> ... the right to external self-determination, which entails the possibility of choosing (or restoring) independence, has only been bestowed upon two classes of peoples (those under colonial rule or foreign occupation), based upon the assumption that both classes make up entities that are inherently distinct from the colonial Power and the occupant Power and that their 'territorial integrity', all but destroyed by the colonist or occupying Power, should be fully restored....

132. The right of colonial peoples to exercise their right to self-determination by breaking away from the "imperial" power is now undisputed, but is irrelevant to this Reference.

133. The other clear case where a right to external self-determination accrues is where a people is subject to alien subjugation, domination or exploitation outside a colonial context. This recognition finds its roots in the *Declaration on Friendly Relations:*

> Every State has the duty to promote, through joint and separate action, realization of the principle of equal rights and self-determination of peoples, in accordance with the provisions of the Charter, and to render assistance to the United Nations in carrying out the responsibilities entrusted to it by the Charter regarding the implementation of the principle, in order:
>
> (a) To promote friendly relations and co-operation among States; and
>
> (b) To bring a speedy end to colonialism, having due regard to the freely expressed will of the peoples concerned; and bearing in mind that subjection of peoples to alien subjugation, domination and exploitation constitutes a violation of the principle, as well as a denial of fundamental human rights, and is contrary to the Charter.

134. A number of commentators have further asserted that the right to self-determination may ground a right to unilateral secession in a third circumstance. Although this third circumstance has been described in several ways, the underlying proposition is that, when a people is blocked from the meaningful exercise of its right to self-determination internally, it is entitled, as a last resort, to exercise it by secession. The *Vienna Declaration* requirement that governments represent "the whole people belonging to the territory without distinction of any kind" adds credence to the assertion that such a complete blockage may potentially give rise to a right of secession.

135. Clearly, such a circumstance parallels the other two recognized situations in that the ability of a people to exercise its right to self-determination internally is somehow being totally frustrated. While it remains unclear whether this third proposition actually reflects an established international law standard, it is unnecessary for present purposes to make that determination. Even assuming that the third circumstance is sufficient to create a right to unilateral secession under international law, the current Quebec context cannot be said to approach such a threshold. As stated by the *amicus curiae,* Addendum to the factum of the *amicus curiae,* at paras. 15–16:

> [TRANSLATION] 15. The Quebec people is not the victim of attacks on its physical existence or integrity, or of a massive violation of its fundamental rights. The Quebec people is manifestly not, in the opinion of the *amicus curia,* an oppressed people.
>
> 16. For close to 40 of the last 50 years, the Prime Minister of Canada has been a Quebecer. During this period, Quebecers have held from time to time all the most important positions in the federal Cabinet. During the 8 years prior to June 1997, the Prime Minister and the Leader of the Official Opposition in the House of Commons were both Quebecers. At present, the Prime Minister of Canada, the Right Honourable Chief Justice and two other members of the Court, the Chief of staff of the Canadian Armed Forces and the Canadian ambassador to the United States, not to mention the Deputy Secretary-General of the United Nations, are all Quebecers. The international achievements of Quebecers in most fields of human endeavour are too numerous to list. Since the dynamism of the Quebec people has been directed toward the business sector, it has been clearly successful in Quebec, the rest of Canada and abroad.

136. The population of Quebec cannot plausibly be said to be denied access to government. Quebecers occupy prominent positions within the government of Canada. Residents of the province freely make political choices and pursue economic, social and cultural development within Quebec, across Canada, and throughout the world. The population of Quebec is equitably represented in legislative, executive and judicial institutions. In short, to reflect the phraseology of the international documents that address the right to self-determination of peoples, Canada is a "sovereign and independent state conducting itself in compliance with the principle of equal rights and self-determination of peoples and thus possessed of a government representing the whole people belonging to the territory without distinction".

137. The continuing failure to reach agreement on amendments to the Constitution, while a matter of concern, does not amount to a denial of self-determination. In the absence of amendments to the Canadian Constitution, we must look at the constitutional arrangements presently in effect, and we cannot conclude under current circumstances that those arrangements place Quebecers in a disadvantaged position within the scope of the international law rule.

138. In summary, the international law right to self-determination only generates, at best, a right to external self-determination in situations of former colonies; where a people is oppressed, as for example under foreign military occupation; or where a definable group is denied meaningful access to government to pursue their political, economic, social and cultural development. In all three situations the people in question are entitled to a right to external self-determination because they have been denied the ability to exert internally their right to self-determination. Such exceptional circumstances are manifestly inapplicable to Quebec under existing conditions. Accordingly, neither the population of the province of Quebec, even if characterized in terms of "people" or "peoples", nor its representative institutions, the National Assembly, the legislature or government of Quebec, possess a right, under international law, to secede unilaterally from Canada.

139. We would not wish to leave this aspect of our answer to Question 2 without acknowledging the importance of the submissions made us respecting the rights and concerns of aboriginal peoples in the event of a unilateral secession, as well as the appropriate means of defining the boundaries of a seceding Quebec with particular regard to the northern lands occupied largely by aboriginal peoples. However, the concern of aboriginal peoples is precipitated by the asserted right of Quebec to unilateral secession. In light of our finding that there is no such right applicable to the population of Quebec, either under the Constitution of Canada or at international law, but that on the contrary a clear democratic expression of support for secession would lead under the Constitution to negotiations in which aboriginal interests would be taken into account, it becomes unnecessary to explore further the concerns of the aboriginal peoples in this Reference.

(2) *Recognition of a Factual/Political Reality: the "Effectivity" Principle*

140. As stated, an argument advanced by the *amicus curiae* on this branch of the Reference was that while international law may not ground a positive right to unilateral secession in the context of Quebec, international law equally does not prohibit secession and, in fact, international recognition would be conferred on such a political reality if it emerged, for example, via effective control of the territory of what is now the province of Quebec.

141. It is true that international law may well, depending on the circumstances, adapt to recognize a political and/or factual reality, regardless of the legality of the steps leading to its creation. However, as mentioned at the outset, effectivity, as such, does not have any real applicability to Question 2, which asks whether a right to unilateral secessions exists.

142. No one doubts that legal consequences may flow from political facts, and that "sovereignty is a political fact for which no purely legal authority can be constituted ...", H.W.R. Wade, "The Basis of Legal Sovereignty", [1995] *Camb. L.J.* 172, at p. 196. Secession of a province from Canada, if successful in the streets, might well lead to the creation of a new state. Although recognition by other states is not, at least as a matter of theory, necessary to achieve statehood, the viability of a would-be state in the international community depends, as a practical matter, upon recognition by other states. That process of recognition is guided by legal norms. However, international recognition is not alone constitutive of statehood and, critically, does not relate back to the date of secession to serve retroactively as a source of a "legal" right to secede in the first place. Recognition occurs only after a territorial unit has been successful, as a political fact, in achieving secession.

143. As indicated in responding to Question 1, one of the legal norms which may be recognized by states in granting or withholding recognition of emergent states is the legitimacy of the process by which the *de facto* secession is, or was, being pursued. The process of recognition, once considered to be an exercise of pure sovereign discretion, has come to be associated with legal norms. See, e.g. European Community Declaration on the *Guidelines on the Recognition of New States in Eastern Europe and in the Soviet Union*, 31 I.L.M. 1486 (1992), at p. 1487. While national interest and perceived political advantage to the recognizing state obviously play an important role, foreign states may also take into account their view as to the existence of a right to self-determination on the part of the population of the putative state, and a counterpart domestic evaluation, namely, an examination of the legality of the secession according to the law of the state from which the territorial unit purports to have seceded. As we indicated in our answer to Question 1, an emergent state that has disregarded legitimate obligations arising out of its previous situation can potentially expect to be hindered by that disregard in achieving international recognition, at least with respect to the timing of that recognition. On the other had, compliance by the seceding province with such legitimate obligations would weigh in favour of international recognition. The notion that what is not explicitly prohibited is implicitly permitted has little relevance where (as here) international law refers the legality of secession to the domestic law of the seceding state and the law of the state holds unilateral secession to be unconstitutional.

144. As a court of law, we are ultimately concerned only with legal claims. If the principle of "effectivity" is no more than that "successful revolution begets its own legality" (S.A. de Smith, "Constitutional Lawyers in Revolutionary Situations" (1968), 7 *West. Ont. L. Rev.* 93, at p. 96), it necessarily means that legality follows and does not precede the successful revolution. *Ex hypothesi*, the successful revolution took place outside the constitutional framework of the predecessor state, otherwise it would not be characterized as "a revolution". It may be that a unilateral secession by Quebec would eventually be accorded legal status by Canada and other states, and thus give rise to legal consequences; but this does not support the more radical contention that subsequent recognition of a state of affairs brought about by a unilateral declaration of independence could be taken to mean that secession was achieved under colour of a legal right.

145. An argument was made to analogize the principle of effectivity with the second aspect of the rule of law identified by this Court in *Manitoba Language Rights Reference, supra,* at p. 753, namely, avoidance of a legal vacuum. In that Reference, it will be recalled, this Court declined to strike down all of Manitoba's legislation for its failure to comply with constitutional dictates, out of concern that this would leave the province in a state of chaos. In so doing, we recognized that the rule of law is a constitutional prin-

ciple which permits the courts to address the practical consequences of their actions, particularly in constitutional cases. The similarity of that principle and the principle of effectivity, it was argued, is that both attempted to refashion the law to meet social reality. However, nothing of our concern in the *Manitoba Language Rights Reference* about the severe practical consequences of unconstitutionality affected our conclusion that, as a matter of law, all Manitoba legislation at issue in that case was unconstitutional. The Court's declaration of unconstitutionally was clear and unambiguous. The Court's concern with maintenance of the rule of law was directed in its relevant aspect to the appropriate remedy, which in that case was to suspend the declaration of invalidity to permit appropriate rectification to take place.

146. The principle of effectivity operates very differently. It proclaims that an illegal act may eventually acquire legal status if, as a matter of empirical fact, it is recognized on the international plane. Our law has long recognized that through a combination of acquiescence and prescription, an illegal act may at some later point be accorded some form of legal status. In the law of property, for example, it is well known that a squatter on land may ultimately become the owner if the true owner sleeps on his or her right to repossess the land. In this way, a change in the factual circumstances may subsequently be reflected in a change in legal status. It is, however, quite another matter to suggest that a subsequent condonation of an initially illegal act retroactively creates a legal right to engage in the act in the first place. The broader contention is not supported by the international principle of effectivity or otherwise and must be rejected.

C. Question 3

In the event of a conflict between domestic and international law on the right of the National Assembly, legislature or government of Quebec to effect the secession of Quebec from Canada unilaterally, which would take precedence in Canada?

147. In view of our answers to Questions 1 and 2, there is no conflict between domestic and international law to be addressed in the context of this Reference.

* * *

153. The task of the Court has been to clarify the legal framework within which political decisions are to be taken "under the Constitution", not to usurp the prerogatives of the political forces that operate within that framework. The obligations we have identified are binding obligations under the Constitution of Canada. However, it will be for the political actors to determine what constitutes "a clear majority on a clear question" in the circumstances under which a future referendum vote may be taken. Equally, in the event of demonstrated majority support for Quebec secession, the content and process of the negotiations will be for the political actors to settle. The reconciliation of the various legitimate constitutional interests is necessarily committed to the political rather than the judicial realm precisely because that reconciliation can only be achieved through the give and take of political negotiations. To the extent issues addressed in the course of negotiation are political, the courts, appreciating their proper role in the constitutional scheme, would have no supervisory role.

154. We have also considered whether a positive legal entitlement to secession exists under international law in the factual circumstances contemplated by Question 1 i.e., a clear democratic expression of support on a clear question for Quebec secession. Some of those who supported an affirmative answer to this question did so on the basis of the recognized right to self-determination that belongs to all "peoples". Although much of the Quebec population certainly shares many of the characteristics of a people, it is not necessary to decide the "people" issue because, whatever may be

the correct determination of this issue in the context of Quebec, a right to secession only arises under the principle of self-determination of peoples at international law where "a people" is governed as part of a colonial empire; where "a people" is subject to alien subjugation, domination or exploitation; and possibly where "a people" is denied any meaningful exercise of its right to self-determination within the state of which it forms a part. In other circumstances, peoples are expected to achieve self-determination within the framework of their existing state. A state whose government represents the whole of the people or peoples resident within its territory, on a basis of equality and without discrimination, and respects the principles of self-determination in its internal arrangements, is entitled to maintain its territorial integrity under international law and to have that territorial integrity recognized by other states. Quebec does not meet the threshold of a colonial people or an oppressed people, nor can it be suggested that Quebecers have been denied meaningful access to government to pursue their political, economic, cultural and social development. In the circumstances, the national Assembly, the legislature or the government of Quebec do not enjoy a right at international law to effect the secession of Quebec from Canada unilaterally.

155. Although there is no right, under the Constitution or at international law, to unilateral secession, that is secession without negotiation on the basis just discussed, this does not rule out the possibility of an unconstitutional declaration of secession leading to a *de facto* secession. The ultimate success of such a secession would be dependent on recognition by the international community, which is likely to consider the legality and legitimacy of secession having regard to, amongst other facts, the conduct of Quebec and Canada, in determining whether to grant or withhold recognition. Such recognition, even if granted, would not, however, provide any retroactive justification for the act of secession, either under the Constitution of Canada or at international law.

156 The reference questions are answered accordingly.

Judgment accordingly.

QUESTIONS

1. In what circumstances did the Canadian Supreme Court conclude that "a people" had a right to unilateral secession from a state under international law?
2. What guidance did the Court give on the meaning of "peoples"?
3. What do you understand the Court to mean by the "effectivity principle"?
4. Would a wider acceptance of the right to secession lead to political instability or help to prevent the bloodshed of civil war?

The International Court of Justice also discussed self-determination in its decision refusing to reach the merits in the *Case Concerning East Timor* (Portugal v. Australia), 1995 I.C.J. 90:

> 29. . . .
>
> In the Court's view, Portugal's assertion that the right of peoples to self determination, as it evolved from the Charter and United Nations practice, has an *erga omnes* character, is irreproachable. The principle of self-determination of peoples has been recognized by the United Nations Charter and in the jurisprudence of the Court (see *Legal Consequences for States of the Continued Presence of South Africa in Namibia (South West Africa) notwithstanding Security Council Resolu-*

> *tion 276 (1970), Advisory Opinion, I.C.J. Reports 1975,* pp. 31–33, paras. 54–59); it is one of the essential principles of international law.
>
> * * *
>
> 31. . . .
>
> For the two parties [Portugal and Australia], the Territory of East Timor remains a non-self-governing territory and its people has the right to self-determination.... Furthermore, the Security Council in its resolutions 384 (1975) and 389 (1976) has expressly called for respect for "the territorial integrity of East Timor as well as the inalienable right of its people to self-determination in accordance with General Assembly Resolution 1514 (XV)."

See also Judge Weeramantry's dissenting opinion in the *Case Concerning East Timor* (Portugal v. Australia), 1995 I.C.J. 90, at p. 142 ff.

More recently, in October, 2008, the General Assembly adopted a resolution drafted by Serbia requesting an advisory opinion from the ICJ on the following question: "Is the unilateral declaration of independence by the Provisional Institutions of Self-Government of Kosovo in accordance with international law?" The Court has fixed time limits for receiving statements and comments as April and July 2009[7] so it looks as if the Court is planning to issue an advisory opinion on this important issue.

State Responsibility

States have responsibility for a variety of obligations imposed upon them by international law. The nature of these obligations has provoked much controversy and is largely beyond the scope of this book. The International Law Commission, which consists of thirty four members elected by the General Assembly, is required to work towards "encouraging the progressive development of international law and its codification...."[8] The Commission has been working for many years on a series of draft articles on State Responsibility which may evolve into a comprehensive treaty. See also Humanitarian Intervention: Duty to Protect, chapter X.

A State's Capacity to Bring International Claims on Behalf of Individuals

Although the topic of State Responsibility will not be covered in any detail in this book, the ability of a state to bring claims on behalf of individuals will be covered briefly. Professor Rebecca Wallace defines state responsibility in international law as the liability

> of one state to another for the non-observance of the obligations imposed by the international legal systems. A state may incur liability for injury to the de-

7. G.A. Res. 10764; U.N. GAOR, 63rd Sess.; U.N. Doc. A/RES/63/3 (Oct. 8, 2008).
8. U.N. Charter, art 13, para. 1(a). For current information on the work of the International Law Commission, go to: http://www.un.org/law/ilc.

fendant state itself. This may be, for example, for breach of a treaty obligation, or for injury to the defendant State's nationals or their property.[9]

When an individual is injured by his/her own state a remedy, if any is available, must be sought through the national court system. When an individual is injured in or by a state, other than his/her own state, the injury may be the result of actions of private parties or it may be the result of actions by the state, its instrumentalities or agencies. If the injury is caused by the state then the individual must seek redress, in the first instance, through the judicial system of that state. If the injury is caused by a private party in the foreign state, generally the state will not be liable for the private party's actions. Any remedy must be sought through the foreign court system. If, however, the foreign state fails to provide a remedy or fails to prosecute offenders with due diligence then the individual may have a claim against the foreign state. Similarly, where a foreign state fails to control the unlawful actions of its own citizens (such as a band of terrorists) when it was reasonable to expect that the state would control such citizens, and the unlawful activity injures an alien, then the state may incur liability.

If an individual has a claim against a foreign state and all efforts to receive a remedy in the foreign state have failed, then the individual may ask his/her own state to take up the claim at the international level. Whether the state agrees to do this is left entirely to the discretion of the state. International law does not require a state to espouse any claims on behalf of its citizens. Obviously minor, isolated claims are much more unlikely to be pursued at the international level than major claims or multiple claims presenting the same issue.

Nationality of the Claimant

States may only bring claims on behalf individuals who are citizens of that state. Throughout the world there are a variety of ways that states confer citizenship, through birth in the territory, through consanguinity, through naturalization upon the fulfillment of certain conditions, after successful claims of political asylum or even because a state would like an athlete on its national team. International law does not set down any requirements for the conferring of citizenship,[10] but international law does require a certain level of relationship between the individual and the state before the state is permitted to bring an international claim on behalf of an individual as the case below reveals.

Nottebohm Case
(Liechtenstein v. Guatemala)

1955 I.C.J. 4

Note

Friedreich Nottebohm was born in Germany in 1881 and was a German citizen from his birth until 1939, shortly after the outbreak of World War II. From 1905 he had spent

9. Rebecca M. M. Wallace, International Law 187 (5th ed. 2005).

10. A state may not confer citizenship after birth without the individual's consent. See, Restatement Third, §211, cmt. d on Involuntary Nationality and Reporter's Note 2 (1987).

considerable time in Guatemala where he pursued his business interests. He also possessed assets in the United States. He visited Germany from time to time and also visited his brother who lived in Liechtenstein. After the outbreak of war he applied for naturalization in Liechtenstein and after eleven days received his citizenship. The usual residency requirements were waived.

After war was declared, the United States confiscated his property as an enemy alien. He was arrested in Guatemala and deported to the U.S. where he was interned. Guatemala also confiscated his property. After his release in 1946, Nottebohm resided in Liechtenstein. Both Guatemala and the United States had joined the European war effort against Germany in 1941. Liechtenstein had remained a neutral country.

Opinion of the Court

By the Application filed on December 17th, 1951, the Government of Liechtenstein instituted proceedings before the Court in which it claimed restitution and compensation on the ground that the Government of Guatemala had 'acted towards the person and property of Mr. Friedreich Nottebohm, a citizen of Liechtenstein, in a manner contrary to international law'. In its Counter-Memorial, the Government of Guatemala contended that this claim was inadmissible on a number of grounds, and one of its objections to the admissibility of the claim related to the nationality of the person for whose protection Liechtenstein had seised the Court.

It appears to the Court that this plea in bar is of fundamental importance and that it is therefore desirable to consider it at the outset.

Guatemala has referred to a well-established principle of international law, which it expressed in [its] Counter-Memorial, where it is stated that 'it is the bond of nationality between the State and the individual which alone confers upon the State the right of diplomatic protection'. This sentence is taken from a Judgment of the Permanent Court of International Justice (Series A/B, No. 76, p. 16), which relates to the form of diplomatic protection constituted by international judicial proceedings.

Liechtenstein considers itself to be acting in conformity with this principle and contends that Nottebohm is its national by virtue of the naturalization conferred upon him.

Nottebohm was born at Hamburg on September 16th, 1881. He was German by birth and still possessed German nationality when, in October 1939, he applied for naturalization in Liechtenstein.

In 1905 he went to Guatemala. He took up residence there and made that country the headquarters of his business activities, which increased and prospered; these activities developed in the field of commerce, banking and plantations. Having been an employee in the firm of Nottebohm Hermanos, which had been founded by his brothers Juan and Arturo, he became their partner in 1912 and later, in 1937, he was made head of the firm. After 1905 he sometimes went to Germany on business and to other countries for holidays. He continued to have business connections in Germany. He paid a few visits to a brother who had lived in Liechtenstein since 1931. Some of his other brothers, relatives and friends were in Germany, others in Guatemala. He himself continued to have his fixed abode in Guatemala until 1943, that is to say, until the occurrence of the events which constitute the basis of the present dispute.

On October 9th, 1939, Nottebohm, 'resident in Guatemala since 1905 (at present residing as a visitor with his brother, Hermann Nottebohm, in Vaduz)', applied for admission as a national of Liechtenstein.... He sought dispensation from the condition of three years' residence as prescribed by law, without indicating the special circumstances warranting such waiver. He submitted a statement of the Credit Suisse in Zurich concerning his assets, and undertook to pay ... 12,500 Swiss francs to the State.... On October 20th, 1939, Mr. Nottebohm took the oath of allegiance....

In order to decide upon the admissibility of the Application, the Court must ascertain whether the nationality conferred on Nottebohm by Liechtenstein by means of a naturalization which took place in the circumstances which have been described, can be validly invoked as against Guatemala, whether it bestows upon Liechtenstein a sufficient title to the exercise of protection in respect of Nottebohm as against Guatemala and therefore entitles it to seise the Court of a claim relating to him....

The Court does not propose to go beyond the limited scope of the question which it has to decide, namely whether the nationality conferred on Nottebohm can be relied upon as against Guatemala in justification of the proceedings instituted before the Court. It must decide this question on the basis of international law; to do so is consistent with the nature of the question and with the nature of the Court's own functions.

* * *

Since no proof has been adduced that Guatemala has recognized the title to the exercise of protection relied upon by Liechtenstein as being derived from the naturalization which it granted to Nottebohm, the Court must consider whether such an act of granting nationality by Liechtenstein directly entails an obligation on the part of Guatemala to recognize its effect, namely, Liechtenstein's right to exercise its protection. In other words, it must be determined whether that unilateral act by Liechtenstein is one which can be relied upon against Guatemala in regard to the exercise of protection. The Court will deal with this question without considering that of the validity of Nottebohm's naturalization according to the law of Liechtenstein.

It is for Liechtenstein, as it is for every sovereign State, to settle by its own legislation the rules relating to the acquisition of its nationality, and to confer that nationality by naturalization granted by its own organs in accordance with that legislation. It is not necessary to determine whether international law imposes any limitations on its freedom of decision in this domain. Furthermore, nationality has its most immediate, its most far-reaching and, for most people, its only effects within the legal system of the State conferring it. Nationality serves above all to determine that the person upon whom it is conferred enjoys the rights and is bound by the obligations which the law of the State in question grants to or imposes on its nationals. This is implied in the wider concept that nationality is within the domestic jurisdiction of the State.

But the issue which the Court must decide is not one which pertains to the legal system of Liechtenstein. It does not depend on the law or on the decision of Liechtenstein whether that State is entitled to exercise its protection, in the case under consideration. To exercise protection, to apply to the Court, is to place oneself on the plane of international law. It is international law which determines whether a State is entitled to exercise protection and to seise the Court.

* * *

International arbitrators have decided in the same way numerous cases of dual nationality, where the question arose with regard to the exercise of protection. They have given their preference to the real and effective nationality, that which accorded with the facts, that based on stronger factual ties between the person concerned and one of the

States whose nationality is involved. Different factors are taken into consideration, and their importance will vary from one case to the next: the habitual residence of the individual concerned is an important factor, but there are other factors such as the centre of his interests, his family ties, his participation in public life, attachment shown by him for a given country and inculcated in his children, etc.

Similarly, the courts of third States, when they have before them an individual whom two other States hold to be their national, seek to resolve the conflict by having recourse to international criteria and their prevailing tendency is to prefer the real and effective nationality.

The same tendency prevails in the writings of publicists and in practice. This notion is inherent in the provisions of Article 3, paragraph 2, of the Statute of the Court. National laws reflect this tendency when, inter alia, they make naturalization dependent on conditions indicating the existence of a link, which may vary in their purpose or in their nature but which are essentially concerned with this idea. The Liechtenstein Law of January 4th, 1934, is a good example.

The practice of certain States which refrain from exercising protection in favour of a naturalized person when the latter has in fact, by his prolonged absence, severed his links with what is no longer for him anything but his nominal country, manifests the view of these States that, in order to be capable of being invoked against another State, nationality must correspond with the factual situation.

The character thus recognized on the international level as pertaining to nationality is in no way inconsistent with the fact that international law leaves it to each State to lay down the rules governing the grant of its own nationality. The reason for this is that the diversity of demographic conditions has thus far made it impossible for any general agreement to be reached on the rules relating to nationality, although the latter by its very nature affects international relations. It has been consider that the best way of making such rules accord with the varying demographic conditions in different countries is to leave the fixing of such rules to the competence of each State. On the other hand, a State cannot claim that the rules it has thus laid down are entitled to recognition by another State unless it has acted in conformity with this general aim of making the legal bond of nationality accord with the individual's genuine connection with the State which assumes the defense of its citizens by means of protection as against other States.

The requirement that such a concordance must exist is to be found in the studies carried on in the course of the last thirty years upon the initiative and under the auspices of the League of Nations and the United Nations. It explains the provision which the Conference for the Codification of International Law, held at The Hague in 1930, inserted in Article 1 of the Convention relating to the Conflict of Nationality Laws, laying down that the law enacted by a State for the purpose of determining who are its nationals 'shall be recognized by other States in so far as it is consistent with ... international custom, and the principles of law generally recognized with regard to nationality'. In the same spirit, Article 5 of the Convention refers to criteria of the individual's genuine connections for the purpose of resolving questions of dual nationality which arise in third States.

According to the practice of States, to arbitral and judicial decisions and to the opinions of writers, nationality is a legal bond having as its basis a social fact of attachment, a genuine connection of existence, interests and sentiments, together with the existence of reciprocal rights and duties. It may be said to constitute the juridical expression of the fact that the individual upon whom it is conferred, either directly by the law or as the result of an act of the authorities, is in fact more closely connected with the population of the State conferring nationality than with that of any other State. Conferred by a State, it only entitles that State to exercise protection vis-a-vis another State, if it constitutes a translation into juridical terms of the individual's connection with the State which has made him its national.

* * *

Since this is the character which nationality must present when it is invoked to furnish the State which has granted it with a title to the exercise of protection and to the institution of international judicial proceedings, the Court must ascertain whether the nationality granted to Nottebohm by means of naturalization is of this character or, in other words, whether the factual connection between Nottebohm and Liechtenstein in the period preceding, contemporaneous with and following his naturalization appears to be sufficiently close, so preponderant in relation to any connection which may have existed between him and any other State, that it is possible to regard the nationality conferred upon him as real and effective, as the exact juridical expression of a social fact of a connection which existed previously or came into existence thereafter.

Naturalization is not a matter to be taken lightly. To seek and to obtain it is not something that happens frequently in the life of a human being. It involves his breaking of a bond of allegiance and his establishment of a new bond of allegiance. It may have far-reaching consequences and involve profound changes in the destiny of the individual who obtains it. It concerns him personally, and to consider it only from the point of view of its repercussions with regard to his property would be to misunderstand its profound significance. In order to appraise its international effect, it is impossible to disregard the circumstances in which it was conferred, the serious character which attaches to it, the real and effective, and not merely the verbal preference of the individual seeking it for the country which grants it to him.

At the time of his naturalization does Nottebohm appear to have been more closely attached by his tradition, his establishment, his interests, his activities, his family ties, his intentions for the near future to Liechtenstein than to any other State?

The essential facts are as follows:

At the date when he applied for naturalization Nottebohm had been a German national from the time of his birth. He had always retained his connections with members of his family who had remained in Germany and he had always had business connections with that country. His country had been at war for more than a month, and there is nothing to indicate that the application for naturalization then made by Nottebohm was motivated by any desire to dissociate himself from the Government of his country.

He had been settled in Guatemala for 34 years. He had carried on his activities there. It was the main seat of his interests. He returned there shortly after his naturalization, and it remained the centre of his interests and of his business activities. He stayed there until his removal as a result of war measures in 1943. He subsequently attempted to return there, and he now complains of Guatemala's refusal to admit him. There, too, were several members of his family who sought to safeguard his interests.

In contrast, his actual connections with Liechtenstein were extremely tenuous. No settled abode, no prolonged residence in that country at the time of his application for naturalization: the application indicates that he was paying a visit there and confirms the transient character of this visit by its request that the naturalization proceedings should be initiated and concluded without delay. No intention of settling there was shown at that time or realized in the ensuing weeks, months or years—on the contrary, he returned to Guatemala very shortly after his naturalization and showed every intention of remaining there. If Nottebohm went to Liechtenstein in 1946, this was because of the refusal of Guatemala to admit him. No indication is given of the grounds warranting the waiver of the condition of residence, required by the 1934 Nationality Law, which waiver was implicitly granted to him. There is no allegation of any economic interests or of any activities exercised or to be exercised in Liechtenstein, and no manifestation of any intention whatsoever to transfer all or some of his interests and his business activities to Liechtenstein. It is unnecessary in this connection to attribute much importance to the promise to pay the taxes levied at the time of his naturalization. The only links to be discovered between the Principality and Nottebohm are the short sojourns already referred to and the presence in Vaduz of one of his brothers: but his brother's presence is referred to in his application for naturalization only as a reference to his good conduct. Furthermore, other members of his family have asserted Nottebohm's desire to spend his old age in Guatemala.

These facts clearly establish, on the one hand, the absence of any bond of attachment between Nottebohm and Liechtenstein and, on the other hand, the existence of a long-standing and close connection between him and Guatemala, a link which his naturalization in no way weakened. That naturalization was not based on any real prior connection with Liechtenstein, nor did it in any way alter the manner of life of the person upon whom it was conferred in exceptional circumstances of speed and accommodation. In both respects, it was lacking in the genuineness requisite to an act of such importance, if it is to be entitled to be respected by a State in the position of Guatemala. It was granted without regard to the concept of nationality adopted in international relations.

Naturalization was asked for not so much for the purpose of obtaining a legal recognition of Nottebohm's membership in fact in the population of Liechtenstein, as it was to enable him to substitute for his status as a national of a belligerent State that of a national of a neutral State, with the sole aim of thus coming within the protection of Liechtenstein but not of becoming wedded to its traditions, its interests, its way of life or of assuming the obligations—other than fiscal obligations—and exercising the rights pertaining to the status thus acquired.

Guatemala is under no obligation to recognize a nationality granted in such circumstances. Liechtenstein consequently is not entitled to extend its protection to Nottebohm vis-a-vis Guatemala and its claim must, for this reason, be held to be inadmissible.

For these reasons,

THE COURT,

by eleven votes to three,

Holds that the claim submitted by the Government of the Principality of Liechtenstein is inadmissible.

QUESTIONS

1. Did the Court rule that Liechtenstein had illegally conferred citizenship on Nottebohm?
2. Why were Nottebohm's links with Liechtenstein insufficient to require Guatemala to recognize his Liechtensteinian nationality for the purposes of presenting an international claim before the Court?

3. If Nottebohm had possessed property in Switzerland (also a neutral country in World War II) but had never lived there—would the Court have ruled the same way if Liechtenstein presented a claim against Switzerland?
4. If this case had not arisen in the context of wartime allegiances, do you think the Court would have ruled the same way?

For a case upholding the right of a state to represent a citizen when that citizen's treaty rights have been violated see the *LaGrand Case* (Germany v. United States) 2001 I.C.J. 466 and the *Avena Case* (Mexico v. United States) 2004 I.C.J. 12, pp. 66–76 *supra.*

International Organizations

Inter-Governmental Organizations

An international, inter-governmental organization is an entity created by an agreement between states and having states as its constituent members. The United Nations is a prime example of such an entity. Its principal constituent agreement is the U.N. Charter and membership was opened to all the states that participated in the San Francisco Conference of 1945 and to "all other peaceloving states which accept the obligations contained in the present Charter and, in the judgment of the Organization, are able and willing to carry out these obligations."[11] The extent to which an international organization possesses international capacity (often called personality) will depend, in part, upon the degree of capacity conferred upon it by its constituent documents. Its capacity may also evolve through practice and may be deduced from its overall purposes. To some degree the extent to which an international organization is able to exercise the international capacity conferred upon it by its charter will be determined by the will of its members. Below is a brief description of the status and structure of the United Nations which has almost universal state membership.

The United Nations

International Status

When seeking to determine the international capacity of an organization the first place to look is its constituent documents. The U.N. Charter is largely silent on this matter although article 104 provides: "The Organization shall enjoy in the territory of each of its Members such legal capacity as may be necessary for the exercise of its functions and the fulfilment of its purposes." Similarly article 105 states:

1. The Organization shall enjoy in the territory of each of its Members such privileges and immunities as are necessary for the fulfilment of its purposes.
2. Representatives of the Members of the United Nations and officials of the Organization shall similarly enjoy such privileges and immunities as are necessary for the independent exercise of their functions in connection with the Organization.
3. The General Assembly may make recommendations with a view to determining the details of the application of paragraphs 1 and 2 of this Article or may propose conventions to the Members of the United Nations for this purpose.

---

11. U.N. Charter, art. 4, para. 1.

These two articles only confer capacity on the U.N. and its representatives within the territories of its members. Nothing is said about the general international capacity of the organization or about its capacity in its relations with non-members.

The next place to search for legal capacity of an organization is any agreements it may have entered into with its members. In 1946 the General Assembly adopted the *Convention on the Privileges and Immunities of the United Nations.*[12] This convention is an agreement between the United Nations and each of its members and provides for juridical capacity (Article I), specifically the capacity "(a) to contract; (b) to acquire and dispose of immovable and movable property; (c) to institute legal proceedings." (Article I, Section 1.). It also provides for a broad range of privileges and immunities for the United Nations in order to facilitate its work.[13] Wherever the U.N. has offices it enters into an agreement with the host state under which the host state agrees to grant the U.N., its representatives and officials, various privileges and immunities.[14]

Constituent documents and agreements between an international organization and its members cannot hope to cover the myriad of issues relating to capacity that may arise in the course of the organization's development. Such issues can only be resolved through practice and legal inference. The International Court of Justice was asked to address such issues by the General Assembly in 1948 in the case below.

Reparations for Injuries Suffered in the Service of the United Nations

1949 I.C.J. 174 (Advisory Opinion)

Note

The Swedish national, Count Bernadotte, was the Chief United Nations Truce Negotiator after the Arab-Israeli war which erupted after Israel declared itself a state on May 14, 1948. Count Bernardotte was killed in Jerusalem on September 17, 1948, probably by a militant Zionist group. Israel was not a member of the U.N. at the time. The General Assembly asked the International Court of Justice for its opinion on several issues relating to the U.N.'s international legal capacity to pursue claims arising out of Count Bernadotte's death.

Opinion of the Court

THE COURT, ... gives the following advisory opinion:

On December 3rd, 1948, the General Assembly of the United Nations adopted the following Resolution: ...

---

12. 1 U.N.T.S. 15, 21 U.S.T. 1418, T.I.A.S. No. 6900, adopted by the General Assembly on 13 Feb. 1946, entered into force for the U.S. 29 April 1970.

13. There is also a Convention on the Privileges and Immunities of the Specialized Agencies, which provides privileges and immunities for the U.N. specialized agencies, 33 U.N.T.S. 261, signed 21 Nov. 1947, entered into force, 2 Dec. 1948.

14. See, e.g., Agreement Between the United Nations and the United States of America Regarding the Headquarters of the United Nations, 11 U.N.T.S. 11, T.I.A.S. No. 1676, signed 26 June 1947, entered into force, 21 Nov. 1947.

The General Assembly

Decides to submit the following legal questions to the International Court of Justice for an advisory opinion:

'I. In the event of an agent of the United Nations in the performance of his duties suffering injury in circumstances involving the responsibility of a State, has the United Nations, as an Organization, the capacity to bring an international claim against the responsible *de jure* or *de facto* government with a view to obtaining the reparation due in respect of the damage caused (a) to the United Nations, (b) to the victim or to persons entitled through him?

II. In the event of an affirmative reply on point I (b), how is action by the United Nations to be reconciled with such rights as may be possessed by the State of which the victim is a national?'

* * *

The questions asked of the Court relate to the 'capacity to bring an international claim'; accordingly, we must begin by defining what is meant by that capacity, and consider the characteristics of the Organization, so as to determine whether, in general, these characteristics do, or do not, include for the Organization a right to present an international claim.

Competence to bring an international claim is, for those possessing it, the capacity to resort to the customary methods recognized by international law for the establishment, the presentation and the settlement of claims. Among these methods may be mentioned protest, request for an enquiry, negotiation, and request for submission to an arbitral tribunal or to the Court in so far as this may be authorized by the Statute.

This capacity certainly belongs to the State; a State can bring an international claim against another State. Such a claim takes the form of a claim between two political entities, equal in law, similar in form, and both the direct subjects of international law. It is dealt with by means of negotiation, and cannot, in the present state of the law as to international jurisdiction, be submitted to a tribunal, except with the consent of the States concerned.

When the organization brings a claim against one of its Members, this claim will be presented in the same manner, and regulated by the same procedure. It may, when necessary, be supported by the political means at the disposal of the Organization. In these ways the Organization would find a method for securing the observance of its rights by the Member against which it has a claim.

But, in the international sphere, has the Organization such a nature as involves the capacity to bring an international claim? In order to answer this question, the Court must first enquire whether the Charter has given the Organization such a position that it possesses, in regard to its Members, rights which it is entitled to ask them to respect. In other words, does the Organization possess international personality? This is no doubt a doctrinal expression, which has sometimes given rise to controversy. But it will be used here to mean that if the Organization is recognized as having that personality, it is an entity capable of availing itself of obligations incumbent upon its Members.

To answer this question, which is not settled by the actual terms of the Charter, we must consider what characteristics it was intended thereby to give to the Organization.

The subjects of law in any legal system are not necessarily identical in their nature or in the extent of their rights, and their nature depends upon the needs of the community. Throughout its history, the development of international law has been influenced by the requirements of international life, and the progressive increase in the collective activities of States has already given rise to instances of action upon the international plane by certain entities which are not States. This development culminated in the establishment in June 1945 of an international organization whose purposes and principles are specified in the Charter of the United Nations. But to achieve these ends the attribution of international personality is indispensable.

The Charter has not been content to make the Organization created by it merely a centre 'for harmonizing the actions of nations in the attainment of these common ends' (Article I, para. 4). It has equipped that centre with organs, and has given it special tasks. It has defined the position of the Members in relation to the Organization by requiring them to give it every assistance in any action undertaken by it (Article 2, para.5.), and to accept and carry out the decisions of the Security Council; by authorizing the General Assembly to make recommendations to the Members; by giving the Organization legal capacity and privileges and immunities in the territory of each of its Members; and by providing for the conclusion of agreements between the Organization and its Members. Practice—in particular the conclusion of conventions to which the Organization is a party—has confirmed this character of the Organization, which occupies a position in certain respects in detachment from its Members, and which is under a duty to remind them, if need be, of certain obligations. It must be added that the Organization is a political body, charged with political tasks of an important character, and covering a wide field namely, the maintenance of international peace and security, the development of friendly relations among nations, and the achievement of international co-operation in the solution of problems of an economic, social, cultural or humanitarian character (Article 1); and in dealing with its Members it employs political means. The 'Convention on the Privileges and Immunities of the United Nations' of 1946 creates rights and duties between each of the signatories and the Organization (see, in particular, Section 35). It is difficult to see how such a convention could operate except upon the international plane and as between parties possessing international personality.

In the opinion of the Court, the Organization was intended to exercise and enjoy, and is in fact exercising and enjoying, functions and rights which can only be explained on the basis of the possession of a large measure of international personality and the capacity to operate upon an international plane. It is at present the supreme type of international organization, and it could not carry out the intentions of its founders if it was devoid of international personality. It must be acknowledged that its Members, by entrusting certain functions to it, with the attendant duties and responsibilities, have clothed it with the competence required to enable those functions to be effectively discharged.

Accordingly, the Court has come to the conclusion that the Organization is an international person. That is not the same thing as saying that it is a State, which it certainly is not, or that its legal personality and rights and duties are the same as those of a State. Still less is it the same thing as saying that it is 'a super-State', whatever that expression may mean. It does not even imply that all its rights and duties must be upon the international plane, any more than all the rights and duties of a State must be upon that plane. What it does mean is that it is a subject of international law and capable of possessing international rights and duties, and that it has capacity to maintain its rights by bringing international claims.

The next question is whether the sum of the international rights of the Organization comprises the right to bring the kind of international claim described in the Request for this Opinion. That is a claim against a State to obtain reparation in respect of the damage caused by the injury of an agent of the Organization in the course of the performance of his duties. Whereas a State possesses the totality of international rights and duties recognized by international law, the rights and duties of an entity such as the Organization must depend upon its purposes and functions as specified or implied in its constituent documents and developed in practice. The functions of the Organization are of such a character that they could not be effectively discharged if they involved the concurrent action, on the international plane, of fifty-eight or more Foreign Offices, and the Court concludes that the Members have endowed the Organization with capacity to bring international claims when necessitated by the discharge of its functions.

What is the position as regards the claims mentioned in the request for an opinion? Question I is divided into two points, which must be considered in turn.

* * *

Question I (a) is as follows:

'In the event of an agent of the United Nations in the performance of his duties suffering injury in circumstances involving the responsibility of a State, has the United Nations, as an Organization, the capacity to bring an international claim against the responsible *de jure* or *de facto* government with a view to obtaining the reparation due in respect of the damage caused (a) to the United Nations ... ?'

The question is concerned solely with the reparation of damage caused to the Organization when one of its agents suffers injury at the same time. It cannot be doubted that the Organization has the capacity to bring an international claim against one of its Members which has caused injury to it by a breach of its international obligations towards it. The damage specified in Question I (a) means exclusively damage caused to the interests of the Organization itself, to its administrative machine, to its property and assets, and to the interests of which it is the guardian. It is clear that the Organization has the capacity to bring a claim for this damage. As the claim is based on the breach of an international obligation on the part of the Member held responsible by the Organization, the Member cannot contend that this obligation is governed by municipal law, and the Organization is justified in giving its claim the character of an international claim.

When the Organization has sustained damage resulting from a breach by a Member of its international obligations, it is impossible to see how it can obtain reparation unless it possesses capacity to bring an international claim. It cannot be supposed that in such an event all the Members of the Organization, save the defendant State, must combine to bring a claim against the defendant for the damage suffered by the Organization....

* * *

Question I (b) is as follows:

'... has the United Nations, as an Organization, the capacity to bring an international claim ... in respect of the damage caused ... (b) to the victim or to persons entitled through him?'

In dealing with the question of law which arises out of Question I (b), it is unnecessary to repeat the considerations which led to an affirmative answer being given to Question I (a). It can now be assumed that the Organization has the capacity to bring a claim on the international plane, to negotiate, to conclude a special agreement and to prosecute a claim before an international tribunal. The only legal question which remains to be considered is whether, in the course of bringing an international claim of this kind, the Organization can recover 'the reparation due in respect of the damage caused ... to the victim.... '

The traditional rule that diplomatic protection is exercised by the national State does not involve the giving of a negative answer to Question I (b).

In the first place, this rule applies to claims brought by a State. But here we have the different and new case of a claim that would be brought by the Organization.

In the second place, even in inter-State relations, there are important exceptions to the rule, for there are cases in which protection may be exercised by a State on behalf of persons not having its nationality.

In the third place, the rule rests on two bases. The first is that the defendant State has broken an obligation towards the national State in respect of its nationals. The second is that only the party to whom an international obligation is due can bring a claim in respect of its breach. This is precisely what happens when the Organization, in bringing a claim for damage suffered by its agent, does so by invoking the breach of an obligation towards itself. Thus, the rule of the nationality of claims affords no reason against recognizing that the Organization has the right to bring a claim for the damage referred to in Question I (b). On the contrary, the principle underlying this rule leads to the recognition of this capacity as belong to the Organization, when the Organization invokes, as the ground of its claim, a breach of an obligation towards itself.

The Charter does not expressly confer upon the Organization the capacity to include, in its claim for reparation, damage caused to the victim or to persons entitled through him. The Court must therefore begin by enquiring whether the provisions of the Charter concerning the functions of the Organization, and the part played by its agents in the performance of those functions, imply for the Organization power to afford its agents the limited protection that would consist in the bringing of a claim on their behalf for reparation for damage suffered in such circumstances. Under international law, the Organization must be deemed to have those powers which, though not expressly provided in the Charter, are conferred upon it by necessary implication as being essential to the performance of its duties. This principle of law was applied by the Permanent Court of International Justice to the International Labour Organization in its Advisory Opinion No. 13 of July 23rd, 1926 (Series B., No. 13, p. 18), and must be applied to the United Nations.

Having regard to its purposes and functions already referred to, the Organization may find it necessary, and has in fact found it necessary, to entrust its agents with important missions to be performed in disturbed parts of the world. Many missions, from their very nature, involve the agents in unusual dangers to which ordinary persons are not exposed. For the same reason, the injuries suffered by its agents in these circumstances will sometimes have occurred in such a manner that their national State would not be justified in bringing a claim for reparation on the ground of diplomatic protection, or, at any rate, would not feel disposed to do so. Both to ensure the efficient and independent performance of these missions and to afford effective support to its agents, the Organization must provide them with adequate protection.

This need of protection for the agents of the Organization, as a condition of the performance of its functions, has already been realized, and the Preamble to the Resolution of December 3rd, 1948..., shows that this was the unanimous view of the General Assembly.

For this purpose, the Members of the Organization have entered into certain undertakings, some of which are in the Charter and others in complementary agreements. The content of these undertakings need not be described here; but the Court must stress the importance of the duty to render to the Organization 'every assistance' which is accepted by the Members in Article 2, paragraph 5, of the Charter. It must be noted that the effective working of the Organization—the accomplishment of its task, and the independence and effectiveness of the work of its agents—require that these undertakings should be strictly observed. For that purpose, it is necessary that, when an infringement occurs, the Organization should be able to call upon the responsible State to remedy its default, and, in particular, to obtain from the State reparation for the damage that the default may have caused to its agent....

Upon examination of the character of the functions entrusted to the Organization and of the nature of the missions of its agents, it becomes clear that the capacity of the Organization to exercise a measure of functional protection of its agents arises by necessary intendment out of the Charter.

The obligations entered into by States to enable the agents of the Organization to perform their duties are undertaken not in the interest of the agents, but in that of the Organization. When it claims redress for a breach of these obligations, the Organization is invoking its own right, the right that the obligations due to it should be respected. On this ground, it asks for reparation of the injury suffered, for 'it is a principle of international law that the breach of an engagement involves an obligation to make reparation in an adequate form'; as was stated by the Permanent Court in its Judgment No. 8 of July 26th, 1927 (Series A., No. 9, p. 21). In claiming reparation based on the injury suffered by its agent, the Organization does not represent the agent, but is asserting its own right, the right to secure respect for undertakings entered into towards the Organization.

Having regard to the foregoing considerations, and to the undeniable right of the Organization to demand that its Members shall fulfil the obligations entered into by them in the interest of the good working of the Organization, the Court is of the opinion that, in the case of a breach of these obligations, the Organization has the capacity to claim adequate reparation, and that in assessing this reparation it is authorized to include the damage suffered by the victim or by persons entitled through him.

* * *

The question remains whether the Organization has 'the capacity to bring an international claim against the responsible *de jure* or *de facto* government with a view to obtaining the reparation due in respect of the damage caused (a) to the United Nations, (b) to the victim or to persons entitled through him' when the defendant State is not a member of the Organization.

In considering this aspect of Question I (a) and (b), it is necessary to keep in mind the reasons which have led the Court to give an affirmative answer to it when the defendant State is a Member of the Organization. It has now been established that the Organization has capacity to bring claims on the international plane, and that it possesses a right of functional protection in respect of its agents. Here again the Court is authorized to assume that the damage suffered involves the responsibility of a State, and it is not called upon to express an opinion upon the various ways in which that responsibility might be engaged. Accordingly the question is whether the Organization has capacity to bring a claim against the defendant State to recover reparation in respect of that damage or whether, on the contrary, the defendant State, not being a member, is justified in raising the objection that the Organization lacks the capacity to bring an international claim. On this point, the Court's opinion is that fifty States, representing the vast majority of the members of the international community, had the power, in conformity with international law, to bring into being an entity possessing objective international personality, and not merely personality recognized by them alone, together with capacity to bring international claims.

Accordingly, the Court arrives at the conclusion that an affirmative answer should be given to Question I (a) and (b) whether or not the defendant State is a Member of the United Nations.

* * *

Question II is as follows:

'In the event of an affirmative reply on point I (b), how is action by the United Nations to be reconciled with such rights as may be possessed by the State of which the victim is a national?'

The affirmative reply given by the Court on point I (b) obliges it now to examine Question II. When the victim has a nationality, cases can clearly occur in which the injury suffered by him may engage the interest both of his national State and of the Organization. In such an event, competition between the State's right of diplomatic protection and the Organization's right of functional protection might arise, and this is the only case with which the Court is invited to deal.

In such a case, there is no rule of law which assigns priority to the one or to the other, or which compels either the State or the Organization to refrain from bringing an international claim. The court sees no reason why the parties concerned should not find solutions inspired by goodwill and common sense, and as between the Organization and its Members it draws attention to their duty to render 'every assistance' provided by Article 2, paragraph 5, of the Charter.

Although the bases of the two claims are different, that does not mean that the defendant State can be compelled to pay the reparation due in respect of the damage twice over. International tribunals are already familiar with the problem of a claim in which two or more national States are interested, and they know how to protect the defendant State in such a case.

The risk of competition between the Organization and the national State can be reduced or eliminated either by a general convention or by agreements entered into in each particular case. There is no doubt that in due course a practice will be developed, and it is worthy of note that already certain States whose nationals have been injured in the performance of missions undertake for the Organization have shown a reasonable and co-operative disposition to find a practical solution.

* * *

The question of reconciling action by the Organization with the rights of a national State may arise in another way; that is to say, when the agent bears the nationality of the defendant State.

The ordinary practice whereby a State does not exercise protection on behalf of one of its nationals against a State which regards him as its own national, does not constitute a precedent which is relevant here. The action of the Organization is in fact based not upon the nationality of the victim but upon his status as agent of the Organization. Therefore it does not matter whether or not the State to which the claim is addressed regards him as its own national, because the question of nationality is not pertinent to the admissibility of the claim.

In law, therefore, it does not seem that the fact of the possession of the nationality of the defendant State by the agent constitutes any obstacle to a claim brought by the Organization for a breach of obligations towards it occurring in relation to the performance of his mission by that agent.

FOR THESE REASONS,

The Court is of opinion

On Question I (a):

(I) unanimously,

That, in the event of an agent of the United Nations in the performance of his duties suffering injury in circumstances involving the responsibility of a Member State, the United Nations as an Organization has the capacity to bring an international claim against the responsible *de jure* or *de facto* government with a view to obtaining the reparation due in respect of the damage caused to the United Nations.

(ii) unanimously,

That, in the event of an agent of the United Nations in the performance of his duties suffering injury in circumstances involving the responsibility of a State which is not a member, the United Nations as an Organization has the capacity to bring an international claim against the responsible *de jure* or *de facto* government with a view to obtaining the reparation due in respect of the damage caused to the United Nations.

On Question I(b):

(I) by eleven votes against four,

That, in the event of an agent of the United Nations in the performance of his duties suffering injury in circumstances involving the responsibility of a Member State, the United Nations as an Organization has the capacity to bring an international claim against the responsible *de jure* or *de facto* government with a view to obtaining the reparation due in respect of the damage caused to the victim or to persons entitled through him.

(ii) by eleven votes against four,

That, in the event of an agent of the United Nations in the performance of his duties suffering injury in circumstances involving the responsibility of a State which is not a member, the United Nations as an Organized has the capacity to bring an international claim against the responsible *de jure* or *de facto* government with a view to obtaining the reparation due in respect of the damage caused to the victim or to persons entitled through him.

On Question II:

By ten votes against five,

When the United Nations as an Organization is bringing a claim for reparation of damage caused to its agent, it can only do so by basing its claim upon a breach of obligations due to itself; respect for this rule will usually prevent a conflict between the action of the United Nations and such rights as the agent's national State may possess, and thus bring about a reconciliation between their claims; moreover, this reconciliation must depend upon considerations applicable to each particular case, and upon agreements to be made between the Organization and individual States, either generally or in each case.

QUESTIONS

1. Briefly list the reasons that persuaded the Court that the U.N. has the capacity to bring a claim for reparations for damages to itself incurred through injury to its agent in the performance of his/her duties against
   (a) a member state
   (b) a non-member state.
2. Briefly list the reasons that persuaded the Court that the U.N. has the capacity to bring a claim for reparations for damage caused to its agent (the victim) when he/she suffers injury in the performance of his/her duties against
   (a) a member state
   (b) a non-member state.
3. Why are non-members of the U.N. bound to recognize the international capacity of an organization they did not create?

Structure of the United Nations

The League of Nations, which was founded in 1919 to limit resort to war and to provide a mechanism for settlement of international disputes, collapsed during World War II. After the war, the determination to provide an international organization that could "maintain international peace and security" (U.N. Charter, article 1(1)) bore fruit at the San Francisco conference of 1945 where fifty nations met and the U.N. Charter was drafted. The principal purpose of the U.N. was directed to the maintenance of peace and collective security but the Charter outlined far broader purposes such as developing "friendly relations among nations" (article 1(2)), "equal rights and self-determination of peoples" (article 1(2)), "international cooperation in solving ... economic, social, cultural [and] humanitarian" problems (article 1(3)), and "promoting and encouraging respect for human rights and for fundamental freedoms for all without distinction as to race, sex, language or religion" (article 1(3)). Many of these concepts have become almost common place today (though few are fully realized) but in 1945 they were nothing short of radical. Below is a brief description of the structure of the United Nations.

U.N. Principal Organs

Article 7 of the Charter establishes six principal organs of the U.N.: the General Assembly, the Security Council, the Economic and Social Council, the Trusteeship Council, the International Court of Justice, and the Secretariat.

The General Assembly

The General Assembly is made up of all the member states of the United Nations, now numbering over one hundred and ninety. Each member may have up to five representatives in the Assembly (article 9(2)) but each state has only one vote. Voting is generally by simple majority but "important questions" (article 18(2)) require a two-thirds vote of the members present and voting. "Important questions" are defined in article 18(2) and include such matters as the election of non-permanent members of the Security Council, the expulsion of members and budgetary questions. Clearly, a one-state-one-vote system is far from democratic. The most heavily populated states such as China or India, with over one billion people, have one vote as does Nauru which has about 12,000 people. Numerous suggestions have been made to alter the General Assembly's voting system but no reform has been agreed upon.

The General Assembly "may discuss any questions or any matters within the scope of the present Charter or relating to the powers and functions of any organs provided for in the present Charter and ... may make recommendations to the Members ... or to the Security Council...." (article 10). If the Security Council has a matter under consideration then the General Assembly "shall not make any recommendations with regard to that dispute...." (article 12(1)).

The main work of the General Assembly consists of "initiating studies and making recommendations" (article 13(1)) to promote international political cooperation, to encourage the development of international law,[15] to promote cooperation in the "economic, social, cultural, educational and health fields" (article 13(1)(b)) and to assist in realizing "human rights and fundamental freedoms for all without distinction as to race, sex, language or religion." (article 13(1)(b)). The General Assembly also considers and approves "the budget of the Organization" (article 17(1)). This latter task has been fraught with difficulties over the years as various nations have refused to pay their assessed portions of the budget.

The Security Council

The Security Council has the "primary responsibility for the maintenance of international peace and security...." (article 24(1)). All members of the U.N. "agree to accept and carry out the decisions of the Security Council...." (article 25). The Charter intended that member states would enter into agreements with the Security Council undertaking "to make available to the Security Council ... armed forces, assistance, and facilities ... necessary for the purposes of maintaining international peace and security." (Article 43(1)). In fact no such agreements have been negotiated. Although the United Nations has sent peacekeeping troops to a variety of locations round the globe and has authorized certain states to use all necessary means to quell certain threats to the peace, the troops used on such occasions have been supplied by individual states on an *ad hoc* basis.

States may refer disputes to the Security Council for recommendations on settlement. The Council has the power to "determine the existence of any threat to the peace, breach of the peace, or act of aggression" (article 39) and makes decisions on the measures to be taken. The measures taken can be non forceful actions such as economic sanctions or severance of diplomatic relationships (article 41) or the Security Council may take action "by air, sea, or land forces as may be necessary to maintain or restore international peace and security." (Article 42). The Council provides a forum where states can raise issues implicating threats to the peace. The Security Council has frequently called upon parties to settle their disputes. It has dispatched peace keeping forces, increasingly so in recent years, (e.g., to the former Yugoslavia, and Somalia) and it has authorized state led military actions against states determined to have breached the peace (e.g., Resolutions relating to the Gulf War (1990–91) where the U.S. led a coalition of other states against Iraq after its invasion of Kuwait).

There are fifteen members of the Security Council, five permanent members, China, France, Russia, the United Kingdom and the United States, and nine non-permanent

---

15. The International Law Commission, which consists of thirty four prominent scholars, was established in 1947 to help accomplish this mandate. See p. 269 n. 8.

members elected for two year terms. Members of the Security Council each have one vote. Nine votes are needed to pass a resolution in the Security Council and that vote must include all five permanent members except when voting on procedural matters (article 27). In practice the abstention of a permanent member is not counted as a vote against a resolution. The preeminence accorded to the five permanent members may have given recognition to the major powers in 1945 but certainly does not reflect the distribution of political power today and is not in any way democratic. Again, there have been numerous suggestions on reforming the membership and voting in the Security Council but none has been adopted.

The Economic and Social Council (ECOSOC)

The Economic and Social Council consists of twenty-seven members with nine members elected each year for three year terms. The Council's principal function is to study and report to the General Assembly, the members and the specialized agencies on economic, social, cultural, educational, health and human rights matters.

ECOSOC has established many commissions and committees to report on subjects within its competence. It coordinates the work of the long list of specialized agencies such as the United Nations International Children's Emergency Fund (UNICEF) and the World Health Organization (WHO). It also has the power to give non-governmental organizations consultative status when their expertise would be useful to the work of ECOSOC. The number of organizations granted consultative status now runs to several thousand. Each member of the Council has one vote and a majority of the members present and voting is required to pass a resolution.

The Trusteeship Council

The Trusteeship Council operates under the authority of the General Assembly. The main task of the Council was to move dependent territories towards self-government. It played a major role in the decolonization era which rapidly gathered steam during in 1960s. There are relatively few territories left under its jurisdiction now so that its role is much less significant.

The International Court of Justice

For materials on the structure, competence and jurisdiction of the International Court of Justice see chapter IX.

The Secretariat

Currently there are over fifty thousand members of the U.N. staff located at the U.N. headquarters in New York City and throughout the world at other headquarters. The "chief administrative officer" is the Secretary-General who "shall be appointed by the General Assembly upon the recommendation of the Security Council."[16] In effect this means that no Secretary-General can be appointed without the positive endorsement of the five permanent members of the Security Council. The Secretary-General is the chief officer of a very large bureaucracy. A number of nations have called for a reduction in

16. U.N. Charter, art. 97.

the size of the staff and the Secretary-General's office has effected across-the-board cuts in staffing levels in recent years.

The Secretary-General performs any functions entrusted to him/her by the General Assembly, the Security Council, the Economic and Social Council and the Trusteeship Council and "makes an annual report to the General Assembly on the work of the Organization."[17] The Secretary-General also has the power to "bring to the attention of the Security Council any matter which in his opinion may threaten the maintenance of international peace and security."[18] This latter power permits the Secretary-General to play a prominent role in bringing to world attention international crises. A number of Secretaries-General have undertaken active peace negotiation roles in attempts to resolve international disputes and can be very influential in shaping the world wide agenda for the United Nations.[19]

Members of the Secretariat do not represent their particular countries. The U.N. Charter, article 100, makes it clear that "the staff shall not seek or receive instructions from any government or any other authority external to the Organization." The member states of the U.N. undertake to respect the notion of international responsibility of the staff and agree "not to seek to influence them in the discharge of their responsibilities."[20]

Non-Governmental International Organizations

A non-governmental international organization (NGO) is a private organization made up of individuals or groups with chapters of the organization in more than one country. There has been an enormous proliferation of such organizations, particularly since the 1960s. These organizations address a myriad of topics relating to international issues and they have had a profound impact on the development of international law in such areas as civilian and combatants' rights in armed conflict, human rights, environmental concerns, animal rights, workers and employers rights, marine matters and fishing, health, food and hunger, religious rights and scientific progress.

Article 71 of the U.N. Charter states that the Economic and Social Council (ECOSOC) "may make suitable arrangements for consultation with non-governmental organizations which are concerned with matters within its competence." Several thousand NGOs now have consultative status with ECOSOC.

A few examples of NGOs that have performed critical roles in the international arena are Amnesty International (political repression, death penalty and human rights); the International Committee of the Red Cross/Red Crescent (development of the laws of war and the supply of humanitarian assistance during hostilities or natural disasters); the World Wildlife Fund (species conservation and environmental matters); Greenpeace (environmental matters); and Oxfam (world hunger) and many more. These organizations are often the first to bring issues to international attention and

17. Id. at art. 98.

18. Id. at art. 99.

19. See, e.g., Kofi A. Annan, 'We The Peoples': The Role of the United Nations in the 21st Century (2000).

20. U.N. Charter, art. 100, para. 2.

frequently provide the structure and the energy necessary to formulate and to implement solutions. They have helped draft international treaties and have worked vigorously for their worldwide ratification and enforcement. The NGOs provide the framework for the ordinary person to be intimately involved in international problems and their solutions.

Non-State Groups

Protected Groups

Some international human rights treaties recognize the rights of certain sub-state groups based on factors such as race, ethnicity, religion, culture, gender, age or language.[21] There has also been a concerted effort to establish rights for indigenous peoples in many parts of the world.[22] The right of self-determination is said to attach to "peoples," which has been recognized as being a smaller group than the entire state.[23] Some groups, such as those based on race, possess what might be called "immutable characteristics." Other groups, such as those based on religion, are changeable. All such group characteristics, however, depend upon perceived differences ascribed either by the group itself, or by non-group members, or by both members and non-members of the group. To some extent, the rights (or duties) allocated to the group will also depend upon the perceived need for special treatment. We don't find any particular rights being given to "Caucasian, upper income, college educated males", for example, because such a group has not been seen as needing special protection. Although group rights have now found increasing areas of recognition, particularly in the field of human rights, the recognition of groups being permitted to enforce their rights as a group is only just beginning to emerge.

Non-State Actors

Recently, loosely structured international non-governmental paramilitary organizations have successfully launched attacks on a number of targets throughout the world. The bombing of the twin towers in New York city and the Pentagon in Washington, D.C. in September 2001, by means of hijacking airplanes and crashing them into the targeted buildings was apparently mastered minded by a Osama Bin Laden, who is said to head a world wide organization called Al Qaeda, aimed at eliminating Western influence in certain Islamic states. Almost three thousand people were killed in those attacks. In response, the United States launched an attack on Afghanistan against the Taliban government who, at that time, controlled roughly ninety percent of the country. The United States argued that such an attack was justified as self-defense because the Taliban had permitted Osama Bin Laden to run training camps for Al Qaeda in Afghanistan. The task here has not been to confer rights on such groups or to enable them to enforce

21. See, e.g., International Covenant on Civil and Political Rights, art. 27, 999 U.N.T.S. 171, adopted 16 Dec. 1966, entered into force 23 Mar. 1976; European Framework Convention for the Protection of National Minorities, 2151 U.N.T.S. 243, E.T.S. No. 157, adopted 1 Feb. 1995, entered into force 1 Feb. 1998; Convention on the Elimination of All Forms of Discrimination against Women, 1249 U.N.T.S. 13, adopted 18 Dec. 1979, entered into force 3 Sept. 1981.

22. Peer Zumbansen, John W. Cioffi & Lindsay Krauss, Eds., Indigeneous Peoples and the Law: Comparative and Critical Perspectives (2009).

23. Reference re Secession of Quebec, 2 CAN. S.C.R. 217, para. 124 (1998).

rights, but rather to find an entity who can be held liable for their actions. States that facilitate or acquiesce in their criminal activities may well be held liable under principles of State responsibility. Individuals withing the group may be held criminally responsible under national law, or international law if there is an international tribunal with jurisdiction. International law has not yet found a satisfactory place for these non-state actors in the existing framework of international law.

International Status of Individuals

Before the recognition of individual human rights in international law, states had recognized that they owed certain duties to aliens traveling within their borders. Generally, a state has no obligation to admit aliens to its territory but, if it does so, then it owes the alien a duty of care. If that duty of care is breached, the alien can seek a remedy in the foreign state. If no remedy is forthcoming, then the alien's own state can seek a remedy against the foreign state at the international level. In theory the state pursuing a claim at the international level arising out of a citizen's injury abroad was pursuing a remedy for injury to itself not directly on behalf of the citizen. If a citizen was injured, the theory was that a component of the state had been injured so that the state had suffered an injury.

As the law of human rights developed (see chapter VIII) it became clear that people had personal rights that attached to the individual regardless of his/her status as an alien. Increasingly human rights agreements began to give the individual the right to bring a complaint against the state. In other words, the individual was given the capacity to sue the state for an internationally based claim.

At the same time that the individual was gaining international rights, it began to be recognized that individuals may also have responsibilities for breaches of certain obligations attaching to the individual's conduct. The Nuremburg International Criminal Tribunal, which was set up by the Allies to try war criminals after World War II, was clear that responsibility for war crimes could be attributed to individuals. Sentences punishing wartime commanders were handed down by the Tribunal thus establishing individual responsibility for the commission of international crimes. The International Criminal Court for the Former Yugoslavia and for Rwanda and the newly established permanent International Criminal Court (see chapter IX) are also proceeding on the concept of individual responsibility for international offenses. A number of hybrid national/international courts, such as those in East Timor, Sierra Leone and Cambodia are proceeding on the same assumption.

Individuals are increasingly being accorded international rights and responsibilities. The availability of a forum in which the individual can claim such rights or be prosecuted for the violation of international responsibilities has not moved ahead with the same speed as the acceptance of the notion of individual rights and responsibilities. As a result, the availability of a forum to pursue claims or adjudicate responsibilities depends upon the willingness of states to agree to subject themselves to such suits or to allow such prosecutions to go forward in their national courts and the willingness of the international community to establish and support international or quasi-international tribunals for the adjudication of violations of state or individual responsibilities. Such fora are increasing.

Multi-National Corporations

Corporations are, of course, creatures of national law. Their structure and powers are dictated by domestic legislation. When a corporation operates across state borders, however, it finds itself subject to a variety of international regimes, including everything from taxation to labor standards. A number of transnational corporate activities have now created specialized areas of international law such as the international sale of goods[24] or intellectual property licensing.[25]

When corporations decide to invest in another state, they will often enter into an agreement with the state where the investment is located through an internationalized contract which spells out the terms and conditions of the investment and mandates that disputes arising under the contract will be settled by international arbitration rather than by the domestic courts. These contracts will often seek to protect the corporation's investment from expropriation by the local government. Most states seeking foreign investment now recognize that offering contractual protections to multi-national corporations works to their benefit. Without certain international assurances, corporations may simply not be willing to risk investing in less developed countries.

Codes of conduct[26] for multi-national corporations have also developed around areas such as working conditions for corporate employees or environmental standards for conducting business. Although these Codes are not technically binding, many multinational corporations adopt them in an attempt to meet acceptable standards for conducting transnational business. Corporations that operate in more than one country have become major players in the international arena, employing thousands of workers and creating wealth both for investors and for the countries where they operate.

Suggested Further Readings

Ian Brownlie, Principles of Public International Law, chapters 3, 4, 5 & 21 (7th ed. 2008).

D.J. Harris, Cases and Materials on International Law, chapter 4 (6th ed. 2004).

Sean D. Murphy, Principles of International Law, chapter 2 (2006).

Malcolm N. Shaw, International Law, chapter 5 (6th ed. 2008).

Rebecca M. M. Wallace, International Law, chapter 4 (5th ed. 2005).

---

24. See, e.g., UN Convention on the International Sale of Goods, adopted 11 April 1980, entered into force 1 Jan. 1988, 1489 U.N.T.S. 3.

25. See, e.g., WIPO Copyright Treaty, adopted 20 Dec. 1996, entered into force 6 March 2002, 2186 U.N.T.S. 152.

26. For a comprehensive review of a number of Codes see the special issue: Voluntary Codes of Conduct, 59 J. Bus. Ethics 1–119 (2005).

Chapter VIII

Human Rights

Introduction

The traditional definition of international law was that it concerned the legal relationships between states. That definition excluded the way that a state treated its own citizens or whether individuals, or groups, have international rights and responsibilities. The way a state treated aliens was however considered a subject of international law. If a state permitted aliens (non-citizens) to enter its borders then the state's conduct towards the aliens was governed by international law and a minimum standard of treatment was required. If a state violated those minimum standards, the foreigner's nation could claim a remedy from the host state. With the drafting of the United Nations Charter, the way a state treats its own citizens has become part of the fabric of international law.

What are human rights? There is much disagreement at the outer margins of the concept but in general human rights refer to those rights that attach to individuals by virtue of their personhood and, more recently, by virtue of their membership in a group. The notion of individual rights is certainly not as new as the twentieth century. The end of the eighteenth century saw the proclamation of the French Declaration of the Rights of Man and the Citizen, the American Declaration of Independence, the United States' Constitution and Bill of Rights. These documents speak of the inalienable rights of man[1] and declare that governments are instituted to secure such things as "Life, Liberty and the Pursuit of Happiness"[2] or state that "Men are born and remain free and equal in rights ... [such as] rights of liberty, property, security and resistance to oppression...."[3] It is from these revolutionary ideas of the enlightenment that the modern human rights movement traces its roots.

Prior to World War II there were a few treaties that addressed human rights issues such as the Slavery Convention[4] and the International Convention for the Suppression of Traffic in Women and Children,[5] but there was no systematic approach to the protection of human rights. The way that a state treated its own citizens was considered a matter of domestic concern, not a subject of international law.

---

1. "Man," at the end of the eighteenth century, meant a white, propertied and educated male. It was not until well into the twentieth century that women came within its compass. Partial voting rights were extended to African-Americans by the Fifteenth Amendment to the U.S. Constitution in 1870.

2. U.S. Declaration of Independence (1776).

3. The Declaration of the Rights of Man and the Citizen (1789).

4. 60 L.N.T.S. 253, signed 25 Sept. 1926, entered into force, 9 March 1927. A Supplementary Convention on the Abolition of Slavery, the Slave Trade and Institutions and Practices Similar to Slavery, 266 U.N.T.S. 3, was signed on 7 Sept. 1956 and entered into force on 30 April 1957.

5. 60 U.N.T.S. 416, signed 30 Sept. 1921, entered into force, 28 June 1922; see also 1947 Protocol, 53 U.N.T.S. 13.

The United Nations Charter (1945) and the Universal Declaration of Human Rights (1948) began the process of incorporating human rights into the international legal arena.

Human Rights in the United Nations System

The United Nations Charter

The Preamble to the Charter declares that the people of the United Nations "reaffirm faith in fundamental human rights, in the dignity and worth of the human person, in the equal rights of men and women" and pledge "to promote social progress and better standards of life in larger freedom ... [and to promote] the economic and social advancement of all peoples...." Article 1(3) states that one of the purposes of the United Nations is to promote and encourage "respect for human rights and for fundamental freedoms for all without distinction as to race, sex, language or religion...."

Article 55 states:

> With a view to the creation of conditions of stability and well-being which are necessary for peaceful and friendly relations among nations based on respect for the principle of equal rights and self-determination of peoples, the United Nations shall promote:
>
> (a) higher standards of living, full employment, and conditions of economic and social progress and development;
>
> (b) solutions of international economic, social, health, and related problems; and international cultural and educational co-operation; and
>
> (c) universal respect for, and observance of, human rights and fundamental freedoms for all without distinction as to race, sex, language, or religion.

Article 56 declares:

> All Members pledge themselves to take joint and separate action in co-operation with the Organization for the achievement of the purposes set forth in Article 55.

With a view towards implementing U.N. members' pledges to co-operate in the achievement of human rights, article 13(1)(b) states:

> The General Assembly shall initiate studies and make recommendations for the purpose of: ... (b) promoting international co-operation in the economic, social, cultural, educational, and health fields, and assisting in the realization of human rights and fundamental freedoms for all without distinction as to race, sex, language, or religion.

Article 62(2) authorizes the Economic and Social Council to "make recommendations for the purpose of promoting respect for, and observance of, human rights and fundamental freedoms for all." Article 68 requires the Council to "set up Commissions ... for the promotion of human rights...."[6]

---

6. See also, U.N. Charter, art. 76.

At the time when the Charter was written the concept of human rights was far from clear and members of the United Nations had done no more than pledge co-operation towards the achievement of such rights. Most lawyers would not describe such an undertaking as a legal obligation but rather as a hope or aspiration. Much has happened in the human rights field since 1945 both with respect to defining the human rights norms (mainly by treaty) and with respect to creating various forms of enforcement mechanisms. The international community has frequently expressed its approval of a long list of human rights standards so that today many scholars argue that the core concepts of human rights have become part of customary international law binding on all nations.

The Universal Declaration of Human Rights

One of the first international statements of human rights standards was articulated in a General Assembly Resolution of 1948 known as the Universal Declaration of Human Rights.[7] The resolution was adopted by forty-eight votes in favor, none against and eight abstentions.[8] The Declaration is a grand document specifying a large range of rights. At the time it was written, it too was viewed as aspirational but, because it led to the drafting of more specific treaties and implementation mechanisms, scholars now argue that many of the provisions of the Universal Declaration are now part of customary law.

Some of the rights proclaimed in the Universal Declaration are: being "born free and equal" (article 1); freedom from "discrimination of any kind, such as race, colour, sex, language, religion, political or other opinion, national or social origin, property, birth or other status" (article 2); the "right to life, liberty and the security of person" (article 3); freedom from "slavery or servitude" (article 4); freedom from "torture or ... cruel, inhuman or degrading treatment or punishment" (article 5); "the right to recognition everywhere as a person before the law" (article 6); "equal protection of the law [including] ... protection against any discrimination ... and against any incitement to such discrimination" (article 7); "the right to an effective remedy ... [for violation of] fundamental rights granted by the constitution or by law" (article 8); freedom from "arbitrary arrest, detention or exile" (article 9); "a fair and public hearing by an independent and impartial tribunal ... [to determine] rights and obligations and ... any criminal charges against [the accused]" (article 10); "to be presumed innocent until proved guilty ... in a public trial ... [with] the guarantees necessary for ... defence" (article 11(1)); not to be "held guilty of any penal offence" which did not constitute such an offence "at the time when it was committed" (article 11(2)); freedom from "arbitrary interference with ... privacy, family, home or correspondence ... [or] attacks upon ... honour and reputation" (article 12); "the right to freedom of movement and residence within the borders of each State" (article 13(1)); "the right to leave any country, including [one's] own, and to return to [one's] country" (article 13(2)); "the right to seek and to enjoy in other countries asylum from persecution" (article 14(1)); "the right to a nationality" (article 15); the right not to be "arbitrarily deprived of ... nationality nor denied the right to change ... nationality" (article 15(2)); when of "full age" "the right to marry and to found a family ... entered into only with the free and full consent of the intending

7. G.A. Res. 217A, U.N. GAOR, 3rd Sess., pt. I (Dec. 10, 1948).

8. The eight abstentions were Byelorussia, Czechoslovakia, Poland, Saudi Arabia, South Africa, Ukraine, U.S.S.R. and Yugoslavia.

spouses" (article 16(1) & (2)); "the right to own property" and not to be "arbitrarily deprived of ... property" (article 17(1) & (2)); "freedom of thought, conscience and religion ... [including] teaching, practice, worship and observance" (article 18); "freedom of opinion and expression ... [including the right] to seek, receive and impart information and ideas through any media and regardless of frontiers" (article 19); "freedom of peaceful assembly and association ... [and not to be] compelled to belong to an association" (article 20(1) & (2)); "the right to take part in the government of [one's] country, directly or through freely chosen representatives" (article 21(1)); "equal access to public service" (article 21(2)); "universal and equal suffrage ... secret vote or ... equivalent free voting procedures" (article 21(3)); "the right to social security and ... [the] realization ... of the economic, social and cultural rights indispensable for ... dignity and the free development of ... personality" (article 22); "the right to work, to free choice of employment, to just and favourable conditions of work and to protection against unemployment ... equal pay for equal work ... just and favourable remuneration ensuring ... existence worthy of human dignity and supplemented ... by other means of social protection" (article 23(1), (2) & (3)); "the right to form and join trade unions" (article 23(4)); "the right to rest and leisure, including reasonable limitations of working hours and periodic holidays with pay" (article 24); "the right to a standard of living adequate for ... health and well-being ... including food, clothing, housing and medical care and necessary social services, and the right to security in the event of unemployment, sickness, disability, widowhood, old age or other lack of livelihood in circumstances beyond [one's] control" (article 25(1)); "motherhood and childhood" are declared "entitled to special care and assistance" (article 25(2)); "children, whether born in or out of wedlock, shall enjoy the same social protection" (article 25(2)); "the right to education ... [which] shall be free, at least in the elementary ... stages ... [and] compulsory" (article 26(1)); "technical and professional education ... shall be equally accessible to all on the basis of merit" (article 26(1)); "education shall be directed to the full development of the human personality and to the strengthening of respect for human rights" (article 26(2)); "parents have a right to choose the kind of education that shall be given to their children" (article 26(3)); "the right freely to participate in the cultural life of the community" (article 27(1)); "the right to social and international order" (article 28); the rights and freedoms outlined "shall be subject only to such limitations as are determined by law for the purpose of securing due recognition and respect for the rights and freedoms of others ... and the general welfare in a democratic society" (article 29(2)). This far ranging list of rights and freedoms gave rise to two fundamental human rights treaties: (1) the International Covenant on Civil and Political Rights;[9] (2) the International Covenant on Economic, Social and Cultural Rights.[10]

The International Covenant on Civil and Political Rights

Civil and political rights are often referred to as "first generation" human rights because they were the earliest human rights to receive recognition. Economic, social and

9. 999 U.N.T.S. 171, adopted by the General Assembly on 16 Dec. 1966, G.A. Res. 2200, 21 GAOR, 21st Sess., Supp. No. 16, U.N. Doc. 1/6316, at 52 (1966); entered into force, 23 Mar. 1976, reprinted at 6 I.L.M. 368 (1967).

10. 993 U.N.T.S. 3, adopted by the General Assembly on 16 Dec. 1966, G.A. Res. 2200, U.N. GAOR, 21st Sess., Annex, Supp. 16, U.N. Doc. A/6316, at 490 (1966); entered into force, 3 Jan. 1976, reprinted at 6 I.L.M. 360 (1967).

cultural rights are referred to as "second generation" rights because they were second in line for acknowledgment. Various forms of group rights such as the right to development and self-determination are known as "third generation" rights because they are the most recent rights to receive attention.

Rights and Freedoms under the Civil and Political Rights Covenant

Many of the rights and freedoms articulated in the Civil and Political Rights Covenant reiterate those found in the Universal Declaration. These rights and freedoms include, but are not limited to, "the equal right of men and women to the enjoyment of all civil and political rights" (article 3); "the inherent right to life" (article 6); not to be "subjected to torture" (article 7); not to be "held in slavery" (article 8); "the right to liberty and security of person" (article 9); the right to be "informed of any charges against him [/her if arrested] ... [to] be brought promptly before a judge ... [and to receive a hearing] before a court" (article 9 (2)(3) & (4)); "the right to liberty of movement" (article 12); the right to "be equal before the courts" (article 14); the right to a variety of criminal due process protections (articles 14 & 15); "freedom of thought, conscience and religion" (article 18); "the right to peaceful assembly" (article 21); "freedom of association" (article 22); the right to "marry and to found a family" (article 23(2)); children are given certain protections (article 24); and the right "to vote and be elected at genuine periodic elections" (article 25(b)).

States' Rights to Derogate from Guaranteed Rights and Freedoms

Article 4 of the Covenant does provide that "[i]n time of public emergency which threatens the life of the nation ... States ... may take measures derogating from their obligations under the present Covenant to the extent strictly required by the exigencies of the situation...." However no derogation is permitted from certain articles: the right to life, the right not to be tortured, not to be held in slavery or servitude, not to be imprisoned because of inability to fulfill a contract, not to be held guilty of an offense that did not constitute a crime at the time it was committed; the right to recognition as a person before the law; and the right to freedom of thought, conscience and religion. When a state derogates from the guaranteed rights and freedoms it must inform the Secretary-General of the United Nations.

Enforcement of Rights and Freedoms under the Civil and Political Rights Covenant

Human rights advocates are generally only too aware that there is no comprehensive enforcement mechanism in the international arena.[11] The International Court of Justice, for example, only has jurisdiction over states if the particular state brought before the Court has given its consent to the Court's jurisdiction (see chapter IX). The drafters of the Covenant were eager, therefore, to build in an enforcement mechanism within the four corners of the Covenant itself.

Various articles of the Covenant impose specific obligations upon the states which are parties to the treaty. States are required "to respect and to ensure ... the rights recog-

---

11. For a useful practitioners' guide to human rights procedures see, Hurst Hannum, Guide to International Human Rights Practice (4th ed. 2004).

nized in the present Covenant." (Article 2(1)). States must "take the necessary steps ... to adopt such legislative or other measures as may be necessary to give effect to the rights recognized in the present Covenant." (Article 2(2)). They must also provide "an effective remedy" when the Covenant's rights are violated. (Article 3(a)). These articles make it clear that the drafters of the Covenant intended its provisions to be more than mere aspirations and hopes.

Part IV of the Covenant establishes a Human Rights Committee consisting of eighteen members. The method of nomination and elections of Committee members is articulated in articles 28 through 39. The Committee's principal function is to receive reports on measures which states have taken to implement the Covenant's rights and transmit its comments on those reports back to the states. The obligation for states to submit reports is mandatory "whenever the Committee so requests" (article 40(1)(b)). Obviously the reporting requirement is a relatively weak enforcement mechanism but given the reluctance of most states to submit to any form of international supervision it is a great deal better than nothing.

Article 41 provides an enforcement mechanism with a few more teeth but it is entirely optional. In other words states, parties to the Covenant, are not obliged to submit to article 41 procedures. Article 41 provides that states may submit communications to the Human Rights Committee complaining that another state "is not fulfilling its obligations under the present Covenant." This state-against-state complaint procedure is only available to states who have themselves already agreed that other states may submit complaints against them. The Committee holds closed meetings when considering such complaints and first tries to resolve the dispute by reaching a "friendly solution" but if that is not possible the Committee hears the states' submissions on the matter and issues a report together with any solution reached. If no solution is reached, then the Committee confines its report to "a brief statement of the facts" and the submissions of the parties concerned. If there is still no resolution of the dispute, a Conciliation Commission may be appointed, provided the parties agree, which is empowered to submit a report either spelling out the solution reached or, if that is not possible, setting out "its views on the possibilities of an amicable solution of the matter" (article 42(7)(c)). This report is not binding on the parties but they are required to notify the Chairman "whether or not they accept the contents of the report of the Commission." As you can see, the state-against-state enforcement mechanism is hardly a stringent method of ensuring the rights and freedoms of the Covenant. To date it has never been invoked. Although one hundred and sixty-four states are parties to the Covenant, less than fifty have made declarations accepting the state-against-state procedure under article 41.

Optional Protocols to the Covenant on Civil and Political Rights

There are also two optional protocols to the Covenant. The first Optional Protocol to the International Covenant on Civil and Political Rights[12] was adopted by the U.N. General Assembly in 1966 and entered into force in 1976. Under this Protocol individuals may submit complaints to the Human Rights Committee alleging that their rights under the Covenant have been violated provided they have exhausted all domestic remedies. The Committee receives the individual's "written communication"

12. Optional Protocol to the International Covenant on Civil and Political Rights, 999 U.N.T.S. 171 signed 16 Dec.1966, entered into force 23 March 1976, reprinted at 6 I.L.M. 383 (1967). Currently one hundred and four states are parties to this Protocol.

(article 3), brings that communication to the attention of the accused state, receives any "written explanations" (article 4(2)) submitted by the state and "forward[s] its views to the State party concerned and to the individual." (Article 5(4)). A summary of the Committee's activities under this Protocol appear as part of the Committee's annual report. Over one hundred states are parties to this Protocol and several hundred complaints have been filed under the procedures provided. Two recent cases are excerpted below.

Uteev v. Uzbekistan

Human Rights Committee: 91st Session
Communication No. 1150/2002
Date of Adoption of Views: 26, October 2007 (footnotes omitted)

1.1 The author of the communication is Ms. Roza Uteeva, an Uzbek national of Kazakh origin. She submits the communication on behalf of her brother, Azamat Uteev, also an Uzbek national of Kazakh origin, born in 1981, who at the time of submission of the communication was awaiting execution in Tashkent, after being sentenced to death by the Supreme Court of the Republic of Karakalpakstan (Uzbekistan) on 28 June 2002. She claims that her brother is a victim of violations by Uzbekistan of his rights under article 6; article 7; article 9; article 10; article 14, paragraphs 1, 2, and 3; and article 16, of the Covenant. She is unrepresented.

1.2 When registering the communication on 7 January 2003, and pursuant to rule 92 of its rules of procedures, the Committee, acting through its Special Rapporteur on new communications and interim measures, requested the State party not to carry out the author's brother's execution while his case was under examination. On 16 July 2003, the State party informed the Committee that Mr. Uteev's execution had already been carried out, without however providing the exact date of execution.

Factual background

2.1 On 28 June 2002, Mr. Azamat Uteev was found guilty and sentenced to death by the Supreme Court of the Republic of Karakalpakstan (Uzbekistan), for having murdered with particular violence one Saira Matyakubova (a minor), and having robbed money, jewellery, and other items for a total of 670, 120 Uzbek sum from her parents' apartment, in the morning of 3 April 2002. After having committed the murder and robbery, and in order to conceal his actions, he set fire to the apartment, posing a threat to the life of others, and causing damage to the victim's parents equal to 5,824,000 sum. On 6 August 2002, the judgment was reviewed by the appeal body of the Karakalpakstan Supreme Court, which confirmed the death sentence. On 26 November 2002, the Supreme Court of Uzbekistan also reviewed the case and confirmed the death sentence.

2.2 The author claims that her brother did not commit the murder of which he was convicted. He was beaten and tortured by investigators and thus forced to confess guilt. Furthermore, she claims that her brother's sentence was particularly severe and unfounded and that his punishment did not correspond with his personality. He was positively assessed by his neighbours and documents to this effect were submitted to the court.

2.3 The author refers to a ruling of the Supreme Court of Uzbekistan of 1996, according to which evidence obtained through unlawful methods is inadmissible. This was not respected in her brother's case. She claims that her numerous complaints to different institutions (Presidential administration, Ombudsman, General Prosecutor's Office, Supreme Court of Uzbekistan) about the irregularities committed by the investigators remained unanswered or were simply sent to the same service against whose actions she was complaining about.

2.4 The author contends that in court, her brother claimed that he was innocent and that he was initially interrogated as a witness in relation to the crimes but was later arrested. Officials from the District Unit of the Ministry of Internal Affairs and the Prosecutor's Office beat and tortured him, in the absence of a defence counsel. In describing the methods of torture used, he allegedly claimed that he was forced to wear a gas mask with obstructed air access and was thus prevented from breathing; he was also placed in salt water. According to the author, the court rejected her brother's claims, considering that they constituted a defence strategy to avoid criminal liability.

2.5 According to the author, the investigators and the court examined her brother's criminal case superficially and in a biased manner. In particular, the investigator did everything possible to avoid the engagement of the criminal liability of one Rinat Mamutov (a former colleague of the father of the murdered Matyakubova), who, according to the author, had committed the murder.

2.6 The author claims that pursuant to article 23 of the Uzbek Criminal Procedure Code, it is not incumbent on the accused to prove his/her innocence and any remaining doubts are to his/her benefit. The court, however, did not comply with these requirements in her brother's case. The sentence was based on indirect evidence collected by the investigators that could not be confirmed in court, whereas evidence that could establish Uteev's innocence was lost during the investigation. In particular, the author contends that the record in relation to the examination of the crime scene mentioned that Uteev had stabbed the victim several times with a knife. According to her, her brother's hair, hands and clothes should have disclosed blood marks. However, no expert's examination of his hair, hands, or of the substance under his nails was ever carried out, although this was crucial in establishing his guilt.

The complaint

3.The author claims that her brother is a victim of violations by Uzbekistan of his rights under article 6; article 7; article 9; article 10; article 14, paragraphs 1, 2, and 3; and article 16, of the Covenant.

State party's observations and absence of author's comments thereon

4.1 The State party presented its observations on 16 July 2003 and 12 October 2005. It recalls that the alleged victim was sentenced to death by the Supreme Court of the Republic of Karakalpakstan on 28 June 2002, for robbery, premeditated murder, and deliberate destruction of property causing significant damages. On 6 August 2002, the appeal body of the Karakalpakstan Supreme Court confirmed the sentence. According to the State party, Mr. Uteev's guilt in committing the offences was proven, his illegal acts were duly classified under the law in force, and his punishment was determined after taking into account information on his personality and the public danger of the crimes he had committed. The State party states that the death sentence of the alleged victim has already been carried out, without however providing the exact date of the execution.

4.2 The author did not present comments on the State party's observations, in spite of three reminders.

Non-respect of the Committee's request for interim measures

5.1 When submitting her communication on 7 January 2003, the author informed the Committee that at that point, her brother was on death row. On 3 February 2003, she submitted a written authorization to act on behalf of Mr. Uteev that was signed by him, on 14 January 2003, i.e. subsequently to the transmittal to the State party of the Committee's request not to cary out the alleged victim's execution while his case is under consideration. On 16 July 2003, the State party informed the Committee that the alleged victim's execution had been carried out, without providing the date of execution. The Committee notes that it is uncontested that the execution in question took place despite the fact that the alleged victim's communication had been registered under the Optional Protocol and a request for interim measures of protection had been duly addressed to the State party. The Committee recalls that by adhering to the Optional Protocol, a State party to the Covenant recognizes the competence of the Committee to receive and consider communications from individuals claiming to be victims of violations of any of the rights set forth in the Covenant (in the Preamble and in article 1). Implicit in a State's adherence to the Protocol is an undertaking to cooperate with the Committee in good faith, so as to enable it to consider such communications, and after examination, to forward its Views to the State party and to the individual concerned (article 5, paragraphs 1 and 4). It is incompatible with these obligations for a State party to take any action that would prevent or frustrate the Committee in its consideration and examination of the communication, and in the expression of its final Views.

5.2 Apart from any violation of the Covenant found against a State party in a communication, a State party commits grave breaches of its obligations under the Optional Protocol if it acts to prevent or to frustrate consideration by the Committee of a communication alleging a violation of the Covenant, or to render examination by the Committee moot and the expression of its Views nugatory and futile. In the present case, the author alleges that her brother was denied his rights under various articles of the Covenant. Having been notified of the communication, the State party breached its obligations under the Protocol by executing the alleged victim *before* the Committee concluded its consideration and examination of the case, and the formulation and communication of its Views.

5.3 The Committee recalls that interim measures under rule 92 of its rules of procedure adopted in conformity with article 39 of the Covenant, are essential to the Committee's role under the Protocol. Flouting of the rule, especially by irreversible measures such as, as in this case, the execution of Mr. Azamat Uteev, undermines the protection of Covenant rights through the Optional Protocol.

* * *

Consideration of the merits

7.1 The Human Rights Committee has considered the communication in the light of all the information made available to it by the parties, as provided for under article 5, paragraph 1, of the Optional Protocol.

7.2 The author has claimed that her brother was beaten and tortured by investigators to force him to confess guilt in the murder and other crimes. In court, he retracted his initial confessions made during the investigation, and explained that they were obtained under beatings and torture. The court rejected his claim as constituting a defense strategy aimed at avoiding criminal liability. These allegations were brought to the attention of the Supreme Court of Uzbekistan and were rejected. The Committee recalls that once a complaint against ill-treatment contrary to article 7 is filed, a State party is duty bound to investigate it promptly and impartially. In this case, the State party has not specifically, by the way of presenting the detailed consideration by the courts, or otherwise, refuted the author's allegations nor has it presented any particular information, in the context of the present communication, to demonstrate that it conducted any inquiry in this respect. In these circumstances, due weight must be given to the author's allegations, and the Committee consider that the facts presented by the author disclose a violation of her brother's rights under article 7 and article 14, paragraph 3 (g), of the Covenant.

7.3 In light of the above finding, the Committee does not find it necessary to address separately the author's claim under article 10 of the Covenant.

7.4 The Committee recalls that the imposition of a sentence of death upon conclusion of a trial in which the provisions of the Covenant have not been respected constitutes a violation of article 6 of the Covenant. In the present cases, Mr. Uteev's death sentence was passed in violation of the guarantees set out in article 7 and article 14, paragraph 3 (g), of the Covenant, and thus also in breach of article 6, paragraph 2, of the Covenant.

8. The Human Rights Committee, acting under article 5, paragraph 4, of the Optional Protocol to the International Covenant on Civil and Political Rights, is of the view that the facts before it disclose a violation of the author's brother's rights under article 7 and article 14, paragraph 3 (g), read together with article 6, paragraph 2, of the Covenant.

9. In accordance with article 2, paragraph 3 (a), of the Covenant, the State party is under an obligation to provide Ms. Uteeva with an effective remedy, including compensation. The State party is also under an obligation to prevent similar violations in the future.

10. Bearing in mind that, by becoming a party to the Optional Protocol, the State party has recognized the competence of the Committee to determine whether there has been a violation of the Covenant or not and that, pursuant to article 2 of the Covenant, the State party has undertaken to ensure to all individuals within its territory or subject to its jurisdiction the rights recognized in the Covenant and to provide an effective and enforceable remedy in case a violation has been established, the Committee wishes to receive from the State party, within 180 days, information about the measures taken to give effect to the Committee's Views. The State party is also requested to publish the Committee's Views.

Note

Remember that the Human Rights Committee is not a trial court able to subpoena witnesses and other evidence. It generally has to rely upon information submitted by the complainant and any reply received from the state against which the complaint is brought.

QUESTIONS

1. What rights was Uzbekistan found to have violated.
2. By executing Azamat Uteev while the case was pending before the Human Rights Committee, what obligations did Uzbekistan violate?
3. What effect did the failure of Uzbekistan to investigate the allegations of torture have on the Committee's decision?
4. What remedies did the Committee order?
5. Although complainants can be represented by a lawyer before the Committee, there is no right to have a lawyer provided without cost. Should there be? Who should pay for such legal representation?

Llantoy Huamán v. Peru

Human Rights Committee: Communication No.1153/2003
Date of Adoption of Views: 24 October 2005,
13 Int'l Hum. Rts Rep. 355 (2006) (footnotes omitted)

Views [adopted by the Human Rights Commitee] under article 5 paragraph 4 of the Optional Protocol

1. The author of the communication is Karen Noelia Llantoy Huamán, born in 1984, who claims to be a victim of a violation by Peru of articles 2, 3, 6, 7, 17, 24 and 26 of the International Covenant on Civil and Political Rights. She is represented by the organizations DEMUS, CLADEM and Center for Reproductive Law and Policy. The Optional Protocol entered into force for Peru on 3 October 1980.

Factual background

2.1 The author became pregnant in March 2001, when she was aged 17. On 27 June 2001 she was given a scan at the Archbishop Loayza National Hospital in Lima, part of the Ministry of Health. The scan showed that she was carrying an anencephalic foetus.

2.2 On 3 July 2001, Dr. Ygor Pérez Solf, a gynaecologist and obstetrician in the Archbishop Loayza National Hospital in Lima, informed the author of the foetal abnormality and the risks to her life if the pregnancy continued. Dr. Pérez said that she had two options: to continue the pregnancy or to terminate it. He advised termination by means of uterine curettage. The author decided to terminate the pregnancy, and the necessary clinical studies were carried out, confirming the foetal abnormality.

2.3 On 19 July 2001, when the author reported to the hospital together with her mother for admission preparatory to the operation, Dr. Pérez informed her that she needed to obtain written authorization from the hospital director. Since she was under age, her mother, Ms. Elena Huamán Lara, requested the authorization. On 24 July 2001, Dr. Maximiliano Cárdenas Díaz, the hospital director, replied in writing that the termination could not be carried out as to do so would be unlawful, since under article 120 of the [Peruvian] Criminal Code, abortion was punishable by a prison term of no more than three months when it was likely that at birth the child would suffer serious physical or mental defects, while under article 119, therapeutic abortion was permitted only when termination of the pregnancy was the only way of saving the life of the pregnant woman or avoiding serious and permanent damage to her health.

2.4 On 16 August 2001, Ms. Amanda Gayoso, a social worker and member of the Peruvian association of social workers, carried out an assessment of the case and concluded that medical intervention to terminate the pregnancy was advisable "since its continuation would only prolong the distress and emotional instability of Karen and her family". However, no intervention took place owing to the refusal of the Health Ministry medical personnel.

2.5 On 20 August 2001, Dr. Marta B. Rondón, a psychiatrist and member of the Peruvian Medical Association, drew up a psychiatric report on the author, concluding that "the so-called principle of the welfare of the unborn child has caused serious harm to the mother, since she has unnecessarily been made to carry to term a pregnancy whose fatal outcome was known in advance, and this has substantially contributed to triggering the symptoms of depression, with its severe impact on the development of an adolescent and the patient's future mental health".

2.6 On 13 January 2002, three weeks late with respect to the anticipated date of birth, the author gave birth to an anencephalic baby girl, who survived for four days, during which the mother had to breastfeed her. Following her daughter's death, the author fell into a state of deep depression. This was diagnosed by the psychiatrist Marta B. Rondón. The author also states that she suffered from an inflammation of the vulva which required medical treatment.

2.7 The author has submitted to the Committee a statement made by Dr. Annibal Faúdes and Dr. Luis Tavara, who are specialists from the association called Center for Reproductive Rights, and who on 17 January 2003 studied the author's clinical dossier and stated that anencephaly is a condition which is fatal to the foetus in all cases. Death immediately follows birth in most cases. It also endangers the mother's life. In their opinion, in refusing to terminate the pregnancy, the medical personnel took a decision which was prejudicial to the author.

2.8 Regarding the exhaustion of domestic remedies, the author claims that this requirement is waived when judicial remedies available domestically are ineffective in the case in question, and she points out that the Committee has laid down on several occasions that the author has no obligation to exhaust a remedy which would prove ineffective. She adds that in Peru there is no administrative remedy which would enable a pregnancy to be terminated on therapeutic grounds, nor any judicial remedy functioning with the speed and efficiency required to enable a woman to require the authorities to guarantee her right to a lawful abortion within the limited period, by virtue of the special circumstances obtaining in such cases. She also states that her financial circumstances and those of her family prevented her from obtaining legal advice.

2.9 The author states that the complaint is not being considered under any other procedure of international settlement.

The complaint

* * *

3.3 The author claims a violation of article 6 of the Covenant. She states that her experience had a serious impact on her mental health from which she has still not recovered. She points out that the Committee has stated that the right to life cannot be interpreted in a restrictive manner, but requires States to take positive steps to protect it, including the measures necessary to ensure that women do not resort to clandestine abortions which endanger their life and health, especially in the case of poor women. She adds that the Committee has viewed lack of access for women to reproductive health services, including abortion, as a violation of women's right to life, and that this has been reiterated by other committees such as the Committee on the Elimination of Discrimination against Women and the Committee on Economic, Social and Cultural Rights. The author claims that in the present case, the violation of the right to life lay in the fact that Peru did not take steps to ensure that the author secured a safe termination of pregnancy on the grounds that the foetus was not viable. She states that the refusal to provide a legal abortion service left her with two options which posed an equal risk to her health and safety: to seek clandestine (and hence highly risky) abortion services, or to continue a dangerous and traumatic pregnancy which put her life at risk.

3.4 The author claims a violation of article 7 of the Covenant. The fact that she was obliged to continue with the pregnancy amounts to cruel and inhuman treatment, in her view, since she had to endure the distress of seeing her daughter's marked deformities and knowing that her life expectancy was short. She states that this was an awful experience which added further pain and distress to that which she had already borne during the period when she was obliged to continue with the pregnancy, since she was subjected to an "extended funeral" for her daughter, and sank into a deep depression after her death.

3.5 The author points out that the Committee has stated that the prohibition in article 7 of the Covenant relates not only to physical pain but also to mental suffering, and that this protection is particularly important in the case of minors. She points out that, after considering Peru's report in 1996, the Committee expressed the view that restrictive provisions on abortion subjected women to inhumane treatment, in violation of article 7 of the Covenant, and that in 2000, the Committee reminded the State party that the criminalization of abortion was incompatible with articles 3, 6 and 7 of the Covenant.

3.6 The author claims a violation of article 17, arguing that this article protects women from interference in decisions which affect their bodies and their lives, and offers them the opportunity to exercise their right to make independent decisions on their reproductive lives. The author points out that the State party interfered arbitrarily in her private life, taking on her behalf a decision relating to her life and reproductive health which obliged her to carry a pregnancy to term, and thereby breaching her right to privacy. She adds that the service was available, and that if it had not been for the interference of State officials in her decision, which enjoyed the protection of the law, she would have been able to terminate the pregnancy. She reminds the Committee that children and young people enjoy special protection by virtue of their status as minors, as recognized in article 24 of the Covenant and in the Convention on the Rights of the Child.

3.7 The author claims a violation of article 24, since she did not receive the special care she needed from the health authorities, as an adolescent girl. Neither her welfare nor her state of health were objectives pursued by the authorities which refused to carry out an abortion on her. The author points out that the Committee laid down in its General Comment No. 17, relating to article 24, that the State should also adopt economic, social and cultural measures to safeguard this right. For example, every possible economic and social measure should be taken to reduce infant mortality and to prevent children from being subjected to acts of violence or cruel or inhuman treatment, among other possible violations.

* * *

State party's failure to cooperate under article 4 of the Optional Protocol

4. On 23 July 2003, 15 March 2004 and 25 October 2004, reminders were sent to the State party inviting it to submit information to the Committee concerning the admissibility and the merits of the complaint. The Committee notes that no such information has been received. It regrets that the State party has not supplied any information concerning the admissibility or the merits of the author's allegations. It points out that it is implicit in the Optional Protocol that States parties make available to the Committee all information at their disposal. In the absence of a reply from the State party, due weight must be given to the author's allegations, to the extent that these have been properly substantiated.

Issues and proceedings before the Committee

Consideration of admissibility

* * *

5.5 Concerning the allegations relating to articles 6, 7, 17 and 24 of the Covenant, the Committee considers that they are adequately substantiated for purposes of admissibility, and that they appear to raise issues in connection with those provisions. Consequently, it turns to consideration of the substance of the complaint.

Consideration of the merits

6.1 The Human Rights Committee has considered the present complaint in the light of all the information received, in accordance with article 5, paragraph 1, of the Optional Protocol.

6.2 The Committee notes that the author attached a doctor's statement confirming that her pregnancy exposed her to a life-threatening risk. She also suffered severe psychological consequences exacerbated by her status as a minor, as the psychiatric report of 20 August 2001 confirmed. The Committee notes that the State party has not provided any evidence to challenge the above. It notes that the authorities were aware of the risk to the author's life, since a gynaecologist and obstetrician in the same hospital had advised her to terminate the pregnancy, with the operation to be carried out in the same hospital. The subsequent refusal of the competent medical authorities to provide the service may have endangered the author's life. The author states that no effective remedy was available to her to oppose that decision. In the absence of any information from the State party, due weight must be given to the author's claims.

6.3 The author also claims that, owing to the refusal of the medical authorities to carry out the therapeutic abortion, she had to endure the distress of seeing her daughter's marked deformities and knowing that she would die very soon. This was an experience which added further pain and distress to that which she had already borne during the period when she was obliged to continue with the pregnancy. The author attaches a psychiatric certificate dated 20 August 2001, which confirms the state of deep depression into which she fell and the severe consequences this caused, taking her age into account. The Committee notes that this situation could have been foreseen, since a hospital doctor had diagnosed anencephaly in the foetus, yet the hospital director refused termination. The omission on the part of the State in not enabling the author to benefit from a therapeutic abortion was, in the Committee's view, the cause of the suffering she experienced. The Committee has pointed out in its General Comment No. 20 that the right set out in article 7 of the Covenant relates not only to physical pain but also to mental suffering, and that the protection is particularly important in the case of minors. In the absence of any information from the State party in this regard, due weight must be given to the author's complaints. Consequently, the Committee considers that the facts before it reveal a violation of article 7 of the Covenant. In the light of this finding the Committee does not consider it necessary in the circumstances to made a finding on article 6 of the Covenant.

6.4 The author states that the State party, in denying her the opportunity to secure medical intervention to terminate the pregnancy, interfered arbitrarily in her private life. The Committee notes that a public-sector doctor told the author that she could either continue with the pregnancy or terminate it in accordance with domestic legislation allowing abortions in cases of risk to the life of the mother. In the absence of any information from the State party, due weight must be given to the author's claim that at the time of this information, the conditions for a lawful abortion as set out in the law were present. In the circumstances of the case, the refusal to act in accordance with the author's decision to terminate her pregnancy was not justified and amounted to a violation of article 17 of the Covenant.

6.5 The author claims a violation of article 24 of the Covenant, since she did not receive from the State party the special care she needed as a minor. The Committee notes the special vulnerability of the author as a minor girl. It further notes that, in the absence of any information from the State party, due weight must be given to the author's claim that she did not receive, during and after her pregnancy, the medical and psychological support necessary in the specific circumstances of her case. Consequently, the Committee considers that the facts before it reveal a violation of article 24 of the Covenant.

6.6 The author claims to have been a victim of [a] violation of article 2 of the Covenant on the grounds that she lacked an adequate legal remedy. In the absence of information from the State party, the Committee considers that due weight must be given to the author's claims as regards lack of an adequate legal remedy and consequently concludes that the facts before it also reveal a violation of article 2 in conjunction with articles 7, 17 and 24.

7. The Human Rights Committee, acting under article 5, paragraph 4, of the Optional Protocol to the Covenant, is of the view that the facts before it disclose a violation of articles 2, 7, 17 and 24 of the Covenant.

8. In accordance with article 2, paragraph 3 (a), of the Covenant, the State party is required to furnish the author with an effective remedy, including compensation. The State party has an obligation to take steps to ensure that similar violations do not occur in the future.

9. Bearing in mind that, as a party to the Optional Protocol, the State party recognizes the competence of the Committee to determine whether there has been a violation of the Covenant, and that, under article 2 of the Covenant, the State party has undertaken to ensure to all individuals within its territory and subject to its jurisdiction the rights recognized in the Covenant and to offer an effective and enforceable remedy when a violation is found to have occurred, the Committee wishes to receive from the State party, within 90 days, information about the measures taken to give effect to the present Views. The State party is also requested to publish the Committee's Views.

* * *

Dissenting Opinion By Committee Member

Hipólito Solari-Yrigoyen

[This member of the Committee would also have found a violation of article 6 and stated: "It is not only taking a person's life that violates article 6 of the Covenant but also placing a person's life in grave danger, as in this case. Consequently, I consider that the facts in the present case reveal a violation of article 6 of the Covenant."]

QUESTIONS

1. What provisions of the International Covenant on Civil and Political Rights were found to have been violated by Peru?
2. What effect did Peru's failure to respond have?
3. What remedies did the Human Rights Committee indicate must be provided by Peru?
4. As a party to the ICCPR, must Peru provide arbortion on demand?

Note

This is the first case where there has been a determination that restricting access to an abortion, in the particular circumstances of the case, violated a woman's human rights.

There is also a further protocol to the Civil and Political Rights Covenant entitled the Second Optional Protocol to the International Covenant on Civil and Political Rights, Aiming at the Abolition of the Death Penalty.[13] This protocol provides that "[n]o one within the jurisdiction of a State Party to the present Protocol shall be executed." (Article 1). No derogations from article 1 are permitted (article 6(2)). States can make reservations to the requirement of the abolition of the death penalty when they ratify the Protocol but only "for the application of the death penalty in time of war pursuant to a conviction for a most serious crime of a military nature committed during wartime." (Article 2).

The International Covenant on Economic, Social and Cultural Rights[14]

Many of the rights and freedoms specified in the Economic, Social and Cultural Rights Covenant restate parts of the Universal Declaration. The enforcement mechanisms are similar to the reporting requirements found in the Civil and Political Rights Covenant, but do not provide for the state-against-state or the individual-against-state complaints.

Rights and Freedoms under the Economic, Social and Cultural Rights Covenant

The rights and freedoms protected by this Covenant are: "the right of self-determination ... [to] freely determine ... political status and freely pursue ... economic, social and cultural development." (Article 1(1)). The right to "freely dispose of ... natural wealth and resources" (article 1(2)); "the right to work" (article 6); "the right ... to ... just and favourable conditions of work ... [including] ... remuneration ... safe and healthy working conditions ... equal opportunity ... to be promoted ... rest, leisure and ... limitation of working hours and periodic holidays with pay" (article 7); "the right ... to form trade unions" (article 8(1)(a)); "the right to strike" (article 8(1)(d)); "the right ... to social security" (article 9); the family is described as "the natural and fundamental group unit of society" (article 10(1)); mothers are to be accorded "special protection ... during a reasonable period before and after child birth ... [and] working mothers ... [are to be] accorded paid leave or leave with adequate social security benefits" (article 10(2)); children are to be afforded "special measures of protection" (article 10(3)); states are required to "set age limits ... [for] child labour" (article 10(3)); everyone has the right "to an adequate standard of living for himself and his family, including adequate food, clothing and housing" (article 11(1)); the right "to be free from hunger" (article 11(2)); "the right ... to the enjoyment of the highest attainable standard of physical and mental health" (article 12(1)); "the right ... to education ... [including,

13. 1642 U.N.T.S. 414, adopted by the U.N. General Assembly 15 Dec. 1989, G.A. Res. 44/128, 44 GAOR, 44th Sess., Supp.No. 49 at 207, U.N. Doc. A/44/824 (1989), entered into force 11 July 1991, reprinted at 29 I.L.M. 1464 (1990). Currently there are seventy one parties to this Protocol.

14. *Supra* note 10.

compulsory, free] primary education "(article 13(1) & (2)(a)); "the liberty of parents ... [or] legal guardians to choose for their children schools [other than state run schools] ... to ensure the religious and moral education of their children" (article 13(3)); "the right ... to take part in cultural life ... [and] to enjoy the benefits of scientific progress" (article 15(1)(a) & (b)).

Many of the rights outlined in the Economic, Social and Cultural Rights Covenant obviously depend upon a fairly high level of stable, social organization and a reasonably vibrant economy. No one has yet invented a fool-proof system to ensure social stability or a vibrant economy but clearly measures of enforcement were important to the drafters of the Covenant.

Enforcement of Rights and Freedoms under the Economic, Social and Cultural Rights Covenant

The Covenant contains a number of articles that impose obligations upon the states parties to the Covenant. Those states "shall promote the realization of the right to self-determination" (article 1(3)); states "undertake to take steps ... to the maximum of [their] available resources ... [to achieve] progressively the full realization of the rights recognized in the present Covenant." (Article 2(1)); states "undertake to guarantee that the rights enunciated in the present Covenant will be exercised without discrimination of any kind as to race, colour, sex, language, religion, political or other opinion, national or social origin, property, birth or other status" (article 2(2)); developing countries are permitted to "determine to what extent they would guarantee the economic rights recognized in the present Covenant to non-nationals" (article 2(3)); to ensure the right to work states shall provide "technical and vocational guidance and training programmes" (article 6(2)); to ensure an adequate standard of living states must take measures "to improve methods of production, conservation and distribution of food" (article 11(1) & (2)(a)); to ensure the enjoyment of good health states must take steps to reduce "infant mortality ... improve all aspects of environmental and industrial hygiene ... [to] control epidemic [s] ... [and] assure to all medical service ... in the event of sickness" (article 12); to ensure the right to education states must actively pursue "the development of a school system at all levels" (article 13(e)); if a state does not have a system of compulsory, free primary education it must "within two years ... work out and adopt a detailed plan of action" (article 14). The Covenant recognizes that many of the rights articulated will have to be achieved progressively but attempts to impose a series of obligations that will ensure development towards the achievement of the rights outlined. All of the rights may be subjected "only to such limitations as are determined by law only in so far as this may be compatible with the nature of these rights and solely for the purpose of promoting the general welfare in a democratic society" (article 4).

Article 16 imposes a reporting obligation upon the parties to the Covenant "to submit ... reports on the measures which they have adopted and the progress made in achieving the observance of the rights recognized herein." These reports are submitted to the U.N. Secretary-General who transmits them to the Economic and Social Council for consideration. The Economic and Social Council[15] (ECOSOC) is one of the principal organs of the United Nations. Article 17 also provides that the states "shall furnish

15. U.N. Charter, arts. 7, & 61–72.

their reports in stages, in accordance with a programme to be established by the Economic and Social Council ... [which] may indicate factors and difficulties affecting the degree of fulfillment of obligations under the present Covenant" (article 17(1) & (2)). ECOSOC is authorized to make arrangements with the specialized agencies of the United Nations to receive reports from them on progress being made to achieve the rights specified in the Covenant.[16] The states' reports and the specialized agencies' reports were originally able to be transmitted to the Commission on Human Rights "for study and general recommendation" (article 19). The Commission has now been replaced by the Human Rights Council (see description pp. 310–311).

To fulfill its obligations ECOSOC initially established a Working Group composed of representatives from various governments. This group was eventually dissolved and in 1987 the Committee on Economic, Social and Cultural Rights (CESCR) was established consisting of eighteen members. States now submit a report to this Committee every five years. A number of the United Nations specialized agencies (the ILO, WHO, UNESCO etc.) have assisted the Committee in compiling reports and non-governmental organizations (NGOs) are now permitted to submit written reports to the Committee. The CESCR prepares an annual report and has on occasion criticized various parties for failing to fulfill their obligations under the Covenant.[17] On December 10, 2008, the General Assembly unanimously adopted an Optional Protocol to the ICESCR[18] which grants the Committee the right to hear individual or group complaints against states that are parties to this new Optional Protocol. This Protocol will be open for signature in 2009.

The United Nations Human Rights Council

Until 2006, the Human Rights Commission was a subsidiary body of the Economic and Social Council (ECOSOC). Article 19 of the Covenant on Economic, Social and Cultural Rights provides:

> The Economic and Social Council may transmit to the Commission on Human Rights for study and general recommendation or as appropriate for information the reports concerning human rights submitted by States in accordance with articles 16 and 17, and those concerning human rights submitted by the specialized agencies in accordance with article 18.

The Commission has now been replaced by the Human Rights Council[19] which is based in Geneva, has forty seven members and functions as a subsidiary body of the General Assembly. Its first meeting was held on June 18, 2007 and its main purpose is to examine human rights violations and make recommendations on them. It is charged with reviewing all UN Member states' records on human rights through a system called The Universal Periodic Review. In 2006, the Council decided to examine all of the various mechanism for reviewing human rights that had previously been undertaken by the

16. Id. art. 18.

17. E.g., Rwanda was criticized for failure to submit within two years a plan for the progressive implementation of free, compulsory primary education as required by art. 14. CESCR Report, U.N. ESCOR, 44th Sess., Supp. 4, at 41 (1989).

18. G.A. Res. A/RES/63/117, 10 Dec. 2008.

19. G.A. Res. A/RES/60/251, 15 Mar. 2006.

Human Rights Commission.[20] A Complaint Procedure is being established to examine consistent patterns of gross violations of human rights. Working Groups have been set up to assist the Council. The criteria for a communication to be accepted for examination have been established.

The United Nations High Commissioner for Human Rights

In 1993, the U.N. General Assembly voted to create the position of U.N. High Commissioner for the Promotion and Protection of All Human Rights.[21] José Ayala Lasso, Ecuador's Ambassador to the United Nations, was nominated by the Secretary-General to be the first High Commissioner for Human Rights and assumed his office in April of 1994. Mary Robinson, former President of Ireland, succeeded him in 1997. Louise Arbor, formerly a member of the Supreme Court of Canada and chief prosecutor for the International Criminal Tribunal for the former Yugoslavia and Rwanda, took over the office on July 1, 2004. She has now been succeeded by Navanethem Pillay, a former Judge and President of the International Criminal Tribunal for Rwanda, who took up her post on September 1, 2008. The High Commissioner is given the "principal responsibility for United Nations human rights activities ..."[22] The High Commissioner is directed to "[f]unction within the framework of the Charter of the United Nations, the Universal Declaration of Human Rights, other international instruments of human rights and international law...."[23] but is also required to "respect the sovereignty, territorial integrity and domestic jurisdiction of States...."[24] The Office therefore, has to decide upon the appropriate line between human rights and state sovereignty. The High Commissioner is required to investigate and report upon human rights abuses and to make recommendations to the various U.N. human rights entities with a view to improving the protection of human rights. The Office also has to coordinate all the various informational functions in which the United Nations engages to educate the world about human rights. The former High Commissioner published an ambitious Strategic Plan for 2008–2009[25]

So far the High Commissioners have visited an impressive array of countries and have established regional and country offices throughout the world. The growth of the High Commissioner's staff and the large number of pressing issues addressed by the office, ranging from racial discrimination to violence against women, continues to be impressive.

United Nations Conventions on Specific Topics of Human Rights

There are a growing number of conventions that seek to protect a broad range of human rights. Some of the major treaties are listed below together with their legal cita-

---

20. To examine the Human Rights Council Complaint Procedure, go to: http://www2.ohchr.org/english/bodies/chr/complaints.htm.

21. G.A. Res. 48/141, U.N. GAOR, 48th Sess., Agenda Item 114(b), at 1, U.N. Doc. A/RES/48/141 (1993).

22. Id. at para. 4.

23. Id. para. 3(a).

24. Id.

25. For the text of High Commissioner's Strategic Management Plan: http://www.ohchr.org/Documents/Press/SMP2008-2009.pdf.

tions, the date of entry into force and the enforcement mechanism provided for in the particular treaty (see chart on pp. 313–314).

Regional Human Rights Systems

The most active and rigorous promotion and enforcement of human rights is currently occurring at the regional level in Europe. The United Nations human rights system is important but often lacks stringent enforcement mechanisms because states have been unwilling to submit to a governance structure that is often seen as politically motivated and remote from national life.

The European Human Rights System

The European Convention

The European Convention for the Protection of Human Rights and Fundamental Freedoms[26] was the first treaty to protect human rights at the regional level. The Convention is open to all members of the Council of Europe. The Council was established after World War II to achieve greater European unity and to promote economic and social progress including "the maintenance and further realization of human rights and fundamental freedoms."[27]

The European Convention gives protection to a long list of human rights broadly in the area of civil and political rights, many of them similar to those found in the Universal Declaration and the Covenant on Civil and Political Rights. A number of optional protocols have expanded the list of protected rights. Many of the listed rights are subject to restrictions prescribed by law to protect such interests as national security, public safety and prevention of disorder or crime.

Enforcement of the European Convention

The European Convention on Human Rights and Fundamental Freedoms[28] permits both individual, group, corporate or individual complaints against states (article 34) and complaints by one state against another state (article 33). The enforcement system for the Convention has evolved and altered considerably over time. Originally, the complaint procedures were optional and also had to be vetted by other European institutions. Overtime, the complaint procedures have become mandatory and the main hurdle in approaching the European Court of Human Rights is that remedies in the state against which the complaint is brought must have been exhausted. The member states have the primary responsibility for the enforcement of the Convention with the Court only available where no further relief is available at the state level. The European Court now has the power to tell member states that their own law violates their obligations under the Convention. National law thus has to be repealed or altered to comply with

26. 213 U.N.T.S. 221, signed 4 Nov. 1950, entered into force, 3 Sept. 1953 [hereinafter European Convention].

27. 87 U.N.T.S. 105, art. 1(b) (statute of the Council of Europe).

28. Supra note 26.

Title	Basic Legal Citation	Date of Entry into Force	Enforcement Mechanism
Slavery Convention of 1926	60 L.N.T.S. 253	March 9, 1927	Any party may submit a dispute to the Permanent Court of International Justice (P.C.I.J.)* (article 8) provided the parties to the dispute have accepted the Court's jurisdiction. If the parties have not accepted the Court's jurisdiction then they must choose one of three options: (a) submit the dispute to the P.C.I.J.; (b) submit to a court of arbitration under the 1907 Convention for the Pacific Settlement of International Disputes; or (c) submit to some other court of arbitration.
Supplementary Convention on the of Slavery, the Slave Trade and Institutions Similar to Slavery	266 U.N.T.S. 291	April 30, 1957	Reporting requirement to the U.N. Secretary-General (article 8). Abolition Any party may submit disputes to the I.C.J. (article 10).
Convention on the Prevention and Punishment of the Crime of Genocide	78 U.N.T.S. 277	January 12, 1951	Any party may submit disputes to the I.C.J. (article IX).
International Convention on the Elimination of All Forms of Racial Discrimination	660 U.N.T.S. 195	January 4, 1969	Mandatory reporting obligation to the Committee on the Elimination of Racial Discrimination (article 9). Any party may submit disputes for arbitration by the Committee (article 11). If a dispute is still not settled, any party to the dispute may submit it to the I.C.J. (article 22).
International Convention on the Suppression and Punishment of the Crime of Apartheid	1015 U.N.T.S. 243	July 18, 1976	Mandatory submission of reports to a sub-group of the Commission on Human Rights (article VII). Any party may call on any organ of the U.N. to take action to prevent and suppress the crime of apartheid (article VIII). Any party may submit disputes to the I.C.J. (article XII).
Convention for the Suppression of the Traffic in Persons and of the Exploitation of the Prostitution of Others	96 U.N.T.S. 271	July 25, 1951	Reporting requirement to the U.N. Secretary General (article 21). Any party may submit disputes to the I.C.J. (article 22).
Convention Relating to the Status of Refugees	189 U.N.T.S. 137	April 22, 1954	Any party may submit disputes to the I.C.J. (article 38). Requirement of co-operation with the Office of the High Commissioner for Refugees (article 35).

Title	Basic Legal Citation	Date of Entry into Force	Enforcement Mechanism
Protocol Relating to the Status of Refugees	606 U.N.T.S. 267	October 4, 1967	Any party may submit disputes to the I.C.J. (article IV).
Convention on the Elimination of All Forms of Discrimination against Women	1249 U.N.T.S. 13	September 3, 1981	Mandatory reporting obligation to the Committee on the Elimination of Discrimination against Women (article 18). Any party may submit disputes to arbitration. If the dispute cannot be arbitrated, any party to the dispute may submit it to the I.C.J. (article 29), unless the party against which the complaint is filed submitted a reservation to article 29 refusing to accept the I.C.J.'s jurisdiction under this article.
Convention Against Torture and Other Cruel, Inhuman or Degrading Treatment or Punishment	1465 U.N.T.S. 85 reprinted at 23 I.L.M. 1027 (1984) as amended 24 I.L.M. 535 (1985)	June 26, 1987	Mandatory reporting obligation to the Committee Against Torture (article 19). Optional referral of state-against-state complaints to the Committee (article 21). Optional referral of individual-against-state complaints to the Committee (article 22). Any party may submit disputes to arbitration. If the dispute cannot be arbitrated, any party to the dispute may submit it to the I.C.J. (article 30), unless the party against which the complaint is filed has submitted a reservation to article 30 refusing to accept the I.C.J.'s jurisdiction under this article.
Convention on the Rights of Child	1577 U.N.T.S. 3 (1989), reprinted at 28 I.L.M. 1448 (1989)	September 2, 1990	Mandatory reporting obligation to the Committee on the the Rights of the Child (article 44).
Convention on the Rights of Persons with Disabilities	Doc.A/61/611	May 3, 2008	Reporting requirement to the Committee on the Rights of Persons with Disabilities (articles 34–39). An Optional Protocol allows citizens or groups to bring complaints to the Committee after exhausting national remedies.

* With the demise of the Permanent Court of International Justice, references to the P.C.I.J. automatically became references to the International Court of Justice (I.C.J.) by virtue of article 37 of the Statute of the International Court of Justice.

Convention obligations and remedies must be provided for violations of certain Convention rights. This may sound somewhat dictatorial, but remember that the member states have agreed to this system. They have, by treaty and protocols, freely bound themselves to this system.

The European Court of Human Rights

The European Court of Human Rights consists of "a number of judges equal to that of the Members of the Council of Europe" (article 38). The Court is empowered to sit as a Chamber, consisting of seven judges, or as a Grand Chamber of seventeen judges. Below is a recent decision of a Grand Chamber.

Case of Leyla Şahin v. Turkey

(Application no. 44774/98)
European Court of Human Rights
Grand Chamber
JUDGMENT
STRASBOURG
10 November 2005

In the case of Leyla Şahin v. Turkey,

The European Court of Human Rights, sitting as a Grand Chamber ... Having deliberated in private on 18 May and 5 October 2005, Delivers the following judgment, which was adopted on the last mentioned date:

PROCEDURE

1. The case originated in an application (no. 44774/98) against the Republic of Turkey lodged with the European Commission of Human Rights ("the Commission") under former Article 25 of the Convention for the Protection of Human Rights and Fundamental Freedoms ("the Convention") by a Turkish national, Ms Leyla Şahin ("the applicant"), on 21 July 1998.

* * *

3. The applicant alleged that her rights and freedoms under Articles 8, 9, 10 and 14 of the Convention and Article 2 of Protocol No. 1 had been violated by regulations on wearing the Islamic headscarf in institutions of higher education.

8. In its judgment of 29 June 2004 ("the Chamber judgment"), the Chamber held unanimously that there had been no violation of Article 9 of the Convention on account of the ban on wearing the headscarf and that no separate question arose under Articles 8 and 10, Article 14 taken in conjunction with Article 9 of the Convention, and Article 2 of Protocol No. 1.

9. On 27 September 2004 the applicant requested that the case be referred to the Grand Chamber (Article 43 of the Convention).

10. On 10 November 2004 a panel of the Grand Chamber decided to accept her request (Rule 73).

* * *

THE FACTS

I. THE CIRCUMSTANCES OF THE CASE

14. The applicant was born in 1973 and has lived in Vienna since 1999, when she left Istanbul to pursue her medical studies at the Faculty of Medicine at Vienna University. She comes from a traditional family of practising Muslims and considers it her religious duty to wear the Islamic headscarf.

A. The circular of 23 February 1998

15. On 26 August 1997 the applicant, then in her fifth year at the Faculty of Medicine at Bursa University, enrolled at the Cerrahpaşa Faculty of Medicine at Istanbul University. She says she wore the Islamic headscarf during the four years she spent studying medicine at the University of Bursa and continued to do so until February 1998.

16. On 23 February 1998 the Vice-Chancellor of Istanbul University issued a circular, the relevant part of which provides:

> "By virtue of the Constitution, the law and regulations, and in accordance with the case-law of the Supreme Administrative Court and the European Commission of Human Rights and the resolutions adopted by the university administrative boards, students whose 'heads are covered' (who wear the Islamic headscarf) and students (including overseas students) with beards must not be admitted to lectures, courses or tutorials. Consequently, the name and number of any student with a beard or wearing the Islamic headscarf must not be added to the lists of registered students. However, students who insist on attending tutorials and entering lecture theatres although their names and numbers are not on the lists must be advised of the position and, should they refuse to leave, their names and numbers must be taken and they must be informed that they are not entitled to attend lectures. If they refuse to leave the lecture theatre, the teacher shall record the incident in a report explaining why it was not possible to give the lecture and shall bring the incident to the attention of the university authorities as a matter of urgency so that disciplinary measures can be taken."

17. On 12 March 1998, in accordance with the aforementioned circular, the applicant was denied access by invigilators to a written examination on oncology because she was wearing the Islamic headscarf. On 20 March 1998 the secretariat of the chair of orthopaedic traumatology refused to allow her to enrol because she was wearing a headscarf. On 16 April 1998 she was refused admission to a neurology lecture and on 10 June 1998 to a written examination on public health, again for the same reason.

B. The application for an order setting aside the circular of 23 February 1998

18. On 29 July 1998 the applicant lodged an application for an order setting aside the circular of 23 February 1998. In her written pleadings, she submitted that the circular and its implementation had infringed her rights guaranteed by Articles 8, 9 and 14 of the Convention and Article 2 of Protocol No. 1, in that there was no statutory basis for the circular and the Vice-Chancellor's Office had no regulatory power in that sphere.

19. In a judgment of 19 March 1999, the Istanbul Administrative Court dismissed the application, holding that by virtue of section 13(b) of the Higher Education Act (Law no. 2547 ...) a university vice-chancellor, as the executive organ of the university, had power to regulate students' dress for the purposes of maintaining order. That regula-

tory power had to be exercised in accordance with the relevant legislation and the judgments of the Constitutional Court and the Supreme Administrative Court. Referring to the settled case-law of those courts, the Administrative Court held that neither the regulations in issue, nor the measures taken against the applicant, could be considered illegal.

20. On 19 April 2001 the Supreme Administrative Court dismissed an appeal on points of law by the applicant.

C. The disciplinary measures taken against the applicant

21. In May 1998 disciplinary proceedings were brought against the applicant under paragraph 6 (a) of the Students Disciplinary Procedure Rules ... as a result of her failure to comply with the rules on dress.

22. On 26 May 1998, in view of the fact that the applicant had shown by her actions that she intended to continue wearing the headscarf to lectures and/or tutorials, the dean of the faculty declared that her attitude and failure to comply with the rules on dress were not befitting of a student. He therefore decided to issue her with a warning.

23. On 15 February 1999 an unauthorised assembly gathered outside the deanery of the Cerrahpaşa Faculty of Medicine to protest against the rules on dress.

24. On 26 February 1999 the dean of the faculty began disciplinary proceedings against various students, including the applicant, for joining the assembly. On 13 April 1999, after hearing her representations, he suspended her from the university for a semester pursuant to Article 9 (j) of the Students Disciplinary Procedure Rules....

25. On 10 June 1999 the applicant lodged an application with the Istanbul Administrative Court for an order quashing the decision to suspend her. The application was dismissed on 30 November 1999 by the Istanbul Administrative Court on the ground that, in the light of the material in the case file and the settled case-law on the subject, the impugned measure could not be regarded as illegal.

26. Following the entry into force of Law no. 4584 on 28 June 2000 (which provided for students to be given an amnesty in respect of penalties imposed for disciplinary offences and for any resulting disability to be annulled), the applicant was granted an amnesty releasing her from all the penalties that had been imposed on her and the resultant disabilities.

27. On 28 September 2000 the Supreme Administrative Court held that Law no. 4584 made it unnecessary to examine the merits of the applicant's appeal on points of law against the judgment of 30 November 1999.

28. In the meantime, on 16 September 1999, the applicant abandoned her studies in Turkey and enrolled at Vienna University, where she pursued her university education.

II. RELEVANT LAW AND PRACTICE

A. The Constitution

29. The relevant provisions of the Turkish Constitution provide:

Article 2

> "The Republic of Turkey is a democratic, secular [*laik*] and social State based on the rule of law that is respectful of human rights in a spirit of social peace, national solidarity and justice, adheres to the nationalism of Atatürk and is underpinned by the fundamental principles set out in the Preamble."

Article 4

"No amendment may be made or proposed to the provisions of Article 1 of the Constitution laying down that the State shall be a Republic, the provisions of Article 2 concerning the characteristics of the Republic or the provisions of Article 3."

Article 10

"All individuals shall be equal before the law without any distinction based on language, race, colour, sex, political opinion, philosophical belief, religion, membership of a religious sect or other similar grounds.

Men and women shall have equal rights. The State shall take action to achieve such equality in practice.

No privileges shall be granted to any individual, family, group or class.

State bodies and administrative authorities shall act in compliance with the principle of equality before the law in all circumstances."

Article 13

"Fundamental rights and freedoms may be restricted only by law and on the grounds set out in special provisions of the Constitution, provided always that the essence of such rights and freedoms must remain intact. Any such restriction shall not conflict with the letter or spirit of the Constitution or the requirements of a democratic, secular social order and shall comply with the principle of proportionality."

Article 14

"The rights and freedoms set out in the Constitution may not be exercised with a view to undermining the territorial integrity of the State, the unity of the nation or the democratic and secular Republic founded on human rights.

No provision of this Constitution shall be interpreted in a manner that would grant the State or individuals the right to engage in activities intended to destroy the fundamental rights and freedoms embodied in the Constitution or to restrict them beyond what is permitted by the Constitution.

The penalties to which persons who engage in activities that contravene these provisions are liable shall be determined by law."

Article 24

"Everyone shall have the right to freedom of conscience, belief and religious conviction.

Prayers, worship and religious services shall be conducted freely, provided that they do not violate the provisions of Article 14.

No one shall be compelled to participate in prayers, worship or religious services or to reveal his or her religious beliefs and convictions; no one shall be censured or prosecuted for his religious beliefs or convictions.

Education and instruction in religion and ethics shall be provided under the supervision and control of the State. Instruction in religious culture and in morals shall be a compulsory part of the curricula of primary and secondary schools. Other religious education and instruction shall be a matter for individual choice, with the decision in the case of minors being taken by their legal guardians.

No one shall exploit or abuse religion, religious feelings or things held sacred by religion in any manner whatsoever with a view to causing the social, economic, political or legal order of the State to be based on religious precepts, even if only in part, or for the purpose of securing political or personal interest or influence thereby."

Article 42

"No one may be deprived of the right to instruction and education.

The scope of the right to education shall be defined and regulated by law.

Instruction and teaching shall be provided under the supervision and control of the State in accordance with the principles and reforms of Atatürk and contemporary scientific and educational methods. No educational or teaching institution may be set up that does not follow these rules.

Citizens are not absolved from the duty to remain loyal to the Constitution by freedom of instruction and teaching.

Primary education shall be compulsory for all citizens of both sexes and provided free of charge in State schools.

The rules governing the functioning of private primary and secondary schools shall be regulated by law in keeping with the standards set for State schools.

The State shall provide able pupils of limited financial means with the necessary aid in the form of scholarships or other assistance to enable them to pursue their studies. It shall take suitable measures to rehabilitate those in need of special training so as to render them useful to society.

Education, teaching, research, and study are the only activities that may be pursued in educational and teaching institutions. These activities shall not be impeded in any way ..."

Article 153

"The decisions of the Constitutional Court shall be final. A decision to invalidate a provision shall not be made public without a written statement of reasons.

When striking down a law or legislative decree or a provision thereof, the Constitutional Court may not act as a quasi-legislature by drafting provisions that would be enforceable....

Judgments of the Constitutional Court shall be published immediately in the Official Gazette and shall be binding on the legislative, executive, and judicial organs, the administrative authorities, and natural and juristic persons."

B. History and background

1. Religious dress and the principle of secularism

30. The Turkish Republic was founded on the principle that the State should be secular (*laik*). Before and after the proclamation of the Republic on 29 October 1923, the public and religious spheres were separated through a series of revolutionary reforms: the abolition of the caliphate on 3 March 1923; the repeal of the constitutional provision declaring Islam the religion of the State on 10 April 1928; and, lastly, on 5 February 1937, a constitutional amendment according constitutional status to the principle of secularism (see Article 2 of the Constitution of 1924 and Article 2 of the Constitutions of 1961 and 1982, as set out in paragraph 29 above).

31. The principle of secularism was inspired by developments in Ottoman society in the period between the nineteenth century and the proclamation of the Republic. The idea of creating a modern public society in which equality was guaranteed to all citizens without distinction on grounds of religion, denomination or sex had already been mooted in the Ottoman debates of the nineteenth century. Significant advances in women's rights were made during this period (equality of treatment in education, the introduction of a ban on polygamy in 1914, the transfer of jurisdiction in matrimonial cases to the secular courts that had been established in the nineteenth century).

32. The defining feature of the Republican ideal was the presence of women in public life and their active participation in society. Consequently, the ideas that women should be freed from religious constraints and that society should be modernised had a common origin. Thus, on 17 February 1926 the Civil Code was adopted, which provided for equality of the sexes in the enjoyment of civic rights, in particular with regard to divorce and succession. Subsequently, through a constitutional amendment of 5 December 1934 (Article 10 of the 1924 Constitution), women obtained equal political rights to men.

33. The first legislation to regulate dress was the Headgear Act of 28 November 1925 (Law no. 671), which treated dress as a modernity issue. Similarly, a ban was imposed on wearing religious attire other than in places of worship or at religious ceremonies, irrespective of the religion or belief concerned, by the Dress (Regulations) Act of 3 December 1934 (Law no. 2596).

34. Under the Education Services (Merger) Act of 3 March 1924 (Law no. 430), religious schools were closed and all schools came under the control of the Ministry of Education. The Act is one of the laws with constitutional status that are protected by Article 174 of the Turkish Constitution.

35. In Turkey, wearing the Islamic headscarf to school and university is a recent phenomenon which only really began to emerge in the 1980s. There has been extensive discussion on the issue and it continues to be the subject of lively debate in Turkish society. Those in favour of the headscarf see wearing it as a duty and/or a form of expression linked to religious identity. However, the supporters of secularism, who draw a distinction between the *başörtüsü* (traditional Anatolian headscarf, worn loosely) and the *türban* (tight, knotted headscarf hiding the hair and the throat), see the Islamic headscarf as a symbol of a political Islam. As a result of the accession to power on 28 June 1996 of a coalition government comprising the Islamist Refah Partisi, and the centre-right Doğru Yol Partisi, the debate has taken on strong political overtones. The ambivalence displayed by the leaders of the Refah Partisi, including the then Prime Minister, over their attachment to democratic values, and their advocacy of a plurality of legal systems functioning according to different religious rules for each religious community was perceived in Turkish society as a genuine threat to republican values and civil peace (see *Refah Partisi (the Welfare Party) and Others v. Turkey* [GC], nos. 41340/98, 41342/98, 41343/98 and 41344/98, ECHR 2003-II).

2. The rules on dress in institutions of higher education and the case-law of the Constitutional Court

36. The first piece of legislation on dress in institutions of higher education was a set of regulations issued by the Cabinet on 22 July 1981 requiring staff working for public organisations and institutions and personnel and female students at State institutions to wear ordinary, sober, modern dress. The regulations also provided that female members of staff and students should not wear veils in educational institutions.

37. On 20 December 1982 the Higher Education Authority issued a circular on the wearing of headscarves in institutions of higher education. The Islamic headscarf was banned in lecture theatres. In a judgment of 13 December 1984, the Supreme Administrative Court held that the regulations were lawful, noting:

> "Beyond being a mere innocent practice, wearing the headscarf is in the process of becoming the symbol of a vision that is contrary to the freedoms of women and the fundamental principles of the Republic."

38. On 10 December 1988 transitional section 16 of the Higher Education Act (Law no. 2547) came into force. It provided:

> "Modern dress or appearance shall be compulsory in the rooms and corridors of institutions of higher education, preparatory schools, laboratories, clinics and multidisciplinary clinics. A veil or headscarf covering the neck and hair may be worn out of religious conviction."

39. In a judgment of 7 March 1989 published in the Official Gazette of 5 July 1989, the Constitutional Court held that the aforementioned provision was contrary to Articles 2 (secularism), 10 (equality before the law) and 24 (freedom of religion) of the Constitution. It also found that it could not be reconciled with the principle of sexual equality implicit, *inter alia*, in republican and revolutionary values (see Preamble and Article 174 of the Constitution).

In their judgment, the Constitutional Court judges explained, firstly, that secularism had acquired constitutional status by reason of the historical experience of the country and the particularities of Islam compared to other religions; secularism was an essential condition for democracy and acted as a guarantor of freedom of religion and of equality before the law. It also prevented the State from showing a preference for a particular religion or belief; consequently, a secular State could not invoke religious conviction when performing its legislative function. They stated, *inter alia*:

> "Secularism is the civil organiser of political, social and cultural life, based on national sovereignty, democracy, freedom and science. Secularism is the principle which offers the individual the possibility to affirm his or her own personality through freedom of thought and which, by the distinction it makes between politics and religious beliefs, renders freedom of conscience and religion effective. In societies based on religion, which function with religious thought and religious rules, political organisation is religious in character. In a secular regime, religion is shielded from a political role. It is not a tool of the authorities and remains in its respectable place, to be determined by the conscience of each and everyone ..."

Stressing its inviolable nature, the Constitutional Court observed that freedom of religion, conscience and worship, which could not be equated with a right to wear any particular religious attire, guaranteed first and foremost the liberty to decide whether or not to follow a religion. It explained that, once outside the private sphere of individual conscience, freedom to manifest one's religion could be restricted on public-order grounds to defend the principle of secularism.

Everyone was free to choose how to dress, as the social and religious values and traditions of society also had to be respected. However, when a particular dress code was imposed on individuals by reference to a religion, the religion concerned was perceived and presented as a set of values that were incompatible with those of contemporary society. In addition, in Turkey, where the majority of the population were Muslims, presenting the wearing of the Islamic headscarf as a mandatory religious duty would result in discrimination between practising Muslims, non-practising Muslims and non-believers on grounds of dress with anyone who refused to wear the headscarf undoubtedly being regarded as opposed to religion or as non-religious.

The Constitutional Court also said that students had to be permitted to work and pursue their education together in a calm, tolerant and mutually supportive atmosphere without being deflected from that goal by signs of religious affiliation. It found that, irrespective of whether the Islamic headscarf was a precept of Islam, granting legal recognition to a religious symbol of that type in institutions of higher education was not compatible with the principle that State education must be neutral, as it would be liable to generate conflicts between students with differing religious convictions or beliefs.

40. On 25 October 1990 transitional section 17 of Law no. 2547 came into force. It provides:

> "Choice of dress shall be free in institutions of higher education, provided that it does not contravene the laws in force."

41. In a judgment of 9 April 1991, which was published in the Official Gazette of 31 July 1991, the Constitutional Court noted that, in the light of the principles it had established in its judgment of 7 March 1989, the aforementioned provision did not allow headscarves to be worn in institutions of higher education on religious grounds and so was consistent with the Constitution.

> "... the expression 'laws in force' refers first and foremost to the Constitution ... In institutions of higher education, it is contrary to the principles of secularism and equality for the neck and hair to be covered with a veil or headscarf on grounds of religious conviction.

* * *

3. Application of the regulations at Istanbul University

42. Istanbul University was founded in the fifteenth century and is one of the main centres of State higher education in Turkey. It has seventeen faculties (including two faculties of medicine—Cerrahpaşa and Çapa) and twelve schools of higher education. It is attended by approximately 50,000 students.

* * *

46. On 23 February 1998 a circular signed by the Vice-Chancellor of Istanbul University was distributed containing instructions on the admission of students with beards or wearing the Islamic headscarf (for the text of this circular, see paragraph 16 above).

47. Istanbul University adopted a resolution (no. 11 of 9 July 1998), worded as follows:

> "1. Students at Istanbul University shall comply with the legal principles and rules on dress set out in the decisions of the Constitutional Court and higher judicial bodies.
>
> 2. Students shall not wear clothes that symbolise or manifest any religion, faith, race, or political or ideological persuasion in any institution or department of the university, or on any of its premises.
>
> 3. Students shall comply with the rules requiring specific clothes to be worn for occupational reasons in the institutions and departments at which they are enrolled.

4. Photographs supplied by students to their institution or department [must be taken] from the 'front' 'with head and neck uncovered'. They must be no more than six months old and make the student readily identifiable.

5. Anyone displaying an attitude that is contrary to the aforementioned points or who, through his words, writings or deeds, encourages such an attitude shall be liable to action under the provisions of the Students Disciplinary Procedure Rules."

* * *

D. Comparative law

55. For more than twenty years the place of the Islamic headscarf in State education has been the subject of debate across Europe. In most European countries, the debate has focused mainly on primary and secondary schools. However, in Turkey, Azerbaijan and Albania it has concerned not just the question of individual liberty, but also the political meaning of the Islamic headscarf. These are the only member States to have introduced regulations on wearing the Islamic headscarf in universities.

56. In France, where secularism is regarded as one of the cornerstones of republican values, legislation was passed on 15 March 2004 regulating, in accordance with the principle of secularism, the wearing of signs or dress manifesting a religious affiliation in State primary and secondary schools. The legislation inserted a new Article L. 141-5-1 in the Education Code which provides: "In State primary and secondary schools, the wearing of signs or dress by which pupils overtly manifest a religious affiliation is prohibited. The school rules shall state that the institution of disciplinary proceedings shall be preceded by dialogue with the pupil."

The Act applies to all State schools and educational institutions, including post-baccalaureate courses (preparatory classes for entrance to the *grandes écoles* and vocational training courses). It does not apply to State universities. In addition, as a circular of 18 May 2004 makes clear, it only concerns "... signs, such as the Islamic headscarf, however named, the kippa or a cross that is manifestly oversized, which make the wearer's religious affiliation immediately identifiable".

57. In Belgium there is no general ban on wearing religious signs at school. In the French Community a decree of 13 March 1994 stipulates that education shall be neutral within the Community. Pupils are in principle allowed to wear religious signs. However, they may do so only if human rights, the reputation of others, national security, public order, and public health and morals are protected and internal rules complied with. Further, teachers must not permit religious or philosophical proselytism under their authority or the organisation of political militancy by or on behalf of pupils. The decree stipulates that restrictions may be imposed by school rules. On 19 May 2004 the French Community issued a decree intended to institute equality of treatment. In the Flemish Community, there is no uniform policy among schools on whether to allow religious or philosophical signs to be worn. Some do, others do not. When pupils are permitted to wear such signs, restrictions may be imposed on grounds of hygiene or safety.

58. In other countries (Austria, Germany, the Netherlands, Spain, Sweden, Switzerland and the United Kingdom), in some cases following a protracted legal debate, the State education authorities permit Muslim pupils and students to wear the Islamic headscarf.

59. In Germany, where the debate focused on whether teachers should be allowed to wear the Islamic headscarf, the Constitutional Court stated on 24 September 2003 in a

case between a teacher and the *Land* of Baden-Württemberg that the lack of any express statutory prohibition meant that teachers were entitled to wear the headscarf. Consequently, it imposed a duty on the *Länder* to lay down rules on dress if they wished to prohibit the wearing of the Islamic headscarf in State schools.

60. In Austria there is no special legislation governing the wearing of the headscarf, turban or kippa. In general, it is considered that a ban on wearing the headscarf will only be justified if it poses a health or safety hazard for pupils.

61. In the United Kingdom a tolerant attitude is shown to pupils who wear religious signs. Difficulties with respect to the Islamic headscarf are rare. The issue has also been debated in the context of the elimination of racial discrimination in schools in order to preserve their multicultural character (see, in particular, *Mandla v. Dowell*, The Law Reports 1983, pp. 548–70). The Commission for Racial Equality, whose opinions have recommendation status only, also considered the issue of the Islamic headscarf in 1988 in the *Altrincham Grammar School* case, which ended in a compromise between a private school and members of the family of two sisters who wished to be allowed to wear the Islamic headscarf at the school. The school agreed to allow them to wear the headscarf provided it was navy blue (the colour of the school uniform), kept fastened at the neck and not decorated.

In *R. (On the application of Begum) v. Headteacher and Governors of Denbigh High School* ([2004] EWHC 1389 (Admin)), the High Court had to decide a dispute between the school and a Muslim pupil wishing to wear the *jilbab* (a full-length gown). The school required pupils to wear a uniform, one of the possible options being the headscarf and the *shalwar kameeze* (long traditional garments from the Indian subcontinent). In June 2004 the High Court dismissed the pupil's application, holding that there had been no violation of her freedom of religion. However, that judgment was reversed in March 2005 by the Court of Appeal, which accepted that there had been interference with the pupil's freedom of religion, as a minority of Muslims in the United Kingdom considered that a religious duty to wear the *jilbab* from the age of puberty existed and the pupil was genuinely of that opinion. No justification for the interference had been provided by the school authorities, as the decision-making process was not compatible with freedom of religion.

62. In Spain there is no express statutory prohibition on pupils' wearing religious head coverings in State schools. By virtue of two royal decrees of 26 January 1996, which are applicable in primary and secondary schools unless the competent authority—the autonomous community—has introduced specific measures, the school governors have power to issue school rules which may include provisions on dress. Generally speaking, State schools allow the headscarf to be worn.

63. In Finland and Sweden the veil can be worn at school. However, a distinction is made between the *burka* (the term used to describe the full veil covering the whole of the body and the face) and the *niqab* (a veil covering all the upper body with the exception of the eyes). In Sweden mandatory directives were issued in 2003 by the National Education Agency. These allow schools to prohibit the *burka* and *niqab*, provided they do so in a spirit of dialogue on the common values of equality of the sexes and respect for the democratic principle on which the education system is based.

64. In the Netherlands, where the question of the Islamic headscarf is considered from the standpoint of discrimination rather than of freedom of religion, it is generally tolerated. In 2003 a non-binding directive was issued. Schools may require pupils to wear a uniform provided that the rules are not discriminatory and are included in

the school prospectus and that the punishment for transgressions is not disproportionate. A ban on the *burka* is regarded as justified by the need to be able to identify and communicate with pupils. In addition, the Equal Treatment Commission ruled in 1997 that a ban on wearing the veil during physical education classes for safety reasons was not discriminatory.

65. In a number of other countries (Russia, Romania, Hungary, Greece, the Czech Republic, Slovakia and Poland), the issue of the Islamic headscarf does not yet appear to have given rise to any detailed legal debate.

* * *

THE LAW

I. ALLEGED VIOLATION OF ARTICLE 9 OF THE CONVENTION

70. The applicant submitted that the ban on wearing the Islamic headscarf in institutions of higher education constituted an unjustified interference with her right to freedom of religion, in particular, her right to manifest her religion.

She relied on Article 9 of the Convention, which provides:

"1. Everyone has the right to freedom of thought, conscience and religion; this right includes freedom to change his religion or belief and freedom, either alone or in community with others and in public or private, to manifest his religion or belief, in worship, teaching, practice and observance.

2. Freedom to manifest one's religion or beliefs shall be subject only to such limitations as are prescribed by law and are necessary in a democratic society in the interests of public safety, for the protection of public order, health or morals, or for the protection of the rights and freedoms of others."

A. The Chamber judgment

71. The Chamber found that the Istanbul University regulations restricting the right to wear the Islamic headscarf and the measures taken thereunder had interfered with the applicant's right to manifest her religion. It went on to find that the interference was prescribed by law and pursued one of the legitimate aims set out in the second paragraph of Article 9 of the Convention. It was justified in principle and proportionate to the aims pursued and could therefore be regarded as having been "necessary in a democratic society" (see paragraphs 66–116 of the Chamber judgment).

* * *

C. The Court's assessment

75. The Court must consider whether the applicant's right under Article 9 was interfered with and, if so, whether the interference was "prescribed by law", pursued a legitimate aim and was "necessary in a democratic society" within the meaning of Article 9 § 2 of the Convention.

1. Whether there was interference

76. The applicant said that her choice of dress had to be treated as obedience to a religious rule which she regarded as "recognised practice". She maintained that the restriction in issue, namely the rules on wearing the Islamic headscarf on university premises, was a clear interference with her right to freedom to manifest her religion.

* * *

78. As to whether there was interference, the Grand Chamber endorses the following findings of the Chamber (see paragraph 71 of the Chamber judgment):

> "The applicant said that, by wearing the headscarf, she was obeying a religious precept and thereby manifesting her desire to comply strictly with the duties imposed by the Islamic faith. Accordingly, her decision to wear the headscarf may be regarded as motivated or inspired by a religion or belief and, without deciding whether such decisions are in every case taken to fulfil a religious duty, the Court proceeds on the assumption that the regulations in issue, which placed restrictions of place and manner on the right to wear the Islamic headscarf in universities, constituted an interference with the applicant's right to manifest her religion."

2. "Prescribed by law"

(a) The parties' submissions to the Grand Chamber

79. The applicant said that there had been no "written law" to prohibit students from wearing the Islamic headscarf at university, either when she enrolled in 1993 or in the period thereafter. She explained that under the Students Disciplinary Procedure Rules it was not a disciplinary offence merely to wear the Islamic headscarf (see paragraphs 49 and 50 above). The first regulation to restrict her right to wear the headscarf had been the circular issued by the Vice-Chancellor on 23 February 1998, some four and a half years later.

* * *

(b) The Court's assessment

84. The Court reiterates its settled case-law that the expression "prescribed by law" requires firstly that the impugned measure should have a basis in domestic law. It also refers to the quality of the law in question, requiring that it be accessible to the persons concerned and formulated with sufficient precision to enable them—if need be, with appropriate advice—to foresee, to a degree that is reasonable in the circumstances, the consequences which a given action may entail and to regulate their conduct.

* * *

88. Further, as regards the words "in accordance with the law" and "prescribed by law" which appear in Articles 8 to 11 of the Convention, the Court observes that it has always understood the term "law" in its "substantive" sense, not its "formal" one; it has included both "written law", encompassing enactments of lower ranking statutes (see *De Wilde, Ooms and Versyp v. Belgium*, judgment of 18 June 1971, Series A no. 12, pp. 45–46, § 93) and regulatory measures taken by professional regulatory bodies under independent rule-making powers delegated to them by Parliament (see *Barthold v. Germany*, judgment of 25 March 1985, Series A no. 90, pp. 21–22, § 46), and unwritten law. "Law" must be understood to include both statutory law and judge-made "law" (see, among other authorities, *The Sunday Times v. the United Kingdom (no. 1)*, judgment of 26 April 1979, Series A no. 30, p. 30, § 47; *Kruslin*, cited above, pp. 21–22, § 29 *in fine*; and *Casado Coca v. Spain*, judgment of 24 February 1994, Series A no. 285-A, p. 18, § 43). In sum, the "law" is the provision in force as the competent courts have interpreted it.

89. Accordingly, the question must be examined on the basis not only of the wording of transitional section 17 of Law no. 2547, but also of the relevant case-law.

In that connection, as the Constitutional Court noted in its judgment of 9 April 1991 (see paragraph 41 above), the wording of that section shows that freedom of dress in institutions of higher education is not absolute. Under the terms of that provision, students are free to dress as they wish "provided that [their choice] does not contravene the laws in force".

90. The dispute therefore concerns the meaning of the words "laws in force" in the aforementioned provision.

* * *

92. The Court notes in that connection that in its aforementioned judgment the Constitutional Court found that the words "laws in force" necessarily included the Constitution. The judgment also made it clear that allowing students' "neck and hair to be covered with a veil or headscarf on grounds of religious conviction" in universities was contrary to the Constitution (see paragraph 41 above).

93. That decision of the Constitutional Court, which was both binding ... and accessible, as it had been published in the Official Gazette of 31 July 1991, supplemented the letter of transitional section 17 and followed the Constitutional Court's previous case-law (see paragraph 39 above). In addition, the Supreme Administrative Court had by then consistently held for a number of years that wearing the Islamic headscarf at university was not compatible with the fundamental principles of the Republic, since the headscarf was in the process of becoming the symbol of a vision that was contrary to the freedoms of women and those fundamental principles (see paragraph 37 above).

* * *

98. In these circumstances, the Court finds that there was a legal basis for the interference in Turkish law, namely transitional section 17 of Law no. 2547 read in the light of the relevant case-law of the domestic courts. The law was also accessible and can be considered sufficiently precise in its terms to satisfy the requirement of foreseeability. It would have been clear to the applicant, from the moment she entered Istanbul University, that there were restrictions on wearing the Islamic headscarf on the university premises and, from 23 February 1998, that she was liable to be refused access to lectures and examinations if she continued to do so.

3. Legitimate aim

99. Having regard to the circumstances of the case and the terms of the domestic courts' decisions, the Court is able to accept that the impugned interference primarily pursued the legitimate aims of protecting the rights and freedoms of others and of protecting public order, a point which is not in issue between the parties.

4. "Necessary in a democratic society"

* * *

(b) The Court's assessment

(i) General principles

104. The Court reiterates that, as enshrined in Article 9, freedom of thought, conscience and religion is one of the foundations of a "democratic society" within the meaning of the Convention. This freedom is, in its religious dimension, one of the most vital elements that go to make up the identity of believers and their conception of life, but it is also a precious asset for atheists, agnostics, sceptics and the unconcerned. The pluralism indissociable from a democratic society, which has been dearly won over the centuries, depends on it. That freedom entails, *inter alia*, freedom to hold or not to hold religious beliefs and to practise or not to practise a religion....

105. While religious freedom is primarily a matter of individual conscience, it also implies, *inter alia*, freedom to manifest one's religion, alone and in private, or in community with others, in public and within the circle of those whose faith one shares. Article 9 lists the various forms which manifestation of one's religion or belief may take, namely worship, teaching, practice and observance ...

Article 9 does not protect every act motivated or inspired by a religion or belief....

106. In democratic societies, in which several religions coexist within one and the same population, it may be necessary to place restrictions on freedom to manifest one's religion or belief in order to reconcile the interests of the various groups and ensure that everyone's beliefs are respected (see *Kokkinakis*, cited above, p. 18, § 33). This follows both from paragraph 2 of Article 9 and the State's positive obligation under Article 1 of the Convention to secure to everyone within its jurisdiction the rights and freedoms defined therein.

107. The Court has frequently emphasised the State's role as the neutral and impartial organiser of the exercise of various religions, faiths and beliefs, and stated that this role is conducive to public order, religious harmony and tolerance in a democratic society. It also considers that the State's duty of neutrality and impartiality is incompatible with any power on the State's part to assess the legitimacy of religious beliefs or the ways in which those beliefs are expressed ... and that it requires the State to ensure mutual tolerance between opposing groups (see *United Communist Party of Turkey and Others v. Turkey*, judgment of 30 January 1998, *Reports* 1998-I, p. 27, § 57). Accordingly, the role of the authorities in such circumstances is not to remove the cause of tension by eliminating pluralism, but to ensure that the competing groups tolerate each other (see *Serif v. Greece*, no. 38178/97, § 53, ECHR 1999-IX).

108. Pluralism, tolerance and broadmindedness are hallmarks of a "democratic society". Although individual interests must on occasion be subordinated to those of a group, democracy does not simply mean that the views of a majority must always prevail: a balance must be achieved which ensures the fair and proper treatment of people from minorities and avoids any abuse of a dominant position. Pluralism and democracy must also be based on dialogue and a spirit of compromise necessarily entailing various concessions on the part of individuals or groups of individuals which are justified in order to maintain and promote the ideals and values of a democratic society.... Where these "rights and freedoms" are themselves among those guaranteed by the Convention or its Protocols, it must be accepted that the need to protect them may lead States to restrict other rights or freedoms likewise set forth in the Convention. It is precisely this constant search for a balance between the fundamental rights of each individual which constitutes the foundation of a "democratic society" (see *Chassagnou and Others*, cited above, § 113).

109. Where questions concerning the relationship between State and religions are at stake, on which opinion in a democratic society may reasonably differ widely, the role of the national decision-making body must be given special importance.... This will notably be the case when it comes to regulating the wearing of religious symbols in educational institutions, especially (as the comparative-law materials illustrate—see paragraphs 55–65 above) in view of the diversity of the approaches taken by national authorities on the issue. It is not possible to discern throughout Europe a uniform conception of the significance of religion in society and the meaning or impact of the public expression of a religious belief will differ according to time and context.... Rules in this sphere will consequently vary from one country to another according to national

traditions and the requirements imposed by the need to protect the rights and freedoms of others and to maintain public order.... Accordingly, the choice of the extent and form such regulations should take must inevitably be left up to a point to the State concerned, as it will depend on the specific domestic context ...

110. This margin of appreciation goes hand in hand with a European supervision embracing both the law and the decisions applying it. The Court's task is to determine whether the measures taken at national level were justified in principle and proportionate.... In delimiting the extent of the margin of appreciation in the present case, the Court must have regard to what is at stake, namely the need to protect the rights and freedoms of others, to preserve public order and to secure civil peace and true religious pluralism, which is vital to the survival of a democratic society....

* * *

(ii) Application of the foregoing principles to the present case

112. The interference in issue caused by the circular of 23 February 1998 imposing restrictions as to place and manner on the rights of students such as Ms Şahin to wear the Islamic headscarf on university premises was, according to the Turkish courts (see paragraphs 37, 39 and 41 above), based in particular on the two principles of secularism and equality.

113. In its judgment of 7 March 1989, the Constitutional Court stated that secularism, as the guarantor of democratic values, was the meeting point of liberty and equality. The principle prevented the State from manifesting a preference for a particular religion or belief; it thereby guided the State in its role of impartial arbiter, and necessarily entailed freedom of religion and conscience. It also served to protect the individual not only against arbitrary interference by the State but from external pressure from extremist movements. The Constitutional Court added that freedom to manifest one's religion could be restricted in order to defend those values and principles (see paragraph 39 above).

114. As the Chamber rightly stated (see paragraph 106 of its judgment), the Court considers this notion of secularism to be consistent with the values underpinning the Convention. It finds that upholding that principle, which is undoubtedly one of the fundamental principles of the Turkish State which are in harmony with the rule of law and respect for human rights, may be considered necessary to protect the democratic system in Turkey. An attitude which fails to respect that principle will not necessarily be accepted as being covered by the freedom to manifest one's religion and will not enjoy the protection of Article 9 of the Convention....

* * *

117. The Court must now determine whether in the instant case there was a reasonable relationship of proportionality between the means employed and the legitimate objectives pursued by the interference.

118. Like the Chamber (see paragraph 111 of its judgment), the Grand Chamber notes at the outset that it is common ground that practising Muslim students in Turkish universities are free, within the limits imposed by the constraints of educational organisation, to manifest their religion in accordance with habitual forms of Muslim observance. In addition, the resolution adopted by Istanbul University on 9 July 1998 shows that various other forms of religious attire are also forbidden on the university premises (see paragraph 47 above).

119. It should also be noted that, when the issue of whether students should be allowed to wear the Islamic headscarf surfaced at Istanbul University in 1994 in relation

to the medical courses, the Vice-Chancellor reminded them of the reasons for the rules on dress. Arguing that calls for permission to wear the Islamic headscarf in all parts of the university premises were misconceived and pointing to the public-order constraints applicable to medical courses, he asked the students to abide by the rules, which were consistent with both the legislation and the case-law of the higher courts....

* * *

122. In the light of the foregoing and having regard to the Contracting States' margin of appreciation in this sphere, the Court finds that the interference in issue was justified in principle and proportionate to the aim pursued.

123. Consequently, there has been no breach of Article 9 of the Convention.

* * *

(**Note:** The Court also found there had been no violation of Şahin's right to education as guaranteed by article 2 of Protocol Number 1 to the European Convention on Human Rights and Fundamental Freedoms, nor were there any violations of articles 8, 10 or 14 of the Convention).

FOR THESE REASONS, THE COURT

1. *Holds*, by sixteen votes to one, that there has been no violation of Article 9 of the Convention;

2. *Holds*, by sixteen votes to one, that there has been no violation of the first sentence of Article 2 of Protocol No. 1.

* * *

DISSENTING OPINION OF JUDGE TULKENS

(Translation)
(footnotes omitted)

For a variety of mutually supporting reasons, I did not vote with the majority on the question of Article 9 of the Convention or of Article 2 of Protocol No. 1, which concerns the right to education. I do, however, fully agree with the Court's ruling that the scope of the latter provision extends to higher and university education.

A. Freedom of religion

1. As regards the general principles reiterated in the judgment, there are points on which I strongly agree with the majority (see paragraphs 104–08 of the judgment). The right to freedom of religion guaranteed by Article 9 of the Convention is a "precious asset" not only for believers, but also for atheists, agnostics, sceptics and the unconcerned. It is true that Article 9 of the Convention does not protect every act motivated or inspired by a religion or belief and that in democratic societies, in which several religions coexist, it may be necessary to place restrictions on freedom to manifest one's religion in order to reconcile the interests of the various groups and ensure that everyone's beliefs are respected (see paragraph 106 of the judgment). Further, pluralism, tolerance and broadmindedness are hallmarks of a democratic society and this entails certain consequences. The first is that these ideals and values of a democratic society must also be based on dialogue and a spirit of compromise, which necessarily entails mutual concessions on the part of individuals. The second is that the role of the authorities in such circumstances is not to remove the cause of the tensions by eliminating pluralism, but, as the Court again reiterated only recently, to ensure that the competing groups tolerate each other (see *Ouranio Toxo and Others v. Greece*, no. 74989/01, § 40, ECHR 2005-X).

2. Once the majority had accepted that the ban on wearing the Islamic headscarf on university premises constituted interference with the applicant's right under Article 9 of the Convention to manifest her religion, and that the ban was prescribed by law and pursued a legitimate aim—in this case the protection of the rights and freedom of others and of public order—the main issue became whether such interference was "necessary in a democratic society". Owing to its nature, the Court's review must be conducted *in concreto*, in principle by reference to three criteria: firstly, whether the interference, which must be capable of protecting the legitimate interest that has been put at risk, was appropriate; secondly, whether the measure that has been chosen is the measure that is the least restrictive of the right or freedom concerned; and, lastly, whether the measure was proportionate, a question which entails a balancing of the competing interests

Underlying the majority's approach is the margin of appreciation which the national authorities are recognised as possessing and which reflects, *inter alia*, the notion that they are "better placed" to decide how best to discharge their Convention obligations in what is a sensitive area (see paragraph 109 of the judgment). The Court's jurisdiction is, of course, subsidiary and its role is not to impose uniform solutions, especially "with regard to establishment of the delicate relations between the Churches and the State" (see *Cha'are Shalom Ve Tsedek v. France* [GC], no. 27417/95, § 84, ECHR 2000-VII), even if, in certain other judgments concerning conflicts between religious communities, the Court has not always shown the same judicial restraint (see *Serif v. Greece*, no. 38178/97, ECHR 1999-IX, and *Metropolitan Church of Bessarabia and Others v. Moldova*, no. 45701/99, ECHR 2001-XII). I therefore entirely agree with the view that the Court must seek to reconcile universality and diversity and that it is not its role to express an opinion on any religious model whatsoever.

3. I would perhaps have been able to follow the margin-of-appreciation approach had two factors not drastically reduced its relevance in the instant case. The first concerns the argument the majority use to justify the width of the margin, namely the diversity of practice between the States on the issue of regulating the wearing of religious symbols in educational institutions and, thus, the lack of a European consensus in this sphere. The comparative-law materials do not allow of such a conclusion, as in none of the member States has the ban on wearing religious symbols extended to university education, which is intended for young adults, who are less amenable to pressure. The second factor concerns the European supervision that must accompany the margin of appreciation and which, even though less extensive than in cases in which the national authorities have no margin of appreciation, goes hand in hand with it. However, other than in connection with Turkey's specific historical background, European supervision seems quite simply to be absent from the judgment. However, the issue raised in the application, whose significance to the right to freedom of religion guaranteed by the Convention is evident, is not merely a "local" issue, but one of importance to all the member States. European supervision cannot, therefore, be escaped simply by invoking the margin of appreciation.

4. On what grounds was the interference with the applicant's right to freedom of religion through the ban on wearing the headscarf based? In the present case, relying exclusively on the reasons cited by the national authorities and courts, the majority put forward, in general and abstract terms, two main arguments: secularism and equality. While I fully and totally subscribe to each of these principles, I disagree with the manner in which they were applied here and to the way they were interpreted in relation to the practice of wearing the headscarf. In a democratic society, I believe that it is necessary to seek to harmonise the principles of secularism, equality and liberty, not to weigh one against the other.

5. As regards, firstly, *secularism*, I would reiterate that I consider it an essential principle and one which, as the Constitutional Court stated in its judgment of 7 March 1989, is undoubtedly necessary for the protection of the democratic system in Turkey. Religious freedom is, however, also a founding principle of democratic societies. Accordingly, the fact that the Grand Chamber recognised the force of the principle of secularism did not release it from its obligation to establish that the ban on wearing the Islamic headscarf to which the applicant was subject was necessary to secure compliance with that principle and, therefore, met a "pressing social need".

Only indisputable facts and reasons whose legitimacy is beyond doubt—not mere worries or fears—are capable of satisfying that requirement and justifying interference with a right guaranteed by the Convention. Moreover, where there has been interference with a fundamental right, the Court's case-law clearly establishes that mere affirmations do not suffice: they must be supported by concrete examples (see *Smith and Grady v. the United Kingdom*, nos. 33985/96 and 33986/96, §89, ECHR 1999-VI). Such examples do not appear to have been forthcoming in the present case.

6. Under Article 9 of the Convention, the freedom with which this case is concerned is not freedom to have a religion (the internal conviction) but to manifest one's religion (the expression of that conviction). If the Court has been very protective (perhaps over-protective) of religious sentiment ... it has shown itself less willing to intervene in cases concerning religious practices, ... which only appear to receive a subsidiary form of protection (see paragraph 105 of the judgment). This is, in fact, an aspect of freedom of religion with which the Court has rarely been confronted up to now and on which it has not yet had an opportunity to form an opinion with regard to external symbols of religious practice, such as particular items of clothing, whose symbolic importance may vary greatly according to the faith concerned.

* * *

8. Freedom to manifest a religion entails everyone being allowed to exercise that right, whether individually or collectively, in public or in private, subject to the dual condition that they do not infringe the rights and freedoms of others and do not prejudice public order (Article 9 §2).

As regards the first condition, this could have not been satisfied if the headscarf the applicant wore as a religious symbol had been ostentatious or aggressive or was used to exert pressure, to provoke a reaction, to proselytise or to spread propaganda and undermined—or was liable to undermine—the convictions of others. However, the Government did not argue that this was the case and there was no evidence before the Court to suggest that Ms Şahin had any such intention. As to the second condition, it has been neither suggested nor demonstrated that there was any disruption in teaching or in everyday life at the university, or any disorderly conduct, as a result of the applicant's wearing the headscarf. Indeed, no disciplinary proceedings were taken against her.

* * *

10.... While everyone agrees on the need to prevent radical Islamism, a serious objection may nevertheless be made to such reasoning. Merely wearing the headscarf cannot be associated with fundamentalism and it is vital to distinguish between those who wear the headscarf and "extremists" who seek to impose the headscarf as they do other religious symbols. Not all women who wear the headscarf are fundamentalists and there is nothing to suggest that the applicant held fundamentalist views. She is a young adult woman and a university student, and might reasonably be expected to have a heightened capacity to resist pressure, it being noted in this connection that the judgment fails to provide any concrete example of the type of pressure concerned. The applicant's personal interest in exercising the right to freedom of religion and to manifest her religion by an external symbol cannot be wholly absorbed by the public interest in fighting extremism.

11. Turning to *equality*, the majority focus on the protection of women's rights and the principle of sexual equality.... Wearing the headscarf is considered on the contrary to be synonymous with the alienation of women. The ban on wearing the headscarf is therefore seen as promoting equality between men and women. However, what, in fact, is the connection between the ban and sexual equality? The judgment does not say. Indeed, what is the signification of wearing the headscarf? As the German Constitutional Court noted in its judgment of 24 September 2003, wearing the headscarf has no single meaning; it is a practice that is engaged in for a variety of reasons. It does not necessarily symbolise the submission of women to men and there are those who maintain that, in certain cases, it can even be a means of emancipating women. What is lacking in this debate is the opinion of women, both those who wear the headscarf and those who choose not to.

12. On this issue, the Grand Chamber refers in its judgment to *Dahlab* (cited above), taking up what to my mind is the most questionable part of the reasoning in that decision, namely that wearing the headscarf represents a "powerful external symbol", which "appeared to be imposed on women by a religious precept that was hard to reconcile with the principle of gender equality" and that the practice could not easily be "reconciled with the message of tolerance, respect for others and, above all, equality and non-discrimination that all teachers in a democratic society should convey to their pupils"....

It is not the Court's role to make an appraisal of this type—in this instance a unilateral and negative one—of a religion or religious practice, just as it is not its role to determine in a general and abstract way the signification of wearing the headscarf or to impose its viewpoint on the applicant ... Finally, if wearing the headscarf really was contrary to the principle of equality between men and women in any event, the State would have a positive obligation to prohibit it in all places, whether public or private.

13. Since, to my mind, the ban on wearing the Islamic headscarf on the university premises was not based on reasons that were relevant and sufficient, it cannot be considered to be interference that was "necessary in a democratic society" within the meaning of Article 9 § 2 of the Convention. In these circumstances, there has been a violation of the applicant's right to freedom of religion, as guaranteed by the Convention.

* * *

Note: Judge Tulkens would also have found a violation of the right to education.

Note: The Human Rights Committee decided that Uzbekistan's prohibition on wearing headscarves in universities violated article 18, paragraph 2 of the International Covenant on Civil and Political Rights ["No one shall be subject to coercion which would impair his freedom to have or to adopt a religion or belief of his choice."] *Hudoyberganova v. Uzbekistan*, Human Rights Committee, 82nd Sess., Communication No. 931/2000, 5 Nov. 2004, 12 Int'l Hum. Rt. Rep. 345 (2005).

QUESTIONS

1. What rights did Leyla Şahin complain were being violated by the University (a government institution) and thus by Turkey?

2. Did the Court give sufficient weight to the fact that the events occurred in a university?
3. Do you find the Court's opinion or the Dissenting opinion more persuasive? Why?
4. Why did the Court think that it had to give considerable deference (margin of appreciation) to the Turkish Constitutional Court's decision on the issue?
5. Do you agree with the Dissent's statement: "[E]veryone agrees on the need to prevent radical Islamism.... ?" Wouldn't such a view infringe the right to religious freedom for those who believe in radical Islamism?

Other European Human Rights Conventions

The European Social Charter[29] protects a number of economic and social rights including the right to work, to just conditions of work, fair remuneration, the right to organize, to bargain collectively, to protections against child labour, to protections for employed women, to vocational guidance and training, to protection of health, social security, social and medical assistance, to training for the physically and mentally disabled, to protections for the family and migrant workers. States parties to the Charter are required to submit annual reports on implementation to the European Committee of Social Rights which monitors compliance with the Charter's Obligations.

The European Convention for the Prevention of Torture and Inhuman or Degrading Treatment or Punishment[30] established a Committee whose job it is to visit places of detention in the states who are parties to the Convention and ensure that detainees are not subject to torture or other forms of severe mistreatment. After visiting places of detention (usually prisons) the Committee issues a confidential report.

The Inter-American System

The Organization of American States (OAS) is a regional agency within the United Nations and is governed by the Charter of the Organization of American States[31] which articulates a number of purposes including strengthening "the peace and security of the continent" (article 2(b)). The Inter-American Commission on Human Rights is an organ of the OAS (article 52 (e)) "whose principal function shall be to promote the observance and protection of human rights...." (Article 111). The Commission and the Inter-American Court of Human Rights play a role in the enforcement of the American Convention on Human Rights[32] which is open to all members of the OAS.

---

29. 529 U.N.T.S. 89, signed 18 Oct. 1961, entered into force 26 Feb. 1965, revised 1996, Revised Charter, entered into force 7 Jan. 1999.

30. E. T. S. No. 126, signed 26 Nov. 1987, entered into force 1 Feb. 1989, reprinted at 27 I.L.M. 1152 (1988), text amended by Protocol No. 1, E.T.S. No. 151, and Protocol No. 2, E.T.S. No. 152, both of which entered into force on 1 March 2002.

31. 119 U.N.T.S. 3, 2 U.S.T. 2394, O.A.S. T.S. No. 1-D; OAS Doc. OEA/Ser.A/2 (English) Rev. 2., signed 30 April 1948, entered into force 31 Dec. 1951, reprinted at 25 I.L.M. 529 (1986).

32. 1144 U.N.T.S. 123, O.A.S. Official Records OEA/Ser.K/XVI/1.1, Dec. 65, Rev. 1, Corr. 1, 7 Jan. 1970, signed Nov. 22, 1969, entered into force 18 July 1978, reprinted at 9 I.L.M. 101 (1970), revised by Additional Protocol in the area of Economic, Social, and Cultural Rights, O.A.S.T.S. No. 69, 17 Nov. 1988, entered into force, 16 Nov. 1999; Protocol to Abolish the Death Penalty, O.A.S.T.S. No. 73, 8 June 1990, ratified and in force for eleven member states.

Rights Protected by the American Convention on Human Rights

The American Convention on Human Rights protects a variety of human rights: "the right to recognition as a person before the law" (article 3); "the right to have ... life respected" (article 4) which includes limitations on the death penalty and its prohibition for those under eighteen or over seventy at the time of the commission of the crime and a requirement that it not be carried out on pregnant women (article 4); the right to humane treatment including a prohibition of torture (article 5); freedom from slavery and compulsory labor, except as punishment for a crime (article 6); "the right to personal liberty and security" (article 7); the right to a fair trial including a variety of due process protections (article 8); freedom from the imposition of *ex post facto* laws (article 9); the right to privacy (article 11); "the right to freedom of conscience and religion" (article 12); "the right to freedom of thought and expression" (article 13); the "right of peaceful assembly" (article 15); "the right to associate freely" (article 16); the family is declared to be "the natural and fundamental group unit of society ... entitled to protection" (article 17(1)); "the right ... to marry and raise a family" (article 17(2)); "the right to a given name and to the surnames of [a person's] parents or that of one of them" (article 18); minor children have the right to "measures of protection" (article 19); "the right to a nationality" (article 20); "the right to the use and enjoyment of ... property" (article 21(1)); the right not to "be deprived of ... property except upon payment of just compensation" (article 21(2)); freedom of movement and residence (article 22(1)); "the right to leave any country freely" (article 22(2)); the right not to "be expelled from the territory of the state of which [a person] is a national or be deprived of the right to enter it" (article 22(5)); "the right to seek and be granted asylum in a foreign territory" (article 22(7)); the right not to be "returned to a country ... [where] his right to life or personal freedom is in danger of being violated because of his race, nationality, religion, social status, or political opinions" (article 22(8)); the right to participate in government (article 23); the right "to equal protection of the law" (article 24); the right to recourse to courts for protection against violation of fundamental rights (article 25). The states parties to the Convention "undertake to adopt measures ... with a view to achieving progressively ... the full realization of ... the economic, social, educational, scientific and cultural standards set forth in the Charter ..." (Article 26).

States are permitted to derogate from the guarantee of certain rights but only "[i]n time of war, public danger, or other emergency that threatens the independence or security of a State party ... provided that such [derogations] ... do not involve discrimination on the ground of race, color, sex, language, religion or social origin." (Article 27). There are listed certain rights and freedoms from which states may not derogate: the "Right to Juridical Personality ... Right of Life ... Right to Humane Treatment ... Freedom from Slavery ... Freedom from Ex Post Facto Laws ... Freedom of Conscience and Religion ... Rights of the Family ... Right to a Name ... Rights of the Child ... Right to a Nationality ... Right to Participate in Government ... [and the right to] judicial guarantees essential for the protection of such rights" (Article 27(2)).

Enforcement Mechanisms under the American Convention on Human Rights

The American Convention provides for enforcement by the Inter-American Commission on Human Rights (an OAS organ) which sits in Washington, D.C., U.S.A., and the Inter-American Court of Human Rights, based in San Jose, Costa Rica. The Commission is made up of seven independent members and the Court consists of seven judges "elected in an individual capacity" (article 52(1)).

The Inter-American Commission

The American Convention provides for a compulsory system of individual, group or NGO petitions against any state party to the Convention. (Article 44). These petitions are presented to the Commission (article 44) which then has the responsibility to investigate the allegations, request information from relevant entities, conduct hearings and attempt to reach "a friendly settlement of the matter" (article 48). The Commission has the power to carry out on-site visits as part of its investigations. If a settlement is not reached, the Commission draws up a report "setting forth the facts and stating its conclusions" (article 50). The report is then transmitted to the states concerned (but not to the individual, group or NGO that lodged the complaint). The states concerned are not "at liberty to publish" the report (article 50(2)).

Within a period of three months from the transmittal of the report, the Commission or the state concerned (but not the petitioner) may submit the matter to the Inter-American Court, provided the state has accepted the Court's jurisdiction, which is optional (articles 51 & 62). If the matter is not submitted to the Court then the Commission may "set forth its opinion and conclusions concerning the question submitted for its consideration" (article 51(1)). The Commission can make recommendations to the state concerned and set a time limit in which the state should take measures to remedy the situation (article 51(2)). When the time limit has expired, the Commission decides whether adequate measures have been taken and whether it will publish its report (article 51(3)). This is the extent of the Commission's sanctioning power.

The American Convention also contains an optional state-against-state petition system (article 45). To date only ten parties have deposited acceptances of this provision. The Commission's hearing and reporting system for the state-against-state petitions is essentially the same as individual petitions.

Apart from its authority under the American Convention, the Commission has the authority to hear communications from individuals or NGOs alleging that an OAS member state has violated the American Declaration of the Rights and Duties of Man.[33] This document is similar to the Universal Declaration of Human Rights and was originally meant to serve as a statement of aspiration and hope. In 1967 the OAS Charter was amended to make the contents of the American Declaration equivalent to "fundamental rights" outlined in article 3(k) of the OAS Charter. It is argued that through this amendment the rights outlined in the American Declaration became binding on all OAS members regardless of whether they are parties to the American Convention on Human Rights. When the Commission receives a petition alleging a violation of the Charter it investigates the allegation and issues a report which states the facts, conclusions and any recommendations. Time limits are set for compliance. The only other enforcement power the Commission possesses in the case of non-compliance is to publish

33. O.A.S. Res. XXX, adopted by the Ninth International Conference of American States (March 30–May 2, 1948), Bogota, O.A.S. Off. Rec. OEA/Ser. L/V/I.4 Rev. (1965), reprinted at 43 Amer. J. Int'l L. Supp. 133 (1949).

the report. This area of the Commission's jurisdiction is hotly disputed by some countries, particularly the United States.[34]

The Commission also undertakes investigations into situations where it has reason to believe that there are widespread violations of human rights. If the Commission wishes to undertake in-state investigation, it must receive that state's permission (OAS Charter, article 18). The Commission is authorized to publish any report it makes after such an investigation. It is hoped that the dissemination of such a report will bring pressure upon the offending state to remedy the situation.

The Inter-American Court of Human Rights

The Court can only receive a case once the Commission has submitted its report to the state concerned and either the Commission or the state has referred the case to the Court. The Court will only have jurisdiction to proceed if the state concerned has accepted the Court's jurisdiction under article 62(1) or by special agreement under article 62(3). The Court has both contentious jurisdiction and can also give advice to OAS member states on the compatibility of their domestic laws with American human rights standards (article 64). The Court's judgments are binding on the parties and states "undertake to comply with the judgment of the Court in any case to which they are parties." (Article 68) Below is a decision of the Inter-American Court of Human Rights.

Case of Valle Jaramillo et al. v. Colombia

Judgment of November 27, 2008
(Merits, reparations, and costs)
(Footnotes omitted)

In the case of *Valle Jaramillo et al.*,

the Inter-American Court of Human Rights (hereinafter "the Court" or "the Inter-American Court"), composed of the following judges:

Cecilia Medina Quiroga, President
Diego García Sayán, Vice President
Sergio García Ramírez, Judge
Manuel E. Ventura Robles, Judge
Leonardo A. Franco, Judge
Margarette May Macaulay, Judge, and
Rhadys Abreu Blondet, Judge; ...
delivers this judgement.

I

INTRODUCTION OF THE CASE AND PURPOSE OF THE DISPUTE

1. On February 13, 2007, the Inter-American Commission on Human Rights (hereinafter "the Commission" or "the Inter-American Commission") submitted to the Court, in accordance with the provisions of Articles 50 and 61 of the American Conven-

34. See, e.g., Donald T. Fox, Inter-American Commission on Human Rights Finds United States in Violation, 82 Amer. J. Int'l L. 601 (1988) discussing the U.S. response to *The Death Penalty Cases*, Res. 3/87, Case No. 9647, O.A.S. Ser.L/VII. 71, Doc. 9 (1987).

tion, an application against the Republic of Colombia (hereinafter "the State" or "Colombia"). This application originated from petition No. 12,415, forwarded to the Secretariat of the Commission on August 2, 2001, by the *Grupo Interdisciplinario por los Derechos Humanos* [Interdisciplinary Group for Human Rights] (hereinafter "GIDH").

* * *

2. In its application, the Commission alleged that:

> On February 27, 1998, [...] two armed men entered Jesús María Valle Jaramillo's office in [...] Medellín [where Carlos Fernando Jaramillo Correa and] Nelly Valle [Jaramillo], Jesús María Valle's sister, were also present [...]. [Subsequently, a woman entered and, together with two armed men, proceeded to] tie up and immobilize the hostages [...]. Jesús María Valle was murdered with two shots to his head, [and] died instantly. [...] Following the extrajudicial execution, Mrs. Valle and Mr. Jaramillo Correa were dragged to the lobby, [where] they were threatened with guns [...]. [T]he perpetrators [then] left the office. [...] Carlos Fernando Jaramillo [...] had to go into exile because of his fears owing to the threats he had received. [...] The available evidence indicates that the motive for the murder was to silence the reports of the human rights defender Jesús María Valle about the crimes perpetrated in the municipality of Ituango by members of paramilitary forces in connivance with members of the Army [...]. [A]most nine years have passed [...], three civilians have been convicted *in absentia*, and there are no judicial investigations underway to determine whether State agents bear any responsibility.

3. Based on the above, the Commission alleged that the State is responsible for:

> The [alleged] extrajudicial execution of the human rights defender Jesús María Valle Jaramillo; the [alleged] detention and cruel, inhuman, and degrading treatment that preceded it, to the detriment of Mr. Valle Jaramillo, Nelly Valle Jaramillo, his sister, and Carlos Fernando Jaramillo Correa [...]; the [alleged] lack of investigation and punishment of those responsible for these acts; the [alleged] lack of adequate reparation in favor of the [presumed] victims and their next of kin; and the [alleged] forced displacement that Mr. Jaramillo Correa suffered following the facts.

4. The Commission asked the Court to declare the international responsibility of the State for the violation of:

(a) Articles 4 (Right to Life), 5 (Right to Humane Treatment) and 7 (Right to Personal Liberty) of the American Convention, in relation to Article 1(1) (Obligation to Respect Rights) thereof, to the detriment of Jesús María Valle Jaramillo;

(b) Articles 5 (Right to Humane Treatment) and 7 (Right to Personal Liberty) of the American Convention, in relation to Article 1(1) (Obligation to Respect Rights) thereof, to the detriment of Nelly Valle Jaramillo Jaramillo (hereinafter "María Nelly Valle Jaramillo" or "Nelly Valle Jaramillo") and Carlos Fernando Jaramillo Correa;

(c) Article 22 (Freedom of Movement and Residence) of the American Convention, in relation to Article 1(1) (Obligation to Respect Rights) thereof, to the detriment of Carlos Fernando Jaramillo Correa "and his next of kin"; and

(d) Articles 8(1) (Right to a Fair Trial) and 25 (Right to Judicial Protection) of the American Convention, in relation to Article 1(1) (Obligation to Respect Rights) thereof, to the detriment of Nelly Valle Jaramillo, Carlos Fernando Jaramillo Correa, and "the next of kin" of Jesús María Valle Jaramillo.

Finally, the Commission asked the Court to order the State to adopt various measures of pecuniary and non-pecuniary reparation.

* * *

9. On March 10, 2008, the parties forwarded their respective briefs with final arguments. As requested by the Court, the State transmitted with this brief, *inter alia*, a transcript and recording of statements made by Salvatore Mancuso on January 15 and May 15, 2007, "in relation to General Alfonso Manosalva," as well as a copy of a payment authorization dated February 14, 2008, issued by the Ministry of the Interior and Justice, relating to the settlement agreement signed by the State and some of the alleged victims on April 26, 2007, and approved on September 28, 2007.

* * *

III
Jurisdiction

19. The Court is competent to hear this case in the terms of Article 62(3) of the American Convention, because Colombia has been a State Party to the Convention since July 31, 1973, and accepted the compulsory jurisdiction of the Court on June 21, 1985.

* * *

64. Having examined the probative elements in the case file, the Court will now analyze the alleged violations in the corresponding chapters, considering the facts that have been acknowledged and those that it finds proved. The Court will also consider the pertinent arguments of the parties, bearing in mind the State's acknowledgment of facts and acquiescence.

VI
Violation of Articles 4, 5, and 7 (Right to Life, Right to Humane Treatment, and Right to Personal Liberty) of the American Convention in Relation to Article 1(1) (Obligation to Respect Rights) Thereof

65. The Commission and the representatives alleged that the State is responsible for the violation of the right to life of Jesús María Valle Jaramillo, as well as the right to humane treatment and the right to personal liberty of Jesús María Valle Jaramillo, Nelly Valle Jaramillo, and Carlos Fernando Valle Jaramillo. Additionally, the representatives asked that the Court declare the State responsible for the violation of the right to humane treatment of "the next of kin" of Jesús María Valle Jaramillo and Nelly Valle Jaramillo.

66. According to the Commission and the representatives, "the execution of Jesús María Valle did not occur in a void and was not an isolated case; rather it took place in a specific context as part of a series of murders, harassment, stigmatization, and attacks against individuals and social organizations dedicated to the defense of human rights. The consequences have continued over time owing to the ineffectiveness of the administration of justice in cases such as this." To support these allegations, the Commission indicated, *inter alia*, that "[t]he State authorities themselves declared that the grave situation of vulnerability in which Colombian human rights defenders found themselves generated a increased responsibility of protection for the State […]. In this case, it was reasonable to think that the risk borne by Jesús María Valle Jaramillo merited that the State adopt measures in accordance with this increased responsibility of protection." The Commission also indicated that "the authorities were aware of the risk and adopted measures to deal with it. However, those measures were insufficient […]."

67. In addition, the representatives argued that, "at the time the human rights defender Jesús María Valle Jaramillo was executed, the defense of human rights in Colombia took place in a context of systematic persecution and the absence of measures of protection and guarantees for the full and free exercise of this task, together with a pattern of impunity that [...] still characterizes the investigations undertaken in response to acts of intimidation and violence [...] against human rights defenders in different parts of the country." Furthermore, the representatives indicated that between July 1, 1996, and December 31, 1998, "several human rights defenders were executed in similar circumstances, using a specific *modus operandi.*"

* * *

69. Furthermore, the Commission and the representatives indicated that the illegal and arbitrary detention of Jesús María Valle Jaramillo, Nelly Valle Jaramillo, and Carlos Jaramillo Correa placed them in a situation of vulnerability resulting in the real and imminent danger that their other rights would be violated. According to the representatives, the situation of "absolute defenselessness [...] must have caused them immense anguish, since the outcome was predictable; acts that corresponded to cruel, inhuman, and degrading treatment." In addition, the Commission and the representatives alleged that "the execution of [Jesús María] Valle Jaramillo had a specific and grave impact on the stability of the family, which was deprived of the person who guided and supported it," "because the pain and suffering caused by both his death and the circumstances surrounding the case constitute a violation of the physical and moral integrity of all [his] family."

70. The State acknowledged that "Jesús María Valle Jaramillo was a well-known human rights defender in Antioquia who, as of 1996, had been systematically denouncing what he considered the arbitrary actions and excesses of paramilitary groups," particularly in the municipality of Ituango. The State accepted that, on February 27, 1998, two armed men [entered] Mr. Valle Jaramillo's office in Medellín and shot him with a pistol, killing him instantly. Nelly Valle Jaramillo and Carlos Fernando Jaramillo Correa were also present, and were tied up and later threatened with firearms, following which the armed men told Mr. Jaramillo Correa, "we will spare your life, but you haven't seen us," and left.

* * *

72. In order to analyze Colombia's international responsibility for the violation of Articles 7, 5, and 4 of the Convention, in relation to Article 1(1) thereof, the Court deems it pertinent to structure this chapter as follows: (a) context and international responsibility of the State under the Convention; (b) measures of protection due to human rights defenders such as Jesús María Valle Jaramillo, who are especially vulnerable; (c) the violation of Jesús María Valle Jaramillo's right to personal liberty, to humane treatment, and to life; (d) the violation of Nelly Valle Jaramillo and Carlos Fernando Jaramillo Correa's right to personal liberty and humane treatment; and (e) the violation of the right to humane treatment of the other alleged victims.

A) Context and international responsibility of the State under the Convention

73. As part of its acquiescence, the State acknowledged that Jesús María Valle Jaramillo was a well-known human rights defender. According to the evidence provided, and as established by the Court in the *case of the Ituango Massacres*, as of 1996 and until the time of his death, Jesús María Valle Jaramillo actively denounced the crimes perpetrated by paramilitary elements, as well as the collaboration and acquiescence between the latter and members of the National Army.

74. The Court considers it pertinent to make some observations on the phenomenon of paramilitarism in Colombia, as well as its consequences for those human rights defenders who, like Jesús María Valle Jaramillo, denounced the violations committed by paramilitary elements and some members of the National Army.

* * *

76. [I]t is evident that the State encouraged the creation of "self-defense" groups with specific objectives, but these were overstepped, and the self-defense groups began to function beyond the law. In this regard, the Court has observed that these paramilitary groups are responsible for numerous murders and many of the human rights violations committed in Colombia generally. In addition, numerous links between paramilitary groups and members of the armed forces have been demonstrated before this Court in relation to facts similar to those of the present case, as have omissive attitudes by members of the armed forces in relation to the acts of such groups." In cases such as these, the Court has declared that the Colombian State bears international responsibility for the failure to comply with "its obligation to ensure human rights, [and, thus,] its duty of prevention and protection."

77. In this regard, the Court has recognized that, within the framework of the State's obligation to ensure respect for these rights between individuals, the State's international responsibility may arise when human rights violations committed by third parties or individuals are attributed to it. Hence, the Court has found that:

> This international responsibility may arise also from the acts of individuals, which, in principle, are not attributable to the State. [The obligations *erga omnes* to respect and ensure respect for the norms of protection, which are the responsibility of the States Parties to the Convention,] extend their effects beyond the relationship between State agents and the persons subject to its jurisdiction, since they are also manifest in the positive obligation of the State to adopt the necessary measures to ensure the effective protection of human rights in relations between individuals. The attribution of responsibility to the State for the acts of individuals may occur in cases in which the State fails to comply with the obligations *erga omnes* contained in Articles (1) and 2 of the Convention, owing to the acts or omissions of its agents when they are in the position of guarantors.

78. However, the Court has also recognized that a State cannot be responsible for every human rights violation committed by individuals subject to its jurisdiction. In other words, even though the legal consequences of an act or omission of an individual is a violation of the human rights of another, that violation cannot be automatically attributed to the State, but must be considered in light of the particular circumstances of the case and the way the State has carried out its obligations as guarantor. Indeed, the … *erga omnes* [nature] of the State's Convention obligations do not entail its unlimited responsibility for every act of an individual, because the obligation of the State to adopt preventive measures to protect individuals in their relationships with each other is conditioned by its awareness of a situation of real and imminent risk for a specific individual or group of individuals, and on the existence of the reasonable possibility of preventing or avoiding that danger.

* * *

80.In this regard, the Court has previously indicated that "by contributing to the establishment of these ["self-defense"] groups, the State objectively created a dangerous situation for its inhabitants and did not adopt the necessary and sufficient measures to prevent these groups from continuing to commit acts such as those of the instant case."

* * *

81. The Court finds that the danger created by the State aggravated the situation of vulnerability of human rights defenders who, like Jesús María Valle Jaramillo, denounced the violations committed by paramilitary groups and the armed forces.

B) Measures of protection due to human rights defenders such as Jesús María Valle Jaramillo, who are in a situation of special vulnerability

82. The Court observes that, in its T-590/98 ruling on the application for legal protection based on a violation of constitutional rights, issued on October 20, 1998, the year in which Jesús María Valle Jaramillo was murdered, the Constitutional Court of Colombia stated that, at the time of the events of the instant case, human rights defenders in Colombia faced a grave risk of becoming victims of violence. According to the Constitutional Court, "the activities of Colombian human rights defenders [were] fraught with innumerable dangers," making human rights defenders "a vulnerable sector of society," and imposing upon the State the obligation to "prioritize their protection." Specifically, the Constitutional Court declared that, at the time of Jesús María Valle Jaramillo's death, there was an "unconstitutional state of affairs" in Colombia, owing to the State's failure to protect human rights defenders.

83. It is worth noting that the Colombian Constitutional Court declared the existence of this "unconstitutional state of affairs" based on the reports of various international organizations regarding the vulnerability of human rights defenders in Colombia and the danger they faced.

* * *

87. The Court finds that in order to prevent such situations, States must create the necessary conditions for the effective enjoyment and exercise of the rights established in the Convention. Compliance with this obligation is tied intrinsically to the protection and recognition of the importance of the role of human rights defenders, whose work is essential to strengthen democracy and the rule of law.

90. Consequently, the Court finds that a State has the obligation to adopt all reasonable measures required to guarantee the rights to life, to personal liberty, and to personal integrity of those defenders who denounce human rights violations and who are in a situation of special vulnerability such as the internal armed conflict in Colombia. However, this obligation is conditional upon the State being aware of a real and immediate danger to the said human rights defenders and upon the existence of a reasonable possibility of preventing or avoiding this danger.

91. To this end, the States must implement the necessary measures to ensure that those who denounce human rights violations can carry out their activities freely; to protect human rights defenders when they are threatened in order to avoid attacks on their life and personal integrity; to generate the conditions necessary to eradicate human rights violations by State agents or individuals; to abstain from imposing obstacles to the work of human rights defenders; and investigate effectively and efficiently violations committed against them, in order to combat impunity.

C) Violation of the rights to personal liberty, to humane treatment, and to life (Articles 7, 5, and 4 of the Convention) of Jesús María Valle Jaramillo

* * *

94. It is worth noting that one month before his death, at a meeting at the Army's Fourth Brigade, Jesús María Valle Jaramillo had denounced the collusion between members of the armed forces and the paramilitary groups, particularly about the perpetration of more than 150 murders in Ituango. Moreover, the day before his death, on Feb-

ruary 26, 1998, Jesús María Valle Jaramillo testified about these accusations in the action on defamation and slander filed against him by a member of the Girardot Battalion attached to the Fourth Brigade.... The following day, February 27, 1998, Jesús María Valle Jaramillo was murdered.

95. In light of the foregoing..., the Court finds that Jesús María Valle Jaramillo's declarations, which were intended to alert society to the links between paramilitary groups and some State agents, put his life, liberty, and personal integrity in grave danger. It also finds that the State, although aware of this danger, did not adopt the reasonable measures needed to prevent the violation of these rights.

* * *

97. This Court finds that the facts of the present case created an obligation on the part of the State to investigate with respect to the violation of the right to life, personal integrity, and personal liberty of Jesús María Valle Jaramillo. In previous cases, the Court has recognized that ... the general obligation to guarantee rights indicated in Article 1(1) of the Convention, gives rise to obligations for the State to ensure the free and full exercise of the rights established in the Convention to all persons subject to its jurisdiction. Since its duty as guarantor is related to specific rights, it can be complied with in different ways depending on the right in question and the particular circumstances of the case.

98. The obligation to investigate human rights violations is among the positive measures that the State must adopt to guarantee the rights established in the Convention. Additionally, the State must, if possible, try to reestablish a right that has been violated and, if applicable, repair the damage produced by human rights violations.

* * *

102. Furthermore, the absence of a complete and effective investigation into the facts constitutes a source of additional suffering and anguish for victims and their next of kin, who have the right to know the truth of what happened. This right to the truth requires a procedural determination of the most complete historical truth possible, including the determination of patterns of collective action and of all those who, in different ways, took part in the said violations, as well as their corresponding responsibilities.

103. The next of kin of the victims also have the right to reparations for the damage they have suffered and the States have the obligation to provide them. In this regard, the State has a binding obligation to repair directly those human rights violations for which it is responsible, according to the standards for attributing international responsibility and for reparation established in the Court's case law. Moreover, the State must ensure that satisfaction of the claims for reparation made by victims of human rights violations and their next of kin is not impeded or obstructed by excessively complicated procedures or other obstacles to the reparation of their rights.

104. In this case, the assessment of the obligation to guarantee the rights to life, to humane treatment, and to personal liberty through a serious, complete, and effective investigation into the facts is made in Chapter VIII of this judgment. For the purpose of determining a violation of Articles 4, 5, and 7 of the Convention, in relation to Article 1(1) thereof, it is sufficient to indicate that, in this case, the State has not guaranteed the said rights effectively.

105. In conclusion, in accordance with the State's acknowledgement of responsibility in the instant case, the Court finds that the State did not comply with its duty to adopt the reasonable measures required to guarantee effectively the rights to personal liberty, hu-

mane treatment, and life of Jesús María Valle Jaramillo, who was in grave danger due to the public denunciations he made as part of his work as a human rights defender during Colombia's internal armed conflict. International responsibility for these acts can be attributed to the State, inasmuch as it failed in its obligations to prevent and investigate such acts. Both obligations derive from Articles 4, 5, and 7 of the Convention, considered in relation to Article 1(1) thereof, which obliges the State to ensure the enjoyment of these rights.

106. Based on the above, and bearing in mind the State's acquiescence and acknowledgment of the facts, the Court finds that the State violated the rights to personal liberty, to humane treatment, and to life embodied in Articles 7(1), 5(1) and 4(1) of the American Convention, respectively, in relation to the obligation to respect rights embodied in Article 1(1) thereof, to the detriment of Jesús María Valle Jaramillo.

D) Violation of the right to personal liberty and personal integrity (Articles 7(1) and 5(1) of the Convention) of Nelly Valle Jaramillo and Carlos Fernando Jaramillo Correa

107. Based on the State's acknowledgment of the facts, the Court finds it proved that on February 27, 1998, Nelly Valle Jaramillo and Carlos Fernando Jaramillo Correa were held hostage in Jesús María Valle Jaramillo's office by armed individuals who proceeded to tie up their hands and feet. It has also been established that, after these individuals executed Jesús María Valle Jaramillo, the physical violence against Nelly Valle Jaramillo and Carlos Fernando Jaramillo Correa continued, because they were dragged around the office.

108. Based on these facts, the Court finds it pertinent to reiterate that, according to its case law, freedom must be recognized as a basic human right inherent in the individual that crosscuts the entire American Convention. The Court has also held that the mere threat that an act prohibited by Article 5 of the Convention will be committed, when sufficiently real and imminent, can in itself violate the right to humane treatment. In other words, threatening or creating a situation that threatens a person's life can constitute inhuman treatment in some circumstances at least.

109. In the instant case, the threat to Nelly Valle Jaramillo and Carlos Fernando Jaramillo Correa is evident and is revealed in the most extreme manner possible, as it was a direct threat of death. Both Nelly Valle and Carlos Fernando Jaramillo were tied up and underwent an agonizing and threatening situation that, ultimately, resulted in the death of a third person held hostage with them. The treatment that Nelly Valle Jaramillo and Carlos Fernando Jaramillo Correa received was brutal and violent. In addition, the extrajudicial execution of Jesús María Valle Jaramillo permits the inference that Mrs. Valle Jaramillo and Mr. Jaramillo Correa could fear and anticipate that they would be arbitrarily and violently deprived of their life also, which constituted a violation of their personal integrity.

110. Based on the above, and taking into account the State's acknowledgement of the facts and acquiescence, the Court finds that the State violated the right to personal liberty and to humane treatment recognized in Articles 7(1) and 5(1) of the American Convention, respectively, in relation to the general obligation to protect rights embodied in Article 1(1) thereof, to the detriment of Nelly Valle Jaramillo and Carlos Fernando Jaramillo Correa.

E) Violation of the right to personal integrity (Article 5(1) of the Convention) of other alleged victims

[The Court also found violations of the right to personal integrity (Article 5(1) of the Convention of various other victims]

* * *

VII
Violation of Article 22 (Freedom of Movement and Residence) of the American Convention in relation to Article 1(1) (Obligation to Respect Rights) thereof

133. The Commission and the representatives alleged the violation of the right to freedom of movement and residence of Carlos Fernando Jaramillo Correa and his family, since "as a result of the death threats he received following the events of February 27, 1998, due to his participation as a witness in their investigation and in the legal proceedings, and because the State had placed him in a situation of vulnerability and defenselessness, Carlos Fernando Jaramillo Correa, together with his family, suffered forced displacement within Colombia and, subsequently, exile in another country."

* * *

144. Based on the foregoing, the Court declares that the State is responsible for the violation of the right to freedom of movement and residence established in Article 22(1) of the Convention, in relation to Article 1(1) thereof, to the detriment of Carlos Fernando Jaramillo Correa, his wife, Gloria Lucía Correa, his son, Carlos Enrique Jaramillo Correa, and his daughters, María Lucía Jaramillo Correa and Ana Carolina Jaramillo Correa.

VIII
Violation of Articles 8(1) (Judicial Guarantees) and 25(1) (Judicial Protection) of the American Convention, in relation to Article 1(1) (Obligation to Respect Rights) thereof

* * *

165. Based on the above, the Court finds that even though criminal investigations have been conducted, resulting in the conviction of several private individuals, partial impunity subsists in this case, as the State has acknowledged, to the extent that the whole truth of the facts and all those responsible have not been determined. In addition, the impunity in this case is reflected by the trial and conviction *in absentia* of members of paramilitary groups, who have benefited from the ineffectiveness of the punishment, because the warrants for their arrest have not been executed.

* * *

XIII
Reparations (Application of Article 63(1) of the American Convention)

198. It is a principle of international law that any violation of an international obligation that has resulted in harm entails the obligation to repair it adequately. All aspects of this obligation to make reparations are regulated by international law. The Court has based its decisions in this regard on Article 63(1) of the American Convention.

* * *

[Various amounts of pecuniary and non-pecuniary compensation was either approved by the Court as a result of settlements or ordered by the Court].

* * *

XIV
Operative Paragraphs

252. Therefore,

The Court

Declares,

Unanimously, that:

1. It accepts the State's partial acknowledgement of international responsibility in the terms of paragraphs 20, 35 and 38 of this judgment, and declares a violation of the rights to personal liberty, to personal integrity, and to life, embodied in Articles 7(1), 5(1), and 4(1), respectively, of the American Convention on Human Rights, in relation to the general obligation to ensure rights contained in Article 1(1) thereof, to the detriment of Jesús María Valle Jaramillo, in the terms of paragraphs 105 and 106 of this judgment.

2. It accepts the State's partial acknowledgment of international responsibility in the terms of paragraphs 20, 35 and 38 of this judgment, and declares a violation of the rights to personal liberty and to personal integrity embodied in Articles 7(1) and 5(1), respectively, of the American Convention on Human Rights, in relation to the general obligation to ensure rights contained in Article 1(1) thereof, to the detriment of Nelly Valle Jaramillo and Carlos Fernando Jaramillo Correa, in the terms of paragraph 110 of this judgment.

3. It accepts the State's partial acknowledgment of international responsibility, in the terms of paragraphs 20, 35 and 38 of this judgment, and declares a violation of the right to personal integrity embodied in Article 5(1) of the American Convention on Human Rights, in relation to the general obligation to ensure rights contained in Article 1(1) thereof, to the detriment of María Leticia Valle Jaramillo, Ligia Valle Jaramillo, Luzmila Valle Jaramillo, Magdalena Valle Jaramillo, Romelia Valle Jaramillo, Marina Valle Jaramillo, Darío Valle Jaramillo, Octavio Valle Jaramillo, Alfonso Montoya Restrepo, Luis Fernando Montoya Valle, Gloria Lucía Correa, Carlos Enrique Jaramillo Correa, María Lucía Jaramillo Correa, Ana Carolina Jaramillo Correa, Jesús Emilio Jaramillo Barrera, Adela Correa de Jaramillo, Blanca Lucía Jaramillo Correa, Romelia Jaramillo Correa, Nellyda Jaramillo Correa, José María Jaramillo Correa, Luis Eugenio Jaramillo Correa, Gloria Elena Jaramillo Correa and Adriana María Jaramillo Correa, in the terms of paragraphs 118 to 129 of this judgment.

4. It accepts the State's partial acknowledgment of international responsibility, in the terms of paragraphs 20, 35 and 38 of this judgment, and declares a violation of the right to freedom of movement embodied in Article 22(1) of the American Convention on Human Rights, in relation to the general obligation to ensure rights contained in Article 1(1) thereof, to the detriment of Carlos Fernando Jaramillo Correa, his wife, Gloria Lucía Correa, his son, Carlos Enrique Jaramillo Correa, and his daughters, María Lucía Jaramillo Correa and Ana Carolina Jaramillo Correa, in the terms of paragraph 144 of this judgment.

5. It accepts the State's partial acknowledgment of international responsibility, in the terms of paragraphs 20 and 38 of this judgment, and declares a violation of the rights to judicial guarantees and to judicial protection embodied in Articles 8(1) and 25(1) of the American Convention on Human Rights, in relation to the general obligation to respect rights contained in Article 1(1) thereof, to the detriment of Nelly Valle Jaramillo, Alfonso Montoya Restrepo, Luis Fernando Montoya Valle, Carlos Fernando Jaramillo Cor-

rea, Gloria Lucía Correa, Carlos Enrique Jaramillo Correa, María Lucía Jaramillo Correa, Ana Carolina Jaramillo Correa, Jesús Emilio Jaramillo Barrera, Adela Correa de Jaramillo, Blanca Lucía Jaramillo Correa, Romelia Jaramillo Correa, Nellyda Jaramillo Correa, José María Jaramillo Correa, Luis Eugenio Jaramillo Correa, Gloria Elena Jaramillo Correa, Adriana María Jaramillo Correa, María Leticia Valle Jaramillo, Ligia Valle Jaramillo, Luzmila Valle Jaramillo, Magdalena Valle Jaramillo, Romelia Valle Jaramillo, Marina Valle Jaramillo, Darío Valle Jaramillo and Octavio Valle Jaramillo, in the terms of paragraphs 168 to 170 of this judgment.

6. The State violated the right to personal integrity embodied in Article 5(1) of the American Convention on Human Rights, in relation to the general obligation to ensure rights contained in Article 1(1) thereof, to the detriment of Blanca Inés Valle Jaramillo, Gonzalo de Jesús Jaramillo Correa, Juan Guillermo Valle Noreña, John Jairo Valle Noreña and Luz Adriana Valle Noreña, in the terms of paragraphs 122, 126, 127 and 130 of this judgment

* * *

And Decides,

Unanimously, that:

12. This judgment constitutes *per se* a form of reparation.

13. The State must pay the amounts established in this judgment for pecuniary and non-pecuniary damage, and for reimbursement of costs and expenses, within one year of notification of this judgment, in the terms of paragraphs 207, 210, 216, 224 to 226 and 244 hereof.

14. The State must investigate the facts that gave rise to the violations in the instant case, in the terms of paragraphs 231, 232 and 233 of this judgment.

15. The State must publish once in the official gazette and once in another national newspaper with widespread circulation, paragraphs 2 to 4, 6, 29, 47, 70 to 78, 80 to 97, 104 to 107, 109, 110, 115, 122, 125 to 128, 130, 132, 140 to 144, 147, 160, 161, 165 to 170, 176 to 180, 184, 190, 191, 196, 197 and 200 of this judgment, without the corresponding footnotes but with the titles of the respective chapters, as well as its operative paragraphs, within one year of notification of this judgment, in the terms of paragraphs 227, 231 and 234 hereof.

16. The State must organize a public act to acknowledge its international responsibility for the violations declared in this case at the University of Antioquia within one year of notification of this judgment, in the terms of paragraph 227 and 231 hereof.

17. The State must place a plaque in memory of Jesús María Valle Jaramillo in the Courthouse of the Department of Antioquia within one year of notification of this judgment, in the terms of paragraphs 227 and 231 hereof.

18. The State must provide immediately and free of charge, through its specialized health care institutions, any psychological and psychiatric care required by the victims, in the terms of paragraphs 227, 231 and 238 of this judgment.

19. The State must grant Nelly Valle Jaramillo and Carlos Fernando Jaramillo Correa an educational grant to study or train for a profession, within one year of notification of this judgment, in the terms of paragraphs 227 and 231 hereof

20. The State must guarantee the safety of Carlos Fernando Jaramillo Correa should he decide to return to Colombia, in the terms of paragraph 227 and 231 of this judgment.

Judge Sergio García Ramírez informed the Court of his concurring opinion, which is attached to this judgment.

Done, at San José, Costa Rica, on November 27, 2008, in Spanish and English, the Spanish text being authentic....

QUESTIONS

1. Why was Colombia held responsible for some of the acts of paramilitary groups that were not agents of the State?
2. What obligations did Colombia fail to fulfill?
3. What could Colombia have done to fulfill its obligations?
4. List the types of reparations ordered by the Court.

The African System

The African Charter

The Charter of the Organization of African Unity[34] (OAU) was established in 1963 and created the framework for a regional governmental organization within the African continent. The OAU was disbanded in 2002 and replaced by the African Union (AU) which is based in Addis Adaba, Ethiopia. The AU was established by the Constitutive Act which was adopted in 2000 and came into force for member states in 2001.[35] The African Charter on Human and Peoples' Rights[36] (also known as the Banjul Charter) was adopted by the OAU in 1981 and entered into force in 1986. The African Charter protects a broad range of civil, political, economic, social and cultural rights. Certain rights are fundamentally different from those found in the European or American Conventions. The African Charter protects the right of "[c]olonized or oppressed peoples ... to free themselves from the bonds of domination by resorting to any means recognized by the international community" (article 20(2)); "the right to the assistance of the States parties to the present Charter in their liberation struggle against foreign domination, be it political, economic or cultural" (article 20(3)); "the right to free disposal of ... wealth and natural resources with a view to strengthening African unity and solidarity" (article 21(4)); states "undertake to eliminate all forms of foreign economic exploitation particularly that practiced by international monopolies" (article 21(5)); people are guaranteed "the right to their economic, social and cultural development" (article 22(1)); and states "have the duty ... to ensure the exercise of the right to development" (article 22(2)); people are also guaranteed "the right to a general satisfactory environment favourable to their development" (article 24). A number of duties are given to individuals: individuals are recognized as having "duties towards [the] family and society, the State and other legally recognized communities and the international community" (article 27(1)); "the duty to respect and consider ... fellow beings without discrimination" (article 28); the duty to "preserve the harmonious development of the family" (article 29(1)); "to serve [the] national community" (article 29(2)); "to preserve and strengthen social and national solidarity (article 29(2)); "[t]o work ... and to pay taxes imposed by law" (article

---

34. 479 U.N.T.S. 39, signed 25 May 1963, entered into force 13 Sept. 1963, reprinted at 2 I.L.M. 766 (1963).

35. The Constitutive Act of the AU and current information about the African Union is available at: http://www.africa-union.org/.

36. 1520 U.N.T.S. 217, adopted by the O.A.U. 27 June 1981, entered into force 21 Oct. 1986, reprinted at 21 I.L.M. 59 (1982).

29(6)); to "preserve and strengthen positive African cultural values" (article 29(7)); and to "contribute ... to the promotion and achievement of African unity" (article 29(8)).

Enforcement of the African Charter

The African Union's Constitutive Act establishes a number of operational organs of the AU including The Peace and Security Council which dispatched its first group of cease-fire monitors and military personnel to Sudan in 2004 following widespread attacks by the Janjaweed Militia against the civilian population. The incumbent Chairman of the AU at that time, the President of Nigeria, organized mediation talks between the Sudanese government and the rebels in the late summer of 2004.[37] In March 2009, the Council met to consider the situation in Somalia.

Perhaps the most import organ of the AU concerning human rights, to date, is the African Commission on Human and Peoples' Rights.[38] The Commission has the power to undertake educational activities, appoint Special Rapporteurs, adopt recommendations for governmental action and can hear state versus state complaints. The Democratic Republic of the Congo complained, in 1999, that it had been attacked by Burundi, Rwanda and Uganda. The Commission ruled that article 23 of the Charter (right to peace) had been violated and that the three respondent states had engaged in human rights violations.[39] States are required to make biennial reports to the Commission on progress towards implementation of rights outlined in the Charter (article 62). To date, the reporting obligation has only been compiled with sporadically.

In 1998 the Assembly of the OAU adopted a Protocol to the African Charter for the establishment of an African Court on Human and Peoples' Rights.[40] The Protocol came into force on January 15, 2004 upon the deposit of the fifteenth ratification. Under the Protocol, The Commission, State parties, African Regional Organizations, certain NGOs with observer status at the AU and, provided their country has agreed, individuals can bring suit in the Court. The Court will hear disputes concerning "the interpretation and application of the Charter, this Protocol and any other relevant Human Rights instruments ratified by the States concerned."[41] Some judges were elected by the Executive Council in 2006 and 2008 but no cases have yet been heard.

League of Arab States

The League of Arab States, informally known as the Arab League (AL), was founded in Cairo in 1945. It is a voluntary association of mainly Arabic speaking states based in Cairo, Egypt. Its purpose is to strengthen ties among members by coordinating policies and promoting common interests. The members have established a Joint Defense Council, an Economic Council and a Permanent Military Command as well as a number of Specialized Organizations and Committees with specific areas of concern. In February of 2004, the Yemeni president proposed replacing the AL with a European Union

37. Amil Khan & Mohamed Abdellah, The Boston Globe, Aug. 9, 2004, at A6.
38. The Commission's web site is available at: http://www.achpr.org/english/_info/news_en.html.
39. African Commission, Commumication 227/99, EX.CL/279(1X) Annex IV, at 111ff.
40. The Protocol is available on the website of the African Union, note 33 *supra*.
41. Id. at art. 3.

style Arab Union. In August, 2004, the AL publically opposed any economic sanctions against Sudan or any "forced foreign military intervention in the area."[42] The League has missions in Africa, Asia, the U.S.A. and Europe. The League adopted an Arab Charter on Human Rights in 1994, which was revised in 2004 and entered into force in 2008.[43] It reiterates many of the principles in the Universal Declaration and the ICCPR and the Cairo Declaration on Human Rights in Islam, but all rights are stated to be subject to Islamic Shari'ah (articles 24 & 25). The Charter is to be enforced by an Arab Human Rights Committee (articles 45–48).

The Shanghai Cooperation Organization and the Eurasian Economic Community

Asia does not have an official regional structure and thus has no regional human rights system but the Shanghai Cooperation Organization (SCO) and the Eurasian Economic Community are rapidly developing the scope of their activities and the number of participating countries and might, one day, create a human rights system. The SCO started in 1996 as an intergovernmental organization focussed on military relations between China, Kazakhstan, Kyrgyzstan, Russia and Tajikistan. Uzbekistan was admitted in 2001. India, Iran, Mongolia, and Pakistan have observer status. Afghanistan is part of a contact group. The U.S. applied for observer status but was turned down in 2005. Originally focussed on military and security issues, the SCO has rapidly evolved to tackle social development, drug crimes, terrorism, economic cooperation, transportation, movement of goods, currency and fiscal policies, food production, energy supplies and cultural exchanges.[44]

There is also a Eurasian Economic Community (EAEC) which was established by treaty in 2000[45] and signed by Belarus, Kazakhstan, Kyrgyzstan, Russian and Tajikistan which sets out to deepen "Integration in the Economic and Humanitarian Spheres...."[46] and promote a customs union. Uzbekistan was admitted as a member in 2005, with Armenia, Moldova and Ukraine as observer states.[47] The European Union started out as a purely trade related group. It is possible that the above organizations will eventually encompass human rights.

Enforcement of Human Rights in National (Domestic) Courts

A great number of states have ratified many of the important human rights treaties. All of those states have national court systems, so you may be wondering why individ-

42. As quoted in The Boston Globe, note 37 *supra*. For current information about the Arab League go to: http://www.arableagueonline.org.

43. Revised, May 22, 2004, entered into force, March 15, 2008, reprinted at 12 Int'l Hum. Rts. Rep. 893 (2005).

44. The SCO now has an official web site available in Chinese, Russian and English at: http://www.sectsco.org/EN/.

45. Treaty on the Establishment of the Eurasian Economic Community, 2212 U.N.T.S. I-39321, signed Oct. 10, 2000, entered into force, May 30, 2001.

46. Id. at preamble.

47. For the EAEC web site, go to: http://www.evrazes.com.

uals don't simply seek to enforce their human rights through their own national courts. The answer to this question is somewhat complex and turns upon the status of a treaty in a particular country's legal system as well as the interpretive issue of whether the treaty intended to create an enforceable right or remedy for individuals. It may also be complicated by the scope of sovereign immunity accorded to the government or to government officials in the particular country as well as the integrity of the judicial system.

Self-Execution of Treaties

Some countries follow a doctrine that provides that once treaties are ratified they become part of the national laws, just like enacted statutes. The United States Constitution, for example, provides that: "This Constitution, and the laws of the United States which shall be made in pursuance thereof; and all treaties made, or which shall be made, under the authority of the United States, shall be the supreme law of the land...." (U.S. Constitution, article VI, paragraph 2). Some scholars hold that this language indicates that U.S. treaties were to be regarded as part of U.S. law, that is, they were automatically self-executing and did not need implementing legislation to become effective. Other writers insist that whether a U.S. treaty is self-executing or not depends upon the intention of the United States in ratifying the treaty.[48] Certain U.S. courts have tended to follow this latter approach when resolving the issue,[49] although there are many U.S. cases where the courts have assumed that the treaty is self-executing without even discussing the issue.[50] (See, for example *U.S. v. Alvarez-Machain*, pp. 128–137.) The recent U.S. Supreme Court case, *Medellin v. Texas*, 128 S. Ct. 1346 (2008), exposed a wide division on the Court concerning the methodology to be used to determine whether treaties are self-executing with the majority looking for explicit treaty language indicating self-execution. This approach has been very controversial.

Under the United States Constitution, there are some areas that are within the exclusive law making authority of Congress, such as the appropriation of money or the determination that certain acts constitute a federal crime. When a treaty undertakes to provide monies or declare certain international crimes to be federal offenses, it is generally held that such treaties will need implementing legislation to become effective as U.S. law.[51] In recent years, when giving its consent to the ratification of a treaty, the U.S. Senate has sometimes stipulated that the President shall not ratify the treaty until Congress has passed implementing legislation.[52] After the *Medellin* case, the Senate has sometimes indicated whether it considers a treaty to be self-executing.

---

48. See, Restatement Third, § 111, cmt. h.

49. See, e.g., *Foster v. Neilson*, 27 U.S. (2 Pet.) 253, 314 (1828).

50. See, e.g., *Ware v. Hylton*, 3 U.S. (3 Dall.) 199 (1796); *Fairfax's Devisee v. Hunter's Lessee*, 11 U.S. (7 Cranch) 603 (1813).

51. Other areas where it has been suggested that implementing legislation is necessary are: declaring war, punishing certain activities, raising revenue, imposing tariffs, see Restatement Third, § 111, cmt. i.

52. See, e.g., U.S. Senate reservations to the Convention Against Torture and Other Cruel, Inhuman, or Degrading Treatment or Punishment, G.A. Res. 39/46, U.N. GAOR, 39th Sess., Supp. No. 51, U.N. Doc. A/39/51 (1984) (U.S. Senate advice and consent, 136th Cong. Rec. S. 17491-2 (daily ed. Oct. 27, 1990)).

When an individual seeks to rely upon the provisions of a treaty in national courts, for human rights or other purposes, the first question to be answered is whether the treaty is self-executing. If it is not, then the individual cannot rely upon the treaty as such, although s/he may be able to argue that the treaty is evidence of a customary norm which is binding in the national courts. (Cf., *The North Sea Continental Shelf Cases*, pp. 22–26, *The Paquete Habana*, pp. 5–10.)

If the treaty is self-executing or has been implemented by legislation, the next question to be answered is whether the treaty or the implementing legislation intended to create a right or remedy in favor of the individual bringing the claim. This is often a difficult question to resolve even after a careful reading of the treaty or the legislation. United States courts will seek to discover the meaning of the treaty or legislation in this regard and have fairly liberal views about the type of evidence that may be introduced to throw light upon the drafters' intent.

Negusie v. Holder

Supreme Court of the United States
129 S. Ct. 1159 (2009)
(Footnotes omitted)

(**Note:** The U.S. is party to the Protocol Relating to the Status of Refugees (606 U.N.T.S. 267, 19 U.S.T. 6223) which has been enacted into U.S. law by the Refugee Act of 1980. This treaty and act state that a foreigner who is in the U.S. may be granted asylum if s/he has been persecuted or has "a well-founded fear of persecution [in their home country] on account of race, religion, nationality, membership in a particular social group or political opinion...." 8 U.S.C. § 1101 (a)(42)(A) & 8 U.S.C. § 1158 (b)(1)(A). Also, an alien cannot be removed to a country where her/his "life or freedom would be threatened ... because of the alien's race, religion, nationality, membership in a particular social group or political opinion." 8 U.S.C. § 1231(b)(3)(A). However, the alien cannot claim such protections if s/he has persecuted others on account of their race, religion, nationality, membership in a particular social group or political opinion. 8 U.S.C.1158(b)(2)(A)(i) & 8 U.S.C. § 1231 (b) (3)(B)(i). In this case, Daniel Girmai Neguise, a foreigner in the U.S., was trying to claim rights under the treaty and implementing legislation in U.S. national courts.)

OPINION

Justice KENNEDY delivered the opinion of the Court.

An alien who fears persecution in his homeland and seeks refugee status in this country is barred from obtaining that relief if he has persecuted others.

"The term 'refugee' does not include any person who ordered, incited, assisted, or otherwise participated in the persecution of any person on account of race, religion, nationality, membership in a particular social group, or political opinion." Immigration and Nationality Act (INA), § 101, 66 Stat. 166, as added by Refugee Act of 1980, § 201(a), 94 Stat. 102-103, 8 U.S.C. § 1101(a)(42).

This so-called "persecutor bar" applies to those seeking asylum, § 1158(b)(2)(A)(i), or withholding of removal, § 1231(b)(3)(B)(i). It does not disqualify an alien from receiving a temporary deferral of removal under the Convention Against Torture and Other Cruel, Inhuman or Degrading Treatment or Punishment (CAT), art. 3, Dec. 10, 1984, S. Treaty Doc. No. 100-20, p. 20, 1465 U.N.T.S. 85; 8 CFR § 1208.17(a) (2008).

In this case the Board of Immigration Appeals (BIA) determined that the persecutor bar applies even if the alien's assistance in persecution was coerced or otherwise the product of duress. In so ruling the BIA followed its earlier decisions that found *Fedorenko v. United States,* 449 U.S. 490, 101 S.Ct. 737, 66 L.Ed.2d 686 (1981), controlling. The Court of Appeals for the Fifth Circuit, in affirming the agency, relied on its precedent following the same reasoning. We hold that the BIA and the Court of Appeals misapplied *Fedorenko.* We reverse and remand for the agency to interpret the statute, free from the error, in the first instance.

I

Petitioner in this Court is Daniel Girmai Negusie, a dual national of Eritrea and Ethiopia, his father having been a national of the former and his mother of the latter. Born and educated in Ethiopia, he left there for Eritrea around the age of 18 to see his mother and find employment. The year was 1994. After a few months in Eritrea, state officials took custody of petitioner and others when they were attending a movie. He was forced to perform hard labor for a month and then was conscripted into the military for a time. War broke out between Ethiopia and Eritrea in 1998, and he was conscripted again.

When petitioner refused to fight against Ethiopia, his other homeland, the Eritrean Government incarcerated him. Prison guards punished petitioner by beating him with sticks and placing him in the hot sun. He was released after two years and forced to work as a prison guard, a duty he performed on a rotating basis for about four years. It is undisputed that the prisoners he guarded were being persecuted on account of a protected ground—*i.e.,* "race, religion, nationality, membership in a particular social group, or political opinion." 8 U.S.C. § 1101(a)(42). Petitioner testified that he carried a gun, guarded the gate to prevent escape, and kept prisoners from taking showers and obtaining fresh air. He also guarded prisoners to make sure they stayed in the sun, which he knew was a form of punishment. He saw at least one man die after being in the sun for more than two hours. Petitioner testified that he had not shot at or directly punished any prisoner and that he helped prisoners on various occasions. Petitioner escaped from the prison and hid in a container, which was loaded on board a ship heading to the United States. Once here he applied for asylum and withholding of removal.

In a careful opinion the Immigration Judge, W. Wayne Stogner, found that petitioner's testimony, for the most part, was credible. He concluded that petitioner assisted in persecution by working as an armed guard. The judge determined that although "there's no evidence to establish that [petitioner] is a malicious person or that he was an aggressive person who mistreated the prisoners, ... the very fact that he helped [the government] in the prison compound where he had reason to know that they were persecuted constitutes assisting in the persecution of others and bars [petitioner] from" obtaining asylum or withholding of removal. App. to Pet. for Cert. 16a–17a (citing, *inter alia, Fedorenko, supra*). The judge, however, granted deferral of removal under CAT [Convention Against Torture] because petitioner was likely to be tortured if returned to Eritrea.

The BIA affirmed the denial of asylum and withholding. It noted petitioner's role as an armed guard in a facility where "prisoners were tortured and left to die out in the sun ... on account of a protected ground." App. to Pet. for Cert. 6a. The BIA held that "[t]he fact that [petitioner] was compelled to participate as a prison guard, and may not have actively tortured or mistreated anyone, is immaterial." *Ibid.* That is because "'an alien's motivation and intent are irrelevant to the issue of whether he "assisted" in persecution ... [I]t is the objective effect of an alien's actions which is controlling.'" *Ibid.*

(quoting *Matter of Fedorenko,* 19 I. & N. Dec. 57, 69 (BIA 1984)). The BIA also affirmed the grant of deferral of removal under CAT.

On petition for review the Court of Appeals agreed with the BIA that whether an alien is compelled to assist in persecution is immaterial for persecutor-bar purposes. App. to Pet. for Cert. 2a (citing *Fedorenko,* 449 U.S., at 512, n. 34, 101 S.Ct. 737, 66 L. Ed. 2d 686). We granted certiorari. 552 U.S. ___, 128 S.Ct. 1695, 170 L.Ed.2d 352 (2008).

* * *

B

The parties disagree over whether coercion or duress is relevant in determining if an alien assisted or otherwise participated in persecution. As there is substance to both contentions, we conclude that the statute has an ambiguity that the agency should address[this] in the first instance.

Petitioner argues that the statute's plain language makes clear that involuntary acts do not implicate the persecutor bar because "'persecution'" presumes moral blameworthiness. Brief for Petitioner 23–28. He invokes principles of criminal culpability, concepts of international law, and the rule of lenity. *Id.,* at 28–45. Those arguments may be persuasive in determining whether a particular agency interpretation is reasonable, but they do not demonstrate that the statute is unambiguous....

The Government, on the other hand, asserts that the statute does not allow petitioner's construction. "The statutory text," the Government says, "directly answers that question: there is no exception" for conduct that is coerced because Congress did not include one. Brief for Respondent 11. We disagree. The silence is not conclusive. The question is whether the statutory text mandates that coerced actions must be deemed assistance in persecution. On that point the statute, in its precise terms, is not explicit. Nor is this a case where it is clear that Congress had an intention on the precise question at issue. Cf. *Cardoza-Fonseca, supra,* at 448–449, 107 S.Ct. 1207, 94 L. Ed. 2d 434.

* * *

The persecutor bar in this case, by contrast, was enacted as part of the Refugee Act of 1980. Unlike the DPA, which was enacted to address not just the post war refugee problem but also the Holocaust and its horror, the Refugee Act was designed to provide a general rule for the ongoing treatment of all refugees and displaced persons. As this Court has twice recognized, "'one of Congress' primary purposes' in passing the Refugee Act was to implement the principles agreed to in the 1967 United Nations Protocol Relating to the Status of Refugees, Jan. 31, 1967, 19 U.S.T. 6224, T.I.A.S. 6577 (1968)," as well as the "United Nations Convention Relating to the Status of Refugees, 189 U.N.T.S. 150 (July 28, 1951), reprinted in 19 U.S.T. 6259." *Aguirre-Aguirre,* 526 U.S., at 427, 119 S.Ct. 1439, 143 L. Ed. 2d 590 (quoting *Cardoza-Fonseca,* 480 U.S., at 436–437, 107 S.Ct. 1207, 94 L. Ed. 2d 434).

These authorities illustrate why *Fedorenko,* which addressed a different statute enacted for a different purpose, does not control the BIA's interpretation of this persecutor bar. Whatever weight or relevance these various authorities may have in interpreting the statute should be considered by the agency in the first instance, and by any subsequent reviewing court, after our remand.

* * *

Our reading of these decisions confirms that the BIA has not exercised its interpretive authority but, instead, has determined that *Fedorenko* controls. This mistaken assumption stems from a failure to recognize the inapplicability of the principle of statutory construction invoked in *Fedorenko,* as well as a failure to appreciate the differences in statutory purpose. The BIA is not bound to apply the *Fedorenko* rule that motive and intent are irrelevant to the persecutor bar at issue in this case. Whether the statute permits such an interpretation based on a different course of reasoning must be determined in the first instance by the agency.

III

Having concluded that the BIA has not yet exercised its *Chevron* discretion to interpret the statute in question, "'"the proper course, except in rare circumstances, is to remand to the agency for additional investigation or explanation."'" *Gonzales v. Thomas,* 547 U.S. 183, 186, 126 S.Ct. 1613, 164 L.Ed.2d 358 (2006) *(per curiam)* (quoting *Ventura,* 537 U.S., at 16, 123 S.Ct. 353, 154 L. Ed. 2d 272, in turn quoting *Florida Power & Light Co. v. Lorion,* 470 U.S. 729, 744, 105 S.Ct. 1598, 84 L.Ed.2d 643 (1985)). This remand rule exists, in part, because "ambiguities in statutes within an agency's jurisdiction to administer are delegations of authority to the agency to fill the statutory gap in reasonable fashion. Filling these gaps ... involves difficult policy choices that agencies are better equipped to make than courts." *Nat'l Cable & Telecomms. Ass'n v. Brand X Internet Services,* 545 U.S. 967, 980, 125 S.Ct. 2688, 162 L.Ed.2d 820 (2005).

JUSTICE STEVENS would have the Court provide a definite answer to the question presented and then remand for further proceedings. That approach, however, is in tension with the "ordinary 'remand' rule."

* * *

As the Court said in *Ventura* and reiterated in *Thomas,* "'[t]he agency can bring its expertise to bear upon the matter; it can evaluate the evidence; it can make an initial determination; and, in doing so, it can, through informed discussion and analysis, help a court later determine whether its decision exceeds the leeway that the law provides.'" 547 U.S., at 186–187, 126 S.Ct. 1613, 164 L. Ed. 2d 358 (quoting *Ventura, supra,* at 17, 123 S.Ct. 353, 154 L. Ed. 2d 272). If the BIA decides to adopt a standard that considers voluntariness to some degree, it may be prudent and necessary for the Immigration Judge to conduct additional factfinding based on the new standard. Those determinations are for the agency to make in the first instance.

* * *

We reverse the judgment of the Court of Appeals and remand the case for further proceedings consistent with this opinion.

It is so ordered.

Justice SCALIA, with whom Justice ALITO joins, concurring.

I agree with the Court that "the statute has an ambiguity," *ante,* at 5, with respect to whether an alien who was coerced to assist in persecution is barred from obtaining asylum in the United States. I agree that the agency is entitled to answer that question. *Ibid.* See *Chevron U.S.A. Inc. v. NRDC.,* 467 U.S. 837, 843, 104 S.Ct. 2778, 81 L.Ed.2d 694 (1984). And I agree that a remand is in order, to give the agency an opportunity to clarify whether its affirmative answer was premised on an erroneous view that this Court's decision in *Fedorenko v. United States,* 449 U.S. 490, 101 S.Ct. 737, 66 L.Ed.2d 686 (1981), compelled it. *Ante,* at 11.

I would not agree to remand if I did not think that the agency has the option of adhering to its decision. The majority appears to leave that question undecided, *ante,* at 5 (reserving whether "a particular agency interpretation is reasonable"); two Justices forthrightly disagree and would require the agency to recognize at least some sort of duress exception, *post,* at 7 (STEVENS, J., concurring in part and dissenting in part).

But good reasons for the agency's current practice exist—reasons adequate to satisfy the requirement that an agency act reasonably in choosing among various possible constructions of an ambiguous statute. The statute does not mandate the rule precluding the duress defense but does not foreclose it either; the agency is free to retain that rule so long as the choice to do so is soundly reasoned, not based on irrelevant or arbitrary factors (like the *Fedorenko* precedent).

Justice STEVENS, with whom Justice BREYER joins, concurring in part and dissenting in part.

The narrow question of statutory construction presented by this case is whether the so-called "persecutor bar," 8 U.S.C. §§1101(a)(42), 1158(b)(2)(A)(i), 1231(b)(3)(B), disqualifies from asylum or withholding of removal an alien whose conduct was coerced or otherwise the product of duress. If the answer to that threshold question is "no," courts should defer to the Attorney General's evaluation of particular circumstances that may or may not establish duress or coercion in individual cases. But the threshold question the Court addresses today is a "pure question of statutory construction for the courts to decide." *INS v. Cardoza-Fonseca,* 480 U.S. 421, 446, 107 S.Ct. 1207, 94 L.Ed.2d 434 (1987). For that reason, while I agree with the Court's cogent explanation of why its misguided decision in *Fedorenko v. United States,* 449 U.S. 490, 101 S.Ct. 737, 66 L.Ed.2d 686 (1981), does not govern our interpretation of the persecutor bar, I would provide a definite answer to the question presented and then remand for further proceedings.

* * *

III

The threshold question the Court addresses today is the kind of "pure question of statutory construction for the courts to decide" that we answered in *Cardoza-Fonseca, id.,* at 446, 107 S.Ct. 1207, 94 L. Ed. 2d 434, rather than a fact-intensive question of the kind we addressed in *Aguirre-Aguirre.* Just as we decided the narrow legal question presented in *Cardoza-Fonseca* but did not "attempt to set forth a detailed description of how the 'well-founded fear' test should be applied," 480 U.S., at 448, 107 S.Ct. 1207, 94 L. Ed. 2d 434, I would decide the narrow legal question now before us and remand for the agency to determine how the persecutor bar applies in individual cases

* * *

For reasons similar to those set forth in my dissent in *Fedorenko,* I think it plain that the persecutor bar does not disqualify from asylum or withholding of removal an alien whose conduct was coerced or otherwise the product of duress. Although I agree in full with the Court's conclusion that the majority opinion in *Fedorenko* does not govern our interpretation of the persecutor bar, the differences the Court highlights between the Displaced Persons Act of 1948 (DPA), 62 Stat. 1009, and the Refugee Act of 1980, 94 Stat. 102, only strengthen my conclusion that *voluntary* assistance in persecution is required and that duress and coercion vitiate voluntariness.

The *Fedorenko* Court's construction of the DPA threatened to exclude from the United States concentration camp prisoners who were forced to assist the Nazis in the persecution of other prisoners. In my view, this construction was insupportable—the DPA's exclusion of persons who "assisted the enemy in persecuting civil populations," Constitution of the International Refugee Organization, Annex I, Part II, §2 *(a),* 62 Stat. 3051, did not extend to concentration camp prisoners who did so involuntarily. These prisoners were victims, not persecutors.

Without an exception for involuntary action, the Refugee Act's bar would similarly treat entire classes of victims as persecutors. The Act does not support such a reading. The language of the persecutor bar is most naturally read to denote culpable conduct, and this reading is powerfully supported by the statutory context and legislative history.

* * *

The Convention excludes from the *nonrefoulement* obligation of Article 33 persons who have "committed a crime against peace, a war crime, or a crime against humanity." Convention, Art. 1(F) *(a),* 19 U.S. T., at 6263. It is this exception that the persecutor bar reflects. See, *e.g.,* H.R.Rep. No. 96-608, at 18 (persecutor bar encompasses "exceptions … provided in the Convention relating to aliens who have themselves participated in persecution"); H.R. Conf. Rep. No. 96-781, p. 20 (1980). The language of the Convention's exception is critical: We do not normally convict individuals of *crimes* when their actions are coerced or otherwise involuntary. Indeed, the United Nations Handbook, to which the Court has looked for guidance in the past, states that all relevant factors, including "mitigating circumstances," must be considered in determining whether an alien's acts are of a "criminal nature" as contemplated by Article 1(F). Office of the United Nations High Commissioner for Refugees, Handbook on Procedures and Criteria for Determining Refugee Status 157, 162 (reedited Jan. 1992). Other states parties to the Convention and Protocol likewise read the Convention's exception as limited to culpable conduct. When we interpret treaties, we consider the interpretations of the courts of other nations, and we should do the same when Congress asks us to interpret a statute in light of a treaty's language. See *Zicherman v. Korean Air Lines Co.,* 516 U.S. 217, 226–228, 116 S.Ct. 629, 133 L.Ed.2d 596 (1996). Congress' effort to conform United States law to the standard set forth in the U.N. Convention and Protocol shows that it intended the persecutor bar to apply only to culpable, voluntary acts—and it underscores that Congress did not delegate the question presented by this case to the agency.

* * *

While I would hold that the persecutor bar does not automatically disqualify from asylum or withholding of removal an alien who acted involuntarily, I would leave for the Attorney General—and, through his own delegation, the BIA—the question how the voluntariness standard should be applied. The agency would retain the ability, for instance, to define duress and coercion; to determine whether or not a balancing test should be employed; and, of course, to decide whether any individual asylum-seeker's acts were covered by the persecutor bar. Those are the sorts of questions suited to the agency's unique competencies in administering the INA. The threshold question before the Court is not.

* * *

Justice THOMAS, dissenting.

The "persecutor bar" in the Immigration and Nationality Act (INA) denies asylum and the withholding of removal to any alien who has "ordered, incited, assisted, or otherwise participated in the persecution of any person on account of race, religion, nationality, membership in a particular social group, or political opinion." 8 U.S.C. §§1101(a)(42), 1158(b)(2)(A), 1231(b)(3)(B)(i). The Board of Immigration Appeals

(BIA), principally relying on this Court's decision in *Fedorenko v. United States,* 449 U.S. 490, 101 S.Ct. 737, 66 L.Ed.2d 686 (1981), held that the statute does not require that the persecution be voluntarily inflicted. The Court of Appeals for the Fifth Circuit affirmed.

* * *

In sum, the INA's persecutor bar does not require that assistance or participation in persecution be voluntary or uncoerced to fall within the statute's reach. It instead "mandates precisely" what it says: "[A]n individual's service as a [prison] camp armed guard—whether voluntary or involuntary—ma[kes] him ineligible for" asylum or withholding of removal if the guard's service involved assistance or participation in the persecution of another person on account of a protected ground. *Fedorenko, supra,* at 512, 101 S.Ct. 737. Here, it is undisputed that petitioner served at a prison camp where guards persecuted prisoners because of their religious beliefs. See *ante,* at 2–3 (majority opinion). It also is undisputed that petitioner carried out the persecution by preventing prisoners from escaping and by standing guard while at least one prisoner died from sun exposure. *Ibid.* Petitioner, therefore, "assisted, or otherwise participated" in persecution and thus is statutorily disqualified from receiving asylum or withholding of removal under the INA.

IV

Because I conclude that the INA's persecutor bar applies whether or not petitioner's assistance or participation in persecution was voluntary, and because it is conceded that petitioner assisted and participated in persecution while serving as an armed prison guard in Eritrea, I would affirm the decision of the Court of Appeals. Accordingly, I respectfully dissent

QUESTIONS

1. Would you grant asylum to someone who had persecuted others if the persecutor had been forced to carry out the persecution?
2. Note how the U.S. statute (the Refugee Act) mirrors the language of the Refugee Protocol and Convention.
3. Should national courts look at decisions of foreign courts when deciding how to interpret a treaty?

(**Note:** Compare the above case with *The Prosecutor v. Dražen Erdemovic,* pp. 426–441).

Suggested Further Readings

Ian Browlie, Principles of Public International Law, chapter 35 (7th ed. 2008).

Thomas Buergenthal, Dinah Shelton & David Stewart, International Human Rights in a Nutshell (3d ed. 2002).

Hurst Hannum, Guide to International Human Rights Practice (4th ed. 2004).

D.J. Harris, Cases and Materials on International Law, chapter 9 (6th ed. 2004).

Sean D. Murphy, Principles of International Law, chapter 10 (2006).

Malcolm N. Shaw, International Law, chapters 6 & 7 (6th ed. 2008).

Henry J. Steiner, Philip Alston & Ryan Goodman, International Human Rights in Context (3d ed. 2008).

Rebecca M. M. Wallace, International Law, chapter 9 (5th ed. 2005).

Chapter IX

The Peaceful Settlement of Disputes: Arbitration and International Courts

The Obligation to Settle Disputes

The United Nations Charter requires states to settle their disputes peacefully. Article 33 states:

1. The parties to any dispute, the continuance of which is likely to endanger the maintenance of international peace and security, shall, first of all, seek a solution by negotiation, enquiry, mediation, conciliation, arbitration, judicial settlement, resort to regional agencies or arrangements, or other peaceful means of their own choice.
2. The Security Council shall, when it deems necessary, call upon the parties to settle their disputes by such means.

On the whole states prefer to settle disputes themselves by direct negotiations without the interference of third parties. Negotiations may be undertaken by ministers or their deputies from the states involved or they may be undertaken by the country's respective ambassadors or special envoys.

Other informal methods of dispute settlement, usually involving a third party, are called: *good offices*, where a third party facilitates the negotiations between the parties; *mediation*, where an intermediary operates between the parties to settle the dispute; *conciliation*, where an outside party will study the dispute and may propose a settlement; *commissions of inquiry*, where a commission seeks to establish the factual basis of the dispute and may suggest a framework for settlement.

Arbitration

Arbitration is a more formal, quasi-judicial method of settling disputes and one that has found increasing favor in the international community in recent years. The International Law Commission has defined it as: "a procedure for the settlement of disputes between States by a binding award on the basis of law and as a result of an undertaking voluntarily accepted."[1] In the typical arbitration, the parties will work out an agreement on the structure of the arbitral panel or tribunal, the appointment of the members of the panel, the substantive and procedural law to be applied and the particular dispute,

1. II Y. B. Int'l L. Comm'n 202 (1953).

or group of disputes, to be settled by the arbitral tribunal. In many ways the parties create their own "court" for the settlement of the dispute. You may well ask why the parties do not use an existing court rather than go to the trouble of creating one themselves. The answer lies partly in the lack of any international courts until the twentieth century and their limited jurisdiction and partly in the amount of control that the parties can exercise over the structure and proceedings of an arbitral tribunal. One or more of the parties may not like the substantive or procedural law of existing courts or they may think that the judges would be prejudiced against them, or they may think that the court procedure takes too long or is too expensive. Arbitration generally affords the parties a great deal more flexibility than existing courts. The parties are not obliged to accept any particular procedure, or judge and they can work out the framework for the tribunal to their mutual satisfaction.

Arbitration has a long history but in the modern era the practice has been for states to enter into agreements setting out the specific conditions for the establishment of the arbitral tribunal. Often each state involved in a dispute will be given the right to appoint an arbitrator, and a neutral person or entity, such as the Secretary-General of the United Nations, will also appoint an arbitrator. In the arbitral agreement the parties to the dispute will agree to abide by the arbitrators' decision. Arbitration agreements may relate to a particular dispute such as a territorial dispute[2] or they may relate to a variety of claims arising out of an international dispute.[3]

The Permanent Court of Arbitration was established in 1900 pursuant to the 1899 Hague Convention for the Pacific Settlement of International Disputes.[4] This agreement essentially allows parties to the Convention to nominate up to four arbitrators from which a list of arbitrators is created. The disputants can select judges from the list. The machinery of the "Court" only goes into operation if an arbitral panel is requested. Although the "Court" was relatively active in its early years, it then became relatively quiescent probably because there were many more avenues for the settlement of disputes available, such as the International Court of Arbitration of the International Chamber of Commerce in Paris, France. In recent years, the Court has experienced a resurgence in its use. There are currently eleven pending cases. The United Nations Commission on International Trade has developed the UNCITRAL Arbitration Rules which are widely used in international arbitration. The rapid growth of international trade and finance has necessitated the creation of dispute settlement mechanisms. The 1965 Convention on the Settlement of Investment Disputes[5] between States and Nationals of Other States established the International Center for the Settlement of Investment Disputes in Washington, D.C. The American Arbitration Association (AAA) facilitates arbitrations and has also developed its own set of rules.

2. See e.g., *The Clipperton Island Case* (France v. Mexico) reprinted at 26 Amer. J. Int'l L. 390 (1932).

3. E.g., the Iran-U.S. Claims Tribunal was given authority to hear claims by United States citizens and corporations against Iran and claims by Iranian citizens and corporations against the U.S. as well as inter-state claims. The Tribunal was set up under the Declaration of Algeria, reprinted at 20 I.L.M. 223 ff. (1981).

4. 32 Stat. 1799, T.S. 410, 2 Malloy 2016, revised by the Convention of 1907, 36 Stat. 2199, T.S. 536, 2 Malloy 2220.

5. 575 U.N.T.S. 159, reprinted at 4 I.L.M. 532 (1965).

International Courts

The Permanent Court of International Justice

The Permanent Court was set up under the League of Nations Covenant in 1920 and functioned until the League collapsed in 1946. It operated under a Statute annexed to the Covenant and decided a number of important cases. When the United Nations was established in 1945, the International Court of Justice was established under the United Nations Charter.

The International Court of Justice

The framework of the Court is set out in the United Nations Charter, articles 92–96. The Court is "the principal judicial organ of the United Nations." (Article 92). It functions in accordance with a Statute which is annexed to the U.N. Charter which is said to form "an integral part of the ... Charter." (Article 92). All members of the United Nations are parties to the Court's statute (Article 93(1)) but this *does not* mean that the Court has jurisdiction over all members of the U.N. What it means is that all members of the U.N. are free to submit to the jurisdiction of the Court for the settlement of their international disputes. Under article 94 of the Charter every member of the U.N. "undertakes to comply with the decision of the International Court of Justice in any case to which it is a party." (Article 94(1)). If a state fails to comply with the Court's judgment against it, the other party before the Court "may have recourse to the Security Council, which may, if it deems necessary, make recommendations or decide upon measures to be taken to give effect to the judgment." (Article 94(2)). Although there have been several cases where the losing party has failed to comply with the Court's judgment, the enforcement procedure outlined in article 94 has only been invoked once. Nicaragua went to the Security Council and sought enforcement of the judgment rendered in its favor against the United States in *Military and Paramilitary Activities in and Against Nicaragua*.[6] The United states vetoed the proposed resolution which called for "immediate compliance" with the Court's judgment.[7] Article 95 of the Charter makes it clear that states are free to submit their disputes to any tribunal for settlement and that the International Court of Justice is simply one mechanism available for international legal dispute settlement. Article 96 vests the Court with advisory jurisdiction under which the Court is empowered to issue an advisory opinion when so requested by the General Assembly or Security Council or other duly authorized United Nations organ or agency.

The Composition of the Court

The rules governing the Court are set out in the Statute of the International Court of Justice which is an integral part of the United Nations Charter. There are fifteen judges on the International Court of Justice. Five judges are elected every three years and each judge holds office for nine years and may be re-elected. Judges are nominated by national

6. 1986 I.C.J. 14.
7. U.N. SCOR, 41st Sess., 2718th mtg. at 51, U.N. Doc. S/PV. 2718 (1986).

groups and must receive an absolute majority vote in both the Security Council and the General Assembly. No country is ever permitted to have more than one judge of its nationality on the Court. Generally all the permanent members of the Security Council (China, France, Russia, United Kingdom and United States) have a judge on the Court and the rest of the judges are distributed throughout the various regions of the world.

The Court began sitting in 1946 and has since decided over eighty contentious cases and has issued more than twenty advisory opinions. The disputes resolved have covered a large range of topics such as territorial and border disputes, maritime and continental shelf delimitation, fishing rights, the use of force and intervention, diplomatic relations, hostage taking, rights of asylum and questions of nationality.

The Court has two official languages (French and English) and is located at The Peace Palace at the Hague in The Netherlands. It generally sits as a full Court but under the Rules of the Court it may also establish a special chamber. The chamber procedure was first used in the *Gulf of Maine Area Case* (Canada v. U.S.), 1984 I.C.J. 246, and has been used in five subsequent cases.[8] Article 38 of the Court's statute requires it to apply treaties and conventions recognized by the states appearing before the Court, international custom, the general principles of law and, as subsidiary means, judicial decisions and the teachings of the most highly qualified publicists of the various nations.

The Jurisdiction of the International Court of Justice in Contentious Cases

When one state brings a case against another state in the Court those cases are said to be within the Court's contentious jurisdiction. In other words the Court is asked to resolve a specific dispute between the states involved. Before a state can become a party before the International Court of Justice it must first submit to the Court's jurisdiction. This makes the Court a very different institution from most other courts. In national courts a defendant or respondent cannot choose whether they wish to be there or not. Statutes will spell out the scope of the particular court's jurisdiction and if a party falls under the court's jurisdiction in a case before the court it will do no good for that party to announce that it does not consent to the court's jurisdiction.

How does a state give its consent to the Court's jurisdiction? There are a number of different ways by which a state can express its consent to the Court's jurisdiction which are explained in the Court's Statute. Article 36 of the Statute reads:

> 1. The jurisdiction of the Court comprises all cases which the parties refer to it and all matters specially provided for in the Charter of the United Nations or in treaties and conventions in force.

"[A]ll cases which the parties refer to it (i.e. the Court)...."

Disputing states may decide that they would like the Court to settle the issues giving rise to the dispute. They will then draw up an agreement between them that spells out the precise nature of the dispute, stating that the states involved agree to litigate the issues before the Court for its determination. The special agreement (sometimes called by

8. *Frontier Dispute* (Burkina Faso v. Mali), 1986 I.C.J. 554; *Land, Island and Maritime Frontier Dispute* (El Salvador v. Honduras), and *Application for Revision of the Judgement in El Salvador/Honduras* (Nicaragua intervening), 2003 I.C.J. 392, 1992 I.C.J. 351; *ELSI Case* (U.S. v. Italy), 1989 I.C.J. 15. *Frontier Dispute* (Benin v. Niger), 2005 I.C.J. 90. See generally, Stephen Schwebel, Ad Hoc Chambers of the International Court of Justice, 81 Amer. J. Int'l L. 831 (1987).

its French name of "*compromis*") gives the Court jurisdiction over the parties to the dispute and also defines the scope of the issues to be settled. The Court is not free to explore other areas touching upon the dispute. It may only decide the particular questions presented to it in the special agreement. An example of this type of agreement can be found in the special agreement entered into between the United States and Canada when both states asked the Court to settle the boundaries of the continental shelves and exclusive fishing zones between them in the Gulf of Maine.[9]

"[A]ll matters specially referred to in the Charter of the United Nations. . . ."

In fact there are no matters specially referred to in the Charter which confer jurisdiction on the Court. Why then does article 36 of the Statute refer to such "matters"? The late Professor Michael Akehurst unravelled the confusion for us:

> "The explanation of this paradox is that Article 36(1) of the Statute of the Court was drafted at a time when it looked as if the Charter would provide for compulsory jurisdiction [i.e., states would be required to submit their international disputes to the Court for settlement]; the San Francisco Conference [where the U.N. Charter was drafted] subsequently rejected proposals to provide for compulsory jurisdiction in the Charter, but forgot to delete the cross-reference in the Statute."[10]

"[A]ll matters . . . in treaties and conventions in force."

A good number of treaties currently in force include a provision which states that parties to the treaty agree that, with respect to disputes arising under the treaty, any party to the treaty may bring the dispute to the Court against any other party to the treaty. For example, Article IX of the Convention on the Prevention and Punishment of the Crime of Genocide[11] states:

> Disputes between the Contracting Parties relating to the interpretation, application or fulfilment of the present Convention, including those relating to the responsibility of a State for genocide or any of the other acts enumerated in Article III, shall be submitted to the International Court of Justice at the request of any of the parties to the dispute.

When the Court acquires jurisdiction through the operation of a clause in a treaty it is only empowered to decide issues arising under that treaty. It is not free to decide other issues even though they may be closely related to the treaty issue.[12]

Compulsory Jurisdiction: The Optional Clause

Article 36, paragraphs two through four, of the Court's Statute explain yet another method by which states can submit to the jurisdiction of the Court:

> 2. The parties to the present Statute may at any time declare that they recognize as compulsory *ipso facto* and without special agreement in relation to any other state accepting the same obligation, the jurisdiction of the Court in all legal disputes. . . .

9. *Gulf of Maine Area* (Canada v. United States), 1984 I.C.J. 246.

10. Peter Malanczuk, Akehurst's Modern Introduction to International Law 283 (7th rev. ed. 1997).

11. 78 U.N.T.S. 277, adopted by the G.A. on 9 Dec. 1948, entered into force, 12 Jan. 1951.

12. See, e.g., *Application of the Convention on the Prevention and Punishment of the Crime of Genocide* (Bosnia and Herzegovina v. Yugoslavia (Serbia and Montenegro)) 1993 I.C.J. 3 at 18, para. 35 (request for the indication of provisional measures) & 1993 I.C.J. 325 at 341, para. 36 (further requests for the indication of provisional measures), and 2007 I.C.J. ___ (merits).

3. The declaration referred to above may be made unconditionally or on condition of reciprocity on the part of several or certain states, or for a certain time.

4. Such declarations shall be deposited with the Secretary-General of the United Nations, who shall transmit copies thereof to the parties to the Statute and to the Registrar of the Court.

This means that states can deposit a declaration with the Secretary-General that they accept the Court's jurisdiction for the settlement of international legal disputes they may have with other states that have also accepted the Court's jurisdiction. This type of jurisdiction is often called "compulsory" jurisdiction but you should note that state's are completely free to decide whether they will accept such jurisdiction.

Here are some examples of states' declarations of acceptance of the Court's compulsory jurisdiction:

SWEDEN[13]

[Translation from the French] 6 IV 57.

On behalf of the Royal Swedish Government, I declare that it accepts as compulsory *ipso facto* and without special agreement, in relation to any other State accepting the same obligation, the jurisdiction of the International Court of Justice, in accordance with Article 36, paragraph 2, of the Statute of the said Court, for a period of five years as from 6 April 1957. This obligation shall be renewed by tacit agreement for further periods of the same duration unless notice of abrogation is made at least six months before the expiration of any such period. The above-mentioned obligation is accepted only in respect of disputes which may arise with regard to situations or facts subsequent to 6 April 1947.

New York, 6 April 1957.

(Signed) Claes Carbonnier, Permanent Representative *a. i.* of Sweden to the United Nations.

(Sweden had previously made a declaration on 5 April 1947 which had been made for a period of ten years.)

UNITED STATES OF AMERICA[14]

26 VIII 46.

I, Harry S. Truman, President of the United States of America, declare on behalf of the United States of America, under Article 36, paragraph 2, of the Statute of the International Court of Justice, and in accordance with the Resolution of 2 August 1946 of the Senate of the United States of America (two-thirds of the Senators present concurring therein), that the United States of America recognizes as compulsory *ipso facto* and without special agreement, in relation to any other State accepting the same obligation, the jurisdiction of the International Court of Justice in all legal disputes hereafter arising concerning—

(a) the interpretation of a treaty;
(b) any question of international law;
(c) the existence of any fact which, if established, would constitute a breach of an international obligation;

13. See 1992–93 Y.B.I.C.J. 109. Currently, sixty-six states have accepted the Court's compulsory jurisdiction although many have included limitations in the scope of their acceptance.

14. See 1983–84 Y.B.I.C.J. 90–91.

(d) the nature or extent of the reparation to be made for the breach of an international obligation;

Provided, that this declaration shall not apply to—

(a) disputes the solution of which the parties shall entrust to other tribunals by virtue of agreements already in existence or which may be concluded in the future; or

(b) disputes with regard to matters which are essentially within the domestic jurisdiction of the United States of America as determined by the United States of America; or

(c) disputes arising under a multilateral treaty, unless (1) all parties to the treaty affected by the decision are also parties to the case before the Court, or (2) the United States of America specially agrees to jurisdiction; and

Provided further, that this declaration shall remain in force for a period of five years and thereafter until the expiration of six months after notice may be given to terminate this declaration.

(*Signed*) Harry S. Truman

Done at Washington this fourteenth day of August 1946.

Note

On April 6, 1984 the United States attempted a partial withdrawal from the Court's compulsory jurisdiction[15] discussed in the *Nicaragua Case* pp. 370–379. On October 7, 1985, in the wake of the International Court of Justice's decision in the *Nicaragua Case*, President Ronald Reagan terminated the United States acceptance of compulsory jurisdiction to be effective six months later. Some internationalist in the U.S. are hoping that President Obama will reinstate the U.S. acceptance of the Court's compulsory jurisdiction.

Notice that states only accept the Court's jurisdiction under such declarations "in relation to any other state accepting the same obligation." That clause ensures that states that *have not accepted* the Court's compulsory jurisdiction cannot use such a declaration to sue states that *have accepted* the compulsory jurisdiction. A state that has not accepted the Court's compulsory jurisdiction is not a "state accepting the same obligation" in relation to a state that has accepted the Court's compulsory jurisdiction. This notion of reciprocity can also work against a state that has accepted the Court's compulsory jurisdiction but has appended various exceptions to its acceptance as the *Norwegian Loans Case*[16] demonstrates.

Norwegian Loans Case

International Court of Justice
France v. Norway, 1957 I.C.J. 9

Note

France sued Norway on behalf of French holders of Norwegian bonds. Norway objected to the Court's jurisdiction. France had accepted the Court's compulsory jurisdic-

15. 1984–85 Y.B.I.C.J. 100.
16. (France v. Norway), 1957 I.C.J. 9.

tion but had added the following exception: "This declaration does not apply to differences relating to matters which are essentially within the national jurisdiction as understood by the Government of the French Republic." (Such a clause is often called a self-judging, domestic affairs reservation). In other words France reserved the right to determine that any issue before the Court was not a matter subject to the Court's jurisdiction, despite the fact that article 36(6) of the Court's Statute says: "In the event of a dispute as to whether the Court has jurisdiction, the matter shall be settled by the decision of the Court." Norway had also accepted the Court's compulsory jurisdiction but had not appended a self-judging, domestic affairs reservation. Nonetheless, Norway argued that because she had only accepted the Court's jurisdiction in relation to any other state accepting the same obligation she should be able to invoke the same reservation as France.

Opinion of the Court

Convinced that the dispute which has been brought before the Court by the Application of July 6, 1955, is within the domestic jurisdiction, the Norwegian Government considers itself fully entitled to rely on this right. Accordingly, it requests the Court to decline, on grounds that it lacks jurisdiction, the function which the French Government would have it assume.

[I]n the present case the jurisdiction of the Court depends upon the Declarations made by the Parties in accordance with Article 36, paragraph 2, of the Statute on condition of reciprocity; and that, since two unilateral declarations are involved, such jurisdiction is conferred upon the Court only to the extent to which the Declarations coincide in conferring it. A comparison between the two Declarations shows that the French Declaration accepts the Court's jurisdiction within narrower limits than the Norwegian Declaration; consequently the common will of the Parties, which is the basis of the Court's jurisdiction, exists within these narrower limits indicated by the French reservation....

France has limited her acceptance of the compulsory jurisdiction of the Court by excluding beforehand disputes 'relating to matters which are essentially within the national jurisdiction as understood by the Government of the French Republic.' In accordance with the condition of reciprocity to which acceptance of the compulsory jurisdiction is made subject in both Declarations and which is provided for in Article 36, paragraph 3, of the Statute, Norway, equally with France, is entitled to except from the compulsory jurisdiction of the Court disputes understood by Norway to be essentially within its national jurisdiction....

The Court does not consider that it should examine whether the French reservation is consistent with the undertaking of a legal obligation and is compatible with Article 36, paragraph 6, of the Statute....

The validity of the reservation has not been questioned by the Parties. It is clear that France fully maintains its Declaration, including the reservation, and that Norway relies upon the reservation....

The Court considers that the Norwegian Government is entitled, by virtue of the condition of reciprocity, to invoke the reservation contained in the French Declaration of March 1, 1949; that this reservation excludes from the jurisdiction of the Court the dispute which has been referred to it by the Application of the French Government; that consequently the Court is without jurisdiction to entertain the Application....

For these reasons,

THE COURT,

by 12 votes to three, finds that it is without jurisdiction to adjudicate upon the dispute which has been brought before it by the Application of the Government of the French Republic of July 6, 1955.

INDIVIDUAL OPINION OF JUDGE LAUTERPACHT

[I] consider that as the French Declaration of Acceptance excludes from the jurisdiction of the Court, 'matters which are essentially within the national jurisdiction as understood by the Government of the French Republic'—the emphasis being here on the words 'as understood by the Government of the French Republic'—it is for the reason of that latter qualification an instrument incapable of producing legal effects before this Court and of establishing its jurisdiction. This is so for the double reason that: (a) it is contrary to the Statute of the Court; (b) the existence of the obligation being dependent upon the determination by the Government accepting the Optional Clause, the Acceptance does not constitute a legal obligation. That Declaration of Acceptance cannot, accordingly, provide a basis for the jurisdiction of the Court....

If that type of reservation is valid, then the Court is not in the position to exercise the power conferred upon it—in fact, the duty imposed upon it—under paragraph 6 of Article 36 of its Statute.... The French reservation lays down that if, with regard to that particular question, there is a dispute between the Parties as to whether the Court has jurisdiction the matter shall be settled by a decision of the French Government. The French reservation is thus not only contrary to one of the most fundamental principles of international—and national—jurisprudence according to which it is within the inherent power of a tribunal to interpret the text establishing its jurisdiction. It is also contrary to a clear specific provision of the Statute of the Court as well as to the general Articles 1 and 92 of the Statute and of the Charter, respectively, which require the Court to function in accordance with its Statute.

Now what is the result of the fact that a reservation or part of it are contrary to the provisions of the Statute of the Court? The result is that that reservation or that part of it is invalid. Some examples may usefully illustrate that aspect of the question: What would be the position if in accepting—or purporting to accept—the obligations of Article 36 of the Statute, a State were to exclude the operation of paragraph 6 of that Article not only with regard to one reservation but with regard to all reservations or, generally, with regard to any disputed question of the jurisdiction of the Court?

What would be the position if the Declaration were to make it a condition that the oral proceedings of the Court shall be secret; or that its Judgment shall not be binding unless given by unanimity; or that it should contain no reasons; or that no Dissenting Opinion shall be attached; or that Judges of certain nationality or nationalities shall be excluded; or that, contrary to what is said in Article 38 of its Statute, the Court shall apply only treaties and custom in the sense that it shall not be authorized to apply general principles of law as recognized by civilized States and that if it is unable to base its decision on treaty or custom it shall pronounce a *non liquet*? ...

In accepting the jurisdiction of the Court Governments are free to limit its jurisdiction in a drastic manner. As a result there may be little left in the Acceptance which is subject to the jurisdiction of the Court. This the Governments, as trustees of the interests entrusted to them, are fully entitled to do. Their right to append reservations which are not inconsistent with the Statute is no longer in question. But the question whether that little that is left is or is not subject to the jurisdiction of the Court must be determined by the Court itself....

I arrive at the same conclusion on the second—and different—ground, namely, that having regard to the formulation of the reservation of national jurisdiction on the part of the French Government the Acceptance embodying the 'automatic reservation' is invalid as lacking an essential condition of validity of a legal instrument. This is so for the reason that it leaves to the Party making the Declaration the right to determine the extent and the very existence of its obligation. The effect of the French reservation relating to domestic jurisdiction is that the French Government has, in this respect, undertaken an obligation to the extent to which it, and it alone, considers that it has done so. This means that it has undertaken no obligation. An instrument in which a party is entitled to determine the existence of its obligation is not a valid and enforceable legal instrument of which a court of law can take cognizance. It is not a legal instrument. It is a declaration of a political principle and purpose....

Note

Judge Lauterpacht then considered whether the invalid reservation could be severed from the rest of the French acceptance of jurisdiction so that the acceptance would remain without the domestic self-judging clause. He came to the conclusion that the clause could not be severed from the rest of the acceptance because the self-judging clause was "an essential and deliberate condition of the Acceptance."[17]

Case Concerning Military and Paramilitary Activities in and against Nicaragua Nicaragua v. United States

1984 I.C.J. 392

(Jurisdiction of the Court and Admissibility of the Application)

Note

Nicaragua complained to the Court that the United States was using military force against Nicaragua and intervening in her internal affairs. In particular, Nicaragua accused the United States of laying mines in Nicaraguan harbors and of training, arming, supplying and paying an army of "more than 10,000 mercenaries ... installed ... in ... camps in Honduras along the border with Nicaragua ... [and that the U.S. had] directed their attacks against human and economic targets inside Nicaragua." (For the decision on the merits see pp. 393–401 & 409–416).

The United States disputed the Court's jurisdiction on a number of grounds and also argued that the issues presented to the Court were inadmissible. Nicaragua had argued that she had made a declaration accepting the Permanent Court of International Justice's [P.C.I.J.] compulsory jurisdiction and that Article 36(5) of the International Court of Justice's [I.C.J.] Statute states that:

17. 1957 I. C. J. at 58. See also Vienna Convention on the Law of Treaties, art. 44, 1155 U.N.T.S. 331, signed 23 May 1969, entered into force 27 Jan. 1980, reprinted at 8 I.L.M. 679 (1969).

> Declarations made under Article 36 of the Permanent Court of International Justice and which are still in force shall be deemed, as between the parties to the present statute, to be acceptance of the compulsory jurisdiction of the International Court of Justice for the period which they still have to run and in accordance with their terms.

Nicaragua therefore contended that her acceptance of the P.C.I.J's compulsory jurisdiction is deemed an acceptance of the I.C.J.'s compulsory jurisdiction by virtue of Article 36(5) of the current Court's Statute. The United States had accepted the Court's compulsory jurisdiction in 1946 (see declaration, pp. 366–367) but the U.S. argued that the Nicaraguan acceptance of the P.C.I.J.'s jurisdiction was defective, so that Nicaragua had never accepted the Court's jurisdiction and thus could not bring a case against the U.S., because compulsory jurisdiction is only accepted "in relation to any other state accepting the same obligation...."

Some of the Court's arguments relating to jurisdiction and admissibility are excerpted below:

Opinion of the Court

11. The present case concerns a dispute between the Government of the Republic of Nicaragua and the Government of the United States of America occasioned, Nicaragua contends, by certain military and paramilitary activities conducted in Nicaragua and in the waters off its coasts, responsibility for which is attributed by Nicaragua to the United States. In the present phase the case concerns the jurisdiction of the Court to entertain and pronounce upon this dispute, and the admissibility of the Application by which it was brought before the Court. The issue being thus limited, the Court will avoid not only all expressions of opinion on matters of substance, but also any pronouncement which might prejudge or appear to prejudge any eventual decision on the merits.

12. To found the jurisdiction of the Court in the present proceedings, Nicaragua in its Application relied on Article 36 of the Statute of the Court and the declarations, described below, made by the Parties accepting compulsory jurisdiction pursuant to that Article....

13. The United States made a declaration, ... [accepting the Court's compulsory jurisdiction] on 14 August 1946, containing certain reservations, to be examined below, and expressed to

> remain in force for a period of five years and thereafter until the expiration of six months after notice may be given to terminate this declaration.

On 6 April 1984 the Government of the United States of America deposited with the Secretary-General of the United Nations a notification, signed by the Untied States Secretary of State, Mr. George Shulz, referring to the Declaration deposited on 26 August 1946, and stating that:

> the aforesaid declaration shall not apply to disputes with any Central American State or arising out of or related to events in Central America, any of which disputes shall be settled in such manner as the parties to them may agree.
>
> Notwithstanding the terms of the aforesaid declaration, this proviso shall take effect immediately and shall remain in force for two years, so as to foster the continuing regional dispute settlement process which seeks a negotiated so-

> lution to the interrelated political, economic and security problems of Central America.

This notification will be referred to, for convenience, as the "1984 notification".

14. In order to be able to rely upon the United States Declaration of 1946 to found jurisdiction in the present case, Nicaragua has to show that it is a "State accepting the same obligation" within the meaning of Article 36, paragraph 2, of the Statute. For this purpose, Nicaragua relies on a Declaration made by it on 24 September 1929 pursuant to Article 36, paragraph 2, of the Statute of the Permanent Court of International Justice.

15. The circumstances of Nicaragua's Declaration of 1929 were as follows. The Members of the League of Nations (and the States mentioned in the Annex to the League of Nations Covenant) were entitled to sign the Protocol of Signature of the Statute of the Permanent Court of International Justice, which was drawn up at Geneva on 16 December 1920. That Protocol provided that it was subject to ratification, and that instruments of ratification were to be sent to the Secretary-General of the League of Nations. On 24 September 1929, Nicaragua, as a Member of the League, signed this Protocol and made a declaration under Article 36, paragraph 2, of the Statute of the Permanent Court which read:

[Translation from the French]

> On behalf of the Republic of Nicaragua I recognize as compulsory unconditionally the jurisdiction of the Permanent Court of International Justice.
>
> Geneva, 24 September 1929.
>
> (Signed) T.F. Medina.

16. According to the documents produced by both Parties before the Court, on 4 December 1934, a proposal for the ratification of (*inter alia*) the Statute of the Permanent Court of International Justice and of the Protocol of Signature of 16 December 1920 was approved by the "Ejecutivo" (executive power) of Nicaragua. On 14 February 1935, the Senate of Nicaragua decided to ratify these instruments, its decision being published in *La Gaceta*, the Nicaraguan official journal, on 12 June 1935, and on 11 July 1935 the Chamber of Deputies of Nicaragua adopted a similar decision, similarly published on 18 September 1935. On 29 November 1939, the Ministry of External Relations of Nicaragua sent the following telegram to the Secretary-General of the League of Nations:

[*Translation*]

> (Statute and Protocol Permanent Court International Justice The Hague have already been ratified. Will send you in due course Instrument Ratification. Relations.)

The files of the League of Nations however contain no record of an instrument of ratification ever having been received. No evidence has been adduced before the Court to show that such an instrument of ratification was ever despatched to Geneva.

17. On the basis of these facts, the United States contends, first, that Nicaragua never became a party to the Statute of the Permanent Court of International Justice, and that accordingly it could not and did not make an effective acceptance of the compulsory jurisdiction of the Permanent Court; the 1929 acceptance was therefore not "still in force" within the meaning of the English version of Article 36, paragraph 5, of the Statute of the present Court.

* * *

24. In order to determine whether the provisions of Article 36, paragraph 5, can have applied to Nicaragua's Declaration of 1929, the Court must first establish the legal characteristics of that declaration and then compare them with the conditions laid down by the text of that paragraph.

* * *

26. The Court therefore notes that Nicaragua, having failed to deposit its instrument of ratification of the Protocol of Signature of the Statute of the Permanent Court, was not a party to that treaty. Consequently the Declaration made by Nicaragua in 1929 had not acquired binding force prior to such effect as Article 36, paragraph 5, of the Statute of the International Court of Justice might produce.

27. However, while the declaration had not acquired binding force, it is not disputed that it could have done so, for example at the beginning of 1945, if Nicaragua had ratified the Protocol of Signature of the Statute of the Permanent Court.... It follows that such a declaration as that made by Nicaragua had a certain potential effect which could be maintained indefinitely. This durability of potential effect flowed from a certain characteristic of Nicaragua's declaration: being made "unconditionally", it was valid for an unlimited period.... In sum, Nicaragua's 1929 Declaration was valid at the moment when Nicaragua became a party to the Statute of the new Court; it had retained its potential effect because Nicaragua, which could have limited the duration of that effect, had expressly refrained from doing so.

28. The Characteristics of Nicaragua's declaration have now to be compared with the conditions of applicability of Article 36, paragraph 5, as laid down in that provision. The first condition concerns the relationship between the declarations and the Statute.... Apart from this relationship with the Statute of the Permanent Court, the only condition which declarations have to fulfil is that they should be "still in force" (in English) or "faites pour une durée qui n'est pas encore expirée" (in French). The Parties have devoted much argument to this apparent discrepancy between the two versions, its real meaning and the interpretation which the Court should adopt as correct.

29. The Court must in the first place observe that this is the first time that it has had to take a position on the question whether a declaration which did not have binding force at the time of the Permanent Court is or is not to be numbered among those to which Article 36, paragraph 5, of the Statute of the International Court of Justice applies.

30. Having thus stressed the novelty of the problem, the Court will refer to the following considerations in order to reach a solution. First, it does not appear possible to reconcile the two versions of Article 36, paragraph 5, by considering that both versions refer to binding declarations. According to this interpretation, upheld by the United States, Article 36, paragraph 5, should be read as if it mentioned "binding" declarations. The French text, in this view would be the equivalent of the English text, for logically it would imply that declarations *dont la durée n'est pas encore expirée* are solely those which have acquired binding force. The Court, however, considers that it must interpret Article 36, paragraph 5, on the basis of the actual terms used, which do not include the word "binding" According to the *travaux préparatorires* the word "binding" was never suggested; and if it had been suggested for the English text, there is no doubt that the drafters would never have let the French text stand as finally worded. Furthermore, the Court does not consider the French text to imply that *la durée non expirée* (the unexpired period) is that of a commitment of a binding character. It may be granted that, for a period to continue or expire, it is necessary for some legal effect to have come into ex-

istence. But this effect does not necessarily have to be of a binding nature. A declaration validly made under Article 36 of the Statute of the Permanent Court had a certain validity which could be preserved or destroyed, and it is perfectly possible to read the French text as implying only this validity.

31. It is therefore the Court's opinion that the English version in no way expressly excludes a valid declaration of unexpired duration, made by a State not party to the Protocol of Signature of the Statute of the Permanent Court, and therefore not of a binding character.

* * *

36. This finding as regards the interpretation of Article 36, paragraph 5, must, finally, be compared to the conduct of States and international organizations in regard to this interpretation In that respect, particular weight must be ascribed to certain official publications, namely the *I.C.J. Yearbook* (since 1946–1947), the *Reports* of the Court to the General Assembly of the United Nations (since 1968) and the annually published collection of *Signatures, Ratifications, Acceptances, Accessions, etc., concerning the Multilateral Conventions and Agreements in respect of which the Secretary-General acts as Depositary.* The Court notes that, ever since they first appeared, all these publications have regularly placed Nicaragua on the list of those States that have recognized the compulsory jurisdiction of the Court by virtue of Article 36, paragraph 5, of the Statue. Even if the *I.C.J. Yearbook* has, in the issue for 1946–1947 and as from the issue for 1955–1956 onwards, contained a note recalling certain facts concerning Nicaragua's ratification of the Protocol of Signature of the Statue of the Permanent Court of International Justice, this publication has never modified the classification of Nicaragua or the binding character attributed to its 1929 Declaration—indeed the *Yearbooks* list Nicaragua among the States "still bound by" their declarations under Article 36 of the Statute of the Permanent Court....

* * *

52. The acceptance of jurisdiction by the United States which is relied on by Nicaragua is, as noted above, that dated 14 August 1946. The United States contends however that effect must also be given to the "1984 notification"—the declaration deposited with the Secretary-General of the United Nations on 6 April 1984. It is conceded by Nicaragua that if this declaration is effective as a modification or termination of the Declaration of 14 August 1946, and valid as against Nicaragua at the date of its filing of the Application instituting the present proceedings (9 April 1984), then the Court is without jurisdiction to entertain those proceedings, at least under Article 36, paragraphs 2 and 5, of the Statute. It is however contended by Nicaragua that the 1984 notification is ineffective because international law provides no basis for unilateral modification of declarations made under Article 36 of the Statute of the Court, unless a right to do so has been expressly reserved.

* * *

59. Declarations of acceptance of the compulsory jurisdiction of the Court are facultative, unilateral engagements, that States are absolutely free to make or not to make. In making the declaration a State is equally free either to do so unconditionally and without limit of time for its duration, or to qualify it with conditions or reservations. In particular, it may limit its effect to disputes arising after a certain date; or it may specify how long the declaration itself shall remain in force, or what notice (if any) will be required to terminate it. However, the unilateral nature of declarations does not signify that the State making the declaration is free to amend the scope and the contents of its solemn commitments as it pleases.

60. In fact, the declarations, even though they are unilateral acts, establish a series of bilateral engagements with other States accepting the same obligation of compulsory jurisdiction, in which the conditions, reservations and time-limit clauses are taken into consideration. In the establishment of this network of engagements, which constitutes the Optional-Clause system, the principle of good faith plays an important role. . . .

61. The most important question relating to the effect of the 1984 notification is whether the United States was free to disregard the clause of six months' notice which, freely and by its own choice, it had appended to its 1946 Declaration. In so doing the United States entered into an obligation which is binding upon it vis-á-vis other States parties to the Optional-Clause system. Although the United States retained the right to modify the contents of the 1946 Declaration or to terminate it, a power which is inherent in any unilateral act of a State, it has, nevertheless assumed an inescapable obligation towards other States accepting the Optional Clause, by stating formally and solemnly that any such change should take effect only after six months have elapsed as from the date of notice.

62. The United States has argued that the Nicaraguan 1929 Declaration, being of undefined duration, is liable to immediate termination, without previous notice, and that therefore Nicaragua has not accepted "the same obligation" as itself for the purposes of Article 36, paragraph 2, and consequently may not rely on the six months' notice proviso against the United States. The Court does not however consider that this argument entitles the United States validly to act in non-application of the time-limit proviso included in the 1946 Declaration. The notion of reciprocity is concerned with the scope and substance of the commitments entered into, including reservations, and not with the formal conditions of their creation, duration or extinction. It appears clearly that reciprocity cannot be invoked in order to excuse departure from the terms of a State's own declaration, whatever its scope, limitations or conditions.

63. Moreover, since the Untied States purported to act on 6 April 1984 in such a way as to modify its 1946 Declaration with sufficiently immediate effect to bar an Application filed on 9 April 1984, it would be necessary, if reciprocity is to be relied on, for the Nicaraguan Declaration to be terminable with immediate effect. But the right of immediate termination of declarations with indefinite duration is far from established. It appears from the requirements of good faith that they should be treated, by analogy, according to the law of treaties, which requires a reasonable time for withdrawal from or termination of treaties that contain no provision regarding the duration of their validity. Since Nicaragua has in fact not manifested any intention to withdraw its own declaration, the question of what reasonable period of notice would legally be required does not need to be further examined: it need only be observed that from 6 to 9 April would not amount to a "reasonable time".

* * *

65. In sum, the six months' notice clause forms an important integral part of the United States Declaration and it is a condition that must be complied with in case of either termination or modification. Consequently, the 1984 notification, in the present case, cannot override the obligation of the United States to submit to the compulsory jurisdiction of the Court vis-á-vis Nicaragua, a State accepting the same obligation.

* * *

84. The Court now turns to the question of the admissibility of the Application of Nicaragua. The United States of America contended in its Coutner-Memorial that Nicaragua's Application is inadmissible on five separate grounds, each of which, it is said, is sufficient to establish such inadmissibility, whether considered as a legal bar to adjudication or as "a matter requiring the exercise of prudential discretion in the interest of the integrity of the judicial function". Some of these grounds have in fact been presented in terms suggesting that they are matters of competence or jurisdiction rather than admissibility, but it does not appear to be of critical importance how they are classified in this respect. These grounds will now be examined; but for the sake of clarity it will first be convenient to recall briefly what are the allegations of Nicaragua upon which it bases its claims against the United States.

85. In its Application instituting proceedings, Nicaragua asserts that:

> The United States of America is using military force against Nicaragua and intervening in Nicaragua's internal affairs, in violation of Nicaragua's sovereignty, territorial integrity and political independence and of the most fundamental and universally accepted principles of international law. The United States has created an 'army' of more than 10,000 mercenaries ... installed them in more than ten base camps in Honduras along the border with Nicaragua, trained them, paid them, supplied them with arms, ammunition, food and medical supplies, and directed their attacks against human and economic targets inside Nicaragua.

86. The first ground of inadmissibility relied on by the United States is that Nicaragua has failed to bring before the Court parties whose presence and participation is necessary for the rights of those parties to be protected and for the adjudication of the issues raised in the Application.

* * *

88. There is no doubt that in appropriate circumstances the Court will decline, as it did in the case concerning *Monetary Gold Removed from Rome in 1943*, to exercise the jurisdiction conferred upon it where the legal interests of a State not party to the proceedings "would not only be affected by a decision, but would form the very subject-matter of the decision" (*I.C.J. Reports 1954*, p. 32). Where however claims of a legal nature are made by an Applicant against a Respondent in proceedings before the Court, and made the subject of submissions, the Court has in principle merely to decide upon those submissions, with binding force for the parties only, and no other State, in accordance with Article 59 of the Statute. As the Court has already indicated ... other States which consider that they may be affected are free to institute separate proceedings, or to employ the procedure of intervention. There is no trace, either in the Statute or in the practice of international tribunals, of an "indispensable parties" rule of the kind argued for by the United States, which would only be conceivable in parallel to a power, which the Court does not possess, to direct that a third State be made a party to proceedings.

89. Secondly, the United States regards the Application as inadmissible because each of Nicaragua's allegations constitutes no more than a reformulation and restatement of a single fundamental claim, that the United States is engaged in an unlawful use of armed force, or breach of the peace, or acts of aggression against Nicaragua, a matter which is committed by the Charter and by practice to the competence of other organs, in particular the United Nations Security Council. All allegations of this kind are confined to the political organs of the Organization for consideration and determination; the United States quotes Article 24 of the Charter, which confers

upon the Security Council "primary responsibility for the maintenance of international peace and security". The provisions of the Charter dealing with the ongoing use of armed force contain no recognition of the possibility of settlement by judicial, as opposed to political, means. Under Article 52 of the Charter there is also a commitment of responsibility for the maintenance of international peace and security to regional agencies and arrangements, and in the view of the United States the Contadora process is precisely the sort of regional arrangement or agency that Article 52 contemplates.

* * *

91. It will be convenient to deal with this alleged ground of inadmissibility together with the third ground advanced by the United States namely that the Court should hold the Application of Nicaragua to be inadmissible in view of the subject-matter of the Application and the position of the Court within the United Nations system, including the impact of proceedings before the Court on the ongoing exercise of the "inherent right of individual or collective self-defence" under Article 51 of the Charter. This is, it is argued, a reason why the Court may not properly exercise "subject-matter jurisdiction" over Nicaragua's claims. Under this head, the United States repeats its contention that the Nicaraguan Application requires the Court to determine that the activities complained of constitute a threat to the peace, a breach of the peace, or an act of aggression, and proceeds to demonstrate that the political organs of the United Nations, to which such matters are entrusted by the Charter, have acted, and are acting, in respect of virtually identical claims placed before them by Nicaragua.

* * *

93. The United States is thus arguing that the matter was essentially one for the Security Council since it concerned a complaint by Nicaragua involving the use of force. However, having regard to the *United States Diplomatic and Consular Staff in Tehran* case, the Court is of the view that the fact that a matter is before the Security Council should not prevent it being dealt with by the Court and that both proceedings could be pursued *pari passu*. In that case the Court held:

> In the preamble to this second resolution the Security Council expressly took into account the Court's Order of 15 December 1979 indicating provisional measures; and it does not seem to have occurred to any member of the Council that there was or could be anything irregular in the simultaneous exercise of their respective functions by the Court and the Security Council. Nor is there in this any cause for surprise. (*I.C.J. Reports 1980*, p. 21, para. 40.)

94. The United States argument is also founded on a construction, which the Court is unable to share, of Nicaragua's complaint about the United States use, or threat of the use, of force against its territorial integrity and national independence, breach of Article 2, paragraph 4, of the United Nations Charter. The United States argues that Nicaragua has thereby invoked a charge of aggression and armed conflict envisaged in Article 39 of the United Nations Charter, which can only be dealt with by the Security Council in accordance with the provisions of Chapter VII of the Charter, and not in accordance with the provisions of Chapter VI. This presentation of the matter by the United States treats the present dispute between Nicaragua and itself as a case of armed conflict which must be dealt with only by the Security Council and not by the Court which, under Article 2, paragraph 4, and Chapter VI of the Charter, deals with pacific settlement of all disputes between member States of the United Nations. But, if so, it has

to be noted that, while the matter has been discussed in the Security Council, no notification has been given to it in accordance with Chapter VII of the Charter, so that the issue could be tabled for full discussion before a decision were taken for the necessary enforcement measures to be authorized. It is clear that the complaint of Nicaragua is not about an ongoing armed conflict between it and the United States, but one requiring, and indeed demanding, the peaceful settlement of disputes between the two States. Hence, it is properly brought before the principal judicial organ of the Organization for peaceful settlement.

* * *

99. The fourth ground of inadmissibility put forward by the United state is that the Application should be held inadmissible in consideration of the inability of the judicial function to deal with situations involving ongoing conflict. The allegation, attributed by the United States to Nicaragua, of an ongoing conflict involving the use of armed force contrary to the Charter is said to be central to, and inseparable from, the Application as a whole, and is one with which a court cannot deal effectively without overstepping proper judicial bounds. The resort to force during ongoing armed conflict lacks the attributes necessary for the application of the judicial process, namely a pattern of legally relevant facts discernible by the means available to the adjudicating tribunal, establishable in conformity with applicable norms of evidence and proof, and not subject to further material evolution during the course of, or subsequent to, the judicial proceedings. It is for reasons of this nature that ongoing armed conflict must be entrusted to resolution by political processes.

* * *

101. The Court is bound to observe that any judgment on the merits in the present case will be limited to upholding such submissions of the Parties as have been supported by sufficient proof of relevant facts, and are regarded by the Court as sound in law. A situation of armed conflict is not the only one in which evidence of fact may be difficult to come by, and the Court has in the past recognized and made allowance for this (*Corfu Channel, I.C.J. Reports 1949,* p. 18; *United States Diplomatic and Consular Staff in Tehran, I.C.J. Reports 1980*, p. 10, para. 13). Ultimately, however, it is the litigant seeking to establish a fact who bears the burden of proving it; and in cases where evidence may not be forthcoming, a submission may in the judgment be rejected as unproved, but is not be ruled out as inadmissible *in limine* on the basis of an anticipated lack of proof.

102. The fifth and final contention of the United States under this head is that the Application should be held inadmissible because Nicaragua has failed to exhaust the established processes for the resolution of the conflicts occurring in Central America. In the contention of the United States, the Contadora process, to which Nicaragua is party, is recognized both by the political organs of the United Nations and by the Organization of American States, as the appropriate method for the resolution of the issues of Central America.

* * *

106. With regard to the contention of the United States of America that the matter raised in the Nicaraguan Application was part of the Contadora Process, the Court considers that even the existence of active negotiations in which both parties might be involved should not prevent both the Security Council and the Court from exercising their separate functions under the Charter and the Statute of the Court.

113. For these reasons,

THE COURT,

(1)(a) *finds*, by eleven votes to five, that it has jurisdiction to entertain the Application filed by the Republic of Nicaragua on 9 April 1984, on the basis of Article 36, paragraphs 2 and 5, of the Statute of the Court;

(b) *finds* by fourteen votes to two, that it has jurisdiction to entertain the Application filed by the Republic of Nicaragua on 9 April 1984, in so far as that Application relates to a dispute concerning the interpretation or application of the Treaty of Friendship, Commerce and Navigation between the United States of America and the Republic of Nicaragua signed at Managua on 21 January 1956, on the basis of Article XXIV of that Treaty:

(2) *finds*, unanimously, that the said Application is admissible.

Note

On October 7, 1985, President Ronald Reagan terminated the United States' acceptance of the Court's compulsory jurisdiction. The termination was stated to be effective six months later.

QUESTIONS

1. Do you agree with the Court's decision that it had jurisdiction to decide the case on the merits?
2. What do you understand the term "admissibility" to mean?
3. Do you think that the Court was the best forum for resolving the dispute submitted by Nicaragua against the United States?
4. If you were advising your state (a) whether or not to accept the Court's compulsory jurisdiction and (b) what type of reservations or conditions, if any, to add to the acceptance, what would you advise and why? If your state decided to accept the Court's compulsory jurisdiction would you advise your state to insert a self-judging, domestic reservation?

Currently sixty-six of the member states of the United Nations have accepted the compulsory jurisdiction of the Court and many of those states have appended reservations (or exceptions) to their acceptances. Many hundreds of states are parties to specific treaties with clauses granting the Court jurisdiction to resolve disputes between parties that arise under the particular treaty. Nonetheless many states are reluctant to accept the Court's jurisdiction. Why is this so? A variety of reasons are given by various states. Some states are reluctant to submit to the authority of any outside body. Somehow they regard compliance with judicial decisions rendered by non-national bodies as diminishing their own sovereignty or their own control over the dispute. Some states contend that the decisions of the Court are unpredictable. It may indeed be difficult to predict the outcome in cases where the facts are in dispute or where the issues raised are on the cutting edge of the law but that is always true in all law cases. Developing states may fear that the law applied has largely been made by the developed states and they may not agree with some of the customary rules. All of these fears have elements of validity in them but the main argument in favor of using the Court to settle disputes (or indeed any other method designed to settle disputes peacefully) is that the alternatives often involve the use of force with its inevitable trail of calamities. In an address at Delhi

University in 1959 President Dwight Eisenhower made the point succinctly. He said: "It is better to lose a point now and then in an international tribunal and gain a world in which everyone lives at peace under the rule of law."

Jurisdiction Forum Prorogatum

The Court also has jurisdiction over states if they consent to the Court's jurisdiction by specifically indicating their consent or engaging in conduct from which their consent may be deduced. The principle that a court has jurisdiction if the parties consent to its jurisdiction is known as the doctrine of *forum prorogatum*. For example, a state's consent may be expressed in a letter to the Court[18] or implied from the fact that a state has argued the case on the merits without objecting to the Court's jurisdiction.[19]

The Jurisdiction of the International Court of Justice in Advisory Cases

The Court can also issue opinions when requested to do so by the General Assembly, the Security Council or specialized agencies of the United Nations when authorized to request an opinion by the General Assembly. These opinions fall within the court's *advisory* jurisdiction.

Since 1946 the Court has issued over twenty advisory opinions on topics ranging from the legality of the threat or use of nuclear weapons to the territorial status of South-West Africa (Namibia). Although advisory opinions are not binding in the same way that contentious cases are binding on the parties before the Court, there is no doubt that the body of advisory opinions have been influential not only within the United Nations but also in the development of international law generally.

The Power of the International Court of Justice to Issue Interim Measures of Protection

Under article 41 of the Court's Statute it is given the power "to indicate, if it considers that circumstances so require, any provisional measures which ought to be taken to preserve the respective rights of either party." (Article 41 para. 1). This mechanism allows the parties to request a fairly rapid decision aimed at preventing irreparable harm to a party which might occur if that party had to wait until the Court had deliberated and decided first, whether it had jurisdiction over the case and then, if so, how it would rule on the merits. In interim measures proceedings, the Court first makes what it calls a"*prima facie*" (at first look) decision that there appears to be a basis for the Court's jurisdiction. The Court has stated that it will only issue interim measures of protection if there is an urgency and that failure to issue the orders would result in irreparable prejudice to the rights of one of the parties to the dispute. For example, in the *LaGrand Case*, (Germany v. U.S.) 2001 I.C.J. 466,

18. *Corfu Channel Case* (U.K. v. Albania), 1948 I.C.J. 15 (preliminary objection).

19. *Rights of Minorities in Polish Upper Silesia* (Germany v. Poland) 1928 P.C.I.J. (ser. A) No. 15. at 24–25. See also *Application of the Convention on the Prevention and Punishment of the Crime of Genocide* (Bosnia and Herzegovina v. Yugoslavia (Serbia and Montenegro)), 1996 I.C.J. 595, 621 (preliminary objections) and *Case Concerning Questions of Mutual Assistance in Criminal Matters* (Djibouti v. France), 2008 I.C.J. ___, paras. 60-94.

Walter LaGrand was about to be executed in the United States, so Germany requested, and was granted, interim measures of protection. Before the hearings on jurisdiction or the merits began the Court ordered that: "The United States should take all measures at its disposal to ensure that Walter LaGrand is not executed pending the final decision in these proceedings...."[20] In the *LaGrand Case*, the Court also ruled that interim measures of protection were legally binding. 2001 I.C.J. 466 at paras. 98ff.

Other Major International Courts

The chapter on human rights (chapter VIII) explored various enforcement mechanisms for human rights including regional human rights courts. Some of those regional systems also have a general regional court, such as the European Court of Justice which sits in Luxembourg and has power to decide disputes arising under the constituent documents of the European Union. The United Nations Security Council has created two international criminal courts and has assisted other states, such as East Timor, Sierra Leone and Camboida, in creating quasi-international courts which operate under a mixture of national and international law. In 1998, The United Nations General Assembly convened the conference in Rome, Italy which led to the adoption of the Rome Statute for the establishment of the International Criminal Court (see below). There are also a growing number of *ad hoc* international arbitral tribunals which are created by states to settle particular disputes between them when those disputes cannot otherwise be settled.

The International Criminal Tribunal for the Former Yugoslavia

In the wake of the Balkan war of the 1990s, the international community was concerned to reenforce the idea of individual responsibility for acts contrary to international humanitarian law. After a great deal of debate, the Security Council created an International Criminal Tribunal for the former Yugoslavia. Security Council Resolution 827 establishes the International Criminal Tribunal and states its purpose as "prosecuting persons responsible for serious violations of international humanitarian law committed in the territory of the former Yugoslavia...."[21]

The Security Council asserted that it was acting under the powers conferred upon it by Chapter VII of the United Nations Charter (articles 39–51). Under article 39 the Security Council is empowered "to determine the existence of any threat to the peace, breach of the peace, or act of aggression and [to] ... make recommendations, or decide what measures shall be taken in accordance with Articles 41 and 42, to maintain or restore international peace and security." Article 41 permits the Security Council to "decide what measures not involving the use of force are to be employed to give effect to its decisions...." Although the Security Council had never before used its powers to create an international tribunal, it is arguable that it is within the scope of its Chapter VII powers.[22]

20. Case Concerning the Vienna Convention on Consular Relations (Germany v. U.S.) 1999 I.C.J. 9 (Request for the Indication of Provisional Measures, 3 March 1999).

21. S.C. Res. 827, U.N. SCOR, 48th Sess., U.N. Doc. S/RES 827 (1993) reprinted at 32 I.L.M. 1203 (1993).

22. See *Prosecutor v. Dusko Tadić*, Decision on the Defense Motion for Interlocutory Appeal on Jurisdiction, 1995 I.C.T.Y. No. IT-94-1-AR 72 (App. Chamber Oct. 2, 1995), reprinted at 35 I.L.M. 32, at 48 (1996).

The Secretary-General had been asked to draw up a report on the creation of a court to prosecute international crimes in the Former Yugoslavia and the Security Council adopted the Statute of the International Tribunal which was annexed to the Secretary-General's report. The Tribunal's Statute provides that it shall have the power to prosecute "persons responsible for serious violations of international humanitarian law ..." (article 1); "persons committing or ordering to be committed grave breaches of the Geneva Conventions of 12 August 1949 ..." (article 2); "persons violating the laws or customs of war" (article 3); "persons committing genocide ..." (article 4); and "persons responsible for ... [crimes against humanity] when committed in armed conflict, whether international or internal in character, and directed against any civilian population ..." (article 5).[23] The Tribunal has also adopted rules of procedure and rules of evidence as authorized by article 15 of the Tribunal's Statute.

The Tribunal was established in 1993 and sits in the Hague in The Netherlands. It consists of three trial chambers each with three permanent judges and a maximum of six *ad litem* judges, and an appeals chambers of seven judges. This appeals chamber also serves as the appeals chamber of the Internal Tribunal for Rwanda (see p. ___). The judges are elected by the General Assembly from a list submitted by the Security Council. They "shall be persons of high moral character, impartiality and integrity who possess the qualifications required in their respective countries for appointment to the highest judicial office.... [D]ue account shall be taken of the experience of the judges in criminal law, international law, including international humanitarian law and human rights." (Article 13, Statute of International Tribunal).

The Statute for the Tribunal also required the appointment of a prosecutor and created a Registry to carry out the administrative work of the Court. The Tribunal has indicted one hundred and sixty one people and has completed proceedings against one hundred and sixteen people . There are forty-two on-going proceedings. Only two indictees have not yet been arrested, Ratko Mladić and Goran Hadžic. The Tribunal hopes to complete all trials by 2010 and all appeals by 2011.

The first person to be tried by the Tribunal was Dusko Tadić, a low ranking member of the Serbian military who was accused of a variety of crimes under the Statute. His trial proved to be a fertile ground for testing a number of the controversial aspects of the law of the Tribunal. The most radical attack mounted by Tadić's lawyers was the argument that the Security Council had no authority to create the Tribunal and that therefore the whole proceeding was without legal foundation. Although the trial chamber had determined that it lacked the power to consider the legality of its own creation,[24] the Appeals Chamber was willing to tackle the issue. The Appeals Chamber undertook a thorough investigation of the Security Council's powers under Chapter VII of the United Nations Charter and concluded that "the International Tribunal has been established in accordance with the appropriate procedures under the United Nations Charter...."[25] The particular interpretation that the Appeals Chamber gave to particular articles of the Charter are of less importance than the fact that the Appeals Chamber considered itself empowered to address such questions. Whether the assertion of what is usually called "judicial

23. Statute of the International Tribunal, adopted as part of S.C. Res. 827, reprinted at 32 I.L.M. 1159 at 1192 ff. (1993). See generally, M. Cherif Bassiouni & Peter Manikas, The Law of the International Criminal Court for the Former Yugoslavia (1996); Virginia Morris & Michael Scharf, An Insider's Guide to the International Criminal Tribunal for the Former Yugoslavia (1995).

24. International Criminal Tribunal for the Former Yugoslavia: *Decision in Prosecutor v. Dusko Tadić*, reprinted at 35 I.L.M. 32, at 40 (1996).

25. Id. at 48.

supremacy" (the power of a court to pronounce upon the scope of the powers of the various branches of the U.N. system) will stand the test of time remains to be seen.

In 1996, a Croatian soldier in the Bosnian Serb army, Drazen Erdemovíc, pleaded guilty to the charge of crimes against humanity and was sentenced to ten years in prison. (See *Erdemovic Case* at pp. 426–441). In 1998, the Appeals Chamber reduced his sentence to seven years. In 1997, Tadić was convicted of eleven of the counts brought against him[26] and was sentenced to twenty years in jail.[27] The Tribunal has now completed proceedings in over a hundred cases. Slobodan Milošević, who was first President of Serbia, and then President of Federal Republic of Yugoslavia, was indicted for grave breaches of the Geneva Convention's of 1949, war crimes, genocide and crimes against humanity. He died in 2006 while his trial was still taking place. The Security Council has called upon the Court to complete all proceedings by 2011. The Court's website is located at: www.icty.org.

The International Criminal Tribunal for Rwanda

A tribunal has also been established by the Security Council to prosecuted the atrocities that occurred in Rwanda and neighboring states between January 1st 1994 and December 31st 1994.[28] The structure and composition of the Tribunal is very similar to the Yugoslavian Tribunal, but it sits in Arusha in Tanzania. The Rwanda Tribunal originally functioned with the same prosecutor's office as the Yugoslavian Tribunal but now has its own prosecutorial staff. The Rwanda Tribunal got off to a rocky start with allegations of bureaucratic mismanagement. Those problems appear to have been solved. Twenty-nine cases have been completed. Five detainees were also acquitted. Twenty-three cases are on-going and seven cases are currently on appeal. Eight of the indicted are awaiting trial and thirteen fugitives remain at large. The Tribunal hopes to complete its work by 2010. (See *Aloys Simba Case* at pp. 442–449 *infra.*) The Court's website is located at: www.ictr.org.

The International Criminal Court

Although war criminals were prosecuted after World War II in the trials at Nuremberg and Tokyo, those courts have often been described as victors' courts. They were established by the victorious allies after the Nazi surrender. The Yugoslavian and Rwandan tribunals were established by the international community but only have jurisdiction over crimes relating to conflict in particular geographic areas. For more than fifty years there have been those who have advocated the establishment of a Permanent International Criminal Court.

---

26. *Opinion and Judgment of the International Criminal Tribunal for the Former Yugoslavia in Prosecutor v. Dus ko Tadić*, Case No. IT-94-1-T, May 7, 1997, reprinted at 36 I.L.M. 908 (1997).

27. Id. footnote at 908.

28. S.C. Res. 935, U.N. SCOR, 49th Sess. U.N. Doc. S/RES/935 (1994) established a Commission of Experts to investigate "grave violations of international humanitarian law in the territory of Rwanda, including the evidence of possible acts of genocide...." S.C. Res. 955, U.N. SCOR, 49th Sess. U.N. Doc. S/RES/955 (1994) created "an international tribunal for the sole purpose of prosecuting persons responsible for genocide and other serious violations of international humanitarian law committed in the territory of Rwanda and Rwandan citizens responsible for genocide and other violations committed in the territory of neighboring states between 1 January 1994 and 31 December 1994 and to this end adopt the statute of the International Criminal Tribunal for Rwanda annexed hereto...."

In 1996 the General Assembly convened a Prepatory Committee to draft a treaty to establish a permanent international criminal court. The International Law Commission and the International Institute of Higher Studies in Criminal Sciences in Siracusa, Italy had both produced drafts of texts for the establishment of the Court which were considered by the Prepatory Committee. In 1998, the U.N. General Assembly convened a diplomatic conference in Rome, Italy to establish an International Criminal Court. The draft statute for the Court was finalized at the Rome conference and the treaty went into force on July 1, 2002.[29] To date, one hundred and eight states have deposited their ratifications to the treaty. The Court has been established at The Hague, The Netherlands. The Prosecutor's Office is investigating three situations referred by states and one situation referred by the Security Council. Four arrest warrants have been issued with respect to activities in Uganda. Three cases concern proceedings on activities in the Democratic Republic of the Congo. President Omar Hassan Ahmad Al Bashir of Sudan has been indicted for activities related to the Darfur region. Pre-trial proceedings are continuing with respect to the Central African Republic. The Court's website is located at: www.icc-cpi.int/.

Conclusion

The current era has seen a rapid expansion of the fora available for the settlement of international disputes and a growing willingness on the part of some states to use existing courts, tribunals and other settlement mechanisms to resolve otherwise intractable areas of conflict.[30] At the same time the rate of the outbreak of internal and international hostilities does not appear to have diminished. The trend towards the creation of settlement mechanisms for international disputes is likely to continue, in part because of the exponential explosion in international transactions. International settlement mechanisms have become a functional necessity for the international community. Whether these mechanisms will ultimately contribute to permanent reductions in hostilities remains to be seen.

Suggested Further Readings

Ian Browlie, Principles of Public International Law, chapter 32 (7th ed. 2008).

D.J. Harris, Cases and Materials on International Law, chapter 12 (6th ed. 2004).

Shabtai Rosenne & Yael Ronen, The Law and Practice of the International Court, 1920–2005 (2006).

Malcolm N. Shaw, International Law, chapter 19 (6th ed. 2008).

Rebecca M. M. Wallace, International Law, chapter 12 (5th ed. 2005).

---

29. Rome Statute of the International Criminal Court, 2187 U.N.T.S. 3, adopted 17 July 1998, entered into force 1 July 2002. The treaty is available at the Court's web site: www.icc-cpi.int/.

30. For a very comprehensive account of all the available dispute settlement mechanisms for inter-state disputes see, Karin Oellers-Frahm & Andreas Zimmerman eds., Dispute Settlement in Public International Law (Vols. I and II) (2d ed. 2001).

Chapter X

The Use of Force Including War

Introduction

For as long as history has been recorded individuals and groups have fought, maimed and killed each other. This type of extreme activity is prohibited at the individual level by state criminal law. Carefully fashioned exceptions and defenses to the prohibited acts have arisen over the centuries. When a group organizes itself to attack another group we generally call the activity "war." The attacks may take place between clans, tribes or gangs,[1] and may occur within a nation state or across state lines. When these attacks are launched there will usually be an articulated reason for the show of force which may be based on fact or fancy. International law has generally divided the use of force into: 1) inter-state armed conflict or 2) intra-state armed conflict, although the distinctions are now blurring. Inter-state conflict was generally thought of as one state (or a co-alition) using force against another state (or a col-alition). Intra-state conflict was regarded as conflict between different armed groups within a state which were usually vying for governmental power. Recently, with the rise of international, non-governmental, armed groups, that may operate in several countries, the above categories of conflict are being challenged.

The rules governing inter-state warfare have generally been divided into two categories: the rules that govern when it is permissible to initiate an attack, which has become known as "*jus ad bellum*" and the rules that govern behavior during war, known as "*jus in bello.*" From time to time, most major religions have produced doctrines which define the occasions when fighting a war is justified.[2] Medieval Europe developed elaborate rules governing behavior during war and Shakespeare's Henry V has frequent references to permissible and impermissible activity during war.[3] All of the above doctrines or codes have only been followed by particular groups at particular moments in history. It was not until the end of the nineteenth century and the beginning of the twentieth century that there was any movement to urge the adoption of universal rules governing inter-state warfare. (For rules governing civil wars see pp. 416 & 424–426). By this time, in Europe at least, the power of the Church had been superseded by the power of the secular state. War was an instrument of state policy and was used when seen as promoting the state's interests. Despite early efforts of some international scholars to promote

---

1. "Gang warfare," a feature of city life in most developed states, is regulated under domestic criminal law.

2. See, e.g., R. A. Markus, Saint Augustine's Views on The 'Just War' 1–13, in The Church and War (W.J. Sheils ed. 1983); Just War and Jihad, Historical and Theoretical Perspectives on War and Peace in Western and Islamic Traditions (John Kelsay & James Turner Johnson eds. 1991).

3. See, Theodor Meron, Shakespeare's Henry The Fifth and The Law of War, 86 Amer. J. Int'l L. 1 (1992).

rules governing warfare[4] it is fair to say that, prior to the twentieth century, war was beyond the scope of anything recognizable as law.

The Modern Era

Coercive Measures Not Amounting to Armed Force

States, particularly powerful states, often try to influence the conduct of other states. Influence can take many forms but usually constitutes either the proverbial carrot or stick. The carrot may consist of economic aid or offering favorable trade conditions. The stick may mean engaging in a variety of unfriendly acts which may or may not be illegal.

Retorsions

The term "retorsion" refers to unfriendly, but not illegal, retaliatory actions taken by one state against another in response to actions that are regarded as hostile, unfriendly or not in keeping with the policy aims of the responding states. This type of retaliation can take a variety of forms. It may consist of breaking off trade or diplomatic relations or imposing embargoes on the export or import of goods from or to the offending state. Nationals of the offending state may be denied entry visas. Vessels may be denied entry to ports. Aircraft may be denied rights of overflight. It may even go as far as the massing of troops near the offending state's border but a large troop manoever might constitute an illegal threat of force. One essential element of a retorsion is that the action undertaken is not illegal. For example if State A had a treaty obligation to allow State B to fly over its territory, its suspension of overflight rights would amount to an illegal breach of the treaty and would not be classified as a retorsion.

Reprisals Not Involving the Use of Armed Force

A reprisal is an illegal act taken as a measure of self-help in response to a prior illegal act. Provided the state undertaking the reprisal is correct in its assessment that the other state's prior actions were indeed illegal and provided the reprisal is proportionate to the initial wrongdoing, then the reprisal is not considered unlawful. Reprisals not involving armed force are often called "counter-measures" to distinguish them from armed reprisals. (Armed reprisals are now governed by the U.N. Charter and the customary laws of war.) One arbitral tribunal explained the law of reprisals in this way:

> If a situation arises which, in one State's view, results in the violation of an international obligation by another State, the first State is entitled, ... to affirm its rights through 'counter-measures'....
>
> It is generally agreed that all counter-measures must, in the first instance, have some degree of equivalence with the alleged breach.... It has been observed, generally, that judging the 'proportionality' of counter-measures is not an easy task and can best be accomplished by approximation....

4. E.g., Hugo Grotius, De Juri Belli Ac Pacis (1625) (A.C. Campbell trans., reprinted 1979).

However, the lawfulness of such counter-measures has to be considered still from another viewpoint. It may indeed be asked whether they are valid in general, in the case of a dispute concerning a point of law, where there is arbitral or judicial machinery which can settle the dispute. Many jurists have felt that while arbitral or judicial proceedings were in progress, recourse to counter-measures, even if limited by the proportionality rule, was prohibited. Such an assertion deserves sympathy but requires further elaboration. If the proceedings form part of an institutional framework ensuring some degree of enforcement of obligations, the justification of counter-measures will undoubtedly disappear, but owing to the existence of that framework rather than solely on account of the existence of arbitral or judicial proceedings as such.[5]

Pre-1945 Law on the Use of Armed Force

World War I caused death and suffering on an unprecedented scale. It has been estimated that between ten and thirteen million military personnel died[6] and a further six million were seriously injured.[7] About seven million civilians were killed and roughly twelve million civilians were injured. The League of Nations arose out of the Peace Conference of Paris at the close of World War I in an attempt to provide some international mechanism where nations could meet and discuss their differences and thereby resolve disputes without the necessity of going to war. The Covenant of the League of Nations which was signed in 1919 attempted to govern the procedural steps necessary before going to war. Article 12(1) provides that the members of the League agree that "they will submit [disputes] ... either to arbitration or juridical settlement or to inquiry by the Council, and [that] they agreed in no case to resort to war until three months after the awards by the arbitrators or the judicial decision, or the report by the Council."[8] Members were also obligated not to go to war with another member as long as that member was complying with an arbitral award or judicial decision[9] or with a unanimous report by the Council.[10] The idea behind these requirements was that a cooling off period would benefit all parties to disputes and that a decision by an outside (presumably impartial) body was infinitely preferable to the devastation of conflict. If a member resorted to war contrary to the Covenant, other members were obliged to "subject it to the severance of all trade or financial relations, the prohibition of all intercourse between their nationals and the nationals of the covenant-breaking State, and the prevention of all financial, commercial or personal intercourse...."[11]

Despite the Covenant's high aspirations, the League failed to take decisive action when Italy invaded Abyssinia (Ethiopia) in 1935. Abyssinia reported the invasion to the League's Council and Italy was found in violation of the Covenant. Sanctions were drawn up but the powerful nations prevented embargoes on coal, steel and oil. The lim-

---

5. *Air Services Agreement Case*, (France v. United States), 18 R. I. A. A. 416, paras. 81, 83 & 94 (1978).

6. C.R.M.F. Cruttwell, A History of the Great War, Appendix I, 631–632 (2d ed. 1934).

7. S.L.A. Marshall, American Heritage History of World War I, 344 (Alvin M. Joesephy & Joseph L. Gardner eds. 1964).

8. League of Nations Covenant, art. 12, para. 1.

9. Id. at art. 13, para. 4.

10. Id. at art. 15, para. 6.

11. Id. at art. 16.

ited sanctions imposed proved insufficient and the League took no further action against Italy. With the outbreak of World War II the League ultimately collapsed.

There had also been other movements to outlaw war. In 1928 sixty-three nations had signed the General Treaty for the Renunciation of War,[12] also known as the Kellogg-Briand Pact. The parties condemned "recourse to war for the solution of international controversies, and [they] renounce[d] it as an instrument of national policy in their relationships with one another."[13] They pledged that "the settlement of all disputes or conflicts of whatever nature ... which may arise among them, shall never be sought except by pacific means."[14] These early efforts at renouncing and regulating war proved insufficient to prevent the outbreak of World War II.

The Customary Law of Self-Defence (For spelling of "Defence" see note 24 infra).

The Caroline Incident

2 Moore, Digest of International Law 412 (1906)

Note

In 1837 a rebellion occurred in Canada against the British authorities which at that time still ruled Canada. The leaders of the rebellion had persuaded a number of Americans to assist them. The American group occupied Navy Island in Canadian waters of the Niagara River and from there launched raids upon the Canadian shore and attacked British ships. An American ship called the *Caroline* supplied the insurgents. On December 29, 1837, the *Caroline* was moored at the American port of Schlosser. The British forces seized the *Caroline*, set fire to her and sent her over the Niagara Falls which resulted in the death of at least two Americans. Several other men were never accounted for. A British subject, Alexander McLeod, was arrested and put on trial in New York for his alleged participation in the destruction of the Caroline and the murder of the two Americans. Extensive correspondence on the matter took place between Daniel Webster, the American Secretary of State, and both Mr. Henry Fox, the British Minister and Lord Ashburton, the British Special Emissary. These letters are generally regarded as stating the pre-Charter law of self-defence.

> **Mr. Webster to Mr. Fox (April 24, 1841).** It will be for ... [Her Majesty's] Government to show a necessity of self-defence, instant, overwhelming, leaving no choice of means, and no moment for deliberation. It will be for it to show, also, that the local authorities of Canada, even supposing the necessity of the moment authorized them to enter the territories of The United States at all, did nothing unreasonable or excessive; since the act, justified by the necessity of self-defence, must be limited by that necessity, and kept clearly within it. It must be shown that admonition or remonstrance to the persons on board the *Caroline* was impracticable, or would have been unavailing; it must be shown that day-light could not be waited for; that there could be no attempt at discrimination between the innocent and the guilty; that it would not have been

12. 94 L.N.T.S. 57, signed 27 Aug. 1928, entered into force 24 July 1929.
13. Id. at art. I.
14. Id. at art. II.

enough to seize and detain the vessel; but that there was a necessity, present and inevitable, for attacking her in the darkness of the night, while moored to the shore, and while unarmed men were asleep on board, killing some and wounding others, and then drawing her into the current, above the cataract, setting her on fire, and, careless to know whether there might not be in her the innocent with the guilty, or the living with the dead, committing her to a fate which fills the imagination with horror. A necessity for all this, the Government of The United States cannot believe to have existed.[15]

Lord Ashburton to Mr. Webster (July 28, 1842). It is so far satisfactory to perceive that we are perfectly agreed as to the general principles of international law applicable to this unfortunate case.[16]

QUESTIONS

1. What were the preconditions for the exercise of self-defence articulated by Secretary Webster?
2. The British argued that they were justified in anticipating further attacks by the *Caroline* and that therefore they were entitled to exercise self-defence. Does article 2(4) of the United Nations Charter permit anticipatory self-defence or must an armed attack precede the right to self-defence? (See section on Self-Defence pp. 392–406.)

Post-1945 Law

The six years of World War II heaped further devastation upon Europe and the far East. Here the estimates for deaths are staggering. Total deaths are listed as between fifty to seventy million, with civilian deaths accounting for more than forty-five million.[17] The allied powers emerged determined to establish a world wide framework for ensuring peace. The Charter of the United Nations[18] was signed in San Francisco, U.S.A. in 1945 and declares one of its main purposes to be "to unite our strength to maintain international peace and security, and to ensure ... that armed force shall not be used, save in the common interest...." U.N. Charter, Preamble.

The United Nations Charter Law

Article 2(4) of the Charter provides:

"All Members shall refrain in their international relations from the threat or use of force against the territorial integrity or political independence of any state, or in any other manner inconsistent with the Purposes of the United Nations."

15. 29 British and Foreign State Papers 1137–1138 (1857).
16. 30 British and Foreign State Papers 195–196 (1858).
17. J. Keegan, The Second World War (1989); Rudolph J. Rummel, Statistics of Democide (1997).
18. 3 Bevans 1153, signed June 26, 1945, entered into force Oct. 24, 1945.
19. See *Case Concerning Military and Paramilitary Activities in and against Nicaragua* (Merits) (Nicaragua v. U.S.), 1986 I.C.J. 14, at 100.

Although this article is addressed only to members of the United Nations, it is now considered to be a binding rule of customary international law applicable to all states.[19]

The Meaning of "Force"

Article 2(4) does not use the term "war" but rather refers to "the threat or use of force." Use of force short of war is clearly encompassed by the article, but does the article only refer to military force? What about economic, political, ideological or psychological force? The Preamble to the Charter declares that "armed force shall not be used, save in the common interest...." Article 51 preserves the "right of individual or collective self-defence if an *armed attack* occurs...." (emphasis added). (See section on Self-Defence, pp. 392–406.) In 1970 the General Assembly adopted the *Declaration on Principles of International Law Concerning Friendly Relations and Co-operation Among States in Accordance with the Charter of the United Nations.*[20] This resolution was adopted without vote by consensus but is considered an authoritative statement on the interpretation of certain provisions of the Charter. The Declaration reiterates article 2(4) and elaborates upon the occasions when the threat or use of force is prohibited but it does not address the question of whether force includes non-military force within the scope of the Charter. The Declaration also states that: "Nothing in the foregoing paragraphs shall be construed as enlarging or diminishing in any way the scope of the provisions of the Charter concerning cases in which the use of force is lawful." Certain types of armed and non-armed intervention are prohibited by the Declaration: "No State or group of States has the right to intervene, directly or indirectly, for any reason whatever, in the internal or external affairs of any other State. Consequently, armed intervention and all other forms of interference or attempted threats against the personality of the State or against its political, economic and cultural elements, are in violation of international law." The above sentence and various other sentences in the Declaration address the use of non-military force but in the context of other international obligations such as the obligation not to intervene in the affairs of another state (see section on Civil Wars and the Rule of Non-Intervention p. 416).

A number of developing nations have maintained that "force" includes non-military force but the developed states have resisted this view while conceding that non-military force of various kinds may be outlawed by other principles of international law. In the *Nicaragua Case* it was argued that the United States economic sanctions against Nicaragua constituted a violation of the customary law rule of non-intervention but the Court rejected that view in the particular circumstances of the case.[21]

What Is a Threat of Force?

The issue of what constitutes a "*threat* ... of force" has received little attention. The late Professor Schachter admitted that it was difficult to define what minimum show of force was contemplated by the phrase, particularly in light of the interplay of power politics, but that at least: "A blatant and direct threat of force to compel another state to yield territory or make substantial political concessions (not required by law) would

20. G.A. Res. 2625, U.N. GAOR, 6th Comm., 25th Sess., 1883rd plen. mtg., Agenda Item 85, at 337, U.N. Doc. A/8082 (1970).

21. *Nicaragua v. U.S.*, 1986 I.C.J. 14, at 126.

22. Oscar Schachter, International Law in Theory and Practice 111 (1991).

have to be seen as illegal under Article 2(4), if the words 'threat of force' are to have any meaning."[22] The International Court of Justice refused to find military manoevres held by the U.S. near the Nicaraguan border constituted a threat of force. "The Court is however not satisfied that the manoevres complained of, in the circumstances in which they were held, constituted on the part of the United States a breach, as against Nicaragua, of the principle forbidding recourse to the threat or use of force...."[23]

Legality of the Threat or Use of Nuclear Weapons

International Court of Justice, Advisory Opinion
1996 I.C.J. 226, reprinted at 35 I.L.M. 809 (1996)

Note

The General Assembly of the United Nations submitted the following question to the Court for an advisory opinion: "is the threat or use of nuclear weapons in any circumstances permitted under international law?" The excerpt of the case below focuses on the question of whether the possession of nuclear weapons should be treated as a "threat" to use force under article 2(4) of the U.N. Charter.

Opinion of the Court

* * *

47. In order to lessen or eliminate the risk of unlawful attack, States sometimes signal they possess certain weapons to use in self-defence against any State violating their territorial integrity or political independence. Whether a signaled intention to use force if certain events occur is or is not a "threat" within Article 2, paragraph 4, of the Charter depends upon various factors. If the envisaged use of force is itself unlawful, the stated readiness to use it would be a threat prohibited under Article 2, paragraph 4. Thus it would be illegal for a State to threaten force to secure territory from another State, or to cause it to follow or not follow certain political or economic paths. The notions of "threat" and "use" of force under Article 2, paragraph 4, of the Charter stand together in the sense that if the use of force itself in a given case is illegal—for whatever reason—the threat to use such force will likewise be illegal. In short, if it is to be lawful, the declared readiness of a State to use force must be a use of force that is in conformity with the Charter. For the rest, no State—whether or not it defended the policy of deterrence—suggested to the Court that it would be lawful to threaten to use force if the use of force contemplated would be illegal.

48. Some States put forward the argument that possession of nuclear weapons is itself an unlawful threat to use force. Possession of nuclear weapons may indeed justify an inference of preparedness to use them. In order to be effective, the policy of deterrence, by which those States possessing or under the umbrella of nuclear weapons seek to discourage military aggression by demonstrating that it will serve no purpose, necessitates that the intention to use nuclear weapons be credible. Whether this is a "threat" contrary to Article 2, paragraph 4, depends upon whether the particular use of force envisaged would be directed against the territorial integrity or political independence of a State, or against the Purposes of the United Nations or whether, in the event that it was

23. *Nicaragua v. U.S.*, 1986 I.C.J. 14, at para. 227.

intended as a means of defence, it would necessarily violate the principles of necessity and proportionality. In any of these circumstances the use of force, and the threat to use it, would be unlawful under the law of the Charter.

Must Force be Used for a Particular Object to Violate Article 2(4)?

Article 2(4) prohibits the threat or use of force "against the territorial integrity or political independence of any State. . . ." This raises the question of whether force used for ends other than attacking the territorial integrity or political independence of a state is permitted. For example, can a state use force to rescue a group of its own citizens under imminent threat in another state? Can force be used to promote or protect human rights or democracy or to preserve "peace and security"? To attempt to answer this question it should be remembered that force is also forbidden when it is used "in any manner inconsistent with the Purposes of the United Nations." Article 2(4). The main purposes of the Charter are spelled out in the Preamble and Article 1 and embrace a variety of aims encompassing human rights, equality, justice, social progress, tolerance and friendly relations among nations. The principal purpose appears in article 1(1):

> To maintain international peace and security, and to that end: to take effective collective measures for the prevention and removal of threats to the peace, and for the suppression of acts of aggression or other breaches of the peace, and to bring about by peaceful means, and in conformity with the principle of justice and international law, adjustment or settlement of international disputes or situations which might lead to a breach of the peace.

Since the use of force for any purpose creates an immediate potential for a breach of the peace and since its use cannot be viewed as the peaceful settlement of an international dispute it would appear that the threat or use of force is contrary to article 2(4) unless it falls within specific Charter exceptions. (See also, section on Civil Wars and the Rule of Non-intervention p. 416).

Exceptions to Article 2(4)

Self-Defence[24]

Article 51 provides:

> Nothing in the present Charter shall impair the inherent right of individual or collective self-defence if an armed attack occurs against a Member of the United Nations, until the Security Council has taken measures necessary to maintain international peace and security. Measures taken by Members in the exercise of this right of self-defence shall be immediately reported to the Security Council and shall not in any way affect the authority and responsibility of the Security Council under the present Charter to take at any time such action as it deems necessary in order to maintain or restore international peace and security.

Some authors maintain that the Charter law subsumes all pre-existing law on the use of force and that the entire right of self-defence is spelled out in the Charter. They argue

---

24. Self-defence is spelled with a "c" rather than an "s" in this chapter because the U.N. Charter and other major international instruments relating to the use of force use the English spelling, as does the I.C.J.

that article 51 precludes anticipatory self-defence.[25] Other writers argue that the phrase "inherent right of self-defence" indicates that the Charter intended to incorporate the customary law of self-defence including anticipatory self-defence when facing imminent attack.[26] Without addressing the issue of anticipatory self-defence, the International Court of Justice has recognized that the right to individual and collective self-defence were part of customary international law pre-dating the Charter and that the Charter recognized this by its reference to "the inherent right (or '*droit naturel*') which any State possesses in the event of an armed attack...."[27]

Case Concerning Military and Paramilitary Activities in and against Nicaragua Nicaragua v. United States

1986 I.C.J. 14 (Merits)

Note

In 1979 the left-wing Sandinista government came to power in Nicaragua after a long struggle to overthrow the right-wing Somoza government. The United States government was not happy with these developments and supported the government of El Salvador, one of Nicaragua's northern neighbors. In 1981 the U.S. concluded that Nicaragua was aiding rebel forces in El Salvador and so all economic aid to Nicaragua was suspended. In the case below the Nicaraguan government accused the United States of laying mines in Nicaraguan waters and damaging ships, ports, oil facilities and a naval base. They also accused the U.S. of arming, training and financing the *Contra* forces—a rebel force seeking to overthrow the Sandanistas who were trained in Honduras, across Nicaragua's northern border.

The U.S. disputed the Court's jurisdiction but the Court concluded that it had jurisdiction over the parties and that the case was suitable for adjudication (see pp. 370–379). At that point the United States withdrew from the proceedings before the Court but it had already made it clear that its principal argument justifying its activities was going to be based on the collective self-defence of El Salvador. The U.S. argued that since Nicaragua was attacking El Salvador, she was justified in coming to El Salvador's aid and using coercive measures against Nicaragua.

Nicaragua's main claims against the U.S. were based on violations of the U.N. Charter and the Charter of the Organization of American States as well as the Treaty of Friendship Commerce and Navigation between the two states. The Court was unable to take up the Charter claims because the U.S. had appended an exception to its acceptance of the Court's jurisdiction under which the U.S. reserved the right not to submit to the Court's jurisdiction if a dispute arose under a multi-lateral treaty (which the

25. Hans Kelsen, The Law of the United Nations 914 (1950); Joseph Kunz, Individual and Collective Self-Defense in Article, 51 of the Charter of the U.N., 41 Amer. J. Int'l L. 872, 877 (1947); Louis Henkin, How Nations Behave 141 (2d ed. 1979); Yoram Dinstein, War, Aggression and Self-Defence, 182–183 (2d ed. 1994); Valerie Epps, Rejecting the Supposed Right to Anticipatory Self-Defence, 2 Northeast Asian L. Rev. 1 (2008).

26. D. W. Bowett, Self-Defence in International Law 817 n. 1 (1958).

27. *Nicaragua v. U.S.*, 1986 I.C.J. 14, at para. 193.

Charters were) unless all of the parties to the dispute were before the Court. The U.S. maintained that El Salvador, Honduras and Costa Rica were also parties to the dispute and were not before the Court. The Court found that this exception prevented the Court from deciding the case under the U.N. and O.A.S. Charters. Nevertheless, the Court determined that since the Charter obligations were essentially the same as customary law obligations, the Court would proceed to decide the case under customary law. For purposes of clarity the case is divided into two sections. The first section, directly below, deals with the arguments connected with collective self-defense and the second section, later in the chapter, deals with the arguments addressing the law of non-intervention (see pp. 409–416).

Opinion of the Court

190. A further confirmation of the validity as customary international law of the principle of the prohibition of the use of force expressed in Article 2, paragraph 4, of the Charter of the United Nations may be found in the fact that it is frequently referred to in statements by State representatives as being not only a principle of customary international law but also a fundamental or cardinal principle of such law. The International Law Commission, in the course of its work on the codification of the law of treaties, expressed the view that "the law of the Charter concerning the prohibition of the use of force in itself constitutes a conspicuous example of a rule in international law having the character of *jus cogens*" (paragraph (1) of the commentary of the Commission to Article 50 of its draft Articles (1) of the commentary of the Commission to Article 50 of its draft Articles on the Law of Treaties, *ILC Yearbook*, 1966-II, p. 247). Nicaragua in its Memorial on the Merits submitted in the present case states that the principle prohibiting the use of force embodied in Article 2, paragraph 4, of the Charter of the United Nations "has come to be recognized as *jus cogens*". The United States, in its Counter-Memorial on the questions of jurisdiction and admissibility, found it material to quote the views of scholars that this principle is a "universal norm", a "universal international law", a "universally recognized principle of international law", and a "principle of *jus cogens*".

191. As regards certain particular aspects of the principle in question, it will be necessary to distinguish the most grave forms of the use of force (those constituting an armed attack) from other less grave forms. In determining the legal rule which applies to these latter forms, the Court can again draw on the formulations contained in the Declaration on Principles of International Law concerning Friendly Relations and Co-operation among States in accordance with the Charter of the United Nations (General Assembly resolution 2625 (XXV), referred to above). As already observed, the adoption by States of this text affords an indication of their *opinio juris* as to customary international law on the question. Alongside certain descriptions which may refer to aggression, this text includes others which refer only to less grave forms of the use of force. In particular, according to this resolution:

> "Every State has the duty to refrain from the threat or use of force to violate the existing international boundaries of another State or as a means of solving international disputes, including territorial disputes and problems concerning frontiers of States.
>
> ....
>
> States have a duty to refrain from acts of reprisal involving the use of force.
>
> ....

> Every State has the duty to refrain from any forcible action which deprives peoples referred to in the elaboration of the principle of equal rights and self-determination of that right to self-determination and freedom and independence.
>
> Every State has the duty to refrain from organizing or encouraging the organization of irregular forces or armed bands, including mercenaries, for incursion into the territory of another State.
>
> Every State has the duty to refrain from organizing, instigating, assisting or participating in acts of civil strife or terrorist acts in another State or acquiescing in organized activities within its territory directed towards the commission of such acts, when the acts referred to in the present paragraph involve a threat or use of force."

* * *

193. The general rule prohibiting force allows for certain exceptions. In view of the arguments advanced by the United States to justify the acts of which it is accused by Nicaragua, the Court must express a view on the content of the right of self-defence, and more particularly the right of collective self-defence. First, with regard to the existence of this right, it notes that in the language of Article 51 of the United Nations Charter, the inherent right (or "droit naturel") which any State possesses in the event of an armed attack, covers both collective and individual self-defence. Thus, the Charter itself testifies to the existence of the right of collective self-defence in customary international law. Moreover, just as the wording of certain General Assembly declarations adopted by States demonstrates their recognition of the principle of the prohibition of force as definitely a matter of customary international law, some of the wording in those declarations operates similarly in respect of the right of self-defence (both collective and individual). Thus, in the declaration quoted above on the Principles of International Law concerning Friendly Relations and Cooperation among States in accordance with the Charter of the United Nations, the reference to the prohibition of force is followed by a paragraph stating that:

> "nothing in the foregoing paragraphs shall be construed as enlarging or diminishing in any way the scope of the provisions of the Charter concerning cases in which the use of force is lawful".

This resolution demonstrates that the States represented in the General Assembly regard the exception to the prohibition of force constituted by the right of individual or collective self-defence as already a matter of customary international law.

194. With regard to the characteristics governing the right of self-defence, since the Parties consider the existence of this right to be established as a matter of customary international law, they have concentrated on the conditions governing its use. In view of the circumstances in which the dispute has arisen, reliance is placed by the Parties only on the right of self-defence in the case of an armed attack which has already occurred, and the issue of the lawfulness of a response to the imminent threat of armed attack has not been raised. Accordingly the Court expresses no view on that issue. The Parties also agree in holding that whether the response to the attack is lawful depends on observance of the criteria of the necessity and the proportionality of the measures taken in self-defence. Since the existence of the right of collective self-defence is established in customary international law, the Court must define the specific conditions which may have to be met for its exercise, in addition to the conditions of necessity and proportionality to which the Parties have referred.

195. In the case of individual self-defence, the exercise of this right is subject to the State concerned having been the victim of an armed attack. Reliance on collective self-defence of course does not remove the need for this. There appears now to be general agreement on the nature of the acts which can be treated as constituting armed attacks. In particular, it may be considered to be agreed that an armed attack must be understood as including not merely action by regular armed forces across an international border, but also "the sending by or on behalf of a State of armed bands, groups, irregulars or mercenaries, which carry out acts of armed force against another State of such gravity as to amount to" (*inter alia*) an actual armed attack conducted by regular forces, "or its substantial involvement therein". This description, contained in Article 3, paragraph (g), of the Definition of Aggression annexed to General Assembly resolution 3314 (XXIX), may be taken to reflect customary international law. The Court sees no reason to deny that, in customary law, the prohibition of armed attacks may apply to the sending by a State of armed bands to the territory of another State, if such an operation, because of its scale and effects would have been classified as an armed attack rather than as a mere frontier incident had it been carried out by regular armed forces. But the Court does not believe that the concept of "armed attack" includes not only acts by armed bands where such acts occur on a significant scale but also assistance to rebels in the form of the provision of weapons or logistical or other support. Such assistance may be regarded as a threat or use of force, or amount to intervention in the internal or external affairs of other States. It is also clear that it is the State which is the victim of an armed attack which must form and declare the view that it has been so attacked. There is no rule in customary international law permitting another State to exercise the right of collective self-defence on the basis of its own assessment of the situation. Where collective self-defence is invoked, it is to be expected that the State for whose benefit this right is used will have declared itself to be the victim of an armed attack.

* * *

199. At all events, the Court finds that in customary international law, whether of a general kind or that particular to the inter-American legal system, there is no rule permitting the exercise of collective self-defence in the absence of a request by the State which regards itself as the victim of an armed attack. The Court concludes that the requirement of a request by the State which is the victim of the alleged attack is additional to the requirement that such a State should have declared itself to have been attacked.

200. At this point, the Court may consider whether in customary international law there is any requirement corresponding to that found in the treaty law of the United Nations Charter, by which the State claiming to use the right of individual or collective self-defence must report to an international body, empowered to determine the conformity with international law of the measures which the State is seeking to justify on that basis. Thus Article 51 of the United Nations Charter requires that measures taken by States in exercise of this right of self-defence must be "immediately reported" to the Security Council. As the Court has observed above ... a principle enshrined in a treaty, if reflected in customary international law, may well be so unencumbered with the conditions and modalities surrounding it in the treaty. Whatever influence the Charter may have had on customary international law in these matters, it is clear that in customary international law it is not a condition of the lawfulness of the use of force in self-defence that a procedure so closely dependent on the content of a treaty commitment and of the institutions established by it, should have been followed. On the other hand, if self-defence is advanced as a justification for measures which would otherwise be in breach

both of the principle of customary international law and of that contained in the Charter, it is to be expected that the conditions of the Charter should be respected. Thus for the purpose of enquiry into the customary law position, the absence of a report may be one of the factors indicating whether the State in question was itself convinced that it was acting in self-defence.

201. To justify certain activities involving the use of force, the United States has relied solely on the exercise of its right of collective self-defence. However the Court, having regard particularly to the non-participation of the United States in the merits phase, considers that it should enquire whether customary international law, applicable to the present dispute, may contain other rules which may exclude the unlawfulness of such activities. It does not, however, see any need to reopen the question of the conditions governing the exercise of the right of individual self-defence, which have already been examined in connection with collective self-defence. On the other hand, the Court must enquire whether there is any justification for the activities in question, to be found not in the right of collective self-defence against an armed attack, but in the right to take counter-measures in response to conduct of Nicaragua which is not alleged to constitute an armed attack. It will examine this point in connection with an analysis of the principle of non-intervention in customary international law.

* * *

211. The Court has recalled above ... that for one State to use force against another, on the ground that that State has committed a wrongful act of force against a third State, [it] is regarded as lawful, by way of exception, only when the wrongful act provoking the response was an armed attack. Thus the lawfulness of the use of force by a State in response to a wrongful act of which it has not itself been the victim is not admitted when this wrongful act is not an armed attack. In the view of the Court, under international law in force today—whether customary international law or that of the United Nations system—States do not have a right of "collective" armed response to acts which do not constitute an "armed attack". Furthermore, the Court has to recall that the United States itself is relying on the "inherent right of self-defence" ... but apparently does not claim that any such right exists as would, in respect of intervention, operate in the same way as the right of collective self-defence in respect of an armed attack. In the discharge of its duty under Article 53 of the Statute, the Court has nevertheless had to consider whether such a right might exist; but in doing so it may take note of the absence of any such claim by the United States as an indication of *opinio juris.*

* * *

227. The Court will first appraise the facts in the light of the principle of the non-use of force, examined ... above. What is unlawful, in accordance with that principle, is recourse to either the threat or the use of force against the territorial integrity or political independence of any State. For the most part, the complaints by Nicaragua are of the actual use of force against it by the United States. Of the acts which the Court has found imputable to the Government of the United States, the following are relevant in this respect:

> the laying of mines in Nicaraguan internal or territorial waters in early 1984 ...
>
> certain attacks on Nicaraguan ports, oil installations and a naval base....

These activities constitute infringements of the principle of the prohibition of the use of force, defined earlier, unless they are justified by circumstances which exclude their unlawfulness, a question now to be examined. The Court has also found ... the existence of military manoevres held by the United States near the Nicaraguan borders; and Nicaragua has made some suggestion that this constituted a "threat of force", which is equally forbidden by the principle of non-use of force. The Court is however not satisfied that the manoevres complained of, in the circumstances in which they were held, constituted on the part of the United States a breach, as against Nicaragua, of the principle forbidding recourse to the threat or use of force.

228. Nicaragua has also claimed that the United States has violated Article 2, paragraph 4, of the Charter, and has used force against Nicaragua in breach of its obligation under customary international law in as much as it has engaged in

> recruiting, training, arming, equipping, financing, supplying and otherwise encouraging, supporting, aiding, and directing military and paramilitary actions in and against Nicaragua (Application, para. 26 (a) and (C)).

So as far as the claim concerns breach of the Charter, it is excluded from the Court's jurisdiction by the multilateral treaty reservation. As to the claim that United States activities in relation to the *contras* constitute a breach of the customary international law principle of the non-use of force, the Court finds that, subject to the question whether the action of the United States might be justified as an exercise of the right of self-defence, the United States has committed a prima facie violation of that principle by its assistance to the *contras* in Nicaragua, by "organizing or encouraging the organization of irregular forces or armed bands ... for incursion into the territory of another State", and "participating in acts of civil strife ... in another State," in terms of General Assembly resolution 2625 (XXV). According to that resolution, participation of this kind is contrary to the principle of the prohibition of the use of force when the acts of civil strife referred to "involve a threat or use of force". In the view of the Court, while the arming and training of the *contras* can certainly be said to involve the threat or use of force against Nicaragua, this is not necessarily so in respect of all the assistance given by the United States Government. In particular, the Court considers that the mere supply of funds to the *contras*, while undoubtedly an act of intervention in the internal affairs of Nicaragua, as will be explained below, does not in itself amount to a use of force.

229. The Court must thus consider whether, as the Respondent claims, the acts in question of the United States are justified by the exercise of its right of collective self-defence against an armed attack. The Court must therefore establish whether the circumstances required for the exercise of this right of self-defence are present and, if so, whether the steps taken by the United States actually correspond to the requirements of international law. For the Court to conclude that the United States was lawfully exercising its right of collective self-defence, it must first find that Nicaragua engaged in an armed attack against El Salvador, Honduras or Costa Rica.

230. As regards El Salvador, the Court has found ... that it is satisfied that between July 1979 and the early months of 1981, an intermittent flow of arms was routed via the territory of Nicaragua to the armed opposition in that country. The Court was not however satisfied that assistance has reached the Salvadorian armed opposition, on a scale of any significance, since the early months of 1981, or that the Government of Nicaragua was responsible for any flow of arms at either period. Even assuming that the supply of arms to the opposition in El Salvador could be treated as imputable to the Government of Nicaragua, to justify invocation of the right of collective self-defence in customary international law, it would have to be equated with an armed attack by

Nicaragua on El Salvador. As stated above, the Court is unable to consider that, in customary international law, the provision of arms to the opposition in another State constitutes an armed attack on that State. Even at a time when the arms flow was at its peak, and again assuming the participation of the Nicaraguan Government, that would not constitute such armed attack.

231. Turning to Honduras and Costa Rica, the Court has also stated ... that it should find established that certain trans-border incursions into the territory of those two States, in 1982, 1983 and 1984, were imputable to the Government of Nicaragua. Very little information is however available to the Court as to the circumstances of these incursions or their possible motivations, which renders it difficult to decide whether they may be treated for legal purposes as amounting, singly or collectively, to an "armed attack" by Nicaragua on either or both States. The Court notes that during the Security Council debate in March/April 1984, the representative of Costa Rica made no accusation of an armed attack, emphasizing merely his country's neutrality and support for the Contadora process (S/PV.2529, pp. 13–23); the representative of Honduras however stated that

> my country is the object of aggression made manifest through a number of incidents by Nicaragua against our territorial integrity and civilian population (*ibid.*, p. 37).

There are however other considerations which justify the Court in finding that neither these incursions, nor the alleged supply of arms to the opposition in El Salvador, may be relied on as justifying the exercise of the right of collective self-defence.

232. The exercise of the right of collective self-defence presupposes that an armed attack has occurred; and it is evident that it is the victim State, being the most directly aware of that fact, which is likely to draw general attention to its plight. It is also evident that if the victim State wishes another State to come to its help in the exercise of the right of collective self-defence, it will normally make an express request to that effect. Thus in the present instance, the Court is entitled to take account, in judging the asserted justification of the exercise of collective self-defence by the United States, of the actual conduct of El Salvador, Honduras and Costa Rica at the relevant time, as indicative of a belief by the State in question that it was the victim of an armed attack by Nicaragua, and of the making of a request by the victim State to the United States for help in the exercise of collective self-defence.

* * *

235. There is also an aspect of the conduct of the United States which the Court is entitled to take into account as indicative of the view of that State on the question of the existence of an armed attack. At no time, up to the present, has the United States Government addressed to the Security Council, in connection with the matters the subject of the present case, the report which is required by Article 51 of the United Nations Charter in respect of measures which a State believes itself bound to take when it exercises the right of individual or collective self-defence. The Court, whose decision has to be made on the basis of customary international law, has already observed that in the context of that law, the reporting obligation enshrined in Article 51 of the Charter of the United Nations does not exist. It does not therefore treat the absence of a report on the part of the United States as the breach of an undertaking forming part of the customary international law applicable to the present dispute. But the Court is justified in observing that this conduct of the United States hardly conforms with the latter's avowed conviction that it was acting in the context of collective self-defence as conse-

crated by Article 51 of the Charter. This fact is all the more noteworthy because, in the Security Council, the United States has itself taken the view that failure to observe the requirement to make a report contradicted a State's claim to be acting on the basis of collective self-defence (S/PV.2187).

236. Similarly, while no strict legal conclusion may be drawn from the date of El Salvador's announcement that it was the victim of an armed attack, and the date of its official request addressed to the United States concerning the exercise of collective self-defence, those dates have a significance as evidence of El Salvador's view of the situation. The declaration and the request of El Salvador, made publicly for the first time in August 1984, do not support the contention that in 1981 there was an armed attack capable of serving as a legal foundation for United States activities which began in the second half of that year. The States concerned did not behave as though there were an armed attack at the time when the activities attributed by the United States to Nicaragua, without actually constituting such an attack, were nevertheless the most accentuated; they did so behave only at a time when these facts fell furthest short of what would be required for the Court to take the view that an armed attack existed on the part of Nicaragua against El Salvador.

237. Since the Court has found that the condition *sine qua non* required for the exercise of the right of collective self-defence by the United States is not fulfilled in this case, the appraisal of the United States activities in relation to the criteria of necessity and proportionality takes on a different significance. As a result of this conclusion of the Court, even if the United States activities in question had been carried on in strict compliance with the canons of necessity and proportionality, they would not thereby become lawful. If however they were not, this may constitute an additional ground of wrongfulness. On the question of necessity, the Court observes that the United States measures taken in December 1981 (or, at the earliest, March of that year ...) cannot be said to correspond to a "necessity" justifying the United States action against Nicaragua on the basis of assistance given by Nicaragua to the armed opposition in El Salvador. First, these measures were only taken, and began to produce their effects, several months after the major offensive of the armed opposition against the Government of El Salvador had been completely repulsed (January 1981), and the actions of the opposition considerably reduced in consequence. Thus it was possible to eliminate the main danger to the Salvadorian Government without the United States embarking on activities in and against Nicaragua. Accordingly, it cannot be held that these activities were undertaken in the light of necessity. Whether or not the assistance to the *contras* might meet the criterion of proportionality, the Court cannot regard the United States activities summarized in paragraphs 80, 81 and 86, i.e., those relating to the mining of the Nicaraguan ports and the attacks on ports, oil installations, etc., as satisfying that criterion. Whatever uncertainty may exist as to the exact scale of the aid received by the Salvadorian armed opposition from Nicaragua, it is clear that these latter United States activities in question could not have been proportionate to that aid. Finally on this point, the Court must also observe that the reaction of the United States in the context of what it regarded as self-defence was continued long after the period in which any presumed armed attack by Nicaragua could reasonably be contemplated.

238. Accordingly, the Court concludes that the plea of collective self-defence against an alleged armed attack on El Salvador, Honduras or Costa Rica, advanced by the United States to justify its conduct toward Nicaragua, cannot be upheld; and accordingly that the United States has violated the principle prohibiting recourse to the threat or use of force by the acts listed in paragraph 227 above, and by its assistance to the con-

tras to the extent that this assistance "involve[s] a threat or use of force" (paragraph 228 above).

QUESTIONS

1. What types of action in the Court's view, are sufficient to amount to an armed attack?
2. Why were Nicaragua's activities not sufficient to constitute an armed attack on El Salvador.
3. If State A supplies the rebels in State B with weapons and logistical support, does that constitute an armed attack by State A on State B? Would such action constitute a threat or use of force by State A against State B?
4. What events must occur before State C is permitted to exercise collective self-defence on behalf of State D against State E?
5. What weight did the Court give to the failure of the United States to report its actions on behalf of El Salvador to the Security Council?
6. If State A has used force, not amounting to an armed attack, against State B, does State C have a right to use force against State A by exercising a right to collective forceful counter-measures?
7. What actions of the United States were held to constitute a threat or use of force against Nicaragua?
8. Why did the Court not consider the United States actions against Nicaragua necessary or proportionate in relation to Nicaragua's activities against El Salvador?

Legality of the Threat or Use of Nuclear Weapons

International Court of Justice, Advisory Opinion,
1996 I.C.J. 226, reprinted at 35 I.L.M. 809 (1996)

Note

For the introductory note to this case see p. 391 *supra*.

The excerpt of the case below focuses on Charter law relating to the threat or use of force and self-defence as it relates to nuclear weapons.

Opinion of the Court

* * *

37. The Court will now address the question of the legality or illegality of recourse to nuclear weapons in the light of the provisions of the Charter relating to the threat or use of force.

38. The Charter contains several provisions relating to the threat or use of force. In Article 2, paragraph 4, the threat or use of force against the territorial integrity or political independence of another State or in any other manner inconsistent with the purposes of the United Nations is prohibited. That paragraph provides:

> All Members shall refrain in their international relations from the threat or use of force against the territorial integrity or political independence of any

State, or in any other manner inconsistent with the Purposes of the United Nations.

This prohibition of the use of force is to be considered in the light of other relevant provisions of the Charter. In Article 51, the Charter recognizes the inherent right of individual or collective self-defence if an armed attack occurs. A further lawful use of force is envisaged in Article 42, whereby the Security Council may take military enforcement measures in conformity with Chapter VII of the Charter.

39. These provisions do not refer to specific weapons. They apply to any use of force, regardless of the weapons employed. The Charter neither expressly prohibits, nor permits, the use of any specific weapon, including nuclear weapons. A weapon that is already unlawful *per se*, whether by treaty or custom, does not become lawful by reason of its being used for a legitimate purpose under the Charter.

40. The entitlement to resort to self-defence under Article 51 is subject to certain constraints. Some of these constraints are inherent in the very concept of self-defence. Other requirements are specified in Article 51.

41. The submission of the exercise of the right of self-defence to the conditions of necessity and proportionality is a rule of customary international law. As the Court stated in the case concerning *Military and Paramilitary Activities in and against Nicaragua (Nicaragua v. United States of America) (I.C.J. Reports 1986*, p. 94, para. 176): "there is a specific rule whereby self-defence would warrant only measures which are proportional to the armed attack and necessary to respond to it, a rule well established in customary international law". This dual condition applies equally to Article 51 of the Charter, whatever the means of force employed.

42. The proportionality principle may thus not in itself exclude the use of nuclear weapons in self-defence in all circumstances. But at the same time, a use of force that is proportionate under the law of self-defence, must, in order to be lawful, also meet the requirements of the law applicable in armed conflict which comprise in particular the principles and rules of humanitarian law.

43. Certain States have in their written and oral pleadings suggested that in the case of nuclear weapons, the condition of proportionality must be evaluated in the light of still further factors. They contend that the very nature of nuclear weapons, and the high probability of an escalation of nuclear exchanges, mean that there is an extremely strong risk of devastation. The risk factor is said to negate the possibility of the condition of proportionality being complied with. The Court does not find it necessary to embark upon the quantification of such risks; nor does it need to enquire into the question whether tactical nuclear weapons exist which are sufficiently precise to limit those risks: it suffices for the Court to note that the very nature of all nuclear weapons and the profound risks associated therewith are further considerations to be borne in mind by States believing they can exercise a nuclear response in self-defence in accordance with the requirements of proportionality.

44. Beyond the conditions of necessity and proportionality, Article 51 specifically requires that measures taken by States in the exercise of the right of self-defence shall be immediately reported to the Security Council; this article further provides that these measures shall not in any way affect the authority and responsibility of the Security Council under the Charter to take at any time such action as it deems necessary in order to maintain or restore international peace and security. These requirements of Article 51 apply whatever the means of force used in self-defence.

Case Concerning Oil Platforms (Islamic Republic of Iran v. United States of America)

2003 I.C.J. 161

Note

Iran brought suit against the U.S. claiming that the destruction of three offshore oil platforms in the Persian Gulf by U.S. warships during 1987–1988 constituted a violation of the Treaty of Amity, Economic Relations and Consular Rights between Iran and the U.S. as well as a breach of international law. The U.S. filed a counter-claim alleging that Iran's actions in the Gulf during the same time period had resulted in mining attacks on U.S. flagged or U.S. owned vessels. The U.S. did not deny that the attacks on the oil platforms were carried out by the U.S. military but sought to justify its actions on the basis of self-defence. The Court's discussion of self-defence appears below.

Opinion of the Court

49. In its Counter-Memorial, the United States … argued that Iranian actions during the relevant period constituted a threat to essential security interests of the United States, inasmuch as the flow of maritime commerce in the Persian Gulf was threatened by Iran's repeated attacks on neutral vessels; that the lives of United States nationals were put at risk; that United States naval vessels were seriously impeded in their security duties; and that the United States Government and United States nationals suffered severe financial losses. According to the United States, it was clear that diplomatic measures were not a viable means of deterring Iran from its attacks: "Accordingly, armed action in self-defense was the only option left to the United States to prevent additional Iranian attacks".

50. The Court will thus first concentrate on the facts tending to show the validity or otherwise of the claim to exercise the right of self-defence. In its communication to the Security Council, … the United States based this claim on the existence of

> "a series of unlawful armed attacks by Iranian forces against the United States, including laying mines in international waters for the purpose of sinking or damaging United States flag ships, and firing on United States aircraft without provocation";

it referred in particular to a missile attack on the *Sea Isle City* as being the specific incident that led to the attack on the Iranian platforms.… To justify its choice of the platforms as target, the United States asserted that they had "engaged in a variety of actions directed against United States flag and other non-belligerent vessels and aircraft". Iran has denied any responsibility for (in particular) the attack on the *Sea Isle City*, and has claimed that the platforms had no military purpose, and were not engaged in any military activity.

51.… Therefore, in order to establish that it was legally justified in attacking the Iranian platforms in exercise of the right of individual self-defence, the United States has to show that attacks had been made upon it for which Iran was responsible; and that those attacks were of such a nature as to be qualified as "armed attacks" within the meaning of that expression in Article 51 of the United Nations Charter, and as understood in customary law on the use of force. As the Court observed in the case concerning *Military and Paramilitary Activities in and against Nicaragua*, it is necessary to distinguish "the most grave forms of the use of force (those constituting and armed attack) from other less grave forms" (*I.C.J. Reports 1986*, p. 101, para. 191), since "In the case of individual self-defence, the exercise of this right is subject to the State concerned having been the victim of an armed attack" (*ibid.*, p. 103, para. 195). The United States must also show that its actions were necessary and proportional to the armed attack made on it, and that the platforms were a legitimate military target open to attack in the exercise of self-defence.

52. Since it was the missile attack on the *Sea Isle City* that figured most prominently in the United States contentions, the Court will first examine in detail the evidence relating to that incident. The *Sea Isle City* was a Kuwait tanker reflagged to the United States; on 16 October 1987 it had just ended a voyage under "Operation Earnest Will", ... when it was hit by a missile near Kuwait's Al-Ahmadi Sea Island (or Mina al-Ahmadi) terminal. This incident, which caused damage to the ship and injury to six crew members, was claimed by the United States to be the seventh involving Iranian anti-ship cruise missiles in the area in the course of 1987. The United States asserts that the missile that struck the *Sea Isle City* was launched by Iran from a facility located in the Fao area.

* * *

54. Iran suggests that no credible evidence has been produced that there were operational Iranian missile sites in the Fao area.... [The Court then reviewed in detail the evidence produced by the U.S. that Iran carried out the attacks as well as Iran's theory that perhaps Iraq had carried out the attacks. Iran and Iraq were at war during this period.]

* * *

57. For present purposes, the Court has simply to determine whether the United States has demonstrated that it was the victim of an "armed attack" by Iran such as to justify it using armed force in self-defence; and the burden of proof of the facts showing the existence of such an attack rests on the United States.

* * *

61. In short, the Court has examined with great care the evidence and arguments presented on each side, and finds that the evidence indicative of Iranian responsibility for the attack on the *Sea Isle City* is not sufficient to support the contentions of the United States. The conclusion to which the Court has come on this aspect of the case is thus that the burden of proof of the existence of an armed attack by Iran on the United States, in the form of the missile attack on the *Sea Isle City*, has not been discharged.

* * *

64.... There is no evidence that the minelaying alleged to have been carried out by the *Iran Ajr*, at a time when Iran was at war with Iraq, was aimed specifically at the United States; and similarly it has not been established that the mine struck by the *Bridgeton* was laid with the specific intention of harming that ship, or other United States vessels. Even taken cumulatively, and reserving, as already noted, the question of Iranian responsibility, these incidents do not seem to the Court to constitute an armed attack on the United States, of the kind that the Court, in the case concerning *Military and Paramilitary Activities in and against Nicaragua*, qualified as a "most grave" form of the use of force....

* * *

67. The nature of the attacks on the Salman and Nasr complexes, and their alleged justification, was presented by the United States to the United Nations Security Council in the following terms (letter from the United States Permanent Representative of 18 April 1988, S/19791):

> "In accordance with Article 51 of the Charter of the United Nations, I wish, on behalf of my Government, to report that United States forces have exercised their inherent right of self-defence under international law by taking defensive action in response to an attack by the Islamic Republic of Iran against a United States naval vessel in international waters of the Persian Gulf. The actions taken are necessary and are proportionate to the threat posed by such hostile Iranian actions.

* * *

68. The Court notes that the attacks on the Salman and Nasr platforms were not an isolated operation, aimed simply at the oil installations, as had been the case with the attacks of 19 October 1987; they formed part of a much more extensive military action, designated "Operation Praying Mantis", conducted by the United States against what it regarded as "legitimate military targets"; armed force was used, and damage done to a number of targets, including the destruction of two Iranian frigates and other Iranian naval vessels and aircraft.

74. In its decision in the case concerning *Military and Paramilitary Activities in and against Nicaragua*, the Court endorsed the shared view of the parties to that case that in customary law "whether the response to the [armed] attack is lawful depends on observance of the criteria of the necessity and the proportionality of the measures taken in self-defence"*(I.C.J. Reports 1986*, p. 103, para. 194). One aspect of these criteria is the nature of the target of the force used avowedly in self-defence. In its communications to the Security Council, in particular in that of 19 October 1987 (paragraph 46 above), the United States indicated the grounds on which it regarded the Iranian platforms as legitimate targets for an armed action in self-defence.

* * *

76. The Court is not sufficiently convinced that the evidence available supports the contentions of the United States as to the significance of the military presence and activity on the Reshadat oil platforms; and it notes that no such evidence is offered in respect of the Salman and Nasr complexes. However, even accepting those contentions, for the purposes of discussion, the Court is unable to hold that the attacks made on the platforms could have been justified as acts of self-defence. The conditions for the exercise of the right of self-defence are well settled: as the Court observed in its Advisory Opinion on *Legality of the Threat or Use of Nuclear Weapons*, "The submission of the exercise of the right of self-defence to the conditions of necessity and proportionality is a rule of customary international law"*(I.C.J. Reports 1996 (I)*, p. 245, para. 41); and in the case concerning *Military and Paramilitary Activities in and against Nicaragua*, the Court referred to a specific rule "whereby self-defence would warrant only measures which are proportional to the armed attack and necessary to respond to it" as "a rule well established in customary international law" *(I.C.J. Reports 1986*, p. 94, para. 176). In the case both of the attack on the *Sea Isle City* and the mining of the USS *Samuel B. Roberts*, the Court is not satisfied that the attacks on the platforms were necessary to respond to these incidents. In this connection, the Court notes that there is no evidence that the United States complained repeatedly of minelaying and attacks on neutral shipping,

which does not suggest that the targeting of the platforms was seen as a necessary act. The Court would also observe that in the case of the attack of 19 October 1987, the United States forces attacked the R-4 platform as a "target of opportunity", not one previously identified as an appropriate military target....

77. As to the requirement of proportionality, the attack of 19 October 1987 might, had the Court found that it was necessary in response to the *Sea Isle City* incident as an armed attack committed by Iran, have been considered proportionate. In the case of the attacks of 18 April 1988, however, they were conceived and executed as part of a more extensive operation entitled "Operation Praying Mantis".... The question of the lawfulness of other aspects of that operation is not before the Court, since it is solely the action against the Salman and Nasr complexes that is presented as a breach of the 1955 Treaty; but the Court cannot assess in isolation the proportionality of that action to the attack to which it was said to be a response; it cannot close its eyes to the scale of the whole operation, which involved, *inter alia,* the destruction of two Iranian frigates and a number of other naval vessels and aircraft. As a response to the mining, by an unidentified agency, of a single United States warship, which was severely damaged but not sunk, and without loss of life, neither "Operation Praying Mantis" as a whole, nor even that part of it that destroyed the Salman and Nasr platforms, can be regarded, in the circumstances of this case, as a proportionate use of force in self-defence.

78. The Court thus concludes from the foregoing that the actions carried out by United States forces against Iranian oil installations on 19 October 1987 and 18 April 1988 cannot be justified, under Article XX, paragraph 1*(d)*, of the 1955 Treaty, as being measures necessary to protect the essential security interests of the United States, since those actions constituted recourse to armed force not qualifying, under international law on the question, as acts of self-defence, and thus did not fall within the category of measures contemplated, upon its correct interpretation, by that provision of the Treaty.

* * *

[The Court did not find that the U.S. had breached the Treaty of Amity, Economic Relations and Consular Rights between Iran and the U.S. and thus declined to award reparations to Iran].

QUESTIONS

1. What did the Court require the U.S. to prove before it was willing to examine whether the U.S. had engaged in permissible self-defence?
2. Why did the U.S. fail to convince the Court that its actions were a legitimate use of force in self-defence?

Preemption

In March 2003, the United States initiated armed force against Iraq. The United States sought to justify its attack on the basis of a new doctrine under which it maintained the right to use force preemptively because it stated that it had received "reliable intelligence" that Iraq had "weapons of mass destruction" which Iraq was capable of using against the United States.[28] Later, other justifications were added to the rationale

28. The National Security Strategy of the U.S. (Sept. 17, 2002) available at: http://www.whitehouse.gov/nsc/nss.pdf.

for the attack such as Iraq's violation of Security Council resolutions relating to the conditions imposed on Iraq after Iraq's invasion of Kuwait in 1990. The announcement of the preemption doctrine caused a torrent of debate especially when it became clear that there were no weapons of mass destruction in Iraq and that the "reliable intelligence" data had in fact never been considered "reliable" even by many within the U.S. intelligence agencies.

Previously, scholars who had accepted the argument for anticipatory self-defence had always insisted that the threatened attack must be "imminent." The preemption doctrine either stretches the term "imminent" beyond normal linguistic limits or simply dispenses with the need for any imminence. Any future attack, however remote or speculative, would then justify self-defence. Needless to say, this doctrine is highly controversial. For a reasoned explanation of many scholars' views of this issue in the Iraq war context see: *Agora: Future Implications of the Iraq Conflict,* 97 American Journal of International Law 553–642 (2003).

Reprisals Using Force

Earlier in this chapter a reprisal was defined as "an illegal act taken as a measure of self-help in response to a prior illegal act." (p. 386–387) That earlier section discussed reprisals not involving force. What if a reprisal in fact involves force, such as a bombing raid into a neighboring territory or the dispatch of a commando unit to rescue hostages held by another state? The International Court of Justice has stated that "armed reprisals in time of peace ... are considered to be unlawful."[29] The Court also added that with respect to "belligerent reprisals ... any right of recourse to such reprisals would, like self-defence, be governed *inter alia* by the principle of proportionality."[30] Reprisals that take place during war are also governed by the laws of war including the four Geneva Conventions of 1949.[31]

If a prior illegal action amounted to an armed attack, the prior action would trigger the right to self defence but, as the *Nicaragua* case makes clear, not all armed illegal activities amount to an armed attack giving rise to the right of self-defence.

Although the Security Council has frequently condemned armed reprisals, it remains true that many states engage in armed reprisals. The international community has not created an effective mechanism to redress illegal inter-state acts, with the result that states are often ready to use self-help in the form of armed reprisals at an ever escalating level.[32]

The Rule of Non-Intervention

Article 2(1) of the United Nations Charter declares that: "The Organization is based on the principle of the sovereign equality of all its Members." The principle of the equality of states carries with it the notion that every state is prohibited from interfering

29. *Legality of the Threat or Use of Nuclear Weapons,* 1996 I.C.J. 226, at para. 46, reprinted at 35 I.L.M. at 823 (1996).

30. Id.

31. See e.g., Geneva Convention Relative to the Protection of Civilian Persons in Time of War, art. 18, 75 U.N.T.S. 287, 6 U.S.T. 3516, T.I.A.S. No. 3365, signed 12 August 1949, entered into force 21 Oct. 1950.

32. See generally, D.W. Bowett, Reprisals Involving Recourse to Armed Force, 66 Amer. J. Int'l L. 1 (1972).

in the internal affairs of another state. Interference can take many forms. If it comes in the form of force it is governed by U.N. Charter articles 2(4) and 51 as well as customary law governing the use of force but it may also constitute illegal intervention. If interference does not amount to the use of force, then a state's conduct is governed by the rules relating to non-intervention.

In 1965, the General Assembly issued the *Declaration on the Inadmissibility of Intervention in the Domestic Affairs of States and the Protection of Their Independence and Sovereignty.*[33]

> 1. No State has the right to intervene, directly or indirectly, for any reason whatever, in the internal or external affairs of any other State. Consequently, armed intervention and all other forms of interference or attempted threats against the personality of the State or against its political, economic and cultural elements, are condemned;
>
> 2. No State may use or encourage the use of economic, political or any other type of measures to coerce another State in order to obtain from it the subordination of the exercise of its sovereign rights or to secure from it advantages of any kind. Also, no State shall organize, assist, foment, finance, incite or tolerate subversive, terrorist or armed activities directed towards the violent overthrow of the regime of another State, or interfere in civil strife in another State;
>
> 3. The use of force to deprive peoples of their national identity constitutes a violation of their inalienable rights and of the principle of non-intervention;
>
> 4. The strict observance of these obligations is an essential condition to ensure that nations live together in peace with one another, since the practice of any form of intervention not only violates the spirit and letter of the Charter but also leads to the creation of situations which threaten international peace and security;
>
> 5. Every State has an inalienable right to choose its political, economic, social and cultural systems, without interference in any form by another State;
>
> 6. All States shall respect the right of self-determination and independence of peoples and nations, to be freely exercised without any foreign pressure, and with absolute respect for human rights and fundamental freedoms. Consequently, all States shall contribute to the complete elimination of racial discrimination and colonialism in all its forms and manifestations;
>
> 7. For the purpose of this Declaration, the term "State" covers both individual States and groups of States;
>
> 8. Nothing in this Declaration shall be construed as affecting in any manner the relevant provisions of the Charter of the United Nations relating to the maintenance of international peace and security, in particular those contained in Chapters VI, VII and VIII.

In the *Nicaragua Case* the Court indicated that it considered this Declaration to be an expression of customary law. (See *Nicaragua Case* at para. 203 below.) States do, of

33. G.A. Res. 2131, U.N. GAOR, 20th Sess., Supp. No. 14, at 11, U.N. Doc. A/6620 (1965).

course, try to influence the behavior of other states in a variety of ways. The line between permissible diplomatic influence and illegal intervention is often hard to distinguish.

The International Court of Justice discussed one aspect of intervention in the *Corfu Channel Case*.[34] After British warships had been damaged by mines while exercising their right of innocent passage in Albanian territorial waters that were also designated as an international strait, other British warships were sent back into the Corfu Channel to sweep for mines on a mission named "Operation Retail." The British were convinced that the Albanians had put the mines in the Channel and they argued that they had a right to intervene to acquire and preserve evidence in order to submit it to an international tribunal.

The Court rejected this argument and stated.

> "The Court can only regard the alleged right of intervention as a manifestation of a policy of force, such as has, in the past, given rise to most serious abuses and such as cannot, whatever be the present defects in international organization, find a place in international law....
>
> The United Kingdom ... has further classified "Operation Retail" among methods of self-protection or self-help. The Court cannot accept this defence either. Between independent states, respect for territorial sovereignty is an essential foundation of international relations."[35]

The International Court of Justice also addressed a number of aspects of intervention in the *Nicaragua Case* below.

Case Concerning Military and Paramilitary Activities in and against Nicaragua Nicaragua v. United States

1986 I.C.J. 14 (Merits)

Note

For the introductory note to this case see pp. 393–394.

Opinion of the Court

* * *

202. The principle of non-intervention involves the right of every sovereign State to conduct its affairs without outside interference; though examples of trespass against this principle are not infrequent, the Court considers that it is part and parcel of customary international law. As the Court has observed: "Between independent States, respect for territorial sovereignty is an essential foundation of international relations" (*I.C.J. Reports 1949*, p. 35), and international law requires political integrity also to be respected. Expressions of an *opinio juris* regarding the existence of the principle of

34. 1949 I.C.J. 3.
35. Id. at 35.

non-intervention in customary international law are numerous and not difficult to find. Of course, statements whereby States avow their recognition of the principles of international law set forth in the United Nations Charter cannot strictly be interpreted as applying to the principle of non-intervention by States in the internal and external affairs of other States, since this principle is not, as such, spelt out in the Charter. But it was never intended that the Charter should embody written confirmation of every essential principle of international law in force. The existence in the *opinio juris* of States of the principle of non-intervention is backed by established and substantial practice. It has moreover been presented as a corollary of the principle of the sovereign equality of States. A particular instance of this is General Assembly resolution 2625 (XXV), the Declaration on the Principles of International Law concerning Friendly Relations and Co-operation among States. In the *Corfu Channel* case, when a State claimed a right of intervention in order to secure evidence in the territory of another State for submission to an international tribunal (*I.C.J. Reports 1949*, p. 34), the Court observed that:

> the alleged right to intervention as the manifestation of a policy of force, such as has, in the past, given rise to most serious abuses and such as cannot, whatever be the present defects in international organization, find a place in international law. Intervention is perhaps still less admissible in the particular form it would take here; for, from the nature of things, it would be reserved for the most powerful States, and might easily lead to perverting the administration of international justice itself. (*I.C.J. Reports 1949*, p. 35.)

203. The principle has since been reflected in numerous declarations adopted by international organizations and conferences in which the United States and Nicaragua have participated, e.g., General Assembly resolution 2131 (XX), the Declaration on the Inadmissibility of Intervention in the Domestic Affairs of States and the Protection of their Independence and Sovereignty. It is true that the United States, while it voted in favour of General Assembly resolution 2131 (XX), also declared at the time of its adoption in the First Committee that it considered the declaration in that resolution to be "only a statement of political intention and not a formulation of law" (*Official Records of the General Assembly, Twentieth Session*, First Committee, A/C. 1/SR.1423, p. 436). However, the essentials of resolution 2131 (XX) are repeated in the Declaration approved by resolution 2625 (XXV), which set out principles which the General Assembly declared to be "basic principles" of international law, and on the adoption of which no analogous statement was made by the United States representative.

204. As regards inter-American relations, attention may be drawn to, for example, the United States reservation to the Montevideo Convention on Rights and Duties of States (26 December 1933), declaring the opposition of the United States Government to "interference with the freedom, the sovereignty or other internal affairs, or processes of the Governments of other nations"; or the ratification by the United States of the Additional Protocol relative to Non-Intervention (23 December 1936). Among more recent texts, mention may be made of resolutions AG/RES.78 and AG/RES.128 of the General Assembly of the Organization of American States. In a different context, the United States expressly accepted the principles set forth in the declaration, to which reference has already been made, appearing in the Final Act of the Conference on Security and Co-operation in Europe (Helsinki, 1 August 1975), including an elaborate statement of the principle of non-intervention; while these principles were presented as applying to the mutual relations among the participating States, it can be inferred that the text testi-

fies to the existence, and the acceptance by the United States, of a customary principle which has universal application.

205. Notwithstanding the multiplicity of declarations by States accepting the principle of non-intervention, there remain two questions: first, what is the exact content of the principle so accepted, and secondly, is the practice sufficiently in conformity with it for this to be a rule of customary international law? As regards the first problem—that of the content of the principle of non-intervention—the Court will define only those aspects of the principle which appear to be relevant to the resolution of the dispute. In this respect it notes that, in view of the generally accepted formulations, the principle forbids all States or groups of States to intervene directly or indirectly in internal or external affairs of other States. A prohibited intervention must accordingly be one bearing on matters in which each State is permitted, by the principle of State sovereignty, to decide freely. One of these is the choice of a political, economic, social and cultural system, and the formulation of foreign policy. Intervention is wrongful when it uses methods of coercion in regard to such choices, which must remain free ones. The element of coercion, which defines, and indeed forms the very essence of, prohibited intervention, is particularly obvious in the case of an intervention which uses force, either in the direct form of military action, or in the indirect form of support for subversive or terrorist armed activities within another State. As noted above (paragraph 191), General Assembly resolution 2625 (XXV) equates assistance of this kind with the use of force by the assisting State when the acts committed in another State "involve a threat or use of force". These forms of action are therefore wrongful in the light of both the principle of non-use of force, and that on non-intervention. In view of the nature of Nicaragua's complaints against the United States, and those expressed by the United States in regard to Nicaragua's conduct towards El Salvador, it is primarily acts of intervention of this kind with which the Court is concerned in the present case.

206. However, before reaching a conclusion on the nature of prohibited intervention, the Court must be satisfied that State practice justifies it. There have been in recent years a number of instances of foreign intervention for the benefit of forces opposed to the government of another State. The Court is not here concerned with the process of decolonization; this question is not in issue in the present case. It has to consider whether there might be indications of a practice illustrative of belief in a kind of general right for States to intervene, directly or indirectly, with or without armed force, in support of an internal opposition in another State, whose cause appeared particularly worthy by reason of the political and moral values with which it was identified. For such a general right to come into existence would involve a fundamental modification of the customary law principle of non-intervention.

207. In considering the instances of the conduct above described, the Court has to emphasize that, as was observed in the *North Sea Continental Shelf* cases, for a new customary rule to be formed, not only must the acts concerned "amount to a settled practice", but they must be accompanied by the *opinio juris sive necessitatis.* Either the States taking such action or other States in a position to react to it, must have behaved so that their conduct is

> evidence of a belief that this practice is rendered obligatory by the existence of a rule of law requiring it. The need for such a belief, i.e., the existence of a subjective element, is implied in the very notion of the *opinio juris sive necessitatis.* (*I.C.J. Reports 1969*, p. 44, para. 77.)

The Court has no jurisdiction to rule upon the conformity with international law of any conduct of States not parties to the present dispute, or of conduct of the Parties unconnected with the dispute; nor has it authority to ascribe to States legal views which they do not themselves advance. The significance for the Court of cases of State conduct prima facie inconsistent with the principle of non-intervention lies in the nature of the ground offered as justification. Reliance by a State on a novel right or an unprecedented exception to the principle might, if shared in principle by other States, tend towards a modification of customary international law. In fact however the Court finds that States have not justified their conduct by reference to a new right of intervention or a new exception to the principle of its prohibition. The United States authorities have on some occasions clearly stated their grounds for intervening in the affairs of a foreign State for reasons connected with, for example, the domestic policies of that country, its ideology, the level of its armaments, or the direction of its foreign policy. But these were statements of international policy, and not an assertion of rules of existing international law.

208. In particular, as regards the conduct towards Nicaragua which is the subject of the present case, the United States has not claimed that its intervention, which is justified in this way on the political level, was also justified on the legal level, alleging the exercise of a new right of intervention regarded by the United States as existing in such circumstances. As mentioned above, the United States has, on the legal plane, justified its intervention expressly and solely by reference to the "classic" rules involved, namely, collective self-defence against an armed attack. Nicaragua, for its part, has often expressed its solidarity and sympathy with the opposition in various States, especially in El Salvador. But Nicaragua too has not argued that this was a legal basis for an intervention, let alone an intervention involving the use of force.

209. The Court therefore finds that no such general right of intervention, in support of an opposition within another State, exists in contemporary international law. The Court concludes that acts constituting a breach of the customary principle of non-intervention will also, if they directly or indirectly involve the use of force, constitute a breach of the principle of non-use of force in international relations.

210. When dealing with the rule of the prohibition of the use of force, the Court considered the exception to it constituted by the exercise of the right of collective self-defence in the event of armed attack. Similarly, it must now consider the following question: if one States acts towards another State in breach of the principle of non-intervention, may a third State lawfully take such action by way of counter-measures against the first State as would otherwise constitute an intervention in its internal affairs? A right to act in this way in the case of intervention would be analogous to the right of collective self-defence in the case of an armed attack, but both the act which gives rise to the reaction, and that reaction itself, would in principle be less grave. Since the Court is here dealing with a dispute in which a wrongful use of force is alleged, it has primarily to consider whether a State has a right to respond to intervention with intervention going so far as to justify a use of force in reaction to measures which do not constitute an armed attack but may nevertheless involve a use of force. The question is itself undeniably relevant from the theoretical viewpoint. However, since the Court is bound to confine its decision to those points of law which are essential to the settlement of the dispute before it, it is not for the Court here to determine what direct reactions are lawfully open to a State which considers itself the victim of another State's acts of intervention, possibly involving the use of force. Hence it has not to determine whether, in the event of Nicaragua's having committed any such acts against El Salvador, the latter was lawfully entitled to take any particular counter-measure. It might however be suggested that, in such a situation, the United States might have been permitted to intervene in Nicaragua in the exercise of some right analogous to the right of collective self-defence, one which might be resorted to in a case of intervention short of armed attack.

* * *

239. The Court comes now to the application in this case of the principle of non-intervention in the internal affairs of States. It is argued by Nicaragua that the "military and paramilitary activities aimed at the government and people of Nicaragua" have two purposes:

(a) The actual overthrow of the existing lawful government of Nicaragua and its replacement by a government acceptable to the United States; and
(b) The substantial damaging of the economy, and the weakening of the political system, in order to coerce the government of Nicaragua into the acceptance of United States policies and political demands.

Nicaragua also contends that the various acts of an economic nature, summarized in paragraphs 123 to 125 above, constitute a form of "indirect" intervention in Nicaragua's internal affairs.

240. Nicaragua has laid much emphasis on the intentions it attributes to the Government of the United States in giving aid and support to the *contras*. It contends that the purpose of the policy of the United States and its actions against Nicaragua in pursuance of this policy was, from the beginning, to overthrow the Government of Nicaragua. In order to demonstrate this, it has drawn attention to numerous statements by high officials of the United States Government, in particular by President Reagan, expressing solidarity and support for the *contras*, described on occasion as 'freedom fighters', and indicating that support for the *contras* would continue until the Nicaraguan Government took certain action, desired by the United States Government, amounting in effect to a surrender to the demands of the latter Government. The official Report of the President of the United States to Congress of 10 April 1985, quoted in paragraph 96 above, states that: "We have not sought to overthrow the Nicaraguan Government nor to force on Nicaragua a specific system of government." But it indicates also quite openly that "United States policy toward Nicaragua"—which includes the support for the military and paramilitary activities of the *contras* which it was the purpose of the Report to continue—"has consistently sought to achieve changes in Nicaraguan government policy and behavior".

241. The Court however does not consider it necessary to seek to establish whether the intention of the United States to secure a change of governmental policies in Nicaragua went so far as to be equated with an endeavor to overthrow the Nicaraguan Government. It appears to the Court to be clearly established first, that the United States intended, by its support of the *contras*, to coerce the Government of Nicaragua in respect of matters in which each State is permitted, by the principle of State sovereignty, to decide freely (see paragraph 205 above); and secondly that the intention of the *contras* themselves was to overthrow the present Government of Nicaragua. The 1983 Report of the Intelligence Committee refers to the *contras*' "openly acknowledged goal of overthrowing the Sandinistas". Even if it be accepted, for the sake of argument, that the objective of the United States in assisting the *contras* was solely to interdict the supply of arms to the armed opposition in El Salvador, it strains belief to suppose that a body formed in armed opposition to the Government of Nicaragua, and calling itself the "Nicaraguan Democratic Force", intended only to check Nicaraguan interference in El Salvador and did not intend to achieve violent change of government in Nicaragua. The Court considers that in international law, if one State, with a view to the coercion of another State, supports and assists armed bands in that State whose purpose is to overthrow the government of that State, that amounts to an intervention by the one State in

the internal affairs of the other, whether or not the political objective of the State giving such support and assistance is equally far-reaching. It is for this reason that the Court has only examined the intentions of the United States Government so far as they bear on the question of self-defence.

* * *

242. The Court therefore finds that the support given by the United States, up to the end of September 1984, to the military and paramilitary activities of the *contras* in Nicaragua, by financial support, training, supply of weapons, intelligence and logistic support, constitutes a clear breach of the principle of non-intervention. The Court has however taken note that, with effect from the beginning of the United States governmental financial year 1985, namely 1 October 1984, the United States Congress has restricted the use of the funds appropriated for assistance to the *contras* to "humanitarian assistance" (paragraph 97 above). There can be no doubt that the provision of strictly humanitarian aid to persons or forces in another country, whatever their political affiliations or objectives, cannot be regarded as unlawful intervention, or is in any other way contrary to international law. The characteristics of such aid were indicated in the first and second of the fundamental principles declared by the Twentieth International Conference of the Red Cross, that

> The Red Cross, born of a desire to bring assistance without discrimination to the wounded on the battlefield, endeavours—in its international and national capacity—to prevent and alleviate human suffering wherever it may be found. Its purpose is to protect life and health and to ensure respect for the human being. It promotes mutual understanding, friendship, co-operation and lasting peace amongst all peoples

and that

> It makes no discrimination as to nationality, race, religious beliefs, class or political opinions. It endeavours only to relieve suffering, giving priority to the most urgent cases of distress.

243. The United States legislation which limited aid to the *contras* to humanitarian assistance however also defined what was meant by such assistance, namely:

> the provision of food, clothing, medicine, and other humanitarian assistance, and it does not include the provision of weapons, weapons systems, ammunition, or other equipment, vehicles, or material which can be used to inflict serious bodily harm or death (paragraph 97 above).

It is also to be noted that, while the United States Congress has directed that the CIA and Department of Defense are not to administer any of the funds voted, it was understood that intelligence information might be "shared" with the *contras*. Since the Court has no information as to the interpretation in fact given to the Congress' decision, or as to whether intelligence information is in fact still being supplied to the *contras*, it will limit itself to a declaration as to how the law applies in this respect. An essential feature of truly humanitarian aid is that it is given "without discrimination" of any kind. In the view of the Court, if the provision of "humanitarian assistance" is to escape condemnation as an intervention in the internal affairs of Nicaragua, not only must it be limited to the purposes hallowed in the practice of the Red Cross, namely "to prevent and alleviate human suffering", and "to protect life and health and to ensure respect for the human being"; it must also, and above all, be given without discrimination to all in need in Nicaragua, not merely to the *contras* and their dependents.

244. As already noted, Nicaragua has also asserted that the United States is responsible for an "indirect" form of intervention in its internal affairs inasmuch as it has taken, to Nicaragua's disadvantage, certain action of an economic nature. The Court's attention has been drawn in particular to the cessation of economic aid in April 1981; the 90 percent reduction in the sugar quota for United States imports from Nicaragua in April 1981; and the trade embargo adopted on 1 May 1985. While admitting in principle that some of these actions were not unlawful in themselves, counsel for Nicaragua argued that these measures of economic constraint add up to a systematic violation of the principle of non-intervention.

245. The Court does not here have to concern itself with possible breaches of such international economic instruments as the General Agreement on Tariffs and Trade, referred to in passing by counsel for Nicaragua; any such breaches would appear to fall outside the Court's jurisdiction, particularly in view of the effect of the multilateral treaty reservation, nor has Nicaragua seised the Court of any complaint of such breaches. The question of the compatibility of the actions complained of with the 1956 Treaty of Friendship, Commerce and Navigation will be examined below, in the context of the Court's examination of the provisions of that Treaty. At this point, the Court has merely to say that it is unable to regard such action on the economic plane as is here complained of as a breach of the customary-law principle of non-intervention.

246. Having concluded that the activities of the United States in relation to the activities of the *contras* in Nicaragua constitute prima facie acts of intervention, the Court must next consider whether they may nevertheless be justified on some legal ground. As the Court has stated, the principle of non-intervention derives from customary international law. It would certainly lose its effectiveness as a principle of law if intervention were to be justified by a mere request for assistance made by an opposition group in another State—supposing such a request to have actually been made by an opposition to the regime in Nicaragua in this instance. Indeed, it is difficult to see what would remain of the principle of non-intervention in international law if intervention, which is already allowable at the request of the government of a State, were also to be allowed at the request of the opposition. This would permit any State to intervene at any moment in the internal affairs of another State, whether at the request of the government or at the request of its opposition. Such a situation does not in the Court's view correspond to the present state of international law.

247.... The Court must therefore enquire now whether the activities of the United States towards Nicaragua might be justified as a response to an intervention by that State in the internal affairs of another State in Central America.

248. The United States admits that it is giving its support to the *contras* in Nicaragua, but justifies this by claiming that that State is adopting similar conduct by itself assisting the armed opposition in El Salvador, and to a lesser extent in Honduras and Costa Rica, and has committed transborder attacks on those two States. The United States raises this justification as one of self-defence; having rejected it on those terms, the Court has nevertheless to consider whether it may be valid as action by way of counter-measures in response to intervention. The Court has however to find that the applicable law does not warrant such a justification.

249. On the legal level the Court cannot regard response to an intervention by Nicaragua as such a justification. While an armed attack would give rise to an entitlement to collective self-defence, a use of force of a lesser degree of gravity cannot, as the Court has already observed (paragraph 211 above), produce any entitlement to take col-

lective counter-measures involving the use of force. The acts of which Nicaragua is accused, even assuming them to have been established and imputable to that State, could only have justified proportionate counter-measures on the part of the State which had been the victim of these acts, namely El Salvador, Honduras or Costa Rica. They could not justify counter-measures taken by a third State, the United States, and particularly could not justify intervention involving the use of force.

QUESTIONS

1. What types of evidence persuaded the Court that the principle of non-intervention had become accepted as customary law?
2. What types of interference in a state's internal or external affairs constitutes a violation of the principle of non-intervention?
3. Do states have a right to intervene in other states in support of internal opposition?
4. If State A, without using armed force amounting to an armed attack, unlawfully intervenes in State B's internal affairs what countermeasures may State B take? What countermeasures may State C take on behalf of State B?
5. Why did the Court find that the United States had unlawfully intervened in Nicaragua's internal affairs?
6. Did the United States' supply of humanitarian aid to the *contras* violate principles of non-intervention?

Civil Wars and the Rule of Non-Intervention

The clear import of the Court's opinion in the *Nicaragua Case* is that states have no right to support *rebel* groups in other states even if requested to do so and even if they are convinced that the rebels' cause is just. This prohibition of support for rebels even extends to humanitarian aid unless it is made equally available to government forces.

At the present time international law does not prohibit civil wars. Article 2(4) of the U.N. Charter and the customary laws of war are directed towards the prohibition of international hostilities. The laws addressing the conduct of hostilities do apply to the conduct of civil wars in certain instances. (See section on *Jus in Bello* pp. 423ff.)

May a state support a foreign *government's forces* when that government is threatened by rebel forces? The International Court of Justice appeared to endorse such support in paragraph 246 of the *Nicaragua Case, supra* p. 415. A good number of powerful states have come to the aid of friendly governments threatened by rebels and some states maintain that temporary assistance to restore internal order is not a violation of international law. Some authors disagree and maintain that: "Since international law recognizes the right of revolution, it cannot permit other states to intervene to prevent it."[36] When a state is in the throes of incipient revolution it is often difficult to determine which of several competing groups is "the government" and whether "the government" made any request for assistance. Professor Harris suggests that such difficulties demonstrate "one of the weaknesses of allowing intervention at the request of the constitutional government...."[37]

---

36. Quincy Wright, Subversive Intervention, 54 Am. J. Int'l L. 521, 529 (1960).
37. D.J. Harris, Cases and Materials on International Law 918 (6th ed. 2004).

Intervention in Particular Circumstances

Intervening to Protect Nationals Abroad

When a citizen travels abroad, the state to which s/he travels has an obligation to ensure that the alien is protected at least to the minimum international standard and to ensure that the alien's human rights are not violated (see chapter VIII). Not all states fulfil these obligations of care, so that aliens may find themselves in immediate danger without the time or means to leave the country. The aliens in question may have lived in the foreign country for some time and acquired considerable property which may also be threatened. This type of situation raises the question of whether the alien's state may intervene to protect its nationals and/or their property. Such intervention always necessitates some use of force.

Several recent incursions by states into foreign territory have been justified, at least partly, on the basis of the claimed right to protect nationals or their property abroad; the 1956 invasion of Suez by a joint Anglo-French force in part to protect nationals and their property; the Israeli raid on Entebbe, Uganda, to rescue hijacked Israeli citizens in 1976; the United States 1980 attempt to rescue U.S. hostages held in Iran; the 1983 invasion of Grenada by U.S. military and troops from the Organization of Eastern Carribean States, partly to rescue U.S. nationals stranded during a power struggle between various political factions; and the 1989 invasion of Panama by U.S. military forces, in part to protect U.S. nationals.

All of the above incidents have generated much controversy. There are often arguments about the facts: whether the nationals or their properties were really in any danger. There is also the fundamental question of whether such uses of force violate article 2(4) of the Charter. They certainly entail a "use of force" but it is disputed whether the force is directed "against the territorial integrity or political independence of any state, or [is used] in ... [a] manner inconsistent with the Purposes of the United Nations."

These incursions do not fit easily into article 51's self-defence exception in that no "armed attack" has occurred in the territory of the invading state. Some scholars believe that because anticipatory self-defence was permitted under pre-Charter law and because article 51 speaks of "the inherent" right to self-defence, the right to resort to force in anticipation of an armed attack is permitted by article 51.[38] For these scholars armed reprisals, which is what this type of intervention amounts to, is permissible provided it meets the requirements of necessity and proportionality.

Humanitarian Intervention

Over the years a number of states and various international scholars have maintained that there is a right to military intervention in the affairs of other states where the intervenor is seeking to preserve or promote certain concepts that they regard as central to the framework of international law.[39] Most prevalent among the occasions stated to justify intervention are when the intervenor is seeking to preserve or promote human rights or democracy or peace and security. None of these "rights to intervene" has re-

---

38. Rebecca M. M. Wallace, International Law, at 284 (5th ed. 2005).

39. See W. Michael Reisman, Coercion and Self-Determination: Construing Charter Article 2(4), 78 Amer. J. Int'l L. 643 (1984); contra Oscar Schachter, The Legality of Pro-Democratic Invasion, 78 Amer. J. Int'l L. 645 (1984).

ceived broad acceptance by the international community and thus cannot be regarded as established in customary international law. Nevertheless every time a state does exercise force to intervene in another state to preserve or promote one of the favored interests and is not rebuked by the international community, the state's actions contribute to the development of an accepted state practice. Below are some examples where state military intervention has been justified on one or more of the above grounds.

The 1989 U.S. invasion of Panama occurred shortly after General Noriega had annulled the results of an election thought to have been won by his rival. President Bush wrote a letter to the Speaker of the U.S. House of Representatives in which he outlined a number of justifications for the invasion including "defend[ing] democracy in Panama...."[40] A draft resolution of the Security Council calling for U.S. withdrawal was vetoed by the U.S., the U.K. and France,[41] although the General Assembly did pass a resolution calling the invasion "a flagrant violation of international law."[42]

In 1971 a civil war broke out in Pakistan after East Pakistan had declared itself to be the independent State of Bangladesh. During the ensuing crisis more than one million refugees crossed from East Pakistan into India. India was sympathetic with the Bengalis and gave military assistance to the Bangladesh guerrillas. War broke out between India and Pakistan but two weeks later Pakistan surrendered. Writers have justified India's military assistance and her invasion on several grounds including protecting Bangladesh's right to self-determination. The U.N. General Assembly had called on India to withdraw her forces.[43]

In 1979 Tanzania invaded Uganda in order to topple the brutal regime of Uganda's notorious dictator, Idi Amin. Although Tanzania justified her invasion on the basis of self-defence, others have condoned the military intervention on the basis of protecting human rights.[44]

In 1999 the North Atlantic Treaty Organization (NATO) carried out a seventy-eight day bombing campaign against Yugoslavia in response to perceived wide spread human rights abuses carried out by the Serb dominated government of Yugoslavia against the minority ethnic population of Kosovo Albanians. The legality of this invasion was the subject of much debate. Professor Louis Henkin concluded that: "In my view, the law is, and ought to be, that unilateral intervention by military force by a state or group of states is unlawful unless authorized by the Security Council."[45] Nonetheless, Professor Henkin added that "many—governments and scholars—thought that something had to be done to end the horrors of Kosovo [and] that NATO was the appropriate body to do it...."[46] Professor Ruth Wedgwood thought that "[t]he war over Kosovo ... may ... mark the emergence of a limited and conditional right of humanitarian intervention, permitting the use of force to protect the lives of a threatened population when the decision is taken by ... a responsible multilateral organization and the Security Council does not oppose the action."[47] On the other hand, the late Professor Jonathan Charney

40. Public Papers of the President, 25 Weekly Comp. Press Doc. 1974, Dec. 20, 1989, H.R. Doc. No. 101-127 (1990).

41. 26 U.N. Chronicle No. 1 at 67 (1990).

42. G.A. Res. 44/240, U.N. GAOR, 44th Sess., 88th plen. mtg., U.N. Doc. A/RES/44/240 (1989).

43. G.A. Res. 2793, U.N. GAOR, 26th Sess., Supp. No. 29, at 3 (1971).

44. See e.g., Fernando R. Teson, Humanitarian Intervention: An Inquiry into Law and Morality, 169–175 (1988).

45. Louis Henkin, Kosovo and the Law of Humanitarian Intervention, 93 Amer. J. Int'l L. 824, 826 (1999).

46. Id.

47. Ruth Wedgwood, NATO's Campaign in Yugoslavia, 93 Amer. J. Int'l L. 828 (1999).

was clear in his view that "the NATO intervention through its bombing campaign violated the United Nations Charter and international law."[48]

Yugoslavia filed multiple cases against individual NATO members in the International Court of Justice arguing that the bombing violated international legal norms.[49] The Security Council was asked to condemn NATO's military action but the resolution failed with three votes in favor and twelve against.[50] The Security Council has since endorsed an international civilian and military administration of the Kosovo region.[51]

The Responsibility to Protect

Recently, there has been a great deal of debate and some endorsement of a concept that has come to be known as the "Responsibility to Protect." This concept arises out of the knowledge that the international machinery to authorize the collective use of force, as originally envisioned in the Charter, has not materialized and authorization by the Security Council for states to form co-alitions and use of force for acceptable emergency purposes is seldom granted. Yet because atrocities continue, the argument is made that states with the capacity to act to prevent catastrophes, or to rapidly react after they occur, have a responsibility to offer such assistance, including reconstruction after conflict. Such action is characterized as humanitarian intervention which, although recognizing the Security Council's primary responsibility to act, nonetheless, places responsibility to act on states and "the international community" when the Security Council fails to authorize such protective action. Such proposals are controversial, favoring, as they must, richer and more powerful states. The concept of "The Responsibility to Protect" has been endorsed at the highest U.N. levels[52] but cannot be characterized as customary international law at this time.

The Security Council's Power to Intervene

Article 24 of the U.N. Charter gives the Security Council "primary responsibility for the maintenance of international peace and security...." United Nations members also "agree to accept and carry out the decisions of the Security Council in accordance with the present Charter." Article 25.

---

48. Jonathan Charney, Anticipatory Humanitarian Intervention in Kosovo, 93 Amer. J. Int'l L. 834 (1999).

49. The title of all of the cases filed by Yugoslavia against NATO members is: Legality of Use of Force. *Legality of Use of Force* (Yugoslavia v. Spain) 1999 I.C.J. 761, was dismissed for lack of jurisdiction, as was the case against the U.S., *Legality of Use of Force* (Yugoslavia v. U.S.) 1999 I.C.J. 916. The Court rejected Yugoslavia's request for interim measures of protection, while reserving the issue of the Court's jurisdiction on the merits, in *Legality of Use of Force* (Yugoslavia v. Belgium), 1999 I.C.J. 124 (Order of 2 June 1999). It issued similar orders on the same day in (Yugoslavia v. Canada) 1999 I.C.J. 259; (Yugoslavia v. France) 1999 I.C.J. 363; (Yugoslavia v. Germany) 1999 I.C.J. 422; (Yugoslavia v. Italy) 1999 I.C.J 481; (Yugoslavia v. U.K.) 1999 I.C.J. 826. (The Court's web site also refers to Yugoslavia by its newer name, "Serbia and Montenegro"). Serbia and Montenegro have now become separate States.

50. See Security Council Rejects Demand for Cessation of Use of Force Against Federal Republic of Yugoslavia, UN Press Release SC/6659 (Mar. 26, 1999).

51. S.C. Res. 1244, U.N. Doc. S/RES/1244 (June 10, 1999).

52. See, e.g., International Commission on Intervention and State Sovereignty, The Responsibility to Protect, (2001); A More Secure World: Our Shared Responsibility, Report of the U.N. High-Level Panel on Threats, Challenges and Change, U.N. Doc. A/59/565 (2004); Report of the U.N. Secretary-General, In Larger Freedom: Towards Development, Security and Human Rights for All, U.N. Doc. A/59/2005 (2005); World Summit Outcome, G.A. Res. 60/1/2005; Carsten Stahn, Responsibility to Protect: Political Rhetoric or Emerging Legal Norm?, 101 Amer. J. Int'l L. 99 (2007).

Article 2(7) states a general limitation upon all organs of the United Nations with one exception:

> Nothing contained in the present Charter shall authorize the United Nations to intervene in matters which are essentially within the domestic jurisdiction of any State or shall require the Members to submit such matters to settlement under the present Charter; but this principle shall not prejudice the application of enforcement measures under Chapter VII.

Chapter VI of the U.N. Charter is entitled "Pacific Settlement of Disputes." Under this Chapter the Security Council is given power to investigate disputes between states and to recommend appropriate settlement procedures.

Chapter VII of the Charter first grants the Security Council the power to "determine the existence of any threat to the peace, breach of the peace, or act of aggression and ... [to] make recommendations, or decide what measures shall be taken in accordance with Articles 41 and 42, to maintain or restore international peace and security." Article 39. Article 40 gives the Security Council the power to "call upon the parties concerned [where there has been a threat to the peace, a breach of the peace, or an act of aggression] to comply with such provisional measures as it deems necessary or desirable...."

Article 41 Measures

Under article 41, the Security Council "may decide what measures not involving the use of armed force are to be employed to give effect to its decisions, and it may call upon the Members of the United Nations to apply such measures...." The article goes on to give examples of the types of non-armed force measures that may be employed and mentions "interruption of economic relations and of rail, sea, air, postal, telegraphic, radio and other means of communication, and the severance of diplomatic relations."

The Security Council has used its article 41 powers on numerous occasions and there has been much debate on the effectiveness of such measures. For example, the Security Council ordered increasingly severe economic sanctions against Southern Rhodesia from 1965 through 1968[53] after the white government of Ian Smith had unilaterally declared independence from Britain. These sanctions were not lifted until 1979 when Rhodesia became the independent State of Zimbabwe.[54] Economic sanctions were also applied to South Africa in an attempt to dismantle the government's apartheid policies. In 1963 the Council called for a voluntary arms embargo.[55] When it became clear that the voluntary embargo was not effective, the Council imposed a mandatory arms embargo.[56] More recently the Council has imposed a series of far reaching economic sanctions on Iraq in the wake of its invasion of Kuwait.[57] In 1992, the Security Council ordered Libya to hand over either to Britain or to the U.S. two named suspects in the PAN AM 103 bombing in Lockerbie, Scotland.[58] When Libya did not comply, an arms and air

53. See, e.g., Question Concerning the Situation in Southern Rhodesia, S.C. Res. 221, U.N. SCOR, 21st Sess., 1277th mtg. at 5, U.N. Doc. S/RES/221 (1966); S.C. Res. 232, U.N. SCOR, 21st Sess., 1340th mtg., U.N. Doc. S/RES/232 (1966); S.C. Res. 253, U.N. SCOR, 23rd Sess., 1428th mtg. at 5, U.N. Doc. S/RES/253 (1968).

54. S.C. Res. 460, U.N. SCOR, 34th Sess., 2181st mtg. at 15, U.N. Doc. S/RES/460 (1979).

55. S.C. Res. 181, U.N. SCOR, 18th Sess. 1056th mtg. at 7, U.N. Doc. S/RES/181 (1963).

56. S.C. Res. 418, U.N. SCOR, 32nd Sess. 2046th mtg. at 5, U.N. Doc. S/RES/418 (1977).

57. See, e.g., S.C. Res. 661, U.N. SCOR, 45th Sess., 2933d mtg. at 19, U.N. Doc. S/INF/46 (1990); S.C. Res. 670, U.N. SCOR, 45th Sess. 2943d mtg., U.N. Doc. S/INF/46 (1990).

58. S.C. Res.731, U.N. Doc. S/RES/731 (1992).

embargo was imposed.[59] These sanctions were lifted in 1999 when the accused men were handed over to be tried by a Scottish court located in the Netherlands[60]. An arms embargo has been in place since 2004 on Sudan with respect to activity in the Darfur region.[61] Iran has also been subject to sanctions for its suspected nuclear activity.[62]

Article 42 Measures

If the Security Council determines that article 41 measures are inadequate "it may take such action by air, sea, or land forces as may be necessary to maintain or restore international peace and security. Such actions may include demonstrations, blockade, and other operations by air, sea, or land forces of Members of the United Nations." Article 42. When the U.N. Charter was drafted it was assumed that member states would enter into agreements with the Security Council undertaking to provide standing forces to be used by the Council whenever deemed necessary. Article 43 outlines the mechanism for such agreements. In fact, no state has entered into such an agreement with the Security Council so that there are no permanent U.N. forces. Whenever the Security Council determines that armed force is necessary to maintain or restore international peace and security it asks for states to supply forces on a volunteer basis and agreements are reached between the Security Council and the states supplying forces with respect to the particular action contemplated.

In 1950 North Korea crossed the 38th Parallel into South Korea and hostilities broke out. The Security Council called upon United Nations Members to "furnish such assistance to the Republic of Korea [South Korea] as may be necessary to repel the armed attack and to restore international peace and security in the area."[63] Sixteen states offered assistance and the Security Council recommended that Members providing assistance "make such forces and other assistance available to a unified command under the United States … [who was requested to] designate the commander of such forces … [and] at its discretion to use the United Nations flag in the course of operations against North Korean forces…."[64] The nations supplying forces to assist South Korea made agreements with the United States rather than the United Nations. The use of force had been authorized by the United Nations but it was the United States that led and commanded the expedition from the outset.[65]

The legality of the Korean action has long been debated. Some authors maintain that absent UN forces mustered under article 43, the Security Council has no power to authorize a UN force. Some have argued that the absence of the USSR in the Security Council made the resolutions improper. Article 39 of the Charter gives the Security Council broad powers to decide upon the measures to be taken under article 41 or 42 which can include actions by the forces of member states. Such actions would not

59. S.C. Res. 748, U.N. Doc. S/RES/748 (1992).

60. S.C. Res. 1192, U.N. Doc. S/RES/1192 (1998) and Statement of the President of the Security Council, July 9, 1999, S/PRST/1999/22.

61. S.C. Res. 1556, U.N. Doc. S/RES/1556 (2004) & 1591, U.N. Doc. S/RES/1591 (2005).

62. S.C. Res. 1737, U.N. Doc. S/RES/1737 (2006); 1747 U.N. Doc S/RES/1747 (2007) & 1803 U.N. Doc. S/RES/1803 (2008).

63. S.C. Res. 84, U.N. SCOR, 5th Sess., 474th mtg. at 5, U.N. Doc. S/INF/S Rev. 1 (1950).

64. S.C. Res. 84, U.N. SCOR, 5th Sess., 476th mtg., at 5–6, U.N. Doc. S/INF/4 Rev. 1 (1950).

65. The USSR representative to the Security Council had been absent during the crucial votes on Korea. The Nationalist Chinese delegation had been permitted to take China's seat in the Security Council and the USSR representative had absented himself in protest. The USSR resumed its seat on August 1st 1950 and the Security Council took no further action in the military enterprise.

strictly be the actions of UN forces as such. Almost all of the states involved in the Korean action, however, regarded it as a U.N. action,[66] admittedly led by the United States. The action could also be regarded as the exercise of the right of collective self-defence on behalf of South Korea although the request and reporting requirements outlined in the *Nicaragua Case*[67] were probably not complied with.

After Iraq invaded Kuwait in 1990 the Security Council first imposed economic sanctions[68] and later authorized member states "to use all necessary means to uphold and implement Security Council resolution 660 (1990) [demanding Iraqi withdrawal] ... and to restore international peace and security in the area...."[69] This resolution was presumably permitted under article 39 and there has been no suggestion that the Gulf operation was a UN action as such. A coalition of member state forces led by the United States and Britain removed the Iraqi forces from Kuwait five days after the offensive began on February 24th 1991.

United Nations Peacekeeping Forces

Although there is nothing in the U.N. Charter which specifically authorizes the use of peacekeeping forces (in contrast to forces used to restore peace and security) such forces have been increasingly used in recent years. Technically a force is only dispatched if the host country consents to its presence but if the governmental framework has collapsed this "consent" often occurs in highly confused circumstances. By the end of 1996, sixteen peacekeeping missions were operating under UN authorization.[70] Twenty-nine peacekeeping operations were created between 1988 and 1996. Currently (2009) there are sixteen peacekeeping missions around the world. Over time, these missions have become increasingly complex and often operate in dangerous situations. The expectation is that the demand for such missions will increase.

The legality of assessing expenses for peacekeeping forces was challenged by a number of states who refused to make any financial contributions assessed by the General Assembly under article 17 for peacekeeping forces in the Congo (ONUC) and the Middle East (UNEF). The General Assembly requested an advisory opinion from the International Court of Justice on the legality of the assessed expenses. In the *Certain Expenses of the United Nations Case*[71] the Court ruled that the expenses were legitimate because they were assessed to fulfill the overall purposes of the United Nations, namely "to promote and to maintain ... peaceful settlement of [disputes]...."[72]

Jus In Bello

The law described up to this point in the chapter is called *jus ad bellum*. It is the law concerned with the right to use inter-state force. With few limited exceptions the use of

66. D.W. Bowett, United Nations Forces: A Legal Study 882 n. 22 (1964).

67. See *supra* p. 327.

68. E.g., S.C. Res 661, U.N. SCOR, 45th Sess., 2933d mtg., U.N. Doc. S/RES/661 (1990).

69. S.C. Res. 678, U.N. SCOR, 45th Sess., 2963d mtg., U.N. Doc. S/RES/678 (1990).

70. U.N. Peace-Keeping: Some Questions and Answers (U.N. Dept. Public Information DPI/1851) Sept. 1996 at 1; see generally, Lamin J. Sise, Illusions of a Standing United Nations Force, 28 Cornell Int'l L. J. 645, 646 (1995).

71. 1962 I.C.J. 151.

72. Id. at 171–172.

inter-state force is now prohibited by international law but history teaches us that we do not always obey the law either at the municipal level or the international level. Since at least the middle of the nineteenth century, the modern laws of warfare have sought to create legal norms applicable while armed conflict is in progress regardless of whether the resort to force was permissible or not. Gradually a core code of conduct has developed which seeks to regulate the conduct of war and protect victims of armed conflict both military and civilian. This area of law is called **humanitarian law.** The law that seeks to regulate the types of force used is also found in the various conventions and some customary law that seeks to prohibit and restrict the use of certain weapons. Humanitarian law is closely related to human rights law since much of it seeks to protect military and civilian victims of conflict. Humanitarian law is the principal body of law applying in armed conflict but human rights law continues to apply in conflict unless humanitarian law has a specific rule that would oust the human rights rule. See *Legal Consequencs of the Construction of a Wall in the Occupied Palestinian Territory,* paras. 102–106 (2004 I.C.J. 136) (Advisory Opinion 9 July 2004).

Regulation of the Conduct of Hostilities and Humanitarian Law

President Lincoln is credited with promulgating the first modern comprehensive code regulating the conduct of hostilities during the United States Civil War. The *Lieber Code,* named after its chief author Professor Francis Lieber, was an attempt to codify the laws of war and to prepare them in a booklet that would serve as instructions to commanders in the field.[73] The first Hague Peace Conference convened in 1899 adopted the *Convention Concerning the Laws and Customs of War on Land.*[74] The Second Hague Peace Conference of 1907 revised this Convention and adopted the *Convention concerning the Laws and Customs of War on Land together with appended Hague Regulations.*[75] The *Regulations* were intended to form the basis of army manuals for the states parties to the Convention. These conventions and regulations were generally regarded as expressing the customary law of warfare as it existed at that time. They express the underlying principle behind the laws of warfare namely that force may only be used to achieve military advantage, that unnecessary suffering must be avoided and that if suffering is disproportionate to the military advantage gained its infliction is prohibited. From the middle of the nineteenth century, nations began to adopt conventions prohibiting the use of particular types of weapons. (See section on Weapons Control pp. 449–475).

Thirteen conventions were adopted at the 1907 Hague Conference of which twelve were ratified. These conventions define belligerent status, forbid the use of force against undefended towns, regulate belligerent occupation of territory, set out the rights and responsibilities of neutral states and prohibit the use of arms calculated to inflict unnecessary suffering. The four 1949 Geneva Conventions together with the two 1977 Protocols now represent the current codification of the laws of war.[76]

---

73. Francis Lieber, Instructions for the Government of Armies of the United States in the Field (1863).

74. Signed July 29, 1899, 32 Stat. 1803, T.S. 11 (1901).

75. 36 Stat. 2277, T.S. No. 539, 1 Bevans 631, signed Oct. 18, 1907, entered into force, Jan. 26, 1910.

76. Convention for the Amelioration of the Conditions of the Wounded and Sick in Armed Forces in the Field, signed 12 August 1949, entered into force 21 Oct. 1950, 75 U.N.T.S. 31, 6 U.S.T. 3114; Convention for the Amelioration of the Conditions of Wounded, Sick and Shipwrecked Members of the Armed Forces at Sea, signed 12 August 1949, entered into force 21 Oct. 1950, 75 U.N.T.S.

The four Geneva or "Red Cross" Conventions deal with the treatment of army and navy personnel wounded during combat, the treatment of prisoners of war and the protection of civilians. A number of warlike practices are forbidden such as torture, taking hostages, extra judicial executions, deportation and wanton destruction of property. There are detailed rules on the protection of medical personnel, hospitals and hospital ships and specific protections for noncombatants. The definition of a combatant came under increasing attack as rebel groups and guerrillas began to appear in many hostilities particularly after World War II. Protocol I tried to readjust the definition of combatant in light of the tactics of modern warfare but has remained controversial. The distinction between civilian populations and military personnel remains the bedrock for the provisions providing protection for civilians. Civilians are not to be the object of a military attack. The Hague Convention for the Protection of Cultural Property in the Event of Armed Conflict[77] protects cultural objects and buildings and those objects necessary to civilian survival such as food, livestock and drinking water supplies.

The main criticism leveled again the Geneva Conventions and Protocols is that they are based on the concept of "limited war" where war meant military forces fighting each other, where the distinction between combatants and noncombatants was clear and where resources under the control of military as opposed to civilian control could be distinguished. In a world where "total war" is possible and where an entire nation's effort can be turned towards the war enterprise it is argued that the traditional laws of war no longer make sense. Before you are ready to throw out the customary laws of war, however, it is salutary to remember that all wars since World War II have in fact been limited wars fought with non-nuclear weapons. In many of these conflicts, the distinctions worked out in the conventions largely apply. A second major criticism levelled at the conventions is that many, if not most, current conflicts are the result of civil wars and that the conventions and protocols primarily address inter-state conflicts thus leaving internal conflicts largely unregulated by international law. The rise of international, non-governmental, para-military groups who launch attacks in a variety of locations throughout the world has also challenged the traditional application of the laws of war. The 1949 conventions are indeed primarily concerned with international hostilities. However, each of the four 1949 conventions has what is known as "Common Article 3" which provides:

> *Article 3.* In the case of armed conflict not of an international character occurring in the territory of one of the High Contracting Parties, each Party to the conflict shall be bound to apply, as a minimum, the following provisions:
>
> (1) Persons taking no active part in the hostilities, including members of armed forces who have laid down their arms and those placed *hors de combat* by sickness, wounds, detention, or any other cause, shall in all circumstances be treated humanely, without any adverse distinction founded on race, colour, religion or faith, sex, birth or wealth, or any other similar criteria.

85, 6 U.S.T. 3217; Convention Relative to the Treatment of Prisoners of War, signed 12 Aug. 1949, entered into force 21 Oct. 1950, 75 U.N.T.S. 135, 6 U.S.T. 3316; Convention Relative to the Protection of Civilian Persons in Time of War, signed 12 August 1949, entered into force 21 Oct. 1950, 75 U.N.T.S. 287, 6 U.S.T. 3516; Protocol Additional to the Geneva Conventions of 12 August 1949, and Relating to the Protection of Victims of International Armed Conflicts (Protocol I), signed 8 June 1977, entered into force 7 Dec. 1978, 1125 U.N.T.S. 3, reprinted at 16 I.L.M. 1391 (1977); Protocol Additional to the Geneva Conventions of 12 August 1949, and Relating to the Protection of Victims of Non-International Armed Conflicts (Protocol II), signed 8 June 1977, entered into force 7 Dec. 1978, 1129 U.N.T.S. 609, reprinted at 16 I.L.M. 1442 (1977).

77. 249 U.N.T.S. 215, signed 14 May 1954, entered into force 4 Sept. 1956.

To this end, the following acts are and shall remain prohibited at any time and in any place whatsoever with respect to the above-mentioned persons:

(a) violence to life and person, in particular murder of all kinds, mutilation, cruel treatment and torture;

(b) taking of hostages;

(c) outrages upon personal dignity, in particular, humiliating and degrading treatment;

(d) the passing of sentences and the carrying out of executions without previous judgment pronounced by a regularly constituted court affording all the judicial guarantees which are recognized as indispensable by civilized peoples.

(2) the wounded and sick shall be collected and cared for.

An impartial humanitarian body, such as the International Committee of the Red Cross, may offer its services to the Parties to the conflict.

The Parties to the conflict should further endeavor to bring into force, by means of special agreements, all or part of the other provisions of the present Convention.

The application of the preceding provisions shall not affect the legal status of the Parties to the conflict.

This article provides a standard of treatment for noncombatants, the wounded and prisoners in non international armed conflicts. Protocol II develops these standards further and is specifically applicable to "all armed conflicts [not covered by article 1 to Protocol II] ... which take place in the territory of a High Contracting Party between its armed forces and dissident armed forces or other organized armed groups which, under responsible command, exercise such control over a part of its territory as to enable them to carry out sustained and concerted military operations and to implement this Protocol."[78] The Protocol does not apply to "internal disturbances and tensions, such as riots, isolated and sporadic acts of violence and other acts of a similar nature, as not being armed conflict."[79] Trying to decide when the threshold level of violence has been reached sufficient to trigger the Protocol is obviously difficult.

The Protocol guarantees fundamental protection for noncombatants, the wounded and prisoners. Certain activities are absolutely prohibited such as torture, collective punishments, rape, enforced prostitution and pillage. Special protection is given to children. Prisoners must be treated humanely and no form of penalty may be carried out against prisoners unless pronounced by a court providing the fundamentals of fairness and impartiality.

The law applicable to internal hostilities is clearly in need of further development. Professors Sassoli and Bouvier, the authors of a well known text book on international humanitarian law, state that they begin to see the distinct areas of international and internal armed conflict law moving together:

> "In recent years, the IHL [international humanitarian law] of non-international armed conflicts is however drawing closer to the IHL of international conflicts: through the jurisprudence of the International Criminal Tribunals for the former Yugoslavia and Rwanda based upon their assessment of customary international law; in the crimes defined in the Statute of the International Criminal

78. Protocol I, *supra* note 68, at art. 1.
79. Id. at art. 2.

Court; by States having accepted that both categories of conflicts are covered by recent treaties on weapons and on the protection of cultural objects; under the growing influence of International Human Rights Law and according to the outcome of the ICRC [International Committee of the Red Cross] Study on customary international humanitarian law." (Footnotes omitted).[80]

It remains to be seen whether the nations of the world are prepared to develop or merge these areas of law or to comply with the law once agreed upon.

Since their establishment in the 1990s, the International Criminal Tribunal for the Former Yugoslavia and the International Criminal Tribunal for Rwanda (see pp. 381–383) have issued a number of judgments on a large variety of international humanitarian law issues. Below are excerpts from two cases.

Note: To read the Statute and other rules governing the International Criminal Tribunal for the Former Yugoslavia go to the Tribunal's web site at www.icty.org. Click on Basic Legal Documents.

The Prosecutor v. Drazen Erdemovíc

Case no. IT-96-22-A
Judgement of the Appeals Chamber, 7 October 1997
International Criminal Tribunal for the Former Yugoslavia
(Footnotes omitted)

* * *

I. INTRODUCTION

1. The Appeals Chamber of the International Tribunal for the Prosecution of Persons Responsible for Serious Violations of International Humanitarian Law Committed in the Territory of the Former Yugoslavia since 1991 ("the International Tribunal") is seized of an appeal lodged by Drazen Erdemovíc ("the Appellant") against the Sentencing Judgement rendered by Trial Chamber I on 29 November 1996 ("Sentencing Judgement"). By this Sentencing Judgement, the Trial Chamber sentenced the Appellant to 10 years' imprisonment, following his guilty plea to one count of a crime against humanity, for his participation in the execution of approximately 1,200 unarmed civilian Muslim men at the Branjevo farm near the town of Pilica in eastern Bosnia on 16 July 1995, in the aftermath of the fall of the United Nations "safe area" of Srebrenica.

2. The relevant facts, so far as this appeal is concerned, may be set out as follows. The Appellant was transferred into the custody of the International Tribunal on 30 March 1996 in connection with the Prosecutor's investigations into serious violations of international humanitarian law allegedly committed against the civilian population in and around Srebrenica in July 1995.

* * *

3. The Appellant was indicted on 29 May 1996 on one count of a crime against humanity and on an alternative count of a violation of the laws or customs of war. The Indictment alleged the following facts:

> 1. On 16 April 1993, the Security Council of the United Nations, acting pursuant to Chapter VII of the United Nations Charter, adopted resolution 819, in

80. I Marco Sassòli & Antoine A. Bouvier, How Does Law Protect in War? 250 (2d ed. 2006).

which it demanded that all parties to the conflict in the Republic of Bosnia and Herzegovina treat Srebrenica and its surroundings as a safe area which should be free from any armed attack or any other hostile act. Resolution 819 was reaffirmed by Resolution 824 on 6 May 1993 and by Resolution 836 on 4 June 1993.

2. On or about 6 July 1995, the Bosnian Serb army commenced an attack on the UN "safe area" of Srebrenica. This attack continued through until 11 July 1995, when the first units of the Bosnian Serb army entered Srebrenica.

3. Thousands of Bosnian Muslim civilians who remained in Srebrenica during this attack fled to the UN compound in Potocari and sought refuge in and around the compound.

4. Between 11 and 13 July 1995, Bosnian Serb military personnel summarily executed an unknown number of Bosnian Muslims in Potocari and in Srebrenica.

5. Between 12 and 13 July 1995, the Bosnian Muslim men, women and children, who had sought refuge in and around the UN compound in Potocari were placed on buses and trucks under the control of Bosnian Serb military personnel and police and transported out of the Srebrenica enclave. Before boarding these buses and trucks, Bosnian Muslim men were separated from Bosnian Muslim women and children and were transported to various collection centres around Srebrenica.

6. A second group of approximately 15,000 Bosnian Muslim men, with some women and children, fled Srebrenica on 11 July 1995 through the woods in a large column in the direction of Tuzla. A large number of the Bosnian Muslim men who fled in this column were captured by or surrendered to Bosnian Serb army or police personnel.

7. Thousands of Bosnian Muslim men who had been either separated from women and children in Potocari or who had been captured by or surrendered to Bosnian Serb military or police personnel were sent to various collection sites outside of Srebrenica including, but not limited to a hangar in Bratunac, a soccer field in Nova Kasaba, a warehouse in Kravica, the primary school and gymnasium of "Veljko Lukic-Kurjak" in Grbavci, Zvornik municipality and divers fields and meadows along the Bratunac-Milici road.

8. Between 13 July 1995 and approximately 22 July 1995, thousands of Bosnian Muslim men were summarily executed by members of the Bosnian Serb army and Bosnian Serb police at diverse locations including, but not limited to a warehouse at Kravica, a meadow and a dam near Lazete and divers other locations.

9. On or about 16 July 1995, DRAZEN ERDEMOVÍC and other members of the 10th Sabotage Detachment of the Bosnian Serb army were ordered to a collective farm near Pilica. This farm is located northwest of Zvornik in the Zvornik Municipality.

10. On or about 16 July 1995, DRAZEN ERDEMOVÍC and other members of his unit were informed that bus loads of Bosnian Muslim civilian men from Srebrenica, who had surrendered to Bosnian Serb military or police personnel, would be arriving throughout the day at this collective farm.

11. On or about 16 July 1995, buses containing Bosnian Muslim men arrived at the collective farm in Pilica. Each bus was full of Bosnian Muslim men, ranging from approximately 17 to 60 years of age. After each bus arrived at the farm,

> the Bosnian Muslim men were removed in groups of about 10, escorted by members of the 10th Sabotage Detachment to a field adjacent to farm buildings and lined up in a row with their backs facing DRAZEN ERDEMOVÍC and members of his unit.
>
> 12. On or about 16 July 1995, DRAZEN ERDEMOVÍC did shoot and kill and did participate with other members of his unit and soldiers from another brigade in the shooting and killing of unarmed Bosnian Muslim men at the Pilica collective farm. These summary executions resulted in the deaths of hundreds of Bosnian Muslim male civilians.

4. At his initial appearance on 31 May 1996, the Appellant pleaded guilty to the count of a crime against humanity. The Appellant added this explanation to his guilty plea:

> Your Honour, I had to do this. If I had refused, I would have been killed together with the victims. When I refused, they told me: "If you are sorry for them, stand up, line up with them and we will kill you too." I am not sorry for myself but for my family, my wife and son who then had nine months, and I could not refuse because then they would have killed me. That is all I wish to add.

The Trial Chamber accepted the Appellant's guilty plea and dismissed the second count of a violation of the laws or customs of war.

* * *

8. In his testimony before the Trial Chamber, the Appellant described in detail the facts alleged in paragraphs 9 to 12 of the Indictment (*see* paragraph 3, *supra*). The Trial Chamber summed up his testimony on these facts as follows:

> On the morning of 16 July 1995, Drazen Erdemovíc and seven members of the 10th Sabotage Unit of the Bosnian Serb army were ordered to leave their base at Vlasenica and go to the Pilica farm north-west of Svornik. When they arrived there, they were informed by their superiors that buses from Srebrenica carrying Bosnian Muslim civilians between 17 and 60 years of age who had surrendered to the members of the Bosnian Serb police or army would be arriving throughout the day.
>
> Starting at 10 o'clock in the morning, members of the military police made the civilians in the first buses, all men, get off in groups of ten. The men were escorted to a field adjacent to the farm buildings where they were lined up with their backs to the firing squad. The members of the 10th Sabotage Unit, including Drazen Erdemovíc, who composed the firing squad then killed them. Drazen Erdemovíc carried out the work with an automatic weapon. The executions continued until about 3 o'clock in the afternoon.
>
> The accused estimated that there were about 20 buses in all, each carrying approximately 60 men and boys. He believes that he personally killed about seventy people.

And further on:

> Drazen Erdemovíc claims that he received the order from Brano Gojkovic, commander of the operations at the Branjevo farm at Pilica, to prepare himself along with seven members of his unit for a mission the purpose of which they had absolutely no knowledge. He claimed it was only when they arrived on-site that the members of the unit were informed that they were to massacre hun-

> dreds of Muslims. He asserted his immediate refusal to do this but was threatened with instant death and told "If you don't wish to do it, stand in the line with the rest of them and give others your rifle so that they can shoot you." He declared that had he not carried out the order, he is sure he would have been killed or that his wife or child would have been directly threatened. Regarding this, he claimed to have seen Milorad Pelemis ordering someone to be killed because he had refused to obey. He reported that despite this, he attempted to spare a man between 50 and 60 years of age who said that he had saved Serbs from Srebrenica. Brano Gojkovic then told him that he did not want any surviving witnesses to the crime.
>
> Drazen Erdemovíc asserted that he then opposed the order of a lieutenant colonel to participate in the execution of five hundred Muslim men being detained in the Pilica public building. He was able not to commit this further crime because three of his comrades supported him when he refused to obey.

8. [There appear to be two paragraphs numbered as "8"]. The Appellant also testified to his personal situation and circumstances leading up to and following the crime. In addition, two pseudonymed witnesses testified on behalf of the Defense as to the Appellant's character.

9. The Prosecutor called one witness, Jean-Rene Ruez, an investigator in the Office of the Prosecutor, who testified as to the locations of several execution sites disclosed to him by the Appellant, information which was corroborated by the investigations of the Office of the Prosecutor. In particular, he testified that investigations had confirmed the existence of a mass grave at the Branjevo farm near Pilica, where the Appellant claimed he committed the crime in question. Investigations also confirmed that a massacre may have occurred in a public building in Pilica where, according to the Appellant's testimony, about 500 Muslims were executed on or about 16 July 1995.

10. The Trial Chamber, having accepted the Appellant's plea of guilty to the count of a crime against humanity, sentenced the Appellant to 10 years' imprisonment. This term of imprisonment was imposed by the Trial Chamber having regard to the extreme gravity of the offence and to a number of mitigating circumstances.

a.) *The extreme gravity of the crime*

The Trial Chamber took the view that the objective gravity of the crime was such that "there exists in international law a standard according to which a crime against humanity is one of extreme gravity demanding the most severe penalties when no mitigating circumstances are present."

It also took into account the subjective gravity of the crime, which was underscored by the Appellant's significant role in the mass execution of 1,200 unarmed civilians during a five-hour period, in particular, his responsibility for killing between 10 and 100 people.

It is to be noted that the Trial Chamber also took the view that no consideration could be given to any aggravating circumstances when determining the sentence to be imposed for these crimes because of the extreme gravity *per se* of crimes against humanity.

b.) *The mitigating circumstances*

As regards the mitigating circumstances contemporaneous with the crime, that is the "state of mental incompetence claimed by the Defense [and] the extreme necessity in which [the Appellant] allegedly found himself when placed under duress by the order and threat from his hierarchical superiors as well as his subordinate level within the military hierarchy" the Trial Chamber considered that these were insufficiently proven since the Appellant's testimony in this regard had not been corroborated by independent evidence.

With regard to the mitigating circumstances which followed the commission of the crime, the Trial Chamber took into account the Appellant's feelings of remorse, his desire to surrender to the International Tribunal, his guilty plea, his cooperation with the Office of the Prosecutor, and "the fact that he now does not constitute a danger and the corrigible character of his personality."

The Trial Chamber also accepted, as mitigating factors, the Appellant's young age, 23 years at the time of the crime, and his low rank in the military hierarchy of the Bosnian Serb army.

II. THE APPEAL

A. Grounds of Appeal

11. The Appellant, in the Appellant's Brief filed by Counsel for the Accused Draz en Erdemovíc against the Sentencing Judgement, filed on 14 April 1997 ("Appellant's Brief,") asked that the Appeals Chamber revise the Sentencing Judgement:

a.) By pronouncing the accused Drazen Erdemovíc guilty as charged, but excusing him from serving the sentence on the grounds that the offences were committed under duress and without the possibility of another moral choice, that is, in extreme necessity, and on the grounds that he was not accountable for his acts at the time of the offence, nor was the offence premeditated,....

* * *

C. The Scope of the Appeals Chamber's Judicial Review: Issues Raised Proprio Motu and Preliminary Questions

16. The Appeals Chamber has raised preliminary issues *proprio motu* pursuant to its inherent powers as an appellate body once seized of an appeal lodged by either party pursuant to Article 25 of the Statute. The Appeals Chamber finds nothing in the Statute or the Rules, nor in practices of international institutions or national judicial systems, which would confine its consideration of the appeal to the issues raised formally by the parties. The preliminary issues revolve around the question of the validity of the pleas of guilty entered by the Appellant. This is a question to be decided *in limine*. In pursuance of its *proprio motu* examination of the validity of the Appellant's guilty plea, the Appeals Chamber addressed three preliminary questions to the parties in a Scheduling Order dated 5 May 1997:

1. In law, may duress afford a complete defence* to a charge of crimes against humanity and/or war crimes such that, if the defence is proved at trial, the accused is entitled to an acquittal?

2. If the answer to (1) is in the affirmative, was the guilty plea entered by the accused, at his initial appearance equivocal in that the accused, while pleading guilty, invoked duress?

3. Was the acceptance of a guilty plea valid in view of the mental condition of the accused at the time the plea was entered? If not, was this defect cured by statements made by the accused in subsequent proceedings?

---

* The Tribunal uses the English spelling of "defence" throughout this opinion.

III. REASONS

17. In answering the preliminary questions surrounding the validity of the Appellant's plea, the members of the Appeals Chamber differ on a number of issues, both as to reasoning and as to result. Consequently, the views of each of the members of the Appeals Chamber on particular issues are set out in detail in Separate Opinions which are attached to this Judgement and merely summarized here.

18. The Appeals Chamber, for the reasons set out in the Joint Separate Opinion of Judge McDonald and Judge Vohrah, unanimously finds that the Appellant's plea was voluntary.

19. For the reasons set out in the Joint Separate Opinion of Judge McDonald and Judge Vohrah and in the Separate and Dissenting Opinion of Judge Li, the majority of the Appeals Chamber finds that duress does not afford a complete defence to a soldier charged with a crime against humanity and/or a war crime involving the killing of innocent human beings. Consequently, the majority of the Appeals Chamber finds that the guilty plea of the Appellant was not equivocal. Judge Cassese and Judge Stephen dissent from this view for the reasons set out in their Separate and Dissenting Opinions.

20. However, the Appeals Chamber, for the reasons set out in the Joint Separate Opinion of Judge McDonald and Judge Vohrah, finds that the guilty plea of the Applicant was not informed and accordingly remits the case to a Trial Chamber other than the one which sentenced the Appellant in order that he be given an opportunity to replead. Judge Li dissents from this view for the reasons set out in his Separate and Dissenting Opinion.

21. Consequently, the Appellant's application for the Appeals Chamber to revise his sentence is rejected by the majority. The Appeals Chamber also unanimously rejects the Appellant's application for acquittal.

IV. DISPOSITION

THE APPEALS CHAMBER

1. Unanimously **REJECTS** the Appellant's application that the Appeals Chamber should acquit him;

2. By four votes (Judges Cassese, McDonald, Stephen and Vohrah) to one (Judge Li) **REJECTS** the Appellant's application that the Appeals Chamber should revise his sentence;

3. By four votes (Judges Cassese, McDonald, Stephen and Vohrah) to one (Judge Li) **FINDS** that the guilty plea entered by the Appellant before Trial Chamber I was not informed;

4. By three votes (Judges McDonald, Li and Vohrah) to two (Judges Cassese and Stephen) **FINDS** that duress does not afford a complete defence to a soldier charged with a crime against humanity and/or a war crime involving the killing of innocent human beings and that, consequently, the guilty plea entered by the Appellant before Trial Chamber I was not equivocal;

5. By four votes (Judges Cassese, McDonald, Stephen and Vohrah) to one (Judge Li) **HOLDS** that the case must be remitted to a Trial Chamber, other than the one which sentenced the Appellant, so that the Appellant may have the opportunity to replead in full knowledge of the nature of the charges and the consequences of his plea; and

6. **INSTRUCTS** the Registrar, in consultation with the President of the International Tribunal, to take all necessary measures for the expeditious initiation of proceedings before a Trial Chamber other than Trial Chamber I.

* * *

Antonio Cassese

Presiding

Judges Cassese, Li and Stephen append Separate and Dissenting Opinions to this Judgement.

Judges McDonald and Vohrah append a Joint Separate Opinion to this Judgement.

* * *

JOINT SEPARATE OPINION OF JUDGE MCDONALD AND JUDGE VOHRAH

* * *

III. CAN DURESS BE A COMPLETE DEFENCE IN INTERNATIONAL LAW TO THE KILLING OF INNOCENTS?

32. As to the first preliminary question addressed to the parties in this appeal, "[i]n law, may duress afford a complete defence to a charge of crimes against humanity and/or war crimes such that, if the defence is proved at trial, the accused is entitled to an acquittal?", three factors bear upon this general statement of the issue. Firstly, the particular war crime or crime against humanity committed by the Appellant involved the killing of innocent human beings. Secondly, as will be shown in the ensuing discussion, there is a clear dichotomy in the practice of the main legal systems of the world between those systems which would allow duress to operate as a complete defence to crimes involving the taking of innocent life, and those systems which would not. Thirdly, the Appellant in this case was a soldier of the Bosnian Serb army conducting combat operations in the Republic of Bosnia and Herzogovina at the material time. As such, the issue may be stated more specifically as follows: In law, may duress afford a complete defence to a soldier charged with crimes against humanity or war crimes where the soldier has killed innocent persons?

* * *

3. What is the general principle?

66. Having regard to the above survey relating to the treatment of duress in the various legal systems, it is, in our view, a general principle of law recognized by civilized nations that an accused person is less blameworthy and less deserving of the full punishment when he performs a certain prohibited act under duress. We would use the term "duress" in this context to mean "imminent threats to the life of accused if he refuses to commit a crime" and do not refer to the legal terms of art which have the equivalent meaning of the English word "duress" in the languages of most civil law systems. This alleviation of blameworthiness is manifest in the different rules with differing content in the principal legal systems of the world as the above survey reveals. On the one hand, a large number of jurisdictions recognize duress as a complete defence absolving the accused from all criminal responsibility. On the other hand, in other jurisdictions, duress does not afford a complete defence to offences generally but serves merely as a factor which would mitigate the punishment to be imposed on a convicted person. Mitigation is also relevant in two other respects. Firstly, punishment may be mitigated in respect of offences which have been specifically excepted from the operation of the defence of duress by the legislatures of some jurisdictions. Secondly, courts have the power to mitigate sentences where the strict elements of a defence of duress are not made out on the facts.

It is only when national legislatures have prescribed a mandatory life sentence or death penalty for particular offences that no consideration is given in national legal systems to the general principle that a person who commits a crime under duress is less blameworthy and less deserving of the full punishment in respect of that particular offence.

4. What is the applicable rule?

67. The rules of the various legal systems of the world are, however, largely inconsistent regarding the specific question whether duress affords a complete defence to a combatant charged with a war crime or a crime against humanity involving the killing of innocent persons. As the general provisions of the numerous penal codes set out above show, the civil law systems in general would theoretically allow duress as a complete defence of all crimes including murder and unlawful killing. On the other hand, there are laws of other legal systems which categorically reject duress as a defence to murder. Firstly, specific laws relating to war crimes in Norway and Poland do not allow duress to operate as a complete defence but permit it to be taken into account only in mitigation of punishment. Secondly, the Ethiopian Penal Code of 1957 provides in Article 67 that only "absolute physical coercion" may constitute a complete defence to crimes in general. Where the coercion is "moral," which we would interpret as referring to duress by threats, the accused is only entitled to a reduction of penalty. This reduction of penalty may extend, where appropriate, even to a complete discharge of the offender from punishment. Thirdly, the common law systems throughout the world, with the exception of a small minority of jurisdictions of the United States which have adopted without reservation Section 2.09 of the United States Model Penal Code, reject duress as a defence to the killing of innocent persons.

* * *

(b) The principle behind the rejection of duress as a defence to murder in the common law

70. Murder is invariably included in any list of offences excepted by legislation in common law systems from the operation of duress as a defence. The English common law rule is that duress is no defence to murder, either for a principal offender or a secondary party to the crime. The House of Lords in R. v. Howe and Others overruled the earlier decision of a differently constituted House of Lords in Lynch v. DPP for Northern Ireland in which it was held that duress could afford a defence to murder for a principle in the second degree. Thus, R. v. Howe restored the position of the English common law to the traditional position that duress is not available as a defence to murder generally.

* * *

(c) No consistent rule from the principal legal systems of the world.

72. It is clear from the differing positions of the principal legal systems of the world that there is no consistent concrete rule which answers the question whether or not duress is a defence to the killing of innocent persons. It is not possible to reconcile the opposing positions and, indeed, we do not believe that the issue should be reduced to a contest between common law and civil law.

We would therefore approach this problem bearing in mind the specific context in which the International Tribunal was established, the types of crimes over which it has jurisdiction, and the fact that the International Tribunal's mandate is expressed in the Statute as being in relation to "serious violations of international humanitarian law."

D. The Rule Applicable to this Case

1. A normative mandate for international criminal law

* * *

75. The resounding point from these eloquent passages is that the law should not be the product or slave of logic or intellectual hair-splitting, but must serve broader normative purposes in light of its social, political and economic role. It is noteworthy that the authorities we have just cited issued their cautionary words in respect of domestic society and in respect of a range of ordinary crimes including kidnaping, assault, robbery and murder. Whilst reserving our comments on the appropriate rule for domestic national contexts, we cannot but stress that we are not, in the International Tribunal, concerned with ordinary domestic crimes. The purview of the International Tribunal relates to war crimes and crimes against humanity committed in armed conflicts of extreme violence with egregious dimensions. We are not concerned with the actions of domestic terrorists, gang-leaders and kidnappers. We are concerned that, in relation to the most heinous crimes known to humankind, the principles of law to which we give credence have the appropriate normative effect upon soldiers bearing weapons of destruction and upon the commanders who control them in armed conflict situations. The facts of this particular case, for example, involved the cold-blooded slaughter of 1200 men and boys by soldiers using automatic weapons. We must bear in mind that we are operating in the realm of international humanitarian law which has, as one of its prime objectives, the protection of the weak and vulnerable in such a situation where their lives and security are endangered. Concerns about the harm which could arise from admitting duress as a defence to murder were sufficient to persuade a majority of the House of Lords and the Privy Council to categorically deny the defence in the national context to prevent the growth of domestic crime and the impunity of miscreants.

If national law denies duress as a defence even in a case in which a single innocent life is extinguished due to action under duress, international law, in our view, cannot admit duress in cases which involve the slaughter of innocent human beings on a large scale. It must be our concern to facilitate the development and effectiveness of international humanitarian law and to promote its aims and application by recognizing the normative effect which criminal law should have upon those subject to them. Indeed, Security Council resolution 827 (1993) establishes the International Tribunal expressly as a measure to "halt and effectively redress" the widespread and flagrant violations of international humanitarian law occurring in the territory of the former Yugoslavia and to contribute thereby to the restoration and maintenance of peace.

* * *

2. An exception where the victims will die regardless of the participation of the accused?

79. It was suggested during the hearing of 26 May 1997 that neither the English national cases nor the post-World War Two military tribunal decisions specifically addressed the situation in which the accused faced the choice between his own death for not obeying an order to kill or participating in a killing which was inevitably going to occur regardless of whether he participated in it or not. It has been argued that in such a situation where the fate of the victim was already sealed, duress should constitute a complete defence. This is because the accused is then not choosing that one innocent human being should die rather than another. In a situation where the victim or victims would have died in any event, such as in the present case where the victims were to be executed by firing squad, there would be no reason for the accused to have sacrificed his life. The accused could not have saved the victim's life by giving his own and thus, ac-

cording to this argument, it is unjust and illogical for the law to expect an accused to sacrifice his life in the knowledge that the victim/s will die anyway. The argument, it is said, is vindicated in the Italian case of *Masetti* which was decided by the Court of Assize in L'Aquila. The accused in that case raised duress in response to the charge of having organized the execute [sic] of two partisans upon being ordered to do so by the battalion commander. The Court of Assize acquitted the accused on the ground of duress and said:

> ... the possible sacrifice [of their lives] by Masetti and his men [those who comprised the execution squad] would have been in any case to no avail and without any effect in that it would have had no impact whatsoever on the plight of the persons to be shot, who would have been executed anyway even without him [the accused.]

We have given due consideration to this approach which, for convenience, we will label "the *Masetti* approach." For the reasons given below we would reject the *Masetti* approach.

3. Rejection of utilitarianism and proportionality where human life must be weighed

80. The *Masetti* approach proceeds from the starting point of strict utilitarian logic based on the fact that if the victim will die anyway, the accused is not at all morally blameworthy for taking part in the execution; there is absolutely no reason why the accused should die as it would be unjust for the law to expect the accused to die for nothing. It should be immediately apparent that the assertion that the accused is not morally blameworthy where the victim would have died in any case depends entirely again upon a view of morality based on utilitarian logic. This does not, in our opinion, address the true rationale for our rejection of duress as a defence to the killing of innocent human beings. The approach we take does not involve a balancing of harms for and against killing but rests upon an application in the context of international humanitarian law of the rule that duress does not justify or excuse the killing of an innocent person. Our view is based upon a recognition that international humanitarian law should guide the conduct of combatants and their commanders. There must be legal limits as to the conduct of combatants and their commanders in armed conflict. In accordance with the spirit of international humanitarian law, we deny the availability of duress as a complete defence to combatants who have killed innocent persons. In so doing, we give notice in no uncertain terms that those who kill innocent persons will not be able to take advantage of duress as a defence and thus get away with impunity for their criminal acts in the taking of innocent lives.

* * *

E. Our conclusions

88. After the above survey of authorities in the different systems of law and exploration of the various policy considerations which we must bear in mind, we take the view that duress cannot afford a complete defence to a soldier charged with crimes against humanity or war crimes in international law involving the taking of innocent lives. We do so having regard to our mandated obligation under the Statute to ensure that international humanitarian law, which is concerned with the protection of humankind, is not in any way undermined.

89. In the result, we do not consider the plea of the Appellant was equivocal as duress does not afford a complete defence in international law to a charge of a crime against humanity or a war crime which involves the killing of innocent human beings.

90. Our discussion of the issues relating to the guilty plea entered by the Appellant is sufficient to dispose of the present appeal. It is not necessary for us to engage ourselves

in the remaining issues raised by the parties. We would observe, however, that in rejecting the evidence of the Appellant that he had committed the crime under a threat of death from his commanding officer and consequently in refusing to take the circumstance of duress into account in mitigation of the Appellant's sentence, the Trial Chamber appeared to require corroboration of the Appellant's testimony as a matter of law. There is, with respect, nothing in the Statute or the Rules which requires corroboration of the exculpatory evidence of an accused person in order for that evidence to be taken into account in mitigation of sentence.

91. We would allow the appeal on the ground that the plea was not informed. The case is hereby remitted to another Trial Chamber where the Appellant must be given the opportunity to replead in full knowledge of the consequences of pleading guilty *per se* and of the inherent difference between the alternative charges.

* * *

SEPARATE AND DISSENTING OPINION OF JUDGE CASSESE

* * *

II. DURESS
(OR: THE QUESTION OF WHETHER INTERNATIONAL CRIMINAL LAW UPHOLDS THE COMMON-LAW APPROACH TO DURESS IN THE CASE OF KILLING)

A. *Introduction*

11. I also respectfully disagree with the conclusions of the majority of the Appeals Chamber concerning duress, as set out in the Joint Separate Opinion of their Honours Judge McDonald and Judge Vohrah and on the following grounds:

(I) after finding that *no specific international rule* has evolved on the question of whether duress affords a complete defence to the killing of innocent persons, the majority should have drawn the only conclusion imposed by law and logic, namely that the general rule on duress should apply—subject, of course, to the necessary requirements. In logic, if no exception to a *general* rule be proved, then the general rule prevails. Likewise in law, if one looks for a *special* rule governing a specific aspect of a matter and concludes that no such rule has taken shape, the only inference to be drawn is that the specific aspect is regulated by the rule governing the general matter;

(ii) instead of this simple conclusion, the majority of the Appeals Chamber has embarked upon a detailed investigation of "practical policy considerations" and has concluded by upholding "policy considerations" substantially based on English law. I submit that this examination is *extraneous to the task of our Tribunal.* This International Tribunal is called upon to apply international law, in particular our Statute and principles and rules of international humanitarian law and international criminal law. Our International Tribunal is a court of law; it is bound only by international law. It should therefore refrain from engaging in meta-legal analyses. In addition, it should refrain from relying exclusively on notions, policy considerations or the philosophical underpinnings of common-law countries, while disregarding those of civil-law countries or other systems of law. What is even more important, a policy-oriented approach in the area of criminal law runs contrary to the fundamental customary principle *nullum crimen sine lege.* On the strength of international principles and rules my conclusions on duress differ widely from those of the majority of the

Appeals Chamber. I shall set out below the legal reasons which I believe support my dissent.

12. In short, I consider that: (1) under international criminal law duress may be generally urged as a defence, provided certain strict requirements are met; when it cannot be admitted as a defence, duress may nevertheless be acted upon as a mitigating circumstance; (2) with regard to war crimes or crimes against humanity whose underlying offence is murder or more generally the taking of human life, no special rule of customary international law has evolved on the matter; consequently, even with respect to these offences the general rule on duress applies; it follows that duress may amount to a defence provided that its stringent requirements are met. For offences involving killing, it is true, however, that one of the requirements (discussed at paragraph 42 below)—proportionality—would usually not be fulfilled. Nevertheless, in exceptional circumstances this requirement might be met, for example, when the killing would be in any case perpetrated by persons other than the one acting under duress (since then it is not a question of saving your own life by killing another person, but of simply saving your own life when the other person will inevitably die, which may not be 'disproportionate' as a remedy;) (3) the Appeals Chamber should therefore remit the case to a Trial Chamber on the issue of duress (as well as on the issue that the plea was not informed)....

* * *

16. Let us now turn to the conditions applicable to the defence of duress. The relevant case-law is almost unanimous in requiring four strict conditions to be met for duress to be upheld as a defence, namely:

(I) the act charged was done under an immediate threat of severe and irreparable harm to life or limb;

(ii) there was no adequate means of averting such evil;

(iii) the crime committed was not disproportionate to the evil threatened (this would, for example, occur in the case of killing in order to avert an assault.) In other words, in order not to be disproportionate, the crime committed under duress must be, on balance, the lesser of two evils;

(iv) the situation leading to duress must not have been voluntarily brought about by the person coerced.

In addition, the relevant national legislation supports the principle that the existence in law of any special duty on the part of the accused towards the victim may preclude the possibility of raising duress as a defence.

17. It is worth insisting on the fourth requirement just mentioned, in order to highlight its particular relevance to war-like situations. According to the case-law on international humanitarian law, duress or necessity cannot excuse from criminal responsibility the person who intends to avail himself of such defence if he freely and knowingly chose to become a member of a unit, organization or group institutionally intent upon actions contrary to international humanitarian law.

* * *

D. Application To The Judgement Under Appeal

50. In view of my finding, above, that in exceptional circumstances duress can be urged in defence to a charge of crimes against humanity or war crimes, it follows that the Ap-

pellant's guilty plea was equivocal. Thus, the Trial Chamber should have entered a plea of not guilty and held a trial. Accordingly, I would remit the case to a Trial Chamber for entry of a not-guilty plea and a determination on the issue of whether or not Appellant was acting under duress when he committed the crime, so that he would not be criminally responsible within the meaning of Article 7 of the Statute of the International Tribunal.

Antonio Cassese

Presiding Judge

* * *

SEPARATE AND DISSENTING OPINION OF JUDGE STEPHEN

* * *

1. In this appeal from the sentence of Trial Chamber I of this International Tribunal in the case of Draz en Erdemovíc (the "Appellant"), the facts and circumstances of which appear in greater detail in other Opinions, there are a number of aspects which call for particular consideration. They all concern the Appellant's plea of guilty, a matter to which the Trial Chamber devoted considerable attention in the opening portions of its Sentencing Judgement of 29 November 1996.

* * *

12. The question that immediately arises is whether the Appellant's plea of guilty, when coupled with his statement, subsequently elaborated, that he had acted in accordance with the order of his superior and under threat of immediate death if he did not obey the order given, resulted in such ambiguity in his plea of guilty as would require the Trial Chamber to enter a plea of not guilty and proceed to trial instead of accepting his guilty plea and proceeding to sentence.

13. The Trial Chamber was well aware that the circumstances gave rise to such a question and, at the outset of its Sentencing Judgement, gave its reasons for accepting the Appellant's plea of guilty. It adverted first to Article 7, paragraph 4, of the Statute of the International Tribunal ("Statute") which states that the existence of superior orders provides no defence but may be a ground for mitigation of sentence. It went on to recognize that if coupled with physical and moral duress these factors might not only mitigate the penalty but "depending on the probative value and force which may be given to them" could also constitute a defence as eliminating "the *mens rea* of the offence and therefore the offence itself." In such a case, it concluded, a plea of guilty would be invalidated. It accordingly turned to an examination of what it described as "the elements invoked."

In doing so it observed that, unlike the case of superior orders, the Statute provides no guidance regarding the availability of duress as a defence. This is, of course, correct; the Statute does not, with the sole exception of superior orders, advert at all to what defences are available. It is left to the International Tribunal in the trials it conducts to apply existing international humanitarian law.

14. The Trial Chamber accordingly reviewed decisions of post-Second World War military tribunals, noting that in a number of cases duress was regarded as a complete defence, the absence of moral choice occasioned by imminent physical danger being on occasions recognized as an essential component of duress as a defence. Those decisions, it noted, referred to three factors as essential features for duress to be accepted as a de-

fence, namely the existence of an immediate danger, both serious and irreparable, the absence of any adequate means of escape and the fact that the remedy was not disproportionate to the evil. Reference was also made to two other factors, to an accused's voluntary participation in an enterprise that left no doubt as to its end results and to the respective ranks held by the giver and receiver of a superior order which was manifestly illegal.

15. The Trial Chamber then turned to the facts of the case before it and stated that the Appellant did not challenge the manifestly illegal nature of the order that he was allegedly given and that, according to the case law to which it had referred, in the case of a manifestly illegal order "the duty was to disobey rather than to obey," a duty which could "only recede in the face of the most extreme duress."

* * *

23.... This brings me, then, to that aspect of this appeal upon which I have the misfortune to differ from the Joint Separate Opinion of Judges McDonald and Vohrah, whether duress is in international law a defence to a charge of murder or any charge involving the taking of innocent life. The Prosecution contends that it is not and that, at most, duress can only be a mitigating circumstance. It submits that the overwhelming weight of material garnered from post-Second World War crimes trials establishes that duress can never be raised as a defence to a charge of murder. It acknowledges that the decisions on which it relies are very largely those of tribunals having common law origins but contends that while the common law has provided the source of the doctrine denying duress as a defence to murder, this does nothing to alter the fact that the doctrine is now well established as part of international law.

24. The Prosecution view that the great preponderance of such decisions do in fact establish that in international law duress is no defence to a charge of murder is, I believe, mistaken. His Honour Judge Cassese has dealt with this matter in great detail and I concur in his conclusion that on a close examination of the decisions the Prosecution's contention is not borne out. What the decisions do in my view demonstrate is that in relation to duress the strong tendency has been to apply principles of criminal law derived from analogous municipal law rules of the particular tribunal, and this despite the few divergences from that tendency, as in the *obiter dictum* of the Judge-Advocate in the *Einsatzgruppen* case and the observations of the Judge-Advocate in the *Stalag Luft III* case. The post-Second World War military tribunals do not appear to have acted in relation to duress in conscious conformity with the dictates of international law, as, for example, they have in their treatment of the doctrine of superior orders. It appears to me that it cannot be said that, in applying one principle or another to particular cases, the necessary *opinio iuris sine necessitatis* was present so as to establish any rule of customary international law.

25. I accordingly turn to those "general principles of law recognized by civilized nations," referred to in Article 38(1)(c) of the Statute of the International Court of Justice as a further source of international law.

* * *

26. Were it not for the common law's exceptional exclusion of murder (and in saying this I exclude the case of some American States to which I will later refer,) there would, I think, accordingly be little doubt that duress, albeit hedged around with appropriate qualifications, should likewise be treated in international law as a general principle of law recognized by civilized nations as available as a defence to all crimes. Why this

should be so, not only because of the approach of the civil law but also as a matter of simple justice, is perhaps best illustrated by example, set in a domestic rather than an international humanitarian law context since the former has been the context in which the common law approach has developed.

Were a civilian, going about his lawful business, to be suddenly accosted by an armed man and ordered, under threat of immediate and otherwise unavoidable death and without explanation, then and there to kill a total stranger present at the scene and against whom he can have no conceivable animus, it would be strange justice indeed to deny that civilian the defence of duress. Yet if he obeys the order and kills that total stranger what else is it, according to the common law, but murder to which duress, his only defence, is no defence?

* * *

33. What lies at the core of the common law exception regarding murder is Lord Hale's concept of equivalence, the evil involved in seeking to balance one life against another. That he could not accept; accordingly a person subjected to duress "ought rather to die himself than kill an innocent" when the choice lies between one's own life and that of another. This concept permeates the writing of subsequent common law jurists, who never had to consider the situation in which the choice presented to an accused was not that of one life or another but that of one life or both lives, the very situation which, according to his statements, confronted the present Appellant.

34. The case of *R. v. Dudley and Stephens*, one of necessity rather than duress, was that of shipwrecked sailors, adrift in an open boat in mid-ocean, who killed a boy, one of their number, ate his body and drank his blood to save themselves from death and who raised the defence of necessity when ultimately rescued and tried on a charge of murder. Despite the close connection in principle between necessity and duress, this case in fact has little in common with the present; it was an instance of "his life or mine," much like the oft-cited and hypothetical case of two men in the water and at risk of drowning, and with a plank only big enough to support one of them. The problem which so concerned Lord Coleridge, that of the measure of comparative value of lives, and which he resolved by adopting Lord Hale's dictum that a man ought rather to die himself than kill an innocent, is wholly absent if the innocent are to die in any event.

* * *

52. Highly relevantly to this present appeal, he [Sir John Smith] points out that it has generally been supposed by those opposing duress as any defence to murder "that there is a direct choice between the life of the person under duress and the life of the victim" and adds: "This is by no means always the case ...". It is not, as I have said, the case in the present instance. It is significant that in all the reported cases this question of choice was present, the choice, to be made by the accused, between the victim's life and that of the accused, so that Lord Hale's dictum—that an accused ought rather "to die himself, than kill an innocent" at least has some meaning, whatever else may be said of it. This matter of choice, inherent in the element of proportionality and in the questions of morality which surround it, necessarily plays a prominent part in the reasoning on duress. It features prominently in *R. v. Dudley and Stephens* and again in the later cases to which I have referred. The altogether different situation which faced the Appellant in the present case, according to his account of events, was one in which he believed, in all probability correctly, that no choice of his would alter the fate of the Muslim victims, yet the choice for him was to die alongside them or to live, a situation

not addressed in the reported cases yet clearly falling within the general classification of duress.

* * *

66. It is for the foregoing reasons that I conclude that, despite the exception which the common law makes to the availability of duress in cases of murder where the choice is truly between one life or another, the defence of duress can be adopted into international law as deriving from a general principle of law recognized by the world's major legal systems, at least where that exception does not apply.

67. The stringent conditions always surrounding that defence will have to be met, including the requirement that the harm done is not disproportionate to the harm threatened. The case of an accused, forced to take innocent lives which he cannot save and who can only add to the toll by sacrifice of his own life, is entirely consistent with that requirement.

* * *

Ninian Stephen

Judge

Note

The case was remanded to a new Trial Chamber where Erdemovíc was permitted to replead to the charges. On January 14th, 1998, he pled guilty to the alternative charge of a violation of the laws and customs of war, rather than pleading guilty to the charge of a violation of a crime against humanity to which he had pled guilty at the first hearing. The Prosecutor withdrew the charge of the count of a crime against humanity. After a sentencing hearing, the Trial Chamber sentenced Erdemovíc to five years imprisonment with time deducted for the period already spent in custody.

QUESTIONS

1. The Statute of the International Criminal Tribunal for the Former Yugoslavia (Article 7, paragraph 4) makes it clear that the defense of acting on the orders of a superior officer will not justify a violation of the laws of war but may mitigate the punishment. Do you think a soldier who has killed unarmed civilians should be acquitted when he was ordered to shoot the civilians by a superior officer and was told that he would be shot if he did not carry out the killings?
2. Do you think it makes any difference that Erdemovíc knew that even if he was shot, the unarmed civilians would not be spared?
3. You may wish to compare this case with the analogous provision in the Statute of the International Criminal Court, article 31(d) available at: www.icc-cpi.int/. Compare also *Negusie V. Holder*, pp. 352–358 *supra*.

Note

To read the Statute and other rules governing the International Criminal Tribunal for Rwanda (ICTR) go to the Tribunal's web site at *www.ictr.org/*. Click on Basic Legal Texts.

The Prosecutor v. Aloys Simba

Case no. ICTR-01-76-T
Judgement and Sentence of the Trial Chamber, 13 December 2005
The International Criminal Tribunal for Rwanda
(Footnotes omitted)

Note

The facts of the cases are stated in the Tribunal's opinion. The events described took place in the east African country of Rwanda in 1994. The "Interahamwe" mentioned in the opinion were a rebel group principally drawn from the Hutu ethnic group. During a three month period, the Interahamwe killed about 800,000 people who were either from the Tutsi ethnic group or were thought to be moderate Hutus.

CHAPTER I:

* * *

2. INDICTMENT

4. Under the amended Indictment of 6 May 2004 ("the Indictment"), the Prosecution charged Aloys Simba with four counts, pursuant to Articles 2 and 3 of the Statute: genocide; complicity in genocide; extermination as a crime against humanity; and murder as a crime against humanity. The Indictment, which is set out in full in an Annex to this Judgement, charged the Accused with individual criminal responsibility under Article 6 (1) and (3) for these crimes. At the end of its case, the Prosecution withdrew superior responsibility under Article 6 (3) as a form of responsibility as well as the charges of complicity in genocide and murder as a crime against humanity.

3. SUMMARY OF PROCEDURAL HISTORY

5. Aloys Simba was arrested in Senegal on 27 November 2001. The trial commenced on 30 August 2004 and closed on 8 July 2005. Over the course of thirty trial days, the Prosecution called sixteen witnesses. The Defence case opened on 13 December 2004. During twenty-three trial days, the Defence called twenty witnesses, including the Accused. The procedural history is set out in full in an Annex to this Judgement.

4. OVERVIEW OF THE CASE

6. In the days following the death of President Habyarimana, thousands of Tutsi civilians in Gikongoro prefecture in southern Rwanda fled their homes following attacks by Hutu militiamen. They sought sanctuary at places such as Kibeho Parish, Cyanika Parish, Murambi Technical School, and Kaduha Parish. Attacks against the refugees at these places began with Kibeho Parish on 14 April 1994. On 21 April 1994, Hutu militiamen assisted by local officials and gendarmes launched subsequent attacks against refugees at Murambi, Cyanika, and Kaduha in the course of a period of around twelve hours. At the end of April, attackers from Gikongoro prefecture continued the killings by crossing the Mwogo River into neighbouring Butare prefecture to kill Tutsi civilians who had fled to Ruhashya commune. These five massacre sites are the primary basis of this case.

7. The Prosecution places responsibility for these killings on Aloys Simba, a retired lieutenant colonel and former member of parliament. Simba hails from Musebeya commune, Gikongoro prefecture and became a national hero fighting the "*Inkotanyi*"

[a Tutsi led military/political group] in the 1960s. He is a member of the "comrades of the fifth of July", who participated in the *coup d'état* that brought former President Juvénal Habyarimana to power in 1973, and was well-knownthroughout Rwanda. At the time of the events in 1994, Simba had no formal ties to any government, military, or political structure. He claims that he was an ordinary man who had become a marginal figure in Rwandan society. Simba assumed the role of civil defence adviser to the Prefect of Gikongoro on 18 May 1994. The five massacres are not related to his actions in this position.

8. The Prosecution contends that Simba is one of the principal architects of the five massacres and that he personally participated in their execution by furnishing arms, ordering militiamen and government forces to attack and kill Tutsi.

9. The Defence presented evidence of an alibi that Simba was not in Gikongoro prefecture when the genocide was planned or unfolded and that he played no role in the killings in Butare. According to Simba, in the days following the death of President Habyarimana, he remained in Kigali gathering family, friends, and neighbours in an effort to protect them from the ensuing violence. As Kigali became a war-zone, he evacuated a number of refugees hiding in his home to Gitarama Town where some of them remained with him from 13 until 24 April. He relocated to Gikongoro prefecture on 24 April only after the killings had come to an end in the prefecture. The Defence has also challenged the fairness of the proceedings on grounds of lack of notice and of alleged undue interference with Defence witnesses.

CHAPTER II: FACTUAL FINDINGS

[The Tribunal carefully review all of the evidence produced by the Prosecution and the Defense.]

* * *

CHAPTER III: LEGAL FINDINGS

1. CRIMINAL RESPONSIBILITY

385. The Prosecution seeks to establish Simba's criminal liability for the massacres at Kibeho Parish, Murambi Technical School, Cyanika Parish, Kaduha Parish, and Ruhashya commune under Article 6 (1) of the Statute based on the theory of joint criminal enterprise. Article 6 (1) sets out certain forms of individual criminal responsibility applicable to the crimes falling within the Tribunal's jurisdiction. Article 6 (1) does not make explicit reference to "joint criminal enterprise". However, the Appeals Chamber has previously held that participating in a joint criminal enterprise is a form of liability which exists in customary international law and that it is a form of "commission" under Article 6 (1).

1.1 Elements of Joint Criminal Enterprise

386. Article 6 (1) has been interpreted to contain three forms of joint criminal enterprise: basic, systemic, and extended. At the close of its case, the Prosecution indicated that it is primarily pursuing the basic form. The "basic" form requires that all the co-perpetrators, acting pursuant to a common purpose, possess the same criminal intention.

387. According to settled jurisprudence, the required *actus reus* for each form of joint criminal enterprise comprises three elements. First, a plurality of persons is required. They need not be organised in a military, political or administrative structure. Second, the existence of a common purpose which amounts to or involves the commission of a crime provided for in the Statute is required. There is no necessity for this purpose to

have been previously arranged or formulated. It may materialise extemporaneously and be inferred from the facts. Third, the participation of the accused in the common purpose is required, which involves the perpetration of one of the crimes provided for in the Statute. This participation need not involve commission of a specific crime under one of the provisions (for example, murder, extermination, torture, or rape), but may take the form of assistance in, or contribution to, the execution of the common purpose. The Appeals Chamber in *Kvocka et al.* provided guidance on distinguishing between joint criminal enterprise and other forms of liability, such as aiding and abetting.

388. The required *mens rea* for each form of joint criminal enterprise varies. The basic form of joint criminal enterprise requires the intent to perpetrate a certain crime, this intent being shared by all co-perpetrators. Where the underlying crime requires a special intent, such as discriminatory intent, the accused, as a member of the joint criminal enterprise, must share the special intent.

* * *

393. In most cases, the participants who physically perpetrated the crimes are identified in each section of the Indictment dealing with a particular massacre site by broad category, such as *Interahamwe* or gendarmes, and then further identified with geographic and temporal details. In the context of this case and given the nature of the attacks, the Chamber is not satisfied that the Prosecution could have provided more specific identification. The Indictment alleges Simba's interactions with the attackers in such a way as to reflect concerted action.

* * *

394. With respect to the purpose of the joint criminal enterprise, it is clear that it was to kill Tutsi at Kibeho Parish, Murambi Technical School, Cyanika Parish, and Kaduha Parish in Gikongoro prefecture, as well as in Ruhashya commune in Butare prefecture. This follows from a reading of the Indictment in conjunction with the Pre-trial Brief.

395. The Pre-trial Brief also makes clear that Simba's participation in the joint criminal enterprise encompasses the specific criminal acts pleaded in the Indictment. For his part, Simba is accused of planning the massacres, distributing weapons to attackers, and ordering or instigating others to commit massacres. The Pre-trial Brief also reflects that the time frame of the joint criminal enterprise is from 6 April until 17 July 1994.

396. The Chamber finds that the manner in which the Prosecution has given notice of its theory of joint criminal enterprise in the present case has not in any way rendered the trial unfair.

1.3 Application

397. In its factual findings, the Chamber found that *Interahamwe*, gendarmes, and members of the local population killed thousands of mostly Tutsi refugees at Kibeho Parish, Murambi Technical School, Cyanika Parish, Kaduha Parish, and in Ruhashya commune in Butare prefecture. The Chamber will discuss the nature and extent of Simba's criminal responsibility, if any, for these massacres below.

Murambi Technical School, Cyanika Parish, and Kaduha Parish

398. The massacres at Murambi Technical School, Cyanika Parish, and Kaduha Parish on 21 April commenced around 3.00 a.m. when *Interahamwe* and gendarmes, armed with guns and grenades began the killings at Murambi. Around 6.00 a.m., Prefect Bucyibaruta, Captain Sebuhura, and Bourgmestre Semakwavu replenished ammunition and directed half of the assailants to reinforce the assault at nearby Cyanika Parish. Simba

came to Murambi Technical School around 7.00 a.m. after the other authorities had left. He distributed traditional weapons to the attackers who then continued the killing.

399. Attackers at Murambi Technical School also participated in the massacre at Cyanika Parish, which commenced around 8.00 a.m. Victims at Murambi and Cyanika recounted the presence of *Interahamwe* from Mudasomwa commune at both locations. Defence Witness NGJ2 attested to the movement of the attackers from Murambi to Cyanika. The Chamber has no direct evidence of the presence of Simba or local authorities such as Prefect Bucyibaruta or Captain Sebuhura at Cyanika Parish.

400. Simba arrived at Kaduha Parish around 9.00 a.m. on 21 April where hundreds of attackers had already assembled. Most of the assailants were armed with traditional weapons. However, around fifty gendarmes, former soldiers, and communal policemen carried guns and grenades. Bourgmestre Gashugi had convoked some of this smaller group of well-armed attackers the previous day and brought them to the parish that morning. Simba, invoking the approval of the government, urged the attackers to "get rid of the filth" at the parish. He then distributed guns and grenades to the assailants who proceeded to kill the Tutsi at the parish. There is no reliable evidence placing Prefect Bucyibaruta and Captain Sebuhura at Kaduha on the day of the attack.

401. The three massacres on 21 April at Murambi Technical School, Cyanika Parish, and Kaduha Parish can only be described, in the Chamber's view, as a highly coordinated operation involving local militiamen backed by gendarmes, armed with guns and grenades, and with the organizational and logistical support offered by local authorities and prominent personalities such as Simba who provided encouragement, direction, and ammunition. This operation was conducted over the course of a period of around twelve hours on a single day and involved the killing of thousands of Tutsi concentrated at three geographically proximate locations. Prior planning and coordination is the only reasonable explanation for the manner in which the perpetrators conducted these three massive assaults. The Chamber notes in addition, prior to 21 April, *Interahamwe*, relying principally on traditional weapons, had been largely unsuccessful in attacking refugees at these locations. Therefore, the added elements of coordination, official encouragement, well-armed gendarmes, and the use of guns and grenades proved decisive.

402. In the Chamber's view, the only reasonable inference from the evidence is that a common criminal purpose existed to kill Tutsi at these three sites. The Chamber will discuss the extent to which Simba shared this common purpose below. The Chamber finds that the massive scale and relative efficiency of the slaughter by necessity demanded the involvement of a plurality of persons, each carrying out a particular role at one or more of the massacres. In addition to the physical perpetrators of the crimes, other prominent participants in the enterprise included Simba, Prefect Bucyibaruta, Captain Sebuhura, and Bourgmestre Semakwavu.

403. Simba participated in the joint criminal enterprise through his acts of assistance and encouragement to the physical perpetrators of the crimes at Murambi Technical School and Kaduha Parish. In the Chamber's view, Simba's actions at those two sites had a substantial effect on the killings which followed. Witness KSY noted that the attackers at Murambi continued with renewed enthusiasm after Simba's departure. Moreover, the use of guns and grenades, which Simba distributed at Kaduha Parish, was a decisive factor in the success of these assaults. The Chamber notes that Simba was a respected national figure in Rwandan society and well-known in his native region. Therefore, the assailants at those places would have viewed his presence during the attacks, however brief, as approval of their conduct, particularly after Simba's invocation of the government.

404. In addition, given his stature in Rwandan society, his participation in the joint criminal enterprise would have had a similar effect on other prominent participants such as Prefect Bucyibaruta, Captain Sebuhura, Bourgmestre Semakwavu as well as other local authorities. The only reasonable conclusion on the evidence is that Simba coordinated his actions with these individuals before the attacks. In reaching this conclusion, the Chamber recalls that Simba likely arrived in the prefecture only a few days before the assaults, after fleeing Kigali with his family. At the time, he had no formal ties to the government or to the military. However, on 21 April, he was accompanied by gendarmes and *Interahamwe*. At Kaduha Parish, he invoked the government's request that he return to service, before urging on the attackers. In addition, Simba had a cache of weapons, including firearms and grenades for distribution, which certainly would have come from civilian or military authorities.

405. The Prosecution argues that Simba participated in the planning of the three massacres on 21 April. There is no direct evidence of this. Moreover, the Chamber is not satisfied that this is the only reasonable inference available from the evidence. It is also possible that local authorities formulated a plan of attack and then requested Simba to assist in implementing it.

406. The Chamber finds beyond reasonable doubt that Simba shared the common purpose of killing Tutsi at Murambi Technical School and Kaduha Parish based on his presence and specific actions at the two sites. He also distributed the means to implement the killings during an ongoing massacre at Murambi Technical School. In addition, after leaving the massacre at Murambi, he distributed guns and grenades to assailants at Kaduha Parish and urged them to "get rid of the filth".

407. However, the Chamber has some doubt that he equally shared the common purpose of killing Tutsi at Cyanika Parish. There is no direct evidence linking him to Cyanika Parish or indicating that he knew and accepted that it would also form part of the operation. Accordingly, the Chamber is not satisfied beyond reasonable doubt that Simba also had the shared intention to kill Tutsi at Cyanika Parish or that the killings there would in any way be a foreseeable consequence of his role in the joint criminal enterprise at Murambi Technical School and Kaduha Parish.

408. The question of whether Simba and the other participants in the joint criminal enterprise possessed the requisite *mens rea* for the underlying crime will be addressed in the Chamber's legal findings on genocide and crimes against humanity.

* * *

2. GENOCIDE

411. In Count 1 of the Indictment, the Prosecution has charged Simba with Genocide under Article 2 of the Statute.

412. To find an accused guilty of the crime of genocide it must be established that he committed any of the enumerated acts in Article 2 (2) with the specific intent to destroy, in whole or in part, a group, as such, that is defined by one of the protected categories of nationality, race, ethnicity, or religion. Although there is no numeric threshold, the perpetrator must act with the intent to destroy at least a substantial part of the group. The perpetrator need not be solely motivated by a criminal intent to commit genocide, nor does the existence of personal motive preclude him from having the specific intent to commit genocide.

413. In the absence of direct evidence, a perpetrator's intent may be inferred from relevant facts and circumstances. Factors that may establish intent include the general con-

text, the perpetration of other culpable acts systematically directed against the same group, the scale of atrocities committed, the systematic targeting of victims on account of their membership in a particular group, or the repetition of destructive and discriminatory acts.

414. The Indictment charges Simba with killing or causing serious bodily or mental harm to members of the Tutsi group. However, in its Closing Brief, the Prosecution directs the Chamber only to evidence of killing. Killing members of the group requires a showing that the principal perpetrator intentionally killed one or more members of the group, without the necessity of premeditation.

415. It is not disputed in the present case that Tutsi are members of a protected group under the Statute. The Chamber has found that Simba participated in a joint criminal enterprise to kill Tutsi civilians at Murambi Technical School and Kaduha Parish by providing weapons and lending encouragement and approval to the physical perpetrators. In its findings on criminal responsibility, the Chamber described this assistance as having a substantial effect on the killings that followed. The assailants at these sites killed thousands of Tutsi civilians. Given the manner in which the attacks were conducted, the Chamber finds that the assailants intentionally killed members of a protected group.

416. The Chamber has heard extensive evidence, which it accepts, about the targeting of Tutsi civilians in the days immediately after the death of President Habyarimana. A great many Tutsi sought refuge at Murambi Technical School and Kaduha Parish after Hutu militiamen burned and looted their homes. These Tutsi refugees were slaughtered by the thousands over the course of a period of around twelve hours on a single day. Given the scale of the killings and their context, the only reasonable conclusion is that the assailants who physically perpetrated the killings possessed the intent to destroy in whole or in part a substantial part of the Tutsi group. This genocidal intent was shared by all participants in the joint criminal enterprise, including Simba.

* * *

418. Simba was physically present at two massacre sites. He provided traditional weapons, guns, and grenades to attackers poised to kill thousands of Tutsi. Simba was aware of the targeting of Tutsi throughout his country, and as a former military commander, he knew what would follow when he urged armed assailants to "get rid of the filth". The only reasonable conclusion, even accepting his submissions as true, is that at that moment, he acted with genocidal intent.

419. The Chamber finds beyond reasonable doubt that Simba is criminally responsible under Article 6 (1) of the Statute based on his participation in a joint criminal enterprise to kill Tutsi civilians at Murambi Technical School and Kaduha Parish. Therefore, the Chamber finds Simba guilty on Count 1 of the Indictment for genocide.

3. CRIMES AGAINST HUMANITY (EXTERMINATION)

420. In Count 3 of the Indictment, the Prosecution charges Simba with extermination as a crime against humanity under Article 3 of the Statute.

421. For an enumerated crime under Article 3 to qualify as a crime against humanity, the Prosecution must prove that there was a widespread or systematic attack against the civilian population for national, political, ethnic, racial or religious grounds. Intended to be read as disjunctive elements, "widespread" refers to the large scale of the attack, while "systematic" describes the organized nature of the attack. A perpetrator must have

acted with knowledge of the broader context and knowledge that his acts formed part of the attack, but he need not share the purpose or goals behind the broader attack.

422. The crime of extermination requires proof that an accused participated in a widespread or systematic killing or in subjecting a widespread number of people or systematically subjecting a number of people to conditions of living that would inevitably lead to death. Extermination is distinguishable from murder because it is the act of killing on a large-scale. Although extermination is the act of killing a large number of people, such a designation does not suggest that a numerical minimum must be reached. The mental element for extermination is the intent to perpetrate or to participate in a mass killing.

423. The evidence in this case amply supports the conclusion that there were widespread attacks against the Tutsi population in Gikongoro prefecture in April 1994. Witnesses recounted Hutu militiamen burning and looting Tutsi homes in the days immediately following the death of President Habyarimana on 6 April. Thousands of Tutsi then congregated at parishes and schools. The evidence of the killings at the five massacre sites as well as their massive scale can lead to no other conclusion. Having considered the totality of the evidence, and in particular the evidence concerning the ethnic composition of the individuals who sought refuge at the various sites, the Chamber finds that in April 1994 there was a widespread attack against the civilian Tutsi population of Gikongoro on ethnic grounds.

424. The Chamber finds it inconceivable that Simba, and the other participants in the joint criminal enterprise, did not know during the massacres of 21 April that their actions formed part of a widespread attack against the Tutsi civilian population. Simba was familiar with the situation in Rwanda nationally from his time in Kigali and Gitarama town. Those who sought refuge at his home in Kigali recounted soldiers looking for Tutsi. He passed roadblocks from Kigali to Gitarama town where militiamen threatened his Tutsi passengers. He was warned by Witness MIB that the road to Gikongoro was not safe because assailants were killing Tutsi. The Chamber found that on 21 April, Simba was present at two massacre sites distributing weapons and speaking with assailants. In addition, other prominent participants in the joint criminal enterprise, such as Prefect Bucyibartua, Captain Sebuhura, and Bourgmestre Semakwavu, attended various meetings with local authorities to discuss the lack of security in the region. They were present during the massacres and directed attackers from Murambi Technical School to Cyanika Parish. The assailants who physically perpetrated the massacres also must have been aware of the broader context, particularly given the scale of the atrocities. The evidence of Witness KEL reflects that the Mudasomwa *Interahamwe* had participated in earlier attacks throughout the region. Many of the attackers participated in the killings on 21 April at multiple sites.

425. The assailants at Murambi Technical School and Kaduha Parish killed thousands of Tutsi civilians in what can only be said to be a large-scale killing, which was part of the widespread attack on ethnic grounds. Simba participated in this large-scale killing as a participant in the joint criminal enterprise to kill Tutsi at these two sites by distributing weapons and lending approval and encouragement to the physical perpetrators. In its findings on criminal responsibility, the Chamber described this assistance as having a substantial effect on the killings that followed. Given the manner in which the attacks were conducted, the nature of the weapons used, and the number of victims, the Chamber finds beyond reasonable doubt that Simba and the assailants intentionally participated in a mass killing of members of the Tutsi ethnic group.

426. The Chamber finds beyond reasonable doubt that Simba is criminally responsible under Article 6 (1) of the Statute based on his participation in a joint criminal enter-

prise to kill Tutsi civilians at Murambi Technical School and Kaduha Parish. Therefore, the Chamber finds Simba guilty on Count 3 of the Indictment for extermination as a crime against humanity.

CHAPTER IV: VERDICT

427. For the reasons set out in this Judgement, having considered all evidence and arguments, the Trial Chamber finds unanimously in respect of Aloys Simba as follows:

Count 1: GUILTY of Genocide

Count 3: GUILTY of Crimes Against Humanity (Extermination)

[The Trial Chamber also found Simba NOT GUILTY of Complicity in Genocide and NOT GUILTY of Murder as these counts were withdrawn by the Prosecution. He was sentenced to twenty-five years' imprisonment with credit for the time served since he was arrested. The Appeals Chamber affirmed the Trial Chamber's Judgement on all counts on 27 November 2007: Case No. ICTR-01-76-A].

QUESTIONS

1. Read article 2 and article 6(1) of the ICTR's Statute on the Tribunal's website: www.ictr.org. What did the Tribunal require that the Prosecution prove to satisfy the elements of genocide? Had Simba killed anyone himself?
2. Does there need to be direct evidence of intent to commit genocide? On what facts did the Tribunal rely to prove Simba's genocidal intent?
3. What elements must be shown to demonstrate a joint criminal enterprise? What had Simba done that demonstrated he was part of a joint criminal enterprise?
4. Read article 3 of the ICTR's Statute. What does the Tribunal mean by "Crimes Against Humanity"?
5. What does the Tribunal mean by "Extermination"? Why was Simba found guilty of extermination?

Weapons Control

The great principle of the laws of warfare is that force is only permissible to achieve military advantage and all unnecessary suffering is prohibited. The law distinguishes between combatants and non-combatants and lays down specific protections for civilians. States are not permitted to attack civilians or civilian buildings and may not use weapons that cannot distinguish between military and civilian targets. When it became apparent that certain weapons did not simply kill the enemy but inflicted great suffering in the process, conventions began to outlaw certain types of weapons.

The 1868 Declaration of St. Petersburg prohibited the use of explosive projectiles.[72] The 1899 Hague Conference adopted a Convention forbidding certain weapons[73] and several Declarations regulated the use of expanding (dum-dum) bullets, projectiles and explosives launched from balloons and projectiles diffusing asphyxiating or deleterious

---

72. Declaration Renouncing the Use, in Time of War, of Explosive Projectiles under 400 Grammes Weight, adopted by the International Military Commission of St. Petersburg, Dec. 11, 1868.

73. Convention with Respect to the Laws and Customs of War on Land, 29 July 1899 (Hague II), 32 Stat. 1803.

gases.[74] A later Hague Conference of 1907 adopted Conventions regulating the laying of automatic submarine contact mines[75] and bombardment by naval forces in time of war.[76] The Protocol of 1925 prohibited the use of asphyxiating, poisonous and other gases during time of war and forbade the use of bacteriological methods of warfare.[77]

In 1972 the Convention on the Prohibition of the Development, Production, and Stockpiling of Bacteriological (Biological) and Toxin Weapons and on their Destruction was signed.[78] This Convention entered into force in 1975. In 1993 the principles and objectives of the 1925 Protocol and the 1972 Convention were reaffirmed and updated by a new Convention on the Prohibition of the Development, Production, Stockpiling and Use of Chemical Weapons and on their Destruction.[79] The Convention, which entered into force in 1997, absolutely prohibits the use of chemical weapons "under any circumstance" and requires the destruction of all such weapons and any chemical weapons production facilities.

In 1980 the Convention on Prohibitions or Restrictions on the Use of Certain Conventional Weapons which May be Deemed to be Excessively Injurious or to have Indiscriminate Effects was adopted.[80] Three Protocols were appended to the Convention: The Protocol on Non-Detectable Fragments (Protocol I);[81] The Protocol on Prohibitions or Restrictions on the Use of Mines, Booby-Traps and Other Devices (Protocol II);[82] and the Protocol on Prohibitions or Restrictions on the Use of Incendiary Weapons (Protocol III).[83] A fourth protocol on Blinding Laser Weapons was adopted in 1995 and entered into force in 1998.[84] A fifth Protocol on Explosive Remnants of War was adopted in 2003 and entered into force in 2006.[85]

The international community has also adopted a Protocol on Restrictions on the Use of Mines, Booby-Traps and Other Devices.[86] More recently, in September,1997, the in-

74. Declaration Respecting Expanding Bullets, 29 July 1899 (Hague Declaration III). 187 Consol. T.S. 459, reprinted at 1 Amer. J. Int'l L. Supp. 155, 156 (1907). Declaration to Prohibit for the Term of Five Years the Launching of Projectiles and Explosives from Balloons, and Other Methods of a Similar Nature, 29 July 1899. (Hague Declaration I), 32 Stat. 1839, 187 Consol. T. S. 456 reprinted at 1 Amer. J. Int'l L. Supp. 153 (1907); Declaration Respecting Asphyxiating Gases, 29 July 1899. (Hague Declaration II). 187 Consol. T. S. 453, reprinted at 1 Amer. J. Int'l L. Supp. 157 (1907).

75. Hague Convention No. VIII Relative to the Laying of Automatic Submarine Contact Mines, 18 Oct. 1907, 36 Stat. 2332, T. S. No. 541.

76. Hague Convention No. IX Concerning Bombardment by Naval Forces in Time of War, 18 Oct. 1907, 36 Stat. 2351, T.S. No. 542.

77. 94 L.N.T.S. 65, 26 U.S.T. 571, T.I.A.S. No. 8061, signed 17 June 1925, entered into force 8 Feb. 1928.

78. 1015 U.N.T.S. 163, 26 U.S.T. 583, T.I.A.S. No. 8062, reprinted at 11 I.L.M. 309 (1972), signed 10 April 1972, entered into force 26 March 1975.

79. 1974 U.N.T.S. 45, adopted 3 Sept. 1992, entered into force 29 April 1997. Reprinted at 32 I.L.M. 800 (1993).

80. 1342 U.N.T.S. 137, adopted 10 Oct. 1980, entered into force, 2 Dec. 1983, reprinted at 19 I.L.M. 1523, at 1524 (1980).

81. Protocol I, reprinted at 19 I.L.M. at 1529 (1980).

82. Protocol II, reprinted at id.

83. Protocol III, reprinted at id. at 1534.

84. Protocol IV, adopted 123 Oct. 1995, entered into force, 30 July 1998, Doc. CCW/CONF.I/16 Part I.

85. Protocol V, adopted 28 Nov. 2003, entered into force, 12 Nov. 2006, Doc. CCW/MSP/2003/2.

86. Protocol II as amended, to the Convention on Prohibitions or Restrictions on the Use of Certain Conventional Weapons Which May Be Deemed to Be Excessively Injurious or to Have Indiscriminate Effects, 10 Oct. 1980, 1342 U.N.T.S. 137, reprinted at 35 I.L.M. 1209 (1996).

ternational community endorsed a treaty banning the use of land mines.[87] The Convention was officially opened for signature in December 1997 and rapidly entered force . There are now over one hundred and fifty-six states that have ratified the treaty which entered into force in 1999. Most recently, the Convention on Cluster Munitions was adopted in May 2008.[88]

Nuclear Weapons

The creation of nuclear weapons heralded the possibility of mass destruction on a vast scale. The use of nuclear weapons during WWII by the United States against Japan proved that the devastation of such weapons was indeed unprecedented not only with respect to the numbers of people killed and buildings razed but also with respect to the deadly after effects of radioactive fall-out. The world community has undertaken a number of initiatives to regulate nuclear weapons. These initiatives fall into four main categories: conventions or declarations that limit the spread or use of nuclear weapons; conventions that call for the reduction of nuclear weapons; conventions that declare certain areas of the world nuclear free; and conventions that prohibit the testing of nuclear weapons. Below is a list of some of the more important conventions in this area. The Advisory Opinion of the International Court of Justice on the *Legality of the Threat or Use of Nuclear Weapons* (see pp. 454–475) contains a much more comprehensive list of conventions, resolutions and declarations.

A. Conventions and Declarations that Limit the Spread or Use of Nuclear Weapons.

(I) **Treaty on the Non-Proliferation of Nuclear Weapons.**[89] Under this treaty the parties with nuclear weapons agree not to transfer nuclear weapons or nuclear explosive devices to non-nuclear states and not to assist such states in the manufacture or acquisition of such weapons. The non-nuclear parties agree not to receive such weapons or to manufacture or acquire them. All parties are permitted to develop nuclear energy for peaceful purposes.

The Treaty was extended indefinitely in 1995 and the five declared nuclear weapon states gave various security assurances to the non-nuclear state parties.[90] The 2000 Review Conference examined implementation procedures. The 2005 Conference brought into focus wide disagreements between those who wanted serious progress towards total nuclear disarmament and those who wanted to pursue enforcement actions against non-cooperating member states such as Iran.

(ii) **Declaration on the Prohibition of the Use of Nuclear and Thermo-Nuclear Weapons.**[91] This General Assembly resolution declares that the use of nuclear weapons violates the United Nations Charter.

---

87. Convention on the Prohibition of the Use, Stockpiling, Production and Transfer of Anti-Personnel Mines and on Their Destruction, 2056 U.N.T.S. 211, opened for signature, 3 Dec. 1997, entered into force 1 March 1999, reprinted at 36 I.L.M. 1507 (1997). For more information on the treaty and its implementation go to http://www.icbl.org.

88. Adopted 30 May 2008, not yet in force.

89. 729 U.N.T.S. 161, 21 U.S.T. 483, T.I.A.S. No. 6839, signed 1 July 1968, entered into force 5 March 1970, reprinted at 7 I.L.M. 811 (1968).

90. United Nations, Final Document on Extension of the Treaty on the Non-Proliferation of Nuclear Weapons, U.N. Doc. NPT/CONF. 1995/32 (Part I), reprinted at 34 I.L.M. 959 (1995).

91. G.A. Res. 1653, U.N. GAOR, 16th Sess., Sup. No. 17, U.N. Doc. A/5100 (1961). Adopted by the U.N. General Assembly on Nov. 24, 1961, 55 votes in favor, 20 against, 26 abstentions.

B. Conventions that Call for the Reduction of Nuclear Weapons

(I) **Treaty on the Limitation of Anti-Ballistic Missile Systems (ABM Treaty)** (Now Terminated).[92] Under this treaty between the United States and the U.S.S.R. both parties agreed "not to deploy ABM systems for a defense of the territory of its country...." (article I 2). On December 13, 2001, the United States notified Russia of its intent to withdraw from the treaty in six months in conformity with the treaty's termination procedure. The treaty is no longer in existence.

(ii) Although **The Treaty on the Limitation of Strategic Offensive Arms (SALT II Treaty)**[93] was concluded by the United States and the U.S.S.R. in 1979 it has never been ratified.

(iii) **The Strategic Arms Reduction Treaty (START I)** was an agreement between the United States and the U.S.S.R. which sought to reduce the number of deployed nuclear warheads.[94] It is estimated that it brought about a substantial reduction of strategic nuclear weapons. The treaty was signed on July 31, 1991 shortly before the collapse of the U.S.S.R. An annex stated that Russia, Belarus, Kazakhstan and Ukraine would enforce the treaty. The latter three states have been engaged in transferring their nuclear weapons to Russia. The treaty will expire on December 5, 2009. Another treaty, **The Strategic Arms Reduction Treaty (START II)** was signed by the U.S. and Russia in 1993.[95] The treaty banned multiple independently targetable reentry vehicles (MIRVs) carried on intercontinental ballistic missiles (ICBMs). It never entered into force. After the U.S. withdrew from the ABM Treaty, Russia withdrew from START II.

The Strategic Offensive Reduction Treaty (SORT) commits both the U.S. and Russia to reduce their nuclear weapons to 1700–2200[96] deployed warheads. It was signed on May 24, 2002, entered into force on June 1, 2003 and will end on December 31, 2012. Parties can withdraw after giving three months notice.

C. Conventions that Declare Certain Areas of the World Nuclear Free

(I) **The Antarctic Treaty**[97] Article 1 of this treaty declares that "Antarctica shall be used for peaceful purposes only...." Article V specifically states: "Any nuclear explosions in Antarctica and the disposal there of radio-active waste materials shall be prohibited."

(ii) **Treaty on Principles Governing the Activities of States in the Exploration and Use of Outer Space, including the Moon and Other Celestial Bodies.**[98] Under this treaty the parties "undertake not to place in orbit around the Earth any objects carrying nuclear weapons or any other kinds of weapons of mass destruction, install such weapons

92. 23 U.S.T. 3435, T.I.A.S. No. 7503, signed 26 May 1972, entered into force 3 Oct. 1972, reprinted at 11 I.L.M. 784 (1972) (now terminated).

93. U.S.-U.S.S.R., signed 18 June 1979, S. Exec. Doc., 96th Cong., 1st Sess. (1979) (not in force).

94. START I, signed 31 July 1991, entered into force 5 Dec. 1994, expired 5 Dec. 2009.

95. START II, S. Treaty Doc. No. 103-1, signed 3 Jan. 1993, entered into force, 14 April 2000.

96. SORT, S. Treaty Doc. No. 107-8, signed 24 May 2002, entered into force, 1 June 2003.

97. 402 U.N.T.S. 71, 12 U.S.T. 794, T.I.A.S. No. 4780, signed 1 Dec. 1959, entered into force 23 June 1961, reprinted at 19 I.L.M. 860 (1980).

98. 610 U.N.T.S. 205, 18 U.S.T. 2410, T.I.A.S. No. 6347, reprinted at 6 I.L.M. 386 (1967), signed 27 Jan. 1967, entered into force 10 Oct. 1967.

on celestial bodies, or station such weapons in outer space in any other manner."[99] The testing of any weapons is also forbidden.

(iii) **Treaty for the Prohibition of Nuclear Weapons in Latin America and the Caribbean.**[100] Under this treaty thirty-three countries of Latin America and the Caribbean "undertake to use exclusively for peaceful purposes the nuclear material and facilities which are under their jurisdiction and to prohibit and prevent in their territories: (a) The testing, use, manufacture, production or acquisition by any means whatsoever of any nuclear weapons. . . ." (article 1).

(iv) **South Pacific Nuclear Free Zone Treaty.**[101] The south Pacific Forum, comprising thirteen independent and self-governing states, agreed "not to manufacturer or otherwise acquire, possess or have control over any nuclear explosive device by any means anywhere inside or outside the South Pacific, Nuclear Free Zone. . . ." (article 3).

(v) **African Nuclear-Weapon-Free Zone Treaty.**[102] Under this treaty, which was opened for signature on April 11, 1996, and went into force on December 23, 2003, a large number of African countries have agreed:

> Not to conduct research on, or develop, manufacture, stockpile or otherwise acquire, possess or have control over any nuclear explosive device by any means anywhere. . . .[103] (article 3)

(vi) **Treaty on the Southeast Asia Nuclear Weapon-Free Zone.**[104] Under this Convention all ten countries of Southeast Asia undertake not to "develop, manufacture or otherwise acquire, possess or have control over nuclear weapons ... or test or use nuclear weapons."[105] (Article 3)

(vii) The **Central Asian Nuclear-Weapon-Free-Zone Treaty**[106] commits five central Asian states: "Not to conduct research on, develop, manufacture, stockpile or otherwise acquire, possess or have control over any nuclear weapon. . . ." (article 3(1)(a)). It was signed on September 8, 2006 and all five states have ratified the treaty which entered into force on March 21, 2009.

D. Conventions that Prohibit the Testing of Nuclear Weapons.

(I) **Treaty Banning Nuclear Weapon Tests in the Atmosphere, in Outer Space and Under Water.**[107] A large number of states are now parties to this treaty which prohibits testing nuclear weapons in the atmosphere, outer space or under the water.

---

99. Id. at art. IV.

100. 634 U.N.T.S. 281, 22 U.S.T. 762, opened for signature 14 Feb. 1967, entered into force 25 April 1969; update on status and additional Protocols I and II, reprinted at 28 I.L.M. 1400 (1989).

101. 1445 U.N.T.S. 177, adopted 6 August, 1985, entered into force 11 Dec. 1986, reprinted at 24 I.L.M. 1440 (1985).

102. Opened for signature 11 Apr. 1996, entered into force 23 Dec. 2003, reprinted at 35 I.L.M. 698 (1996).

103. Id. at 707.

104. 1981 U.N.T.S. 129, adopted 15 Dec. 1995, entered into force 27 March 1997, reprinted at 35 I.L.M. 635 (1996).

105. Id. at 640.

106. Available at: http://cns.miis.edu/stories/pdf_support/060905_canwfz.pdf.

107. 480 U.N.T.S. 43, 14 U.S.T. 1313, T.I.A.S. No. 5433, signed 5 August 1963, entered into force 10 Oct. 1963, reprinted at 2 I.L.M. 883 (1963).

(ii) **Comprehensive Nuclear Test Ban Treaty.**[108] One hundred and forty-eight states have already ratified this treaty but it will not go into force until forty-four designated states have ratified the treaty. Thirty-five of the required forty-four states have currently ratified the treaty. Under this convention each state party "undertakes not to carry out any nuclear weapon test explosion or any other nuclear explosion and to prohibit and prevent any such nuclear explosion at any place under its jurisdiction or control." Article I.

International Court of Justice Advisory Opinion on Nuclear Weapons

The General Assembly of the United Nations submitted the following question to the International Court of Justice requesting an advisory opinion: "Is the threat or use of nuclear weapons in any circumstances permitted under international law?" The Court delivered its opinion in the summer of 1996 excerpts of which appear below:

Legality of the Threat or Use of Nuclear Weapons

1996 I.C.J. 226 (Advisory Opinion)
(Footnotes omitted)

Opinion of the Court

* * *

52. The Court notes by way of introduction that international customary and treaty law does not contain any specific prescription authorizing the threat or use of nuclear weapons or any other weapon in general or in certain circumstances, in particular those of the exercise of legitimate self-defence. Nor, however, is there any principle or rule of international law which would make the legality of the threat or use of nuclear weapons or of any other weapons dependent on a specific authorization. State practice shows that the illegality of the use of certain weapons as such does not result from an absence of authorization but, on the contrary, is formulated in terms of prohibition.

53. The Court must therefore now examine whether there is any prohibition of recourse to nuclear weapons as such; it will first ascertain whether there is a conventional prescription to this effect.

54. In this regard, the argument has been advanced that nuclear weapons should be treated in the same way as poisoned weapons. In that case, they would be prohibited under:

(a) the Second Hague Declaration of 29 July 1899, which prohibits "the use of projectiles the object of which is the diffusion of asphyxiating or deleterious gases";
(b) Article 23 (a) of the Regulations respecting the laws and customs of war on land annexed to the Hague Convention IV of 18 October 1907, whereby "it is especially forbidden: ... to employ poison or poisoned weapons"; and
(c) the Geneva Protocol of 17 June 1925 which prohibits "the use in war of asphyxiating, poisonous or other gases, and of all analogous liquids, materials or devices".

---

108. Opened for signature 24 Sept. 1996, G.A. Res. 245, U.N. GAOR, 50th Sess., Annex, Agenda Items 8 & 65, U.N. Doc. A/50/1027 (1996) reprinted at 35 I.L.M. 1439 (1996). Available at: www.ctbto.org.

* * *

55. The Court will observe that the Regulations annexed to the Hague Convention IV do not define what is to be understood by "poison or poisoned weapons" and that different interpretations exist on the issue. Nor does the 1925 Protocol specify the meaning to be given to the term "analogous materials or devices". The terms have been understood, in the practice of States, in their ordinary sense as covering weapons whose prime, or even exclusive, effect is to poison or asphyxiate. This practice is clear, and the parties to those instruments have not treated them as referring to nuclear weapons.

56. In view of this, it does not seem to the Court that the use of nuclear weapons can be regarded as specifically prohibited on the basis of the above-mentioned provisions of the Second Hague Declaration of 1899, the Regulations annexed to the Hague Convention IV of 1907 or the 1925 Protocol (see paragraph 54 above).

57. The pattern until now has been for weapons of mass destruction to be declared illegal by specific instruments. The most recent such instruments are the Convention of 10 April 1972 on the Prohibition of the Development, Production and Stockpiling of Bacteriological (Biological) and Toxin Weapons and on their Destruction—which prohibits the possession of bacteriological and toxic weapons and reinforces the prohibition of their use—and the Convention of 13 January 1993 on the Prohibition of the Development, Production, Stockpiling and Use of Chemical Weapons and on their Destruction—which prohibits all use of chemical weapons and requires the destruction of existing stocks. Each of these instruments has been negotiated and adopted in its own context and for its own reasons. The Court does not find any specific prohibition of recourse to nuclear weapons in treaties expressly prohibiting the use of certain weapons of mass destruction.

58. In the last two decades, a great many negotiations have been conducted regarding nuclear weapons; they have not resulted in a treaty of general prohibition of the same kind as for bacteriological and chemical weapons. However, a number of specific treaties have been concluded in order to limit:

(a) the acquisition, manufacture and possession of nuclear weapons (Peace Treaties of 10 February 1947; State Treaty for the Re-establishment of an Independent and Democratic Austria of 15 May 1955; Treaty of Tlatelolco of 14 February 1967 for the Prohibition of Nuclear Weapons in Latin America, and its Additional Protocols; Treaty of 1 July 1968 on the Non-Proliferation of Nuclear Weapons; Treaty of Rarontonga of 6 August 1985 on the Nuclear-Weapon-Free Zone of the South Pacific, and its Protocols; Treaty of 12 September 1990 on the Final Settlement with respect to Germany);
(b) the deployment of nuclear weapons (Antarctic Treaty of 1 December 1959; Treaty of 27 January 1967 on Principles Governing the Activities of States in the Exploration and Use of Outer Space, including the Moon and Other Celestial Bodies; Treaty of Tlatelolco of 14 February 1967 for the Prohibition of Nuclear Weapons in Latin America, and its Additional Protocols; Treaty of 11 February 1971 on the Prohibition of the Emplacement of Nuclear Weapons and Other Weapons of Mass Destruction on the Sea-Bed and the Ocean Floor and in the Subsoil Thereof; Treaty of Rarontonga of 6 August 1985 on the Nuclear-Weapon-Free Zone of the South Pacific, and its Protocols); and
(c) the testing of nuclear weapons (Antarctic Treaty of 1 December 1959; Treaty of 5 August 1963 Banning Nuclear Weapons Tests in the Atmosphere, in Outer Space and under Water; Treaty of 27 January 1967 on Principles Governing the

Activities of States in the Exploration and Use of Outer Space, including the Moon and Other Celestial Bodies; Treaty of Tlatelolco of 14 February 1967 for the Prohibition of Nuclear Weapons in Latin America, and its Additional Protocols; Treaty of Rarontonga of 6 August 1985 on the Nuclear-Weapon-Free Zone of the South Pacific, and its Protocols).

59. Recourse to nuclear weapons is directly addressed by two of these Conventions and also in connection with the indefinite extension of the Treaty on the Non-Proliferation of Nuclear Weapons of 1968:

(a) the Treaty of Tlatelolco of 14 February 1967 for the Prohibition of Nuclear Weapons in Latin America prohibits, in Article 1, the use of nuclear weapons by the Contracting Parties. It further includes an Additional Protocol II open to nuclear-weapon States outside the region, Article 3 of which provides:

> The Governments represented by the undersigned Plenipotentiaries also undertake not to use or threaten to use nuclear weapons against the Contracting Parties of the Treaty for the Prohibition of Nuclear Weapons in Latin America.

The Protocol was signed and ratified by the five nuclear-weapon States. Its ratification was accompanied by a variety of declarations. The United Kingdom Government, for example, stated that "in the event of any act of aggression by a Contracting Party to the Treaty in which that Party was supported by a nuclear-weapon State", the United Kingdom Government would "be free to reconsider the extent to which they could be regarded as committed by the provisions of Additional Protocol II". The United States made a similar statement. The French Government, for its part, stated that it "interprets the undertaking made in article 3 of the Protocol as being without prejudice to the full exercise of the right of self-defence confirmed by Article 51 of the Charter". China reaffirmed its commitment not to be the first to make use of nuclear weapons. The Soviet Union reserved "the right to review" the obligations imposed upon it by Additional Protocol II, particularly in the event of an attack by a State party either "in support of a nuclear-weapon State or jointly with that State". None of these statements drew comment or objection from the parties to the Treaty of Tlatelolco.

(b) the Treaty of Rarontonga of 6 August 1985 establishes a South Pacific Nuclear Free Zone in which the Parties undertake not to manufacture, acquire or possess any nuclear explosive device (Art. 3). Unlike the Treaty of Tlatelolco, the Treaty of Rarontonga does not expressly prohibit the use of such weapons. But such a prohibition is for the States parties the necessary consequence of the prohibitions stipulated by the Treaty. The Treaty has a number of protocols. Protocol 2, open to the five nuclear-weapon States, specifies in its Article 1 that:

> Each party undertakes not to use or threaten to use any nuclear explosive device against:
> (a) Parties to the Treaty; or
> (b) any territory within the South Pacific Nuclear Free Zone for which a State that has become a Party to Protocol I is internationally responsible.

China and Russia are parties to that Protocol. In signing it, China and the Soviet Union each made a declaration by which they reserved the "right to reconsider" their obligations under the said Protocol; the Soviet Union also referred to certain circumstances in which it would consider itself released from those obligations. France, the United Kingdom and the United States, for their part, signed Protocol 2 on 25 March 1996, but have not yet ratified it.

(c) as to the Treaty on the Non-Proliferation of Nuclear Weapons, at the time of its signing in 1968 the United States, the United Kingdom and the USSR gave various security assurances to the non-nuclear-weapon States that were parties to the Treaty. In resolution 255 (1968) the Security Council took note with satisfaction of the intention expressed by those three States to

> "provide or support immediate assistance, in accordance with the Charter, to any non-nuclear-weapon State Party to the Treaty on the Non-Proliferation ... that is a victim of an act of, or an object of a threat of, aggression in which nuclear weapons are used".

On the occasion of the extension of the Treaty in 1995, the five nuclear-weapon States gave their non-nuclear weapon partners, by means of separate unilateral statements on 5 and 6 April 1995, positive and negative security assurances against the use of such weapons. All the five nuclear-weapon States first undertook not to use nuclear weapons against non-nuclear-weapon States that were parties to the Treaty on the Non-Proliferation of Nuclear Weapons. However, these States, apart from China, made an exception in the case of an invasion or any other attack against them, their territories, armed forces or allies, or on a State towards which they had a security commitment, carried out or sustained by a non-nuclear-weapon State.

60. Those States that believe that recourse to nuclear weapons is illegal stress that the conventions that include various rules providing for the limitation or elimination of nuclear weapons in certain areas (such as the Antarctic Treaty of 1959 which prohibits the deployment of nuclear weapons in the Antarctic, or the Treaty of Tlatelolco of 1967 which creates a nuclear-weapon-free zone in Latin America), or the conventions that apply certain measures of control and limitation to the existence of nuclear weapons (such as the 1963 Partial Test-Ban Treaty or the Treaty on the Non-Proliferation of Nuclear Weapons) all set limits to the use of nuclear weapons. In their view, these treaties bear witness, in their own way, to the emergence of a rule of complete legal prohibition of all uses of nuclear weapons.

61. Those States who defend the position that recourse to nuclear weapons is legal in certain circumstances see a logical contradiction in reaching such a conclusion. According to them, those Treaties, such as the Treaty on the Non-Proliferation of Nuclear Weapons, as well as Security Council Resolutions 255 (1968) and 984 (1995) which take note of the security assurances given by the nuclear-weapon States to the non-nuclear-weapon States in relation to any nuclear aggression against the latter, cannot be understood as prohibiting the use of nuclear weapons, and such a claim is contrary to the very text of those instruments. For those who support the legality in certain circumstances of recourse to nuclear weapons, there is no absolute prohibition against the use of such weapons. The very logic and construction of the Treaty on the Non-Proliferation of Nuclear Weapons, they assert, confirm this. This Treaty, whereby, they contend, the possession of nuclear weapons by the five nuclear-weapon States has been accepted, cannot be seen as a treaty banning their use by those States; to accept the fact that those States possess nuclear weapons is tantamount to recognizing that such weapons may be used in certain circumstances. Nor, they contend, could the security assurances given by the nuclear-weapon States in 1968, and more recently in connection with the Review and Extension Conference of the Parties to the Treaty on the Non-Proliferation of Nuclear Weapons in 1995, have been conceived without its being supposed that there were cir-

cumstances in which nuclear weapons could be used in a lawful manner. For those who defend the legality of the use, in certain circumstances, of nuclear weapons, the acceptance of those instruments by the different non-nuclear-weapon States confirms and reinforces the evident logic upon which those instruments are based.

62. The Court notes that the treaties dealing exclusively with acquisition, manufacture, possession, deployment and testing of nuclear weapons, without specifically addressing their threat or use, certainly point to an increasing concern in the international community with these weapons; the Court concludes from this that these treaties could therefore be seen as foreshadowing a future general prohibition of the use of such weapons, but they do not constitute such a prohibition by themselves. As to the treaties of Tlatelolco and Rarontonga and their Protocols, and also the declarations made in connection with the indefinite extension of the Treaty on the Non-Proliferation of Nuclear Weapons, it emerges from these instruments that:

(a) a number of States have undertaken not to use nuclear weapons in specific zones (Latin America; the South Pacific) or against certain other States (non-nuclear-weapon States which are parties to the Treaty on the Non-Proliferation of Nuclear Weapons);
(b) nevertheless, even within this framework, the nuclear-weapon States have reserved the right to use nuclear weapons in certain circumstances; and
(c) these reservations met with no objection from the parties to the Tlatelolco or Rarontonga Treaties or from the Security Council.

63. These two treaties, the security assurances given in 1995 by the nuclear-weapon States and the fact that the Security Council took note of them with satisfaction, testify to a growing awareness of the need to liberate the community of States and the international public from the dangers resulting from the existence of nuclear weapons. The Court moreover notes the signing, even more recently, on 15 December 1995, at Bangkok, of a Treaty on the Southeast Asia Nuclear-Weapon-Free Zone, and on 11 April 1996, at Cairo, of a treaty on the creation of a nuclear-weapons-free zone in Africa. It does not, however, view these elements as amounting to a comprehensive and universal conventional prohibition on the use, or the threat of use, of those weapons as such.

64. The Court will now turn to an examination of customary international law to determine whether a prohibition of the threat or use of nuclear weapons as such flows from that source of law. As the Court has stated, the substance of the law must be "looked for primarily in the actual practice and *opinio juris* of States" (*Continental Shelf (Libyan Arab Jamahiriya/Malta), Judgment, I.C.J. Reports 1985*, p. 29, para. 27).

65. States which hold the view that the use of nuclear weapons is illegal have endeavoured to demonstrate the existence of a customary rule prohibiting this use. They refer to a consistent practice of non-utilization of nuclear weapons by States since 1945 and they would see in that practice the expression of an *opinio juris* on the part of those who possess such weapons.

66. Some other States, which assert the legality of the threat and use of nuclear weapons in certain circumstances, invoked the doctrine and practice of deterrence in support of their argument. They recall that they have always, in concert with certain other States, reserved the right to use those weapons in the exercise of the right to self-defence against an armed attack threatening their vital security interests. In their view, if nuclear weapons have not been used since 1945, it is not on account of an existing or nascent custom but merely because circumstances that might justify their use have fortunately not arisen.

67. The Court does not intend to pronounce here upon the practice known as the "policy of deterrence". It notes that it is a fact that a number of States adhered to that practice during the greater part of the Cold War and continue to adhere to it. Furthermore, the Members of the international community are profoundly divided on the matter of whether non-recourse to nuclear weapons over the past fifty years constitutes the expression of an *opinio juris*. Under these circumstances the Court does not consider itself able to find that there is such an *opinio juris*.

68. According to certain States, the important series of General Assembly resolutions, beginning with resolution 1635 (XVI) of 24 November 1961, that deal with nuclear weapons and that affirm, with consistent regularity, the illegality of nuclear weapons, signify the existence of a rule of international customary law which prohibits recourse to those weapons. According to other States, however, the resolutions in question have no binding character on their own account and are not declaratory of any customary rule of prohibition of nuclear weapons; some of these States have also pointed out that this series of resolutions not only did not meet with the approval of all of the nuclear-weapon States but of many other States as well.

69. States which consider that the use of nuclear weapons is illegal indicated that those resolutions did not claim to create any new rules, but were confined to a confirmation of customary law relating to the prohibition of means or methods of warfare which, by their use, overstepped the bounds of what is permissible in the conduct of hostilities. In their view, the resolutions in question did no more than apply to nuclear weapons the existing rules of international law applicable in armed conflict; they were no more than the "envelope" or *instrumentum* containing certain pre-existing customary rules of international law. For those States, it is accordingly of little importance that the *instrumentum* should have occasioned negative votes, which cannot have the effect of obliterating those customary rules which have been confirmed by treaty law.

70. The Court notes that General Assembly resolutions, even if they are not binding, may sometimes have normative value. They can, in certain circumstances, provide evidence important for establishing the existence of a rule or the emergence of an *opinio juris*. To establish whether this is true of a given General Assembly resolution, it is necessary to look at its content and the conditions of its adoption; it is also necessary to see whether an *opinio juris* exists as to its normative character. Or a series of resolutions may show the gradual evolution of the *opinio juris* required for the establishment of a new rule.

71. Examined in their totality, the General Assembly resolutions put before the Court declare that the use of nuclear weapons would be "a direct violation of the Charter of the United Nations"; and in certain formulations that such use "should be prohibited". The focus of these resolutions has sometimes shifted to diverse related matters; however, several of the resolutions under consideration in the present case have been adopted with substantial numbers of negative votes and abstentions; thus, although those resolutions are a clear sign of deep concern regarding the problem of nuclear weapons, they still fall short of establishing the existence of an *opinio juris* on the illegality of the use of such weapons.

72. The Court further notes that the first of the resolutions of the General Assembly expressly proclaiming the illegality of the use of nuclear weapons, resolution 1653 (XVI) of 24 November 1961 (mentioned in subsequent resolutions), after referring to certain international declarations and binding agreements, from the Declaration of St. Petersburg of 1868 to the Geneva Protocol of 1925, proceeded to qualify the legal nature of nu-

clear weapons, determine their effects, and apply general rules of customary international law to nuclear weapons in particular. That application by the General Assembly of general rules of customary law to the particular case of nuclear weapons indicates that, in its view, there was no specific rule of customary law which prohibited the use of nuclear weapons; if such a rule had existed, the General Assembly could simply have referred to it and would not have needed to undertake such an exercise of legal qualification.

73. Having said this, the Court points out that the adoption each year by the General Assembly, by a large majority, of resolutions recalling the content of resolution 1653 (XVI), and requesting the member States to conclude a convention prohibiting the use of nuclear weapons in any circumstance, reveals the desire of a very large section of the international community to take, by a specific and express prohibition of the use of nuclear weapons, a significant step forward along the road to compete nuclear disarmament. The emergence, as *lex lata*, of a customary rule specifically prohibiting the use of nuclear weapons as such is hampered by the continuing tensions between the nascent *opinio juris* on the one hand, and the still strong adherence to the practice of deterrence on the other.

* * *

74. The Court not having found a conventional rule of general scope, nor a customary rule specifically proscribing the threat or use of nuclear weapons *per se*, it will now deal with the question whether recourse to nuclear weapons must be considered as illegal in the light of the principles and rules of international humanitarian law applicable in armed conflict and of the law of neutrality.

75. A large number of customary rules have been developed by the practice of States and are an integral part of the international law relevant to the question posed. The "laws and customs of war"—as they were traditionally called—were the subject of codification undertaken in The Hague (including the Conventions of 1899 and 1907), and were based partly upon the St. Petersburg Declaration of 1868 as well as the results of the Brussels Conference of 1874. This "Hague Law" and, more particularly, the Regulations Respecting the Laws and Customs of War on Land, fixed the rights and duties of belligerents in their conduct of operations and limited the choice of methods and means of injuring the enemy in an international armed conflict. One should add to this the "Geneva Law" (The Conventions of 1864, 1906, 1929 and 1949), which protects the victims of war and aims to provide safeguards for disabled armed forces personnel and persons not taking part in the hostilities. These two branches of the law applicable in armed conflict have become so closely interrelated that they are considered to have gradually formed one single complex system, known today as international humanitarian law. The provisions of the Additional Protocols of 1977 give expression and attest to the unity and complexity of that law.

76. Since the turn of the century, the appearance of new means of combat has—without calling into question the longstanding principles and rules of international law—rendered necessary some specific prohibitions of the use of certain weapons, such as explosive projectiles under 400 grammes, dum-dum bullets and asphyxiating gases. Chemical and bacteriological weapons were then prohibited by the 1925 Geneva Protocol. More recently, the use of weapons producing "non-detectable fragments", of other types of "mines, booby traps and other devices", and of "incendiary weapons", was either prohibited or limited, depending on the case, by the Convention of 10 October 1980 on Prohibitions or Restrictions on the Use of Certain Conventional Weapons Which May Be Deemed to Be Excessively Injurious or to Have Indiscriminate Effects. The provi-

sions of the Convention on "mines, booby traps and other devices" have just been amended, on 3 May 1996, and now regulate in greater detail, for example, the use of anti-personnel land mines.

77. All this shows that the conduct of military operations is governed by a body of legal prescriptions. This is so because "the right of belligerents to adopt means of injuring the enemy is not unlimited" as stated in Article 22 of the 1907 Hague Regulations relating to the laws and customs of war on land. The St. Petersburg Declaration had already condemned the use of weapons "which uselessly aggravate the suffering of disabled men or make their death inevitable". The aforementioned Regulations relating to the laws and customs of war on land, annexed to the Hague Convention IV of 1907, prohibit the use of "arms, projectiles, or material calculated to cause unnecessary suffering" (Art. 23).

78. The cardinal principles contained in the texts constituting the fabric of humanitarian law are the following. The first is aimed at the protection of the civilian population and civilian objects and establishes the distinction between combatants and non-combatants; States must never make civilians the object of attack and must consequently never use weapons that are incapable of distinguishing between civilian and military targets. According to the second principle, it is prohibited to cause unnecessary suffering to combatants: it is accordingly prohibited to use weapons causing them such harm or uselessly aggravating their suffering. In application of that second principle, States do not have unlimited freedom of choice of means in the weapons they use.

The Court would likewise refer, in relation to these principles, to the Martens Clause, which was first included in the Hague Convention II with Respect to the Laws and Customs of War on Land of 1899 and which has proved to be an effective means of addressing the rapid evolution of military technology. A modern version of that clause is to be found in Article 1, paragraph 2, of Additional Protocol I of 1977, which reads as follows:

> In cases not covered by this Protocol or by other international agreements, civilians and combatants remain under the protection and authority of the principles of international law derived from established custom, from the principles of humanity and from the dictates of public conscience.

In conformity with the aforementioned principles, humanitarian law, at a very early stage, prohibited certain types of weapons either because of their indiscriminate effect on combatants and civilians or because of the unnecessary suffering caused to combatants, that is to say, a harm greater than that unavoidable to achieve legitimate military objectives. If an envisaged use of weapons would not meet the requirement of humanitarian law, a threat to engage in such use would also be contrary to that law.

79. It is undoubtedly because a great many rules of humanitarian law applicable in armed conflict are so fundamental to the respect of the human person and "elementary considerations of humanity" as the Court put it in its Judgment of 9 April 1949 in the *Corfu Channel* case (*I.C.J. Reports 1949*, p. 22), that the Hague and Geneva Conventions have enjoyed a broad accession. Further these fundamental rules are to be observed by all States whether or not they have ratified the conventions that contain them, because they constitute intransgressible principles of international customary law.

80. The Nuremberg International Military Tribunal had already found in 1945 that the humanitarian rules included in the Regulations annexed to the Hague Convention IV of 1907 "were recognized by all civilized nations and were regarded as being declaratory of the laws and customs of war" (International Military Tribunal, *Trial of the Major War Criminals*, 14 November 1945–1 October 1946, Nuremberg, 1947, Vol., 1, p. 254).

81. The Report of the Secretary-General pursuant to paragraph 2 of Security Council resolution 808 (1993), with which he introduced the Statute of the International Tribunal for the Prosecution of Persons Responsible for Serious Violations of International Humanitarian Law Committed in the Territory of the Former Yugoslavia since 1991, and which was unanimously approved by the Security Council (resolution 827 (1993)), stated:

> In the view of the Secretary-General, the application of the principle *nullum crimen sine lege* requires that the international tribunal should apply rules of international humanitarian law which are beyond any doubt part of customary law . . .
>
> The part of conventional international humanitarian law which has beyond doubt become part of international customary law is the law applicable in armed conflict as embodied in: the Geneva Conventions of 12 August 1949 for the Protection of War Victims; the Hague Convention (IV) Respecting the Laws and Customs of War on Land and the Regulations annexed thereto of 18 October 1907; the Convention on the Prevention and Punishment of the Crime of Genocide of 9 December 1948; and the Charter of the International Military Tribunal of 8 August 1945.

82. The extensive codification of humanitarian law and the extent of the accession to the resultant treaties, as well as the fact that the denunciation clauses that existed in the codification instruments have never been used, have provided the international community with a corpus of treaty rules the great majority of which had already become customary and which reflected the most universally recognized humanitarian principles. These rules indicate the normal conduct and behaviour expected of States.

83. It has been maintained in these proceedings that these principles and rules of humanitarian law are part of *jus cogens* as defined in Article 53 of the Vienna Convention on the Law of Treaties of 23 May 1969. The question whether a norm is part of the *jus cogens* relates to the legal character of the norm. The request addressed to the Court by the General Assembly raises the question of the applicability of the principles and rules of humanitarian law in cases of recourse to nuclear weapons and the consequences of that applicability for the legality of recourse to these weapons. But it does not raise the question of the character of the humanitarian law which would apply to the use of nuclear weapons. There is, therefore, no need for the Court to pronounce on this matter.

84. Nor is there any need for the Court [to] elaborate on the question of the applicability of Additional Protocol I of 1977 to nuclear weapons. It need only observe that while, at the Diplomatic Conference of 1974–1977, there was no substantive debate on the nuclear issue and no specific solution concerning this question was put forward, Additional Protocol I in no way replaced the general customary rules applicable to all means and methods of combat including nuclear weapons. In particular, the Court recalls that all States are bound by those rules in Additional Protocol I which, when adopted, were merely the expression of the pre-existing customary law, such as the Martens Clause, reaffirmed in the first article of Additional Protocol I. The fact that certain types of weapons were not specifically dealt with by the 1974–1977 Conference does not permit the drawing of any legal conclusions relating to the substantive issues which the use of such weapons would raise.

85. Turning now to the applicability of the principles and rules of humanitarian law to a possible threat or use of nuclear weapons, the Court notes that doubts in this respect have sometimes been voiced on the ground that these principles and rules have

evolved prior to the invention of nuclear weapons and that the Conferences of Geneva of 1949 and 1974–1977 which respectively adopted the four Geneva Conventions of 1949 and the two Additional Protocols thereto did not deal with nuclear weapons specifically. Such views, however, are only held by a small minority. In the view of the vast majority of States as well as writers there can be no doubt as to the applicability of humanitarian law to nuclear weapons.

86. The Court shares that view. Indeed, nuclear weapons were invented after most of the principles and rules of humanitarian law applicable in armed conflict had already come into existence; the Conferences of 1949 and 1974–1977 left these weapons aside, and there is a qualitative as well as quantitative difference between nuclear weapons and all conventional arms. However, it cannot be concluded from this that the established principles and rules of humanitarian law applicable in armed conflict did not apply to nuclear weapons. Such a conclusion would be incompatible with the intrinsically humanitarian character of the legal principles in question which permeates the entire law of armed conflict and applies to all forms of warfare and to all kinds of weapons, those of the past, those of the present and those of the future. In this respect it seems significant that the thesis that the rules of humanitarian law do not apply to the new weaponry, because of the newness of the latter, has not been advocated in the present proceedings. On the contrary, the newness of nuclear weapons has been expressly rejected as an argument against the application to them of international humanitarian law:

> "In general, international humanitarian law bears on the threat or use of nuclear weapons as it does of other weapons.
>
> International humanitarian law has evolved to meet contemporary circumstances, and is not limited in its application to weaponry of an earlier time. The fundamental principles of this law endure: to mitigate and circumscribe the cruelty of war for humanitarian reasons." (New Zealand, Written Statement, p. 15, paras. 63–64).

None of the statements made before the Court in any way advocated a freedom to use nuclear weapons without regard to humanitarian constraints. Quite the reverse; it has been explicitly stated,

> "Restrictions set by the rules applicable to armed conflicts in respect of means and methods of warfare definitely also extend to nuclear weapons" (Russian Federation, CR 95/29, p. 52);
>
> "So far as the customary law of war is concerned, the United Kingdom has always accepted that the use of nuclear weapons is subject to the general principles of the *jus in bello*" (United Kingdom, CR 95/34, p. 45); and
>
> "The United States has long shared the view that the law of armed conflict governs the use of nuclear weapons—just as it governs the use of conventional weapons" (United States of America, CR 95/34, p. 85).

87. Finally, the Court points to the Martens Clause, whose continuing existence and applicability is not to be doubted, as an affirmation that the principles and rules of humanitarian law apply to nuclear weapons.

88. The Court will now turn to the principle of neutrality which was raised by several States. In the context of the advisory proceedings brought before the Court by the WHO concerning the *Legality of the Use by a State of Nuclear Weapons in Armed Conflict*, the position was put as follows by one State:

> "The principle of neutrality, in its classic sense, was aimed at preventing the incursion of belligerent forces into neutral territory, or attacks on the persons or ships of neutrals. Thus 'the territory of neutral powers is inviolable' (Article 1 of the Hague Convention (V) Respecting the Rights and Duties of Neutral Powers and Persons in Case of War on Land, concluded on 18 October 1907); 'belligerents are bound to respect the sovereign rights of neutral powers ...' (Article 1 to the Hague Convention (XIII) Respecting the Rights and Duties of Neutral Powers in Naval War, concluded on 18 October 1907), 'neutral states have equal interest in having their rights respected by belligerents ...' (Preamble to Convention on Maritime Neutrality, concluded on 20 February 1928). It is clear, however, that the principle of neutrality applies with equal force to transborder incursions of armed forces and to the transborder damage caused to a neutral State by the use of a weapon in a belligerent State." (*Legality of the Use by a State of Nuclear Weapons in Armed Conflict*, Nauru, Written Statement (I), p. 35, IV E.)

The principle so circumscribed is present as an established part of the customary international law.

89. The Court finds that as in the case of the principles of humanitarian law applicable in armed conflict, international law leaves no doubt that the principle of neutrality, whatever its content, which is of a fundamental character similar to that of the humanitarian principles and rules, is applicable (subject to the relevant provisions of the United Nations Charter), to all international armed conflict, whatever type of weapons might be used.

90. Although the applicability of the principles and rules of humanitarian law and of the principle of neutrality to nuclear weapons is hardly disputed, the conclusions to be drawn from this applicability are, on the other hand, controversial.

91. According to one point of view, the fact that recourse to nuclear weapons is subject to and regulated by the law of armed conflict does not necessarily mean that such recourse is as such prohibited. As one State put it to the Court:

> "Assuming that a State's use of nuclear weapons meets the requirements of self-defence, it must then be considered whether it conforms to the fundamental principles of the law of armed conflict regulating the conduct of hostilities" (United Kingdom, Written Statement, p. 40, para 3.44);
>
> "the legality of the use of nuclear weapons must therefore be assessed in the light of the applicable principles of international law regarding the use of force and the conduct of hostilities, as is the case with other methods and means of warfare" (United Kingdom, Written Statement, p. 75, para. 4.2(3)); and
>
> "The reality ... is that nuclear weapons might be used in a wide variety of circumstances with very different results in terms of likely civilian casualties. In some cases, such as the use of a low yield nuclear weapons against warships on the High Seas or troops in sparsely populated areas, it is possible to envisage a nuclear attack which caused comparatively few civilian casualties. It is by no means the case that every use of nuclear weapons against a military objective would inevitably cause very great collateral civilian casualties." (United Kingdom, Written Statement, p. 53, para. 3.70; see also United States of America, Oral Statement, CR 95/34, pp. 89–90.)

92. Another view holds that recourse to nuclear weapons could never be compatible with the principles and rules of humanitarian law and is therefore prohibited. In the

event of their use, nuclear weapons would in all circumstances be unable to draw any distinction between the civilian population and combatants, or between civilian objects and military objectives, and their effects, largely uncontrollable, could not be restricted, either in time or in space, to lawful military targets. Such weapons would kill and destroy in a necessarily indiscriminate manner, on account of the blast, heat and radiation occasioned by the nuclear explosion and the effects induced; and the number of casualties which would ensue would be enormous. The use of nuclear weapons would therefore be prohibited in any circumstance, notwithstanding the absence of any explicit conventional prohibition. That view lay at the basis of the assertions by certain States before the Court that nuclear weapons are by their nature illegal under customary international law, by virtue of the fundamental principle of humanity.

93. A similar view has been expressed with respect to the effects of the principle of neutrality. Like the principles and rules of humanitarian law, that principle has therefore been considered by some to rule out the use of a weapon the effects of which simply cannot be contained within the territories of the contending States.

94. The Court would observe that none of the States advocating the legality of the use of nuclear weapons under certain circumstances, including the "clean" use of smaller, low yield, tactical nuclear weapons, has indicated what, supposing such limited use were feasible, would be the precise circumstances justifying such use; nor whether such limited use would not tend to escalate into the all-out use of high yield nuclear weapons. This being so, the Court does not consider that it has a sufficient basis for a determination on the validity of this view.

95. Nor can the Court make a determination on the validity of the view that the recourse to nuclear weapons would be illegal in any circumstance owing to their inherent and total incompatibility with the law applicable in armed conflict. Certainly, as the Court has already indicated, the principles and rules of law applicable in armed conflict—at the heart of which is the overriding consideration of humanity—make the conduct of armed hostilities subject to a number of strict requirements. Thus, methods and means of warfare, which would preclude any distinction between civilian and military targets, or which would result in unnecessary suffering to combatants, are prohibited. In view of the unique characteristics of nuclear weapons, to which the Court has referred above, the use of such weapons in fact seems scarcely reconcilable with respect for such requirements. Nevertheless, the Court considers that it does not have sufficient elements to enable it to conclude with certainty that the use of nuclear weapons would necessarily be at variance with the principles and rules of law applicable in armed conflict in any circumstance.

96. Furthermore, the Court cannot lose sight of the fundamental right of every State to survival, and thus its right to resort to self-defence, in accordance with Article 51 of the Charter, when its survival is at stake.

Nor can it ignore the practice referred to as "policy of deterrence", to which an appreciable section of the international community adhered for many years. The Court also notes the reservations which certain nuclear-weapon States have appended to the undertakings they have given, notably under the Protocols to the Treaties of Tlatelolco and Rarotonga, and also under the declarations made by them in connection with the extension of the Treaty on the Non-Proliferation of Nuclear Weapons, not to resort to such weapons.

97. Accordingly, in view of the present state of international law viewed as a whole, as examined above by the Court, and of the elements of fact at its disposal, the Court is

led to observe that it cannot reach a definitive conclusion as to the legality or illegality of the use of nuclear weapons by a State in an extreme circumstance of self-defence, in which its very survival would be at stake.

98. Given the eminently difficult issues that arise in applying the law on the use of force and above all the law applicable in armed conflict to nuclear weapons, the Court considers that it now needs to examine one further aspect of the question before it, seen in a broader context.

In the long run, international law, and with it the stability of the international order which it is intended to govern, are bound to suffer from the continuing difference of views with regard to the legal status of weapons as deadly as nuclear weapons. It is consequently important to put an end to this state of affairs; the long-promised complete nuclear disarmament appears to be the most appropriate means of achieving that result.

99. In these circumstances, the Court appreciates the full importance of the recognition by Article VI of the Treaty on the Non-Proliferation of Nuclear Weapons of an obligation to negotiate in good faith a nuclear disarmament. This provision is worded as follows:

> "Each of the Parties to the Treaty undertakes to pursue negotiations in good faith on effective measures relating to cessation of the nuclear arms race at an early date and to nuclear disarmament, and on a treaty on general and complete disarmament under strict and effective international control."

The legal import of that obligation goes beyond that of a mere obligation of conduct; the obligation involved here is an obligation to achieve a precise result—nuclear disarmament in all its aspects—by adopting a particular course of conduct, namely, the pursuit of negotiations on the matter in good faith.

100. This twofold obligation to pursue and to conclude negotiations formally concerns the 182 States parties to the Treaty on the Non-Proliferation of Nuclear Weapons, or, in other words, the vast majority of the international community.

Virtually the whole of this community appears moreover to have been involved when resolutions of the United Nations General Assembly concerning nuclear disarmament have repeatedly been unanimously adopted. Indeed, any realistic search for general and complete disarmament, especially nuclear disarmament, necessitates the co-operation of all States.

101. Even the very first General Assembly resolution, unanimously adopted on 24 January 1946 at the London session, set up a commission whose terms of reference included making specific proposals for, among other things, "the elimination from national armaments of atomic weapons and of all other major weapons adaptable to mass destruction". In a large number of subsequent resolutions, the General Assembly has reaffirmed the need for nuclear disarmament. Thus, in resolution 808 A(IX) of 4 November 1954, which was likewise unanimously adopted, it concluded

> "that a further effort should be made to reach agreement on comprehensive and co-ordinated proposals to be embodied in a draft international disarmament convention providing for: ... (b) The total prohibition of the use and manufacture of nuclear weapons and weapons of mass destruction of every type, together with the conversion of existing stocks of nuclear weapons for peaceful purposes."

The same conviction has been expressed outside the United Nations context in various instruments.

102. The obligation expressed in Article VI of the Treaty on the Non-Proliferation of Nuclear Weapons includes its fulfillment in accordance with the basic principle of good faith. This basic principle is set forth in Article 2, paragraph 2, of the Charter. It was reflected in the Declaration on Friendly Relations between States (resolution 2625 (XXV) of 24 October 1970) and in the Final Act of the Helsinki Conference of 1 August 1975. It is also embodied in Article 26 of the Vienna Convention on the Law of Treaties of 23 May 1969, according to which "[e]very treaty in force is binding upon the parties to it and must be performed by them in good faith".

Nor has the Court omitted to draw attention to it, as follows:

> "One of the basic principles governing the creation and performance of legal obligations, whatever their source, is the principle of good faith. Trust and confidence are inherent in international co-operation, in particular in an age when this co-operation in many fields is becoming increasingly essential." (*Nuclear Tests (Australia v. France), Judgment of 20 December 1974, I.C.J. Reports 1974*, p. 268, para. 46.)

103. In its resolution 984 (1995) dated 11 April 1995, the Security Council took care to reaffirm "the need for all States Parties to the Treaty on the Non-Proliferation of Nuclear Weapons to comply fully with all their obligations" and urged

> "all States, as provided for in Article VI of the Treaty on the Non-Proliferation of Nuclear Weapons, to pursue negotiations in good faith on effective measures relating to nuclear disarmament and on a treaty on general and complete disarmament under strict and effective international control which remains a universal goal."

The importance of fulfilling the obligation expressed in Article VI of the Treaty on the Non-Proliferation of Nuclear Weapons was also reaffirmed in the final document of the Review and Extension Conference of the parties to the Treaty on the Non-Proliferation of Nuclear Weapons, held from 17 April to 12 May 1995.

In the view of the Court, it remains without any doubt an objective of vital importance to the whole of the international community today.

104. At the end of the present Opinion, the Court emphasizes that its reply to the question put to it by the General Assembly rests on the totality of the legal grounds set forth by the Court above (paragraphs 20 to 103), each of which is to be read in the light of the others. Some of these grounds are not such as to form the object of formal conclusions in the final paragraph of the Opinion; they nevertheless retain, in the view of the Court, all their importance.

105. For these reasons,

THE COURT,

(1) By thirteen votes to one,

Decides to comply with the request for an advisory opinion:

IN FAVOUR: *President* Bedjaoui; *Vice-President* Schwebel; *Judges* Guillaume, Shahabuddeen, Weeramantry, Ranjeva, Herczegh, Shi, Fleischhauer, Koroma, Vereshchetin, Ferrari Bravo, Higgins;

AGAINST: *Judge* Oda.

(2) *Replies* in the following manner to the question put by the General Assembly:

A. Unanimously,

There is in neither customary nor conventional international law any specific authorization of the threat or use of nuclear weapons;

B. By eleven votes to three,

There is in neither customary nor conventional international law any comprehensive and universal prohibition of the threat or use of nuclear weapons as such;

IN FAVOUR: *President* Bedjaoui; *Vice-President* Schwebel; *Judges* Oda, Guillaume, Ranjeva, Herczegh, Shi, Fleischhauer, Vereshchetin, Ferrari Bravo, Higgins;

AGAINST: *Judges* Shahabuddeen, Weeramantry, Koroma.

C. Unanimously,

A threat or use of force by means of nuclear weapons that is contrary to Article 2, paragraph 4, of the United Nations Charter and that fails to meet all the requirements of Article 51, is unlawful;

D. Unanimously,

A threat or use of nuclear weapons should also be compatible with the requirements of the international law applicable in armed conflict, particularly those of the principles and rules of international humanitarian law, as well as with specific obligations under treaties and other undertakings which expressly deal with nuclear weapons;

E. By seven votes to seven, by the President's casting vote,[109]

It follows from the above-mentioned requirements that the threat or use of nuclear weapons would generally be contrary to the rules of international law applicable in armed conflict, and in particular the principles and rules of humanitarian law;

However, in view of the current state of international law, and of the elements of fact at its disposal, the Court cannot conclude definitively whether the threat or use of nuclear weapons would be lawful or unlawful in an extreme circumstance of self-defence, in which the very survival of a State would be at stake;

IN FAVOUR: *President* Bedjaoui; *Judges* Ranjeva, Herczegh, Shi, Fleischhauer, Vereschetin, Ferrari Bravo;

AGAINST: *Vice President* Schwebel; *Judges* Oda, Guillaume, Shahabuddeen, Weeramantry, Koroma, Higgins.

F. Unanimously,

There exists an obligation to pursue in good faith and bring to a conclusion negotiations leading to nuclear disarmament in all its aspects under strict and effective international control

President BEDJAOUI, Judges HERCZEGH, SHI, VERESHCHETIN and FERRARI BRAVO append declarations to the Advisory Opinion of the Court.

Judges GUILLAUME, RANJEVA and FLEISCHHAUER append separate opinions to the Advisory Opinion of the Court.

---

109. Under the Statute of the International Court of Justice, when a vote is evenly divided, the President of the Court may cast a second deciding vote, art. 55.

Vice-President SCHWEBEL, Judges ODA, SHAHABUDDEEN, WEERAMANTRY, KOROMA and HIGGINS append dissenting opinions to the Advisory Opinion of the Court.

DISSENTING OPINION OF VICE-PRESIDENT SCHWEBEL

More than any other case in the history of the Court, this proceeding presents a titanic tension between State practice and legal principle. It is accordingly the more important not to confuse the international law we have with the international law we need. In the main, the Court's Opinion meets that test. I am in essential though not entire agreement with much of it, and shall, in this opinion, set out my differences. Since however I profoundly disagree with the Court's principal and ultimate holding, I regret to be obliged to dissent.

The essence of the problem is this. Fifty years of the practice of States does not debar, and to that extent supports, the legality of the threat or use of nuclear weapons in certain circumstances. At the same time, principles of international humanitarian law which antedate that practice govern the use of all weapons including nuclear weapons, and it is extraordinarily difficult to reconcile the use—at any rate, some uses—of nuclear weapons with the application of those principles.

* * *

[C]ontemporary events ... demonstrate the legality of the threat or use of nuclear weapons in extraordinary circumstances.

Desert Storm

The most recent and effective threat of the use of nuclear weapons took place on the eve of "Desert Storm". The circumstances merit exposition, for they constitute a striking illustration of a circumstance in which the perceived threat of the use of nuclear weapons was not only eminently lawful but intensely desirable.

Iraq, condemned by the Security Council for its invasion and annexation of Kuwait and for its attendant grave breaches of international humanitarian law, had demonstrated that it was prepared to use weapons of mass destruction. It had recently and repeatedly used gas in large quantities against the military formations of Iran, with substantial and perhaps decisive effect. It had even used gas against its own Kurdish citizens. There was no ground for believing that legal or humanitarian scruple would prevent it from using weapons of mass destruction—notably chemical, perhaps bacteriological or nuclear weapons—against the coalition forces arrayed against it. Moreover, it was engaged in extraordinary efforts to construct nuclear weapons in violation of its obligations as a Party to the Non-Proliferation Treaty.

General Norman Schwarzkopf stated on 10 January 1996 over national public television in the United States on "*Frontline*":

> "My nightmare scenario was that our forces would attack into Iraq and find themselves in such a great concentration that they became targeted by chemical weapons or some sort of rudimentary nuclear device that would cause mass casualties.
>
> That's exactly what the Iraqis did in the Iran-Iraq war. They would take the attacking masses of the Iranians, let them run up against their barrier system, and when there were thousands of people massed against the barrier system, they would drop chemical weapons on them and kill thousands of people." (*Frontline*, Show #1408, "The Gulf War," *Transcript of Journal Graphics, Inc., Part II*, p. 5.)

To exorcise that nightmare, the United States took action as described by then Secretary of State James A. Baker in the following terms, in which he recounts his climactic meeting of 9 January 1990 in Geneva with the then Foreign Minister of Iraq, Tariq Aziz:

> "I then made a point 'on the dark side of the issue' that Colin Powell had specifically asked me to deliver in the plainest possible terms. 'If the conflict involves your use of chemical or biological weapons against our forces,' I warned, 'the American people will demand vengeance. We have the means to exact it. With regard to this part of my presentation, that is not a threat, it is a promise. If there is any use of weapons like that, our objective won't just be the liberation of Kuwait, but the elimination of the current Iraqi regime, and anyone responsible for using those weapons would be held accountable.'
>
> "The President had decided, at Camp David in December, that the best deterrent of the use of weapons of mass destruction by Iraq would be a threat to go after the Ba'ath regime itself. He had also decided that U.S. forces would not retaliate with chemical or nuclear response if the Iraqis attacked with chemical munitions. There was obviously no reason to inform the Iraqis of this. In hope of persuading them to consider more soberly the folly of war, I purposely left the impression that the use of chemical or biological agents by Iraq could invite tactical nuclear retaliation. (We do not really know whether this was the reason there appears to have been no confirmed use by Iraq of chemical weapons during the war. My own view is that the calculated ambiguity how we might respond has to be part of the reason.)" (*The Politics of Diplomacy—Revolution, War and Peace, 1989–1992* by James A. Baker III, 1995, p. 359.)

In "*Frontline*", Mr. Baker adds:

> "The president's letter to Saddam Hussein, which Tariq Aziz read in Geneva made it very clear that if Iraq used weapons of mass destruction, chemical weapons, against United States forces that the American people would—would demand vengeance and that we had the means to achieve it." (*Loc. cit., Part I,* p. 13.)

Mr. Aziz is then portrayed on the screen immediately thereafter as saying:

> "I read it very carefully and then when I ended reading it, I told him, 'Look, Mr. Secretary, this is not the kind of correspondence between two heads of state. This is a letter of threat and I cannot receive from you a letter of threat to my president,' and I returned it to him." (*Ibid.*)

At another point in the program, the following statements were made:

> "NARRATOR: The Marines waited for a chemical attack. It never came.
>
> TARIQ AZIZ: We didn't think that it was wise to use them. That's all what I can say. That was not—was not wise to use such kind of weapons in such kind of a war with—with such an enemy." (*Loc. cit., Part II,* p. 7.)

In the Washington Post of 26 August 1995, an article datelined United Nations, 25 August was published as follows:

> "Iraq has released to the United Nations new evidence that it was prepared to use deadly toxins and bacteria against U.S. and allied forces during the 1991 Persian Gulf War that liberated Kuwait from its Iraqi occupiers, U.N. Ambassador Rolf Ekeus said today.

"Ekeus, the chief U.N. investigator of Iraq's weapons programs, said Iraqi officials admitted to him in Baghdad last week that in December 1990 they loaded three types of biological agents into roughly 200 missile warhead and aircraft bombs that were then distributed to air bases and a missile site.

"The Iraqis began this process the day after the U.N. Security Council voted to authorize using 'all necessary means' to liberate Kuwait, Ekeus said. He said the action was akin to playing 'Russian roulette' with extraordinarily dangerous weapons on the eve of war.

"U.S. and U.N. officials said the Iraqi weapons contained enough biological agents to have killed hundreds of thousands of people and spread horrible diseases in cities or military bases in Israel, Saudi Arabia or wherever Iraq aimed the medium-range missiles or squeaked a bomb-laden aircraft through enemy air defenses.

"Ekeus said Iraqi officials claimed they decided not to use the weapons after receiving a strong but ambiguously worded warning from the Bush administration on Jan. 9, 1991, that any use of unconventional warfare would provoke a devastating response.

"Iraq's leadership assumed this meant Washington would retaliate with nuclear weapons, Ekeus said he was told. U.N. officials said they believe the statement by Iraqi Deputy Prime Minister Tariq Aziz is the first authoritative account for why Iraq did not employ the biological or chemical arms at its disposal.

* * *

Thus there is on record remarkable evidence indicating that an aggressor was or may have been deterred from using outlawed weapons of mass destruction against forces and countries arrayed against its aggression at the call of the United Nations by what the aggressor perceived to be a threat to use nuclear weapons against it should it first use weapons of mass destruction against the forces of the coalition.... It rather demonstrates that, in some circumstances, the threat of the use of nuclear weapons—as long as they remain weapons unproscribed by international law—may be both lawful and rational.

* * *

DISSENTING OPINION OF JUDGE KOROMA

It is a matter of profound regret to me that I have been compelled to append this Dissenting Opinion to the Advisory Opinion rendered by the Court, as I fundamentally disagree with its finding—secured by the President's casting vote—that:

> "in view of the current state of international law, and of the elements of fact at its disposal, the Court cannot conclude definitively *whether the threat or use of nuclear weapons would be lawful or unlawful in an extreme circumstance of self-defence, in which the very survival of a State would be at stake*".

This finding, in my considered opinion, is not only unsustainable on the basis of existing international law, but, as I shall demonstrate later, is totally at variance with the weight and abundance of material presented to the Court. The finding is all the more regrettable in view of the fact that the Court had itself reached a conclusion that:

> "the threat or use of nuclear weapons would generally be contrary to the rules of international law applicable in armed conflict, and in particular the principles and rules of humanitarian law".

A finding with which I concur, save for the word "generally". It is my considered opinion based on the existing law and the available evidence that the use of nuclear weapons in any circumstance would be unlawful under international law. That use would at the very least result in the violation of the principles and rules of international humanitarian law, and would therefore be contrary to that law.

* * *

With regard to the elements of fact, the Court noted that the radiation released by a nuclear explosion would affect health, agriculture, natural resources and demography over a wide area and that such weapons would be a serious danger to future generations. It further noted that ionizing radiation has the potential to damage the future environment, food and marine ecosystems, and to cause genetic defects and illness in future generations.

Also in this regard, the Government of Japan told the Court that the yields of the atomic bombs detonated in Hiroshima on 6 August 1945 and in Nagasaki on 9 August 1945 were the equivalent of 15 kilotons and 22 kilotons of TNT respectively. The bomb blast produced a big fireball, followed by extremely high temperatures of some several million degrees centigrade, and extremely high pressures of several hundred thousand atmospheres. It also emitted a great deal of radiation. According to the delegation, the fireball, which lasted for about 10 seconds, raised the ground temperature at the hypocentre to somewhere between 3,000 [degrees] C and 4,000 [degrees] C, and the heat caused the scorching of wood buildings over a radius of approximately 3 kilometers from the hypocentre. The number of houses damaged by the atomic bombs was 70,147 in Hiroshima and 18,409 in Nagasaki. People who were within 1,000 m of the hypocentre were exposed to the initial radiation of more than 3.93 Grays. It is estimated that 50 percent of people who were exposed to more than 3 Grays die of marrow disorder within two months. Induced radiation was emitted from the ground and buildings charged with radioactivity. In addition, soot and dust contaminated by induced radiation was dispersed into the air and whirled up into the stratosphere by the force of the explosion, and this caused radioactive fallout back to the ground over several months.

According to the delegation, the exact number of fatalities was not known, since documents were scarce. It was estimated, however, that the number of people who had died by the end of 1945 amounted to approximately 140,000 in Hiroshima and 74,000 in Nagasaki. The population of the cities at the time was estimated at 350,000 in Hiroshima and 240,000 in Nagasaki. The number of people who died of thermal radiation immediately after the bomb blast, on the same day or within a few days, was not clear. However, 90 to 100 percent of the people who were exposed to thermal radiation without any shield within 1 k of the hypocentre, died within a week. The early mortality rates for the people who were within 1.5 k to 2 k of the hypocentre were 14 percent for people with a shield and 83 percent for the people without a shield. In addition to direct injury from the bomb blast, death was caused by several interrelated factors such as being crushed or buried under buildings, injuries caused by splinters of glass, radiation damage, food shortages or a shortage of doctors and medicines.

Over 320,000 people who survived but were affected by radiation still suffer from various malignant tumors caused by radiation, including leukemia, thyroid cancer, breast cancer, lung cancer, gastric cancer, cataracts and a variety of other after-effects. More than half a century after the disaster, they are still said to be undergoing medical examinations and treatment.

* * *

In the light of the foregoing the Court, as well as taking cognizance of the unique characteristics of nuclear weapons when used, reached the following conclusion; that nuclear weapons have a destructive capacity unmatched by any conventional weapon; that a single nuclear weapon has the capacity to kill thousands if not millions of human beings; that such weapons cause unnecessary suffering and superfluous injury to combatants and non-combatants alike; and that they are unable to distinguish between civilians and combatants. When recourse is had to such weapons, it can cause damage to generations unborn and produce widespread and long-term effects on the environment, particularly in respect of resources necessary for human survival. In this connection, it should be noted that the radioactive effects of such weapons are not only similar to the effects produced by the use of poison gas which would be in violation of the 1925 Geneva Gas Protocol, but are considered even more harmful.

The above findings by the Court should have led it inexorably to conclude that any use of nuclear weapons is unlawful under international law, in particular the law applicable in armed conflict including humanitarian law.

* * *

DISSENTING OPINION OF JUDGE WEERAMANTRY

* * *

(j) Potential to destroy all civilization

Nuclear war has the potential to destroy all civilization. Such a result could be achieved through the use of a minute fraction of the weapons already in existence in the arsenals of the nuclear powers.

As Former [U.S.] Secretary of State, Dr. Henry Kissinger, once observed, in relation to strategic assurances in Europe:

> "The European allies should not keep asking us to multiply strategic assurances that we cannot possibly mean, or if we do mean, we should not want to execute because if we execute, *we risk the destruction of civilization.*"

So, also, Robert McNamara, United States Secretary of Defense from 1961 to 1968, has written:

"Is it realistic to expect that a nuclear war could be limited to the detonation of tens or even hundreds of nuclear weapons, even though each side would have tens of thousands of weapons remaining available for use? The answer is clearly no."

Stocks of weapons may be on the decline, but one scarcely needs to think in terms of thousands or even hundreds of weapons. Tens of weapons are enough to wreak all the destructions that have been outlined at the commencement of this opinion.

Such is the risk attendant on the use of nuclear weapons—a risk which no single nation is entitled to take, whatever the dangers to itself. An individual's right to defend his own interests is a right he enjoys against his opponents. In exercising that right, he cannot be considered entitled to destroy the village in which he lives.

* * *

V. Some General Considerations

1. Two Philosophical Perspectives

This opinion has set out a multitude of reasons for the conclusion that the resort to nuclear weapons for any purpose entails the risk of the destruction of human society, if not of humanity itself . It has also pointed out that any rule permitting such use is inconsistent with international law itself.

Two philosophical insights will be referred to in this section—one based on rationality, and the other on fairness.

In relation to the first, all the postulates of law presuppose that they contribute to and function within the premise of the continued existence of the community served by that law. Without the assumption of that continued existence, no rule of the law and no legal system can have any claim to validity, however attractive the juristic reasoning on which it is based. That taint of invalidity affects not merely the particular rule. The legal system, which accommodates that rule, itself collapses upon its foundations, for legal systems are postulated upon the continued existence of society. Being part of society, they must themselves collapse with the greater entity of which they are a part. This assumption, lying at the very heart of the concept of law, often recedes from view in the midst of the nuclear discussion.

Without delving in any depth into philosophical discussions of the nature of the law, it will suffice for present purposes to refer briefly to two tests proposed by two pre-eminent thinkers about justice of the present era—H.L.A. Hart and John Rawls.

Hart, a leading jurist of the positivistic school, has, in a celebrated exposition of the minium content of natural law, formulated this principle pithily in the following sentence:

> "We are committed to it as something presupposed by the terms of the discussion; for our concern is with social arrangements for continued existence, not with those *of a suicide club.*"

His reasoning is that:

> "there are certain rules of conduct which any social organization must contain if it is to be viable. Such rules do in fact constitute a common element in the law and conventional morality of all societies which have progressed to the point where these are distinguished as different forms of social control."

International law is surely such a social form of control devised and accepted by the constituent members of that international society—the nation States.

Hart goes on to note that:

> "Such universally recognized principles of conduct which have a basis in elementary truths concerning human beings, their natural environment, and aims, may be considered the *minimum content* of Natural Law, in contrast with the more grandiose and more challengeable constructions which have often been proffered under that name."

Here is a recognized minimum accepted by positivistic jurisprudence which questions some of the more literal assumptions of other schools. We are down to the common denominator to which all legal systems must conform.

To approach the matter from another standpoint, the members of the international community have for the past three centuries been engaged in the task of formulating a set of rules and principles for the conduct of that society—the rules and principles we call international law. In so doing, they must ask themselves whether there is a place in that set of rules for a rule under which it would be legal, for whatever reason, to eliminate members of that community or, indeed, the entire community itself. Can the international community, which is governed by that rule, be considered to have given its acceptance to that rule, whatever be the approach of that community—positivist, natural law, or any other? Is the community of nations, to use Hart's expression a "suicide club"?

This aspect has likewise been stressed by perceptive jurists from the non-nuclear countries who are alive to the possibilities facing their countries in conflicts between other States in which, though they are not parties, they can be at the receiving end of the resulting nuclear devastation. Can international law, which purports to be a legal system for the entire global community, accommodate any principles which make possible the destruction of their communities?

* * *

Another philosophical approach to the matter is along the lines of the "veil of ignorance" posited by John Rawls in his celebrated study of justice as fairness.

If one is to devise a legal system under which one is prepared to live, this exposition posits as a test of fairness of that system that its members would be prepared to accept it if the decision had to be taken behind a veil of ignorance as to the future place of each constituent member within that legal system.

A nation considering its allegiance to such a system of international law, and not knowing whether it would fall within the group of nuclear nations or not, could scarcely be expected to subscribe to it if it contained a rule by which legality would be accorded to the use of a weapon by others which could annihilate it. Even less would it consent if it is denied even the right to possess such a weapon and, least of all if it could be annihilated or irreparably damaged in the quarrels of others to which it is not in any way a party.

One would indeed be in a desirable position in the event that it was one's lot to become a member of the nuclear group but, if there was a chance of being cast into the non-nuclear group, would one accept such a legal system behind a veil of ignorance as to one's position? Would it make any difference if the members of the nuclear group gave an assurance, which no one could police, that they would use the weapon only in extreme emergencies? The answers to such questions cannot be in doubt. By this test of fairness and legitimacy, such a legal system would surely fail.

Such philosophical insights are of cardinal value in deciding upon the question whether the illegality of use would constitute a minimum component of a system of international law based on rationality or fairness. By either test, widely accepted in the literature of modern jurisprudence, the rule of international law applicable to nuclear weapons would be that their use would be impermissible.

Fundamental considerations such as these tend to be overlooked in discussions relating to the legality of nuclear weapons. On matter so intrinsic to the validity of the entire system of international law, such perspectives cannot be ignored.

* * *

QUESTIONS

1. Do you agree with the Court's conclusion that there is no "comprehensive and universal conventional prohibition on the use, or the threat of use of ... [nuclear] weapons as such"?

2. Why does the Court determine that there is no customary rule of international law proscribing the threat or use of nuclear weapons *per se*? What sort of evidence might have convinced the Court that there was such a rule?
3. The Court notes that "nuclear weapons were invented after most of the principles and rules of humanitarian law applicable in armed conflict had already come into existence...." (paragraph 86). Similarly the principles of neutrality were also largely laid down before nuclear weapons were invented. How then does the Court conclude that the rules of humanitarian law and the principles of neutrality, nonetheless, apply to nuclear weapons?
4. Does the Court hold that states may use nuclear weapons when exercising the right of self-defense under article 51 of the U.N. Charter?
5. What exactly are the continuing obligations of states parties to the Treaty on the Non-Proliferation of Nuclear Weapons under article VI of that Treaty?
6. Did Judge Schwebel's evidence relating to the Gulf War persuade you that the threat to use nuclear weapons is sometimes permissible? If so, under what circumstances is such a threat permissible?
7. Judge Koroma concluded that the use of nuclear weapons always violates international law because of their indiscriminate devastation. Do you agree?
8. Are you convinced by Judge Weeramantry's notion that because nuclear weapons have the potential to destroy everything, including all legal systems, law cannot possibly condone nuclear weapons? What are the minimum mandatory assumptions that law must adopt if it is to survive as a system for governing human behavior?

Suggested Further Readings

Ian Browlie, Principles of Public International Law, chapter 33 (7th ed. 2008).

Leslie C. Green, The Contemporary Law of Armed Conflict (3d ed. 2008).

D.J. Harris, Cases and Materials on International Law, chapter 11 (6th ed. 2004).

Sean D. Murphy, Principles of International Law, chapter 14 (2006).

Marco Sassoli & Antoine A. Bouvier, How Does Law Protect in War? (2nd ed. 2006).

Malcolm N. Shaw, International Law, chapters 20 & 21 (6th ed. 2008).

Rebecca M. M. Wallace, International Law, chapter 11 (5th ed. 2005).

Treaty Index

(The date listed is the date of adoption or signing)

General Assembly Resolutions Index

Security Council Resolutions Index

General Index